D0842927

uptown
conversation

uptown

conver

columbia university press   new york

the new jazz studies

sation

edited by robert g. o'meally, brent hayes edwards, and farah jasmine griffin

Columbia University Press
Publishers Since 1893
New York   Chichester, West Sussex
Copyright © 2004 Robert G. O'Meally, Brent Hayes Edwards, and Farah Jasmine Griffin

Library of Congress Cataloging-in-Publication Data

Uptown conversation : the new jazz studies / edited by Robert G. O'Meally, Brent Hayes
   Edwards, and Farah Jasmine Griffin.
       p. cm.
    Includes index.
    ISBN 0-231-12350-7 — ISBN 0-231-12351-5
     1. Jazz—History and criticism. I. O'Meally, Robert G., 1948– II. Edwards, Brent Hayes.
 III. Griffin, Farah Jasmine.

ML3507.U68 2004
781.65′09—dc22

                                                                                2003067480

∞

Columbia University Press books are printed on permanent and durable acid-free paper.
Printed in the United States of America
c 10 9 8 7 6 5 4 3 2 1
p 10 9 8 7 6 5 4 3 2 1

contents

part 2

acknowledgments

We would like to thank the Ford Foundation, which has provided funding for the Jazz Study Group since its inception. We are particularly grateful to the program officers and administrators at Ford who have collaborated with the group, including Sheila Biddle, Alison R. Bernstein, Gertrude Fraser, and Mararet B. Wilkerson. We would also like to thank the Louis Armstrong Educational Foundation, the Romare Bearden Foundation, and the Office of University Seminars at Columbia University. Our editor at Columbia University Press, Jennifer Crewe, has been endlessly supportive of this project as it has developed, and Susan Pensak has shepherded the book through the copyediting process with extraordinary patience and a fine eye for detail. In addition, we thank the many scholars, writers, and artists who have participated in Jazz Study Group events during the past decade as well as the musicians and intellectuals who have visited the group. This book would have been impossible without the contribution of the indefatigable assistants who have helped to organize the meetings and conferences of the Jazz Study Group: J. C. Sylvan, Donia Allen, Nicole Stahlmann, Elda Tsou, Jeffrey O'Neal, Carolyn Appel, Jenny Wasserman, Dave Ellenbogen, Jennifer White, and Maxine Gordon.

uptown
conversation

ROBERT G. O'MEALLY, BRENT HAYES EDWARDS, AND FARAH JASMINE GRIFFIN

Introductory Notes

Our new century is witnessing the development of jazz studies as a new field in the liberal arts curriculum at the college and graduate school levels—and with implications for students at all levels. Jazz is not new at the university in the United States. For at least fifty years there have been maverick efforts as well as established classes tracing jazz's beginnings and development; and for years there have been courses teaching students to play. (One of the wondrous oddities of our current moment is that the best advice to a serious jazz player in training is not to drop out and study in New York's nightclubs but to attend one of the several conservatories where excellent jazz instruction, by accomplished jazz artists, is richly available. At Berkelee or the Manhattan School would-be Mileses and Sarahs can major in jazz.)

What is new here is the conviction that jazz is not just for players and aficionados who can count the horns and boxes of the music "from Bunk to Monk," as the expression goes; but that knowing about jazz and its cultural settings is part of what it means to be an educated woman or man in our time—this regardless of a student's own specific major or field. Certainly this does mean that citizens of the new century should know who Bunk Johnson and Thelonious Monk are, that they should be able to trace a crisscross line from early cornettists and trumpeters to brass players of our own era and from early jazz pianists and composers through Monk and beyond. Jazz experts love to chart the ingredients that jazz lovers listen for: Where is the melody? Where is the harmony? What are the colors? How to define the polyrhythmical universe in which jazz reigns, the complex rhythmical play? Where's the music's sense of momentum called swing? Where is the dance-beat orientation? Where is the individuality of sound? Does the soloist "tell the story?" Where is the call and response? The sense of conversation? Where is the improvisation? The bluesiness? The "Latin tinge?" The sense of a jazz tradition, the artwork as archive? How to chart the will to spirituality? The vocal qualities of the instruments, the instrumental sound of the voices? What is the magic that makes a piece with only one or two of these qualities somehow a "jazz" piece any-how? And, by the way: Why do so many musicians, including veteran percussion-ist-composer Max Roach and trombonist-composer George Lewis, disapprove of the word *jazz*? How is such a word constricting? What might such a label leave out of what Roach and Lewis do as artists?

These questions of definition, history, and form will always be part of jazz stud-ies. Getting a small part of the answers to such questions right can be the work of a lifetime. But what more is there to explore?

Uptown Conversation asserts that jazz is not only a music to define, it is a *cul-ture*. Which is to say that not only might one study Bunk and Monk as individual musicians in a broad stream of musicians who influenced them and by whom they in turn were influenced. One also can consider the immeasurably complex worlds through which they moved, and which they helped to shape. What would cultural historians—with their insistent drive to questions of nationality, race, sexuality, gender, economics, and politics—say about the extraordinarily complex terrains of the New Orleans of Bunk Johnson, the North Carolina and West Side Manhattan of Thelonious Monk? Of these artists' other geographical travels? What did their images, including mistaken conceptions of who they were, tell us about the cul-tures that mythologized them?

How did these jazz musicians influence not just musicians but other artists of their era and milieu: the poets and novelists, painters and sculptors, photographers and filmmakers, dancers and choreographers who regularly heard them play and of-ten shared with them a sense of common project? One thinks of Jackson Pollock dancing to the music as he spun the drips of paint on canvasses placed on the stu-dio floor; of Langston Hughes writing detailed instructions to the musicians he hoped would accompany performances of his poetry; of Romare Bearden's beauti-fully turned stage and costume designs for Alvin Ailey and Dianne McIntyre, whose improvisatory jazz dance workshop was called Sounds in Motion; of the drummer Jo Jones in an interview naming as key influences a series of tap dancers he admired; of Stanley Crouch, stirring his high-powered essays in a room where jazz drums stand at the center, the old dream-kit inspiration; of Ralph Ellison, who kept in touch with his beginnings as a musician in Oklahoma City through hour-long conversations with his childhood friend the singer Jimmy Rushing; of Toni Morrison reading her brilliant prose to improvisations by Max Roach and the dancer Bill T. Jones; of the pianist Jason Moran playing at the Studio Museum in Harlem, where he introduced his group as including Beauford Delany, whose paintings hung on the wall near the bandstand—vigorous call and recall across the art forms.

What is a jazz painting? A jazz novel? What is jazz poetry? What is jazz dance? What is a jazz film? What are the sources of jazz as an art form? What are the sources and meanings of art? What work does the music do for the whole community?

With such questions now we are talking about jazz "across the curriculum"—as our colleagues in English departments say about teaching students to write: not just the province of Ph.D.s in English but of the whole liberal arts faculty.

There are other questions, too, once jazz steps outside the music building: What are jazz's implications for the student of law? What issues of copywriting and licensing apply here? How does one protect the intellectual property rights of an improvised jazz solo? Are there *styles* in jazz that have something to teach the law profession? What about business? Business schools typically hold up the symphonic conductor as an important model for someone running a business: cuing, keeping time, building toward climaxes and endings. What could a jazz orchestra, typically without a conductor standing in front of the band, tell a business student about how to swing together, to improvise without losing the time or the sense of ensemble? What could the Duke Ellington Orchestra, which endured from the early 1920s till the artist's death (and still exists today, led by Duke's great-grandson Paul) teach the business world? What economic and political forces have shaped jazz? Who buys jazz? What is its audience? What are the economics of being a "sideman," not a group leader but "just" a player in the band? What are the economics of being Albert "Tootie" Heath—to pick an example of a masterful drummer not known for his own leadership of bands?

Appropriately enough, *Uptown Conversation* derives from the ongoing meetings of a group of scholars and artists who have been attempting to function as a kind of band or scholarly jazz orchestra. These essays are the work of the Jazz Study Group, a scholarly seminar that has met at Columbia University two or three times a year over a period of eight years. A collective of more than thirty members based primarily but not exclusively in the New York metropolitan area, the Jazz Study Group has been a dynamic springboard for the new jazz studies emerging in the past decade.

Uptown Conversation may be regarded as a kind of sequel to our seminar's first book project, *The Jazz Cadence of American Culture* (1998): an anthology of seminal works on jazz and jazz's influence on its sister art forms—classic interviews, definitional texts, and landmark essays by Ralph Ellison, Zora Neale Hurston, Amiri Baraka, and others. Following through on that first book's effort to define a new field of jazz studies across the curriculum, *Uptown Conversation* now records some of the best work, virtually none of it published before, by new voices in this vital emerging field. If the single most striking feature of this book is its robust interdisciplinarity, it thus reflects the composition and working methods of the group itself, which has included a remarkable range of participants: musicians, literary critics, social historians, art and dance historians, musicologists, archivists, film scholars, anthropologists, sociologists, journalists, poets, and visual artists. The aim of this book is that of the seminar, which has pursued, through dialogues between participants from a wide variety of disciplinary perspectives, new methods of studying the history of jazz, its social contexts and broad cultural ramifications.

A number of the essays included here were first developed as presentations at meetings of the Jazz Study Group, literally as parts of conversations held in uptown Manhattan. In order to provide as much space as possible for dialogue and discussion, the topics at these meetings have been deliberately broad and speculative: the jazz voice; women in jazz; Thelonious Monk; musician and icon; jazz and the visual arts; jazz and film; jazz and dance; jazz and poetry; jazz and spirituality; the criticism of Albert Murray and jazz aesthetics; jazz and Africa; jazz and photography; musicians' collectives in Chicago and Detroit. Held over two-day periods, our meetings typically have been structured around one or two formal presentations by group members, followed by free-flowing conversation. In the afternoons we have regularly invited guests to answer questions about their work, to give demonstrations of various techniques or styles, and sometimes to perform. Such visitors during the last few years have included musicians, writers, curators, critics, and dancers: we have hosted Kenny Washington, Amiri Baraka, Geri Allen, Max Roach, Jim Hatch and Camille Billops, George Wein, Marion Coles, Jimmy Slyde, Robert Farris Thompson, Nathaniel Mackey, Randy Weston, Albert Murray, Gerald Cyrus, Chuck Stewart, Daniel Dawson, David Pleasant, Abbey Lincoln, and George Lewis.

Other papers collected here originated as presentations at public events: the conference at Columbia University in May 2000 called "Rhythm-a-ning: A Symposium in Jazz Culture," the symposia for scholars and journalists held at the 2000 Newport Jazz Festival on "The Meanings of Jazz," the conference at the 2001 Verizon Music Festival in New York on "Where Jazz Comes From." While these events—or the speakers series organized for the past three years at the Center for Jazz Studies at Columbia University, drawing on a number of members—have been the most visible face of the Jazz Study Group, the group has also had an impact in ways that are equally important. Mentoring has been another goal of the group: four contributors to this volume are recent Ph.D.s who first joined as graduate students writing their dissertations.

At a number of meetings the discussions have returned to a constellation of concerns at the heart of jazz and of the jazz studies project—*the processes of collaboration itself:* the lessons that we as scholars seek to learn from the music, about modes and methods of working together. How does one approach a long-term collective project? How does one learn to listen, and then to respond as much to a pattern of silences as to what has been said? How do we make room for spontaneity while adhering to the discipline of organized interaction—find the flash of the moment while attending to the rigors of the *longue durée*? How does one learn to critique in a manner that constructs and advances a dialogue rather than shutting it down? To hear an interlocutor's devotion to an unfamiliar vocabulary, a peculiar perspective, as an invitation or a provocation instead of a barricade? How can we be a better working scholarly band?

Some of our most important work has been accomplished at a level that to some would seem mundane: exchanging packets of reading and listening material before each meeting, sharing bibliographies and course syllabi, offering commiseration and encouragement, emailing one another with queries or requests. These practices have emerged out of a shared approach to interdisciplinarity, a sense that modes of crossing barriers must be elaborated out of the practice of crossing—improvised, that is, rather than imposed in a preset method. Some of that shared knowledge is evident in the text that came—after a number of group conversations around the need for such a teaching tool—to comprise *The Jazz Cadence of American Culture*. Other traces show up in the essays that follow here, if not primarily in projects written as outright collaborations, then in the footnotes and acknowledgments of the work individual members have pursued, the sense of conversation, piece by piece. .

The essays are loosely organized around a series of interwoven themes. The collection opens with a number of essays on jazz historiography, considerations of the political stakes of telling the story of the music and its cultural import. These include both salutary attempts to come to terms with the legacies of collectives and coalitions in the music's experimental wing (George Lewis's much needed and thorough overview of the Association for the Advancement of Creative Musicians, Salim Washington's unraveling of the very notion of an "avant garde," or George Lipsitz's polemical juxtaposition of Ken Burns's documentary *Jazz* and Horace Tapscott's Pan-Afrikan Arkestra) and revisionary takes on some of the most familiar figures in the canon: Thelonious Monk, Miles Davis, Duke Ellington, Louis Armstrong.

One of the key developments in new jazz studies has been its forthright attention to transnational concerns—in terms of impact, performance spaces, symbolic resonance and transmission, and practitioners—and a second grouping of essays consider the ways jazz travels, and the ways that outernational settings have in turn transformed the music. Issues of interdisciplinarity in the music are then breached through a number of particular archives, particular cross-fertilizations and links between jazz and creative expression in other media: the visual arts, literature, electronica. The point in this work is not so much to echo old assumptions about the ways that a novelist emulates or evokes a saxophonist but more to suggest that certain aesthetic issues, certain modes and structural paradigms, show up in a number of media—or, more precisely, operate at the edges of media, at what one might term the interface of sound and script and pigment. Rather than simply supposing that a visual artist or a writer tries to capture the quality of Charlie Parker's horn, this work strives to evaluate the ways that a variety of art forms are shaped by, as one painter put it, "*a brush with the blues*."

This volume both builds upon and departs from decades of insightful writing about jazz music. In two important essays prior to this volume, "Jazz Criticism: Its Development and Ideologies" and "Constructing the Jazz Tradition," John Gennari and Scott DeVeaux document the major trends in jazz criticism over the last century. While the earliest forms of criticism were faced with the task of legitimating jazz as a genuine art form, later writers debated critical approaches: Should the critic focus on the technical accomplishments of a particular artist? Should he or she focus on the political, economic, cultural, and social context out of which the music emerges? Both Gennari and DeVeaux demonstrate how the next generation of critics focused on the development of jazz styles through the construction of a linear history focusing on key innovators.

Uptown Conversation is strongly influenced by a variety of developments in the academy: by African American studies, cultural studies, literary studies, the new musicology, and by insights of poststructuralism. Fine examples of this new wave of jazz scholarship include two anthologies, *Representing Jazz* and *Jazz as Discourse*, edited by Krin Gabbard, Eric Porter's recent *What Is This Thing Called Jazz?* and Sherrie Tucker's *Swing Shift*. The essays of *Uptown Conversation* join these works by focusing on moments, meetings, gatherings, gestures, and scenes. Urging us to look past the familiar, the essayists ask that we consider jazz in conversation with other genres of music and other art forms. At times they ask us to look at jazz musicians as thinkers, activists, writers of prose and poetry, and visual artists. They challenge any notion of a strictly linear development of singular jazz styles and insist that we look around or behind the Giants of Jazz to consider less well-known figures as well as the communities that surround, support, and imbibe the music. These writers do not construct a triumphant narrative of jazz as representative of a democracy lacking in disruption and dissent and counternarratives. Most important, they inspire us to listen to music we thought we knew, to discover new artists and sounds, and to anticipate possibilities in the name of a freshly invigorated field.

robert g. o'meally, brent hayes edwards, and farah jasmine griffin

part 1

GEORGE LIPSITZ

Songs of the Unsung:
The Darby Hicks History of Jazz

Nobody agrees on anything about jazz (except that it survived beautifully and blos-
somed), but everybody thinks they know all about it, anywhere in the world. There is an in-
teresting ownership of jazz.
          —Toni Morrison

Beware of the prevailing view of "jazz" as some kind of history lesson that you have to sit
through because it's good for you. . . . Understand that this is a living art form whose
most esteemed practitioners are continually evolving and engaging with the world around
them.
          —Vijay Iyer

They get to think in a memory kind of way about all this Jazz; but these people don't
seem to know it's more than a memory thing. They don't seem to know it's happening
right here where they're listening to it, just as much as it ever did in memory.
          —Sidney Bechet

New members of Harlan Leonard's Territory jazz band in the 1940s began to hear
about Darby Hicks as soon as they were hired. None of them recognized his name,
but evidently the musicians in their new band knew him well. "Oh yes, I heard
about you, " a band veteran would say upon being introduced to the new recruit,
"Darby Hicks told me that you can't play a lick." If a musician failed to hit a high
note or adjust to a key change, someone would always say, "Darby Hicks would
have nailed that." Even worse, Darby Hicks seemed to know them. Senior members of the band would pull newcomers aside and confide to them, "Darby Hicks

was talking about you last night, man. He was saying some terrible things about you, and about your sister, and about your mother, and even about your grandmother too." At this point the initiate often reached the breaking point and exploded in anger, vowing to settle things with Darby Hicks directly by challenging him to a fight.

Darby Hicks did not exist. The musicians made up a name they could use to tease newcomers, to initiate them into the band with an in-joke. Eventually the new band members would become insiders and play the same trick on those who joined the aggregation after them. The "Darby Hicks" story worked because musicians are competitive, proud, and sensitive to peer pressure, because reputations have professional and personal consequences. The story served a disciplinary function for the band as well, placing newcomers on notice that they were being watched, evaluated, and judged. Whatever the new band members thought of their own talent when they entered the band, they soon learned that they had not measured up to the standards of Darby Hicks. Whatever music they were about to play did not matter, because it could never be as good as the music Darby Hicks had already played.[1]

Ken Burns's film *Jazz* has more than a little of Darby Hicks in it, although the name is never mentioned. Its opening and establishing shot presents the high-rise buildings of New York City's skyline illuminated at night during the 1920s as the sounds of automobile horns transform into the sounds of the brass horns of a jazz ensemble. This opening serves to prefigure a connection between black music and modernity as a central focus of the film. A second connection becomes evident immediately as Wynton Marsalis's voice provides a sound bridge to a close-up of his face. Marsalis declares, "Jazz objectifies America," and then explains that jazz music is something that can tell us who "we" are. The trumpet virtuoso then identifies collective improvisation as jazz's core concept and key achievement. He notes that Bach improvised while playing his own compositions on the keyboard, but relegates that accomplishment to a secondary level because Bach did not improvise with other musicians as jazz artists must do. Thus, in rapid order in its first three scenes, *Jazz* (the film) links jazz (the music) to three key signifiers: modernity, America, and the apex of artistic genius.

The opening scenes of *Jazz* brilliantly encapsulate much of what follows during more than twenty hours of film stretched over ten episodes. Burns and his fellow filmmakers compress the infinitely diverse and plural practices that make up the world of jazz into one time—modernity, one place—"America," and one subjectivity—the heroic artist who turns adversity and alienation into aesthetic triumph. As the opening shots of the New York skyline suggest, the film depicts jazz as the quintessential creation of modernity, an art form shaped by the technological and social complexities of the twentieth-century city.

A linear developmental narrative traces the journey of jazz across space, from its origins in the rural areas of the southern U.S. and Europe to the racially mixed and ethnically diverse cities of the twentieth century. The same developmental narrative governs the growth of jazz's key styles from the foundational ensemble style pioneered by Dixieland innovators in New Orleans during the 1910s and

1920s to the section-playing, written arrangements, powerful sounds, and rhythms of swing bands in Kansas City, Chicago, and New York during the 1930s, to ultimate fulfillment in the sophisticated styles of bebop players in New York and Los Angeles in the 1940s and 1950s. The film presents jazz as an art form that emerged from urbanization and industrialization, that fused folk forms with modern improvisation, and that echoed the upheavals of modernity with artistry oriented toward originality and innovation. In this narrative, jazz had a beginning, a middle, and an end.

Jazz music not only has its designated proper time in this film, but it also occupies a discrete physical space: the geographic and juridical boundaries of the United States of America. Jazz music's importance in this film comes from its identity as the most important art form to originate in the United States, from its value as a metaphorical representation of the tensions between diversity and unity that define "American" society. When Wynton Marsalis begins the film proclaiming that "jazz objectifies America" and that it can tell us who "we" are, the audience is being interpellated as national subjects, as "Americans." But as *Jazz* proceeds, we see that Marsalis's comments mean even more, that in this film jazz has metonymic rather than merely metaphorical significance. It not only reflects the nation, it somehow constitutes it. In this film, the story of jazz is also the story of America. The ability of black and white jazz musicians to blend European and African musical traditions into a new synthesis despite the rigidly racist and segregated nature of the nation's social (and musical) institutions is what makes jazz music quintessentially American.

As a means of staking a claim by blacks for inclusion in the celebratory nationalism of the American nation that has routinely excluded them, this narrative strategy makes sense. It urges white nationalists to acknowledge the importance of black people to the national project, while allowing blacks to see themselves as key contributors to a project in which all Americans presumably take pride. In addition, *Jazz* pays homage to artists who deserve to be honored while it recalls a history that very much needs to be told. Yet by telling the story as a narrative about modern time and American space, the film necessarily, and regrettably, occludes other temporal and spatial dimensions of jazz that also need to be illuminated.

The privileged time of modernity and the privileged space of America come together in *Jazz* to draw attention to a privileged social subject: the heroic creative artist. Louis Armstrong serves as the anchor of this project, the prototypical genius who played better (louder, higher, longer) than anyone else and whose creative innovations influenced everyone else. The film's narrative voices use the word *genius* again and again, frequently by connecting Armstrong, Ellington, or Parker to Bach, Mozart, Beethoven or some other recognized genius of the classical canon.

In this formulation, each instrument has its own history and its own exemplary performer. Louis Armstrong perfects the possibilities of the trumpet. Lester Young and Charlie Parker define the limits of artistry on the tenor saxophone. Multi-instrumentalism is only a footnote to this story. Yet in the lives of individual musicians a dialogic history of moving from one instrument to another has often led to innovations undreamed of by single instrument players. Lionel Hampton and Lester Young explored scales extensively when they took up melodic instruments (vibes and saxophones) because they started out as drummers who had not had to think very much about harmony and melody. Under the tutelage of his father, Young learned to play clarinet, piano, flute, and piccolo. The unique sounds that Lester Young coaxed out of the tenor owed much to his previous playing on the C Melody and alto saxophones.[2]

Within the heroic narrative the particularities of black experience and American white supremacy serve as little more than dramatic background for the emergence of individuals who turn adversity into aesthetic perfection through their art. Wynton Marsalis describes the triumphs over adversity by Armstrong and the other geniuses of jazz as part of a universal process that takes place in all societies. Consequently, for Marsalis, racism's relationship to jazz is only as the historically specific obstacle to genius that these artists faced, more part of a general pattern than a constitutive force. "It happened to be racism," in this case Marsalis observes, "but it is always something."

The narrative strategies deployed by the producers of *Jazz* are understandable, logical, and part of a long and honorable tradition. They reflect the efforts by Houston Baker and Paul Gilroy to claim a central place for African Americans in the history of modernism. They echo the insistence of Albert Murray on "the inescapably mulatto" character of "American" culture and on the inalienable contributions by blacks to the national narrative. They continue the claims made by Billy Taylor, Grover Sales, Reginald Buckner, and many others for the canonization of jazz as "America's classical music." Yet, like any historical narrative, the evidence and arguments advanced in *Jazz* are partial, perspectival, and interested. In telling its own truths about time, place, and subjectivity, the film directs our attention away from the many other temporalities, spaces, and subject positions that are central to the story of jazz.

It is not incorrect to view jazz as an exemplary modernist creation of the twentieth-century city, but doing so suppresses other temporalities and spaces equally responsible for the art. The migrant to the city who fashions a new art out of alienation is a recurrent story in the history of modernism, but to tell the story that way privileges the community of artistic practices that migrants create in the city over the community of shared historical experience they leave behind and, in some cases, even bring with them to the metropolis. When Lee Young moved to Los Angeles from New Orleans, Mutt Carey took him into his band without an audition because he already had a long history with the Young family that included walking Lee Young to grade school when they both lived in New Orleans.[3] Black migrants to urban areas have rarely been afforded the luxury of cutting off contact with their previous places of residence. Black urban life has always entailed secondary migrations from regional gateway cities like Memphis, New Orleans, and Atlanta to large metropolitan centers like Chicago, Los Angeles, and New York. Survival strategies often required moving back and forth between cities, maintaining contacts with family and friends in the countryside, using the dispersal of the black population as a way to counter shortages of opportunities and resources in any one place.[4]

In the version of modernity described in *Jazz*, art becomes a specialized and autonomous activity detached from tradition, something created by alienated individuals rather than historical communities. Modernist aesthetics place the value of a work of art in the work itself, not in the broader social relations and practices that shape artistic creation and reception. The aestheticization of alienation is seen as an end in itself, as an episode in the history of art rather than as an individual and collective strategy for living better in the world by calling new realities into being through performance.

This celebration of modernism masks the creative tensions in black culture between modernity and tradition. As Farah Jasmine Griffin explains in her brilliant analysis of the African American "migration narrative," black artists' enthusiasm for modernity has often been tempered by the pull of the past, by the power of "talkative ancestors" warning against a form of freedom based upon detachment from tradition. The honor that elite white artists and critics reserve for high modernism understandably generates a desire among African Americans to celebrate the dynamic presence of African Americans within it. But this prestige comes at a high price when it diverts attention away from the even more impressive African American tradition of refusing to be absorbed completely by either tradition or modernity, but instead to fashion a dynamic fusion built upon a dialectical relationship between the past and present.[5]

It is not incorrect to view jazz as a quintessential expression of U.S. national identity, as an art form that emerged from contacts between European and African musical traditions on the North American continent. But the added prestige that jazz seems to acquire from its association with celebratory nationalism comes at the expense of appreciating jazz's capacity to create identities far more fluid and flexible than the citizen-subject of the nation state.

Duke Ellington may be quintessentially "American" to Wynton Marsalis and Ken Burns, but when the South African pianist Abdullah Ibrahim started playing with the Ellington band in Switzerland he did not think of his boss as a citizen of any particular nation, but rather as "the wise old man in the village—the extended village."[6] Charlie Parker and Dizzy Gillespie invoked Africa as well as America when they performed with dancer Asadata Dafora and an assortment of Cuban and African drummers at New York benefits for the African Academy of Arts and Research in the 1940s. Mary Lou Williams and Dafora staged a two-day Carnegie Hall show in 1945 structured around the links between African and Western music and dance.[7]

The story of jazz as a joint creation of black and white Americans does little to help us understand how light-skinned Puerto Ricans like Louis "King" Garcia and Miguel Angel Duchesne wound up playing for white bandleaders Benny Goodman, Tommy Dorsey, and Paul Whiteman while dark-skinned Puerto Ricans played with bands led by Fletcher Henderson and Noble Sissle. Can a celebratory equation between jazz and "America" lead us to a productive understanding of Rafael Hernandez who played in James Reese Europe's African American Fifteenth Regimental Band in France during World War I, but with the Trio Borinquen (made up of two Puerto Ricans and a Dominican) in Cuba, Mexico, New York, and San Juan in the succeeding decades? Are we still dealing with "American" culture when Sidney Bechet moves to France, Albert Nicholas to Egypt, Buck Clayton to China, Randy Weston to Morocco, Art Blakey to Kenya, Hampton Hawes to Japan, and Teddy Weatherford to India? Did Django Reinhardt cease being Belgian by playing jazz? Did Toshiko Ayoshi cease being Japanese? Does music made in America (the continent) by Machito, Tito Puente, Mongo Santamaria, or Carlos "Patato" Valdes count as jazz in America (the country)? Does the celebratory America of *Jazz* prepare us adequately for the Charles Mingus compositions "They Trespass the Land of the Sacred Sioux," "Remember Rockefeller at Attica," or "Once There Was a Holding Corporation Called Old America?"

It is not incorrect to view jazz as a crucible of heroic artistry. Jazz musicians have discursively transcoded the hard facts of slavery, migration, industrialization, and urbanization in U.S. history into aesthetically rich and complex creations. Their harmonious balance between individual soloists and collective improvisation provides a metaphorical solution to one of the recurrent dilemmas of social life in the U.S.—how to encourage individuality without selfishness and how to encourage civic mindedness without totalitarianism. The formal complexities of jazz composition, the risks and rewards of collective improvisation, and the artistic virtuosity demonstrated by its most accomplished performers make jazz a logical and suitable site for the exploration of art as transcendence and existential fulfillment.

Yet this emphasis on the heroic individual depends upon hierarchies that are not universally accepted among jazz artists and audiences. The history of Western culture is replete with linear developmental narratives that attach art forms to celebratory nationalisms and to canons of great works and artists, but it does not necessarily follow that placing jazz within that pantheon elevates it or even helps explain it. Jazz's emphasis on immediacy, on involvement, and on engagement encourages a sensibility entirely at odds with the romanticization of the alienated artist that is so central to the Western tradition. The jazz sensibility prizes connection rather than canonization, it finds value in the social relations that playing and listening creates rather than in the notes and chords and rhythms all by themselves. As New Orleans drummer Baby Dodds emphasized when speaking about how social connection rather than social alienation permeated the spirit of the bands in which he played, "When the leader of an orchestra would hire a new man there was no jealousy in the gang. Everybody took him in as a brother, and he was treated accordingly. If a fellow came to work with anything, even a sandwich or an orange, the new man would be offered a piece of it. That's the way they were. They believed in harmony."[8]

Some musicians left successful orchestras to return to communities that offered them a greater sense of social connection. That sensibility is what informed Horace Tapscott's decision to leave the Lionel Hampton Band in the late 1950s and devote the remaining forty years of his life to playing and teaching in community based art and music collectives. Sun Ra summarized this school of thought eloquently when he explained, "Musicians often play wonderful things, bring together wonderful sounds, but it doesn't mean a thing. Not for themselves, not for other people. Everyone says that's wonderful, that's the work of a great musician. Of course, that's true, but what's the significance of it? People don't get better because of the music even though they certainly need help. I believe that every artist should realize that. That his work has no meaning whatsoever unless he helps people with it."[9]

The story of jazz artists as heroic individualists also overlooks the gender relations structuring entry into the world of playing jazz for a living. Women musicians Melba Liston, Clora Bryant, and Mary Lou Williams can only be minor supporting players in this drama of heroic male artistry. Bessie Smith and Billie Holiday are revered as interpreters and icons but not acknowledged for their expressly musical contributions. Although *Jazz* acknowledges the roles played by supportive wives and partners in the success of individual male musicians, the broader structures of power that segregated women into "girl" bands, that relegated women players to local rather than national exposure, that defined the music of Nina Simone or Dinah Washington as somehow outside the world of jazz are never systematically addressed in the film, although they have been investigated, analyzed, and critiqued in recent books by Eric Porter, Sherrie Tucker, and Ingrid Monson, among others.[10]

Moreover, the separation of music from other art forms obscures the broader creative activities in which musicians have been engaged. The creation of new social relations through art has taken many unexpected forms for jazz musicians, not all of them limited to playing music. In the early 1960s, Charlie Mingus worked with Max Roach and Jo Jones on plans to open a "school of arts, music, and gymnastics" in New York.[11] Reed player Roscoe Mitchell, trombonist Lester Lashley, and trumpeter Bobby Bradford were also accomplished painters, while painter/collagist Romare Bearden composed songs including "Seabreeze," which he wrote with Billy Eckstine.[12] The mingling between members of different races celebrated in *Jazz* did not occur easily or unproblematically in most places. For example, in Oklahoma City, interracial dances did not take place until the Young Communist League deliberately crossed the color line in 1932 by promoting an interracial dance featuring the Blue Devils in that city's Forest Park.[13]

Tenor saxophonist Lester Young and clarinetist Wilton Crawley sometimes found the English language inadequate for their purposes, expressing their creativity by inventing and speaking languages that they made up. One day Crawley accidentally boarded a train filled with mental patients and spoke to them so successfully the authorities took him to the sanitarium too. Young's original wordplay complemented the originality of his artistry on the saxophone. The same person who signaled other musicians to go to the "bridge" of a song by shouting "George Washington," who said "I feel a draft" to indicate that he was picking up bad vibrations, and who indicated a conversation was over by saying "doom" also used different fingerings and variations in density and tone to make his playing mimic the sounds of vernacular speech.[14]

The pure musicality of artistic innovators in *Jazz* emerged out of a performance tradition that often privileged participation and sensation over cerebral virtuosity. Crawley would disassemble his clarinet during choruses and juggle all six pieces in the air while tap dancing.[15] Charley Siegals entertained audiences at Langford's nightspot in Minneapolis in 1927 by playing the trumpet in the style of Louis Armstrong with one hand while mimicking the style of Earl Hines on piano with the other hand.[16] In the early days of his career, Lester Young delighted carnival audiences by dancing the Charleston while he played the saxophone. He amazed his band mates during the days he played with Count Basie's Orchestra by turning the mouthpiece of the saxophone upside down and holding the instrument over his head as if it were a pipe that he was smoking. At one recording session in 1947, the assembled musicians watched in amazement as Young sat across the room from them on the other side of the studio during fifteen of the sixteen-bar introduction they devised to "East of the Sun." Then, halfway through the sixteenth bar, Young jumped into the air "like a gazelle" and ran over to the microphone to begin an amazing solo.[17]

Even within music, jazz does not exist in a vacuum isolated from other genres. Horace Tapscott's neighbors in Houston included rhythm and blues musicians Floyd Dixon, Amos Milburn, and Johnny Guitar Watson.[18] Lester Young's work with Johnny Otis and others in small combos after World War II developed the core musical features of rhythm and blues, yet Young also insisted repeatedly that he admired the singing of pop performers including Frank Sinatra and Jo Stafford.[19] Preston Love and Tapscott worked together in the West Coast Motown band backing up Diana Ross, the Temptations, the Four Tops, and other Motown acts when they toured California, Oregon, and Washington during the 1960s and 1970s.[20] The dancing performed by the Motown acts on these tours was choreographed by Cholly Atkins under the supervision of stage manager Maurice King, a former jazz saxophone player who first met Preston Love backstage at the Apollo Theatre in New York in 1944 when Love played alto saxophone for the Lucky Millinder Orchestra and King managed the International Sweethearts of Rhythm.[21]

Trumpeter Phil Cohran played rhythm and blues in Jay McShann's band when that group was the house band for Don Robey's Duke and Peacock record labels in Houston, and he also played behind blues singer Walter Brown. Later Cohran worked with jazz composer Oliver Nelson and played trumpet in Sun Ra's Arkestra before founding the Afro Arts Theatre in Chicago to produce plays, poetry, films, theatre, dance, and music. The Artistic Heritage Ensemble started by Cohran later became the Pharaohs, who in turn provided the nucleus for the rhythm and blues jazz fusion group Earth, Wind, and Fire. Cohran invented an amplified *mbira* that he called the "frankiphone" (named after his mother "Frankie" Cohran). Earth, Wind, and Fire's Maurice White never played music with Cohran, but he heard him play many times and became skilled on the electric thumb piano because of his admiration for Cohran's playing.[22]

The grand narrative of modernity, nationalism, and alienated artistry presented by *Jazz* is understandable and plausible but incomplete. Yet its perspectival partiality is not random, but rather a way of serving a pernicious set of interests. The film purports to honor modernist innovation, social struggle, and artistic indifference to popular success, yet its own form is calculatedly conservative and commercial. *Jazz* is a "Darby Hicks" history of jazz that interpellates viewers as consumers rather than creators. The important history of jazz has already happened, it tells us. Jazz's consummate artists are already known and its effects already incorporated into the glory of the nation state. There is nothing left for viewers to do but to honor—and, more important, to *purchase*—relics and souvenirs of an art greater than ourselves. Darby Hicks has decreed that all the great art has already happened.

Consequently, the film is a spectator's story aimed at generating a canon to be consumed. Viewers are not encouraged to make jazz music, to support contemporary jazz artists, or even to advocate jazz education. But they are urged to buy the nine-part home video version of *Jazz* produced and distributed by Time Warner AOL, the nearly twenty albums of recorded music on Columbia/Sony promoting the show's artists and "greatest hits," and the book published by Knopf as a companion to the broadcast of the television program underwritten by General Motors. Thus a film purporting to honor modernist innovation actually promotes nostalgic satisfaction. The film celebrates the centrality of African Americans to the national experience but voices no demands for either rights or recognition on behalf of contemporary African American people. The film venerates the struggles of alienated artists to rise above the formulaic patterns of commercial culture, but comes into existence and enjoys wide exposure only because it works so well to augment the commercial reach and scope of a fully integrated marketing campaign linking "educational" public television to media conglomerates.

Horace Tapscott's autobiography, *Songs of the Unsung*, offers an alternative to the Darby Hicks history of jazz. Even the titles of the two works reflect the profound difference between them: *Jazz* is encyclopedic, comprehensive, and canonical, while *Songs of the Unsung* searches for the obscured, the underappreciated, and the as yet unknown. Tapscott's opening sentences do not reference the New York skyline of *Jazz,* but instead start the story in the segregated hospital named after Confederate leader Jefferson Davis in Houston, Texas where he was born. Tapscott does not designate the modernist city of immigrant and exiled artists meeting each other through their work as the crucible of jazz, but instead details the ways in which his neighbors in the Houston ghetto (and later in Los Angeles) nurtured and sustained a musical culture. The film *Jazz* opens with Wynton Marsalis claiming that "jazz objectifies America," while *Songs of the Unsung* starts with Tapscott telling us that with his birth he "was locked here on this earth." While *Jazz* delivers a story about heroic individuals, Tapscott's autobiography delineates a collective world "where everyone was family," where the goal was to "gain some respect as a whole people," where "we had to learn things in groups," and where "how many mentors you'd have in a day was impossible to count."[23]

Songs of the Unsung presents jazz as the conscious product of collective activity in decidedly local community spaces. The modernist city and the nation pale in significance in Tapscott's account in comparison to the home, the neighborhood, and the community. Physical spaces far more specific than the "city" shaped his encounter with music, and these spaces had meaning because they were connected to a supportive community network. Tapscott remembers his mother placing the family piano inside the front door of their home in Houston "so when you came in my house, you had to play the piano to get to the couch."[24] The family moved to Los Angeles in 1943 when Horace was nine, and his mother immediately connected him to resources in the black community. As soon as they got off the train at Union Station she arranged to have them taken to meet Horace's new teacher, Harry Southard, a barber who lived at 52nd and Central. "We hadn't gotten to the house yet," Tapscott recalls in wonder. "I don't know where I live. And before we get there I'm introduced to my music teacher."[25]

Like many of his fellow musicians, Tapscott drew inspiration from the city itself, from the sights and sounds on Central Avenue, the ghetto's main thoroughfare in those days. It was not just that a network of neighborhood musicians played together in high school bands and orchestras and then became employed in Central Avenue clubs, but rather that the avenue itself pulsated with the sounds of jazz. Buddy Collette and Charles Mingus lived on 96th Street and 108th Street, respectively, but often had to take a streetcar to rehearse with bands downtown. Mingus would frequently carry the bass on his back to 103d Street where he and Collette could catch the Pacific Electric interurban Red Cars downtown. Collette recalled, "Mingus was so excited about playing, he'd get on the car and zip the cover off his bass, and we'd start jamming on the streetcar. . . . He was always a very open guy with his thoughts: 'Let's play! Are we gonna play today?' And I'd say 'Well, OK,' and get the alto out, and the conductor and the motorman would wave—they didn't mind."[26]

Like so many of the artists described in *Jazz*, Horace Tapscott immigrated to a big city and found fellowship within a community of musicians. But the subject position he developed from those experiences was the polar opposite of the isolated heroic individual artist celebrated by *Jazz*. He learned to think of himself as a responsible part of a larger collectivity. After he graduated from high school, his mother and sister saved up money to send him to the prestigious Julliard School of Music in New York, his sister's share coming from the money she had been saving for her own college education. But Tapscott turned down their offer because he felt he would be giving up too much by leaving his community. "No thank you," he told them. "I appreciate it. I love you. But I have the best right here. You already put me in the best atmosphere, and I can't leave. It was SWU, 'Sidewalk University,' because these cats would be on your case all the time."[27]

Tapscott's sense of the links between "place" and "people" influenced the most important decision of his life. On tour with the Lionel Hampton Band, surrounded by great musicians and performing with them every night, making more money than he had ever made before, he realized he was miserable. He felt that audiences didn't really listen to the music the band played, and that the musicians were wasting their talents playing only the things that would bring them another recording date or another tour. He decided to get off the road, go home to Los Angeles, and set up a new kind of space capable of giving rise to a different kind of subjectivity.

Back in Los Angeles, Tapscott started the Pan Afrikan People's Orchestra, or, as he called it, the Ark (short for Arkestra, a spelling he borrowed from Sun Ra). The Ark was a locally based group set up to preserve, teach, show, and perform the music of black Americans and Pan-African music, "to preserve it by playing it and writing it and taking it to the community" (80). The members of the Ark taught music, theatre, poetry, art, and dance to their neighbors in South Central Los Angeles. They played concerts in the parks, in auditoriums, and in their own rehearsal space. They played every day, rarely for money, but somehow they supported themselves. "Everybody became part of the scene," Tapscott recalls. "No one was left out, and everyone felt like they were a part of it. There were people who had a lot to say and didn't have anyplace to say it" (106).

The Ark revolved around the arts, but it advanced an understanding of the arts that embedded them in the everyday life of the community. At some performances, the admission charge was a can of beans. Ark members would deliver personally the food they collected to people who were hungry "and somebody else would be happy because they'd have something to eat that day" (197). Professional artists with global reputations donated their services to the Ark including William Marshall, Marla Gibbs, and Rahsaan Roland Kirk (who told Tapscott that his mission was to see to it that every kid in the neighborhood learned to play two horns at once). But Tapscott did not acknowledge that the Ark was a success until one day when for some reason the group could not hold its usual noisy rehearsals or performances. A wino on Central Avenue stopped him and asked, "Hey man, where's our band?" By calling it "our" band, the derelict expressed the community's sense of ownership of the Ark, and to Tapscott, nothing could do more to honor their efforts (89, 143, 148).

Eager to expand their activities beyond the Arkestra, Tapscott and his group started calling themselves the Underground Musicians Association (UGMA), and later the Union of God's Musicians and Artists Ascension (UGMAA). They recognized that their pro-black and pro-Africa sentiments made them unwelcome in white supremacist America, "because we played and talked about being black, about Africa, about preserving our culture, it scared them," he recalls (88). But it was not just race consciousness that made the UGMA seem subversive, it was their distance from the heroic individualism so celebrated in *Jazz*. Tapscott observes,

> In those early days, UGMA became a very dangerous commodity to the community, because of our comradeship and because of what we were saying about what was happening in the community. People started caring about each other and that was dangerous. We watched each other's back and took care of each other as a group. That became intimidating, to the point where we were called a gang or a 'perversion against the country.' Everywhere we went, the whole group would be with me. We'd be in cars, four or five of us, all the time, and we'd go to places together, not only to play but also to listen. (IBID.)

The sense of collectivity that UGMA cultivated was not only physical. The group ran classes for children in reading, writing, and spelling as well as instruction in playing instruments, singing, and drawing. They were rooted in their local community, but from that vantage point they developed a global perspective. Newspapers from all over the world appeared at the UGMA house, and visiting speakers provided firsthand reports of struggles by oppressed people around the globe. "Our concern was our particular area and black people," Tapscott recalls, but we sympathized with people's struggles around the world" (90). Saying that "jazz objectifies America" as Wynton Marsalis did would not necessarily be a compliment to jazz from Tapscott's perspective. Instead, in his account, America becomes the local point of entry into a wider world. For example, remembering concerts that he played with pianist Andrew Hill in Oakland, California, Tapscott recalls "this young Chinese kid sitting up front and bowing to me. . . . He said his name was Jon Jang" (182). Tapscott relates that moment as the start of his friendship with Jang, now one of the world's leading composers. They collaborated on the 1998 Asian American Jazz Festival, for which Tapscott wrote an original piece, "The Two Shades of Soul." Tapscott claims, "Chinese music has never been foreign to me, because I can hear a lot of things within it." But, by way of elaboration, he then makes a social point, remembering, "When I was growing up in Houston, there was a Chinese guy who used to run the local food store across the street from us and who would let us have food when we needed it just by signing a piece of paper. He was the first Asian I'd seen in my life. I've never forgotten that and have always felt a kind of kinship with the Chinese people" (ibid.).

The new spaces created by the Ark encouraged the formation of new subject positions. Tapscott did not believe that autonomy was a proper goal for art—quite the contrary. His compositions and playing (first on the trombone and later on the piano) drew upon a rhythmic complexity he gleaned from everyday life, from the way people walked down the street to the rhythmic patterns of work. "Every time I write something, it's about what I've been a part of or seen," he maintained. "If the community changes, then so goes the music" (200).

Songs of the Unsung presents a story about jazz that contains no linear developmental narrative, no canon of great art or artists, and no embrace of modernist time or American space. It rejects the idea of the isolated and alienated artist, investing meaning in the power of art to transform social relations and our sense of the self. "Our music is contributive, rather than competitive," Tapscott insisted, and a contributive person is someone far less likely to be hurt by Darby Hicks than a competitive one would be.

To fans of *Jazz*, Horace Tapscott's story probably seems eccentric and parochial, little more than an engaging footnote to the real history of the art. But the particularities of Tapscott's tale should not detract our attention from the more general truths it contains. Racism might just be the particular historical obstacle in the way of artistic genius to Wynton Marsalis, but it is a part and parcel of the music business to Horace Tapscott. From his perspective, the music industry does not just happen to reflect a legacy of racism that exists outside it in the broader society, rather one of the core functions of the music industry and its categories is to produce and reproduce racism every day. Collective improvisation may be a wonderful artistic metaphor for social relations in Wynton Marsalis's universe, but it is a form of social organization and oppositional struggle in Horace Tapscott's world.

Modernist time, American space, and heroic artistry cannot be considered universal simply because they claim universal validity. Preston Love, Horace Tapscott's band mate in the Motown West Coast touring band of the 1960s, provides a perspective very similar to Tapscott's in his splendid autobiography *A Thousand Honey Creeks Later: My Life in Music From Basie to Motown and Beyond*.[28] Unlike the linear development of jazz from New Orleans to Chicago to New York that Ken Burns and Wynton Marsalis use to connect jazz to the modernist city, Love tells the history of jazz from the vantage point of a working musician in Honey Creek, Iowa; Guthrie, Oklahoma; Big Spring, Texas; Alma, Nebraska; St. Cloud, Minnesota; and Roswell, New Mexico. He recognizes Minneapolis and Albuquerque as key venues in the life of Lester Young. Love pays proper tribute to jazz greats he encountered in his life as a musician—Jo Jones, Freddie Green, Lester Young, Count Basie, and Dizzy Gillespie—but he also argues for the value of spontaneous moments when unheralded players reached extraordinary heights, like the chord changes that he heard George Salisbury play one night at the College Inn in Boulder, Colorado, the alto saxophone solo by Frank Sleet on Jimmy Witherspoon's "T'Ain't Nobody's Business," and Buster Coates's innovative playing on electric bass in small jazz clubs in Amarillo, Texas and Clovis, New Mexico in 1955.[29]

The life and career of Sun Ra also testifies to the limits of thinking about jazz as coterminous with modernist time, American space, and artistic heroism. Sun Ra refused to acknowledge that he had a birthday or even a year in which he was born, demurring, "Me and time never got along so good—we just sort of ignore each other."[30] Although observers noted his close resemblance to Herman "Sonny" Blount, born in Birmingham, Alabama on May 22, 1914, Sun Ra did not claim Alabama, America, or even the planet Earth as his space. "I had this touch of sadness in the midst of other people's parties," he explained. "Other people were having a good time, but I would have a moment of loneliness and sadness. It puzzled me, therefore I had to analyze that, and I decided I was different, that's all. I might have come from somewhere else."[31] He claimed "somewhere else" was outer space, perhaps Saturn. He encapsulated his strategic disidentification with modernist time, American space, and artistic individualism all in one sentence when he told an interviewer, "Liberty, too, is not all it's cracked up to be; even the liberty bell is cracked, for that matter, and it was liberty that led people to the use of crack."

Of course, the versions of jazz narrated by Horace Tapscott, Sun Ra, and Preston Love are also partial, perspectival, and interested. The collectivity Tapscott celebrates included women, but in subordinate and secondary roles. Sun Ra's Arkestra was a dictatorship, not a democracy, an aggregation in which the band leader determined what clothes band members could wear, what instruments they would play, and even what color the walls would be in the hotel rooms where they stayed. Preston Love's pantheon includes Billie Holiday, Aretha Franklin and Big Mama Thornton but not Melba Liston, Clora Bryant, Alma Hightower, or Vi Redd.

At stake here is not just an issue of a comprehensive mainstream narrative versus the eccentric tales told by imaginative outsiders. Our entire understanding of music may hinge on what kinds of histories we valorize. Christopher Small rightly urges us to learn from the great African traditions that inform jazz music, to "learn to love the creative act more than the created object," and to not let our respect for the relics of the past inhibit our capacity to create culture relevant to our own experiences.[32] The history of jazz as creative act rather than created object can be represented in an infinitely diverse and plural number of equally true narratives.

Instead of the linear progression from genius to genius and the constant references to Bach that propelled Ken Burns's film, it would be possible to present the history of jazz through many different narratives, perhaps as a history of rhythmic time created in unexpected places. This is a history that might include the Whitman Sisters as well as the Four Step Brothers, Josephine Baker and Mae Barnes as well as Buck and Bubbles, Shorty Snowden and Big Bea as well as Stretch Jones and Little Bea.

Instead of modernist time, this would be a history of dance time, starting with ragtime, not as a showcase for the personal "genius" of Scott Joplin but as a site where African attitudes toward rhythm (and polyrhythm) became prominent in U.S. popular culture. The difference between the rhythmic concepts in ragtime's right-hand melodies and left-hand bass accompaniment and the genre's additive rhythms (eight semiquavers divided into 2/3s and 1/2s) evidenced a taste for multiple patterns at the same time that it opened the door for future rhythmic innovations.[33] Rather than the era that gave rise to Dixieland and swing, the 1920s and 1930s could be see as a movement from the fox-trot to the jitterbug and lindy hop.[34] More than a way to distribute music more effectively to a broader audience, the development of electrical recording techniques would be seen as a shift that enabled bass and drums to replace tuba and banjo as the key sources of rhythm. Such a story would feature the tap dancing of John "Bubbles" Sublette, who was dancing "four heavy beats to the bar and no cheating" fourteen years before the Count Basie band came east and popularized swing.[35] This narrative would honor the moment in 1932 when Bennie Moten began to generate a different kind of rhythm and momentum for dancers by replacing the banjo with the guitar and substituting the string bass for the tuba.[36] The transition from swing to bop in this story would not focus on the emergence of the saxophone over the trumpet or the small ensemble over the big band as much as it would highlight how string bass players and frontline instrumentalists began to assume responsibility for keeping time so that drummers could be free to experiment with polyrhythms and provide rhythmic accents for soloists.[37]

The distinctive creators of "dance time" would not be the virtuoso instrumentalists of modernist time but rather virtuoso "conversationalists" like drummer Max Roach and dancers Earl Basie (better known by his stage name, Groundhog) and Baby Laurence. "I learned a lot listening to Hog's feet," Roach acknowledged, explaining that the multiple tones and variations in pitch that he produced on the drums were simulations of how Groundhog dropped his heels and stamped his feet. For his part, Groundhog claimed that "Max taught me how to drum paradiddles when he was working with Benny Carter. I lie in bed and listen to a metronome for two hours every night, inventing new combinations. I don't like to repeat a step unless it's necessary to help the audience catch on."[38] Roach usually reserved his collaborations with Baby Laurence for an "encore" in which the drummer and dancer would exchange rhythms through "call and response."[39]

Horace Tapscott took some of his time signatures from the rhythms that he encountered on Central Avenue, not in the performances of other musicians, but in the pace of people carrying out their everyday chores and tasks. "When I'm walking down the street I might do something in five or I might do something in six that could run into five," he explained, adding, "I might see somebody walking and think what time is that. Every day, you see different patterns and rhythms going on, and it's just paying attention to what's around you."[40]

From the perspective of modernist time, Sun Ra's contributions to jazz might seem small. But from the vantage point of dance time, his attitudes toward rhythm make him an important part of a broader collective artistic effort to change the relationships between the drums and the rest of the orchestra, to put the drums up front. He objected to composers who wrote melodies but left it up to the musicians playing drums, bass, and piano to provide the rhythm. "For me," he explained, the note is in my mind at the same time as the rhythm, My music is a music of precision. I know exactly the rhythm that must animate my music, and only this rhythm is valid."[41] His band once included as many as five drummers, not to mention the bells, congas, tympani, timbales, and other rhythm instruments that he distributed to horn and reed players.[42] During the recording session that ultimately produced *Island of the Sun*, one of the Arkestra's regular drummers could not play the rhythm that Sun Ra wrote for him. The composer and band leader asked the drummer's female companion, a dancer, to play the part and she got it immediately.[43]

When critics described his music as "far out," Sun Ra replied that "there's humor in all my music. It always has rhythm. No matter how far out I may be, you can always dance to it."[44] Such a history might even have room for the rhythmic and sonic achievements of hip hop, techno, electronica, and other contemporary forms built around the sounds of drums, bass guitars, and the fat sonic booms of Roland TR-808 drum machines.

By telling the history of jazz through the dialogic and collective inventions and improvisations of dancers and drummers, as part of a process that moved the drums "up front," we would have a useful alternative to the heroic narrative of modernist time, American space, and artistic virtuosity authored by Ken Burns, Wynton Marsalis, Stanley Crouch, and Albert Murray. Both histories are "true" in the sense that they rely on presenting verified facts in a linear chronology and fashion a developmental narrative about changing forms of musical expression. But the two stories lead us in very different directions. The heroic narrative is designed as a genealogy of elitist blackness. It was consciously designed to counter the perceived excess of democratic thinking among black intellectuals, as Marsalis argued when he contended that black professionals "are so gullible and worried about being accused of not identifying with the man in the street that they refuse to discern with the interest in quality that makes for a true elite."[45] This black elite, like the white elite it hopes to join, derives its legitimacy precisely from its distance from the majority of the population. For Wynton Marsalis, "the biggest problem with democracy, and with our education, is that every opinion becomes law and fact, just because it exists. . . . Yet we mustn't forget that beneath all those opinions there is an underlying truth and reality."[46]

One might also say, however, that "all those opinions" evidence multiple, conflicting, and contradictory realities and truths. Efforts to identify and honor a classical black tradition in a country historically ruled by elite whites follow an understandable and ideologically overdetermined logic. Yet there is more to be learned from the history and enduring creativity of black music than this. Los Angeles newspaper editor Charlotta Bass used to urge her constituents to look beyond the desire to see "dark faces in high places," to think about how the exclusion of blacks from full citizenship and social membership in U.S. society was symptomatic of larger problems that could not be cured by integration alone, that called instead for fundamentally new ways of knowing, thinking, and being. The true genius of black music has not been confined to the production of individual "geniuses," but rather has been manifest in the plurality of new social relationships that the music has helped bring into being. The created objects and creative artists celebrated in *Jazz* do not tell us enough about the broader African American imagination and activism that gave them determinate shape. As Vincent Harding explains, "This people has not come through this pain in order to attain equal opportunity with the pain inflictors of this nation and this world. It has not been healed in order to join the inflictors of wounds. There must be some other reason for pain than equal opportunity employment with the pain deliverers."[47]

With its compression of modernist time, American space, and artistic struggle, the opening sequence of Ken Burns's *Jazz* captures a part of the truth about the history of jazz. But I suggest we turn to another compression of time, space, and struggle for an even truer and more useful understanding. It occurs in a story that Clora Bryant tells in an oral history interview about jazz on Central Avenue, a story that encapsulates more of the actual history of jazz in this country than all ten episodes of *Jazz*. Bryant related how hard it was to get paid by Curtis Mosby, owner of Central Avenue's Club Alabam. Mosby promised musicians good wages but was slow to keep his promises. Some times he would pay the right amount to keep in good standing with the musicians' union, but then demand kickback from artists before he'd let them play again. As Bryant tells it, one night blind singer Al Hibbler came to the club to demand money that Mosby owed him. "You'd better give me my money or I'll shoot you," Hibbler screamed, drawing a pistol from his pocket. Then evidently remembering that his vision was impaired, Hibbler shouted, "Say something so I'll know where you are."[48]

One joke about one artist and one club owner on one night in one city might not seem like an adequate substitute for the monumental reach and scope of *Jazz*. But Al Hibbler's anger helps us see a side of the music business and the American dream that was largely absent from Ken Burns's film. It may be true that jazz objectifies America, but it does so at least as powerfully through the promises that it breaks as the ones it keeps. Even Darby Hicks knew that.

1. There have been at least two people named Darby Hicks in show business, a Cajun singer and a dancer from Chicago, but *this* Darby Hicks comes from the folklore of the streets—a character who sleeps with other men's wives and girlfriends, something like the "Jody" character in the folklore of U.S. military personnel in the mid-twentieth century.

2. Douglas Henry Daniels, *Lester Leaps In: The Life and Times of Lester "Pres" Young* (Boston: Beacon, 2002), 69, 72, 101, 128.

3. Ibid., 33.

4. See, for example, Earl Lewis, *In Their Own Interests: Race, Class, and Power in Twentieth-Century Norfolk, Virginia* (Berkeley: University of California Press, 1991).

5. Farah Jasmine Griffin, *Who Set You Flowin'? The African American Migration Narrative* (New York: Oxford University Press, 1995).

6. Karen Bennett, "An Audience with Dollar Brand," *Musician*, March 1990, 41

7. Eric Porter, *What Is This Thing Called Jazz? African American Musicians as Artists, Critics, and Activists* (Berkeley: University of California Press, 2002), 78.

8. Quoted in Daniels, *Lester Leaps In*, 34.

9. John F. Szwed, *Space Is the Place: The Lives and Times of Sun Ra* (New York: Da Capo, 1997), 236.

10. Porter, *What Is This Thing Called Jazz?* 26–32; Sherrie Tucker, *Swing Shift: "Al-Girl" Bands of the 1940s* (Durham: Duke University Press, 2000); Ingrid Monson, "The Problem with White Hipness: Race, Gender, and Cultural Conceptions in Jazz Historical Discourse," *Journal of the American Musicological Society* 48 (Fall 1995): 397–422.

11. Porter, *What Is This Thing Called Jazz?* 135.

12. Robin D. G. Kelley, "Dig They Freedom: Meditations on History and the Black Avant Garde," *Lenox Avenue* 3 (1997): 18.

13. Daniels, *Lester Leaps In*, 130.

14. Ibid., 383, 158–59.

15. Marshall and June Stearns, *Jazz Dance: The Story of American Vernacular Dance* (New York: Da Capo, 1994), 234.

16. Daniels, *Lester Leaps In*, 94.

17. Ibid., 154, 158, 273.

18. Tapscott, *Songs of the Unsung*, 14.

19. Daniels, *Lester Leaps In*, 102.

20. Tapscott, *Songs of the Unsung*, 129–30.

21. Preston Love, *A Thousand Honey Creeks Later: My Life in Music from Basie to Motown and Beyond* (Hanover and London: Wesleyan/University Press of New England, 1997), 161. Tapscott, *Songs of the Unsung*, 129–30.

22. Clovis E. Semmes, "The Dialectics of Cultural Survival and the Community Artist: Phil Cohran and the Afro-Arts Theater," *Journal of Black Studies* 24.4 (June 1994): 449, 451, 452, 457, 458.

23. Tapscott, *Songs of the Unsung*, 1, 4, 27.

24. Ibid., 13.

25. Ibid., 18.

26. Robert Gordon, *Jazz West Coast* (London: Quartet, 1986), 38.

27. Tapscott, *Songs of the Unsung*, 29.

28. Love, *A Thousand Honey Creeks Later*.

29. Ibid., 57, 235, 144.

30. Szwed, *Space is the Place*, 5

31. Ibid., 6

32. Christopher Small, *Music of the Common Tongue: Survival and Celebration in African American Music* (Hanover: Wesleyan/University Press of New England, 1998), 72.

33. Ibid., 269.

34. Stearns, *Jazz Dance*, 1.

35. Ibid., 215.

36. Ibid., 325.

37. Lewis Erenberg, *Swingin' the Dream: Big Band Jazz and the Rebirth of American Culture* (Chicago: University of Chicago Press, 1998), 229.

38. Stearns, *Jazz Dance*, 345.

39. Jacqui Malone, *Steppin' on the Blues* (Urbana: University of Illinois Press, 1996), 95, cited in John Mowitt, *Percussion: Drumming, Beating, Striking* (Durham: Duke University Press, 2002), 88.

40. Tapscott, *Songs of the Unsung*, 178–79.

41. Szwed, *Space Is the Place*, 235.

42. Ibid., 143.

43. Ibid., 113.

44. Ibid., 236.

45. Cited in Porter, *What Is This Thing Called Jazz?* 310.

46. Cited ibid., 307.

47. Vincent Harding, "Responsibilities of the Black Scholar to the Community," in Darlene Clark Hine, ed., *The State of Afro-American History: Past, Present, and Future* (Baton Rouge: Louisiana State University Press, 1986), 281.

48. Clora Bryant, Buddy Collette, William Green, Steven Isoardi, Jack Kelson, Horace Tapscott, Gerald Wilson, and Marl Young, *Central Avenue Sounds: Jazz in Los Angeles* (Berkeley: University of California Press, 1998), 356.

SALIM WASHINGTON

"All the Things You Could Be by Now": *Charles Mingus Presents Charles Mingus* and the Limits of Avant-Garde Jazz

The entire history of jazz, with its rapid advancements of styles and genres, could be understood as an avant-garde movement. As historians attempt to frame jazz as the quintessential American music, it has become a symbol of United States culture and is beginning to gain some of the intellectual prestige and institutional support previously reserved for the European art music tradition. As the more celebrated cultural and educational institutions of the country help jazz gain the reputation of a respectable, bourgeois art, its official face accepts an increasingly restrictive view of what is "real jazz" and what is not. This is not only a matter of personnel and repertoire but also of aesthetic criteria and social/political orientation. The emerging canon of jazz history frames jazz as an American music rather than as an African American music.[1] No widely accepted jazz history text denies that the music is an African American creation, or that most of its innovators have been black. In many dominant narratives, however, certain black social and aesthetic practices are routinely marginalized, if not rendered invisible. One way that these important emphases tend to be lost or misrepresented is by severing the avant-garde character from the mainstream of the music. Rather than explain avant-garde aesthetics as a primary *principle* of the music, jazz writers and critics have often chosen to isolate the avant-garde as a *style* practiced by a fringe element of the jazz community.[2]

With the normative influence of repertoire bands like the Lincoln Center Jazz Orchestra, recording canons such as the Smithsonian jazz compilations, and "official" histories such as Ken Burns's film documentary *Jazz*, there is a diminution of the perceived connection between jazz's canonical performances and recordings and its avant-garde tradition, a maneuver that has caused a profound misreading of the aesthetic values of the music. This essay looks at Charles Mingus's 1960 recording *Charles Mingus Presents Charles Mingus* as an example of how an established jazz musician can fruitfully engage the history of the music without relinquishing the aesthetic and ethical concerns traditionally associated with the jazz avant-garde.

An Avant-Garde Tradition: Jazz's First Century

Jazz at its best has always been a perpetual avant-garde movement in at least two ways. Jazz musicians have conducted a continuous search for expansion of the formal parameters available for artistic expression and have often related these breakthroughs in "structures of feeling" to a simultaneous yearning for progress in the concomitant social arrangements of its society. Still a young art, jazz has almost built-in aesthetic preferences for the new sound or novel approach. This century has seen an astonishing rate of development in jazz's musical parameters, including orchestration, instrumental and vocal timbre, harmony, and rhythm, making the jazz enterprise an exciting terrain for formalists. Nevertheless, the ongoing project to create a canonical history of the music has made it easier to posit a *permanent* avant-garde in jazz music than it has to support the notion of jazz as a *perpetual* avant-garde tradition.

More than an artistic expression, jazz, writ large, is a set of cultural products and *processes* that provide insight into the way African Americans do and feel things even as it models their higher aspirations simply as a part of humanity. Its most compelling claim to be avant-garde in the best sense is that it has modeled an artistic and aesthetic vision that seeks a more democratic and egalitarian social praxis. The permanent avant-garde is ostensibly more narrowly defined primarily according to its formal properties and not by its spiritual intent, political content, or social-aesthetic agency.

The attempt to posit an apolitical aesthetic for the avant-garde by certain canon makers and institutions that are seeking to define the tradition, however, is in itself a political stance. As long as jazz's putative political content is confined to a liberal democratic vision that valorizes the triumph of the assertive, ingenious individual, it can be touted as representative of American ideals. Within these limits even the troubling, racialized subjectivity of black jazz artists can be useful in this regard as witnessed by the State Department's willingness to employ artists such as Louis Armstrong and Dizzy Gillespie as cultural ambassadors fighting on the perceptual front of the Cold War. The cultural range of black jazz artists is necessarily wide and certainly includes musicians whose allegiance to American liberalism is less laden with tricksterlike irony than is the case with these two trumpeters. Wynton Marsalis's wholesale adoption of the American nationalism espoused by Albert Murray and Stanley Crouch, as evidenced by Marsalis's various writings and his commentary and voice-overs in *Jazz* is a case in point.

While the underrepresentation of black cultural and intellectual achievement in the U.S. is a serious issue, what is at stake here is not the ethnicity of jazz musicians or the various racial subtexts attending the making of jazz icons. Rather, with this erasure, representations of the music's aesthetic/social criteria and meanings are even more vulnerable to distortion. For instance, I think of my own musical experiences growing up in the Church of God in Christ where the profundity of a musical experience was measured by the extent to which it facilitated bringing down the Holy Ghost and not by technical considerations such as a musician's virtuosity.[3] In this setting, if the music enhances the purpose of the social event and helps the people attain greater involvement in it, *then* it is good music. Without this "anointing," it is just music. This type of criteria for accessing art is quite different from the model of the heroic improviser (or, sticking to the paradigm more closely, the composer) who overcomes his or her alienation to create masterpieces of modernity. Oftentimes, for black people—and this is the case for jazz as much as it is for "gospel"—the success of the music/dance/spiritual event is determined by all the participants of the event and not simply the person formally designated as "the artist." When the artists who were officially frozen as the permanent avant-garde tried to invoke this aesthetic in their music and philosophy, they were often dismissed as "crow-jim" racists.[4]

The historiography of jazz, with notable exceptions, adopts a "great man" theory of art primarily because it frames the music as an extension of American modernity and valorizes the heroic individual who sublimates his alienation to create triumphant art that give testament to (usually) his genius. Black musicians in America are not immune to American modernism but are not as bound by it, as the historical accounts would suggest, either. As Farah Jasmine Griffin elucidates in her study of black migration narratives, *Who Set You Flowin'?* African Americans are not such traditionalists that they live in the past, but black folk thought invokes "talkative ancestors." She explains that since black thought, and even black genius, is not valorized by other folk, black folk have had to keep their ancestors alive even as they embrace modernity.[5] This dual focus is very self-consciously present in much of the music that became tagged as a permanent jazz avant-garde. Consider, for example, the slogan of the Art Ensemble of Chicago (AEC), "Great Black Music, Ancient to the Future." So, while the AEC revived polyphony and chants in their music, they do not do so in the fashion of the great repertory ensembles. Importantly, the AEC does *not* sound like a New Orleans band or a traditional West African ensemble, though they definitely invoke the spirits of those times and places. When the importance of this avant-garde aesthetic that converses with the ancestors is minimized within the historical account, it is easy to lose sight of the social force toward which black music normally aspires. By interpreting the innovations of emerging jazz artists as primarily a revolt against constricting forms and hackneyed expressions, critics and historians deemphasize the extent to which the work of these artists engages in an ideological battle against the political status quo.

The most subtle, and most powerful, opposition to the players whose music precipitated the present-day compartmentalization of jazz's avant-garde spirit openly acknowledges the importance of a host of social, cultural, and economic factors. Several authors discuss the social ramifications of the music with great insight while maintaining the importance of considering the *craft* of the art form first in jazz criticism.[6] Their dismissal of jazz's official avant-garde does not stem from their inability to see the social/aesthetic nexus in the music, but rather from their specific ideological differences with both black nationalism and Marxism.[7] This point goes to the heart of the difference between the historical (European) avant-garde and the jazz avant-garde tradition. The historical avant-garde, in its seeking to shake up the foundations of the art world, strove to separate itself from the traditions upon which they were commenting. By contrast, jazz artists—of all stripes—have not tried to flaunt their prestige and artistic standing or mock the sacred aura of the art world, but have instead been preoccupied with attaining the prestige that European art music routinely enjoys.[8] Ideological battles between musicians and critics and others in the jazz industry did not begin with the young musicians of the 1960s, and black jazz musicians have a glorious history of progressive politics and have consistently expressed antiracist and anti-imperialist ideas going as far back to such founding fathers as Duke Ellington and Sidney Bechet. When musicians began to formally declare their ideological alliance with Marxism and/or black nationalism, however, they were viewed as a separatist artistic movement in a sense that was akin to what happened with the historical avant-garde.[9] Thus, as jazz moves closer to a mainstream American institutional presence, the avant-garde aspects of its expression are ultimately calcified in conception, reduced to a style, and hence rendered more limited (more conservative) in its possible valences with the contemporaneous social world. By contrast, the perpetual avant-garde is about a certain attitude toward constant innovation, motivated in part by a desire for greater justice in the world. It is important to note that there is not necessarily a linear relationship between the views of the canon makers and the careers of musicians they try to exclude. Thus, certain critics used their authoritative positions to censure the expressions and careers of politically explicit artists like Abbey Lincoln for some time, while their diatribes unwittingly supported the careers of others, like Archie Shepp, even if only through increasing his notoriety and marketability by creating controversy. A similar irony may be found in the fact that in the present era the critical authority sanctioning the exclusion of an official avant-garde in jazz is headed by black Americans who prefer to emphasize individual heroism rather than the revolutionary potential or social engagement with the music.

Because jazz music (re)presents a perpetual avant-garde in both the formal/artistic sense of the term and in the social/aesthetic dimension, every major development in the music's history is associated with significant social change in the history of the nation and of African Americans in particular. The emergence of jazz as a mature art form, for example, occurs during the 1890s, a period that represents simultaneously both the nadir of African American history and perhaps its most pervasive cultural flowering.[10] Each subsequent wave of the great migrations (to use one dominant theme of African American history), out of the rural areas into industrial centers, from the South, "out West," and "up North," witnessed a progression of new artistic activity, especially in the music. In each case these musical innovations were accompanied by similar strides taking place in the social arrangements of black folks and the nation in general. Thus, the increased mobility and changed social and familial arrangements of African Americans during the postbellum period helped set the stage for the individualistic, peripatetic possibilities of the blues.[11] The 1920s new take on the amalgamation of various classes, geographies, and "races" in the U.S. subsequent to increased industrialization, the great migration, the blues craze, and the success of the jazz recording industry all contributed to making jazz a national music. These new forms and ways of performing were later studied and further transformed by composers and arrangers such as Don Redman, Jelly Roll Morton, Bubber Miley, and Duke Ellington.[12]

The next (and larger) wave of the migration, associated with World War II, witnessed similar pockets of social militancy, political organization, and cultural innovation that obtained during the earlier migrations. Both the cult of respectability and the defiant militancy that black political activists observed during the 1940s and 1950s segment of the civil rights movement had its analogue in the bebop musicians, who were at once transgressive and bourgeois.[13] At this juncture the jazz world experienced a great bifurcation between modern jazz (bebop) and black popular music (rhythm and blues). Sharing similar social spaces and the same cultural moment led to a preponderance of commonalties between the two musics, however. Formally, both bebop musicians and rhythm and blues musicians showed a strong preference for blues and "rhythm changes" as song types, and many musicians crossed over from one genre to the other, as did of course many listeners. The bebop scene was associated with greater social equality and fraternization between blacks and whites in the jazz community and continued the tradition of integration on the bandstand that had begun earlier during the swing era. While rhythm and blues was still more closely tied to black people and their terpsichorean outlook on the world, it too made inroads into mainstream culture, its very designation replacing the more segregated term *race music*.

During the 1960s the largest wave of black migration out of the South occurred, and, not surprisingly, the social and cultural changes that took place during this time were perhaps on a grander scale. If the ethos of the bebop revolutionaries reflected the patriotic yet alienated stance that produced the double V slogan of the World War II era, then the worldview of the free jazz movement was informed by, among other things, decolonization, the black power movement, the counterculture, and the antiwar movement of the Vietnam era. In each of these historical moments the musical innovations introduced into jazz were cutting-edge musical significations of the fight for freedom, not merely from staid musical conventions but also against political injustice.[14]

The music's ties to black America's social history are not limited to the progressive strains of the culture. During the politically conservative 1980s, the black bourgeoisie tripled in size and gave rise to a generation of black, conservative, superachievers. Intellectuals like Glen Loury and Thomas Sowell and public figures such as Clarence Thomas and Ward Connerly distanced themselves not only from the parochial excesses of black nationalism that black conservatives love to ridicule but also from such mainstream black political desiderata as affirmative action. A parallel rise in prominence of a neoconservative movement in jazz centered on the celebrity of Wynton Marsalis, who as spokesperson and as a musician helped revitalize the jazz tradition and bring it to the attention of mainstream America in a compelling fashion. Perhaps the most powerful jazz musician in history (in terms of institutional sponsorship and in his celebrity as a "serious" artist), Marsalis attracted young practitioners to the art and helped jazz to gain mainstream respectability. The acceptance of jazz as America's "classical" music came at a time when the black bourgeoisie was thriving and finally considered an infrangible part of the nation. At the same time, poverty grew pervasive and persistent for large numbers of blacks that were so barred from access to middle-class lifestyles and privileges they were dubbed the underclass.[15] The widespread acceptance of middle-class black America seemed to involve a tacit agreement to sacrifice the social mobility of this underclass and to render it relatively invisible and silent through a curious mixture of Moynihan-like dismissals of "tangles of pathology" andWashingtonian "bootstrap ideology." Ironically, the attitudes and aesthetics of this class produced the most vibrant and influential cultural movement of the age, hip hop. Hip hop music, especially rap, has kept alive the oppositional stance and attitude in black music at a time when jazz is on the verge of losing its transgressive edge during its bid for mainstream respectability.

Some musicians who were associated with the jazz avant-garde in earlier decades also flourished during the 1980s, though with less fanfare than that which accompanied the neoconservatives. Henry Threadgill, David Murray, and other graduates of the 1970s New York loft scene comprised a group of free-bop musicians who combined the syntax of mainstream jazz (bebop based) with the vocabularies of free jazz. Their music represented an alternative to the neo-hardboppers while at the same time encapsulating a move toward the center by erstwhile avant-garde performers. The move inside by "out" musicians[16] like Lester Bowie, who formed Brass Fantasy, a band that played renditions of pop tunes, was in part a matter of artistic vision and maturity. It can also be understood as a concession to the realities of the contemporaneous jazz industry.

From Perpetual to Permanent: The Post 1960s Jazz Avant-Garde

Of course, the avant-garde tradition did not die in jazz in the late twentieth century any more than did the revolutionary potential in social movements. Today one can point to Graham Haynes, William Parker, David S. Ware, Deidre Murrray, Charles Gayle, Mixashawm, and Pheeroan Aklaff, to name but a few musicians who maintain this type of artistic vision as jazz grows into its second century. This aspect of the jazz scene has become increasingly an underground phenomenon. One of the ways that it has been contained to a growing extent is to explain jazz as a specific set of practices, subsequently using litmus tests to determine which performances are "straight ahead" or "avant-garde" or "commercial."

The music that has become the permanent avant-garde flowered during the 1960s. The music of the holy quadrumvirate of free jazz, Cecil Taylor, Ornette Coleman, Albert Ayler, and John Coltrane, was not fundamentally opposed to a jazz mainstream but had its roots in the music that preceded it. At the time of its emergence the "New Thing" was simply a continuation of the perpetual avant-garde tradition of the music and was no more self-consciously revolutionary than the bebop of "modern music" movement. Nevertheless, the New Thing did have features that emphasized its revolutionary status. Nor did these musicians make the political connotations of their music more explicit than did previous artists, including Duke Ellington in his *Black Brown, and Beige* suite, Max Roach in the *Freedom Now Suite,* Billie Holiday in her "Strange Fruit," or Sun Ra in his metaphysical musings. The degree to which these political yearnings were made explicit in the music at the formal level, however, has in some ways rendered the New Thing a permanent avant-garde, if only because many of the practices seemingly stretched the Western systems of organization to their limits. Some musicians tried to free themselves symbolically from the hegemony of Euro-America through such means as subverting the expectations of functional tonality, abandoning tempered intonation, improvising with free meter and free tonal structures, new instrumental techniques, etc. The non-Western emphasis was underscored by incorporating musical influences from various African, Latin American, and Asian cultures.

It is the putative failure to reinvent traditional practices that causes the music that represented the New Thing of the 1960s to be stigmatized in some quarters. Because some of these musicians did not demonstrate competence in more conventional styles, their craftsmanship is in question, and, consequently, "avant-garde" is a label that connotes to many an artistic cul-de-sac played by musicians who lack the technical and conceptual rigor to continue to break new ground. The prevalence of this train of thought has caused the jazz avant-garde to be understood as a style rather than a process. Consequently, musicians such as Charles Gayle, and Matthew Shipp, whose styles are indebted to Albert Ayler and Cecil Taylor respectively, tend to be regarded as "avant-garde" even though these playing styles and techniques have been with us for four decades. Reified as a style, the now titled avant-garde is widely considered irrelevant to the true tradition, despite the fact that this genre of jazz continues to inspire generations of musicians. Whereas in the early 1960s some conservative jazz critics disparaged figures like Coltrane and Eric Dolphy for being "antijazz" in spirit, some critics and musicians of the 1980s and 1990s, following Marsalis's lead; dismiss this genre as not really being jazz music at all, good or bad, but rather an extension of European music (!).

In tandem with the historiographical creation of a permanent jazz avant-garde, bebop is simultaneously reified as the classical textus receptus of the modern jazz tradition.[17] Bebop conventions such as the harmonic language, rhythms, phrasing, and compositional and arranging practices are now found in the playing of virtually every established jazz musician, young or old. There was a time when a jazz musician could be unconventional enough to play with modernists without trying to copy their language (think of Pee Wee Rusell's idiosyncratic clarinet stylings with the likes of Eric Dolphy or Max Roach). In the present era musicians who make only marginal references to the conventions of modern music are held in suspicion. In the highly competitive world of jazz, with its macho cutting contests, it is bebop and its derivatives that are called upon to determine those who can "really" play and those who cannot. On the one hand, today there is greater acceptance of the fact that there always exists a multiplicity of jazz styles; various genres of jazz have transcended generational signification(s) to become available practices that not only coexist but influence each other. And so, for example, a swing enthusiast or even a "traditional jazz" or Dixieland fan is no longer considered a "moldy fig," as they were called by bebop supporters in the 1940s. On the other hand, despite this postmodern heteroglossia, bebop remains the dominant language of jazz improvisers, and musicians who do not at least demonstrate their capabilities in this arena run the risk of being dismissed as instrumentalists whose music "is more like condiments than food."[18]

A prime example can be found in saxophonist/bass clarinetist David Murray. During the height of his considerable popularity and critical acclaim, young jazz musicians debated whether his music was "really" jazz.[19] Despite Murray's obvious debt to such canonical players as Ben Webster and Paul Gonsalves, the fact that Albert Ayler's style is fundamental to Murray's conception caused the neo-hard-boppers to hold his musicianship under suspicion. While this debate was going on, *Down Beat* magazine published a transcription of Murray's solo on "Body and Soul," a song that has been a proving ground for tenor saxophonists since Coleman Hawkins's important 1939 rendition. Anyone unable to *hear* the form in Murray's solo could read the music and *see* that Murray did indeed follow the changes of the harmonically sophisticated ballad. This did little to silence the debate, however, because ultimately those who accused players such as Murray of not being able to play changes were really casting aspersions on his ability to do so *utilizing the rhythms, melodic clichés, and cadential patterns, of bebop*. Making bebop the litmus test of jazz authenticity affects the canonization of jazz figures and has already begun to impoverish the music's historiography.

Charles Mingus: The Avant-Garde's Reluctant Father

Despite Ekkhard Jost's perceptive essay in his *Free Jazz*, Mingus is rarely associated with the avant-garde. Before becoming a bandleader, Mingus played with Louis Armstrong, Duke Ellington, and Charles Parker, *the* central figures of jazz history. An innovative bassist, bandleader, composer, and arranger, Mingus anticipated a great majority of the discoveries of acknowledged avant-garde jazz musicians, however, in some cases by years or even decades. The way he blended these innovations with traditional techniques and repertoire kept all formal possibilities open and, like the music of his mentor, Ellington, resists easy categorization. His arrangements did not lend themselves to being perceived as stylistically fixed renditions to the same degree as the music of the major figures of the New Thing. In fact, Mingus's music represents the ideal of the perpetual avant-garde because he never relinquished the other aspects of his musical personality to make way for the new as did our quadrumvirate of universally acknowledged avant-garde innovators.

Mingus described himself as a disciple of Charles Parker, but his musical personality was too strong and his muse too varied to ever be dominated by bebop alone.

Within the group of America's greatest composers, which includes Charles Ives, Aaron Copeland, Duke Ellington, and Thelonious Monk, Mingus is the youngest, most modern, most versatile, and the least well known. Mingus is truly one of our representative composers because of the unusual breadth of his musical influences, the depth with which he assimilated them, and the degree to which he synthesized them into a personal voice, avoiding both simple mimicry and post-modern pastiche. His music is informed by the diverse jazz styles of Jelly Roll Morton (e.g., "Jelly Roll"), Duke Ellington (his sensitive treatment of "Mood Indigo" or his Strayhornesque "Duke Ellington's Sound of Love"), and Charles Parker ("Reincarnation of a Love Bird" or almost any of his improvisations), along with the gospel sounds of the Holiness Church ("Wednesday Night Prayer Meeting" or "Better Get Hit in Your Soul"), and certain aspects of Western art music, including Impressionism ("Adagio Ma Non Troppo" and especially the tone poems of Richard Strauss ["The Chill of Death"]). His assimilation of Western art music into his own sound is usually far more compelling than the rather self-conscious efforts of the third stream movement. Similarly, his appropriation of the sounds and techniques of gospel music seem more powerful and less cliché ridden than the gospel inflections of most of the hardbop composers.

The ability to incorporate such disparate styles into a recognizable voice allowed him to introduce new music forms and new approaches to jazz improvisation and composition. Ultimately, the combined legacy of his writing, playing, and bandleading amounts to a reevaluation of the relationship between the composer and the improviser, between the writer and the performing ensemble, and thus interrogates the very fabric of American musical practice in a fundamental way. This is why each Mingus ensemble sounds radically different from all others. Even when playing the same songs with different bands, rarely are they played the same way. The arrangements are different, the tempos and rhythmic patterns are usually played around with, and the forms of the compositions are variable. The willingness to make all his compositions and ensembles a work in progress (hence the name of many of his groups, the Jazz Workshop) meant that though there are certain recognizable Mingus traits—accelerandos, rhythmic shifts, collective improvisations, vamps—different bands and their differing renditions of his classics are sometimes not even remotely similar. There is not the consistency of expectation that one might have of bandleaders like Art Blakey or Horace Silver. His oeuvre is arguably more varied even than that of Duke Ellington.

Second, his music expresses the political concerns associated with the official jazz avant-garde. Through the titles of his compositions, for example, Mingus frequently placed political ideas squarely on the table. By the late 1950s some jazz musicians through their composition titles began to publicly identify with post-colonial African nations, jazz artists such as Jackie McLean played for fundraisers supporting civil rights groups, and a few musicians (Sonny Rollins, Abbey Lincoln, and Max Roach) risked censure by making recordings that explicitly referenced the contemporary freedom fight of African Americans. However, very few established jazz musicians have so consistently sported politically provocative titles such as "Meditations on Integration," "Fables of Faubus," "Remember Rockefeller at Attica," "Free Cellblock F, 'Tis Nazi USA," "Don't Let Them Drop the Atom Bomb on Me," "Haitian Fight Song," "They Trespass the Land of the Sacred Sioux," and "Once There Was a Holding Corporation Called Old America" as did Mingus. Nor did symbolism exhaust his political engagement. For instance, in 1960 with Max Roach he co-led the alternative Newport Rebels Festival in protest of the exclusionary policies of George Wein. The atmosphere of the alternative festival is documented in the later recording, *Newport Rebels,* and fruitfully combines musicians of different generations (Eric Dolphy and Roy Eldridge, for example) who were considered to be on opposite sides of the artistic divide in jazz.[20] He founded two record companies in an attempt to get musicians to tackle the source of their oppression within the political economy of the jazz industry. He published open letters to both musicians and critics revealing strong opinions about his beloved art form and the figures who created it or exerted influence upon it. He also published what is perhaps the most literarily ambitious autobiography of any jazz figure, *Beneath the Underdog,* where he not only tackled the social milieu and political ramifications of the music but also dealt with psychoanalytic theory and fictionalized philosophical discussions about aesthetics and ontology with trumpeter Theodore "Fats" Navarro. Mingus's literary work is as complex and multivariate as his music; the book is written with at least three narrative voices and changes from reportage to fantasy as quickly as he shifts between tempos and various rhythmic feels in his compositions.[21]

Having started his recording career with Louis Armstrong in 1943, Mingus reached a musical maturity before the generation of musicians that came to be known as the jazz avant-garde by twenty years. Mingus, with one of the broadest backgrounds of any musician, remained deeply suspicious of the sincerity and competence of any so-called avant-garde musician who had not proven mastery of traditional forms. Yet he produced many pieces that dealt with most of the new music's pet musical concerns and problems. For instance, he was the best polyphonic writer for big band since Ellington, as can be heard on his ten-melody masterpiece "Don't Be Afraid, the Clown's Afraid Too."[22] While most postbebop bands that improvised collectively were stylistically indebted to either Ornette Coleman's *Free Jazz* or John Coltrane's *Ascension,* Mingus's ensembles frequently employed collective improvisation in diverse styles, ranging from 1910s New Orleans ("Eat That Chicken") to 1960s free-blowing New York style, with many stops in between. As a writer Mingus frequently opened up the forms of his compositions to allow for extemporized vamps and collective improvisations, as he does, for instance, during the free-blowing solos of Don Pullen and George Adams on "Sues Changes" and "Orange Was the Color of Her Dress, Then Silk Blue."[23] This is one way that he ensures that each ensemble will give a fresh interpretation of his music. While apparently some musicians rebelled and resorted to his written parts, Mingus, like Thelonious Monk, preferred to teach his compositions by ear. This allowed the sidemen to interpret the music more naturally and freely. Playing arco bass along with Eric Dolphy on flute, he subtly utilized microtones in his composition "Meditations on Integration" (also known as "Praying with Eric").[24] The passage containing the duet is but one "movement" in an extended piece that mostly uses tempered tuning. All of these techniques, open-ended forms for extended collective improvisations, the focus on orality, and nontempered tunings, became the specialty of later groups identified as avant-garde and "out" musicians. The important difference in Mingus's use of these techniques is not just that he used them earlier but that he used them as procedures available for the presentation of a wider spectrum of music. They were not primarily used for shock value, nor were they regarded as revelations, but rather as specific solutions for an ever changing set of musical contexts.

Mingus on occasion used poetry with his music, as did the more politically minded members of the acknowledged avant-garde. He could write the poetry himself, as he did in "The Chill of Death" (first released almost three decades after its first recording), or collaborate with a distinguished poet such as Langston Hughes.[25] In his recording *The Clown* Jean Shepherd improvised the story line of Mingus's poem as the musicians played the suite.[26] These collaborations eventually produced hybrid forms in which the musical, improvisatory, and textual aspects were in dialogue with each other, exceeding earlier efforts by the beatniks in which the poetry and the music remained discrete elements. They are a direct precursor to the more integrated efforts made during the Black Arts movement. One of the masterpieces of this tradition, Amiri Baraka's "In the Tradition," recorded with jazz musicians David Murray and Steve McCall, is a direct heir to the example of Mingus.[27]

Charles Mingus Presents Charles Mingus: An Answer to the Permanent Avant-Garde

Ornette Coleman's music exerted a strong influence on Mingus's performance practices despite his skepticism about the saxophonist's technique. Always finding those musicians who wore the label *avant-garde* somewhat dubious when it came to mastery of the fundamentals, even his praise for Coleman contained harsh criticism. In a *Down Beat* interview with Leonard Feather, Mingus acknowledged Coleman's relevance with decidedly mixed praise:

Now aside from the fact that I doubt he can even play a C scale . . . in tune, the fact remains that his notes and lines are so fresh. So when [disc jockey] Symphony Sid played his record, it made everything else he was playing, even my own record that he played, sound terrible. I'm not saying everybody's going to have play like Coleman. But they're going to have to stop playing Bird.[28]

Mingus' disdain for the avant-garde was further explained in his "An Open Letter to the Avant-Garde."[29] He relayed a humorous incident in which he asks Ellington to make an avant-garde recording with himself, Dizzy Gillespie, Clark Terry, Thad Jones, and others "who could really play." To Mingus's delight, Ellington replied: "Why should we go back that far? Let's not take music back that far, Mingus. Why not just make a modern record?"[30] In this letter Mingus is brutal, naming names, as when he accuses Pharoah Sanders of having a lot of gimmicks. He claimed that "what they call avant-garde [is] . . . old fashion[ed] music because it's played by beginners, by people trying to learn how to play, or trying to wonder what to play to be different." The main point that Mingus drives home in this essay, rightly I think, is that the real avant-garde is not necessarily represented by the musicians with such reputations, but by musicians like himself, Duke Ellington, and Clark Terry. His bitterness shows in the same essay where he wrote: "I wanted to show what would happen if some musicians who could really play the chord changes, who could really play a tune and not get lost, were to improvise and play free—everybody do what they want to do to outdo the avant-garde."

Ultimately, with Eric Dolphy's help, Mingus was able to combine his traditional musicianship with Ornette Coleman's revolutionary concepts to produce some of his most experimental and multifaceted performances. As Brian Priestley points out, the first Dolphy/Mingus collaboration was probably made undeservedly obscure because it coincided with Ornette Coleman's New York debut.[31] If *Money Jungle* was Mingus's opportunity to showcase Duke Ellington outmodernizing the moderns, then *Charles Mingus Presents Charles Mingus* is the recording where Mingus self-consciously takes on the official jazz avant-garde on its own terrain. Coleman's influence on Mingus is most evident in this recording. It combined hard-driving jazz with experimental forms and approaches to improvisation that required all of the emotional depth and virtuosity available with the stellar lineup of Mingus, Dolphy, Ted Curson, and Dannie Richmond. With Dolphy, his favorite and most sympathetic colleague, Mingus was able to put forth an answer to the challenge represented by Coleman's music. This album also highlights the degree to which Mingus self-consciously addressed both cultural and political issues through his music. Using creative song titles, short monologues, pointed lyrics, innovative compositions, and daring arrangements, Mingus blends his musical and extramusical messages into a well-integrated whole that treats several serious subjects while allowing plenty of space for humor. While this recording was made a full decade after Mingus had begun experimenting with modal playing and collective improvisation, the breadth and depth of his usage of these and other techniques makes *Charles Mingus Presents Charles Mingus* one of the most compelling examples of why Mingus is a father of the jazz avant-garde. It contains the most explicit examples of Mingus's political views as well as his outspoken sentiments about the conditions under which he usually performed his music. It also showcases his ability to transform traditional music forms and standard materials into new expressions and is a compendium of methods for expanding the resources available to the small jazz ensemble.

One reason that this particular recording reveals so much about the political aspect of Mingus's avant-garde impulse is the prevalence of his own words as either introductions to, or as integral parts of, the songs themselves. Nowhere in Mingus' corpus is this more evident than in the lyrics to Mingus's "Original Fables of Faubus." Columbia Records (who released the first recorded version) would not release "Fables of Faubus" in its original form, with the lyrics. On the Candid version Mingus and Dannie Richmond sang the following lyrics in protest of Arkansas governor Orval E. Faubus and his attempt to prevent integration at Little Rock's Central High School:

> Oh, Lord, don't let 'em shoot us!
> Oh, Lord, don't let 'em stab us!
> Oh, Lord, don't let 'em tar and feather us!
> Oh, Lord, no more swastikas!
> Oh, Lord, no more Ku Klux Klan!
>
> Name me someone who's ridiculous, Dannie.
> Governor Faubus!
> Why is he so sick and ridiculous?
> He won't permit us in his schools.
> Then he's a fool!
>
> Boo! Nazi Fascist supremacists!
> Boo! Ku Klux Klan (with your evil plan)
> Name me a handful that's ridiculous, Dannie Richmond.
> —Faubus—Rockefeller—Eisenhower
> Why are they so sick and ridiculous?
> Two, four, six, eight: They brainwash and teach you hate.
> H-E-L-L-O—Hello!

Interestingly, the Candid version not only contains the lyrics but also sports a more raucous and avant-garde *musical* performance. The usual changes in mood and tempo that one expects from Mingus are much more prominent in the Candid version, and the emotion and inspiration behind the song are much more visceral. The Columbia version sounds tame and controlled by comparison, whereas the music of the Candid version contains the same bravado and daring that are found in the 1959 lyrics. Here is an excellent example of the ways in which, even if the same compositions are performed, they often sound like completely new ones when played by a different version of Mingus's Jazz Workshop.[32] "Fables" also highlights a fact that Mingus considered important—that he is a "spontaneous composer." His compositions are "within the category of one feeling, or rather, several feelings expressed as one," even though they typically show "changes in tempo and changes in mode, yet the variations on the theme still fit into one composition."[33] Because these compositions retain a "spontaneous" character, the changes and variations within a single performance are altered further between different performances and with different bands.

Other verbal interludes may have less direct bearing on the music itself but lend insight into the extramusical dimension of Mingus's art. Although *Charles Mingus Presents Charles Mingus* was recorded in a studio, Mingus added chatter and commentary as if he were addressing an audience at a live club date. The "nightclub chatter" contains admonitions against loud noises, sounds of cash registers, and boisterous conversations. These annoyances are the bane of many a performer, but are especially grievous during the (relatively quiet) bass solos. We know from similar passages in Mingus's autobiography, *Beneath the Underdog,* that he hated the lack of attention paid during his bass solos by musicians and audience members alike. His juxtaposition of intruding cash registers with the most poignant and sensitive moments of the performance slyly introduces a critique of some of the obvious drawbacks to the capitalist-inspired conditions that obtained in jazz clubs. This incipient critique was limited to interlude material between songs, much in the fashion of Mingus alumni Rahsaan Roland Kirk. However, these remarks are amplified through the irony of including them in a studio recording. Live recordings (as well as countless anecdotes) reveal that Mingus was also wont to include such commentary during his introductions to songs in front of real audiences. Such harangues could include topics ranging from Mingus's dissatisfaction with George Wein's arrangement of the 1964 tour with his greatest band, to his disappointment and anger toward Dolphy for deciding to leave the ensemble, to his famous introduction to "Meditations on Integration" where he makes a plea for someone to provide black people with "wirecutters" to free themselves from metaphorical concentrations camps "before someone else gets some guns to us."[34]

After introducing these concerns in his introductory chatter, Mingus announces that the first composition will be titled "Folk Forms, No. 1" on the album, in contrast to "Opus." Mingus did use the term *opus* on later recordings, perhaps to emphasize that all his music was not programmatic. Here he is signifying on the difference between the respect afforded symphonic musicians and jazz musicians, especially given his repeated entreaties for his "audience" to not applaud or make noises until the end of the composition. "Folk Forms, No. 1" is a blues. In this slow blues the quartet for twelve minutes presents seemingly endless variations on the ensemble's approach to the same material. In addition to his usual juxtaposition of 4/4 and 6/8 time feels, the quartet is broken into various combinations of duets and trios, where each instrumental voices assumes differing roles. The relationship between horn and rhythm instrument is frequently inverted here, the horn[s] providing accompaniment to the drum or bass's melody. Despite the nontempered passages, and the weird voicings and rhythmic devices, the entire piece is tightly controlled and logically developed. This performance brings to mind another work of art by an outspoken musician in Mingus's generation who admonished the out players even as he engaged them. Yusef Lateef wrote a play, "The Out Game," that featured characters by the name of "Sonny," "Coleman," "Shepp," and "LaShay."[35] In the play Coleman, Shepp, and LaShay (Prince Sasha?) speak dadaistic, nonsense syllables and nonsequiturs. There are some themes like love that seem decipherable, but the dialogue is mostly gibberish. At the end of the play Sonny comes out of a limousine and shows them where it's at, playing a slow blues on a tenor saxophone. After taking center stage, still playing, Sonny returns to the limo with the other characters in tow. Lateef's play is complicated by the multiple meanings that could be ascribed to the image of Sonny Rollins and his followers playing in a limousine. Could Lateef be commenting on the capitulation of Sonny Rollins and the others to the capitalistic interests of the music industry? Maybe not. Rollins's position as a preeminent jazz musician was secure, and he stood to gain neither prestige nor money from his association with the out players. Perhaps it is merely a reference to Sonny Rollins's actual mode of transportation (he has been known to ride in a limousine or two). Or perhaps Lateef, who grew up in one of Detroit's most notorious ghettos, uses the limousine as a symbol denoting accomplishment and ease. Combined with the blues (a slow blues), the limousine becomes a sign of working-class jazz royalty; a symbol of the increased communicative power out players' music would possess in the wisdom of a player like Rollins. Presumably, Sonny Rollins (who made the recording *Our Man in Jazz* with Ornette Coleman's sidemen Don Cherry, Charlie Haden, and Billy Higgins) teaches the well-meaning but meandering moderns to begin with the blues and to mine it for deeper under-standing of the music. In similar fashion, Mingus (as did his idol, Ellington) revis-ited the blues often for fresh approaches to the music, and begins his "set" on *Charles Mingus Presents Charles Mingus* with "Folk Forms, No. 1" in what could be seen as a didactic pose.

Continuing to pretend that he is speaking to an audience at the end of his "set," Mingus's sense of humor comes to the fore as begins his composition "All the Things You Could Be by Now if Sigmund Freud's Wife Was Your Mother" with the following chatter:

> And now, ladies and gentlemen, you have been such a wonderful audi-ence. We have a special treat in store for you. This is a composition dedi-cated to all mothers. And it's titled "All the Things You Could Be by now if Sigmund Freud's Wife was Your Mother." Which means if Sigmund Freud's wife was your mother, all the things you could be by now. Which means nothing. You got it? Thank you. [Counting the tune off] One. One, two, three . . .

Based upon the standard "All the Things You Are," "All the Things You Could Be" is a radical reworking and extension of the original materials, which are barely rec-ognizable in the finished product. In fact, when I have played this piece for college students many of them initially believe that the high energy of the performance is due to a reckless abandon that allows for emoting without intelligent decisions. Here we have Mingus's deepest joke revealed not in the title but in this example of virtuoso musicians outdoing the avant-garde. "All the Things You Could Be," for all its wildness and freshness of expression, is not susceptible to the criticism that Mingus leveled in his open letter to the avant-garde: "noise, squeaks and hollers, yells, banging bells, with no continuity to it, with no recapitulation with no form."

The band comes in at a fast pace with a thirty-six-bar introductory melody. The standard upon which it is based, "All the Things You Are," is also thirty-six bars long rather than the standard thirty-two.[36] The introduction does not adhere to the harmonic sequence of the standard, however, and is in conception and exe-cution much like the first Ornette Coleman records on Atlantic Records, which were just being released at the time. The Ornette-isms abound. The ensemble is a pianoless quartet with alto saxophone and trumpet on the front line playing unisons in the manner that Ornette Coleman and Don Cherry established. The melody, frenetic and startling, is played mostly in unison, and contains abrupt cut-off points followed by ironically simple cadences to the tonic key. The treatment of the rest of the composition shows the kind of arrangement that is typical of Mingus and includes tempo changes, metric changes, and collective improvisation. This kaleidoscopic array of feels and patterns is successful because of the unusually tight synchrony between Mingus and his inveterate colleague, drummer Dannie Richmond. The apparently telepathic communication between the two made abrupt time changes, accelerandos, and the like occur seamlessly.[37] To the uninitiated, this performance seems wild and almost uncontrolled, but it is actually quite well thought out. Space limitations do not allow for a detailed musical analysis, but the song can be represented by the following scheme:

> Melody I (played fast in the style of Ornette Coleman quartet of the late-1950s):
> 8 bar phrase (A)
> 8 bar phrase (A')
> 8 bar phrase (B)
> 12 bar phrase (A")
> Melody II (a sections played fast, each eight bar phrase cut in half, over the first half the rhythm section plays an ascending figure, the second half traditional walking over the harmonies of the standard "All the Things You Are"):
> 4 bar phrase (ascending)   4-bar phrase (standard) (A)
> 4 bar phrase (ascending)   4-bar phrase (standard) (A)
> (B Section is played slowly. The trumpet plays the melody, the saxophone plays a counterpoint line, the bass plays an obbligato, the drums play sparsely)
> 8-bar phrase (slowly, without clearly articulated pulse) (B)
> 4-bar phrase (ascending)   8-bar phrase (standard) (A')

In the space of two choruses of the song, Mingus takes the band through four different time/rhythmic feels, and two complete melodies, before starting the two improvisations by Curson and Dolphy. During the solos there are further changes; those during Curson's trumpet solo are as follows:

> Trumpet solo chorus I (the changes are the standard harmonies from "All the Things You Are." The A sections are played in 6/8 time, and very fast. B section is played very slowly in 4/4 time. The drums and bass play "stop time" during the B section, that is one heavy accent on the first beat of every measure only.)
> 8 bar phrase (6/8 time, very fast) (A)
> 8 bar phrase (6/8 time, very fast) (A)
> 8 bar phrase (4/4 time, stop time, slow) (B)
> 12 bar phrase (6/8 time, very fast) (A')
> Trumpet solo chorus II (this chorus is played in the standard fashion. The bass

walks a 4/4 in medium fast tempo and the drums give standard, straight-ahead accompaniment).

Trumpet solo chorus III (this chorus is played as a collective improvisation between the bass, drums, and trumpet. The bass and the trumpet are in the foreground, and the drums are played sparsely, as if punctuating the ideas of the other two soloing instruments).

Trumpet solo chorus IV (this chorus is played in the same fashion as chorus II, though Mingus stretches the time more during the bridge, but he does so in tension with the underlying swing, more like a conceptual counterpoint than an alternate time feel).

The saxophone solo has a similar development, after which only the first, Coleman-like melody is played, with an extended cadence or tag at the end. Curson holds the final note while Dolphy plays a series of cadences going through the cycle of fifths. Moving upwards in fifths rather than going through the more usual cycle of fourths (downward in fifths), the tag suggests that there is no final resolution.

This tribute to Coleman is in reality more of an answer to Coleman's challenge, in the sense of one-upmanship. There is the apocryphal story that Mingus told in which he sponsored an avant-garde concert performed behind a curtain for a special audience of jazz critics. When the critics give their rave reviews of the daring performance, he pulls back the curtain to reveal a bunch of kids playing on instruments that they had been given immediately prior to the performance. The story is meant to be a scathing put down of the reputed "anything goes" attitude of free jazz. That Mingus was able to glean ideas about presentation and freedom from such players without sacrificing the discipline and virtuosity of earlier musical styles is evident in the performances of "All the Things You Could Be." The solos are largely free of bop clichés, but each instrumentalist clearly demonstrates that he is able to execute harmonically complex ideas with rhythmic fluency, the apotheosis of playing bebop. All of the events are followed simultaneously with split second timing by the various members of the ensemble, and thus reveals the planning and rehearsal necessary to realize this performance. There is nothing haphazard or arbitrary at all about this faux craziness.

Mingus includes on this album another song, "What Love," that owes very little to bebop in conception or execution, though it is based very loosely on the standard "What Is This Thing Called Love?" favored by bebop players. (Charles Parker transformed it into "Hot House.") In "What Love" the organization of the small jazz ensemble is democratized, a consistent trend in jazz throughout the century. The distinction between front line (trumpet, alto saxophone) and rhythm section (bass, drums) is blurred; no longer is one the accompaniment to the other. Rather, each instrument plays a role in the music whose prominence and importance used to be reserved for the instruments carrying the melody. During the statement of the melody by the horns, the bass part is largely contrapuntal. As is typical of many Mingus's melodies, the bass line is phrased in eighth notes, liberally sprinkled with quarter-note triplets. At times Mingus plays the roots of the chord changes, at others his line is melodic, with a rhythmic density that is at par-ity with the horn lines. Curson's trumpet and Dolphy's bass clarinet play in unison with a plaintive melody that is similar in mood to Ornette Coleman's masterpiece, "Lonely Woman." The drums do not play time; rather they provide accents and accompaniments that follow the contours of the melody but do not articulate a pulse or meter. The piece is in metered time, for the most part, but here the rhythm section is not responsible for making it explicit. During the trumpet solo Dolphy in effect joins the rhythm section, playing rhythms and melodies that are apparently part of a written arrangement, helping to outline the harmonies. Again, the song has several short movements, first a drone in the bass, with very brief sections of swing played by the bass and drums, followed by unaccompanied trumpet, followed by another very abstract, arranged accompaniment with bass and bass clarinet playing in counterpoint and the drums providing punctuations to the ensemble's statements. Mingus takes an unaccompanied bass solo, during which he follows the form of the song. When the drums enter at the end of the bass solo, the bass goes to a drone as Dolphy begins his bass clarinet solo.

Eric Dolphy's solo is the climax of the piece, and may be the most startling performance of the album. The bass clarinet solo begins with the same arrangement as the trumpet solo, and then suddenly there is a duet between bass and bass clarinet. Eventually there is an interruption in the form, and the two instruments "talk." They begin with quasi-normal musical phrases and, gradually, using idiosyncratic phrasing and expanded timbral qualities, approximate actual speech patterns rather than normal musical syntax. The conversation includes banter sections with back and forth vituperations and overlapping parts as well as longer soliloquies. There are relatively calm moments of repose as well as instances of "arguments" with screeching and overblowing on the bass clarinet and slapping and bending the strings on the bass. By the end of the conversation/duet, each instrument has long left tempered tuning and any conventional sense of melodic invention.[38] Just as the listener becomes lost in this world of instrumental speech, suddenly a musical cue from the bass brings the band back together for the final statement of the melody, which is repeated at the end. The last chorus of the melody is faster and features a lush and complicated countermelody for the bass clarinet. As in the first statement, the bass alternates between its own countermelody and brief periods of conventional swinging, walking bass lines that outline the harmonic changes.

If "All the Things You Could Be" showcases Mingus's response to Coleman's wing of the jazz avant-garde, "What Love" demonstrates what a composer and arranger of Mingus's stature could make of the innovations later made famous by saxophonists like Pharoah Sanders and Albert Ayler. Both saxophonists were masters of the altissimo register of their instruments and introduced speechlike utterances, including shrieks and screams, in their improvisations. Recall that Mingus rather uncharitably (and, I think, unfairly) implied that these saxophonists lacked musical thought and relied upon gimmicks. Mingus sidestepped the possibility of this kind of criticism when he utilized their techniques in his music, because these innovations were juxtaposed to, or even in dialogue with, earlier styles of jazz improvisation.[39]

The compositions performed on *Charles Mingus Presents Charles Mingus* could be studied profitably by any musician interested in expanding his or her techniques in avant-garde expression. The relative uniqueness of this recording in Mingus's discography underscores that one of his most enduring contributions to American music was his ability to constantly shift his musical expression, allowing not only for his own musical will but for the full expression of each member of specific ensembles. By insisting on this kind of interaction he added unprecedented flexibility to the tradition of American orchestras. The dynamic between written music and improvised music, eagerly embraced and perpetually worried in Charles Mingus's oeuvre, creates tensions that involve the marriage in art between the Dionysian urges and Apollonian control that Nietzsche called for in *The Birth of Tragedy*.[40] While he identified himself more as a composer than he did as a bassist, his approach to composing made virtuosic demands upon performers and helped change the way that bands improvised or interacted with "fixed" compositions as much as did Ornette Coleman or John Coltrane. His place in jazz is assured because he never allowed his desire to display his emotions corrupt the control of his craft or lessen his discipline. Nor did he let the need for precision and clarity of ideas derail him from his mission to present the perpetual avant-garde in American music.

NOTES

1. This is a thorny problem that needs to be theorized more rigorously. African Americans, as Albert Murray points out, are as American as anyone else. Yet, as Dubois remarked famously a century ago, black people have often stood apart from the mainstream of America by law and by custom. African American culture often does in fact represent American values, but just as often it voices dissent from America and almost always presents a critique of mainstream viewpoints and practices that are deemed unjust. Blacks hold views across the entire spectrum of political thought, and several are leaders in the movement to deemphasize the salience of race in social and cultural matters. Thus, it is not altogether ironic that the most celebrated representative of jazz of today, Wynton Marsalis, is a black man who argues that jazz contains "Negro attitude," that it is metaphorically and metonymically American, and that antiblack racism is merely a background obstacle, not a constitutive element of the art form. See Lipsitz, "Songs of the Unsung," this volume.

2. See, for example, Radano, "The Jazz Avant-Garde."

3. I include this autobiographical detail in part in response to Guthrie P. Ramsey's provocative call for scholars of black music to reveal something of their own reasons for entering the field. He argues that the field is potentially impoverished since the relationship of the scholars to the music they study is not investigated with the rigor used to analyze and deconstruct the relationship of black musicians to their musical output. See Ramsey, "Who Hears Here?"

4. See, for example, Gitler, review of *Straight Ahead* by Abbey Lincoln. See also Kofsky, "The State of Jazz Criticism"; and Jones, "Jazz and the White Critic."

5. Griffin, *Who Set You Flowin'?* This is also discussed briefly in Lipsitz, "Songs of the Unsung."

6. The best of these would include Ralph Ellison, Albert Murray, and Stanley Crouch. This wing of jazz criticism is the dominant one, and reached its apotheosis in Ken

Burns's documentary film, *Jazz*. The viewpoints of the other major wing of jazz criticism, which includes such figures as Sidney Finkelstein, Amiri Baraka, and Kalamu ya Salaam, was not represented in the film. See Finkelstein, *Jazz;* Baraka, *Black Music,* "The 'Blues Aesthetic'"; Jones, *Blues People;* and Salaam, *African American Review.* See also O'Meally, *Living with Music;* Murray, *Stomping the Blues, The Omni-Americans, The Hero and the Blues,* and any of Stanley Crouch's numerous jazz articles and reviews in *Village Voice.*

7. Perhaps one of the most egregious examples of a critic using his authoritative position to censure the expressions and careers of artists with these political leanings would be the above-cited review of Abbey Lincoln's *Straight Ahead* recording by Ira Gitler. But more thoughtful and thoroughgoing rejections of black nationalism in jazz can be found in Early, "Ode to John Coltrane," or any number of essays written by jazz critic Stanley Crouch.

8. For an interesting discussion of how this affects avant-garde gestures made by jazz musicians, see Gabbard, "The Quoter and His Culture."

9. Gabbard, ibid.; and Radano, "The Jazz Avant-Garde." For examples of the rhetoric that helped to isolate certain musicians as a permanent avant-garde, see Shepp, "An Artist Speaks Bluntly"; and Braxton, *Tri-Axium Writings.*

10. The social history of the era includes the installation of the black codes, the final dismantling of Reconstruction, and the banishing of the freedmen's hopes for economic and political independence through the debt peonage system and socially sanctioned, extralegal terrorism. Alternatively, the nadir also witnessed the aboveground emergence of the black church, the building of national institutions for political agitation, the formation of fraternal societies, burial societies, charitable organizations, and so on. Incredibly, with jazz, blues, and ragtime, African Americans produced not just one but three music forms that forever changed the cultural landscape of the nation.

11. See for example, Jones, *Blues People;* Oliver, *The Story of the Blues;* and Harrison, *Black Pearls.*

12. Not every jazz composer was as self-consciously programmatic in intent as were composer counterparts in the Harlem Renaissance. Nevertheless, Ellington, the most important and most enduring of these composers, was very aware that he was creating a body of music that reflected the variegated moods and attitudes of black Americans. On the ambitions of the black composers of the Harlem Renaissance, see Floyd, *Black Music in the Harlem Renaissance;* and Spencer, *The New Negroes and Their Music.*

13. On the "politics of respectability," see Higginbotham, *Righteous Discontent.* Higginbotham is analyzing an earlier time period, but her observations are mostly valid for the mid-century movement as well. For a sense of the scope of the bebop revolt in sound and style, see Lott, "Double V, Double-Time."

14. The music's ties with the social history of black migration patterns are also reflected by its demographics. The goals and actions of the civil rights movement were mainly in the South, but the black power movement's epicenter eventually settled in places like Detroit, New York, and California. The New Thing was also a mostly nonsouthern phenomenon despite the fact that many of the key figures were southern born. The Texan saxophonist Ornette Coleman assembled his visionary band in Los Angeles and brought it to national attention in New York. John Coltrane was reared in North Carolina but began his professional career in Philadelphia and lived in New York during his last years when he was considered a proponent of free jazz. Furthermore, most of the collective actions and groups associated with the jazz avant-garde of the time were

formed outside the South. The "October Revolution" in jazz took place in New York. The Association for the Advancement of Creative Musicians (AACM) was founded in Chicago, the Black Artist Group (BAG) in St. Louis, the Artist Collective in Detroit, and Horace Tapscott's Pan-Afrikan Peoples Orchestra in Los Angeles. See Litweiler, *The Freedom Principle*; Braxton, *Tri-Axium Writings*; Wilmer, *As Serious As Your Life*; and Tapscot, *Songs of the Unsung*.

15. See Wilson, *The Declining Significance of Race*.

16. The jazz avant-garde musicians of the 1960s and 1970s used the spatial metaphors "outside" and "inside" to describe the experimental and the established styles of jazz respectively. See Such, *Avant-Garde Jazz Musicians*.

17. This is true despite the recognition that figures predating bebop are essential. The jazz neoconservatives have made especially strong cases, for example, that young musicians should know the music of Duke Ellington and Louis Armstrong.

18. This is the language used by Wynton Marsalis to describe trumpeter Lester Bowie in a *Down Beat* blindfold test.

19. The leader on scores of albums, Murray is a founding member of the World Saxophone Quartet and during the 1980s and 1990s led a critically acclaimed octet, a big band, and numerous smaller bands. The author has heard many students at Berklee College of Music (some of whom went on to become widely acclaimed young lions) express grave doubts about his status as a jazz musician because of his idiosyncratic approach to playing changes.

20. Jazz Artists Guild, *Newport Rebels*.

21. Mingus, *Beneath the Underdog*. See also Saul, "Outrageous Freedom."

22. Mingus, *Let My Children Hear Music*.

23. Mingus, *Changes One and Two*.

24. Mingus, *Charles Mingus at Town Hall with Eric Dolphy*.

25. Mingus, Hughes, and Feather, *Weary Blues*; Mingus, *A Modern Jazz Symposium of Music and Poetry*.

26. Mingus, *The Clown*.

27. Baraka, "In the Tradition."

28. Quoted in Priestly, *Mingus*, pp. 109–10.

29. Mingus, "An Open Letter to the Avant-Garde."

30. Ellington and Mingus did record a modern album with drummer Max Roach in 1962: Ellington, *Money Jungle*.

31. Eric Dolphy was certainly Mingus's favorite sideman and the most able interpreter of Mingus' variegated moods next to drummer Dannie Richmond. Mingus was even angry that Dolphy wanted to leave his band in 1964. The 1964 band, with Richmond, Dolphy, Jaki Byard, Clifford Jordan, and Johnny Coles, was probably pound for pound Mingus's best ensemble. That is, they presented a composite of the writer and the performers that was extremely compelling.

32. The Columbia version can be heard on Mingus, *Better Get It in Your Soul*.

33. Mingus, *Let My Children Hear Music*.

34. Mingus, *Town Hall Concert*.

35. Yusef Lateef, "The Out Game," in Lateef, *Something Else*.

36. For examples of Mingus's own penchant for highly unusual song forms in his compositions see appendix B in Priestley, *Mingus*, 1982.

37. In fact, the almost symbiotic thinking between these two men undoubtedly contributed mightily to Mingus's compositional style; it would have been easier to con-

ceive such kaleidoscopic changes if the composer had a rhythm section that could perform them reliably.

38. Mingus claimed to be able to communicate actual sentences that were intelligible, especially to Eric Dolphy. Amazingly, alto saxophonist and Mingus alumni Charles McPherson confirmed this story to the author at a workshop held at Berklee College of Music in 1991.

39. It is important to note that at the time of this recording Pharoah Sanders and Albert Ayler had not yet reached the national jazz scene and Eric Dolphy was really a pioneer when it came to producing these sounds. Sanders, in the latter phases of his career (mostly after Mingus's death), has shown remarkable affinity for more mainstream styles of jazz performance, especially for ballads. On the other hand, Albert Ayler's attempt to incorporate popular styles into his music at the end of his career, such as his *New Grass* recording on Impulse! A9175, 1968, produced his worst and most forgettable music.

40. Nietzsche, *The Birth of Tragedy*.

WORKS CITED

Baraka, Amiri. *Black Music*. New York: Morrow, 1967.
———— "The 'Blues Aesthetic' and the 'Black Aesthetic': Aesthetics as the Continuing Political History of a Culture." *Black Music Research Journal* 2.2 (Fall 1991).
———— "In the Tradition." *New Music/New Poetry*. India Navigation, 1981.
Braxton, Anthony. *Tri-Axium Writings*. Vols. 1–3. Synthesis Music, 1985.
Early, Gerald. "Ode to John Coltrane: A Jazz Musician's Influence on African-American Culture." *Antioch Review* 57.3 (Summer 1999): 371–85.
Ellington, Duke. *Money Jungle*. United Artists, UAJ14017.
Finkelstein, Sidney. *Jazz: A People's Music*. New York: International, 1988 [1948].
Floyd, Samuel. *Black Music in the Harlem Renaissance: A Collection of Essays*. Knoxville: University of Tennessee Press, 1990.
Gabbard, Krin. "The Quoter and His Culture." In Reginald Buckner and Steven Weiland, eds., *Jazz in Mind: Essays on the History and Meanings of Jazz*, pp. 92–111. Detroit: Wayne State University Press, 1991.
Gitler, Ira. Review of Abbey Lincoln, Straight *Ahead. Down Beat*, March 15, 1962, p. 21.
Griffin, Farah Jasmine. *Who Set You Flowin'? The African American Migration Narrative*. New York: Oxford University Press, 1995.
Harrison, D. D. *Black Pearls: Blues Queens of the 1920s*. New Brunswick: Rutgers University Press, 1988.
Higginbotham, Evelyn Brooks *Righteous Discontent: The Women's Movement in the Black Baptist Church, 1880–1920*. Cambridge: Harvard University, 1993.
Jazz Artists Guild. *Newport Rebels*. Candid SMJ6187, 1960.
Jones, LeRoi. *Blues People: Negro Music in White America*, New York: Morrow, 1963.
————"Jazz and the White Critic." In Amiri Baraka, ed., *Black Music*. New York: Morrow, 1967.
Kofsky, Frank. "The State of Jazz Criticism." *Jazz*, May 1965.
Lateef, Yusef. , *Something Else: The Writings of the Yusef Lateef Quartet*. New York: Autophysiopsychic Partnership, 1973.
Lipsitz, George. "Songs of the Unsung: The Darby Hicks History of Jazz," this volume.
Litweiler, John. *The Freedom Principle: Jazz After 1958*. New York: Da Capo, 1984.

Lott, Eric. "Double V, Double-Time: Bebop's Politics of Style." *Callaloo: A Journal of African-American Arts and Letters* 11.3 (Summer 1988): 597–605.

Mingus, Charles. *A Modern Jazz Symposium of Music and Poetry*. Bethlehem BCP-6026, 1958.

———— "An Open Letter to the Avant-Garde." *Changes*, June 1973; repr. and abridged in Charles Mingus, *More Than a Fake Book: Mingus*, p. 119. New York: Jazz Workshop, 1991.

———— *Beneath the Underdog: His World as Composed by Mingus*. New York: Vintage, 1971.

———— *Better Get It in Your Soul*. Columbia CL 1370, 1958.

———— *Changes One and Two*. Atlantic SD1677, SD1678, 1974.

———— *Charles Mingus at Town Hall with Eric Dolphy*. Jazz Workshop JWS-9, 1964.

———— *Charles Mingus Presents Charles Mingus*. Candid, 1960.

———— *The Clown*. Atlantic 1260, 1957.

———— *Town Hall Concert*. JWS 005, 1964.

Mingus, Charles, Langston Hughes, and Leonard Feather. *Weary Blues*. Verve 841 660–2, 1958.

Murray, Albert. *The Hero and the Blues*. New York: Vintage, 1995 [1973].

———— *The Omni-Americans: Some Alternatives to the Folklore of White Supremacy*. New York: Outerbridge and Dienstfrey, 1970.

———— *Stomping the Blues*. New York: McGraw-Hill, 1976.

Nietzsche, Friedrich. *The Birth of Tragedy*. New York: Dover, 1995.

Oliver, Paul. *The Story of the Blues*. Philadelphia: Chilton, 1969.

O'Meally, Robert G., ed., *Living with Music: Ralph Ellison's Jazz Writings*. New York: Modern Library, 2001.

Priestly, Brian. *Mingus: A Critical Biography*. New York: Da Capo, 1982.

Radano, Ronald M. "The Jazz Avant-Garde and the Jazz Community: Action and Reaction." *Annual Review of Jazz Studies* 3 (1985): 71–79.

Ramsey, Guthrie P., Jr., "Who Hears Here? Black Music, Critical Bias, and the Musicological Skin Trade." *Musical Quarterly* 85.1 (Spring 2001): 1–52.

Salaam, Kalamu ya, ed. *African American Review* 29.2 (Summer 1995). "Special Issue on the Music."

Saul, Scott. "Outrageous Freedom: Charles Mingus and the Invention of the Jazz Workshop." *American Quarterly* 53.3 (September 2001): 387–419.

Shepp, Archie." An Artist Speaks Bluntly." *Down Beat*, December 16, 1965, pp. 11–42.

Spencer, Jon Michael. *The New Negroes and Their Music: The Success of the Harlem Renaissance*. Knoxville: University of Tennessee Press, 1997.

Such, David G. *Avant-Garde Jazz Musicians: Performing "Out There."* Iowa City: University of Iowa Press, 1993.

Tapscot, Horace. *Songs of the Unsung: The Musical and Social Journey of Horace Tapscot*. Durham: Duke University Press, 2001.

Wilmer, Valerie. *As Serious as Your Life: The Story of the New Jazz*. Westport, Conn.: Hill, 1980.

Wilson, William Julius. *The Declining Significance of Race: Blacks and Changing American Institutions*. Chicago: University of Chicago Press, 1978.

GEORGE LEWIS

Experimental Music in Black and White: The AACM in New York, 1970–1985

Since its founding on the virtually all-black South Side of Chicago in 1965, the African American musicians' collective known as the Association for the Advancement of Creative Musicians (AACM) has played an unusually prominent role in the development of American experimental music. The composite output of AACM members explores a wide range of methodologies, processes, and media; AACM musicians have developed new ideas about timbre, sound, collectivity, extended technique and instrumentation, performance practice, intermedia, the relationship of improvisation to composition, form, scores, computer music technologies, invented acoustic instruments, installations, and kinetic sculptures.[1]

In a 1973 article two early AACM members, trumpeter John Shenoy Jackson and cofounder and pianist/composer Muhal Richard Abrams, asserted that "the AACM intends to show how the disadvantaged and the disenfranchised can come together and determine their own strategies for political and economic freedom, thereby determining their own destinies" (Abrams and Jackson 1973:72). This optimistic declaration, based on notions of self-help as fundamental to racial uplift, cultural preservation, and spiritual rebirth, was in accord with many other challenges to traditional notions of order and authority that emerged in the wake of the Black Power movement.

The AACM's goals of individual and collective self-production and promotion challenged racialized limitations on venues and infrastructure, serving as an example to other artists in rethinking the artist/business relationship. A number of organizations in which African American musicians took leadership roles, including the early twentieth-century Clef Club, the short-lived Jazz Composers Guild, the Collective Black Artists, and the Los Angeles–based Union of God's Musicians and Artists Ascension, or Underground Musicians Association (UGMAA/UGMA), preceded the AACM in attempting to pursue these self-help strategies. The AACM, however, has become the most well-known and influential of the post-1960 organizations, and is still active almost forty years later.[2]

The Art Ensemble of Chicago (AEC), which emerged from the AACM and has been active in one form or another from 1969 to the present, is one of the groups that most radically exemplifies AACM-style collectivity, or, in the words of Samuel Floyd, "individuality within the aggregate" (Floyd 1995:228). The five members of the classic Art Ensemble—saxophonists Joseph Jarman and Roscoe Mitchell, trumpeter Lester Bowie, bassist Malachi Favors Maghostous, and drummer Famoudou Don Moye—represent a multivoiced, internationalist vision, exemplifying theorist Kobena Mercer's notion of "plural and heterogeneous black identities" (Mercer 1994:53–66).

The AEC's percussionist, Famoudou Don Moye, explains the necessity of acting in concert in order to move beyond simple strategies of resistance: "Along with defiance you have organization. There have been moments of defiance throughout the history of the music, but the strength of the effort and the strength of the cooperation between the musicians and their unity of effort is what enables us to survive. Anytime the musicians are not strong in their unity, the control factor goes over to the *other* side" (Beauchamp 1998:56).

The first activities of AACM artists in New York City, occurring roughly between 1970 and 1985, played a crucial and very public role in the emergence during this period of now standard musical and critical discourses of genre mobility and musical hybridity. As AACM trumpeter Lester Bowie asserted, not long after the dawn of postmodernism, "We're free to express ourselves in any so-called idiom, to draw from any source, to deny any limitation. We weren't restricted to bebop, free jazz, Dixieland, theater or poetry. We could put it all together. We could sequence it any way we felt like it. It was entirely up to us" (Beauchamp 1998:46). Having emerged from the jazz tradition, which had already problematized the border between popular and high culture, AACM musicians, by actively seeking dialogue with a variety of traditions, had placed themselves in an excellent position to recursively intensify and extend the blurring and possible erasure of this and other boundaries—or, as Charlie Parker is reputed to have said, "Man, there's no boundary line to art."

To the extent that AACM musicians challenged racialized hierarchies of aesthetics, method, place, infrastructure, and economics, the organization's work epitomizes the early questioning of borders by artists of color that is only beginning to be explored in serious scholarship on music. Indeed, it may fairly be said that the AACM has received far less credit for this role in challenging borders of genre, practice, and cultural reference than members of subsequently emerging experimental music art worlds. In particular, the so-called downtown improvisors and the "totalist" composers, two loosely-structured musical communities largely framed and coded as white by press reception, articulated similar discourses of mobility, extending them to an alliance with rock that undoubtedly furthered their respective causes (see Gann 1997:320–23, 355–56).

The corporate-approved celluloid description of the AACM in the recent Ken Burns blockbuster film contrasts markedly with the situation in the real world, where the AACM's international impact has gone far beyond "white college students—in France" (see Ken Burns's *Jazz*, episode 10). While most studies that extensively reference the AACM appear to be confined to an examination of the group's influence within an entity culturally identified as the "world of jazz," the musical influence of the AACM has extended across borders of race, geography, genre, and musical practice and must be confronted in any nonracialized account of experimental music. To the extent that "world of jazz" discourses cordon off musicians from interpenetration with other musical art worlds, they cannot account for either the breakdown of genre definitions or the mobility of practice and method that informs the present-day musical landscape.

In New York the example of the AACM expanded the range of thinkable and actualizable positions for a generation of black experimental artists, such as Anthony Davis and James Newton, and the various artists who emerged from the M-BASE collective, such as Steve Coleman, Graham Haynes, Geri Allen, Robin Eubanks, and Greg Osby. Finally, the AACM's work challenged the white-coded American experimental music movement to move beyond ethnic particularism toward the recognition of a multicultural, multiethnic base, with a variety of perspectives, histories, traditions, and methods.

This study of the AACM in New York is intended to illustrate some of the strategies black musicians used in negotiating the complex, diverse, and unstable environment of contemporary musical experimentalism. Presenting a brief summary of the group's origins, initial goals, and activities in Chicago, the essay contextualizes the period by referencing a set of core AACM ideologies, including notions of collectivity, the management of difference and innovation via individualism, the importance of composition, the promulgation of a nurturing atmosphere, and border crossing. Given this preparatory context, we then follow the consequences of the attempts by AACM members to hew to these ideologies and practices in the stressful musical environment of New York City in the 1970s and 1980s. Here critical reception and the members' own views of their activities coalesce to provide some understanding of the effects of AACM activities on the musical world as a whole.[3]

In this essay I draw in part on my own experiences and history as an AACM member who was active in that environment, but rather than advancing a straightforward version of my own oral narrative—a slave narrative, if you will—I try to create a critical history as well, placing my perspectives in intersection with published reports and interviews from the period. In that spirit I also would inform the reader that, rather than speaking for the AACM, I present my own perspective, in the hope that others will consider their own understandings alongside it.

The Crucible of Chicago

In the spring of 1965 a number of Chicago musicians received a postcard from four of their mid-career colleagues—pianists Jodie Christian and Richard Abrams, drummer Steve McCall, and trumpeter Philip Cohran—calling for a general meeting and specifying fourteen issues to be discussed in relation to forming a new organization for musicians. The meeting was held on May 8, 1965, at Cohran's home on East 75th Street, near Cottage Grove Avenue on Chicago's South Side. The proceedings were conducted using more or less standard parliamentary procedure and were recorded on audiotape. Each participant stated his or her name for identification purposes before speaking. The participants were diverse in age, gender, and musical direction.[4] Some of the meeting participants had taken part in the rehearsals of Abrams's Experimental Band from 1961–64 (Radano 1993:77–80). Cohran in particular had found sustenance in the work of Sun Ra (Shapiro 2001), with whom he had performed until Ra's departure for New York in 1961. Others were more traditionally minded; in fact, the individual work of many of these musicians was too diverse to make sense of an experimental/traditional binary.

The wide-ranging discussions in these early meetings, in which musicians spoke frankly among themselves, rather than to any outside media, evince nothing so much as an awakening of subalterns to the power of speech. Already on display was the radical collective democracy that later became a central aspect of AACM ideology. What the taped evidence does *not* support, however, is the understandable but erroneous notion, advanced by most critical reception, that the AACM was formed in order to promote or revise "new jazz," "the avant-garde," or "free music." Rather, with the very first order of business, the focus of the meeting was on finding ways to foster the creation and performance of a generalized notion of what the musicians called "original music." I include here some excerpts from the discussion:

RICHARD ABRAMS: First of all, number one, there's original music, *only.* This will have to be voted and decided upon. I think it was agreed with Steve and Phil that what we meant is original music proceeding from the members in the organization.

PHILIP COHRAN: I think the reason original music was put there first was because of all of our purposes of being here, this is the primary one. Because why else would we form an association? By us forming an association and promoting and taking over playing our own music, or playing music period, it's going to involve a great deal of sacrifice on each and every one of us. And I personally don't want to sacrifice, make any sacrifice for any standard music.

STEVE MCCALL: We've all been talking about it among ourselves for a long time in general terms. We'll embellish as much as we can, but get to what you really feel because we're laying a foundation for something that will be permanent.

MELVIN JACKSON [bassist]: Original music, I feel, is really based on the individual. It doesn't necessarily mean that I care to play all original music, which would be all my music.

ROSCOE MITCHELL: I think, you know, it's time for musicians to, you know, let go of other people and try to start, you know, finding themselves. Because everybody in this room here is creative. I mean, I think we should all try to go into ourselves and stretch out as far as we can, and do what we really want to do.

GENE EASTON [saxophonist]: The [post]cards originally said "creative music" and what picture I hold is that creative music can only be original anyway, in a true creative sense. "Original," in one sense, means something you write in the particular system that we're locked up with now in this society. We express ourselves in this system because it's what we learned, and if you don't express in the system that is known, you're ostracized. But as we learn more of other systems of music around the world we're getting closer to the music that our ancestors played—sound-conscious musicians, finding a complete new system that expresses *us*. Because there are far better systems, and I feel that we will be locked up for the rest of our days in this system unless we can get out of it through some means such as this.

FRED BERRY [trumpeter]: Now before we vote on whether or not we're going to play original music there has to be a clear-cut definition in everyone's mind of what original music is.

RICHARD ABRAMS: We're not going to agree on what exactly original music means to us. We'll have to limit—now—the word "original" to promotion of ourselves and our own material to benefit ourselves (AACM 1965a).

At the next meeting on May 15, the discussion evolved toward an exploration of how "original music" might interface with the venues and infrastructure system that these musicians were about to challenge and eventually outgrow:

JULIAN PRIESTER [trombonist]: Taking into consideration economic factors involved, as musicians we're going to be working in front of the public, and different people, club owners or promoters . . .

RICHARD ABRAMS: No, no, we're not working for club owners, no clubs. Not from this organization. This is strictly concerts. See, there's another thing about us functioning as full artistic musicians. We're not afforded that liberty in taverns. Everybody here knows that (AACM 1965b).

The new organization moved quickly to fashion a formal organization, with bylaws, offices such as president, vice president, treasurer, recording secretary, and business manager, and a board of directors. During meetings a philosophy of collective, one person/one vote governance included debating procedures in which members were addressed as "Mrs.," "Mister," and "Miss." The first board of directors—singers Floradine Geemes and Sandra Lashley, Philip Cohran, Jodie Christian, drummer Jerol Donavon, Peggy Abrams, and Richard Abrams—was charged with creating a name for the new group.

Jacques Attali has asserted that the emergence of "free jazz" was provoked by "the organized and often consensual theft of black American music" (Attali 1989:138). Certainly this understanding of the political, economic, and aesthetic situation for black music extended right into the naming of the new organization. At a May 27 meeting the board settled on two choices. Ultimately, the name *Association of Dedicated Creative Artists* did not receive as much support as the second and eventual choice, but a question arose as to whether the name should refer to "creative music" or "creative musicians." Cohran's exposition settled the matter: "If the association is to advance the creative musicians, they are the ones who need advancing. . . . We can all create music and somebody else can take it and use it, and the music is still . . . [general laughter] . . . The musicians are the ones who need the help" (AACM 1965c).

The name *Association for the Advancement of Creative Musicians* and the acronym *AACM* were adopted unanimously at the next general meeting on May 29, and by August of that year the organization was chartered by the state of Illinois as a nonprofit, tax-exempt corporation. The documents submitted as part of the charter request included a set of nine purposes to which the membership continues to subscribe in 2003:

1. To cultivate young musicians and to create music of a high artistic level for the general public through the presentation of programs designed to magnify the importance of creative music
2. To create an atmosphere conducive to artistic endeavors for the artistically inclined by maintaining a workshop for the express purpose of bringing talented musicians together
3. To conduct a free training program for young aspirant musicians
4. To contribute financially to the programs of the Abraham Lincoln Centre, 700 E. Oakwood Blvd., Chicago, Ill., and other charitable organizations
5. To provide a source of employment for worthy creative musicians
6. To set an example of high moral standards for musicians and to uplift the public image of creative musicians
7. To increase mutual respect between creative artists and musical tradesmen (booking agents, managers, promoters and instrument manufacturers, etc.)
8. To uphold the tradition of cultured musicians handed down from the past
9. To stimulate spiritual growth in creative artists through recitals, concerts, etc., through participation in programs (AACM 1965d).

In early August of 1965 an "open letter to the public" introducing the new organization and announcing its first concerts appeared in the Chicago *Defender*, the important African American newspaper. Written by Richard Abrams and pianist Ken Chaney, the letter declared that" the ultimate goal is to provide an atmosphere that is conducive to serious music and performing new unrecorded compositions. . . .The aim is universal in appeal and is necessary for the advancement, development and understanding of new music" ("Creative Musicians Sponsor" 1965; Abrams and Chaney 1965). The language of the announcement, which uses terms that recall high-culture, pan-European "classical music" culture—"new music," "serious music"—already distances the organization from jazz-oriented signifiers.

At first AACM-sponsored concerts took place weekly in the black community. The first two concerts were held at the now defunct South Shore Ballroom on 79th Street near Stony Island Avenue on the South Side of Chicago. The first AACM concert, featuring the Joseph Jarman Quintet with bassist Charles Clark, drummer Leonard Smith, saxophonist Fred Anderson, and trumpeter Bill Brimfield, took place on August 16, 1965. The second event on August 23 featured Philip Cohran's Artistic Heritage Ensemble, including Gene Easton and pianist and singer Claudine Myers ("Creative Musicians Present" 1965). The concerts took place at 8 P.M., the standard time for concert music events. Production values for the early events were guided by the goal of creating "an atmosphere conducive to serious music," including concert-style seating, the printing and distribution of advertising, attempts to obtain appearances on radio, advance ticket sales, and overall stage and venue management. All these activities were handled by the musicians themselves.[5]

The Abraham Lincoln Centre, a local community-assistance institution, was host to a regular series of AACM concerts, as well as the Saturday general body meeting. Other AACM events, as well as non-AACM events featuring AACM members, took place in galleries, churches, and, indeed, in lounges and taverns, whose atmosphere the music tended to transform toward a concert orientation. Musicians of the AACM performed on both the South Side and the then mainly white North Side of Chicago. Later, students and faculty members at the University of Chicago in the Hyde Park area, a bastion of relative whiteness within the otherwise black South Side, began organizing events with AACM musicians in university concert halls and other spaces, a development that cannot be overestimated in its impact on winning new and larger audiences, including a broadening in terms of race, class, and other demographic factors.

By 1966, however, attendance at meetings had declined considerably, as the optimistic financial projections of the early months were now being tempered by the difficulties of presenting and promoting events with extremely limited means (AACM 1965e, 1966). Soon afterward, however, an influx of new members transformed the organization into what is known as the AACM today. The new members, some of whom have come to be viewed as the organization's "first wave," included trumpeters John Shenoy Jackson, Lester Bowie, and Leo Smith, drummer Alvin Fielder, pianist Christopher Gaddy, saxophonists Maurice McIntyre, John Stubblefield, John Powell, Abshalom Ben Shlomo, and Anthony Braxton, bassists Mchaka Uba and Leonard Jones, violinist Leroy Jenkins, poet David Moore (later Amus Mor), singers Fontella Bass (of "Rescue Me" fame) and Sherri Scott, trombonist Lester Lashley, and vibraphonist Gordon Emanuel, who was later ousted in a contentious meeting that resulted in the organization's membership becoming completely African American (Radano 1993:90 n. 45).

The first articles on the AACM in the United States began to appear as early as 1966 (Welding 1966b; "Jazz Musicians Group" 1966). International attention was not long in coming: between October of 1966 and December of 1968 a series of ten detailed and highly enthusiastic reports on "The New Music," by the young Chicago-based producer-critics Chuck Nessa, John Litweiler, and University of Chicago microbiologist Terry Martin, appeared in the Canadian journal *Coda*.[6] In 1968 Martin published the first major European article on the AACM, in the English journal *Jazz Monthly* (Martin 1968). In 1966 the first commercial recording by an AACM composer, Roscoe Mitchell's *Sound*, was released by an independent Chicago-based firm, Delmark Records (Mitchell 1966), and in May of 1967 Philip Cohran released two seven-inch recordings of his music on his own Zulu Records label (Cohran 1967). As early as 1968 the now landmark series of Delmark and Nessa recordings of AACM music by Abrams, Jarman, Mitchell, and Bowie were becoming known in Europe (James 1968; Cooke 1968a, 1968b; Harrison 1969; "Press Release" 1969a).

AACM members manifested a strong belief in the importance and the inevitable success of the collective mission, even in the face of the tragic deaths of two of its youngest members, Christopher Gaddy in 1968 ("Final Bar" 1968) and Charles Clark in 1969 ("Final Bar" 1969). Serious financial problems, both for the organization and for most individual members, had not forestalled the fulfillment of one of the organization's stated purposes, the founding of the AACM School of Music. The collective gathered on Saturdays at 9:00 A.M., first to conduct the AACM School's free classes in theory, composition, and various instruments (still conducted each Saturday as of 2003) and then for rehearsals and meetings.

An unpublished, fictional journal/narrative by pianist Claudine Myers, written around this time, depicts some of the dreams and aspirations of an organization in harmony. The narrative's dramatic setting is a Saturday afternoon at the Abraham Lincoln Centre, where AACM members are going about their creative business in an optimistic, hopeful spirit. Musicians such as Maurice McIntyre, Leo Smith, and Anthony Braxton appear among the playfully drawn "characters," and nicknames are used for others such as John Stubblefield ("Stub"), Fontella Bass ("Fonnie"), and Roscoe Mitchell ("The Rock"). Since the narrative carried the eponymous byline of one "Ariae," a certain "Claudine" herself appears as a character:

I. Walked in the auditorium. Stub was playing the piano; Anthony Braxton sweeping. Leo was cleaning the office. Claudine proceeded to The Rock's desk. She told Leo that she was going to study with Anthony to learn his theories on notation, sounds . . . Leo said, "Get your own thing. You don't need someone else's. No one can say I'm playing someone else's thing."

II. While Maurice's group is rehearsing, Rock, Braxton and Leo enter. "We're stealing your song, Rock. You've got a hit!" (They were speaking of Rock's composition, "Rock Suite"). Rock replied, "When we get our own record company, we'll put it on a 45."

III. Anthony came down with his contrabass clarinet, "The Rock" had his bass sax. Later Fonnie and Claudine sang and played the piano. Fonnie and Claudine threw in a little 500 Rummy to make the day complete (smile)   (MYERS 1968[?]).

Individualism, Self-Realization, and Atmosphere

AACM members have been connected with a vast range of musical styles, including jazz, blues, gospel, r&b, rock, funk, computer music, and pan-European classical and contemporary forms. Attempts by critics to identify a unitary "AACM style," however, appear to have been largely generalized from the methods of a few of the more prominent early members. For Muhal Richard Abrams, "there is no uniform musical style of the AACM. . . . The style of the AACM consists above all in encouraging people to be self-assured. That is our style" (Jost 1982:189). In 1977 the jazz critic Whitney Balliett quoted an unnamed AACM musician's answer to a query about "the" AACM sound: "If you take all the sounds of all the A.A.C.M. musicians and put them together, that's the A.A.C.M. sound, but I don't think anyone's heard that yet" (Balliett 1977:92).

There was, in fact, strong resistance within the AACM to overarching dogmas. As Anthony Braxton observed, "the diversity of its composite investigation has been the strength of the organization" (Braxton 1985:420). The management of difference was indeed a critical element in maintaining the life of the organization, since not only musical directions but also social and political philosophies held by individual members varied widely. As a result, AACM meetings could be very contentious, and extremely heated debate was common.

Informing AACM practice to a much deeper extent than one sympathetic scholar's notion of "aesthetic spiritualism" (Radano 1993:100–5) were the AACM ideologies of "individualism," "self-realization," and "atmosphere." In AACM parlance the term *individualism* generally connoted a conflation of personality and innovation. As expressed by Muhal Richard Abrams at a 1990 symposium on the AACM, "The AACM inspires individuals to be individuals" (De Lerma 1990:17). This focus on the individual is consistent with African American musical practice generally. The notion of "sound" becomes "one's own sound," connected not with deracinated, autonomous analytic morphologies but with notions of individual expression, agency, personal responsibility, uniqueness, and the avoidance of imitation. After all, the thinking goes, one's own sound—by definition—constitutes something as new to the world as one's very own birth and cannot therefore have been heard before. As Max Roach maintained, "Our music isn't one that demands, 'Okay, we're going to turn out a group of Charlie Parkers. . . . We allow each other the luxury of being an individual. . . . He receives the highest praise if he does break through, but in the sense that he's an individual like Parker, not that he *sounds* like him" (Parks 1973:64).

While celebrating the individual, members of the AACM, practically without exception, tended to see their membership in the collective as equally important to their creative lives. "The organization," as it was commonly called, constituted the foundation of an "atmosphere" that was crucial to the nurturing of creative difference within collectivity. Original member Fred Anderson felt that "it's about everybody getting a possibility to express themselves. . . . Because when you create that kind of atmosphere, then you know that something will come out of it" (Jost 1982:208).[7] Saxophonist Chico Freeman, who would become a part of the AACM's "second wave," felt that "the purpose of the AACM remains to try to create an atmosphere where we can try to reach our own individual potentials" (Gans 1980:47).

The investigations of individual musicians were viewed as being unbound by constructions of genre, method, tradition, or race. As Joseph Jarman put it, "If you're a writer, it's your responsibility to find out everything you possibly can so that you can find out what words are about. If you're going to be a musician, it's your responsibility to find out everything you possibly can about every form of music in the whole universe." Issuing an oblique, yet pointedly universal challenge to the policing and channeling of black musical artists, Jarman goes on to advocate an artistic and intellectual mobility that freely crossed musical borders: "Now that may be a new concept because up until the late '60s, we were always categorized, and it was only possible for you to self-realize certain situations. But then we began to realize that if you began to self-realize, you became a universal property, and then you must use the whole spectrum of conscious reality" (Kostakis 1977:4). In a very real sense this intellectual diversity and methodological catholicity is a question of sheer survival. If the subaltern cannot speak, then he or she is certainly obliged to listen.

The Three Waves and the Move to Paris

The evolution of the AACM's membership has been described by many writers as a succession of waves, or groups of individuals, who came together at a particular point in time in the geographic space of Chicago. Many of these musicians, from the first two waves in particular, became crucial actors in the mid-1970s AACM "invasion" of New York City, and it is to these musicians that I want to pay particular attention.

The first wave consisted of two parts. First, there were the founding and original members who attended the initial organizational meetings and organized the first concerts. Those first-wave members who were later active in New York included cofounders Steve McCall and Richard Abrams as well as original members Fred Anderson, Roscoe Mitchell, Amina Claudine Myers, Malachi Favors, Thurman Barker, Joseph Jarman, and Maurice McIntyre. Within two years of its founding the AACM began to attract a second part of this first wave, including Leo Smith, Lester Bowie, saxophonist Henry Threadgill, Anthony Braxton, John Stubblefield, Leroy Jenkins, and bassist Fred Hopkins.

The organization's artistically successful example of how black musicians could assert control over their destinies had already inspired saxophonists Oliver Lake and Julius Hemphill to take leading roles in the founding of the other important Midwestern collective, the Black Artists Group (BAG) of St. Louis, in 1968. The mandate adopted by BAG was even more radically ambitious in organizing not only musicians but visual and performance artists, writers, and choreographers. The organization established schools that featured instruction in visual art, movement, theater, and music. Its membership included visual and performance artists Patricia and Emilio Cruz, trombonist Joseph Bowie (the younger brother of AACM trumpeter Lester Bowie), trumpeters Baikida E. J. Carroll and Floyd LeFlore, theater artists Portia Hunt and Malinke Robert Elliott, dance artist Georgia

Collins, cellist Abdul Wadud, painter Oliver Jackson, drummer Charles Bobo Shaw, poets K. Curtis Lyle and Ajule Rutlin, and saxophonists James Jabbo Ware, J. D. Parran, and Hamiet Bluiett. Between 1969 and 1971 BAG and AACM members developed a series of exchange concerts in which each collective presented its members' work in the other's home city (cf. Litweiler 1969; Black Artists Group 1970[?]; Lipsitz 2000; Looker 2001).[8]

By 1969 the minds of many AACM members were on widening the audience for their music still further. For several members moving to New York, the traditional Mecca for jazz musicians—as so many Chicago musicians had done before them—proved less attractive than exploring international opportunities. These members decided to take the AACM message to Paris.

Since the early 1960s the French capital had become perhaps the most accommodating of any city in the world to the new black American music.[9] For AACM musicians working in Paris presented a clear statement that becoming known in the wider world beyond the United States could be just as effective as being accepted in the largest American city. By presenting their music in Paris first, the AACM members helped to expand the range of conceivable options for their fellow Chicago musicians beyond the fascination with New York that tended to define the career trajectory for many Chicago musicians.[10]

Within days of their arrival in Paris in June of 1969, four AACM members, Roscoe Mitchell, Joseph Jarman, Malachi Favors, and Lester Bowie, billing themselves as the Art Ensemble of Chicago, caused an immediate sensation with the first of their regular performances at the Theatre du Lucernaire in the Montparnasse district. The group's unusual hybrid of energy, multi-instrumentalism, humor, silence, found sounds, and homemade instruments—and, most crucially, extended collective improvisation instead of heroic individual solos—proved revelatory to European audiences ("Press Release" 1969b). Following closely on the heels of the Art Ensemble were Leroy Jenkins, Leo Smith, and Anthony Braxton, who arrived in Paris that same month and quickly garnered important notice for their work as well. By 1972 BAG artists Oliver Lake, Julius Hemphill, Floyd LeFlore, and Joseph Bowie had joined the expatriate music community in Paris, receiving similar acclaim for their work.

Press reception in France was voluminous and overwhelmingly positive; between 1969 and 1974 citations of the work of the Paris-based AACM and BAG musicians abound in the pages of the two major French jazz magazines, *Jazz* and *Jazz Hot*. Already in October of 1969 a photo of Joseph Jarman on the cover of *Jazz Hot* announced a feature story on the AACM. On Christmas Eve 1969 Jarman's full-page poem (Jarman 1969:14) was published in *Le Monde*, the major French newspaper, on the occasion of the release of the Art Ensemble's Paris-recorded album, *People in Sorrow* (Art Ensemble of Chicago 1969).

Writer Daniel Caux describes the complexity of the scene facing concertgoers at the first AEC performance at the Lucernaire:

The stage of this curious, 140-seat theater is nearly entirely overrun by a multitude of instruments: xylophones, bassoon, sarrusophone, various saxophones, clarinets, banjo, cymbals, gongs, bells, bass drum, balafon, rattles etc. . . . The first night, listeners were surprised to see Joseph Jarman, his naked torso and his face painted, passing slowly through the aisles murmuring a poem while the bassist Malachi Favors, wearing a mask of terror, screamed curses at Lester Bowie, and Roscoe Mitchell operated various car horns.   (1969A:8)

Despite the group's slogan, "Great Black Music," the variegated visual and sonic iconography of the Art Ensemble came from around the world (see Lewis 1998). Jarman explains:

> We were representing history, from the Ancient to the Future. . . . Malachi always represents the oldest entity . . . he would look like an African/Egyptian shaman. . . . Moye was really in the midst of the African tradition. . . . Not a single African tradition, but a total African tradition. . . . I was Eastern oriented. These three were the pantheistic element of Africa and Asia. Roscoe represented the main-stream sort of shaman, the Urban Delivery Man. . . . Lester was always the investigator, wearing cook clothes, which is healing, creating energy and food.
>
>   (1998:74–75)

Creating relationships with more established experimentalists proved far easier in Paris than in New York. Jarman observed in an October 1969 interview in *Jazz Hot*, "We really tried to meet these people in New York, but apparently, there are some difficulties" (Caux 1969b).[11] Steve McCall, the very first AACM member to visit Europe, provided entrée for the newcomers into the expatriate and itinerant musicians' community in Paris (Beauchamp 1998:74). McCall also provided a link to the first wave of European free jazz musicians, such as German vibraphonist Gunter Hampel and Dutch saxophonist Willem Breuker.[12]

AACM members living in Europe vigorously promoted the AACM name and philosophy as they presented performances throughout the continent. Interviews with European-based AACM members in French journals brought other, still relatively unknown Chicago-based members to the attention of European promoters and journalists, preparing the ground for future generations of AACM members to receive a hearing. These interviews also invariably mentioned the AACM itself as an important source of strength and nurturance. By the late 1970s both the promotional and musical efforts bore fruit; in 1977 the entire December/January 1978/79 issue of *Jazz Hot* was devoted to the AACM (Dossier AACM 1978–79).

Nonetheless, by 1971 most of the AACM expatriates had left Europe. While it is impossible to generalize about the reasons for their departure, in 1998 Lester Bowie remembered that "we wanted to go back to the States because we wanted to be home. . . . To me it ain't no gas to be French. I like being an American Negro" (Beauchamp 1998:43). Those who came back to Chicago found their AACM colleagues, such as Claudine Myers (now Amina Claudine Myers), Henry Threadgill, Muhal Richard Abrams, Maurice McIntyre, and Thurman Barker, continuing to hold meetings and present AACM concerts.[13] In addition, a number of new members had appeared, including saxophonists Chico Freeman, Douglas Ewart, Edward Wilkerson, and Mwata Bowden, percussionist Kahil El-Zabar, trumpeters Malachi Thompson and Rasul Siddik, vocalist Iqua Colson, pianist Adegoke Steve Colson, and myself as a trombonist. This so-called second wave of AACM musicians had been enculturated into the set of values developed in the AACM's self-realized atmospheric hothouse: economic and musical collectivity, a composer-centered ideology, methodological diversity, and freedom of cultural reference.

But not all the sojourners returned to Chicago. In fact, a kind of AACM diaspora began to form, with some musicians trying to become established on the East Coast, in California, and in the South, while others moved to Midwestern rural environments distant from major cities. Some musicians attempted to replicate the AACM experience in their local communities. Leo Smith helped found the Creative Musicians Improvisors Forum in Connecticut, Roscoe Mitchell moved to a farmhouse near a small Michigan town and founded the Detroit-based Creative Arts Collective, along with guitarist A. Spencer Barefield, saxophonist Anthony Holland, drummer Tani Tabbal, and bassist Jaribu Shahid.

Back in France, Lester Bowie waxed enthusiastic, stating his intention to "establish the AACM everywhere, in every corner of the universe" (Caux 1969b:17). Now both the tremendous publicity cachet and the depth of new professional associations gained from the Paris experience provided a springboard for a small coterie of AACM members to try to seek performance opportunities in another particularly vital corner of the universe—New York City.

Scouting the Territory: New York, Spring 1970

When Anthony Braxton and Leroy Jenkins returned from Europe in 1970 to pursue an encounter with New York City, performance opportunities and press coverage were relatively sparse. Nonetheless, these AACM musicians performed with many of the more established experimentalists of the period such as Marion Brown, Rahsaan Roland Kirk, Sam Rivers, Chick Corea, Ornette Coleman, and Archie Shepp. In many cases these encounters simply extended the relationships AACM members had initiated in Paris.

The first wave of New York–based AACM musicians presented their own work in concert programs of both contemporary notated music and improvised music. In May of 1970 promoter Kunle Mwanga organized perhaps the first AACM concert in New York, at the Washington Square Methodist Church (Peace Church) in the West Village. Featured was the Creative Construction Company, consisting of Leroy Jenkins, Anthony Braxton, Muhal Richard Abrams, Steve McCall, Leo Smith, and Chicago-born bassist Richard Davis (Palmer 1975; Primack 1976).[14] By 1973 Anthony Braxton managed to garner notice in the *New York Times* for an Alice Tully Hall performance of his chamber work "L-J-637/C" (Henahan 1973). The year before, he had followed in the footsteps of Ornette Coleman by renting Town Hall for a performance of his work.

Between 1972 and 1974 the fortunes of AACM members in New York began to change, with so-called major-label recording contracts for the Art Ensemble of Chicago in 1972 (Atlantic), and for Anthony Braxton in 1974 (Arista). In July of 1973 the first New York concert of the Art Ensemble of Chicago took place at Columbia University's Wollman Auditorium as part of promoter George Wein's Newport Jazz Festival. The *New York Times*'s advance article for the festival was written by Robert Palmer, a member of an emerging critical advance guard that was promulgating new ways of writing about improvised music in the New York press.

Palmer described some of the Art Ensemble's musical methods as reminiscent of various elements of black jazz and r&b traditions, but avoided traditional jazz journalism's tendency to deploy historical jazz icons as a means of quickly, yet all too neatly, contextualizing a particular performer's work within a constructed jazz tradition. Rather, evoking a postmodernist sensibility, the article descriptively expanded the frame of reference, comparing the Art Ensemble's work to "developments in the visual arts; themes, variations, solos and ensemble passages alternate in a continuous flow that is comparable to a collage of apparently disparate objects and images" (Palmer 1973:30).

Black Music of Two Worlds

Samuel Gilmore's sociological analysis of the New York "concert music world" of the early 1980s (i.e., ostensibly excluding jazz, pop, or other "vernacular" genres) draws upon the methods of symbolic interactionism to identify three major art world divisions—uptown, midtown, and downtown—that even by the early 1970s were fairly well defined, if "imagined," communities. While, at this writing, the terms *uptown, midtown,* and *downtown* are still used in New York, it must be emphasized that in the 1970s, as now, the art worlds to which they refer interpenetrated one another to a considerable extent to form an overall "art music" scene in New York.

Gilmore sees the term *midtown* as denoting major symphony orchestras, touring soloists, and chamber groups active in large, well-funded, commercially oriented performing spaces, such as Lincoln Center and Carnegie Hall. *Uptown* refers to academically situated composers "of whom the public has rarely heard . . . but who win the Pulitzer Prize every year" (Gilmore 1987:213). For Gilmore these representative uptown composers included Milton Babbitt, Charles Wuorinen, and Elliott Carter; representative performance ensembles included the Group for Contemporary Music, then directed by composers Harvey Sollberger and Charles Wuorinen, and Speculum Musicae, which then featured the versatile and insightful pianist Ursula Oppens.

Gilmore identifies the term *downtown* as referring to "the composer/performer, living in small performance lofts in Soho, Tribeca, and near alternative performance spaces in Greenwich Village." Representative venues included the Kitchen, the multidisciplinary performance space founded in 1971 by the video artists Steina and Woody Vasulka, which by 1975 had become a central part of New

York's new music scene, intermedia artist Phill Niblock's Experimental Intermedia Foundation, and later Roulette, founded by trombonist Jim Staley and sound artist David Weinstein.

Representative composers active in this downtown art world included John Cage, Philip Glass, Philip Corner, Robert Ashley, and La Monte Young. These artists, and others in their circle, might be brought under the heading of "Downtown I," to distinguish their putative post-Cage commonality from the post-1980 construction of downtown, or "Downtown II," most prominently represented by saxophonist John Zorn, vocalist Shelley Hirsch, sound artist David Moss, and guitarists Fred Frith, Eugene Chadbourne, and Elliott Sharp, among many others.[15] Both Downtown I and Downtown II are generally racially coded in press accounts as white, and by the late 1980s such accounts routinely portrayed Downtown II as the logical successor to Downtown I's connection with pan-European high culture.

Between 1973 and 1977 a sudden and dramatic shift was occurring in experimental music in New York, in which the AACM was to play a crucial role. Part of this shift was occurring in the critical domain. The younger *Times* music writers, including Robert Palmer, John Rockwell, and Jon Pareles, were acquainted with a wide range of musical aesthetics and practices and thus less invested in maintaining traditional taxonomies. In a review of Lincoln Center's 1974 New and Newer Music Festival, Rockwell announced (some might say "warned of") changes in the relationship of jazz with "serious contemporary music." Rockwell contrasts the standard bebop-era image of "somber-looking black men wearing berets," playing in "dim, smoky clubs," with that of "short-haired white people peering industriously through their spectacles at densely notated pages of . . . genteelly complex music in genteelly academic environments." The writer goes on to note that the border between "experimental jazz" and contemporary music was routinely being crossed in the "downtown" environment. "For several years in downtown lofts, the same faces have been turning up among the performers at avant-garde jazz concerts and avant-garde 'serious' new-music concerts" (Rockwell 1974:33).

Rockwell went on to present an optimistically color-blind analysis of the situation: "The National Endowment for the Arts, the New York State Council on the Arts [and] the Guggenheim Foundation are just as likely to give their grants to Ornette Coleman as to Charles Wuorinen" (33). Of course, the real situation was far less sanguine. In 1971 the Jazz and People's Movement, organized by Rahsaan Roland Kirk, Roswell Rudd, and Archie Shepp, had staged a "play-in" at the offices of the John Simon Guggenheim Foundation in New York, "demanding an end to the obvious and blatant racist policies . . . in the allocation of awards" ("Guggenheim to Mingus" 1971). Indeed NEA funding for music was hypersegregated according to racialized categories of "jazz-folk-ethnic" and "music," with the latter category apparently intended to denote, to recall Rockwell's phrase, "short-haired white people" creating "genteelly complex music in genteelly academic environments."

In 1973 the NEA disbursed over \$225,000 to 165 individuals and organizations applying to its "jazz-folk-ethnic" category. Composition grants for commissioning new works were provided; no grant exceeded \$2,000, including those given to such important artists as pianist Cedar Walton, saxophonist Clifford Jordan, and composer Duke Jordan. Several AACM members received grants, including Lester Bowie ($750), Malachi Favors ($1,000), Joseph Jarman ($1,000), Leroy Jenkins ($2,000), Roscoe Mitchell ($1,000), Don Moye ($1,000), Leo Smith ($1,000), and trumpeter Frank Gordon ($1,500) ("Jazz Grants" 1973:46). The next year the new "composer-librettist" category—as it happens, one of the less well-funded among the several categories under which pan-European music could be supported—was allocated nearly twice the amount allotted to the jazz-folk-ethnic category, with grants of $10,000 to George Rochberg and John Harbison. Other grants were received by Vladimir Ussachevsky ($7,500), Charles Wuorinen ($3,500), Morton Subotnick ($7,000), Charles Dodge ($4,500), Steve Reich ($2,000), Otto Luening ($6,000), and Barbara Kolb ($2,000) ("$407,276 in Grants" 1974:75).[16]

Despite the obvious presence of the border in terms of financial support, in other respects many of the changes Rockwell had announced were in the air. The New and Newer Music taking place at Ornette Coleman's Prince Street performance loft Artists House, which he had been renting since 1970, featured works by Coleman, Carla Bley, and Frederic Rzewski—"successive evenings of jazz and classical avant-garde, and works that fuse the two" (Rockwell 1974:33). By 1975 black experimental music was starting to be featured at such midtown venues as Carnegie Recital Hall.

Gary Giddins and Peter Occhiogrosso, and later Stanley Crouch, writing for both the *Village Voice* and the now defunct *Soho Weekly News*, were becoming instrumental in covering this newest black experimental music, which they discursively folded into the previous decade's conception of "avant-garde jazz." Their articles came sporadically, perhaps every other month or so; certainly there was no concentrated, dedicated press coverage of these black experimentalists that could be considered analogous to composer Tom Johnson's weekly *Voice* columns on Downtown I, which were instrumental in furthering the careers of Robert Ashley, Steve Reich, Meredith Monk, Philip Glass, Pauline Oliveros, Glenn Branca, and others.[17]

Even a small amount of publicity for a musician, however, is like an infusion of life-giving oxygen in outer space—or as Art Blakey is said to have observed, "If you don't appear, you disappear." Partially as a result of this press coverage, word was getting back to AACM members in Chicago through the musician's grapevine that New York was beckoning, with potential opportunities far beyond what was available in Chicago at the time.

The Final Invasion

Between 1975 and 1977, it seemed to a Chicago-based musician like myself that one was hearing something exciting about New York every week. Glowing, if often apocryphal, reports came back from New York about playing with famous musicians, enthusiastic audiences, opportunities for foreign travel, and so on. At the same time, it was becoming clear to many who tried that it was not very realistic to try to organize events in New York from afar using the same techniques one used for finding work in other American cities. As one person concluded a conversation with me over the phone, "Are you in New York? No? Well, we'll talk when you get here."

In a sense, the pressure was becoming unbearable, and perhaps these hopeful signs served to "set people flowin," to borrow Farah Jasmine Griffin's phrase about African American migration narratives (Griffin 1995). After the fashion of a river overflowing its banks, members of the AACM's second wave, along with the Chicago-based remnants of the first wave—including, most importantly, founder Muhal Richard Abrams—moved to New York, seemingly en masse. Joining those already on the East Coast, this grand wave, including Kalaparusha Maurice McIntyre, Lester Bowie, Amina Claudine Myers, Henry Threadgill, Steve McCall, Fred Hopkins, Chico Freeman, Malachi Thompson, Iqua Colson, Adegoke Colson, and myself, all moved to Manhattan or the New York area during this time. Members of BAG, including Charles Bobo Shaw, Baikida E. J. Carroll, Oliver Lake, Julius Hemphill, Hamiet Bluiett, J. D. Parran, Joseph Bowie, Patricia Cruz, Emilio Cruz, and James Jabbo Ware, had all arrived in New York before this mass migration, forming a powerful group of Midwestern colleagues.

In addition to this contingent, there was a group of new and exciting Californians, in large part the products of pianist Horace Tapscott's UGMAA, such as saxophonists Arthur Blythe and David Murray, flutist James Newton, and trumpeter Lawrence "Butch" Morris. Also a product of the UGMAA was the writer Stanley Crouch (Tapscott 2001), who presented many of the new experimentalists in his role as music director at the loft/club, on the Bowery, the Tin Palace (Dubin 1982:5) as well as in his own upstairs loft at the same Bowery location, dubbed "Studio Infinity."

The new music of the AACM, BAG, and the Californians was in the process of becoming widely influential. Robert Palmer wrote of the AACM and BAG that

> their originality becomes more and more evident. Their improvisation ranges from solo saxophone recitals to little-tried combinations of horns, rhythm instruments and electronics. They have rendered the clamorous playing characteristic of much of New York's jazz avant-garde all but obsolete with their more thoughtful approaches to improvisational structure and content. (PALMER 1976:18)

The arrival in New York of AACM cofounder Muhal Richard Abrams provided an occasion for perhaps the most extensive *Village Voice* article on the AACM's growing influence on black experimentalism. In a May 1977 article Giddins declared that "[Abrams's] presence here is a crest on the wave of immigrant musicians recently arrived from St. Louis, Los Angeles, and especially Chicago." The article's focus on the history of the AACM sought "to get to the bottom of why an inner-city organization from the Midwest founded in 1965 should revitalize New York's music scene a decade later." Giddins observed that "a distinguishing characteristic of the new movement is that it isn't a movement at all, at least not one with closed stylistic parameters" (Giddins 1977:46). The writer's quote from Leo Smith summarized well the intentions of this nonmovement: "[The AACM] represents the control of destiny for the music and the artist" (ibid.:48).

Some AACM members were ambivalent about being based in New York. Those New York–based members who did comment on their experiences in the city valued above all their access to colleagues of the highest quality and proximity to business opportunities. In a French-language interview in 1977 Abrams said that "it's good for work. In the United States, New York is an important market; if you want to be known beyond your local area, sooner or later you have to have business in New York" (Bourget 1977:22). Kalaparusha was of the same opinion: "New York is a business center, the capital of the music business, that's all. That's why most musicians who want to live from their work are in New York" (Marmande 1977:33).

On the other hand, in an interview with Valerie Wilmer, Amina Claudine Myers noted that many of the promotional strategies and collegialities that had worked in the Chicago days of the AACM were far less effective in the very different and unfamiliar environment of New York: "In Chicago when I wanted to do a concert, I'd just set it up. I'd go out and put up my flyers. Now you can do this in New York but it's definitely not that easy. Chicago has a large black population but New York is altogether a different thing. The pressures are much different" (Wilmer 1979:6). Some of these pressures were gender-related: "I was always encouraged, except for one time. That was in New York about two years ago when I ran across a male ego. . . . I ran across some real games that some of the men musicians played in New York" (Wilmer 1979:5).

Furthermore, even as they acknowledged the central role that New York has traditionally played in musicians' aspirations, AACM members tended to challenge that role where it conflicted with their ideals of methodological mobility. As in Chicago, some AACM artists in New York viewed the jazz community as it was then constructed to be only a part of their overall reference base. Pursuing membership to varying degrees in a panoply of sociomusical and career networks, including those traditionally centering on high-culture "art music," AACM musicians in New York articulated a definitional shift away from rigidly defined and racialized notions of lineage and tradition toward a more fluid, dialogic relationship with a variety of musical practices that problematized the putative jazz label as it was applied to them. For these musicians pan-European contemporary music was not a distant, disembodied influence, nor was it something to be feared, avoided, or worshipped. Rather, musicians articulated participation across genres, as well as exchanges of musical methods. Advancing a notion of hybridity and mobility across and through media, traditions, and materials meant not only the freedom to draw from a potentially infinite number of musical sources but also the freedom to explore a diverse array of infrastructures and modes of presentation.

In May of 1977 the AACM, seeking to do in New York what some of its members had done in Paris—that is, bring to the fore AACM musicians who were not as well known—collaborated with the late Taylor Storer, then a student worker at Columbia University's radio station, WKCR, to produce an ambitious four-day concert series at Wollman Auditorium. Already one of New York's most adventurous radio stations, WKCR was programming a wide variety of musics that rarely received a hearing through commercial outlets. As a preview of the festival, billed "Chicago Comes to New York," the station broadcast ninety consecutive hours of music, interviews, and unpublished recordings of AACM members (Palmer 1977:34).

Thus, one sunny Chicago afternoon, a contingent of AACM members and associates loaded their instruments and suitcases onto a rented Greyhound-style bus bound for New York. Onboard were a large number of musicians who had seldom performed in New York up to that time or who were just then trying to become established there.[18] On the final evening of the "Chicago Comes to New York" event, the AACM Orchestra, conducted by Muhal Richard Abrams, gave a performance of a single untitled work lasting one and one-half hours. The work, which including all the members who had been present, included an instrumental complement of eight reeds, two trumpets, two trombones, four percussionists, three pianists, and three singers (Balliett 1977:96).

This work, as well as the festival as a whole, was the subject of a long, searching article in the *New Yorker*, written by veteran jazz writer Whitney Balliett, that presented a context and history of the AACM as he saw it. The article, which reports on each of the concerts in great detail, provides what is perhaps one of the most meticulous and richly contextualized accounts of AACM musical performances to appear in any American publication. Describing some of the music heard in the ninety-hour radio broadcast as "beautiful, infuriating, savage, surrealistic, boring, and often highly original," the writer described his conception of the AACM's composite vision: "The broadcast revealed a ferocious determination to bring into being a new and durable music—a hard-nosed utopian music, without racial stigmata, without clichés, and without commercialism" (Balliett 1977:92).

The Loft Period

In New York the most radical experimental work was taking place in small performance lofts and other alternative spaces. The so-called loft jazz network developed for most of the same reasons as the "downtown new music" loft movement; it was part of the general move among experimental musicians of various genres to develop alternative spaces that avoided the codes and genre policing of conventional jazz and classical performance. Thus Ornette Coleman's Artists House was started for many of the same reasons as the Kitchen—namely (recalling the AACM press release of 1965), "to provide an atmosphere that is conducive to serious music." Both art worlds needed alternative spaces in order to get their experimental work before the public, expanding the set of positions available for the music.

The venues and social networks to which these new spaces constituted "alternatives," however, were vastly different according to genre and, frequently, race as well. Until the mid-1960s "serious", i.e., pan-European new music, including the early work of John Cage and the New York School, was conceived largely for traditional concert halls, a legacy bequeathed by the previous generations of midtown and uptown within this overall art world. Countering the dominant upper-class ideology, which maintained that such halls were the venue of choice for "serious" music—and, incidentally, only for that music and no other, younger white artists of the 1960s began experimenting with gallery spaces, specially designed site-specific spaces, outdoor spaces, and the like.[19]

For the black musicians, on the other hand, the "club," rather than the concert hall, had been heavily ideologized as the ideal, even the genetically best-suited space for their music. Early on, however, black experimentalists realized that serious engagement with theater and performance, painting, poetry, electronics, and other interdisciplinary expressions that require extensive infrastructure would be generally rendered ineffective or even impossible by the jazz club model. In this light the supposed obligation to perform in clubs began to appear as a kind of unwanted surveillance of the black creative body.

By 1976 the loft was being touted in the New York alternative press as the new jazz club, inheriting from its predecessor minimal infrastructure and the related discourse of "intimacy." Indeed, some of the early lofts sought to emulate traditional jazz club environments, with tables, drink minimums, and smoking, but many others provided versions of a concert environment, with concert seating and, at times, light refreshments (Giddins 1976:82). Musician-organized or directed lofts included the La Mama Children's Workshop Theater, where La Mama founder Ellen Stewart worked with BAG drummer Charles Bobo Shaw, pianist John Fischer's "Environ," drummer Rashied Ali's Studio 77 ("Ali's Alley"), and, perhaps the most adventurous and long-lived of the improvisors' lofts, Sam and Bea Rivers's Studio Rivbea.

Loft proprietors would often band together to present "alternative" festivals that featured musical approaches that were either excluded or poorly represented by the ordinarily "mainstream" jazz policy of the Newport Jazz Festival. The five-LP collection *Wildflowers: The New York Loft Jazz Sessions*, recorded at Studio Rivbea's 1976 Spring Music Festival and originally released in 1977 (Various Artists 1977a, 1977b, 1977c, 1977d, 1977e, 2000 [1977]) constitutes a handy summary of some of the ideas and practices about improvisation that were being explored during this period by the loosely associated group of musicians dubbed the "loft generation"— a term whose ephemerality the musicians are no doubt quite grateful for today.

On these recordings the newcomers from the Midwest and the West, who were now being touted in the New York, European, and Asian press as part of an emerging "loft jazz" movement, were heavily represented. Among the AACM newcomers featured were Roscoe Mitchell, Anthony Braxton, Kalaparusha Maurice McIntyre, Don Moye, Leo Smith, and myself as trombonist, as well as the collective Air, with Henry Threadgill, Fred Hopkins, and Steve McCall. From the BAG diaspora (the group itself had disbanded in 1972) there was Abdul Wadud, Charles Bobo Shaw, Oliver Lake, Julius Hemphill, and Hamiet Bluiett.[20]

In his regular monthly column for the now defunct men's magazine *Players* (a kind of African American *Playboy*), Stanley Crouch, who performed on drums in several of the performances on *Wildflowers*, reviewed the live performances that the recordings later documented. Crouch hailed the new music on these recordings as "significant for its variety, its craftsmanship, and finally, its often breathtaking beauty and clarity of its artistry." For Crouch Hemphill was "masterful," while Mitchell's performance was "almost as exciting and great as anything I've heard from Coltrane, Rollins and Ornette Coleman" (Crouch 1977:6).

It can fairly be said that the loft period provided entry-level support for an emerging multiracial network of musicians. Key players in this network included not only the Californians, BAG, and the AACM but many others, both black and white.[21] Many of these musicians deeply resented the reduction of the diversity of their approaches to the term *loft jazz*. Chico Freeman's reaction was typical: "Then, and I don't know where it came from, somebody came up with this term, 'loft jazz.' Not just me, but every musician who was involved in it vehemently opposed that" (Tesser 1980:28). Not only was there little or no agreement as to what methods or sounds were being described by the term but, as bassist Fred Hopkins related in a 1984 interview, "the funniest thing was, the musicians never considered it a *movement*" (Whitehead 1984:24). Musicians pointed out that this label, by framing their music as requiring minimal infrastructural investment, was used to disconnect them from more lucrative economic possibilities. A 1977 *Voice* article reported the concerns of musicians that "constant press association with lofts has undermined their commercial viability with European promoters, since lofts have come to be synonymous with percentage-of-the door payments" (Giddins 1977a:76).

Nonetheless, critics defended the label and felt confident in assigning musicians to this amorphous category while at the same time admitting its descriptive inadequacies. For instance, in countering what he viewed as "misconceptions," Giddins asserted the tautology that "there is neither a loft nor an AACM style of jazz. Loft jazz is any jazz played in a loft." With this the taxonomic policing mechanism that at once connected the signifiers *AACM, loft,* and *jazz* created a tightly bound, multiply mediated corset that the AACM's mobility and border-crossing strategies were already shredding.

At any rate, by the early 1980s the loft jazz phenomenon was all but dead in New York, the victim of competition for the attention of the new musicians from better-funded, higher-infrastructure New York spaces, such as Broadway producer Joseph Papp's Public Theatre, midtown spaces such as Carnegie Recital Hall, and downtown lofts such as the Kitchen, all of which had engagement policies that mirrored to some extent those of the lofts (Keepnews 1979). Even rock spaces such as CBGB briefly featured loft jazz veterans alongside the "art rock" of groups like the Theoretical Girls. Moreover, the more established artists could obtain work at traditional club spaces, such as Sweet Basil and the Village Gate, to say nothing of the expanded opportunities then becoming available in Europe. Also important were issues of individual support; it is not difficult to imagine that it could have proved daunting for individual musicians such as Sam Rivers to compose and perform new work while directing an ongoing concert series.

Beyond a Binary

As early as 1975, it was becoming increasingly unclear exactly whose purview it would be to chronicle and critique the new hybrid music. *Voice* writer Gary Giddins mused openly on how the blurring of boundaries that was taking place across ethnic and genre divides was affecting critical commentary. He begins with an admission: "I know something of John Cage's theories, but virtually nothing of his music as a living thing. This is pretty strange when you consider how many of the people I write about acknowledge Cage as an influence" (Giddins 1975:106). Giddins goes on to acknowledge the asymmetrical power dynamic symbolized by the separation of genres in his own newspaper, with its twin headings of "Music," i.e., reviews of work from the high culture West, and "Riffs," the low-culture, diminutively-imaged Rest.

Noticing that "much avant-garde music, whether jazz or classicist, is moving in similar directions," the article suggested that Tom Johnson, then the *Voice's* "downtown" critic, might move outside of his normative "Music" purview to investigate Anthony Braxton, while he, as a "Riffs" columnist, would discover Philip Glass. Giddins even invokes a version of the one-drop rule to speculate (perhaps with a naive humor) about what would happen if Glass and Braxton made a recording together: "Since black blood is more powerful than white, as any mulatto will attest, Braxton would presumably render Glass non-Music and both would be filed as a Riff."

Eventually, Giddins and Johnson, among many others, would be obliged to journalistically encounter music that incorporated references outside their usually defined spheres of study. In particular, it was becoming obvious that AACM events were presented in a great diversity of spaces—jazz and new music lofts, clubs, concert halls, and parks. Inevitably, just as the black community of Chicago broke out of the South Side Bantustan to which restrictive covenants and discriminatory law had confined its members, the AACM was destined to run roughshod over many conventional assumptions about infrastructure, reference, and place.

At first, these determined efforts to produce new music that blurred boundaries and exhibited multiplicity of reference were lauded, particularly in the jazz press. An important bellwether of jazz fashion and commercial impact are the two annual *Down Beat* magazine popularity polls—one a compilation of the opinions of "recognized" critics, published in the summer, the other a mail-in poll for readers and subscribers, appearing just before the December holidays. In 1971 perhaps the first AACM musicians to be recognized in these polls were Lester Bowie, Joseph Jarman, Roscoe Mitchell, and Malachi Favors. The Art Ensemble of Chicago was also recognized, and Anthony Braxton and Leroy Jenkins, who were then based in New York, were also listed. Over the next couple of years Jarman took first place in one of these polls, Muhal Richard Abrams was mentioned for the first time, and the Art Ensemble, Braxton, Kalaparusha and Jenkins were all winners.

In 1976 the number of AACM and BAG musicians listed in these polls rose markedly. Often listed in multiple categories, new names, such as those of the trio Air, Fred Hopkins, Henry Threadgill, Julius Hemphill, Leo Smith, Oliver Lake, Hamiet Bluiett, Don Moye, Joseph Bowie, and my own, all appeared. In 1977

Braxton's *Creative Orchestra Music 1976* (Braxton 1976) was the Critics' Poll "Record of the Year," and over the next few years Amina Claudine Myers, Steve McCall, Abdul Wadud, Douglas Ewart, and Chico Freeman found places in the poll listings. In 1980 Air's *Air Lore* (Air 1979) was also selected as the critics' record of the year; other new names, such as the World Saxophone Quartet of Lake, Hemphill, Bluiett, and David Murray, were appearing as well.[22]

Thus it would appear that, at least at first, the business gamble of so many Midwestern musicians paid off. In time, however, some aspects of the evolution of their music met with considerable resistance from a variety of entrenched sectors of New York's jazz and new music communities. Bogged down in binary systems—black/white, jazz/classical, high culture/low culture—critical reception in particular eventually became quite often frankly dismissive of the extensive engagement with extended form, electronics and computers, graphic scores, and traditionally notated works (with or without improvisation) realized by AACM musicians in particular.

Moreover, the cultural and methodological issues that informed the work of AACM composers were often obscured by discussions of whether or not the music was truly "jazz." A *Voice* review of a 1978 Leroy Jenkins concert at Carnegie Recital Hall became the occasion for critic Giddins to confront some of the same questions that had dogged Ellington forty years earlier: "How does this music relate to the jazz tradition? At what point can jazz be wrenched from its idiomatic integrity?" (Giddins 1978a:68).

A related trope informing critical reception on the jazz side articulated concerns about the "authenticity" of hybrid musics—particularly those that incorporate sources from jazz's great competitor, pan-European classical music. Reviewing a Muhal Richard Abrams recording, Giddins expressed "some sympathy for the complaint that extra-jazz influences water down the idiom" (Giddins 1978b:63). In 1979 Rafi Zabor wrote that "one of the hazards this music may be facing now is the ingestion of a fatal dose of root-devouring Western intellectual hunger" (Zabor 1979:73). Peter Occhiogrosso, reviewing a Roscoe Mitchell concert in 1978, declared that Mitchell's work was "uninspired, boring music, music that belongs in the conservatory, music that will hopefully soon go the way of third stream, electronic music and conceptual art. . . . [It] should be left to academics and people like Philip Glass" (Occhiogrosso 1978:111).

Engaging the Third Stream: The Creolization of Composition

Attali notes that the emergence of so-called free jazz represented "a profound attempt to win creative autonomy" (Attali 1989:138). In challenging the policing of the creative black body and asserting freedom of reference, Ornette Coleman was acknowledged by a number of early AACM members as one of the critical forerunners in asserting this autonomy. In Abrams's view "Ornette is the only one that really had been an inspiration for the whole field. . . . Ornette was the first to take the risk" (Vuisje 1978:196). Coleman, then as now, sought to involve himself not so much in "extending the boundaries of jazz" but in erasing the barriers placed around African American creativity generally and around his work in particular. Seeing himself very early on as in international dialogue with musicians from every field, Coleman's string trios and quartets, as well as his orchestral work *Skies of America* (1972), challenged notions of black nonentitlement to the infrastructural means of experimental music production and to the impulse of experimentalism itself.

At first Coleman's compositions became associated with the Third Stream practices of composer and conductor Gunther Schuller; some AACM practices would later be described as congruent with this tradition. While Third Stream infrastructure may well have been attractive in the undercapitalized field of jazz, its ideology was much less so, with its reification of racialized notions of classical and jazz methodology that, as John Coltrane observed, was "an attempt to create something, I think, more with labels, you see, than true evolution" (Kofsky 1970:240). By 1974 John Rockwell could quote conductor Dennis Russell Davies to the effect that the new jazz-classical mixes were not like "the old so-called 'Third Stream.'" For Carla Bley, quoted in the same article, Third Stream practice meant that "the old forms of jazz were put together with the old forms of the other" (Rockwell 1974:33). As Bley clearly implies, by this time Third Stream concepts of musical form had already been overtaken by more radical experiments in indeterminacy and other forms of real-time music-making, notably the work of Christian Wolff, Earle Brown, Morton Feldman, John Cage, and Pauline Oliveros. For many black artists, as "a metaphor for jazz reaching outside itself and incorporating other elements, to broaden and diversify" (Ratliff 2001:E1), Third Stream could be viewed as a form of liberal racial uplift. To white artists and audiences Third Stream could propose a sublimated image of "miscegenation" with jazz as a source of renewal of the European tradition, proposing a way out of the dilemma of the alienated listener, for which European high modernist composition was being blamed.[23]

Post-1960s African American artists like Coltrane, however, were understandably reluctant to commit to a musical movement in which their culture was considered a junior partner. Most crucially, the Third Stream movement failed to realize or support the complexity of black musical culture's independent development of a black experimentalism that, while in dialogue with white high culture, was, like the New Negroes of the Harlem Renaissance, strongly insistent upon the inclusion of the black vernacular, including the imperative of improvisation. Moreover, unlike the Third Stream movement, this independent black experimentalism challenged the centrality of pan-Europeanism to the notion of the experimental itself, instead advancing the notion that experimentalism was becoming "creolized."

In this light the focus in standard histories on the role of improvisor, a trope that has become standard in the historiography and criticism of black American music, cannot account for the diversity of black musical subjectivity exemplified by the AACM. As we can see from the following meeting excerpt, the dominant focus of the AACM as strongly *composer*-centered was fostered right from the start, eventually leading to the extensive engagement with notation in so many AACM members' works.

RICHARD ABRAMS: Now, for the benefit of those who were not here last week, we decided that we in this organization will play only our own music—original compositions or material originating from the members within the group.

JULIAN PRIESTER: It would seem to be that if you put too many restrictions on the activities at this point, you're going to put a lot of obstacles in your way. For instance, to me, everyone in here is not a composer, so right there you exclude them.

RICHARD ABRAMS: No, no one's excluded, you see. You may not be Duke Ellington, but you got some kind of ideas, and now is the time to put 'em in. Wake yourself up. This is an awakening we're trying to bring about (AACM 1965b).

In the context of the 1970s, Abrams' reference to bringing about "an awakening" through composition recognizes that this simple assertion by Afro-Americans—defining oneself as a composer—was a challenge to the social and indeed the economic order of both the music business and the aesthetics business. Moreover, the reference to Ellington is understandable on a number of levels, given the fact that throughout his career Ellington's image of himself as a composer working with and through African American forms was constantly challenged, stigmatized, and stereotyped.[24] Moreover, even African American composers who had grown up with so-called classical training were similarly burdened with ethnic stereotyping and channeling. Thus, Ellington could be viewed as a symbol not only of excellence and innovation but of optimistic perseverance. Moreover, as some AACM composers explored the more restricted, Dahlhausian notion of composition as a dialectic with notation (Dahlhaus 1972:9), modernist black classical composers such as Ulysses Kay, Olly Wilson, Talib Rasul Hakim, and Hale Smith provided models for emulation and vindication.[25]

Like the modernist black composers, AACM composers often sought to place their work in dialogue with diasporic traditions and histories from both Africa and Europe. At the same time, the ongoing binary opposition between composition and improvisation, present as an important trope in both modernist and postmodernist pan-European practice, lacked any real force among AACM composers, who were often drawn to collage and interpenetration strategies that blended, opposed, or ironically juxtaposed the two disciplines. Thus, as with Ellington, as well as later white American experimentalism, the definition of composition could be a fluid one, appropriating and simultaneously challenging and revising various pan-European models, dialoguing with African, Asian, and Pacific music traditions, and employing compositional methods that did not necessarily privilege either conventionally notated scores or the single, heroic creator figure so beloved by jazz historiography.

Roscoe Mitchell's recording of *The Maze* (Mitchell 1978) featured a meditative composition for eight percussionists—or, rather, eight musicians who introduced the AACM-based version of "little instruments," found objects and homemade instruments, to contemporary percussion practice. Muhal Richard Abrams's recording *1QOA+19* (Abrams 1978a) juxtaposed complex written passages with propulsive rhythms, while his *Lifea Blinec* (Abrams 1978b) presented multi-instrumental, text-sound, and electronic textures. Leo Smith recorded a long-form notated work for trumpet and three harps, *The Burning of Stones* (Smith 1979). Chico Freeman (1977) was working with post-bebop jazz quartets, while the trio Air was recasting older, pre–New Orleans African American forms. And my own work, including *Chicago Slow Dance* (Lewis 1977), combined minimalism, open improvisation, electronic tape, and live electronics.

This kind of engagement with composition, following theorist Kobena Mercer, "critically appropriates elements from the master-codes of the dominant culture and *creolizes* them, disarticulating given signs and rearticulating their symbolic meaning otherwise" (Mercer 1994:62).According to Mercer, "critical dialogism"

> has the potential to overturn the binaristic relations of hegemonic boundary maintenance by multiplying critical dialogues *within* particular communities and *between* the various constituencies which make up the "imagined community" of the nation. . . . Such dialogism shows that our "other" is already inside each of us, that black identities are plural and heterogeneous. (65)

Indeed both the overturning of "hegemonic boundary maintenance" and the affirmation of heterogeneous black identity were critical elements of the projects of both Ellington and the AACM. The frequent disclaimers by black musicians of the classification "jazz" can be seen as an expression of this desire for genre and methodological mobility. As Ellington remarked in 1962, after a lifetime of evading labels, "Let's not worry about whether the result is jazz or this or that type of performance. Let's just say that what we're all trying to create, in one way or another, is music" (Tucker 1993:326).

Black Classical Composers (and Black Cultural Critics)

Experimental musicians who were familiar with the important earlier work of the influential critic and activist Amiri Baraka might have been particularly surprised at the vehemence with which he denounced the hybrid new music of the AACM in a collection of his 1980s critical essays, *The Music*. Baraka disparages an unnamed violinist (probably Leroy Jenkins) as a member of what he calls the "Tail Europe" school, whose members were presumably unduly influenced by European modernism. According to Baraka, the project of "Tail Europe" was to "take music on a tired old trip, deliberately trying to *declass* the music, transforming it into a secondary appendage of European concert music, rather than the heroic expression of the folk and classical music of the African-American majority as well as the spirit of a progressive and populist high art." Baraka holds up the work of saxophonist David Murray as an example of "redefining the spiritual aesthetic of a whole people," while another unnamed saxophonist—almost certainly Anthony Braxton—"wants to show us that he's heard Berg and Webern and Stockhausen . . . showing white folks how intelligent he (they) is" (Baraka and Baraka 1987:260).

Even at the time that it was written, this updated Dionysian/Apollonian binary, along with its evocation of the "heroic" and "the majority," is difficult to understand as anything other than a certain nostalgia for a bygone moment. Jazz had by this time long since ceased to be a music of the black majority, but here the music is reenlisted in the quest for what Andrew Ross calls the "Golden Fleece of the intellectuals' century-long search for a democratic people's art that was both organic and post-agrarian" (Ross 1989:93). Moreover, this discussion points to the fact that, despite the best efforts of black scholars such as Eileen Southern and longtime New York *Amsterdam News* music critic Raoul Abdul, the black classical composer has been almost entirely ignored by black cultural critics. The reasons for this disavowal are complex, even as Southern warned in 1973, "If we black folk are serious about our commitment to the rediscovery and the redefining of our heritage in the fine arts, our scholars must take upon themselves the responsibility for developing an appropriate and exemplary literature" (6).

This responsibility has not, for the most part, been taken up by the field of academic popular culture studies, which, by downplaying or even actively disparaging the utility, purpose, and influence of those indigenously black musics that are not obviously or predominantly based in or represented as mass culture, has been unable to account for the full diversity of black musical engagement. Thus, in the age of globalized megamedia, to the extent that certain oppositional black musical forms have been generally ignored or dismissed by academic theorists, the idea is thereby perpetuated that black culture, as academically defined and studied, is in fact corporate-approved culture and that there is no necessary noncommercial space for black musical production.

The implication here is that academics accept the notion that the set of positions for studies of black music, as well as for black musicians themselves, is properly defined by the economic and demographic imperatives of media corporations. In contextualizing the development of African American music, this intellectual climate supports Andrew Ross's commercial/social Darwinist framing of soul music as having forged "a more successful cultural union" (Ross 1989:97). In fact, Ross's critique of "avant-garde jazz" as having "gone beyond the realm of popular taste" (Ross 1989:97) moves well past Baraka's in advancing the notion that marginalized, oppositional, subaltern, corporate-ignored or otherwise nonmainstream forms of black cultural production should be ignored, if not altogether erased.

In this context, the entry into classical music by black composers, rather than bourgeois accommodation, becomes an oppositional stance. In fact, the very existence of the black classical composer not only problematizes dominant conceptions of black music but challenges fixed notions of high and low, black and white. For the most part, black classical composers active since 1930, coming out of the tradition of William Grant Still, have never been as dismissive of popular music as their white colleagues. Black classical music making, from Still's *Afro-American Symphony* (1930) to Hale Smith's *Ritual and Incantations* (1975), continued to reference elements of vernacular black life, both in recognition of the continuing dialogue between black culture and European traditions and articulation of the composers' connection to an African diasporic sonic culture whose worldwide influence throughout the twentieth century and into the twenty-first can hardly be overstated.

Baraka's 1980s definition of the directions in African American music as overdetermined by "wherever the masses of the African-American people have gone" (Baraka and Baraka 1987:177) recapitulates the thrust of his 1966 essay, "The Changing Same (r&b and New Black Music)," an anthem for the more prescriptive aspects of the then emerging Black Aesthetic (Jones 1968:180–211). In such an atmosphere the African American composer trained in the Western European "art" tradition is troped as a tragic mulatto figure—shunned by white-dominated systems of cultural support and supposedly a nonfactor in black culture as well.

It seemed plain enough to Muhal Richard Abrams, however, that "there are different types of black life, and therefore we know that there are different kinds of black music. Because black music comes forth from black life" (Vuisje 1978:199). What the Baraka of the mid-1980s did not notice was a certain reversed dynamic relative to the 1960s, when resistance to dominant narratives included a strategy of refusal of the "bourgeois" values of classical music in favor of the advocacy of vernacular musics such as jazz, blues, and r&b. Attali's notion of the economy of repetition, however, identifies the deployment of an amorphous construction of the masses as useful precisely for the same dominant economic interests who have, according to need, alternately exploited and erased black musical expression. Far from articulating resistance or class struggle, those who import the bourgeois-versus-vernacular binary dialectic unblinkingly into the complex world of black musical expression now risk serving as the ventriloquist's dummy for corporate megamedia.

A conception of black cultural history that is forced to deny engagement with or influence from pan-European traditions would look absurd if it were applied to black writers or visual artists. Such a perspective cannot account for the complexity of experience that characterizes multiple, contemporary black lives. Thus, this particular formulation of resistance, in advancing (strategically) essentialist notions of black music practice and reference, enforced an aesthetic rigidity that minimized the complexity and catholicity of a composite black musical tradition that includes Nathaniel Dett, James Reese Europe, Will Marion Cook, Florence Price, Ulysses Kay, Olly Wilson, Dorothy Rudd Moore, Hale Smith, Primous Fountain III, Wendell Logan, and Jeffrey Mumford.

A trope that uses overly broad strokes to posit a classical-jazz binary cannot account for those who, like Sun Ra, John Coltrane, Miles Davis, Bud Powell, and many others, were extremely respectful of and eager to learn from the achievements in pan-European music—and all other musics—while rejecting Western aesthetic hegemony. On this view the AACM's engagement with Europe was simply the next step in a long history of exchange that, as with AACM composers like Roscoe Mitchell, Joseph Jarman, Henry Threadgill, Malachi Favors, Anthony

Braxton, and others, included formal academic study. Describing the scene at an early, pre-AACM rehearsal of Muhal Richard Abrams's Experimental Band, a group widely seen as a direct predecessor of the AACM, Jarman remembered that his early compositions, influenced by his training with Dr. Richard Wang at Wilson Junior College in Chicago, were "real deep into Anton Webern and the concentrated elements of compositional form" (Jarman 1998). Jarman's story was hardly atypical; of course, white experimentalism was widely discussed, along with other world musics, particularly among the members of the AACM's first wave, a fact that should be unsurprising.

AACM musicians pursued not only practices of exchange and creolization but also strategies of deauthorization, as expressed in Lester Bowie's signifying:

> I mean most Europeans' background is one of wars and colonization of Africa. I mean really, they've dogged a lot of people. And they have this kind of presumed intelligence, they presume that they're really cultured. And they are in a certain sense, but in other ways they're really barbaric, crude. Most western nations are like that. They didn't get to be big western nations walking on roses or no shit like that. I mean they became France by cutting off motherfuckers' heads. (BEAUCHAMP 1998:43)

Thus I would advance the notion that what is particularly striking about some AACM music is not how much it sounded like white European and American experimentalism but how little. Reading many of the "Tail Europe"–style critiques, it became clear to musicians that many jazz critics were simply not prepared for the full impact of the postmodern multi-instrumentalism of the AACM, with its tremendous range of references from around the world. Moreover, if we can take Giddins's and even Baraka's remarks as symptomatic, the high modernist and postmodernist music being performed in New York in the 1970s and 1980s, from Sollberger to Ashley to Reich to Oliveros to Rzewski, was unfamiliar to many jazz writers, even those who were living in New York. In the final analysis, those who thought that Anthony Braxton sounded like Karlheinz Stockhausen or Anton Webern could not be said to have truly heard much of either.

The AACM's radical individualism allowed multiple notions of the future of music to coexist. Thus AACM musicians had been inculcated into a set of values that saw constructed distinctions between musicians, such as those advanced by Baraka between Murray and Braxton, as a form of divide-and-conquer, regardless of the race of the person articulating them. Thus, Steve McCall, one of Baraka's frequent 1980s collaborators, nonetheless said this about New York jazz writers: "Something that irritates me about many people who write about jazz here is the fact that they think that when they praise one music, then they have to downgrade another. I don't like that at all! Because that is completely unnecessary" (Jost 1982:122).

Accordingly, those who were looking for divisions between AACM members based on the Tail Europe issue were undoubtedly disappointed in Lester Bowie's response to an interviewer's claim that Anthony Braxton, Douglas Ewart, and myself "ignore a whole lot of the cultural background of jazz": "There's a whole branch of that, I call it neo-classical. They're in touch with this kind of thing and I feel it's very valid and very cool. . . . They are developing other areas that are just as valid and just as culturally expressive of our time and age. The music is spreading to encompass all of these areas" (Coppens 1979:14).

Where Baraka sees overt class struggle in the composition, performance, appreciation, analysis, and critical writing about the music (Baraka and Baraka 1987:260), I would maintain that, on this very view, the AACM represents an indigenous working-class attempt to open up the space of popular culture to new forms of expression, blurring the boundaries between popular and high culture. As African American musicians sought the same mobility across the breadth of their field that (for example) African American writers and visual artists were striving for, engagement with contemporary pan-European music became a form of boundary-blurring resistance to efforts to restrict the mobility of black musicians, rather than a capitulation to bourgeois values. AACM musicians felt that experimentalism in music need not be bound to particular ideologies, methods, or slogans. Instead, it could take many forms, draw from many histories (including the blues), confront different methodological challenges, and manifest a self-awareness as being in dialogue with the music of the whole earth. Thus Lester Bowie could affirm the excellence of his colleagues while locating himself solidly in a different area within this vast field of musical riches: "I am from a different kind of thing. I deal purely with ass-kicking. Period. Just good old country ass-kicking" (Coppens 1979:14).

New Music and Hybridity

John Cage's "History of Experimental Music in the United States," part of his early, widely influential 1961 manifesto, *Silence* (Cage 1961:67), continues to serve as a "readymade" touchstone for later histories and reference works, including Nyman (1999), Johnson (1989), Kostelanetz (1993), Rubin (1994), and Cameron (1996). These and other historical accounts, reviews, and retrospectives tended to define "experimental music" in terms of a set of acceptable methodologies, people, sites, and venues available to pan-European high-culture music. Musics by people of color (in particular, the high-culture musics of Asia) were most often framed as "sources."

The development of a notion of "experimental" and "American" that excludes the so-called bebop and free jazz movements, perhaps the most influential American experimentalist musics of the latter part of the twentieth century, is highly problematic. This discursive phenomenon can be partly accounted for in terms of the general absence of discourses on issues of race and ethnicity in criticism on American experimentalism. In later years this aspect of denial in new music's intellectual environment tended to separate it from both post-1960s jazz and from other contemporary work in visual art, literature, and dance. More centrally, it could be said that part of white-coded experimentalism's ongoing identity formation project depended upon an Othering of its great and arguably equally influential competitor, the jazz tradition, which is also widely viewed (and views itself) as explicitly experimental. The transcribed "orature" of musicians endorsing the importance of exploration, discovery, and experiment is quite vast and easy to access; it spans virtually every era of jazz music and includes nearly every improvisor of canonical stature before the rise of Wynton Marsalis in the mid-1980s.[26] Even as both uptown and downtown musics of the 1980s sought to challenge prevailing wisdom in so many areas, the dominant response of white American experimentalism to the hybridity represented by the AACM displayed an ongoing fealty to the erasure of African American cultural production from the very definition of experimental.[27]

This stance was radically challenged by the diversity movement in experimental music. For Attali free jazz "eliminated the distinctions between popular music and learned music, broke down the repetitive hierarchy" (Attali 1989:140). As I have noted, the AACM's revision of the relationship between composition and improvisation lies on an unstable fault line between the new black music and the new white music, a border that was brought to light as the work of AACM, BAG, and other black experimentalist composers began to receive limited exposure in some of the same venues, and support from some of the same sources, as white experimental composers. Thus, for a short period between 1976–78, trombonist Garrett List, as music director of the Kitchen, was particularly active in moving toward a nonracialized, barrier-breaking conception of new music. Members of the new generation of black experimentalists, such as Anthony Braxton, Leo Smith, Oliver Lake, and the Art Ensemble of Chicago were presented in Kitchen concerts during List's tenure, though few of these events were ever reviewed. By 1980 my own two-year tenure as music director of the Kitchen could be viewed as shifting the debate around border crossing to a stage where whiteness-based constructions of American experimentalism were being fundamentally problematized.

Both the Voice and the Times announced the new Kitchen regime in bold letters. The Times presented a large picture of the new music director in its Sunday "Arts and Leisure" section, accompanied by the Kitchen's Wales-born director Mary MacArthur (Rockwell 1980). Voice writer Tom Johnson's review of my first curated event described a double bill of a collaboration between synthesist Tom Hamilton and Black Artists Group woodwind improvisor J. D. Parran, followed by a John Zorn "opera" for improvisors, Jai Alai. For Johnson the salient feature of this event was expressed in the headline: "The Kitchen Improvises" (Johnson 1980). Johnson admitted that while the previous Kitchen concert policy had been a valuable forum for "many fine minimalist works requiring long spans of time and complete composer control," it had nonetheless "tended to shut out new music involving improvising groups" (72). Thus the writer predicted that the direction of the Kitchen's programming, "assuming that these opening concerts are symptomatic, is to open the door to new forms of improvising." Nonetheless, the jazz side of the Voice took little, if any, notice of events at the Kitchen. A full five years after the earlier musings of Gary Giddins (1975) about border crossing, the venue was still not considered part of the jazz "turf."

My presence at the Kitchen was an artifact of an era in which African American musical histories and practices came into dialogue with white-coded American experimentalism's methods, practices, and, not incidentally, its sources of support, right in the center of one of the most publicly charged arenas in the world. The Kitchen, with its relatively extensive infrastructure, its large presentation and commissioning budgets, and its commitment to experimental work, had a long history of supporting complex projects that other spaces would not or could not bring to fruition. The new curatorial direction promised to make that infrastructure welcoming to African American artists who sought to present that kind of demanding hybrid work. Perhaps realizing this, Johnson goes on to warn his readers that the apparent broadening of scope and altering of focus was going to require some adjustments, particularly in dialogue with a cultural institution whose overall budget at the time was over half a million dollars: "When it is decided that previously neglected formats will open the season at a place like the Kitchen, that means a lot. It's not just someone's opinions but an actual fact, and everyone concerned must adjust to it" (Johnson 1980:72).[28]

The new hybridity reflected in the Kitchen's programming was part of an emerging challenge to journalistic, critical, social, and historical discourses that presented as entirely natural the musical separation of black and white, low and high, uptown and downtown, popular and serious, "Music" and "Riffs." Lacking a language adequate to the task of describing and contextualizing the new diversity, critical reception eventually settled on the notion that the Kitchen was now "concentrating" on jazz, which seemed putatively defined as "new music by black people, and/or which featured improvisation"—a framing that updated, but ultimately preserved the old racializations. While the number of Kitchen events featuring African Americans or improvised music had indeed increased sharply from prior years, concentration was far too strong a term; the complement of artists presented could not be subsumed under any generalizations about ethnicity, race, gender, or musical method.[29]

Eventually, the *Voice*, which had faithfully covered Kitchen events for years, virtually ceased covering them. The *Soho Weekly News* followed suit until its demise in 1981, preferring (mostly negative) articles about its "uptown" relatives to boundary-crossing engagement with black forms that had started to come under attack on the jazz side of the paper. *Voice* jazz critics practically never ventured to the Kitchen. Gregory Sandow, the eventual replacement for Tom Johnson, bravely stepped into the breach to review a 1981 Julius Hemphill/Anthony Davis double bill, where he discovered that "the new music crowd found at the Kitchen on other nights stayed away" (Sandow 1981).

There are several reasons for the asymmetrical dynamic regarding critical support for experimental forms in New York. First, critical commentary on the work of the Downtown I avant-garde was most often written by composers who were regarded as members of that community. As a result most *Voice* articles were not simply nonadversarial but were, in a sense, insider reports, where the voices of the artists themselves were always centered. With the support of a sympathetic publisher, the clear purpose was to build a community, even as the articles tended to implicitly define Downtown I's methodological, ethnic, and class boundaries. In contrast, writing on black experimental music came not from among the musicians themselves but from a cadre of more or less professional writers. Few black musicians had the kind of relatively unmediated access to publication the white experimentalists enjoyed; for a brief period, guitarist Vernon Reid, later a founding member of the Black Rock Coalition and the important heavy metal band Living Colour, wrote *Voice* reviews.

However, resistance to diversity, while dominant, was hardly monolithic. The central role of leadership exercised by musicians themselves was vital in envisioning the end of "hegemonic boundary maintenance." The Creative Music Studio (CMS), located in Woodstock, New York, was a grassroots initiative of vocalist Ingrid Berger and her partner, Karl Berger, a vibraphonist and academically trained philosopher who had performed with Eric Dolphy (Sweet 1996). Inspired by both Black Mountain College and trumpeter Don Cherry's cross-cultural vision of new music, the Bergers' creolizing conception brought together members of various experimentalisms. This hybrid conception from the 1970s constituted one obvious model for John Zorn's 1986 declaration that "we should take advantage of all the great music and musicians in the world without fear of musical barriers" (McClary 2000:148).

A typical visitor to CMS might encounter a conversation or performance among a diverse array of musicians, including members of the AACM, such as Roscoe Mitchell and Woodstock neighbor Anthony Braxton, Indian flutist G. S. Sachdev, Japanese Zen shakuhachi artist Watazumi-doso, Senegalese drummer Aiyb Dieng, Brazilian multi-instrumentalist Nana Vasconcelos, and composer and improvisor Pauline Oliveros, a CMS neighbor and frequent participant, who collaborated there with the African American choreographer Ione in creating an opera about Angolan Queen Nzinga's resistance to Portuguese colonial domination. Other area residents, such as bassist Dave Holland and drummer Jack DeJohnette, were regular visitors and instructors, as were the members of the best-known of the live electronic music ensembles, Musica Elettronica Viva. These politically engaged composer-performers—pianists Alvin Curran and Frederic Rzewski, synthesizer player Richard Teitelbaum, and trombonist Garrett List—had for many years actively sought alliances with improvisors from different traditions, recognizing early on that musicians of all backgrounds and ethnicities were exchanging sounds, styles, materials, and methodologies (cf. Teitelbaum 1972).

The high point of the early diversity movement produced the New Music America (NMA) Festival, perhaps one of the first attempts to codify, in a performance network, an avant-garde that drew from a wide variety of sources. The festival's immediate predecessor was 1979's "New Music, New York," a week-long series of concerts and symposia sponsored by the Kitchen during composer Rhys Chatham's tenure as music curator. Beginning in 1980 the New Music America Festival sought to expand on the success of "New Music, New York," aiming at the creation of nothing less than an annual national showcase for experimental music. Over the fourteen-year lifespan of the festival large-scale festivals were held in such major cities as Chicago, San Francisco, Miami, and Montreal, among others.

While a 1992 monograph summarizing New Music America's history is suitably multicultural in tone and presentation (Brooks 1992:10), the rhetoric of inclusion never quite caught up to the reality. The fifty-four composers listed in advertisements for the original "New Music, New York" constituted a veritable catalog of Downtown I artists; just three, however, were African American: Don Cherry, Leo Smith, and myself ("Advertisement for New Music, New York Festival"1979). Thus, at several of the panel discussions accompanying the New York festival, criticisms were made concerning the overwhelming whiteness of the version of experimental music being presented as "diverse." The few nonwhite composers featured, however, exercised influence far out of proportion to their numbers, not least because, for perhaps the very first time, their presence obliged the "downtown" artworld to touch upon, however gingerly, the complex relationship between race, culture, music, method, and art world rewards. Anticipating the furor, *Voice* reviewer Johnson, while admitting that "the festival was clearly weighted toward white musicians," felt nonetheless that this had "more to do with recent history than with overt racism" (Johnson 1979:89). Johnson's acknowledgment that "the black-dominated loft jazz scene has evolved right alongside the white-dominated experimental scene throughout this decade" was perhaps the first such admission to appear in any New York paper.

For Johnson, however, an attempt by the Kitchen to engage with this black experimental music "would be far more patronizing than constructive. . . . A truly ecumenical festival of new music in New York would have to include some of the klezmer musicians . . . along with shakuhachi players, kamancheh players, Irish groups, Balkan groups, and so on" (79). This strategy of unfurling the banners of pluralism and color blindness to mask this astonishing conflation of diverse musics under the heading of "Other" begs questions of affinity, collaboration, and competition between black and white experimentalism that were already being articulated all over New York, right under the noses of media commentators supposedly "representing" both camps.

In any event, AACM and BAG artists constituted a clear majority of the very few African American composers featured in New Music America events over the succeeding years. For NMA 1980 in Minneapolis, the only African Americans invited were the Art Ensemble of Chicago, a duo of Oliver Lake and Leroy Jenkins, and former SUNY Buffalo Creative Associate Julius Eastman, out of forty-seven events listed. Despite the presence of two AACM members (Douglas Ewart and myself) on the advisory board of the Chicago-based 1982 NMA festival, of the approximately sixty-five presented just four performances by African Americans were featured. These included an orchestral work by Muhal Richard Abrams and chamber works by Douglas Ewart and Roscoe Mitchell ("Advertisement for New Music America Festival" 1981). Particularly telling, in the founding city of the AACM itself, with an African American population of over 40 percent, was a panel discussion, titled "New Music and Our Changing Culture," in which all the participants—David Behrman, John Cage, Dan Graham, Ben Johnston, Marjorie Perloff, and Christian Wolff—were white.

In the Tradition?

The mid-1980s saw the rise of the neoclassical movement in jazz, which placed musicians, critics, and audiences on the horns of at least two dilemmas: between tradition and innovation and between classical music and jazz. Trumpeter Wynton Marsalis, who possessed expertise in both jazz and classical traditions, soon emerged as the leading spokesperson for this movement. Marsalis, who had already won Grammy awards in both classical and jazz categories—in the same year—began working with New York's Lincoln Center, home to the Metropolitan Opera and the New York Philharmonic, to produce a series called "Classical Jazz," a series title that seemed tailored to Marsalis's rapidly growing public image. In fact, Alina Bloomgarden, a Lincoln Center employee, had been promoting the idea as far back as 1983; for the post of "artistic advisor," she recruited Marsalis, who in turn recruited writer Stanley Crouch (Porter 2002:311–12).[30]

Up to this point the most unusual aspect of the debate over borders between classical music and jazz was that its most publicly prominent conceptual leadership came disproportionately from the black experimental music community. A 1987 *New York Times* article by Jon Pareles, viewing Marsalis's double releases of classical concertos and jazz recordings as "superficial" and "a gimmick," framed AACM composers Roscoe Mitchell and Anthony Braxton, along with Ornette Coleman, James Newton, Anthony Davis, and Butch Morris, as "experimental hybrids [who] have to battle on both the jazz and classical fronts" but were nonetheless key to the emergence of a new synthesis of classical music and jazz (Pareles 1987).

The alacrity with which this interpretation of classical-jazz fusion was simply swept from the chessboard is fascinating to review. The promulgation of a revisionist canon that emphasized a unitary, "classic" tradition of jazz eventually took on an institutionalized cast with the 1991 creation of Jazz at Lincoln Center (JALC), arguably the most heavily funded jazz institution ever to exist. The JALC approach to the classicization of jazz had its antecedents in many earlier classicizing projects, but this new version sought not to problematize or transgress barriers between jazz and classical music, as the AACM and others had tried to do, but to uphold and nurture them. In a critical discursive shift, the term *classical* became less a description of a musical tradition than of an attitude—one of reverence and preservation.

Stanley Crouch, formerly one of the most vocal supporters of the 1970s black experimentalists, had shifted ground by the early 1980s. Influenced by the heroic modernism of writer Albert Murray, Crouch became heavily critical of the new music (Crouch 1979) and declared in the liner notes to a Marsalis recording of "jazz standards" that the new challenge for black musicians would be "to learn how to redefine the fundamentals while maintaining the essences that give the art its scope and grandeur" (quoted in Porter 2002:304).

Ironically, JALC's articulation of membership in the "canon" (at least up to 1960) would be fully congruent with that of the first-wave AACM members, who had all grown up revering the same artists—Louis Armstrong, Jelly Roll Morton, Art Tatum, Duke Ellington, Charlie Parker, Thelonious Monk, and others—that the neoclassicists held dear. For years, prior to coming to New York, Henry Threadgill had been combing the Joplin repertoire, Muhal Richard Abrams was mining and recasting stride, and Roscoe Mitchell was making ironic references to r&b. Moreover, the issue of "standard music" versus "original music" had also been a central aspect of the discussions in the initial meeting of the AACM on May 8, 1965. Bringing up the question of the policing of black creativity, Roscoe Mitchell asserts that "probably most of the people in this room do want to play their own music, but they don't get a chance to do it because somebody on the gig is telling you to play this or play that" (AACM 1965a). Steve McCall's thoughtful, ecumenical reasoning about the need for a new organization is especially valuable:

> The standard music, we've all played it, and not taking nothing away from no form of music at all. But for *this* organization, you know, for the promoting of having cats to write, you know, like the original charts, original compositions, and getting together and presenting, in concert; and as a means of a livelihood, you dig, like making some money, getting out of your things, the things that we all create among ourselves. Being at a concert just for standard music, you know, there doesn't have to be this kind of a group for that kind of thing. (AACM 1965A)

As McCall noted, "The standard music, we've all played it." Thus one can imagine the puzzlement of AACM experimentalists when a new breed of New York–based journalists, critics, and musicians advanced the claim that those who had been creating the new music had "no respect for tradition." The fact that the new musicians chose definition over redefinition, by presenting their own music as they had done since their Chicago days, now became an issue for much critical reception; in fact, the presentation of "original music" was now used as prima facie confirmation of this "lack of respect." For some this "evidence" made the "no respect" claim easier to substantiate than the simultaneous recycling of the older canard that the "free" musicians "couldn't play," since many AACM musicians had worked with some of the most traditionally respected musicians—Mercer Ellington performing Muhal Richard Abrams's Duke Ellington arrangements, Lester Bowie with Albert King, Leo Smith with Little Milton, Pete Cosey with Miles Davis, Steve McCall with Dexter Gordon, Amina Claudine Myers with Gene Ammons and Sonny Stitt, my work with Count Basie and Gil Evans, and so on.

A signal difference between the pre- and post-Marsalis framings of African American musical tradition, however, was that the AACM musicians were taking what was up to that time an unchallenged view—that the jazz music now regarded as "classical" was originally the product of innovation, i.e., "finding one's own sound." On this view the musician's attitude of experiment and self-realization was one of the crucial reasons for the importance of the work itself. A 1995 article on Marsalis in the *New York Times Magazine* questions this view, accusing those who valorized innovation of appealing to outdated notions of "progress" in the arts:

> Have we had progress in poetry, in the novel, in painting or in dance? I don't think so. . . . The way to strengthen one's ability to tell the difference between progress and evolution is to study the canon—that music

which has had the longest and deepest influence—because the canon contains the evolutionary signposts and implies how jazz can spiral outward without losing its identity. . . . One of the most important missions of Jazz at Lincoln Center is to lay down a foundation for the future of jazz by presenting important works from the canon with all the passion and intelligence that can be brought to bear. (CONROY 1995)31

While the new canon seemed lacking in a number of important respects, such as the apparent exclusion of the work of people like Ornette Coleman, Cecil Taylor, post-"Ascension" Coltrane, and other black experimental musicians, Farah Jasmine Griffin points out that "had Marsalis not struck such a conservative stance, whereby some of the most innovative practitioners are left out of the jazz canon, it is highly unlikely he would have been able to acquire the resources necessary to do the kind of work on behalf of the music that he has done" (Griffin 2001:143–44). Certainly, in the severely undercapitalized field of jazz, the advent of JALC, with the massive resources to which Griffin refers, had much the same effect as the introduction of a Wal-Mart into a community of Mom-and-Pop businesses.[32] Taking advantage of a regularly supportive media presence, as well as backing from major corporations for his music and his JALC events, Marsalis eventually took on a role as authoritative spokesperson for the future of music itself, assuming as his primary mission the creation of an atmosphere in which jazz was finally due to be treated with the "same respect" as classical music.

Prominent black intellectuals who had generally been associated with progressive political stances signed on. Some, like Cornel West, did so enthusiastically,[33] while others, like Amiri Baraka, acknowledged a certain ambivalence. In a 1995 German-language interview Baraka avows that "I want to be completely honest there—I would rather hear Wynton Marsalis in an Ellington concert than what [Lester] Bowie or [Henry] Threadgill do. Even when I value them for certain things that they have brought into being." In the very next breath Baraka emphasizes the issue of self-determination, which the AACM had also sought to bring forth—an idea with which Baraka himself, with his long history of political activism, had inspired many:

> Yes, they [Bowie and Threadgill] should have regular stages too, and I wish that Sonny Rollins had one. But the problem will present itself as long as we do not have our own independent institutions. Until then I can only say: It is to be welcomed that the Afro-American tradition is being preserved by Wynton Marsalis. I would even describe his work in these times as progressive. (BROECKING 1995:111)

Despite Baraka's assertion that "there is no point on which we agree" (ibid.), on the issue of black experimental music aesthetics he and Stanley Crouch find common ground in their disapprobation of black music that exhibits too much "European influence"—a criticism that, given their own—and Marsalis's—use of European tropes, appears particularly curious, even contradictory. Thus it became evident that this "progressive" motif of preservation and protection did not extend to the products of the black experimentalists. As early as 1982, discussions of black new music were beginning to disappear from the New York "alternative" press. AACM-oriented ideas of diversity, mobility, and innovation came under withering attack, not only from an emerging politically and culturally neoconservative aesthetic movement but from the black political left wing as well.

Criticisms of Marsalis's approach to the canon were generally dismissed by a supremely supportive New York press, and naysayers were admonished to (as the title of a 1995 *New York Times Magazine* piece had it) "Stop Nitpicking a Genius" (Conroy 1995). Nonetheless, many musicians were resistant to the new regime. Even as he was being widely touted as an up-and-coming "Young Lion in the Tradition," composer Anthony Davis, who collaborated extensively with a number of AACM artists, expressed the views of many when he was widely quoted as saying that the notion of "tradition" was being used "essentially as a vehicle for conservatism" and "as a means of maintaining the status quo, of limiting your own personal connection" (Van Trikt 1985:5).

A number of AACM musicians, moreover, detected (correctly) the hand of corporate megamedia stirring the new traditionalism's soup kettle. Roscoe Mitchell warned that

> what we've seen happen between the 60s and now is the commercial machine expanding and dominating the scene. . . . We've seen the institutionalizing of so-called "jazz." We've seen a general turning away of new ideas and sounds. . . . [Young musicians] are getting these messages from the media that they should do such-and-such to re-create the tradition. But the tradition will never be re-created as strongly as it was by the people who invented it. (BAKER 1989:19)

Indeed the marketing strategy around the heavily advertised and corporate-supported Ken Burns film *Jazz* exhibited a remarkable synergy, with videos, DVDs, and CDs bearing the "Ken Burns Jazz" logo available immediately following the airing of the first episode.[34] Thus Mitchell was certainly expressing a common view, neatly encapsulated in a 1994 *New York Times* headline announcing a "Classical Jazz" event: "Jazz, Classical, Art, Business: A Series Wraps All Into One" (Watrous 1994).

It is worth noting that up to this point in time Lincoln Center had never been a significant long-term supporter of musical experimentalism; why so many people in the jazz community thought that a Lincoln Center jazz program would be any different might be explained with reference to a certain lack of experience with the histories and practices of this and other high-culture institutions. Moreover, despite Marsalis's reputation as an interpreter in both jazz and classical idioms, his public pronouncements regarding method and canon have somehow been essentially limited to the jazz side of his work. Further, within that sphere, black musicians, for the most part, have been the exclusive targets of both his critiques and those emanating from his mentors, Crouch and Murray.

In contrast to the ideologically charged atmosphere on Lincoln Center's jazz side, its classical side has tended to avoid extensive public critiques of experimental music in its chosen, European-based tradition. In fact, composers seen as "fringe" elements were quietly supported, even as it was acknowledged that the public was not necessarily excited about their music. To keep donations flowing, patrons were discouraged from attending new music events (Hersh 1980).

Thus, by the mid-1980s, when one of the new black experimentalists presented an event deemed to fall outside the social or methodological frame of jazz, neither the jazz writers nor the new music writers would cover it. In the jazz press those among the black experimentalists who "refused to swing" or were "too European" were routinely savaged, with little hope of succor from the "new music" press, which simply ignored them as it had done earlier. Black composers framed as "jazz" who dared to present transgressive new work at spaces like the Kitchen would be covered only when they chose to return to their "natural" home in a local club. As Attali says of free jazz, the work of these musicians was "contained, repressed, limited, censored, expelled" (Attali 1989:140).

However, the increasingly interdisciplinary and multicultural landscape in which present-day artists find themselves wreaks havoc with the logic of those who would confine African American musicians to nativist (re)presentations of a narrowly constructed "blues idiom" while arrogating to themselves the right to consider Picasso, Rothko, de Kooning, Proust, Joyce, Eliot, Melville, Kerouac, Burroughs, Wagner, Schoenberg, and Stravinsky salient to their deliberations. Throughout the past century African American musical artists have pursued an ongoing engagement not only with Eurological forms but with the world of art and music as a whole, in full awareness of their position in a world of art-making traditions. As with the work of earlier generations of African American artists, the current generation is free to assimilate sounds from all over the world, even as they situate their work in a complexly articulated African American intellectual, social, and sonic matrix. In this regard Julius Hemphill's challenge to the tradition bandwagon is particularly apt: "Well, you often hear people nowadays talking about the tradition, tradition, tradition. But they have tunnel vision in this tradition. Because tradition in African-American music is as wide as all outdoors. . . . Music is much bigger than bebop changes. I don't feel like being trapped in those halls of harmony" (McElfresh 1994).

Epilogue

Before the 1950s, European high culture was the primary standard for high culture in America. Contemporary classical musicians were under particular pressure because of the very frequent assertions by important European musicians, including Bartók, Milhaud, Ravel, Dvořák, and Stravinsky, that jazz, rather than European-based American classical music, represented "the core of American music" as well as the most likely source of new musical ideas for a truly native American music.[35] As Ravel asserted in 1928, "I am waiting to see more Americans appear with the honesty and vision to realize the significance of their popular product, and the technic and imagination to base an original and creative art upon it" (Oja 2000:296).

Today, we find Ravel still waiting for that bus, as American experimental music from Cowell to Cage has advanced a whiteness-based musical nativism that situates itself historically, ethnically, and methodologically in dialogue with an overall pan-European tradition and tries to erase any connection with black American culture (Lewis 1996:98–99; Oja 2000:297–360). Even as the various forms of black experimentalism—bebop, free improvisation, free jazz, and the hybrid work of the AACM—have emerged as serious competitors for the mantle of high art, the assertion that "jazz is America's classical music" continues to be discouraged. As we glimpse the new century, white-coded American experimentalism's gradual willingness to consider some aspects of a multicultural, multiethnic, and even partly internationalist revision of its definition is at variance with its continued disavowal of specifically African American perspectives, histories, traditions, methods, and people.

One might want to question, however, the desirability or utility of a "classical" music to a postmodern, post–Cold War, postcolonial America. Given such a focus, strategies of classicization become disclosed as aspects of competition over capital, both symbolic and actual. Positively put, however, a larger and perhaps more fruitful question might concern what an American classical music might sound like in a postcolonial world. Certainly such a new music would need to draw upon the widest range of traditions while not being tied to any one. Perhaps, as Attali would have it, such a music would exist "in a multifaceted time in which rhythms, styles, and codes diverge, interdependencies become more burdensome, and rules dissolve"—a "new noise" (Attali 1989:138–40). Thus, as the new century approached, AACM musicians continued to present their radical approaches to diversity, even in the face of the loss of several of its members, including cofounder Steve McCall in 1982 and trumpeter Lester Bowie in 1999. The collective established an AACM New York chapter in 1982 to complement its original base in Chicago and continued to organize and present its own events in both cities.

In 1977 Muhal Richard Abrams predicted that the AACM's influence would empower other musicians and groups: "A lot of people will pick up on the example and do very well with it. A lot of people that are not AACM people. Now who those people will be a couple of years from now, who knows?" (Giddins 1977:48). This prediction proved prescient, as New York experimental music movements emerging in the late 1980s, such as the movements of Downtown II and "totalism,"[36] adopted the language of diversity. Improvisor and composer John Zorn, arguably the most well-known artist to emerge from Downtown II, connects this articulation of diversity directly with the AACM, an important influence on his work. In discovering Braxton and the Art Ensemble, Zorn notices that "the guy's [Braxton] got a great head, he's listening to all this different music. It all connected up" (Gagne 1993:511). Echoing longstanding AACM premises, Zorn declared that "I want to break all these hierarchies: the idea that classical music is better than jazz, that jazz is better than rock. I don't think that way" (Watrous 1989).

Downtown II artists, who were never subjected to the discourses of canonization and "roots" that were being used to police the work of black experimental musicians, were able to take full advantage of their relative freedom from cultural arbitration. Thus contemporaneous commentary on Zorn and other Downtown II artists celebrated this diversity of sonic reference in their work, even as comparable efforts by black experimentalists were being routinely condemned. In 1988 John Rockwell found no particular difficulty in declaring that Zorn not only "transcends categories; better, he's made a notable career crashing them together and grinding them to dust" (Rockwell 1988). In contrast, a 1982 Rockwell piece could insist of Anthony Braxton that, "however much he may resist categories, Mr. Braxton's background is in jazz, which means an improvisatory tradition" (Rockwell 1982), an evocation in a single sentence of the eugenicist power of the one-drop rule that revokes rather than celebrates Braxton's mobility.

Moreover, unlike the black artists who preceded and influenced them, Downtown II artists are routinely framed as transcending race as well as genre. By 1989 a *Times* reviewer could declare that the repertory of Zorn's "Naked City" project

> mirrors a typically modern sensibility, in which the culture of our grandparents—whether it's defined by race, religion or nationality—is abandoned, or at least tempered, in favor of the possibilities of endless information. Eclecticism isn't simply a position for some composers: it's the only position. It's the only culture that makes sense to them, that they can depend on—a culture of musical literacy.   (WATROUS 1989)

Downtown II's press coding as white, however, is not only at variance with this image of transcendence but seems to have little basis in either New York City's geography or musical affinities. African American saxophonist Greg Osby's acerbic observation neatly encapsulates the issue: "I played with all the downtown cats but nobody called *me* a downtown cat"—a statement that some AACM members could have made twenty years before (Nai 2001:16).

To the extent that both Downtown I and II failed to challenge either the dominant culture's generally high levels of investment in white positional diversity, or its complementary disinvestment in black subjectivity, they cannot form the basis for a cosmopolitan, globalized, hybrid, transgressive American experimentalism that confronts the challenges to musical form, transmission, and reception represented by the permeability of borders, the dynamics of postcolonialism, and the decline of the nation-state. In that regard, as Attali notes, the work of John Cage, while certainly announcing "the end of music as autonomous activity," nonetheless presents "not the new mode of musical production, but the liquidation of the old" (Attali 1989:138–40).

A recent article by jazz critic Bill Shoemaker (2000) described an already emerging postjazz, post–new music economic network for improvised music that moves beyond gatekeeping authorities, aiming toward the creation of an environment where canonizing pronouncements are both powerless and meaningless. This network can be described in the same terms as those used by theorists Michael Hardt and Antonio Negri to discuss the antiglobalization movement, which for them constitutes a new form of challenge to centralized authority. For Hardt and Negri, the movement "is not defined by any single identity, but can discover commonality in its multiplicity" (Hardt and Negri 2001). Similarly, Muhal Richard Abrams declared more than twenty years ago:

> First we make for ourselves an atmosphere, in which we can survive, in spite of this environment—simply through that which we have in common. We have something in common! For example, we are in agreement that we should further develop our music. Whatever else we do outside of our central development, we will not let this central development be destroyed. (JOST 1982:194)

Ultimately, the AACM's gamble on New York can be viewed as pointing the way toward a mobile, boundary-crossing experimentalism that exemplifies these notions of commonality in multiplicity and individuality within the aggregate. The example of the AACM has been central to the coming canonization not of a new musical aesthetic with defined borders but of a new kind of musician who works across genres with fluidity, grace, discernment, and trenchancy. After nearly forty years of a living AACM presence, the significance of what these new musicians have done up to now, as well as what they might create in the future, is only now beginning to be understood.

NOTES

I am grateful to Muhal Richard Abrams, Jason Stanyek, and Doug Mitchell for their helpful comments. I am also indebted to Wolfram Knauer, Arndt Weidler, and the Jazz-Institut Darmstadt for their tremendous support in allowing me to create an extensive photocopy library of contemporaneous reviews from American, British, German, Dutch, Italian, and French journals. I would also like to thank Mary Lui, now assistant professor of History at Yale University, for access to the Larayne Black Archive at the Chicago Historical Society; and Deborah Gillaspie, the curator of the Chicago Jazz Archive at the University of Chicago, for access to the Jamil B. Figi Collection.

1. A first-person account of the AACM is found in Braxton (1985:410–39). Other accounts of the AACM's early activity, philosophies and musical approaches are to be found in Jost (1975); Wilmer (1992 [1977]); Litweiler (1984); and Radano (1993).

2. For a useful starter bibliography on musicians' collectives, see Gray (1991:41–57).
    For an account of the Clef Club's goals and activities, see Badger (1995). Contemporaneous accounts of the work of the Jazz Composers' Guild include Levin (1965) and Heckman (1965); for a brief personal account of the guild's practice of collective governance, see Bley and Lee (1999:91–97). Briefer references to the guild are found in Wilmer (1992 [1977]:213–15); Litweiler (1984:138–39); and Jost (1991:213–14). For an extended look at the UGMAA, see Tapscott and Isoardi (2001).

3. From time to time I cite the theorist and economist Jacques Attali, whose brief section on free music in his chapter on "Composing" offers a number of insights that dramatically reflect the contemporary situation (1989:133–58). Attali's influential exposition on the musical implications of the "political economy of repetition," or the mass reproduction and centralization of music, explicitly includes the AACM as emblematic

of the project of using music to build a new culture. I am sure that I am not the first to observe that Attali's notion of "composition," proposed in the hope of finding an exit from the Adornonian nightmare of repetition, resembles, in fact, not composition as we know it in the West but improvisation: "Music is no longer made to be represented or stockpiled, but for participation in collective play, in an ongoing quest for new, immediate communication, without ritual and always unstable. It becomes nonreproducible, irreversible" (ibid.:141).

4. Present at this first meeting were, among others, bassists Charles Clark, Betty Dupree, Melvin Jackson, Malachi Favors (later Maghostous), and Reggie Willis, drummers Jerol Donavon (later Ajaramu) and Steve McCall, singers Floradine Geemes, Sandra Lashley, and Conchita Brooks, trumpeter Fred Berry, saxophonists Troy Robinson, Eugene Easton, Jimmy Ellis, Maurice McIntyre (later Kalaparusha), Joseph Jarman (later Shaku), Roscoe Mitchell, and Gene Dinwiddie, trombonists Julian Priester and Lester Lashley, and pianists Jodie Christian, Willie Pickens, Claudine Myers (later Amina), Bob Dogan, Ken Chaney, and Richard Abrams (later Muhal).

5. Other concert spaces included the Abraham Lincoln Centre (a community-service organization in the so-called Bronzeville district on the South Side), St. John's Grand Lodge on South Ingleside, and later the Parkway Community House on East 67th Street.

6. See Nessa (1966); Martin (1966–67, 1968); and Litweiler (1967a, 1967b, 1967c, 1967d, 1968a, 1968b, 1968c).

7. Translations of Jost (1982) and Broecking (1995), from the original German, Vuisje (1978) from the original Dutch, and Caux (1969a, 1969b), Bourget (1977), and Marmande (1977), from the original French, are by the author.

8. This information was also compiled in part from a Black Artists Group program brochure (Black Artists Group 1970[?]), which contained the organization's operating budget.

9. The classic French treatise on the "new thing," clearly influenced by Leroi Jones's *Blues People* (1963), is Carles and Comolli's *Free Jazz/Black Power* (2000 [1971]).

10. Despite the fact that black experimental musicians had an enormous and lasting impact on Parisian cultural life, their activities are hardly mentioned in American historical accounts of the period (e.g., Stovall 1996), an omission that seems particularly curious given the congruence of these musicians' histories with Paris's traditional relationship with black expatriate artists and intellectuals. For an overview of the activities of black Americans in Paris that includes these musicians to some extent, one might try the difficult-to-locate Fabre and Williams (1996).

11. In Europe AACM members developed collaborative and personal relationships with many residents and frequent visitors to the continent, including trombonist Grachan Moncur III, pianists Bobby Few, Mal Waldron, Dave Burrell, Burton Greene, and Cecil Taylor, trumpeters Clifford Thornton and Jacques Coursil, saxophonists Archie Shepp, Jimmy Lyons, Ornette Coleman, Dewey Redman, Kenneth Terroade, Arthur Jones, Steve Lacy, Robin Kenyatta, Byard Lancaster, Noah Howard, and "The Rev." Frank Wright, drummers Muhammad Ali, Philly Joe Jones, Arthur Taylor, Ed Blackwell, Andrew Cyrille, and Sunny Murray, and bassists Alan Silva and Earl Freeman. See Beauchamp (1998) for first-person reminiscences by Art Ensemble members about the Paris period.

12. Other musicians active in the French-based wing of the emerging European free jazz movement included drummers Francois Tusques, Aldo Romano and Claude Delcloo

(who originally invited the Art Ensemble to Paris), trumpeter Bernard Vitet, German pianist Joachim Kühn, then resident in France, saxophonist/clarinetist Michel Portal, and bassists Beb Guerin, Barre Phillips, and Jean-Francois Jenny-Clark. Perhaps the most thorough historical account of European free jazz activity can be found in Jost (1987).

13. This fact casts some doubt on Radano's assertion (1993:142) that the Paris trip occasioned the collapse of AACM unity.

14. A recording of the concert was released in two volumes (Creative Construction Company 1975, 1976).

15. The terms *Downtown I* and *Downtown II* were created by my graduate student at the University of California, San Diego, Michael Dessen, and myself. For a recent collection of the writings of artists associated with Downtown II, see Zorn (2000).

16. According to Giddins (1978a) the NEA disbursed $6,650,000 for symphony orchestras, $3,400,000 for opera, $310, 000 for "contemporary performance of new music," $475,000 for "composers and librettists" (excluding "jazz" composers), and $640,000 for all forms classified as jazz, of which $80,000 went for "jazz composition" and $100,000 for "jazz performance." According to Pasler (1987), NEA music composition grants (and, not surprisingly, the music panel assignments) tended to rotate among a small coterie of white academics. Gilmore (1993) notes that in 1987 "minorities"— African Americans, Native Americans, Asian-Americans, and Latin Americans combined—received 6.3 percent of all grants for music. As Weathers (1973) shows, many black musicians in New York, such as the important bassist Reggie Workman of the Collective Black Artists, saw these discrepancies as a form of discrimination.

17. For a nearly complete collection of over five hundred pages of reprinted *Voice* articles on Downtown I, see Johnson (1989).

18. These included percussionists Ajaramu, Thurman Barker, and Kahil El-Zabar, saxophonists Douglas Ewart, Edward Wilkerson, Mwata Bowden, and Wallace McMillan, pianist Adegoke Steve Colson, bassists Felix Blackmon, Leonard Jones, and Brian Smith, singers Iqua Colson and Bernard Mixon, bassoonist James Johnson, trumpeters Frank Gordon and John Shenoy Jackson, and myself and Martin "Sparx" Alexander as trombonists. Among the members who had become established in New York, there was the trio Air (Henry Threadgill, Fred Hopkins, and Steve McCall) as well as the trio of Anthony Braxton, Leo Smith and Leroy Jenkins.

19. See Goldberg (1988) for a standard account of this interdisciplinary movement away from traditional spaces.

20. Other new performers included pianist Anthony Davis, guitarist Michael Gregory Jackson, drummer Paul Maddox (now Pheeroan ak Laff), and saxophonist David Murray. Those newcomers were augmented by members of the existing New York experimental improvisation scene such as pianist Dave Burrell, trombonists Grachan Moncur III and Roswell Rudd, drummers Jerome Cooper, Andrew Cyrille, Barry Altschul, and Sunny Murray, saxophonists Sam Rivers, Byard Lancaster, Ken McIntyre, Marion Brown, Frank Lowe, Jimmy Lyons, and David S. Ware, trumpeters Olu Dara, Ahmed Abdullah, and Ted Daniel, guitarist Bern Nix, and vibraphonist Khan Jamal.

21. These included pianists Michelle Rosewoman and Marilyn Crispell, saxophonists Jemeel Moondoc, Daniel Carter, Marty Ehrlich, and Charles Tyler, trombonists Craig Harris and Ray Anderson, drummers John Betsch and Ronald Shannon Jackson, guitarists James "Blood" Ulmer, Jean-Paul Bourelly, and James Emery, bassists Mark Dresser, Jerome Harris, John Lindberg, Wilber Morris, William Parker, and Mark Helias,

clarinetist John Carter, cellist Diedre Murray, violinists Jason Hwang and Billy Bang, and vibraphonist Khan Jamal.

22. The poll information was obtained from *Down Beat* critics' and readers' polls between 1971 and 1980.

23. For an account of the "crisis of the listener" and proposed solutions relating to jazz, see Pleasants (1955, 1962). As it happens, Henry Pleasants, whose books championed jazz as the American music of the future, had served as the CIA station chief in Bonn in the 1950s (Martin 2000).

24. For example, while John Hammond recognized that Ellington, with his extended work "Black, Brown and Beige" was "trying to achieve something of greater significance," the producer clearly felt that something more was needed from the composer: "No one can justly criticize him for this if he keeps up the quality of his music for dancing" (Tucker 1993:173).

25. A number of AACM members, including Roscoe Mitchell, Joseph Jarman, Wadada Leo Smith, Muhal Richard Abrams, Amina Claudine Myers, Anthony Braxton, and, later, Henry Threadgill and the present author, have engaged extensively with this mode of composition. An early public inkling of AACM engagement with pan-European experimentalism occurred with the 1966 Joseph Jarman/John Cage midnight concerts at the Harper Theater in Chicago's Hyde Park, which received a highly unfavorable review in *Down Beat* (Welding 1966a:35).

26. See, for instance, the important interviews with African American improvisors published by drummer Arthur Taylor (1993 [1977])

27. See Chatham (1992) and Nyman (1999). In the second edition of his canonical history of experimental music, Nyman was particularly defensive, even defiant, about the fact that it made no effort whatsoever to redress the lack of cultural and ethnic diversity of the first edition. While admitting that a sequel to his book "would have to be less ethnocentric," Nyman maintained that were he writing the first edition today he "would *not* do it any differently" (1999:xviii).

28. For similar estimates of the Kitchen's 1980 budget, see Rockwell (1980).

29. Information compiled from Kitchen concert announcement mailers printed during my term as music curator (between September 1980 and June 1982) shows that the Kitchen's music program presented, among others, Tom Hamilton, John Zorn, Bertram Turetzky, Rae Imamura, Carles Santos, Derek Bailey, Evan Parker, Takehisa Kosugi, Stuart Dempster, William Hellermann, Eliane Radigue, Julius Hemphill, Anthony Davis, Julius Eastman, Michael Byron, William Hawley, Amina Claudine Myers, Arnold Dreyblatt, Gerry Hemingway, Robert Moran, Glenn Branca, Dick Higgins, Jackson MacLow, Ned Sublette, John Morton, Arlene Dunlap/Daniel Lentz, Jamaican Music Festival, John Morton, Carl Stone, Trans Museq (Davey Williams and LaDonna Smith), Roscoe Mitchell, Peg Ahrens, Defunkt, Tona Scherchen-Hsiao, the Ethnic Heritage Ensemble (Kahil El-Zabar, Edward Wilkerson, and Joseph Bowie), Frederic Rzewski, Rhys Chatham, Ingram Marshall, Douglas Ewart, Muhal Richard Abrams, Robert Ashley, Diamanda Galas, Anthony Braxton, Gerald Oshita, and Joan LaBarbara.

30. For a thoughtful history of Marsalis and neoclassicism, see Porter (2002). For a forthright, first-person declaration of the purposes and strategies envisioned at the time regarding the promulgation of a revised canon for jazz, see Marsalis 1988. Herman Gray (1997) has advanced the notion that Marsalis's advocacy of a highly selective version of a jazz canon recapitulates a neoconservative version of the strategies of both

prescription and resistance promulgated by the Black Aesthetic movement of the 1970s.

31. For further elaboration on these issues from a similar viewpoint, see Piazza 1997.

32. As the saxophonist Jimmy Heath remarked, on the eve of a "Classical Jazz" concert featuring his music, "There were grants before, from the government, but nothing like this. The budget, which, I might add, is probably minuscule compared to the classical budget, is still bigger than anything I'm used to, and Lincoln Center itself has an aura of prestige. It's all very helpful to musicians and to the music" (Watrous 1994).

33. For West, Marsalis, like Louis Armstrong, Ella Baker, W. E. B. DuBois, and Martin Luther King Jr., among others, is one of a new breed of "intellectual freedom fighters, that is, cultural workers who simultaneously position themselves within (or alongside) the mainstream while clearly aligned with groups who vow to keep alive potent traditions of critique and resistance." Going further, West exhorts cultural workers to "take clues from the great musicians or preachers of color who are open to the best of what other traditions offer yet are rooted in nourishing subcultures that build on the grand achievements of a vital heritage" (1993:27).

34. Film and music scholar Krin Gabbard (2000:B18) acidly comments that "some of my more cynical friends in jazz circles have pointed out that the only musicians we see in Burns's finale are the ones with major-label recording contracts." However, the extensive sponsorship for jazz events at Lincoln Center has by no means been limited to media corporations.

35. For a contemporary view see Small (1987).

36. For a description of "totalism," see Gann (1997).

WORKS CITED

AACM. 1965a. Audiotape of AACM meeting, May 8, Chicago. Collection of Muhal Richard Abrams.

——— 1965b. Audiotape of AACM meeting, May 15, Chicago. Collection of Muhal Richard Abrams.

——— 1965c. Audiotape of AACM meeting, May 27, Chicago. Collection of Muhal Richard Abrams.

——— 1965d. "State of Illinois Charter, Association for the Advancement of Creative Musicians," August 5, Chicago.

——— 1965e. Audiotape of AACM meeting, October 2, Chicago. Collection of Muhal Richard Abrams.

——— 1966. Audiotape of AACM meeting, January 15, Chicago. Collection of Muhal Richard Abrams.

Abrams, Muhal Richard, and John Shenoy Jackson. 1973. "Association for the Advancement of Creative Musicians." *Black World* 23.1 (November): 72–74.

Abrams, Richard, and Ken Chaney. 1965. Press Release, August [?]. Archives of the AACM, Chicago.

Advertisement for New Music, New York Festival. 1979. *EAR* 5.2 (Summer).

Advertisement for New Music America Festival. 1981. *EAR* 6.2 (February-March): 29

Attali, Jacques. 1989. *Noise: The Political Economy of Music*. Trans. Brian Massumi. Minneapolis: University of Minnesota.

Badger, Reid. 1995. *A Life in Ragtime: A Biography of James Reese Europe*. New York: Oxford University Press.

Baker, Paul. 1989. "Roscoe Mitchell: The Next Step." *Coda*, no. 228 (October/November): 18–21.

Balliett, Whitney. 1977. "Jazz: New York Notes." *New Yorker* (June 20): 92–97.

Baraka, Amiri, and Amina Baraka. 1987. *The Music: Reflections on Jazz and Blues*. New York: William Morrow.

Beauchamp, Lincoln T. Jr. 1998. *Art Ensemble of Chicago: Great Black Music—Ancient to the Future*. Chicago: Art Ensemble of Chicago.

Black Artists Group. 1970[?]. Program brochure with operating budget. St. Louis, Mo.

Bley, Paul, with David Lee. 1999. *Stopping Time: Paul Bley and the Transformation of Jazz*. Quebec: Vehicule.

Bourget, Jean-Loup. 1977. "Muhal Richard Abrams: Entretien avec l'un de principaux inventeurs des nouveaux sons venus de Chicago." *Jazz* (France), no. 256 (July–August): 22–25.

Braxton, Anthony. 1985. *Tri-Axium Writings*. Vol. 1. Dartmouth: Synthesis/Frog Peak.

Broecking, Christian. 1995. *Der Marsalis-Faktor: Gespräche über afroamerikanische Kultur in der neunziger Jahre*. Waakirchen-Schaftlach (Switzerland): Oreos Verlag.

Brooks, Iris. 1992. "New Music America History: A Caterpillar or a Butterfly?" In *New Music Across America*, edited by Iris Brooks, pp. 6–11. Valencia and Santa Monica: California Institute of the Arts/High Performance.

Burns, Ken, dir. 2000. *Jazz*. Washington, D.C.: Florentine Films/WETA/ BBC.

Cage, John. 1961. *Silence*. Middletown: Wesleyan University Press.

Cameron, Catherine M. 1996. *Dialectics in the Arts: The Rise of Experimentalism in American Music*. Westport, Conn.: Praeger.

Carles, Philippe, and Jean-Louis Comolli. 2000 [1971]. *Free Jazz/Black Power*. Paris: Gallimard.

Caux, Daniel. 1969a. "Le delire et la rigueur de l'Art Ensemble de Chicago." *Jazz Hot*, no. 252 (July-August): 8.

——— 1969b. "A.A.C.M. de Chicago." *Jazz Hot*, no. 254 (October): 16–19.

Chatham, Rhys. 1992. "Five Generations of Composers at the Kitchen." In *The Kitchen Turns Twenty: A Retrospective Anthology*, edited by Lee Morrissey, pp. 7–22. New York: Kitchen Center.

Cohran, Philip T. 1967. Press Release, May 26. Collection of Jamil B. Figi, Chicago Jazz Archive, Regenstein Library, University of Chicago.

Conroy, Frank. 1995. "Stop Nitpicking a Genius." *New York Times Magazine* (June 25): 28–31, 48, 54, and 70.

Cooke, Jack. 1968a. Review of Lester Bowie recording of *Numbers 1, 2. Jazz Monthly* (June): 16.

——— 1968b. Review of Richard Abrams, *Levels and Degrees of Light*, and Joseph Jarman, *Song For. Jazz Monthly* (December): 11–12.

Coppens, George. 1979. Lester Bowie. *Coda*, nos. 164–65: 12–15.

Creative Musicians Present Artistic Heritage Ensemble. 1965. *Chicago Defender* (August 11–17).

Creative Musicians Sponsor Artists Concert Showcase. 1965. *Chicago Defender* (August 7).

Crouch, Stanley. 1977. "New York Jazz Notes." *Players* (July): 5–7.

——— 1979. "Bringing Atlantis Up to the Top." *Village Voice* (April 16): 65–67.

Dahlhaus, Carl. 1972. "Was heisst Improvisation?" *Neue Zeitschrift für Musik* 133:9–23.

De Lerma, Dominique-Rene, ed. 1990. *The Impact Of The AACM in the Twentieth Century: A Panel Discussion*. Unpublished transcript, Center for Black Music Research, Chicago.

Dossier AACM. 1978–79. *Jazz Hot* (France), nos. 356–357 (December–January).

Dubin, Larry. 1982. "Steve McCall." *Coda*, no. 182 (February): 4–6.

Fabre, Michel, and John A. Williams. 1996. *A Street Guide to African-Americans in Paris*. Paris: Cercle d'Etudes Afro-Americaines.

"Final Bar." 1968. *Down Beat* (April 18): 14.

———— 1969. *Down Beat* (May 29): 10.

Floyd, Samuel A. Jr. 1995. *The Power of Black Music: Interpreting Its History from Africa to the United States*. New York: Oxford University Press.

"$407,276 in Grants to Go to Composers." 1974. *New York Times* (February 11): 75.

Gabbard, Krin. 2000. Ken Burns's "Jazz": Beautiful Music, but Missing a Beat. *Chronicle of Higher Education* 47.16 (December 15): B18.

Gagne, Cole. 1993. *Soundpieces 2: Interviews with American Composers*. Metuchen, N.J.: Scarecrow.

Gann, Kyle. 1997. *American Music in the Twentieth Century*. New York: Schirmer.

Giddins, Gary. 1975. "Weather Bird: Riffing About Music." *Village Voice* (February 3): 106–7.

———— 1976. "Weather Bird: Up from the Saloon—Lofts Celebrate Alternate Jazz." *Village Voice* (June 7): 82.

———— 1977a. "Inside Free Jazz: The AACM in New York." *Village Voice* (May 30): 46–48.

———— 1977b. "Weather Bird: Goings on About Town." *Village Voice* (August 29): 76.

———— 1978a. Weather Bird: American Money For American Music. *Village Voice* (January 2):68.

———— 1978b. Leroy Jenkins's Territorial Imperative. *Village Voice* (April 24):68.

———— 1978c. The ABCs of Muhal's Life Line. *Village Voice* (June 19):63–64.

———— 1980. Chico Freeman: New Music from the Source. *Jazz Forum* (June): 44–49.

Gilmore, Samuel. 1987. "Coordination and Convention: The Organization of the Concert World." *Symbolic Interaction* 10.2: 209–27.

———— 1993. "Minorities and Distributional Equity at the National Endowment for the Arts." *Journal of Arts Management, Law and Society* 23.2 (Summer):137–73.

Goldberg, RoseLee. 1988. *Performance Art: From Futurism to the Present*. New York: Abrams.

Gray, Herman. 1997. "Jazz Tradition, Institutional Formation, and Cultural Practice: The Canon and the Street as Frameworks for Oppositional Black Cultural Politics." In *From Sociology to Cultural Studies*, edited by Elizabeth Long, pp. 351–73. Malden, Mass.: Blackwell.

Gray, John. 1991. *Fire Music: A Bibliography of the New Jazz, 1959–1990*. New York: Greenwood.

Griffin, Farah Jasmine. 1995. *Who Set You Flowin': The African-American Migration Narrative*. New York: Oxford University Press.

———— 2001. *If You Can't Be Free, Be a Mystery: In Search of Billie Holiday*. New York: Free.

"Guggenheim to Mingus; Protest at Foundation." 1971. *Down Beat* (May 22): 8.

Hardt, Michael, and Antonio Negri. 2001. What the Protesters in Genoa Want. *New York Times* (July 20): A21.

Harrison, Max. 1969. Review of Roscoe Mitchell, *Congliptious*. *Jazz Monthly* (June): 28–29.

Heckman, Don. 1965. "Caught in the Act: The Jazz Composers Guild." *Down Beat* (February 1): 37–38.

Henahan, Donal. 1973. "The New and Newer Music Fails to Impress at Tully." *New York Times* (January 27): 20.

Hersh, Burton. 1980. "The Secret Life of Lincoln Center." *Town and Country* 134.4997 (January): 71–72,109–13.

James, Michael. 1968. Review of Lester Bowie, *Numbers 1, 2. Jazz Monthly* (June): 16.

Jarman, Joseph. 1969. "Gens en peine: L'Art Ensemble de Chicago vous offre cette musique pour Noël." *Le Monde* (December 24): 14.

———— 1998. Interview with the author, Brooklyn, N.Y., June 28.

"Jazz Grants." 1973. *Down Beat* (October 25): 46.

"Jazz Musicians Group in Chicago Growing." 1966. *Down Beat* (July 28): 11.

Johnson, Tom. 1979. "New Music, New York, New Institution." *Village Voice* (July 2): 88–89.

———— 1980. "The Kitchen Improvises." *Village Voice* (September 24–30): 72.

———— 1989. *A Voice for New Music: New York City 1972–1982*. Eindhoven: Het Apollohuis.

Jones, Leroi [Amiri Baraka]. 1963. *Blues People*. New York: William Morrow.

———— 1968. *Black Music*. New York: William Morrow.

Jost, Ekkehard. 1975. *Free Jazz*. Vienna: Universal Edition

———— 1982. *Jazzmusiker: Materialen zur Soziologie der afro-amerikanischen Musik*. Frankfurt am Main: Ullstein Materialen.

———— 1987. *Europas Jazz, 1960–80*. Frankfurt am Main: Fischer Taschenbuch.

———— 1991. *Sozialgeschichte des Jazz in den USA*. Frankfurt am Main: Wolke.

Keepnews, Peter. 1979. "Public Domain." *Soho Weekly News* (September 27): 23–24, 50.

Kofsky, Frank. 1970. *Black Nationalism and the Revolution in Music*. New York: Pathfinder.

Kostakis, Peter. 1977. Joseph Jarman. *Coda* (December): 2–4.

Kostelanetz, Richard. 1993. *Dictionary of the Avant-Gardes*. Chicago: a cappella.

Levin, Robert. 1965. "The Jazz Composers Guild: An Assertion of Dignity." *Down Beat* (May 6): 17–18.

Lewis, George. 1996. "Improvised Music After 1950: Afrological and Eurological Perspectives." *Black Music Research Journal* 16.1 (Spring): 91–122.

———— 1998. "Singing Omar's Song: A (Re)Construction of Great Black Music. *Lenox Avenue: A Journal of Interartistic Inquiry* 4:69–92.

Lipsitz, George. 2000. Like a Weed in a Vacant Lot: The Black Artists Group in St. Louis. In *Decomposition: Post-Disciplinary Performance*, edited by Sue-Ellen Case, Philip Brett, and Susan Leigh Foster, pp. 51–61. Bloomington: Indiana University Press

Litweiler, John. 1967a. "Altoists and Other Chicagoans." *Coda* (March): 28.

———— 1967b. "The Chicago Scene." *Coda* (May): 36.

———— 1967c. "Summer in Fun City." *Coda* (September): 15.

———— 1967d. "The Chicago Scene." *Coda* (November): 34.

———— 1968a. "The New Music." *Coda* (March): 33.

———— 1968b. "The New Music." *Coda* (July): 35.

———— 1968c. "The New Music." *Coda* (December): 35–37.

———— 1969. Review of Oliver Lake/Julius Hemphill event. *Down Beat* (June 12): 34–35.

———— 1984. *The Freedom Principle: Jazz After 1958*. New York: Da Capo.

Looker, Ben. 2001. "'Poets of Action': The St. Louis Black Artists Group, 1968–1972." *Gateway-Heritage* 22.1 (Summer): 16–27.

McClary, Susan. 2000. *Conventional Wisdom*. Berkeley: University of California Press.

McElfresh, Suzanne. 1994. "Julius Hemphill." *Bomb* (Fall): 46–49.

Marmande, Francis. 1977. "Kalaparusha, Alias Maurice McIntyre." *Jazz* (France), no. 260 (December): 32–33.

Marsalis, Wynton. 1988. "What Jazz Is—And Isn't." *New York Times* (July 31): 21, 24.

Martin, Douglas. 2000. "Henry Pleasants, Eighty-Nine, Spy Who Knew His Music." *New York Times* (January 14): B11.

Martin, Terry. 1966–67. "Chicago—the Avant Garde." *Coda* (December–January): 21.

——— 1968. "The Chicago Avant-Garde." *Jazz Monthly* (March): 12–18.

Mercer, Kobena. 1994. "Diaspora Culture and the Dialogic Imagination." *Welcome to the Jungle: New Positions in Black Cultural Studies*. New York: Routledge.

Myers, Amina Claudine ["Ariae"]. 1968[?]. "A day in the life . . ." Unpublished MS, collection of Amina Claudine Myers.

Nai, Larry. 2001. Interview with Greg Osby. *Cadence* (May): 5–16.

Nessa, Chuck. 1966. "New Music Report." *Coda* (October/November): 20.

Nyman, Michael. 1999. *Experimental Music: Cage and Beyond*, 2d ed. New York: Schirmer.

Occhiogrosso, Peter. 1978. "Don't Stop the Carnival, Just Keep It Out of the Classroom." *Soho Weekly News* (September 21): 84, 111.

Oja, Carol. 2000. *Making Music Modern: New York in the 1920s*. New York: Oxford University Press.

Palmer, Robert. 1973. Pop: Newport Newcomers. *New York Times* (June 10): 30.

——— 1975. Liner notes to *Creative Construction Company*, vol 1. Muse MR 5071.

——— 1976. "New Jazz from the Midwest Moves East." *New York Times* (May 9):18.

——— 1977. "WKCR Will Start Ninety Straight Hours of Jazz Tonight." *New York Times* (May 14): 34

Pareles, Jon. 1987. "Pop View: Classical and Jazz Artists Meet Halfway. *New York Times* (March 15): 2:27.

Parks, Carole A. 1973. "Self-Determination and the Black Aesthetic: An Interview with Max Roach." *Black World* 23.1 (November): 62–71.

Pasler, Jann. 1987. "Musique et institution aux États-Unis." *Inharmoniques* no. 2 (May): 104–34.

Piazza, Tom. 1997. *Blues Up and Down: Jazz in Our Time*. New York: St. Martin's.

Pleasants, Henry. 1955. *The Agony of Modern Music*. New York: Simon and Schuster.

——— 1962. *Death of a Music? The Decline of the European Tradition and the Rise of Jazz*. London: Jazz Book Club.

Porter, Eric. 2002. *What Is This Thing Called Jazz: African-American Musicians as Artists, Critics, and Activists*. Berkeley: University of California Press.

Press Release. 1969a. *Jazz Hot*, no. 250 (May): 12.

Press Release. 1969b. *Jazz* (France), no. 168 (July–August): 14.

Primack, Bret. 1976. Leroy Jenkins: Gut-Plucking Revolutionary. *Down Beat* (November 16): 23–24, 50–51.

Radano, Ronald M. 1993. *New Musical Figurations: Anthony Braxton's Cultural Critique*. Chicago: University of Chicago Press.

Ratliff, Ben. 2001. A Pleasant Swim with Gunther Schuller, the Man Who Named the Third Stream. *New York Times* (March 20): E1.

Rockwell, John. 1974. "Face of Jazz Is Changing Visibly." *New York Times* (June 4): 33.

——— 1980. "A New Music Director Comes to the Avant-Garde Kitchen." *New York Times* (September 14): 2:23.

——— 1982. "Jazz: Two Braxton Programs." *New York Times* (April 23): C23.

——— 1988. "As Important as Anyone in His Generation. *New York Times* (February 21): 2:27.

Ross, Andrew. 1989. *No Respect: Intellectuals and Popular Culture*. London: Routledge.

Rubin, Nathan. 1994. *John Cage and the Twenty-Six Pianos: Forces in American Music from 1940–1990*. Moraga, Cal.: Sarah's.

Sandow, Gregory. 1981. "But Is It Art?" *Village Voice* (March 4–10): 63.

Shapiro, Peter. 2001. "Blues and the Abstract Truth: Phil Cohran." *Wire* (May): 28–31.

Shoemaker, Bill. 2000. "Avant-Garde." *Jazziz* (September): 60–62.

Small, Christopher. 1987. *Music of the Common Tongue*. New York: Riverrun.

Southern, Eileen. 1973. "Music Research and the Black Aesthetic." *Black World* 23.1 (November): 4–13.

Stovall, Tyler. 1996. *Paris Noir: African Americans in the City of Light*. Boston: Houghton Mifflin.

Sweet, Robert E. 1996. *Music Universe, Music Mind: Revisiting the Creative Music Studio, Woodstock, New York*. Ann Arbor: Arborville.

Tapscott, Horace. 2001. *Songs of the Unsung: The Musical and Social Journey of Horace Tapscott*. Ed. Steven Isoardi. Durham: Duke University Press.

Taylor, Arthur. 1993 [1977]. *Notes and Tones: Musician-to-Musician Interviews*. New York: Da Capo.

Teitelbaum, Richard. 1972. World Band. In *Soundings* 1, edited by Peter Garland, pp. 21–33. Self-published.

Tesser, Neil. 1980. "Von and Chico Freeman: Tenor Dynasty." *Down Beat* (July): 24–28.

Tucker, Mark. 1993. *The Duke Ellington Reader*. New York: Oxford University Press.

Van Trikt, Ludwig. 1985. "Henry Threadgill: An Interview." *Cadence* 11.9 (September): 5–7, 28.

Vuisje, Bert. 1978. *De Nieuwe Jazz: Twintig Interviews Door Bert Vuisje*. Baarn (Netherlands): Bosch and Keuning.

Watrous, Peter. 1989. "John Zorn Takes Over the Town." *New York Times* (February 24): C23.

———— 1994. "Jazz, Classical, Art, Business: A Series Wraps All Into One." *New York Times* (August 2): C15.

Weathers, Diane. 1973. "The Collective Black Artists." *Black World* 23.1 (November): 72–74.

Welding, Pete. 1966a. Review of Joseph Jarman/John Cage event. *Down Beat* (January 13): 35.

———— 1966b. Review of Roscoe Mitchell concert. *Down Beat* (May 19).

West, Cornel. 1993. *Keeping Faith: Philosophy and Race in America*. New York: Routledge.

Whitehead, Kevin. 1984. "Fred Hopkins." *Coda*, no. 196: 23–26.

Wilmer, Valerie. 1992 [1977]. *As Serious As Your Life: The Story of the New Jazz*. New York and London: Serpent's Tail.

———— 1979. "Amina Claudine Myers." *Coda*, no. 169:4–6.

Wilson, John S. 1972. "Braxton Performs on Alto Saxophone." *New York Times* (May 24): 55.

Zabor, Rafi. 1979. "Funny, You *Look* Like a Jazz Musician." *Village Voice* (July 2): 72–73.

Zorn, John, ed. 2000. *Arcana: Musicians on Music*. New York: Granary.

DISCOGRAPHY

Abrams, Muhal Richard. 1978a. *1QOA+1*. Black Saint BSR 0017 (LP).

———— 1978b. *Lifea Blinec*. Arista Novus AN3000 (LP).

Air. 1979. *Air Lore*. Arista Novus AN3014 (LP).

Art Ensemble of Chicago. 1969. *People in Sorrow*. Nessa N-3 (LP).

Braxton, Anthony. 1976. *Creative Orchestra Music 1976*. Arista AL4080 (LP).

Creative Construction Company. 1975. *Volume I*. Muse MR 5071 (LP).

———— 1976. *Volume II*. Muse MR 5097 (LP).

Freeman, Chico. 1977. *Chico*. India Navigation IN 1031 (LP).

Lewis, George. 1977. *Chicago Slow Dance*. Lovely Music VR1101 (LP).

Mitchell, Roscoe. 1966. *Sound*. Delmark DD-408 (CD).

———— 1978. *L-R-G; The Maze; SII Examples*. Nessa N-14/15 (LP).

Various Artists. 1977a. *Wildflowers: The New York Loft Jazz Sessions*. Vol. 1. Casablanca/Douglas NBLP 7045 (LP).

———— 1977b. *Wildflowers: The New York Loft Jazz Sessions*. Vol. 2. Casablanca/Douglas NBLP 7046 (LP).

———— 1977c. *Wildflowers: The New York Loft Jazz Sessions*. Vol. 3. Casablanca/Douglas NBLP 7047 (LP).

———— 1977d. *Wildflowers: The New York Loft Jazz Sessions*. Vol. 4. Casablanca/Douglas NBLP 7048 (LP).

———— 1977e. *Wildflowers: The New York Loft Jazz Sessions*. Vol. 5. Casablanca/Douglas NBLP 7049 (LP).

———— 1979. *Spirit Catcher*. Nessa N-19 (LP).

———— 2000 [1977]. *Wildflowers: The New York Loft Jazz Sessions*. Vols. 1–5. KnitClassics 3037 (CD).

FARAH JASMINE GRIFFIN

When Malindy Sings:
A Meditation on Black Women's Vocality

Picture the following:

1.   Marian Anderson singing at the Lincoln Memorial in 1939.
2.   Whitney Houston singing "The Star-Spangled Banner" at the Super Bowl in 1992 during the Gulf War.
3.   Aretha Franklin singing "The Star Spangled Banner" at the 1992 Democratic National Convention.
4.   Santita Jackson singing "The Star Spangled Banner" at inaugural events for William Jefferson Clinton, January 20, 1997.
5.   The anonymous black woman who sang at the first public memorial for the victims of the Oklahoma bombing.
6.   Jessye Norman singing at an event at New York University Law School's Tishman Auditorium in support of Clinton before his impeachment, December 14, 1998. (Toni Morrison speaking at the same event.)
7.   The anonymous black woman singing "Amazing Grace" immediately following the Littleton, Colorado shootings or the Texas church shootings.
8.   Chaka Khan singing at the close of the Republican National Convention in Philadelphia, August 2000.
9.   Related but distinct: Mahalia Jackson at the 1963 March on Washington.
10.   Related but Distinct: Fannie Lou Hamer at the 1964 Democratic National Convention in Atlantic City.

I say picture because these images and our memories of them are as much about the spectacle as the sound. The recognizably black woman—singing rather than speaking—is a familiar sight for American audiences. While each instance, each woman, each voice is unique—these women do not "sound" alike—the physicality is familiar. The woman stands before a crowd in front of a microphone, mouth open, positioned to sing.

The patriotism of the first eight moments is striking. Each occurs when the nation is trying to present an image of itself to itself and to the world. On at least three of these occasions the black woman's voice is the clarion call following heinous displays of American racism and its ugly relatives. The last two scenes are also created in response to American racism, but they signal a challenge to, a critique of the United States.

Marian Anderson sings at the Lincoln Memorial because the Daughters of the American Revolution refuse to allow her to sing at Convention Hall. The Oklahoma federal building was bombed by avowed white supremacists. The shooters in the Littleton, Colorado tragedy espoused racist beliefs. The other instances are not quite as explicit, but just as ironic. Whitney Houston rallies the nation behind a war that has nothing to do with democracy, behind an army made up of the poor, disproportionately poor blacks, whites and Latinos who turn to the military because the nation denies them employment and educational opportunities. Jessye Norman serenades a president who, though more comfortable in the presence of black people than his predecessors, ended "welfare as we knew it" and in so doing sank thousands of poor women and children into greater poverty; a president who, as a candidate, left the campaign trail so that he could execute a retarded black man; a president responsible for silencing the voices of two black women—Lani Guinier and Jocelyn Elders. Nonetheless he is a president with unprecedented popularity amongst a large number of African Americans. He has even been called (not without controversy) the so-called first black president.

Only Mahalia Jackson's and Fannie Lou Hamer's voices were used to rally the troops for social struggle. Because the vision proposed by Marian Anderson on the steps of the Lincoln Memorial had not been born by the 1960s, Jackson's was a voice insisting on a hearing, standing between the Washington Monument and the Lincoln Memorial as the illegitimate daughter of the American Revolution, demanding a seat at the table. Fannie Lou Hamer's voice helped folks to withstand the police batons and fire hoses of the segregationist South. Hers was also the voice raised as witness to the hypocrisy of the 1964 Democratic Convention in Atlantic City. Bernice Johnson Reagan picked up where Mrs. Hamer left off when she sang with the SNCC Freedom Singers and has continued to do so as the founding member of Sweet Honey in the Rock. In the 1960s Abbey Lincoln's articulate screams on Max Roach's "Freedom Now Suite," and Nina Simone's defiant "Mississippi Goddam!!" joined Aretha's call for "Respect" to provide not just the sound track but the announcement of a new militancy. Unlike Mahalia at the March on Washington, these women made demands, not requests. Black audiences endowed them with the responsibility of communicating black frustration, anger, aspiration, and hope.

Approximately two decades following Mahalia Jackson's appearance at the

March on Washington, in 1997 Santita Jackson sang at the inauguration of Bill Clinton and implied that the demand was heard; that we are now one big, unified, biracial family. The younger Jackson sang for a party for which her father is a powerful operative and in which her brother would become an elected official. Perhaps the most cynical of these images (for I do not believe they are all cynical), is Chaka Khan appearing as part of a parade of colored faces performing multiculturalism at a convention whose delegates were overwhelmingly white and whose platform offered little to the majority of black Americans. (Ironically, it did produce a powerful, speaking black woman cabinet member in Condeleeza Rice.)

These various images demonstrate the way the black woman's voice can be called upon to heal a crisis in national unity as well as provoke one. As scholars such as Benedict Anderson have noted, the nation is a fictive construct of community. The image of the "mother of the nation" is one that allows this construct to figure itself as reproduced. But the spectacle of the singing black woman at times of national crisis does not represent the "mother of the nation"; instead that spectacle sometimes invokes a figure that can make no claims on the family unit, though she is "just like one of the family." A figure that serves the unit, who heals and nurtures it but has no rights or privileges within it—more mammy than mother. Here I am not suggesting that the individual women themselves chose to serve as mammies but instead that this figure of the singing black woman is often similar to the uses of black women's bodies as nurturing, healing, life and love giving for the majority culture. This representation of the voice is in stark contrast to representations of that voice in the service of disenfranchised black people, as a voice that poses a challenge to the United States revealing its democratic pretense as a lie. And, yet, this image contains both these possibilities.

Certainly, racism is as American as the African American women's vocal tradition. Perhaps more so, in fact, because it is central to the founding of the nation; whereas the voice, that peculiar black voice, is in it but not of it at the nation's beginning. Since Marian Anderson, the voice and the spectacle of the singing black woman often has been used to suggest a peacefully interracial version of America. In the majority of these spectacles there is the suggestion that the black woman singer pulls together and helps to heal national rifts. This singing spectacle offers an alternative vision of a more inclusive America. It may not be representative of the United States as it is, but it projects an image of what participants long for it to become. On the other hand, the black woman's singing voice can signal a crisis in the spectacle of national unity; it can even invoke such a crisis by mobilizing dissent and forging a space of resistance. Representations of the voice suggest that it is like a hinge, a place where things can both come together and break apart.[1]

What other American voice resonates in this way, mobilizes in this way, evokes a picture of national unity at times of crisis and yet is also capable of invoking a crisis in a tenuous national unity as well? How does a vocal tradition that first emerged in the creation and service of an oppressed people end up in service to a nation that has been hostile to the aspirations of black people? Of course, "the voice" is not stable and unchanging. It varies in tone, timbre, and meaning; it changes according to artist, time, and context.

What follows is more meditation than theory, more questions than conclusions on the meanings of black women's singing. Here I am focusing on representations of black women singers across genres including gospel, jazz, opera, and rhythm and blues over a period of one hundred years. First I will review the language early white observers and later black writers have used to define the sound and the power of black American singing voices in order to situate the voice historically and to demonstrate its place in narratives of nation. In so doing I will try to tease out the meanings with which this voice has been invested. I will then explore an alternative myth of a black woman's singing—a myth of origin for other forms of black expressivity, especially jazz. These myths are also myths of origin for a black nation, where the originary voice is rendered as female but represented by males. My project shares much with and has benefited a great deal from the brilliant work of Lindon Barrett in *Blackness and Value: Seeing Double*. We are both concerned with the black singing voice as "a site of the active production of meaning."[2]

How Shall We Sing The Lord's Songs In a Strange Land?

> By the rivers of Babylon,
> There we sat down
> Yea, we wept when we remembered Zion.
> We hanged our harps upon the willows
> In the midst thereof.
> For there they that carried us away captive
> Required of us a song:
> And they that wasted us required of us mirth,
> Saying,
> Sing us one of the songs of Zion.
> How shall we sing the Lord's songs
> In a strange land?
>
> —PSALM 137

Black Americans have long seen parallels between our own situation and that of the Old Testament Jews, captives exiled in Babylon. "How can we sing the Lord's songs in a strange land?" But sing they did and in so doing created one of the richest vocal traditions the world has known. Black women's voices are central to that tradition.

Before I am accused of essentialism, let me clarify what I mean by the black woman's voice. First, I am here most interested in the way that voice has been described. I am as concerned with the image as I am with the sound. Second, I do not mean the voice that comes out every time any black woman anywhere opens her mouth to sing. Nor do I want to imply that there is something in the structure of the black diaphragm, neck, throat, and tongue, teeth, or mouth that contributes to a certain vocalization. No, I don't mean a black voice as markedly different as skin color or texture of hair. Instead I am talking of a cultural style. A particularly New World style with roots in West Africa. (The centrality of the singing voice is something shared with many West African societies from which the enslaved were taken.)[3] In the United States it is a style transformed, nurtured, and developed in the tradition of the spirituals, field hollers, and work songs and sustained in black church and/or blues and jazz venues.[4]

One finds the most in-depth discussions about the existence and origins of "the black voice" in opera. (For some time black singers were considered interlopers in the field, prompting one critic, the German Dr. Geerd Heinsen, to claim that the black voice was "too Negroid for the French vocal line."[5]) Here we find adjectives used to describe singing voices: "rich," "dark," "heavy," "throaty." These are adjectives borrowed from colors and textures—things that appeal to senses other than sound—a practice Roland Barthes found particularly irritating.[6] Students of black music such as Zora Neale Hurston, Christopher Smalls, Amiri Baraka, Nathaniel Mackey, Brent Edwards, and Robert O'Meally encourage us to think less in terms of adjectives and more in terms of verbs when describing black cultural practices including singing. These writers stress functions, effects, and processes in their descriptions of black music. They use words like stretching, reaching, conversing, sliding, imitating, swinging, rocking.[7]

According to Eileen Southern, during the early days of the nation black singing was described as "distinctive for its high intensity and use of such special effects as falsetto, shouts, groans and gutteral tones. A strong, clear voice was favored, but Europeans generally described the sounds of the African voice as 'a rud noyse,' 'a strong nasal sound,' or 'very loud and shrill'" (14). These descriptions assert the unfamiliarity of the voice, the "otherness" of it. In these descriptions black voices are *other* as in *foreign*. The black voice is part of the black body; the black body was deemed the very antithesis of all that was white and therefore human.

Many white American observers writing during the Civil War contributed to this discourse on the black voice. They stressed the impossibility of notating black American singing on the Western scale. Lucy Kim Garrison, coeditor of *Slave Songs in the United States*, observed:

> It is difficult to express the entire character of these Negro ballads by mere musical notes and signs. The odd turns made in the throat and the curious rhythmic effect produced by single voices chiming in at different irregular intervals, seem almost as impossible to place on the scale as the singing of birds or the tones of an Aeolian Harp.[8]

Her coeditor William Allen lamented:

> What makes it all the harder to unravel a thread of melody out of this strange network is that, like birds, they seem not infrequently to strike sounds that cannot be precisely represented by the gamut and abound in "slides from one note to the another and in turns and cadences not in articulated notes."[9]

Numerous others cautioned about the impossibility of "writing out" or finding "musical characters to represent" black singing. In both instances we get black singing compared to the singing of birds. Birds are part of the natural world; for many whites black people were thought to be closer to the natural world. Bird's songs are beautiful, mysterious, and functional. Furthermore, they are not thought to be the products of intellect, though recognized as a complex form of communication.

Interestingly, from the anonymous composers of the spirituals and folk tales to later poets such as Paul Laurence Dunbar and Abbey Lincoln, black people have likened themselves to birds: birds in flight, birds incapable of flight, caged birds, free birds, but most especially singing birds. For the white observer black singing is birdlike because it escapes categorization. It does not attend to the rules of Western literacy or notation. Nathaniel Mackey refers to this as the "fugitive spirit" of black music in its refusal to "be mapped, captured, notated."[10] Perhaps this is why the black singing voice not only struck an unfamiliar chord but at times a threatening one as well. Lindon Barrett writes:

> Notations of the disturbing acoustic qualities of the diaspora singing voice often accompany the misrecognition of its cultural significance and its dismissal as a meaningful artefact. . . . In New World slave societies affront to Western aesthetic sensibilities one often finds a further corollary in fears concerning the potential threat posed by the singing voice to Western sociality or polity. . . . The singing voice proves a disturbing announcement of the vacuity of African and African diasporic cultures, but nevertheless, also an announcement of a threat to Western societies and psyches. (63)

(A brief aside: Not all black observers were as distinct from whites that heard the voices for the first time. Rebecca Primus, a freeborn Northern black woman who established a school for the freedmen on the Eastern Shore of Maryland, was one black listener who found black southern singing strange and unfamiliar.)

In addition to the distinctive, different sound of black singing, observers also noted the strange effect that sound had on listeners. Eileen Southern writes, "American literature contains numerous references to female slaves of colonial times who kept young audiences spellbound, and adults too with their ancient tales." In all these cases the voice is unfamiliar, uncanny, almost otherworldly. (Years later this would hold true for jazz vocalists such as Billie Holiday, Shirley Horne, Carmen McRae, and Cassandra Wilson, all of whom possess the power of holding audiences spellbound with their "stories.") It is a voice capable of casting spells. It is certainly a voice concerned with its connection to the world of the spirit, its ability to invoke the presence of the divine. So the sound heard as "other," as in "foreign," is also a sound that is "other" like the mystery that is God.[11]

In the instances cited by Southern, it is not just a matter of the voice but the way it tells the tale; the form in which it relays the message. The tone of the voice, its inflections, its register, the cadence, the pauses and silences—these are all as important and in some instances more important than the words themselves. Patti LaBelle's version of "Isn't It a Shame" is an example of a vocalist's ability to render meaning without words. In the midst of a song that mourns the end of a relationship, Labelle stops singing lyrics altogether and begins to moan. The pain about which she sings is beyond conventional speech. She moans a melody that tells a familiar tale of loss and desperate loneliness. It starts with a simple phrase, climaxes in a moan that is almost a holler, before resolving to a whimper. At this point the voices of the other two singers, Nona Hendryx and Sarah Dash, come in to help lift her back up, providing aural support so that she can stand and reenter the realm of language and lyrics.

Now of course I don't want to suggest that Patti Labelle and those unnamed black women cited by Southern represent one invariable, unchanging style, but rather that there is a tradition that values experimentation and risk taking in form as well as content. It is a tradition that seeks to, in fact needs to, communicate beyond words when they are no longer capable of rendering meaning. I imagine this was especially important for persons who were forced to speak in a tongue that was not their native one.

Interestingly, in other cultures "blackness" has been used as a descriptor of certain voices and not of the singers. This quality of "vocal darkness" usually comes from cultures where the pitch of the speaking voice is lower.[12] However, in an essay titled "Cante Moro," the Spanish poet García Lorca offered a meditation on the "dark sounds" of the music of the Romany people, another dark-skinned oppressed people, known as "gypsies." Both Ralph Ellison and Nathaniel Mackey have drawn links between these dark or Moorish sounds, flamenco, and black American blues. In the United States "vocal darkness" is associated with an oppressed minority, identifiable by their skin color; we hear a whole range of meaning in the voices of black singers. For instance, anyone familiar with the racial history of the United States will probably hear irony as well as patriotism when Ray Charles sings "America"; it is not a matter of his individual politics but the vocal tradition out of which he sings, the voice. This is a voice that resounds with echoes of the cotton and tobacco fields, chain gangs and railroad, juke joints and storefront church.

The black church has been the primary site for the development of a distinctive black singing style and tradition. Ralph Ellison describes that style and tradition in his essay "As the Spirit Moves Mahalia," noting that Mahalia Jackson's voice is part of an art form that "depends upon the employment of the full expressive resources of the human voice."[13] Gospel music seems to contain most of the elements identified with black singing. The gospel quality has come to characterize other types of singing associated with black people most especially rhythm and blues and soul as well as jazz. Portia Maultsby notes that across genre black vocalists

> bring intensity to their performances by alternating lyrical, percussive, and raspy timbres; juxtaposing vocal and instrumental textures; changing pitch and dynamic levels; alternating straight with vibrato tones and weaving moans, shouts, grunts, hollers, and screams into the melody.[14]

To experience the growl, falsetto, humming, and moaning in one song listen to Andy Bey sing "You'd Be So Nice to Come Home To," Nina Simone sing "Be My Husband," Sweet Honey in the Rock or Shirley Caesar sing anything. "Be My Husband" is based on a traditional African American work song. It provides an excellent example because the lack of elaborate instrumentation allows us to hear the dips, curves, bends, and flights of Simone's voice. At one point her voice shifts focus from melody to rhythm—keeping time like a hammer or hoe might have. Here she demands, there she pleads: She is both strength and vulnerability. When not singing we can hear an audible breathiness reminding us that the voice is situated in the body. At times she will substitute her voice with clapping hands, again embodying the song. Instead of hiding the breathing, denying the body of the singer in an effort to mimic an out-of-body spiritual transcendence, here we have a reminder of the relationship between body, breath, and spirit; a reminder that transcendence is acquired through the manipulation of bodily functions (chanting, singing, breathing, shouting, dancing).

While the black church is the training ground for many of our most well-known singers, from Miss Anderson to Dinah Washington, Sarah Vaughan, Aretha and Whitney, it is not the sole repository of this sound. One can hear many of these qualities in the voice of Billie Holiday, a Catholic girl who didn't have the huge voice of her sisters but did have a certain way of approaching a note that is also born of this tradition. Billie Holiday, whether singing "Strange Fruit" or "Lover Man," exposed our national and personal frailties, obsessions and secrets. In her voice, first and foremost, we hear an almost brutal honesty.

Descriptions of black singing, particularly black women's singing, have been especially important to black writers. Frederick Douglass's classic description articulates a theory of the relationship between black singing and the social and political condition of black people's lives:

> They would make the dense old woods, for miles around, reverberate with their wild songs, revealing at once the highest joy and the deepest sadness. They would compose and sing as they went along consulting neither time nor tune. The thought that came up, came out—if not in the word, in the sound;—and as frequently in the one as in the other. They would sometimes sing the most pathetic sentiment in the most rapturous tone, and the most rapturous sentiment in the most pathetic tone. . . . They would sing, as a chorus, to words which to many would seem unmeaning jargon, but which, nevertheless, were full of meaning to themselves. I have sometimes thought that the mere hearing of those songs would do more to impress some minds with the horrible character of slavery than the reading of whole volumes of philosophy on the subject would do. . . . They were tones loud, long, and deep. . . . Every tone was a testimony against slavery, and a prayer to God for deliverance from chains . . . to those songs I trace my first glimmering conception of the dehumanizing character of slavery.

Douglass sets the tone that future black writers would employ in their own attempts to represent and interpret black singing. There is the secretive and communal nature of the performance, in the woods (in contrast to the public entertaining function of singing the songs for an audience of whites). There is the emphasis on the meaning conveyed in the sound and on the sound as more representative of the people's condition than words in a book. And yet the only access we have to the sound is his written effort to describe it. The most elaborate articulation of this aesthetic comes nearly a century later in the work of Leroi Jones, especially his important *Blues People* (1963).

Toward the end of Toni Morrison's novel *Beloved*, an army of black women march to 124—the house where former slave Sethe, her daughter Denver, and the ghost of slavery, Beloved, reside. Once there, their voices rise in a wall of sound that exorcises the ghost.

> Where the yard met the road, [Sethe and Beloved] saw the rapt faces of thirty neighborhood women. Some had their eyes closed; others looked at the hot, cloudless sky. Sethe opened the door and reached for Beloved's hand. Together they stood in the doorway. . . . Women searched for the right combination, the key, the code, the sound that broke the back of words. Building voice upon voice until they found it and when they did it was a wave of sound wide enough to sound deep water and knock the pods off Chestnut trees. It broke over Sethe and she trembled like the baptized in its wash. (261)

The ocean of sound, a virtual force of nature, that which continues to communicate when language breaks down, baptizes Sethe. Black women singing in unison confront the evil legacy of white supremacy and the slave trade, fight it and, in this instance, win. In a text so obsessed with dismembered and abused black bodies and psyches, the voice emerges as that part of the body and psyche best suited for creating and healing community. In this text the physical violence of slavery and its aftermath dismembers black bodies, but the discourse of slavery that deconstructs and categorizes black people as inhuman is as substantial and even longer lasting than physical violence ("list her animal characteristics on one side her human on the other," Schoolteacher instructs his "pupils"). Slavery and white supremacy enact physical and discursive dismemberment; the voices of singing black women dismember the ghost of slavery and break the back of words both in order to communicate beyond them and to destroy their power over black bodies. And it is this dual action—the breaking of physical and discursive bonds—that precipitates the healing. (*Beloved* the novel might be likened to a song that attempts to do the same thing.)

There are numerous literary and historical examples of how black women's voices or representations of black women's voices not only soothed white children with lullabies but also healed, nurtured, sustained black people. Importantly, all these discussions of black women's singing focus as much on the listener as they do on the singer. In other words, voices create an aural space where listeners can momentarily experience themselves as outside of themselves, as "home" or as "free." This space can be simultaneously political, spiritual, and sensual.[15] It is the context of the listening or the hearing that embodies the voice with meaning.

Black singing helped black people gather the strength to fight when they had no weapons; it invited and prepared the way for visitations from ancestors and the Holy Ghost. It saved the souls of sinners and made the saved backslide. It laid the foundation for diverse artistic visions. It expressed their longing for safety, for shelter, for love, for divine retribution, and for freedom.

It is this understanding of the meaning and function of black women's singing that informs a century-old myth that situates a black women's voice as the origin of black male literary and musical productivity and as the originary, founding sound of the New World Black Nation.

When Malindy Sings: A Myth of Origin

G'way an' quit dat noise, Miss Lucy—
Put dat music book away;
What's de use to keep on tryin'?
Ef you practise twell you're gray,
You cain't sta't no notes a-flyin'
Lak de ones dat rants and rings
F'om de kitchen to de big woods
When Malindy sings.

You ain't got de nachel o'gans
Fu' to make de soun come right,
You ain't got de tu'ns an' twistin's
Fu' to make it sweet an' light.
Tell you one thing now, Miss Lucy,
An' I'm tellin' you fu' true,
When hit comes to raal right singin',
'T'ain no easy thing to do . . .

Y' ought to hyeah dat gal a-wa'blin';
Robins, la'ks an' all dem things.
Heish dey moufs an' hides dey faces
When Malindy sings.

She jus spreads huh mouf and hollahs,
Come to Jesus, twell you hyeah
Sinnahs' tremblin' steps and voices,
Timid-lak a-drawin' neah;
Den she tu'ns to "Rock of Ages"
Simply to de cross she clings,

An' you fin' yo' teah's a-drappin;
When Malindy sings

Who dat say dat humble praises
Wif de Master nevah counts?
Heish you mouf, I heyea dat music,
Ez hit rises up an' mounts
Floatin by de hills an' valleys
Way above dis buryin' sod,
Ez hit makes its way in glory
To de very gates of God!
Oh, hit's sweetah dan de music
Of an edicated band;

An' hit's dearah dan de battle's
Song o' triumph in de lan'
It seems holier dan evenin'
When de solemn chu'ch bell rings,
Ez I sit an' ca'mly listen
While Malindy sings . . .

— PAUL LAURENCE DUNBAR,
"WHEN MALINDY SINGS," 1895

112

"In the beginning there were no words. In the beginning was the sound, and they all knew what that sound sounded like." This statement comes from one of our greatest wordsmiths—Toni Morrison. Not light at the beginning, but a universe of sound: Birds, wind, water, and the human voice, a woman's voice, and, depending on the teller of the tale, a black woman's voice. A number of writers and musicians identify a moment of hearing that voice as an epiphany: a moment that leads suddenly to insight, understanding, and a hearing of the potential of one's own artistic voice (if not at the moment of hearing, then later, upon reflection, certainly at a signal point in the text). This sound, which is not captured, is represented by the artist in poetry, prose, and music. While it is often the singing of men and women that constitute the moment of epiphany, it seems most often to be the woman's voice that structures the myth.

Let us now turn to four such instances: W. E. B. Du Bois in *Souls of Black Folk*, Jean Toomer in *Cane*, and Miles Davis/Quincy Troupe in *Miles: The Autobiography* (later elaborated in Troupe's *Quincy and Me*). We will close with Cassandra Wilson's contribution to or revision of this myth. There are numerous other examples that will not be examined here but two of the most significant are worth noting before we move on. James Baldwin famously attributes Bessie Smith's recordings with helping him to access the language and tone of his first novel, *Go Tell It on the Mountain*. August Wilson asserts hearing Smith's recordings of "Nobody in Town Can Bake a Sweet Jellyroll Like Mine" was a birth, a baptism, a resurrection and a redemption all rolled up in one. It was the beginning of my consciousness that I was a representative of a culture and the carrier of some very valuable antecedents. With my discovery of Bessie Smith and the blues I had been given a world that contained my image, a world at once rich and varied, marked and marking, brutal and beautiful and at crucial odds with the larger world that contained it and preyed and pressed it from every conceivable angle.[16]

But here, we shall focus on three sons of the North or Midwest who encounter the sound of black singing in the South and in whom it strikes some ancient cultural memory. (Du Bois hears concertized spirituals at Fisk, Toomer hears the singing in rural Sparta, Georgia where he has gone to work in a school, and Davis in rural Arkansas where he visits his grandfather's farm. Wilson is a daughter of the South who hears her own voice in Miles's horn.) Consequently, one mythical source of black modernity is the haunting voice of a black woman.[17] By calling these encounters mythical I am by no means suggesting they did not happen, that they are not situated in history; in fact it is possible that they happened so much, that the tale is told so often it is recognizable, familiar, and therefore easy to invoke. But I am most interested in the rendering of the tale and in the cultural work of the telling.

Scholars Leslie C. Dunn and Nancy A. Jones identify "myths of vocal gender" throughout Western culture. The sirens who lure men to death are but one of the many archetypal figures that "anchor the female voice in the female body" and confer upon it "conventional associations of femininity with nature and matter, with emotion and irrationality." Dunn and Jones write that from classical myth to nineteenth-century opera [we find] a fantasy of origins "that serves to explain and justify the placing, or rather displacing, of the female voice in a patriarchal culture through its alignment with the material, the irrational, the pre-cultural, and the musical." This voice is then contained "within a textuality identified as masculine, thus opposing her literal, embodied vocality to his metaphorical, disembodied 'voice'" (p. 7). To this list I would like to add the singing New World black woman whose voice, linked to nature, inspires cultural memory in the hearer and sets him on his own path of creative discovery.

The title of this section (and of this essay) is taken from Paul Laurence Dunbar's classic dialect poem, "When Malindy Sings," first published in 1895, later set to music by Oscar Brown Jr. and performed and recorded by the extraordinary Abbey Lincoln. The poem sets up many of the tropes of the myth of origin that appear in the later works I mention above. (Of course Douglass's description precedes even this, as does Lucy McKim Garrison's.) First, we read of someone trying to describe Malindy's voice—we never hear that voice, neither speaking nor singing. The poet's persona relays it to us, and we know this witness is black because of the use of dialect. So Malindy's voice, which sends notes a flying, the voice that rings from the kitchen to the woods, a voice based in her so called natural organs, is set in opposition to written Western music—the lines and dots. When Malindy sings, musicians with instruments stop playing and even the mocking bird is intimidated. Her voice goes "to de very gates of God!" Dunbar formalizes the description of a black woman's voice as of nature and of the divine, as racially essential based in biological difference, as incapable of capture in notation. He is not the first to give these kinds of descriptions, but he sets them in poetry in a way that has implications for our myth of origin. We, as readers, as hearers far away from the plantation, have access to this voice only through the words of the learned male poet who represents it to us in the voice of someone who has heard it. So we are twice removed from Malindy's song, which has become the basis and inspiration for the poem.

In 1903 W. E. B. Du Bois closes his classic *Souls of Black Folk* with a meditation on the meaning of black music: "The Sorrow Songs." Of the spirituals he writes:

> The songs are indeed the siftings of centuries; the music is far more ancient than the words, and in it we can trace here and there signs of development. My grandfather's grandmother was seized by an evil Dutch trader two centuries ago; and coming to the valleys of the Hudson and Housatonic, black, little, and lithe, she shivered and shrank in the harsh north winds, looked longing at the hills, and often crooned a heathen melody to the child between her knees. . . . The child sang it to his children and they to their children's children, and so two hundred years it has traveled down to us and we sing it to our children, knowing as little as our fathers what its words may mean, but knowing well the meaning of its music. This was primitive African music; . . . the voice of exile.

Du Bois gives the songs a lineage that is almost Biblical in nature. It is ancient in origin and historically situated in the terror of the slave trade. Here we see the careful construction of the myth. His grandfather's grandmother is African. She is black, little, and lithe. The landscape of New England is utterly foreign to her, and, out of a longing for home, she looks to the hills and sings in an unknown tongue. This moment of passing the tradition on to the child between her knee initiates a familial and racial tradition. Malindy's forbear is here not just a black woman who can sing but an African woman who is most importantly a mother: Mother of a New World race. Du Bois adds another dimension to the tale—we know little of what the words mean, but that doesn't matter because the meaning is in the sound and only the initiated can hear. The lyrics he reproduces are:

> Do bana coba gene me, gene me!
> Do bana coba, gene me, gene me!
> Bend' nuli, nuli, nuli, nuli, bend'le.

As Du Bois renders these lyrics and transcribes the melody on the pages of *Souls*, they appear as a modified blues form, with the repetition of the first two lines before the resolution of the third. Furthermore, he transcribes the song in the complex, dark key of D-flat, one of the keys favored by African American improvisers. In *Souls* Du Bois claims his grandmother was Bantu. However, scholars and linguists have not been able to locate these lyrics within a Bantu language group. Du Bois's biographer David Levering Lewis notes that the closest translation seems to have come from a Wolof song from Senegambia—a song about confinement and captivity: "gene me, gene me, [gene ma, gene ma,]" "Get me out, get me out, get me out." Significantly, a large number of the enslaved Africans brought to the Americas came from the Senegambia region. Some scholars have drawn a connection between the musics of this region and the blues forms that developed in the United States (especially in Mississippi Delta).[18] While here Du Bois's grandmother is a "little black Bantu" living in New England, in other versions of the tale told in *Dusk of Dawn* and elsewhere Du Bois attributes the song to his great grandfather's wife or to another ancestor named Violet. In all cases the song is transmitted by a black woman.

Twenty years after Du Bois, Jean Toomer draws from his experience in Sparta, Georgia to render the black woman's singing voice as an indelible part of a changing landscape and a dying era. In his autobiographical writings Toomer recalled hearing the voices in Georgia:

> A family of back-country Negroes had only recently moved into a shack not too far away. They sang. And this was the first time I'd ever heard the folk-songs and spirituals. They were rich and sad and joyous and beautiful. . . . I realized with deep regret, that the spirituals, meeting ridicule, would be certain to die out.

Here Toomer recalls the voices of a family, not of a woman or of women. He also notes that the spirituals represented a dying tradition: one that he sought to preserve in *Cane*, which he called a swan song. These voices float above and through the narratives and poems of *Cane*. In "Blood Burning Moon," the story that closes the first southern section of the book, Louisa, a young woman torn between two lovers, one black and one white, begins to sing as she goes to meet the black Tom. Her song is a foreboding and a foreshadowing of Tom's murder of her white lover and his own eventual lynching by a white vigilante mob.

> The slow rhythm of her song grew agitant and restless. Rusty black and tan spotted hounds, lying in the dark corners of the porches or prowling around back yards, all over the countryside dogs barked and roosters crowed as if heeding a weird dawn or some ungodly awakening. They put their noses in the air and caught its tremor. They began plaintively to yelp and howl. Chickens woke up and cackled. Intermittently, woman sang lustily.

Here again the voice is otherworldly not because it is from another planet, because it is part of an unseen world that parallels our own rational one. It is both spiritual and material, both mystical and natural. As with Dunbar before him, Toomer represents the voice carried by the breeze, held by the trees, creating a mystical landscape and leading directly to the ears of God. It is a prophetic voice, yet it is one that we cannot hear, that is only brought to us in the work of the literate male poet. It is his source and his inspiration, contained and refined for our consumption.

By the time Miles Davis and Quincy Troupe construct Davis's life story, they are able to contribute to this myth of origin by situating Miles as the hearer of her song, and in so doing they help to construct him as a mythic figure. The mythical voice comes at the end of a chapter where Davis and Troupe chronicle Davis's musical origins. The chapter has situated him as a child of black privilege: professional, college educated parents, his mother the musician who played violin and piano, his grandmother an organ teacher. So his musical lineage is maternal before he meets the great musical fathers who will shape him. "I got my looks from my mother and also my love of clothes and sense of style. I guess you could say I got whatever artistic talent I have from her also" (14). It is a world that witnesses the 1917 race riot to which he attributes some of his distrust of some white people (although his neighborhood was integrated). At the close of the chapter he highlights two formative experiences: listening to a radio show called *Harlem Rhythms* (it was around this time he started taking music lessons.) and hearing a black churchwoman sing.

At the end of the first chapter of the *Miles: The Autobiography* we are told:

> But before the lessons, I also remember how the music used to sound down there in Arkansas, when I was visiting my grandfather, especially at the Saturday night church. Man that shit was a motherfucker. I guess I was about six or seven. We'd be walking on these dark country roads at night and all of a sudden this music would seem to come out of nowhere, out of them spooky-looking trees that everybody said ghosts lived in. . . . I remember a man and a woman singing. . . . Shit, that music was something especially that woman singing. But I think that kind of sound in music, that blues, church, back-road funk kind of thing, that southern, mid-western, rural sound and rhythm. I think it started getting into my blood on them spook-filled Arkansas back-roads after dark when the owls came out hooting. So when I started taking music lessons I might have already had some idea of what I wanted my music to sound like.
>
> Music is a funny thing when you really come to think about it. Because its hard to pinpoint where it all began for me But I think some of it had to have started on that Arkansas road. (29)

Ending the first chapter this way is as much a political and aesthetic choice as it is a genealogical one. The paragraph starts emphatically with "But before the lessons" (a preliterate state). And then we get a description that elaborates upon that of Toomer and Du Bois. From a country road, a country church, the woman isn't described nor is her voice, really, but its eerie, haunting sound and its connection with nature again seem to act as a conduit between different realities. So Davis situates this supernatural, southern, black female sound as the source of his own. Mu-

116

sic lessons will help to structure and distill that voice, and once again the male artist will become our only access to that earlier, more "primitive sound."

Three different renderings of the myth of origin for a written and musical art form. The myth then becomes structured in history and helps to create a myth about the hearer. In Quincy Troupe's *Miles and Me* Troupe returns to this story and elaborates upon it in a way that only a poet familiar with the tropes of the tradition might do. The quotation is lengthy by necessity. Troupe writes:

> The lonely voice of an old black church woman singing plaintively in the dusky glow of a backwater country evening, somewhere few come to, save mosquitoes or rats or evil white men dressed in bed sheets, carrying guns and flaming crosses.
>
> In the midnight air the trains never seem to stop whistling past their wheels humming. The roads are unpaved, empty, and eerie in the twilight just before the hants come out to enter everybody's imagination and shut down those dusty roads. The voice of the old black woman floats above the shadows and trees, disembodied yet whole. It rides up there and cruises alongside the night birds circling above some unseen church or log cabin, in some out-of-the-way location back in the bushes, hidden. The voice also circles. Plaintive. Haunting. Achingly real.
>
> And if you had the privilege of hearing that voice, perhaps you wouldn't file it away as anything special, something to imitate and relate to for the rest of your life—a reference point for your own life's experiences, making you sensitive, alert, cognizant of other beautiful, necessary things. But that's the way Miles heard it.
>
> Perhaps the voice would remind you of a lonely trumpet sound. But maybe you wouldn't know that what you heard was special because you couldn't see that old Black woman's face. And, if you could have met her, you might have been too busy watching her chew on some snuff to see the wisdom in her old eyes. But Miles did see that face, saw it when he heard her voice. He saw the whole scene, took it all in. Knew that it was real and special and filed it away for later use. (2–3)

This rendering situates the young boy Miles in the midst of a Toomeresque landscape. The mythic tropes are catalogued: an old black churchwoman's voice, ghosts, nightriders, and trains. This is the landscape that produced the blues. It is an age-old myth with historically specific resonance. The voice again floats above the trees—"disembodied"—removed from its source. It is "plaintive" "haunting," "achingly real." The authenticity (real) is guaranteed by its proximity to violence and terror (achingly). And the young boy Miles is special from the very beginning because in hearing the voice he can see the face. And, as if seeing the face of God, he is forever changed, is himself touched with a bit of divinity and chosen to pass it along through his horn. To hear the voice is to witness the history. To embody the voice, to play it, to represent it, is to bear witness to that history. The Miles of these passages situates the origin of one of the most original, recognizable, and innovative sounds in the music within a matrilineal lineage that is black and southern.

Long before his death Miles Davis was a mythic figure. This mythology provides a way of dealing with the complexities of the historical, the human Miles. By situating his musical origins in this particular cultural narrative, he becomes as inaccessible as that old black woman's voice, or accessible primarily as inspiration, as mythical ancestral figure who himself floats above as the source of others' creativity. Nowhere is this more evident than in Cassandra Wilson's "Traveling Miles," which ironically returns the sound to the mythical source—the voice of a outhern black woman.

Now of course this particular southern black woman is herself an accomplished musician who had to master the complexity of Miles's music before lending her interpretation to his myth as well as her own emerging one.

Within the lyrics and the music of her CD, *Traveling Miles*, Cassandra Wilson conjures Miles the ancestor, who is not unlike the legendary wandering blues men; but he is also the urban jazz sophisticate. He travels from country roads to Seventh Avenue, from Manhattan to the Nigerian city and mythical land of the Yoruba deities—Ile Ife, from this world to the world beyond:

Traveling Miles

born with the lightning and thunder
sound descending proud and bright
restless as the wind
singing god in the night.
traveling miles
crossing time
shifting style
traveling miles . . . and miles

you can hear him humming on a country road
as the shadows grow to night
swinging through seventh avenue
underneath the city lights

ringing out with no fear or doubt
we can live our dream right now
right now

This moment he sits at the crossroads like Esu, the next he is born of lightening and thunder like Shango. His horn, like the voice of the old black woman, emanates from the landscape and through the heavens. Though the music, lyrics, and stories they tell invoke Davis, Wilson is the teller of this tale, the conjurer of this set. Davis paved the road she travels to this space: a space she creates by producing, writing lyrics, composing music, and singing. She is in full control of the narrative.

The very first song on the CD is Miles's "Run the VooDoo Down," for which she provides lyrics. The CD closes with a VooDoo reprise, and this time Wilson is accompanied by West African vocalist Angelique Kidjo, who is from Benin. So not only do we have the voice of the black southern woman, but she is in dialogue, conversation with a voice that represents Du Bois's African forbear. The duet between the two women dominates: sung in English and in Yoruba, the song returns the sound to the "source": the black woman's voice. And yet these are thoroughly contemporary voices whose meeting is made possible by the circulation of global musical culture. The song, like the spiritual tradition it invokes, makes connections between Africa and the Americas and provides a context for contemporary Africans and African Americans (broadly defined) to forge a common cultural identity. In other words, it isn't about sources and origins at all. Kidjo calls in Yoruba; Wilson responds in Yoruba. Eventually the women's voices overlap and it becomes impossible to distinguish the call from the response. Finally, Wilson answers in the first-person blues narrative with which she opens the CD. Through her rendering of Davis's music, which he claims has its origin in the absent black woman's voice, Wilson reclaims the authority of the female voice, locating it not only as a mythical point of origin but as an ongoing participant in the construction of the music we call jazz. (An earlier and quite extraordinary attempt to render the black female voice as central to the making of improvisatory music while also acknowledging important connections between Africa and the Americas is Amina Claudine Myers's masterpiece, "African Blues" [*Amina Claudine Myers Salutes Bessie Smith*, 1980]).

Blue Notes and Butterflies

Significantly, in both instances the black woman's voice that calls into being a version of the United States as it wishes itself to be and the black woman's voice as the source of black artistic creativity, the voice expresses a quality of longing: longing for home, for love, for connection with God, for heaven, for freedom. It also seems to be a conduit between what and where we are and what and where we want to be.

Perhaps it makes perfect sense that this black voice in the United States has become a quintessential American voice. It parallels the development of the nation. It is one of its founding sounds, and the singing black woman one of its founding spectacles. But because it develops alongside and not fully within the nation, it maintains a space for critique and protest. Here I am reminded of Jacques Attali, who writes that the "appropriation and control" of music "is a reflection of its power. . . . With music is born power and its opposite: subversion." He asserts, "Music, the quintessential mass activity, like the crowd, is simultaneously a threat and a necessary source of legitimacy: trying to channel it is a risk that every system of power must run."[19] The spectacle of the singing black woman at times of crisis as well as the myth of the black woman's voice as the source of and represented by black male creativity are both evidence of this attempt to channel the power and subversive potential of music.

If we consider the ways that the American State Department selected jazz to represent national culture abroad during the Cold War, even as the government continued to deny black Americans full citizenship at home, or the contemporary global circulation of contemporary hip hop culture, then the black woman's voice as representative American voice doesn't seem so ironic after all. When we consider the United States's uncanny ability to co-opt and commodify voices of dissent, it doesn't appear so contradictory.

However, contemporary uses of black women vocalists at times of national crisis is not always an act of cynical co-optation. (Nonetheless, because there is more than cynical co-optation does not mean that vigilance vis-à-vis this possibility can let up in moments of profound healing.) If this voice soothed white children in the early days of the nation, then it nurtured whites in the same way those black women nannies and mammies did and thereby became a mark of their identity as well, even as they deny it or view it with condescension. For black Americans, black women's singing has articulated our most heartfelt political, social, spiritual, and romantic longings and in so doing has given us a sense of ourselves as a people beyond the confines of our oppression.[20] Furthermore, because of its ability to express human longing for love, freedom, and spiritual meaning, this voice is representative of much of the human condition whether it be a people's longing for home or freedom or a nation's longing for an idealized vision of itself.

This was especially evident in a memorial service following the events of September 11, 2001. As part of a number of ecumenical services that took place around the city of New York, Riverside Church hosted an afternoon of dance, music, and prayer on September 16, 2001. Lillias White, an extraordinary African American vocalist who has appeared on Broadway, sang Duke Ellington's "Come Sunday." Throughout his career Ellington and his collaborator Billy Strayhorn often used singers for wordless vocals in their extended compositions. Singers such as Adelaide Hall and Kay Davis were used like instruments in these works and produced exciting and unique performances. Ellington was steeped in the classic studies of black life and culture (at his death he is said to have had a library of eight hundred volumes on African American history), so it is not surprising that in his own epic work inspired by that history, *Black, Brown, and Beige*, the black female voice would come to occupy a central place. In the first section of the extended work, "Black," Ellington offered "Come Sunday," a spiritual. At its initial performance Johnny Hodges provided the exquisite saxophone solo, but subsequently Ellington added words and invited Mahalia Jackson to sing them. Her rendition was recorded in 1958. Ellington later wrote, "This encounter with Mahalia Jackson had a strong influence on me and my sacred music, and also made me a much handsomer kind in the right light" (Ellington. *Music Is My Mistress*) "Come Sunday" returns in his later sacred concerts; he even recorded an especially beautiful version with the white Swedish vocalist Alice Babs.

Listening to versions of "Come Sunday," reading accounts of Ellington's writing and presenting it make it clear that *Black, Brown, and Beige* was not only an effort to "create a tone parallel to the history of the American Negro," as Ellington has said, but that it was also a gift to the world. As an astute student of African American history and a major contributor to its culture, Ellington knew that history and the cultural traditions it has produced can be healing balms during times of uncertainty. This is one of the reasons why we so often turn to black musical traditions during times of national crisis. When Lillias White made her offering of Ellington's "Come Sunday" she helped to articulate national pain and confusion, and one had the sense that, like Malindy, her voice took those concerns to the very ears of God. The "my people" of "Come Sunday" was initially meant to be the descendants of U.S.-born slaves, an oppressed minority. However, in this instance it not only articulated the confusion and pain of the diverse peoples of the United States but also of "God's People"—at any given moment the inhabitants of the United States, Jews, black Americans, Palestinians, Iraquis, or Afro-Colombians— any people suffering the consequences of violence and oppression.

The moment White's voice joined the air, like the blue notes it rendered, it was a voice that brought with it a specific, collective blue-black history, capable of expressing human desire. As with butterflies (whose beauty is born of fierce, difficult, and dangerous struggle),[21] that voice and those of us transported inside its sound are *momentarily* transcendent, ephemeral, beautiful, and, for a time, free before returning to a reality that might still be filled with danger and struggle.

NOTES

I am grateful to Brent Edwards, Michael Awkward, Daphne Brooks, Barbara Savage, W. S. Tkweme, Vijay Iyer, Krin Gabbard, and Salim Washington for reading and/or commenting upon earlier versions of this essay. I also wish to thank members of the Jazz Study Group of the Center for Jazz Studies, Columbia University.

1. This listing is iconic and not empirical. In other words, I have not done an empirical investigation of how many times black women have sang at all moments of national crisis, but, instead, I am interested in moments that stand out in the national memory.

2. See Barrett, *Blackness and Value*, p. 76.

3. See Maultsby, "West African Influence and Retentions in U.S. Black Music" and "Africanisms in African-American Music"; Southern, *The Music of Black Americans*; Stuckey, *Slave Culture*.

4. In *Black Power* Richard Wright writes of his disappointment in a Ghanaian church choir because they don't sound like African American singers. He cites Dunbar's poem to describe the kind of singing he prefers: "I'd much rather have heard the kind of singing that Paul Laurence Dunbar described in his poem: "When Malindy Sings": "She just opens her mouth and hollers, / 'Come to Jesus,' 'til you hear / Sinners' trembling steps and voices / Timidlike a-drawing near;- / Then she turns to 'Rock of Ages,' / Simply to the Cross she clings, / And you find your tears a-dropping / When Malindy sings. But that Gold Coast hymn evoked in me merely a cough of embarrassment behind my cupped palms" (p. 148). Richard Wright, *Black Power: A Record of Reactions in a Land of Pathos* (New York: Harper Perennial, 1995).

5. Story, *And So I Sing*, p. 186. According to Story, "Black singers (but not all them) have been said to possess inordinate ranges and indescribably warm, dark sound." She notes,

"In the high voices the lower end of the black voice is deeper, richer, more voluptuously shaped than that of many white singers." Joan Sutherland feels that black singers have "beautifully rich, mellifluous and warm sound . . . with great sympathy, a loving sound." Story interviewed Barbara Moore, chair of the Voice Department at Dallas Southern University, who explained that the black singing voice is actually the result of speech patterns and culture. According to Moore, most of her black "students grew up listening to and emulating the decidedly low-voiced inflection of gospel singing and rhythm and blues." For Moore the "dark quality may be an extension of the speaking voice." Consequently, she says her black students are much less likely than the white ones to explore the top range of their voices. This may be the case, although it doesn't explain the clarity of coloratura soprano Kathleen Battle.

6. Roland Barthes, "The Grain of the Voice" in Barthes, *Responsibility of Forms.*

7. See Mackey, "Other"; Leroi Jones, *Blues People: Negro Music in White America* (New York: Morrow, 1963), Zora Neale Hurston, "The Sanctified Church (Berkeley: Turtle Island, 1981), Brent Edwards, "The Seemingly Eclipsed Window of Form: James Weldon Johnson's Prefaces," *The Jazz Cadence of American Culture* edited by Robert G. O'Meally. New York: Columbia University Press, 1998." Robert O'Meally, *The Jazz Singers: A Smithsonian Collection*

8. Quoted in Mackey, "Other," p. 269.

9. Ibid. Mackey also quotes Henry Spaulding in 1863 who wrote, "The most striking of their barbaric airs would be impossible to write out." See also Stuckey, *Slave Culture,* pp. 81–83.

10. Mackey, "Other," p. 269.

11. Nathaniel Mackey identifies black singing as part of a larger universe of black linguistic practices "that accent variance [and] variability." He calls these practices "othering practices" that "implicitly react against and reflect critically upon the different sort of othering to which their practitioners, denied agency in a society by which they are designated other, have been subjected." See Mackey, "Cante Moro."

12. See Story, *And So I Sing.* Story contends that "blackness as a description of the voice is not necessarily racial . . . it is a quality of vocal darkness, found in the sound of the Russian Feodor Chaliapin and the Italian Ezio Pinza. But a case is made for the particularly identifiable sound of certain geographic regions. . . . The Italianate, the Welsh, and the Slavic sounds all are determined by what the individual culture, through language and ethnic tradition, determines is beautiful" (p. 187).

13. Ellison, "As the Spirit Moves Mahalia."

14. Maultsby, "Africanisms in African-American Music," p. 92.

15. I am reminded here of the voices of Patti Labelle, Nona Hendryx, and Sarah Dash on "You Turn Me On": three women's voices, overlapping, all-powerful, bursting outside of language. It recalls Michael Poizat's rendering of the opera diva's voice as one where "the body's libidinal drives emerge in sound unmediated by language, producing a sensation of radical loss, whereby castration, difference and subjectivity are annulled." Dunn and Jones, in *Embodied Voices,* write that this "experience of loss threatens the stability of the patriarchal order" (p. 9).

16. Wilson, "Preface to *Three Plays.*"

17. So this is not about jazz per se except to the extent that there are some streams of jazz that are related to forms of artistic and intellectual production that find their inspiration in African American expressive culture. Let me say that while I do not have time to focus on them here I might also include George Gershwin on the Sea Islands or

Frederick Delius at the St. John's River in Florida who is said to have heard black plantation workers singing at night and described that moment as "a truly wonderful sense of musicianship and harmonic resource in the instinctive way in which they treated a melody and hearing their singing in such romantic surroundings it was then that I first felt the urge to express myself in music" (Jack Sullivan, p. 19).

18. Sam Floyd writes:

> The impetus, tone and emotional quality of the blues may have come from Senegambia. Michael Coolen (1991, 3) has shown, for example, that Senegambians suffered inordinately from the slave trade, due to their convient proximity to the Senegal and Gambia rivers, on which "slave factories" were located and where ships arrived to pick up human cargo. The consequent large concentration of Senegambian slaves in America . . . is the reason for the structural and tonal similarities between the blues and the Senegambian fodet, which (1) uses cyclical form, with phrases played or sung to an "alternated use of tonic and secondary tonal centers," (2) commonly has AAB text structure, (3) makes use of a vocal practice in which the song begins on a high pitch and "gradually moves to lower pitches at the end," and (4) contains a low level of virtuosity with the option of a "hot" performance always avilable(16). This description, obviously, could be applied as accurately to the blues.   (THE POWER OF BLACK MUSIC, 75)

See also "From Mali to Mamie: The History of the Blues," part 1, *Southern Cross the Dog* (Winter 2003), pp. 13–16: "Because of its proximity to Spain and Portugal, the chief slave-trding countries, most of the first slaves necessarily came from this region on the West Coast of Africa. This is the locus of the griot tradition and the strongest strain in the American Blues Tradition, with an emphasis on solo vocals. . . . Stringed instruments—predecessors to the banjo and the guitar—dominate the instrumentation, as does a distinct middle Eastern influence (again a matter of geography) that results in long droning melody lines" (p. 14).

19. Attali, *Noise*, p. 14.

20. Barrett convincingly argues that for Black Americans the singing voice "provides a primary means by which African Americans may exchange an expended, valueless self in the New World for a productive recognized self. It provides one important means of formalizing and celebrating an existence otherwise proposed as negative and negligible" (*Blackness and Value*, p. 57).

21. Here I am speaking metaphorically. I am not comparing the sound of White's voice to the "sound" of a butterfly.

REFERENCES

Attali, Jacques. *Noise: The Political Economy of Music*. Minneapolis: University of Minnesota Press, 1985

Barrett, Lindon. *Blackness and Value: Seeing Double*. Cambridge: Cambridge University Press, 1999.

Barthes, Roland. *Responsibility of Forms: New Critical Essays on Music, Art and Representation*. New York: Hill and Wang, 1985.

Crowther, Bruce and Mike Pinfold. *Jazz Singing: From Ragtime to New Wave*. New York: Blandford, 1986.

Davis, Miles, with Quincy Troupe. *Miles: The Autobiography* New York : Simon and Schuster, 1990.

Dunn, Leslie and Nancy A. Jones, eds. *Embodied Voices: Representing Female Vocality in Western Culture*. Cambridge: Cambridge University Press, 1994.

Ellison, Ralph. "As the Spirit Moves Mahalia." In *Shadow and Act*. New York: Random House, 1965.

Floyd, Samuel. *The Power of Black Music: Interpreting Its History from Africa to the United States*. New York: Oxford University Press, 1995.

Holloway, Karla F. C. "The Lyrical Dimensions of Spirituality: Music, Voice, and Language in the Novels of Toni Morrison." In Leslie Dunn and Nancy A. Jones, eds., *Embodied Voices: Representing Female Vocality in Western Culture*. Cambridge: Cambridge University Press, 1994.

Kerman, Cynthia Earl. *The Lives of Jean Toomer: A Hunger for Wholeness*. Baton Rouge: Louisiana State University Press, 1987.

Mackey, Nathaniel. "Other: From Noun to Verb." *Discrepant Engagement: Dissonance, Cross-Culturality, and Experimental Writing*. Cambridge: Cambridge University Press, 1993.

———— "Cante Moro." In Adalaide Morris, ed., *Sound States: Innovative Poetics and Acoustical Technologies*, pp. 194–212. Chapel Hill and London: University of North Carolina Press.

Maultsby, Portia. "Africanisms in African-American Music." In Joseph E. Holloway, ed., *Africanisms in American Culture*. Bloomington: Indiana University Press, 1990.

———— "West African Influence and Retentions in U.S. Black Music: A Sociocultrual Study." In Irene V. Jackson, ed., *More Than Dancing: Essays on Afro-American Music and Musicians*. Westport, Conn.: Greenwood, 1985.

Morrison, Toni. *Beloved: A Novel*. New York: New American Library, 1988 [1987].

Reagon, Bernice Johnson and Sweet Honey in the Rock. *We Who Believe in Freedom: Sweet Honey in the Rock . . . Still on the Journey*. New York: Anchor, 1993.

Southern, Eileen. *The Music of Black Americans: A History*. New York: Norton, 1971.

Story, Rosalyn. *And So I Sing: African-American Divas of Opera and Concert*. New York: Warner, 1990.

Stuckey, Sterling. *Slave Culture*. New York: Oxford University Press, 1987.

Sullivan, Jack. *New World Symphonies: How American Culture Changed European Music*. New Haven: Yale University Press, 1999.

Tolbert, Elizabeth. "The Voice of Lament: Female Vocality and Performative Efficacy in the Finnish-Karelian itkuvirsi." In Leslie Dunn and Nancy A. Jones, eds., *Embodied Voices: Representing Female Vocality in Western Culture*. Cambridge: Cambridge University Press, 1994.

Toomer, Jean. *Cane*. New York: Liveright, 1975 [1923].

Troupe, Quincy. *Miles and Me*. Berkeley: University of California Press, 2000.

Wilson, August. "Preface to *Three Plays*." In Robert G. O'Meally, ed., *The Jazz Cadence of American Culture*. New York: Columbia University Press, 1998.

DISCOGRAPHY

Barnwell, Ysaye. *Singing in the African American Tradition: Choral and Congregational Vocal Music*. Homespun Tapes LTD (Cassette), 1989.

farah jasmine griffin

Ellington, Duke and Mahalia Jackson. *Black, Brown, and Beige* Sony; ASIN: BooooolMY (CD), 1999 [1958].

Labelle. *Nightbirds*. Sony Boooo02532 (CD), 1995 [1974].

Myers, Amina Claudine. *Amina Claudine Myers Salutes Bessie Smith*. Leo Records Boooo281VN (CD), 1996.

Simone, Nina. *Nina Simone Sings Nina*. Polygram Records 314 529 867–2 (CD), 1996.

Wilson, Cassandra. *Traveling Miles*, Blue Note D128340 (CD), 1999.

JOHN GENNARI

Hipsters, Bluebloods, Rebels, and Hooligans: The Cultural Politics of the Newport Jazz Festival, 1954–1960

Baby baby, have you heard the news?
Got festival eyes, got the Newport Blues

Newport Newport, gonna have a ball
If you ain't there baby, you ain't nowhere at all

Rhode Island in summer, Newport in July
I'm gonna dig that festival, and here's the reason why

Music makes me baby, makes me want to move
Swingin' in society, in a high-class groove

Flyin' down to Newport, man I wanna swing
With the real nobility: The Duke, The Count, The King

So come on down to Newport, if you wanna be confused
A panel of professors, will authenticate the blues

— MARSHALL STEARNS,

ON OCCASION OF THE FIRST NEWPORT JAZZ FESTIVAL,

1954

It's a gloomy day at Newport
It's a gloomy, gloomy day.
It's a gloomy day at Newport,
It's a gloomy, gloomy day.
It's a gloomy day at Newport,
The music's going away.

—LANGSTON HUGHES,

ON OCCASION OF THE CLOSING OF THE NEWPORT JAZZ FESTIVAL,

1960

At the Newport Jazz Festival on the fourth of July weekend in 1960, thousands of white youths described by *Life* magazine as "more interested in cold beer than in hot jazz" spilled from the jazz concerts into Newport's downtown, attacking policemen, kicking in store windows, and manhandling the town's residents and visitors. Press reports noted that many of the drunken rioters screamed racial epithets while rampaging through town. State police used billy clubs and tear gas to stem the riot, then called on the marines for help in restoring order. When the air cleared, over two hundred of the marauders found themselves in local jails, while more than fifty of their victims required medical attention. One witness told the *Providence Journal*: "I've experienced fear twice in my life. Once was in combat during World War II; the other was Saturday night in Newport." Scheduled to end on Sunday night, the festival was ordered shut down on Sunday afternoon by the Newport city council. The last act was a program of blues narrated by Langston Hughes. Anticipating the city council's action, Hughes penned a set of lyrics on a Western Union sheet. He handed them to Otis Spann, who sang them slowly as the crowd quietly departed.[1]

Among a rash of press reports on the riot, one commentator blamed the allure of Newport, a "resort area which hold[s] a fascination for the square collegian who wants to ball without running the risk of mom and dad stumbling across his prostrate form on somebody's lawn." Mordantly noting the contrast between the Newport gentry "in the front row with their Martini shakers" and the youngsters "squatting in the back, their heads between their knees, upchucking their beer," journalist Murray Kempton wondered, "Was ever anything in America at once so fashionable and so squalid?" To many who had embraced Newport as jazz's City on a Hill, a sterling model of New England brahmin philanthropy, more disconcerting than the spectacle of loutish yahoos profaning the festival was the rioters's identity. These were not switchblade-wielding rebels without a cause, nor pothead beatniks in overalls. These "young hooligan herrenvolk of the Eastern seaboard," as *Village Voice* jazz critic Robert Reisner dubbed the rioters, were students from the elite colleges, fraternity brothers on a fast track to the corporate boardroom. "You could tell the students from Harvard and Yale," wagged one man on the street: "They were throwing only *imported* beer bottles."[1]

Hooliganism wasn't the only turbulence that swept through the 1960 festival. That same weekend a group of musicians led by Charles Mingus and Max Roach, aggrieved by festival management techniques and programming policies, organized an alternative, or "rebel," festival in another part of town. Claiming that the main festival reeked of Jim Crow, finding its supporters' embrace of jazz suffocating rather than liberating, the rebels literally constructed their own bandstand, printed their own handbills, and erected tents on their own guerrilla concert site. Seizing the rhetoric and imagery of the *salon des refusés*, the rebel festival fancied itself a virtuous self-governing republic of artists pitted against a corrupt empire of profiteering booking agents, promoters, and hoteliers.

The *Voice*'s Reisner deemed it "a case of getting back to the jazz truth," a matter of artists "renew[ing] their creative faculties by embracing poverty." Max Roach characterized the event as an effort to "prove that the musician can produce, present, and participate [by and for] himself"—an idea that Mingus and Roach had enacted earlier in the 1950s through owning and managing their own label, Debut Records. Proceeds collected in a noncoercive passing of the hat established a fund for fighting economic injustices plaguing musicians such as onerous cabaret card laws and unemployment taxes. A correspondent from *Time,* struck by the political significance of the rebellion, unsuccessfully lobbied his editors to get his dispatch in the magazine's national affairs section rather than the music section. "This is an extension of the sit-ins," he told them. "[It's] a sit-out."[2]

The 1960 youth riot and the musicians's rebellion at Newport mocked and challenged a jazz establishment that had played a crucial role in shaping the music's postwar public image. Part of a growing cultural infrastructure that included college concert bookings, a burgeoning LP trade, self-consciously intellectual journals, and U.S. State Department tours, the Newport Jazz Festival signified jazz's affiliation with the "mainstream," the symbolic popular center of the Cold War political imaginary. At the same time, in jazz's version of end-of-ideology ideology, mainstream commentators and gatekeepers evangelized the music as a force of racial harmony and bourgeois normalcy, sanitizing jazz of its affiliations with political radicalism and racial and bohemian subcultures. Noting jazz's appeal to everyone from "a pneumatic drill operator to a little old grandma knitting in a rocking chair," the *New York Post* claimed that one did not have to be a "rootless drifter of the Beat generation," a "boozer," or a "weedhead," to appreciate "America's only true native art." Contrasting jazz with "such popular lunacies as rock and roll," the *Post* counted among the jazz listening public "doctors, lawyers, housewives, and even Congressmen." In a similar vein, *Variety* approvingly noted that in John Foster Dulles's State Department "the hipsters have virtually been given striped pants and sent overseas as ambassadors of good will."[3]

The Newport Jazz Festival was both a symbol and an agent of this mainstreaming of jazz in the mid to late 1950s, and its story brings to light a lively contest over jazz's meaning and public image. As I narrate the story of the festival in its first seven years, I want to highlight several intersecting story lines that underscore the complex cultural politics of jazz in this period. The first is the effort on the part of the festival's promoters and supporters, drawing on the cultural capital, material resources, and physical beauty of Newport, to endow jazz with new images of respectability and aesthetic worth, to trumpet the music as a uniquely American cultural product, and to expand the music's audience as much as possible.

Contributing to this effort—sometimes in alliance with the festival's local producers, sometimes not—were the national and international media (some representing jazz for the very first time) and an assortment of artists, intellectuals, and critics. The second story line focuses on the vexed relations between Newport's producers and a few influential jazz critics who had supported the festival in its first years but turned against it as the festival grew in size and began to feature popular acts that transgressed the critics's notions of jazz authenticity and purism. The third story line focuses on how the jazz musicians themselves interacted with the producers and the critics in negotiating their positions at the festival. This story line complicates and enriches the first two, demonstrating how commercial considerations and artistic ones were always enmeshed with each other. The fourth story line, one that concerns racial politics, shadows all the others. It focuses on the ambivalent experience of black jazz musicians, intellectuals, and fans who assented to the Newport festival's mission and enjoyed its interracial bonhomie but who also encountered racism in the public and private spaces of the town. While allied with jazz's white patrons in seeking to capitalize on the opportunities represented by jazz's new status as a serious American art, these African Americans simultaneously asserted jazz's significance as a crucible of black cultural memory, agency, and autonomy and looked for ways to increase their economic control over the music.

The Newport Jazz Festival began with great fanfare in 1954, ballyhooed by its energetic founders—the Boston jazz promoter George Wein and Newport gentry up-and-comers Elaine and Louis Lorillard—as the American equivalent of the Athenian and Elizabethan national theaters: a grand event celebrating a popular art form indigenous to the nation. "We could make Newport the jazz center of the world," Wein excitedly told the *New Yorker*'s Lillian Ross. "What Salzburg is to Mozart! What Bayreuth is to Wagner! What Tanglewood is to classical music! That's what we could make Newport be to jazz!" The Lorillards—Elaine a former Madison Avenue fashion illustrator, Louis the heir to a tobacco fortune—lost face with the starchiest of their blueblood neighbors, but it didn't take long for Newport burghers to see that jazz was freshly minted cultural capital, a homegrown cosmopolitan form breathing new life over faded Euro-gentility.[4]

One document that dramatizes the cultural transformations wrought by the Newport Jazz Festival is the 1956 movie *High Society*, a musical comedy that signifies on the plot changes of *The Philadelphia Story*. Bing Crosby plays a well-heeled Newport slacker named Dexter, a jazz buff inspired by Louis Lorrilard's efforts to sell the local bluebloods on jazz. In a famous scene Crosby's Dexter cuts into a society ball waltz to introduce Louis Armstrong and his band, which up until this point in the film had provided background music for the romantic contretemps between Dexter and his fiancée, played by Grace Kelly. Crosby and Armstrong launch into an extraordinary rendition of "Now You Has Jazz." Crosby, in brilliant voice, easily relieves the audience of its elitist prejudices. But the really memorable performance is Armstrong's. Constrained by a Hollywood formula in which the black musician serves to authenticate a white star's knowing hipness—Armstrong

plays similar roles opposite Danny Kaye in *A Song is Born* (1948) and Paul Newman in *Paris Blues* (1961)—Armstrong deftly unmasks the film's neominstrel
scheme, purloining Crosby's crystalline vocal lines into a glare of hot trumpet and
signature rasp-scat.[5]

The real-life festival itself was no less exciting and colorful. On the inaugural
weekend of July 16 and 17, 1954, Newport's narrow streets thronged, *Time* reported, "with loud-shirted bookie types from Broadway, young intellectuals in need of
haircuts, crew-cut Ivy Leaguers, sailors, Harlem girls with extravagant hairdos, and
high school girls in shorts. They were cats. From as far away as Kansas they had
come to hear a two-day monster jazz festival." Fourteen thousand attended the Saturday and Sunday evening concerts at the Newport Casino (in a band shell designed by Hso Wen Shih, architect, acoustic designer, and erudite jazz buff who
later served as publisher of the *Jazz Review*). A thousand showed up for the Sunday
afternoon panel discussion on "The Place of Jazz in American Culture." The panel—moderated by the "jazz priest" Father Norman O'Conner, with presentations
by Allan Merriam, anthropology professor at Northwestern University, Henry
Cowell, music professor at the Peabody Institute, Marshall Stearns, English professor at Hunter College and founder of the Institute of Jazz Studies, and Willis James,
folklorist and ethnomusicology professor at Spelman College—symbolized jazz's
rising legitimacy among intellectuals. Local newspaper notices from the *Sacramen-
to Bee* to the *Roanake Times* testified to the festival's national scope. Such was the
rapture of the European press that when Wein arrived in France on a business trip
that fall, French jazz enthusiasts received him as *un homme formidable*.[6]

Wein had established his reputation as a savvy and musically literate jazz impresario at his Boston jazz nightclubs, Storyville and Mahogany Hall. Son of
Boston's best-known plastic surgeon, Wein's own premedical studies foundered in
the late 1940s when his love for jazz and his budding entrepreneurial skills came
together to point him toward a new career. As a pianist, Wein had played traditional jazz behind trumpeter Max Kaminsky at the Ken Club and clarinettist Edmond Hall at the Savoy. He became a promoter when he formed a combo called
"George Wein's Danceable Jazz Featuring Edmond Hall" and toured the New England college circuit. In 1950 Wein launched Storyville on $5,000 cobbled togeth-
er from his G.I. benefits and a loan from his mother. The suggestion to name the
club after the legendary jazz and red-light district of New Orleans came from
Wein's friend Nat Hentoff, at that time host of a popular jazz radio program in
Boston and an aspiring jazz writer. "We grew up together and we hung out together at the Savoy," Wein said recently about his relationship with Hentoff. "Nat introduced me to my wife [Joyce Wein]. I was playing the music, but he knew more
about the history. I'd listen to his radio program, hear Bessie Smith for the first
time—that sort of thing." Hentoff wrote the notes for the first concert Wein produced in Boston, at Jordan Hall, and he wrote a narrative script for the first Newport Jazz Festival—a condensed history of jazz—that was read by master of ceremonies Stan Kenton.[7]

In a profile of Wein in *Esquire* in 1955, George Frazier told a story about one
night at Storyville when Wein still served as house pianist. Drummer Jo Jones,

known both for his good-natured disposition and for his rhythmic perfectionism, found Wein's block chords and comping technique unforgivably clumsy. "George, you gotta make up your mind whether you want to run a night club or play piano. I'm sorry man, but I just can't use you," Jones told him, then cashiered him off the bandstand in what is surely one of the high points in the history of jazz labor-management relations. In the same *Esquire* profile, Frazier quoted Wein as saying that "the worst enemies of jazz are often the musicians themselves"—an argument for the Newport festival's "respectability-by-osmosis" uplift strategy. Some musicians found this attitude patronizing. Worried that Dizzy Gillespie's comic stage antics might profane the solemn rites of the opening night concert, Wein asked the trumpeter to affect a more serious pose. "In my most snobbish manner I decided to ask Dizzy to cut the clowning and just concentrate on his music," Wein contritely wrote in a 1956 *Playboy* article about the festival. "Seeing his goateed jaw drop several inches once I had made my suggestion was one of the most painful experiences of my life," Wein remembered. "I really hit him below the belt and I think it wrecked the entire festival for him." Offended by Wein's heavy-handed gesture, Gillespie redoubled his merry-andrewish efforts. Wearing a wrinkled brown suit and brandishing his signature vertical-belled trumpet, Gillespie paused in his performance, took the mike, and in a tone of mocking gravity introduced the members of his band—to each other. Upon resuming, Gillespie pulled a small camera out of his pocket and spent the rest of the set photographing members of the press.[8]

In planning for the Newport festival, Wein traded on his reputation, in Frazier's words, as "one of the very few night-club operators who is liked and trusted by musicians of violently conflicting schools of jazz." While his own tastes ran to early jazz and swing, Wein had hired Mingus, Charlie Parker, Max Roach, and other bebop players to play at Storyville. "We want to throw modern, swing, and Dixieland together—even have the guys playing them together," Wein described his Newport programming philosophy. "As long as there's a common beat, every guy can play solo his own style. One big happy family." Wein's "one big happy family" was a more sentimental, middlebrow version of what jazz critics had begun to call the jazz tradition or, even more tellingly, the "jazz mainstream," a kind of jazz vital center that jibed with the consensual politics of the era. The inaugural concerts began with a front line of Eddie Condon's Dixieland associates backed by the swing rhythm section of drummer Jo Jones and bassist Milt Hinton. The Modern Jazz Quartet, Dizzy Gillespie Quintet, and Gerry Mulligan Quartet shared a section with Billie Holiday. A tribute to Count Basie was followed by Gillespie and the George Shearing Quintet. Lennie Tristano and Lee Konitz segued into the Gene Krupa Trio. Stan Kenton—whom Wein had enlisted as master of ceremonies after Duke Ellington was unable to reschedule another engagement—led a closing night jam session involving all the artists.[9]

Newport festival programs and publicity campaigns featured chamber-of-commerce-style rhetoric about "the great Newport doctrine of helping new people and new ideas." This publicity linked the 1950s canonization of jazz to a Newport legacy of social, intellectual, and artistic reform. Dizzy Gillespie and John Lewis joined a pageant of freedom seekers stretching back to the Vikings who found shelter in

Newport waters two centuries before Columbus, the proprietors of the tall sailing ships that carved out global trade routes (no mention, of course, of the triangle trade in African slaves), and the patriots of 1776. "Tonight Newport went back to its beginning," intoned society columnist Cleveland Amory at a party at the Lorillard's after the inaugural concert. "Back to the time when it hummed with artists, writers, schoolteachers, ministers, and freedom." Institute of Jazz Studies director Marshall Stearns, in a festival program essay titled "Jazz Comes of Age" that foreshadowed his role as a consultant for the State Department tours, credited the music's global popularity to an antitotalitarian ethos that "transcend[s] rules and regulations" and "offers a common ground on which the conflicting claims of the individual and the group may be resolved."[10]

Stearns was a highly respected pioneering jazz scholar, while Amory's faith in the Newport crusade to "prove that jazz deserved something better than smoke-filled dives and zoot-suited patrons" might have struck a chord with jazz modernists looking for a reprieve from the hurly-burly jazz life. All the same, boosterish claims about Newport's noble history and jazz's democratic ideology gave little solace to black musicians and fans who were turned away at Newport's Viking Hotel. A 1955 *Time* dispatch on the second festival, reporting that "cats, hipsters, vipers, and even a few moldy figs swarmed the stately mansions of Newport," told one side of the story; *Ebony*'s coverage, noting that pianist Billy Taylor had been refused service at a hotel bar, told another. In other cases racial insensitivities registered more subtly as screwball comedy–style faux pas. At the postconcert party at the Lorillard's, Lillian Ross reported in the *New Yorker*, a local old-line matron boasted to Modern Jazz Quartet bassist Percy Heath about "the old, lush days of Newport" when "every house had a large staff of liveried servants."[11]

Concerns about racist incidents in Newport dominated the festival board of directors' meeting in 1955. Jazz critics Leonard Feather and Barry Ulanov, citing incidents of racial discrimination at the Viking Hotel and other local establishments, made a motion to move the festival out of Newport. They also called for a loud publicity campaign shaming the town's burghers for their affront to the democratic principles enshrined in the music. As editors of *Metronome* in the 1940s, Feather and Ulanov were known not just as supporters of bebop but also as liberals with a four-square commitment to racial equality. It was John Hammond, however, the jazz record producer, social critic, and political organizer who had shepherded the careers of Billie Holiday, Count Basie, Benny Goodman, and others while also taking up the cause of the Scottsboro Nine and agitating against Jim Crow in the U.S. military (among other of his liberal commitments), who remained the jazz critic most identified with this issue. Hammond had an especially strong interest in the fate of jazz and race relations in Newport. Here Hammond's reformist zeal was a personal matter—literally. His mother was a Vanderbilt, his forbears the bulwark of the Newport aristocracy. Long engaged in a drama of class treason, Hammond now reveled in seeing his commitment to jazz and black causes delivered on the doorsteps of his family. Responding to Feather and Ulanov's motion, Hammond said:

I think the fact that the . . . jazz festival was held in Newport, the most unlikely place, is essential. I think that if we had tried to have this festival any place else we would find that 80% of our publicity from the past and our good will would be dissipated. . . . I think many of us who are on this advisory committee have been fighting for jazz for a long time. We have no particular love for Newport—I less than almost anybody here [what] with family, relatives and forbears all coming from Newport. It is a kind of society and a kind of life [that I] abhor. Yet in one sense of the word we have brought democracy to Newport, which was that last place in the world where it could have been expected to be found in America.[12]

The festival stayed in Newport and its advisory board continued to be dominated by white liberals. The inclusion of black members on the board—musicians Louis Armstrong and Duke Ellington, novelist and critic Ralph Ellison, and *Ebony* magazine editor Alan Morrison—symbolized the pluralist aspirations of the enterprise. Through the mid-1950s a significant number of black writers, intellectuals, college students, and middle-class vacationers (many from nearby Martha's Vineyard) attended the festival. Ellison, Willis James, Langston Hughes, James Baldwin, and Sterling Brown participated in the panel discussions. Civil rights activist Julian Bond remembers the festival as an important social event for his circle of college friends in the late 1950s. In the New York *Amsterdam News* and other black newspapers festival coverage ran not just in the entertainment section but also in the social pages, where it exemplified the cultivated leisure of the black bourgeoisie.

Amsterdam News reporter Melvin Tapley, covering the 1957 festival, challenged black middle-class leaders to throw more support behind jazz. "I only wish that some of our people with the loot," Tapley wrote, "our doctors, lawyers, and business executives . . . would establish some sort of preservation society, like the Newport nabobs, for our own artists before our cultural bank account is overdrawn and squandered by the 'Great White Father' promoters." Langston Hughes sounded the same note in a private letter to Arna Bontemps. Noting that "half of cullud Harlem" was in Newport for the 1958 festival (and singling out for praise a jazz dance seminar led by Marshall Stearns and S. I. Hayakawa's lecture on the blues with a demonstration by singer Jimmy Rushing), Hughes wrote that "cullud ought to be in on some of this jazz PROMOTING instead of just the playing." This desire for greater black control of cultural production was something Hughes and others had advocated for years and would continue to pursue in years to come. But this didn't prevent Hughes from strategically embracing the mission of the Newport sponsors. "For giving jazz its golden crown at Newport," Hughes wrote in the *New York Post* in 1963, "the Lorrillards themselves deserve a crown." Writing in the public forum of a mainstream newspaper column during a time of increasing civil rights agitation, Hughes celebrated the Newport festival as a shining example of racial equality: "From its beginnings the board of the Newport Jazz Festival insisted that the Festival be completely democratic and interracial. Audiences, performers and (after a few early adjustments) all Newport hotels, restaurants and places of public accommodation were happily integrated without regard to race, color, age, sex or previous conditions of unhepness."[13]

Like Hughes, musicians well understood the social significance and influence of the Newport Jazz Festival. In 1956 the Duke Ellington orchestra was mired in a slump, its low ratings in fan polls and struggle for steady work a sad sign of the decline of the swing band movement Ellington had pioneered in the 1930s. Sensing an opportunity to recapture the public imagination by premiering a new piece at that year's festival, Ellington composed "The Newport Suite." While the festival opened on Thursday night, Ellington was scheduled for Saturday night and remained in New York until that day. George Wein was at an after-concert party at the Lorrillard's on late Thursday night when he was summoned to the phone for a call from Ellington.

> I don't know how the hell he knew where I was. But he was clearly very excited. He said, "What's happening up there? What's the mood?" I told him we were all waiting for him, looking forward to Saturday night. I asked him what he was going to do. He said "I thought we'd do the medley ["Newport Festival Suite"] and maybe some other stuff." I said to him: "Edward, here I am working my fingers to the bone to perpetuate the genius that is Ellington and I'm not getting any cooperation from you. You better come in here swinging."[14]

The good feeling behind this mock jousting dissipated a bit on Saturday night. When four of Ellington's musicians were late, Wein decided to run other acts while waiting for the missing players. The players soon arrived, but the band had to wait for three hours to take the stage. An irritated Ellington groused to Wein, "What are we—the animal act, the acrobats?" Finally, the clock nearing midnight, the band opened with "The Newport Festival Suite," followed by "Diminuendo and Crescendo in Blue," two medium tempo blues Ellington had written in 1937 spliced together with a "wailing interval" by tenor saxophonist Paul Gonsalves.

Ellington kicked off "Diminuendo and Crescendo in Blue" with four unremarkable introductory choruses. As drummer Sam Woodyard and bassist Jimmy Woode dug a deep groove and the horns leaned hard into their exuberant ensemble choruses, Ellington started verbally instigating the band, shouting out, "Uh-huh! Come on! Yeah!" Jo Jones, who earlier in the evening had backed up pianist Teddy Wilson and was now standing in a runway below the left front of the stage, joined Ellington in pushing the band harder, hollering encouragement and rhythmically swatting the edge of the stage with a rolled-up copy of the *Christian Science Monitor.*

Gonsalves stood and launched into his solo. Three choruses in, a platinum blonde in one of the front boxes broke loose from her escort and started spinning wildly, whirling-dervishlike, around the field. Ten choruses in, half the audience was jitterbugging in the aisles, the other half standing on their seats, cheering and clapping with mounting fervor. As the crowd energy surged and a possessed Gonsalves shut his eyes and pressed on, Wein and the local police grew agitated, fearful that a riot might break out. Wein and one of the officers tried to signal to Ellington to stop. In the heat of the moment Ellington shook his finger at Wein and shouted, "Don't be rude to the artists."

Gonsalves's Olympian twenty-seven-chorus solo has subsequently entered jazz legend as an endlessly fetishized performance: in aficionado circles there are people who can provide you the matrix number of a 1951 studio recording of "Diminuendo and Crescendo in Blue" in which Gonsalves took only *twenty-six* choruses. The Columbia recording of the entire Newport Ellington set, *Ellington at Newport,* went on to become Ellington's best-selling LP. A cover story in *Time* magazine called Ellington's Newport performance the "big news . . . that the whole jazz world had hoped to hear: [that] the Ellington band was once again the most exciting thing in the business."[15]

The story of this galvanic performance usually figures as a kind of stock scene of jazz scripture connoting nothing less the resurrection of the messiah. Those less given to hagiography might interpret the event as a triumph of African American performative culture, an eruption of spontaneous jam session–styled energy trumping the containment strategies of the jazz establishment. Yet one might also discern in Ellington's wry rebuke of George Wein the practiced gesture of a celebrity with a well-earned position of influence among national media elites, a savvy operator who knew how to work with promoters like Wein to advance his own interests. It wasn't just Ellington who discovered the career-enhancing possibilities of a Newport appearance. The year before Miles Davis, after a five-year struggle with heroin addiction, had ended a conspicuous absence from the jazz world with a triumphant appearance at Newport with Thelonious Monk. On the strength of glowing reviews of the performance, Davis was able to secure a lucrative recording contract with Columbia. Along with recording deals, musicians profited from Newport media exposure that projected a new kind of image of the jazz musician to the broad American public. In a foreshadowing of the sartorial image-making campaigns for the jazz "young lions" of recent years, fashion editors from *Vogue, Esquire, Ebony,* and *Playboy* descended on Newport in July, embracing jazz musicians as exemplars of bourgeois style. A 1955 *Vogue* photo spread on the second Newport festival featured John Lewis, described as a "well-adjusted Othello," Charles Mingus, "a handsome, solid-looking man . . . with a deep, brooding voice," Dave Brubeck, "an amiable-faced young man with a great wide-jawed grin and black-rimmed spectacles," and Count Basie, pictured seated at a grand piano suavely ornamented by "two cool blue notes," a pair of young and pretty white New York women outfitted in satin evening dresses.[16]

The feature-length documentary film *Jazz on a Summer's Day* marked a new conjunction of jazz, advertising, and modernist visual aesthetics. Shot at the 1958 festival and released to high praise at international film festivals in 1960, the film was produced and directed by Bert Stern, a successful New York advertising photographer venturing into movie making for the first time. Stern, according to critic Jerry Tallmer, had no more knowledge of jazz than Robert Oppenheimer. What he did have, however, was a sense of Newport as a landscape for a new jazz aesthetic. "Too many movies have given jazz an association with violence, narcotics, electric chairs, and murder," Stern explained. "We tried to show the form and beauty of jazz by various devices, such as wave and water effects, children playing, and reflections." Featuring a cinematographic purity of color reported to have "knocked every New York critic out of his seat," Stern's film interweaves festival performances with shots of a racially integrated audience, several dowagers in rococo dress surveying the strange Newport scene, a rooming house roof party, a Dixieland combo of Yale men spiriting through town in a Jazz Age roadster, a solitary young woman on a morning walk of the beach. Tallmer praised the documentary as a "rambling free-form mood poem" that captured the "eternal bold youth of everything," the "ordinary uncomplicated joyousness of sitting around and getting beautifully muzzy on beer as these guys blow these horns through the bright midday and the long afternoon and the soft enfolding evening of a rich little green little seaside town . . . far out of this world."[17]

Stern's artistic sensibility confounded the film's music director George Avakian, who felt that on-site fussing over camera angles and postproduction sleight of hand detracted from the film's value as a musical document. Indeed, the music in the film often functions as background for Stern's highly stylized vignettes. Throughout Anita O'Day's hypercool mannerist introduction to "Sweet Georgia Brown" the camera lingers on a woman in the audience deeply immersed in a paperback copy of *Camille* and a female photographer trying to keep her hat on as she focuses her lens. Thelonious Monk takes the stage and delineates a spare, pointillist sketch out of the head of "Blue Monk," providing the segue for a montage of the America's Cup yacht trials being held in Newport Bay. The languorous tempo of Louis Armstrong's "Up the Lazy River" is underscored by a recurring close-up of a man in the audience snapping his fingers just a shade behind the beat.[18]

Jazz on a Summer's Day is full of artifice: the yacht trials actually took place later in the summer, the audience shots were reconstructed in a New York studio over the winter. But the film's very quality of self-conscious artiness was itself a telling point, a symptom of jazz's association with the rarified discourses of modern art. One of the revealing subtexts of the film is the contrast it draws between Armstrong's old-time image of the good-natured entertainer and the modern jazz musicians's preferred image of a serious, nonaccomodating artist. The film historian Donald Bogle has argued that to young blacks coming of age in the 1950s Armstrong's glowing musicianship provided little inoculation against the embarrassment of his Uncle Tommish eye-popping, shucking and jiving, and too-friendly banter with white costars. Unfairly and with little appreciation of Armstrong's gift for subversive mimicry, jazz purists often winced at the Sambo inflections of Armstrong's comic persona. In 1958, when Leonard Feather ran a reader-response survey in *Down Beat* to the question "What was the worst thing that happened to jazz in the last year?" the most common response was Louis Armstrong's appearance at the Newport Jazz Festival. Even so staunch an Armstrong partisan as Ralph Ellison lamented—in a letter to Albert Murray—that at the 1957 festival Armstrong "was wearing his ass instead of his genius." In *Jazz on a Summer's Day*'s footage of the

1958 festival, Armstrong is shown mugging with Voice of America disk jockey Willis Conover, the festival master of ceremonies, before performing "Up the Lazy River" and his perennial "Rocking Chair" vocal duet with Jack Teagarden. Though the audience appears to love the broadly grinning Satchmo, the filmed performance offers no window into Armstrong's complex psyche—no hint, for instance, of the burden he was carrying for having boldly defied his friend and manager Joe Glaser by speaking out against Arkansas governor Orville Faubus during the 1957 school desegregation crisis. That sort of image—one of the jazz artist with a complicated inner life—is reserved for the modernists. A long passage in the film that captures Chico Hamilton and his sidemen in rehearsal is lit in a film-noirish chiascuro, much like Blue Note album cover photographs of the period—an image that suggested deep emotion, anxiety, and searching intensity. When Conover introduces Thelonious Monk, he archly describes the pianist as a kind of existentialist misanthrope:[19]

> [And now], one of the complete originals of music. A man who lives his music, a man who thinks his music, and it's possible to say he lives and thinks of little else. We can't describe him exactly as daring, because he is unconcerned with any opposition to his music. He concerns himself with such elements as the quarter-tone, which he doesn't find in our Western scale, so he'll strike two adjacent keys on the piano to imply the missing note between. Ladies and gentlemen, Thelonious Monk.

To his credit George Wein programmed postbebop players and even the late 1950s avant-garde—Monk, Chico Hamilton, Cecil Taylor, Max Roach, Charles Mingus, Jimmy Guiffre—despite his own retro tastes, audience diffidence, and a hammering in the general press. Harold Schoenberg, the New York *Times*'s classical music critic, panned the modernists at the 1955 festival (Lee Konitz, the Modern Jazz Quartet, Miles Davis, Charles Mingus) as "dissonant, tight, overintellectual, and nonmelodic," preferring the "earthy and low-down . . . anti-intellectual" fare of Louis Armstrong and Jimmy Rushing. Roger Maren, writing in the *Reporter* that same year, also preferred the "rarely pretentious" traditionalists to modern players who "often give the impression that they are members of a metaphysical cult rather than simply entertainers." Maren found the whole Newport scene too serious. Expecting to find a raucous crowd shouting "Go, man, go," he was disappointed to encounter an atmosphere "resembling Tanglewood's or Salzburg's," a festival program and souvenir booklet whose typography "echoed the experimental art of the 1920s," a "professor [Stearns] comparing Bessie Smith to the Wife of Bath," and song titles like "Epistrophy" and "Fugetta." "The word 'semantic' was used so many times at the Festival with so many odd meanings," Maren complained, "that it took on a new semantic value." (In 1958 gospel singer Mahalia Jackson raised similar concerns about the festival's more cerebral dimensions. After listening to a panel discussion on "Jazz and American Life" involving Ralph Ellison, Langston Hughes, Marshall Stearns, Sterling Brown, and S. I. Hayakawa, Jackson said, "There's been too much analysin' here and not enough heart.")[20]

Nat Hentoff and Whitney Balliett, then tyro jazz critics on the make, condemned Maren in a pair of blistering letters to the editor. Hentoff, at that time the New York editor of *Down Beat,* soon would team up with a fellow grad school casualty, lapsed literary New Critic Martin Williams, in launching the *Jazz Review,* jazz criticism's analogue to the *Partisan Review* and other high modernist journals. Whitney Balliett, then a book reviewer and Talk of the Town scribe at the *New Yorker,* soon would start a regular jazz column at that magazine. This new generation of jazz critics, caught up in their own campaign for legitimation as intellectuals, linked their writerly agendas to the fate of the embattled jazz modernists. Balliett's letter to the *Reporter* diagnosed a malignant symmetry in Maren's Newport analysis: Maren's dismissal of Charles Mingus's aspirations as a jazz composer, Balliett noted, came just two paragraphs before he "takes jazz critics to task for using terms like 'counterpoint,' 'atonality,' and 'polytonality.'"[21]

At issue here—as ever in jazz criticism—was the question of what constitutes real jazz, whether the latest stylistic developments were authentically rooted in the already canonized tradition, and what kind of environment and performing posture were appropriate for the music's presentation. When Wein caught promoter's fever, enlarging the festival each year and aiming to pull in the burgeoning rock 'n' roll youth audience, he became a ripe target for the critics's purist righteousness. Whitney Balliett started turning on Wein in 1956, decrying a "fat hand of bigness" that had begun to strangle the festival in 1955 after it moved from the Casino to Freebody Park, a municipal baseball facility where crowds of twenty thousand and up convened in the coming years. In his liner notes for the LP *Ellington at Newport,* Columbia Records producer George Avakian took pains to suggest that the audience's behavior during "Diminuendo and Crescendo in Blue," while impassioned, was "no rock 'n' roll reaction." The allusion called to mind the epidemic of highly publicized disruptions at rock 'n' roll concerts that season, including a flare-up in September 1956 at a Fats Domino concert at a Newport naval base that resulted in the hospitalization of a dozen black and white servicemen. Avakian's language linked the rhetoric of Cold War domestic containment to jazz's mounting high-culture pretensions. "Despite the unbridled enthusiasm [during Ellington's performance]," he wrote, "there was a controlled, clean quality to the crowd."[22]

Clean or not, the Newport audience from 1957 on encountered a regular diet of acts that jazz critics and purists took as a personal affront, a challenge to their canon-formation endeavors. Whatever one might think about the Four Freshmen, the Kingston Trio, Pat Suzuki, and Eartha Kitt, the indictment ran, they did not belong at a festival that had originally defined itself by its curatorial embrace of the *jazz* tradition. Of the critics, interestingly, it was the old lions John Hammond and Marshall Stearns who encouraged a pluralist outreach to the new popular music. Hammond prevailed on Wein to present Chuck Berry at the 1958 festival, backed by members of a Count Basie reunion band. This half-way covenant between Kansas City 4/4 swing and backbeat-driven rock 'n' roll appears in *Jazz on a Summer's Day* footage to confound the musicians and not quite jell into a compelling rhythmic groove. Many in the audience, however, found Berry's rocking guitar and patented duckwalk reason enough to get on their feet and dance, which they continued to do when Mahalia Jackson's infectious gospel beat capped off the concert. Avakian, who was also Jackson's producer at the time, and who thought the dancing a sacrilege against the gospel matriarch's religious purity, was highly displeased.[23]

So was Melvin Tapley of the New York *Amsterdam News*, who criticized both the Newport impresarios and Jackson herself for "desecrat[ing] music born of our religious beliefs." Ralph Ellison, for his part, was less concerned with a bleeding of the line between the sacred and the secular than with preserving the "authentic" character of Jackson's gospel music. In a 1958 *Saturday Review* essay on Jackson, Ellison lamented the singer's appearance at the 1957 Newport festival singing the "Come Sunday" movement of Duke Ellington's *Black, Brown, and Beige Suite*. Calling the performance "a most unfortunate marriage and an error of taste," Ellison contrasted Ellington's "impression" of a Sunday service with the "real thing"— Jackson singing at Newport's Afro-American Episcopal Church on Sunday morning, much more effectively evoking "the shared community of experience" that defines the black church. Ellison was even more censorious in a letter to Albert Murray, carping not only about Louis Armstrong's embarrassing performance but also about an appearance by "that creep Eartha Kitt and some non-jazz dancers." "The whole circus sounds as though it was rather limp," Ellison reported. "I guess you can't throw too many musicians and hep cats manque together too many times and have it come out listenable."[24]

These pleas for purity—whether the white critics' anticommercialism or black critics' briefs for authentic black culture—were thrown up against a rising juggernaut. By the end of the 1950s the $20,000 two-day festival of 1954 seemed dilettantish: in 1959 the festival—though still a nonprofit venture bankrolled by Louis Lorrillard—spent $265,692 to employ forty-three groups and individuals in a variety of activities, including tours of the United States and eight foreign countries. The combined audience for these Newport Jazz Festival productions was estimated at over a quarter million people. Critics loudly scorned this growth policy. Richard Gehman excoriated the festival management for treating jazz as a "huge supermarket" set up for the benefit of a "vast and generally tasteless public." Dan Morgenstern characterized jazz festivals as "three-ring circuses, crass commercial supermarkets of jazz, cold and uninspired variety shows, and unseemly mixtures of pretentiousness and sham." Wein's old friend Nat Hentoff rued that Newport had become "a money-grubbing enterprise of the same category as any giant midway staffed with shell games, taffy candy, freak shows and thrill rides." [25]

Shaken by such attacks, the festival board of directors had tried mounting a counterassault. In 1958 the board distributed a letter to magazine editors defending the festival for bringing jazz to a bigger public and accusing the critics of elitism:

> Do Gehman, Balliett, and Hentoff typify an alarming trend in jazz criticism today?—are they the foremost spokesmen for that element which is dismayed by popular success for what they consider (privately or subconsciously) to be the proper concern only of "experts"? Thus, while on the one hand they lament the American neglect of its own native music, they

deliberately foster contempt for those who would make it accessible to the public.[26]

Hentoff was hardly a disinterested observer, especially in regard to the rebel festival's racial critique. Of all the Cold War–era white critics deeply invested in the jazz-as-serious-art mission, he was the one who won the most respect from musicians for his commitment to the black freedom movement. He covered the protests and Freedom Rides of the late 1950s and early 1960s, engaged in fundraising efforts for the Student Non-Violent Coordinating Committee (SNCC), and was one of the few white journalists to maintain a trusting relationship with Malcolm X. In 1957 Hentoff was fired from his editor's position at *Down Beat* after protesting the absence of blacks on the magazine's staff and for hiring a black secretary without his superiors's approval. This concern for black equality colored his relationship with the Newport festival. Contra Langston Hughes's sunny account of Newport equality, Hentoff asserted that Jim Crow was still a problem in Newport, citing the complaints of several black musicians who claimed to have been turned away from motels in 1959 and 1960. Hentoff grew exasperated at what he regarded to be the festival's unconscionable refusal to address this problem head on. He complained: "The lame automatic response by Festival officials to criticism of Jim Crow in Newport was, 'Well there'd be Jim Crow anywhere we went. Besides, our musical director is married to a Negro.'" What Hentoff did not mention in this account—published first in 1960 in *Commonweal* and then in 1961 in his book *The Jazz Life*—is that he himself had introduced George Wein to the black woman who became his wife, back when the two men were on better terms.[27]

At a time when jazz was being exported around the globe and trumpeted as the world's first universal art, the fact is that the jazz world itself was a small one, small enough that personal relationships really mattered. One of the musicians who'd had trouble getting a motel room was Charles Mingus. Acutely sensitive to racism, Mingus interpreted this snubbing as part of the same Jim Crow arrangement under which the festival payed him less than Benny Goodman. (According a report in the *Providence Daily Bulletin*, Mingus had agreed to appear at the 1960 festival for $700, but later asked for $5,000 after discovering that Benny Goodman had been paid $7,500 for his appearance at the 1958 festival. Wein pointed out that Goodman had played an entire evening's program and had to pay a seventeen-man band plus singer Jimmy Rushing.) Mingus was notorious for ripping into jazz critics, but he was on good terms with Hentoff, who not only had been writing supportively about Mingus but, as an artists-and-repertory producer, had been recording him for the Candid label. In Mingus's memoir *Beneath the Underdog* he describes Hentoff as "a very sensitive cat . . . one of the few white guys you could really talk to"—and, to prove it, Mingus includes in the book a series of letters he exchanged with Hentoff during the late 1950s, including one written during his stay in the Bellvue psychiatric ward. When Mingus enlisted Hentoff's help in securing a location for the alternative festival, Hentoff turned to Elaine Lorillard, who was recently divorced from Louis, had been voted off of the festival board of directors, and was receptive to the idea of protesting the venality and treachery of the main festival. She introduced Hentoff and Mingus to Nicholas Cannarozzi, owner of the Cliff Walk Manor, a seaside establishment that proved very congenial to the protester's purposes.[28]

The rebel festival included one pick-up group led by swing-era titans Coleman Hawkins and Jo Jones and another by the hardbop trumpeter Kenny Dorham, Max Roach's quintet, the Charles Mingus Jazz Workshop, and the Ornette Coleman Quartet. Throughout the weekend the groups and players reshuffled into different combos. The program ran from Thursday through Monday, outlasting the main festival. Hentoff in *Commonweal*, Whitney Balliett in the *New Yorker*, and Robert Reisner in the *Village Voice* all sang the praises of the music and the setting. Balliett described the event as a "pure and simple . . . virtually handmade . . . wind-driven affair" that served as a perfect antidote to the main festival's "notorious mastadon ways." Hentoff noted that Jo Jones had also broken with George Wein because he thought the main festival was giving short shrift to the young modern players. "The big festival forgot about the music," Jones said, "but these little kiddies—he pointed to several modernists on the stand—have got to have a chance to be heard. That's one reason we did this." Balliett's review implied that the congenial ambience of the event inspired some of the musicians's best playing to date. A spontaneous grouping of Mingus, Roach, Dorham, Julian Priester (Roach's trombonist), and Coleman "provoked Mingus into one of the best solos he has ever played." Summing up the weekend, Balliett wrote: "The Thursday concert at Cliff Walk Manor had an attendance of ten. By Sunday hundreds were on hand. Throughout there was a catching bonhomie between all present, and this, together with Roach's effortless emceeing, gave the event an unfailing smoothness and graciousness. Best of all, there wasn't an impresario in sight."[29]

The sorting out of what happened in Newport in 1960 hinged on the juxtaposition of the two local events—the youth riot and the musicians's rebellion—within a framework that was defined by the larger social revolution unfolding in U.S. culture. Hentoff invoked the moral authority of the civil rights movement in coupling his condemnation of the riot with his support for the rebellion. He noted that none of the many black college students in town for the festival had joined the rioting: they had seen the efficacy of nonviolent direct action during the southern sit-ins, and, besides, the rioters seemed bereft of a cause or commitment any higher than their own freedom. A *New York Herald-Tribune* editorial made this case by putting the Newport riot into a broader political and global context:

> In capitals around the world, desperately earnest students lately have been demonstrating, often rioting, for causes. Some of these have been good causes, some bad; it is as if a contagion of violent fervor were overleaping national boundaries and spreading from university to university. But these young Americans [the Newport rioters] had no cause. They were rioting for nothing but the perverse pleasure of violence. Theirs was a hedonism gone wild, and an irresponsible animal self-indulgence that reflects discredit on their generation.[30]

At a time when the spirit of "freedom" inspired bold new directions in jazz as well as bracing political activism in domestic civil rights and international anticolonialism campaigns, here were the most privileged white kids in the world asserting their freedom to turn a serious cultural event into a frat house debauch. Tempting as it might be to read the riot as entirely a case of racial backlash—to argue, that is, that the rioters were acting primarily out of resentment toward the Newport festival's aura of liberal interracialism and its spotlighting of black cultural excellence—the facts suggest a slightly more tempered interpretation. A similar if less convulsive disturbance, very likely involving some of the same New England college students, had broken out at a Kingston Trio concert a year earlier at the Music Inn in Lenox, Massachusetts. Preppie hooliganism, it seemed, was all the rage, a cultural tremor whose reverberations could drown out dulcet three-part harmony just as easily as down-home twelve-bar blues.[31]

Still, the sound of racial epithets in the Newport air gave this particular riot special resonance. For Hentoff and others invested in the hope that jazz should rise above America rather than capitulate to its worst impulses, this sound was of a piece with the general deterioration of the festival in recent years—years, for these observers, in which the high artistry of jazz and the noble righteousness of the civil rights cause stood as indictments of both mass culture decay and social quiescence. Along these lines, Hentoff's friend Murray Kempton characterized Newport 1960 in terms that linked highbrow purism with social justice: "Jazz has [become] so vogued and Kerouacked as to be unheard . . . and nowhere [is] its presentation more nauseating than at Newport. But whenever either a musician or a sensitive observer complain[s] about these conditions, Newport's sponsors answer in tones of personal righteousness that sound like the letter Woolworth's sends people who want to know why a Negro can't get a cup of coffee at its lunch counter."[32]

Such clamors of outrage packed resonance precisely because of the jazz establishment's uneven response to both the civil rights movement and the jazz avant-garde. Both *Down Beat* and *Metronome* took pains to defend the Newport promoters, casting the youth riot and the musicians's rebellion as twinned acts of heedless irresponsibility. Canadian-born jazz writer Gene Lees, then editor of *Down Beat*, voiced the most intemperate version of this position. Lees made much of a rumor that Mingus had threatened to kill George Wein and throw acid in the face of Louis Lorillard—a literalist misreading of Mingus's Theater of the Absurd-ish agit-prop that fueled Lees's argument that the musician's rebellion was nothing more than a sideshow for self-pitying malcontents. In Lees's view, Mingus was an angry man "whose career has known many frustrations," while the musicians who joined him in the rebellion "had reputations as men with problems—eccentrics, to be kind about it." Lees also attacked Hentoff as "a some time jazz writer and full-time opponent of almost everything."[33]

Gene Lees was right to feel discomfited by the rebels. Theirs was a bold protest against the jazz establishment he represented, a regime whose self-congratulatory liberalism framed the music as a "cause" whose "acceptance" was more important than the fortunes and feelings of the musicians themselves. In challenging jazz's racially structured power relations, the event foreshadowed the black freedom movement's turn to more assertive demands for cultural and economic autonomy. At the same time, I've tried to suggest that race was operating at Newport in 1960 in more nuanced ways, and on more levels, than a straightforward cultural resistance model will enable us to see. The alternative festival reached out to Newport's cosmopolitan, multiracial contingent of intellectuals and middle-class jazz consumers and connoisseurs while showing great skill in appropriating for its own purposes the artistic discourse of critics like Hentoff and Balliett. That discourse was permeated with a Cold War intellectual distrust of youth culture, an anxiety that in this case focused on transgressions of taste and decorum among the white audience. By going to such great lengths to condemn the riot, jazz critics and purists exposed the fiction of a unified American cultural mainstream. In doing so, they resisted the mass popularization of jazz, elevating artistic values over unchecked audience growth.

"Jazz doesn't belong to Nat Hentoff and Whitney Balliett; it belongs to the world," George Wein said recently in a discussion of his battles with critics in the early years of the Newport Jazz Festival. "I thought that if I could bring more people into Newport to hear the music, maybe some of them would become real jazz fans. I'm really no different than the critics. We both have ideals about the music. I've always been concerned about getting respect for the music. But I did know one thing: if the world outside of the small jazz community didn't get exposure to the music, it was going to be a minuscule thing." Guided by this rationale, Wein is not only unapologetic about programming nonjazz music at jazz festivals; he sees this approach as necessary to the economic viability of both the festivals and jazz itself. "The direction that jazz festivals have taken started that night [in Newport in 1958] with Chuck Berry," he said. "You go to festivals all over Europe and you hear all kinds of music. Without that variety, there wouldn't be jazz festivals. A festival doesn't exist without people. Even though something may be non-profit, as the first seven years of Newport were, it doesn't mean there are limitless funds to keep it going. The necessity to maintain a level of bottom-line success is always there."[34]

Chastened by the events of 1960, George Wein stayed away from Newport in 1961. He returned in 1962 with a festival called "Newport '62: The Meaning of Jazz" and with a new organizational structure. No longer was the festival a nonprofit corporation headed by Louis Lorrillard; no longer was there a board and advisory panel. Wein was now completely in charge. He has remained so ever since, moving the festival to New York in 1972, rechristening it the Kool Jazz Festival and later the JVC Jazz Festival as his corporate sponsorship has shifted. In the early 1960s Wein also continued to run the Newport Folk Festival, which he had launched in 1959. Later he started the New Orleans Jazz and Heritage Festival, now a huge two-week affair that offers jazz, blues, rhythm and blues, zydeco, and an assortment of world ethnic music. Through the 1970s and early eighties Wein's penchant for booking big-ticket attractions for the JVC festival—swing-oriented big bands and name singers for the older audience, fusion and r&b for the younger—irked New York jazz critics who favored giving more attention to the many less well-known avant-garde musicians who got little exposure beyond the city's creatively thriving but financially struggling downtown loft scene. Wein's New York festival has always been big enough to accommodate some adventurous programming on its margins, however. Swallowing his own distaste for Ornette Coleman's orchestral works, Wein gave Coleman's symphony *Skies of America* its New York premier at the 1972 festival and reprised it in 1997 with a performance by Coleman and the New York Philharmonic at Avery Fisher Hall. Still, Wein makes no bones about his jazz babbitry. "I have two [programming] criteria—I used to have three," he told one interviewer. "I program the music I love, and I program the music that sells. I used to also do music that would give me credibility with the critics. I've given up on the third."[35]

After the Newport Jazz Festival's opening year "one big happy family" program, it soon became Wein's assumption that the jazz mission demanded a broad mainstream audience development strategy, and that this strategy in turn required the box office clout of a few big-name stars to subsidize the presentation of a wider range of lesser known artists. Jazz had just a few such stars, and increasingly Wein deemed it necessary to venture outside the jazz mainstream for big box office attractions (Chuck Berry, Ray Charles, Aretha Franklin, and the like) that helped underwrite less popular acts. The problem in the early years at Newport was that Wein was operating with a nonprofit business plan while the more famous musicians—who had scuffled long and hard for the opportunity—saw the festival as a chance to cash in. Many demanded fees double and triple what they were receiving for club dates. In 1960 Wein voiced his frustration with these musicians and their management: "The original concept at Newport was to give *all* of jazz as big an audience as possible. That is not going to happen. Now the big artists are taking all the money. We are spending more than ever before and getting less." Unable to see how his own growth-oriented policy contributed to setting the trap that he now found himself in, Wein complained that his increasing overhead costs (publicity, staff, year-round organizational work) made it necessary for him to tilt his programming toward recognizable stars.[36]

In 1988 a young impresario named Michael Dorf launched What is Jazz? an alternative, avant-oriented festival centered at the Knitting Factory, then a ramshackle joint on the edge of the punk-chic East Village. In programming, attitude, and ambience, What is Jazz? was a guerrilla war against Wein's regime and concept; it was also a symbol of the level of cultural capital that jazz has accrued in recent decades due in no small measure to Wein's efforts. By the 1990s, with Wein's JVC festival and the new Lincoln Center jazz program focused on mainstream audience development, a space had opened up for an edgier programming strategy aimed at hip, moneyed New York yuppies. This is the cultural turf that Dorf has exploited with an eclectic, postmodern mix of avant-garde and mainstream jazz, world music, and progressive rock. Critic Gene Santoro has suggested that, despite their differences of age and taste, Wein and Dorf have much in common: they're "both smart, short, Jewish, from well-off backgrounds, balding, pragmatic, driven, obviously ambitious and able to translate entrepreneurial dreams about sound into reality." In 1989 and 1990 the two forged a tentative alliance, with Wein bringing a few of Dorf's Knitting Factory programs uptown to Carnegie and Avery Fisher Halls. Poor ticket sales redoubled Wein's faith in the status quo, and he pulled out of the deal. But Wein has big musical ears and savvy promotional instincts, and in recent years he has absorbed some of the acts that Dorf nurtured at the Knitting Factory. Dorf, for his part, took notes on Wein's modus operandi, learning some lessons about how to pitch jazz in the corporate marketplace—valuable lessons at a time when jazz continues to gain cachet with upscale consumers.[37]

Throughout his long career, Wein has struggled with the perception of the producer as an enemy of the musician. He readily admits to instances of friction but takes pride in the friendly rapport he enjoys with most musicians he has worked with over the years. "I can't think of one of the older musicians who's still around who I'm not friendly with," he said. "There's the recognition that we're on the same team, fighting the good fight. But it takes a few years to establish that. There's a point in the relationship—most of them, anyway—where I gain their trust. Before I gain their trust there are many problems. After I gain their trust they're with me for the rest of their life. Miles [Davis] was with me until the day he died. [Thelonious] Monk was with me, [Charles] Mingus was with me. And I can name others. You gain their trust. I never gained Sarah Vaughan's trust even though I worked with her for many, many years. I should have, I always treated her well, but she always thought I paid Ella [Fitzgerald] more money than I did her."[38]

Challenging both Gene Lees's and Nat Hentoff's accounts of the convulsive events of 1960, Wein claims to have been sympathetic to the rebels's cause and only laments that the riot stole their thunder. He attributes the riot in small part to his festival's effort to attract a younger audience, but in the main to the town's greediness in enacting liquor licensing policies that encouraged the high school and college students to booze up. "If we didn't have the riot," Wein said, "the rebel festival would have meant more than it did. It would have been incorporated into the main festival the same way [later] I incorporated the Knitting Factory into the JVC festival. I always thought that way." Wein thinks Lees's 1960 account, with its emphasis on Mingus's menacing posture, missed the real story. "Mingus might have cussed me out in public," Wein said, "but we were good friends and we understood each other. I was a P.R. person, and Charlie was too. Charlie and Max saw a chance to grab a lot of publicity—don't forget that they had a record deal for the rebel festival—and they grabbed it. They were smart. It was a smart maneuver. I *never* rejected it or was upset about it." Nat Hentoff is skeptical: "To the best of my knowledge George didn't try to block the rebel festival, but he certainly didn't support it." Whatever the truth of Wein's thinking about the Newport rebels in 1960, it is notable that when Wein came back to Newport in 1962, his festival program included Charles Mingus and Max Roach. Mingus was even one of the speakers on a panel discussion of "The Economics of the Jazz Community." And in the days leading up to the festival, Mingus's band and George Wein's band played together at the Cliff Walk Manor.[39]

It was a small world. Circulating within this small world, however, were all the forces that were transforming American culture. Jazz had brought hipsters and blue bloods together in Newport in the late 1950s. It had attracted intellectuals, fashion editors, and filmmakers, all fascinated by the music and its players. In 1960 the rebels and the hooligans delivered something else: a foreshadowing of things to come both in the jazz world and beyond, a preview of both purposeful grassroots organizing work and terrifying disorder that would compete for attention in the national imagination during the most turbulent decade of the century.

Finally, there was the music. Charles Mingus, Max Roach, and the other rebels were not *just* registering their impatience with a patronage arrangement they deemed condescending or unjust ; they were trying to find a serious audience for an artistically adventurous and intellectually challenging music. It was for this reason, in fact, that Mingus and Roach insisted that their effort was less a rebellion than a vindication of Newport's original mission. Surveying the scene at the Sunday afternoon concert at the Cliff Walk Manor in 1960, gratified by the audience's attention and enjoying the sound of jazz cushioned by the ocean waves, Mingus mused, "This is what jazz at Newport was supposed to be."[40]

NOTES

This essay is abstracted from a chapter of my book *Canonizing Jazz: An American Art and Its Critics*, forthcoming from the University of Chicago Press.

1. A valuable source on the history of the festival is Burt Goldblatt, *Newport Jazz Festival: The Illustrated History* (New York: Dial, 1977). The 1960 riot was extensively covered in the jazz and general press. See Gene Lees, "The Trouble," *Down Beat*, August 18, 1960, pp. 20–24; Thomasina Norford, "Newport Freezes Jazz Festival," *New York Amsterdam News*, July 23, 1960, pp. 1,34; Nat Hentoff, "Bringing Dignity to Jazz," in *The Jazz Life* (New York: Da Capo, 1961 [1975]), pp. 98–116; "The Wild Newport Stomp," *Life*, July 18, 1960, pp. 37–38; Hsio Wen Shih, "Jazz in Print," *Jazz Review*, September/October 1960, pp. 32, 34–35; Whitney Balliett, "Musical Events," *New Yorker*, July 16, 1960, pp. 84–88; Robert Reisner, "The Newport Blues," *Village Voice*, July 7, 1960, p. 23; Ken Sobol, "Beatnik, Stay Home," *Village Voice*, July 14, 1960, pp. 7, 12. The *Providence Journal* quote is cited in Hentoff's account, p. 107.

2. The "square collegian" quote is from an unsigned entry in *Down Beat*, September 15, 1960, p. 11. The Kempton quote is cited by Hentoff, "Bringing Dignity to Jazz," p. 104. "young hooligan herrenvolk" is from Reisner, "The Newport Blues." "only imported beer bottles" is from Lees, "The Troubles," p. 22.

3. Reisner, "The Newport Blues." The *Time* reporter's communication with his editors is cited by Hentoff, "Bringing Dignity to Jazz," p. 109.

4. Don Nelson, "Cool But Not Crazy," *New York Post*, July 27, 1958, p. 27; Mike Gross, "Jazz's New 'Commercial' Beat," *Variety*, January 7, 1959, p. 32.

5. Lillian Ross, "You Dig It Sir?" *New Yorker*, July 1954; reprinted in *Jam Session: An Anthology of Jazz*, ed. Ralph Gleason (New York: Putnam, 1958), p. 252.

6. For an excellent discussion of Armstrong's film work, see Krin Gabbard, *Jammin' at the Margins: Jazz and the American Cinema* (Chicago: University of Chicago Press, 1996), pp. 204–238.

7. News clippings on the 1954 festival and on festivals in subsequent years can be consulted at the Institute of Jazz Studies (Rutgers University, Newark) in the file labeled "Newport Jazz Festival." Other valuable published accounts of the early years of the festival include George Frazier, "Blue Notes and Blue Stockings," *Esquire*, August 1955,

pp. 55–58; Lillian Ross, "You Dig It Sir?"; George Wein, "The Newport Jazz Festival: Notes from the Gent Who Started It All," *Playboy*, July 1956, pp. 21–25. The reference to Wein's reception in Europe is from Frazier, "Blue Notes," p.56. The panel discussions involving academics were not original to Newport. Beginning in 1950, Marshall Stearns had hosted a series of seminars at the Music Inn in Lenox, Massachusetts that he called "Jazz Roundtables," at which academics, journalists, and musicians discussed and debated the origins, definition, and cultural meanings of jazz. I discuss these roundtables, which were also tied in with Stearns's foundational work at the Institute of Jazz Studies, in *Canonizing Jazz*.

8. Frazier, "Blue Notes," pp. 55, 56; John Gennari interview with George Wein, August 17, 2000.

9. Frazier, "Blue Notes," p. 55; Wein, "The Newport Jazz Festival," p. 22. In my interview with Wein he confirmed the accuracy of Frazier's story about Jo Jones. "Jo Jones taught me a lot about rhythm," Wein said. "Jo said to me 'for crying out loud George, everything you play is like the Charleston. You need to stop comping the Charleston and learn how to swing." John Gennari interview with George Wein, August 17, 2000.

10. Frazier, "Blue Notes," p. 56; Ross, "You Dig It Sir?" p. 250.

11. 1954 Newport Jazz Festival Program; Ross, "You Dig It Sir?" p. 258.

12. "Jam in Newport," *Time*, July 25, 1955, p. 65; "Newport Jazz Festival," *Ebony*, October 1955, pp. 10–12; Ross, "You Dig It Sir?" p. 259.

13. Minutes of the Newport Festival Executive Advisory Committee meeting, December 9, 1955. Institute of Jazz Studies vertical file "Newport Jazz Festival 1955."

14. Melvin Tapley, "Emotional and Musical Fireworks at Newport Jazz," *New York Amsterdam News*, July 13, 1957, p. 16; Langston Hughes letter to Arna Bontemps, dated July 9, 1958, in *Arna Bontemps-Langston Hughes Letters, 1925–1967*, ed. Charles H. Nichols (New York: Paragon House, 1990), p. 374; Langston Hughes, "Jazz," *New York Post*, June 28, 1963, p. 32.

15. John Gennari interview with George Wein, August 17, 2000.

16. John Hasse, *Beyond Category: The Life and Genius of Duke Ellington* (New York: Simon and Schuster, 1993), pp. 318–22; "Mood Indigo and Beyond," *Time*, August 20, 1956, pp. 54–62; George Avakian, liner notes to *Ellington at Newport* (Columbia CL 934, 1956), reprinted in *Setting the Tempo: Fifty Years of Great Jazz Liner Notes*, ed. Tom Piazza (New York: Anchor, 1996), pp. 80–85.

17. Nat Hentoff's interview with Miles Davis in the November 2, 1955 issue of *Down Beat* was one plank in Davis's effort to regain the public spotlight. Gary Carner's headnotes to his reprint of this interview in *The Miles Davis Companion* offer an excellent summary of the significance of Davis's 1955 Newport appearance. Gary Carner, ed., *The Miles Davis Companion: Four Decades of Commentary* (New York: Schirmer, 1996): p. 58. "Jazz Dossier," *Vogue*, September 15, 1955.

18. The Stern quote is from George Hoefer, "Jazz on a Summer's Day," *Down Beat*, March 17, 1960, p. 19. Other quotations in the paragraph are from Jerry Tallmer, "Jazz on a Summer's Day," *Evergreen Review*, September/October 1960, pp. 126–30.

19. John Gennari interview with George Avakian, September 20, 1992.

20. Donald Bogle, "Louis Armstrong: The Films," in *Louis Armstrong: A Cultural Legacy*, ed. Marc H. Miller (Seattle: University of Washington Press, 1994), pp. 172–175; Leonard Feather, "Feather's Nest," *Down Beat*, April 17, 1958, p. 58; Ralph Ellison letter to Albert Murray, dated August 17, 1957, in *Trading Twelves: The Selected Letters of Ralph Ellison and Albert Murray*, ed. Albert Murray and John Callahan (New York:

Modern Library, 2000), p. 175. For this allusion to the Blue Note record covers, I'm indebted to Burton Peretti's discussion in *Jazz in American Culture* (Chicago: Ivan Dee, 1997), pp. 117–18.

21. Harold Schoenberg, "Jazz Comes of Age in Newport," *New York Times*, July 18, 1955, p. C12; Roger Maren, "A Few False Notes at Newport," *Reporter*, September 8, 1955, pp. 41–44. Mahalia Jackson is quoted in Sheldon Meyers, "Publishing Jazz Books: The Prospects Are Bright," *Publisher's Weekly*, August 11, 1958, p. 29.

22. Nat Hentoff and Whitney Balliett, letters to the editor, *Reporter*, October 20, 1955, p. 7.

23. Whitney Balliett, "Jazz at Newport: 1956," *Saturday Review*, July 28, 1956, p. 25; George Avakian, liner notes to *Ellington at Newport*. For discussion of the riot at the Fats Domino concert, see Brian Ward, *Just My Soul Responding: Rhythm and Blues, Black Consciousness, and Race Relations* (Berkeley: University of California Press, 1998), pp. 113–14.

24. John Gennari interview with George Avakian, September 20, 1992.

25. Melvin Tapley, "Emotional and Musical Fireworks at Newport Jazz," p. 15–16. "Why whites will continue to insist on dragging our religious music in with jazz because it has a rhythm they are intrigued by, and why dedicated Negro artists consent to help them 'lump' the two together . . . is an interesting question," wrote Tapley. Ralph Ellison, "As the Spirit Moves Mahalia," in *Shadow and Act* (New York: Random House, 1964), pp. 218–19. Ellison, *Trading Twelves*, p.175.

26. These data on the size and finances of the festival are taken from "Summer Folk and Classical and Jazz Festivals" (unsigned), *Metronome*, July 1960, p. 12. The criticism of the festival is from Richard Gehman, "The Newport 'News' of 1957," *Saturday Review*, July 28, 1957, p. 36; Dan Morgenstern, "Jazz Festivals: Why Some Are and Some Aren't," *Metronome*, July 1961, p. 10; and Hentoff, *The Jazz Life*, pp. 101–02.

27. I found a draft copy of this letter at the Institute of Jazz Studies in the vertical file labeled "Newport, 1958." The copy has hand-written marginalia that I believe to be the work of Marshall Stearns, although there is no indication who authored the letter.

28. Hentoff, *The Jazz Life*, p.105.

29. John Gennari interview with Nat Hentoff, November 5, 1995; Charles Mingus, *Beneath the Underdog: His World as Composed by Mingus*, ed. Nel King (New York: Vintage, 1971), pp. 325–54. The *Providence Evening Bulletin* report on Mingus's fee arrangement is cited by Burt Goldblatt, *Newport Jazz Festival: The Illustrated History*, p. 72.

30. Whitney Balliett, "Musical Events," pp. 84–87; Hentoff, *The Jazz Life*, p. 109; Reisner, "The Newport Blues."

31. Hentoff, *The Jazz Life*, p. 111.

32. Reporting on the Kingston Trio concert, the *Berkshire Eagle* spoke of "a discontented mob . . . a bunch of rowdies shoving ushers and innocent bystanders around." Cited by Seth Rogovoy, "The Life and Times of Music Inn," *Berkshire Magazine*, Summer 1995, p. 40.

33. Hentoff, *The Jazz Life*, pp. 104–5, 111.

34. Lees, "The Trouble," pp. 20–24.

35. John Gennari interview with George Wein, August 17, 2000.

36. Christopher Lydon interview with George Wein on radio program "The Connection," WBUR (Boston), July 14, 1997.

37. George Wein, "Guest Editor: George Wein," *Metronome*, July 1960, p. 5.

38. Gene Santoro, "JazzFest Madness," *Nation*, August 24/September 1, 1997, p. 46.
39. John Gennari interview with George Wein, August 17, 2000.
40. John Gennari interview with George Wein, August 17, 2000; John Gennari interview with Nat Hentoff, August 22, 2000.
41. Mingus quoted by Hentoff, *The Jazz Life*, p. 109.

DISCOGRAPHY

Ellington, Duke. *Ellington at Newport*. Columbia LP (recorded July 7, 1956); Sony CD 4058, 1999.

Mingus, Charles, Max Roach, Eric Dolphy, Roy Eldridge, Jo Jones (Jazz Artists Guild). *Newport Rebels*. Candid LP 9022 (recorded November 11, 1960); Candid CD 79042, 1991.

FILMOGRAPHY

High Society. Dir. Charles Walters. USA, 1956.
Jazz on A Summer's Day. Dir. Bert Stern. USA, 1959.
Paris Blues. Dir. Martin Ritt. USA, 1961.
A Song is Born. Dir. Howard Hawks. USA, 1948.

MARK TUCKER

Mainstreaming Monk: The Ellington Album

He is, I think, a major jazz composer, the first since Duke Ellington.   —Martin Williams

No jazz composer besides Ellington himself has written such strongly characterized pieces.   —Lewis Porter and Michael Ullman with Edward Hazell

Monk took much of his style from Ellington and he would like to have been an accomplished pianist who could have articulated in the fashion of Ellington.   —Clark Terry

Ellington defined 101 arranging concepts and focused on sound. The sound was the important thing. Thelonious did the same thing.   —Larry Ridley

I continue to feel that to properly appreciate Monk's work and his position in jazz history it is essential to understand that he stands in a direct line of succession from Morton and Ellington.   —Orrin Keepnews

Duke Ellington's name comes up often in discussions of Thelonious Monk. The links between the two musicians seem so close as to be self-evident and irrefutable. Both excelled as composers in a musical tradition known for its emphasis on improvisation. Both were distinctive pianists who displayed stylistic affinities—a percussive attack, a penchant for dissonance, a shared interest in Harlem stride. Both belonged to a select group of exceptional figures in jazz—Jelly Roll Morton, John Lewis, and Charles Mingus also come to mind—who put their individual stamp on the ensembles that performed their works. Both created unique worlds of sound that set them apart from their contemporaries. Though their personalities and careers may have been poles apart, Monk and Ellington, so the literature on jazz reminds us repeatedly, were kindred spirits.

Ellington thought so too, apparently. He first heard Monk's music, according to trumpeter Ray Nance, in the summer of 1948. Nance was traveling with Ellington and a small group of musicians on a short tour of England, and had taken with him a portable gramophone. As Nance told Stanley Dance in a 1966 interview: "I was on my way to Bournemouth, Hampshire, by train, and in my compartment I put on one of my Thelonious Monk records. Duke was passing by in the corridor, and he stopped and asked, 'Who's that playing?' I told him. 'Sounds like he's stealing some of my stuff,' he said. So he sat down and listened to my records, and he was very interested. He understood what Monk was doing" (Dance 1981:139).[1]

In later years Ellington and his orchestra occasionally appeared at festivals that featured Monk on the same bill. On one occasion, the 1962 Newport Jazz Festival, Monk sat in with the Ellington orchestra to play his own "Monk's Dream" and the Billy Strayhorn homage "Frère Monk," the latter a twelve-bar blues with a vaguely Monkian head and dissonant riff figures, including flatted-fifth chords in the last chorus. Both pieces were recorded by Ellington (without Monk) in September 1962 but not issued until the 1980s.[2] They serve to reinforce the notion of musical kinship between Monk and Ellington—a relationship that Monk himself had invited listeners to consider seven years earlier.

It was July 1955 when Monk—a thirty-seven-year-old pianist and composer still not widely known to the public—made his debut recording for the Riverside label, released under the title *Thelonious Monk Plays Duke Ellington* (Riverside RLP 12–201). Backed by bassist Oscar Pettiford and drummer Kenny Clarke, the enigmatic, reclusive Monk interpreted eight compositions by the popular, internationally acclaimed Ellington. Nearly all were standards frequently performed by singers and instrumentalists: "Sophisticated Lady," "I Got It Bad (And That Ain't Good)," "Solitude," "Mood Indigo," "It Don't Mean a Thing If It Ain't Got That Swing, "I Let a Song Go Out of My Heart," and the Ellington-Juan Tizol collaboration "Caravan." The exception was "Black and Tan Fantasy," a piece dating from 1927 that was closely identified with the Ellington orchestra and seldom played by others. Three years later, in 1958, the LP was repackaged and reissued by Riverside with a painting by Henri Rousseau, "The Repast of the Lion," reproduced on the cover. In the liner notes to that reissue, Orrin Keepnews—coproducer and co-owner of Riverside with Bill Grauer Jr.—stated that *Thelonious Monk Plays Duke Ellington* had "proved to be a pioneering album," inaugurating a series of recordings that "met with ever-increasing success and near-unanimous acclaim," and ushering in a period when "Thelonious' increasing[ly] frequent appearances at concerts, festivals and night clubs helped bring him more and more firmly to the fore" (Keepnews [1958]).

Accessible and straightforward, moderate in tone and conservative by design, Monk's Ellington album offers a thirty-five-minute-plus set of pleasurable listening that holds appeal for admirers of both musicians. For historians, though, the recording takes on added layers of significance. It marks one of the rare occasions when Monk addressed the music of Ellington[3]—or any other composer in jazz, for that matter—and thus presents an opportunity to search for points of connection between these two figures. It occurs at a transitional moment in Monk's career, as he moved from relative obscurity into a period of increasing fame and widespread recognition that would peak (during his lifetime) in the mid-1960s. And, with startling directness, the recording attests to the formation in the 1950s of a jazz "mainstream," a critical and historical construct that would prove a powerful force in the way jazz was played, discussed, and sold—so powerful, in fact, that even a rugged iconoclast like Monk could be swept along by its current.

The Ellington album emerged during a difficult and frustrating time for Monk. Four years earlier, in 1951, he and pianist Bud Powell had been arrested on drug charges. (Monk would later declare innocence in the matter.) Powell made bail and was released, but Monk could not and wound up spending sixty days in jail (Gourse 1997:85–87). Worse was to follow, for after Monk got out of jail his cabaret identification card was revoked. This card, issued by the New York City police department, permitted musicians and entertainers to work in nightclubs serving alcohol (see Chevigny 1991:57–68). Without a cabaret card for the next half-dozen years, Monk performed little in Manhattan. Occasionally he took jobs in Brooklyn, the Bronx, and out of town. He also appeared sporadically at clubs in Greenwich Village (the Open Door, for example) and Harlem. Mostly he stayed home in his apartment on West 63rd Street with his wife Nellie and their two young children. Nellie worked to support the family. Her husband, meanwhile, played piano, composed, and socialized with other musicians. His legendary reclusiveness was noted in the program for a concert he gave in Massachusetts in 1955: "Rarely seen, Monk is the Greta Garbo of jazz, and his appearance at any piano is regarded as a major event by serious followers of jazz" (Smith 1958:68).

Monk's recording activity during the first half of the 1950s was slight. In 1952 he signed with the Prestige label. Over the next several years he went into the studio only a few times with his own groups; he had one record date in 1953 with saxophonist Sonny Rollins, another the following year with the Miles Davis All Stars (which yielded his much discussed solo on "Bags' Groove," included on *The Smithsonian Collection of Classic Jazz*). In 1954 Monk went to Paris and recorded for the first time as solo pianist.

Monk's low profile and sluggish career may explain why in 1955 he decided to leave Prestige and try his luck with Riverside, a small, independent label that Keepnews and Grauer had launched in 1953. Now Monk had a chance to make a fresh start by recording his first twelve-inch album. He might have seized the opportunity to unveil new compositions or to revisit some of his best-known compositions, like "'Round Midnight," "Well, You Needn't," and "Epistrophy." Instead he turned to a set of standards by Ellington, a figure whose music Monk had never recorded before and was not known to feature in live performances. To understand how this came about, it may help to recall the general state of jazz in the 1950s as a backdrop for the agenda—both aesthetic and commercial—that Keepnews and Grauer had set for Riverside.

When Monk made his Ellington album in 1955, jazz was characterized both by stylistic pluralism and an emerging sense of consolidation. By this point in the music's history, critics had identified and labeled an array of styles, ranging from "traditional" New Orleans jazz and big-band swing to the postwar sounds of bebop, cool jazz, and hard bop. At the same time, there was a dawning sense that these styles all belonged to some vast and overarching jazz tradition. While critics in the 1940s had argued vigorously about what constituted the "real jazz," in Hugues Pannasié's phrase, in the 1950s this fierce partisanship slowly gave way to a broader, more inclusive conception of the music—a period of detente before free jazz and fusion would explode on the scene in the 1960s, dashing any hope of consensus.

Evidence for this relatively new conception of the "jazz tradition"—at once heterogenous yet cohesive—took many different forms. It surfaced in historical accounts of the music such as Marshall Stearns's *The Story of Jazz* (1956) and Nat Shapiro and Nat Hentoff's *Hear Me Talkin' to Ya* (1955), and in the pages of *The Jazz Review* (1958–1961), a periodical that gave serious consideration to jazz from all eras. It was reflected in a television special like "The Sound of Jazz" from 1957, which placed older and younger musicians side by side—Henry "Red" Allen, Count Basie, and Billie Holiday next to modernists like Monk and Jimmy Giuffre. And the development could also be seen in a new term, *mainstream*, that entered the jazz vocabulary in the second half of the 1950s. Mainstream denoted a kind of "common practice" in jazz. It was apparently introduced into jazz parlance by the British-born critic Stanley Dance (Collier 1988:75).[4] For Dance, mainstream referred to jazz that did not fit either the "traditional" or "modern" (i.e., bebop) categories. In 1958 he produced a series of albums for the Felsted label that appeared under the rubric "Mainstream Jazz." In the liner notes to one of these LPs, Dance defined mainstream as "jazz of a 'central' kind, a music not inhibited by any particular instrumental combination, but emphasizing the twin virtues of communicable emotional expression and swing" (Dance 1958). The "mainstream" figures he cited included bandleaders Ellington and Count Basie, pianist Earl Hines, saxophonist Coleman Hawkins, and trumpeter Buck Clayton. The "swing" label, in fact, could have covered all these figures, but since their careers by now stretched beyond the swing era into the 1950s, Dance suggested "mainstream" as a replacement.[5]

Very soon, though, the term *mainstream* became more inclusive than Dance had intended, as he acknowledged in 1998: "It wasn't long before I realized that bebop had become mainstream, so I quit using the term I'm credited with coining altogether" (Dance 1998). Partly this development reflected the length of time bebop had been part of the jazz scene and the degree to which its stylistic conventions had been assimilated by younger musicians. But looking at the careers of some of the first generation of bebop musicians during the 1950s, it is clear that a general mainstreaming process was affecting the reception of an idiom that only a few years earlier had seemed strange, daring, and controversial. Charlie Parker, for example, had begun recording with strings and winning critics' polls. Dizzy Gillespie was selected by the State Department in 1956 to take a big band overseas on a mission of Cold War cultural diplomacy. Sarah Vaughan had graduated from the bop-tinged bands of Earl Hines and Billie Eckstine to record pop songs with lush orchestral backgrounds for Columbia and later Mercury. Such increasing recognition and commercial success, however, had eluded Monk: by 1955 he had not budged from his position on the far shores of mainstream jazz practice.

Riverside owners Orrin Keepnews and Bill Grauer, meanwhile, were starting to respond to the consensus politics taking shape within the jazz community. Passionate fans of traditional jazz, they had launched their record label in 1953 with reissues of music by Louis Armstrong, Jelly Roll Morton, and other early jazz figures, together with contemporary performances by Dixieland revival bands. In 1954, though, Riverside started reaching out to young "modern" players, beginning with pianist (and Monk protégé) Randy Weston in an all-Cole Porter album (*Cole Porter: In a Modern Mood*). With Weston, Keepnews and Grauer adopted the successful "songbook" formula recently introduced by producer Norman Granz in albums by the Oscar Peterson Trio that were devoted individually to Porter, Gershwin, Ellington, and other leading American songwriters (de Wilde 1997:103). This kind of "tribute" disc (more recently called "concept album") marked an early phase of a canonization process that would gain momentum in the years to follow, serving as the prototype for the songbook albums by Ella Fitzgerald and Sarah Vaughan and remaining popular in the 1990s—witness the string of single-composer discs recorded by saxophonist Joe Henderson for Verve, treating the music of Billy Strayhorn, Antonio Carlos Jobim, Miles Davis, and Gershwin's *Porgy and Bess*.

The songbook album, then, became a tool for mainstreaming jazz. For Riverside it presented a way to seek common ground among different groups of listeners—connoisseurs of "modern" jazz who might want to give Weston a hearing, "traditionalists" who liked jazz treatments of older popular songs, and perhaps even Cole Porter and musical theater fans curious to hear fresh instrumental versions of familiar repertory. Such middle-of-the-road programming became Keepnews and Grauer's initial strategy for Monk, as well. The stakes were higher, though, since Monk—unlike the emerging artist Weston—had already developed a reputation (among aficionados, at least) as someone whose music was difficult and uncompromising. Keepnews later would acknowledge this in liner notes to Monk's third Riverside album, *Brilliant Corners* of 1957, writing that "we at Riverside feel very strongly that the whole emphasis on the exceedingly far-out and 'mysterious' nature of Monk's music has been seriously overdone in past years" and explaining that the decision to have Monk record only standards on his first two albums "was fully deliberate, a plot to seduce non-followers of Monk into giving him a hearing." Keepnews insisted "there was no musical compromise, but there was at least the handle of a familiar melody to begin with" (Keepnews 1957). Nearly thirty years later, in his 1986 notes for a reissue box set of Monk on Riverside, Keepnews elaborated on this point, suggesting why Ellington in particular had been selected for Monk's Riverside debut:

> [Grauer] and I had decided that our initial goal was to reverse the widely-held belief that our new pianist was an impossibly obscure artist; therefore, we would start by avoiding be-bop horns and intricate original tunes. We

proposed an all-Ellington trio date; certainly Duke was a universally respected figure and major composer with (as my 1948 article had noted)[6] a valid musical connection with Monk. He agreed without hesitation, despite claiming to be largely unfamiliar with Ellington's music.

(KEEPNEWS 1986A)

The above explanation offered by Keepnews raises a number of points that deserve individual attention:

ORIGIN OF THE PROJECT   "We proposed an all-Ellington trio date . . ." Did Keepnews and Grauer suggest that Monk make the Ellington album? In an interview conducted by critic Ira Gitler in 1957, Monk and his manager Harry Colomby imply otherwise—or at least seek to dispel the impression that Monk had been coerced into the project:

> GITLER: "Since you went with Riverside, you have recorded one LP of Ellington tunes and another of 'standards' [*The Unique Thelonious Monk*]. I enjoyed them very much, but I prefer to hear you play your own music. . . . How did you feel about doing the two Riverside albums?"
>
> MONK: "I wanted to do it. I felt like playing, that's all. I know that Duke started playing some of his numbers more than he had as I recall."
>
> COLOMBY: "Some critics said it was Riverside's idea."
>
> GITLER: "I remember that. Knowing Monk, I know he wouldn't do anything he didn't want to do." (Gitler 1957)[7]

In this exchange Colomby and Monk defend the vaunted principal of artistic freedom in jazz: no one, they assert, could tell Monk what to play.[8] Keepnews has emphasized the same point: "Some unfriendly reviewers . . . felt we had 'forced' him to play Ellington (which should show how little they understood Thelonious and his artistic stubbornness)" (Keepnews 1986b). Nevertheless, it does seem likely that the idea for Monk to play Ellington, as Keepnews maintains, came from Riverside's owners. Given his precarious status as performer and recording artist in 1955, Monk must have realized it was to his advantage to accept the suggestion. Unlike the Ellington band's performance of "Monk's Dream" in 1962, then, *Thelonious Monk Plays Duke Ellington* was no act of homage but an attempt to make Monk appealing to conservative-minded jazz fans (and perhaps the general public) who otherwise might not give him a hearing.

THE RATIONALE   "Our initial goal was to reverse the widely-held belief that our new pianist was an impossibly obscure artist; therefore, we would start by avoiding be-bop horns and intricate original tunes." Even when Monk played standards in a trio setting, though, the results did not always prove readily accessible or promote "easy listening." This was apparent from earlier recordings Monk had made for Blue Note and Prestige. On "These Foolish Things," for example, with Gary Mapps on bass and Max Roach on drums, Monk states the

EXAMPLE 1   Thelonious Monk, "These Foolish Things" (1952), first chorus, mm. 1–4 (piano only).

melody forcefully in the right hand, adding minor-second dissonances to acidify the tune and lampoon the sentiment (example 1). Nothing so extreme or daring occurs on the Ellington album. Why? Because the Ellington pieces did not invite such a harshly mocking approach? Or because was Monk reining in his adventurous tendencies in an effort to reach a broader audience? Whatever the reason, it is clear from Monk's previous recordings that simply "avoiding be-bop horns and intricate original tunes" could not guarantee tamer, more conventional performances. And it is likely that other factors—Monk's comfort level during the Ellington record date, his personal chemistry with bassist Pettiford and drummer Clarke, and his new working relationship with Keepnews and Grauer at Riverside—strongly shaped the outcome of his performances in the studio.

THE ELLINGTON CONNECTION   "Duke was a universally respected figure and major composer with (as my 1948 article had noted) a valid musical connection with Monk." What was Monk's "valid musical connection" to Ellington? In his 1948 *Record Changer* profile Keepnews had separated out Monk from the other beboppers, claiming that the pianist carried on the tradition of earlier great jazz figures from the past, especially Ellington. Both musicians, Keepnews wrote, had "created a band style molded around his own ideas," preferred to work with the same musicians instead of pick-up groups, and believed in regular rehearsals. As a result, Monk's records "sound purposeful and coordinated instead of like a cutting duel between comparative strangers" (Keepnews 1948:5). In Keepnews's view, then, Monk's "connection" to Ellington had more to do with general principles of working with a band than with shared musical traits or a common vocabulary.

MONK'S KNOWLEDGE OF ELLINGTONIA   "He agreed without hesitation, despite claiming to be largely unfamiliar with Ellington's music." How well-acquainted with Ellington's music was Monk when he recorded the album in 1955? Did he know it primarily as a listener, or had he also previously learned and performed a number of works by Ellington as a pianist? Answers to these questions are elusive. To return for a moment to 1948, when Monk was receiving more press coverage because of his Blue Note releases—in Keepnews's *Record Changer* article that year, he quoted Monk as saying that "no written music [had] sounded right" to him when he was developing as a musician. Keepnews qualified the remark in the same sentence, however, adding his opinion that Monk had "obviously listened intently to the Ellington band of that day [i.e., 1930s]" (Keepnews 1948:20). In another 1948 article (with interview excerpts) by journalist Ira Peck, Monk brought up Ellington's name while discussing his own work at Minton's Playhouse in Harlem: "In order to play we had to make up our own tunes. Just like Duke Ellington had to make up his own music and sounds to express himself" (Peck 1948). When asked about big bands that same year by writer George T. Simon, though, Monk made no mention of Ellington: "[Stan] Kenton tries too hard for effects, though some of them are good. Actually, the only good-sounding band I've heard in years is Claude Thornhill's. I'd like Diz[zy Gillespie]'s band if they played the music right" (Simon 1948:35). It is not clear from these journalistic accounts, then, how closely Monk was following Ellington's career in the 1940s; Monk's comment to Simon, though, if accurate, suggests distance from Ellington's musical world.

That distance also surfaces in Keepnews's account of Monk's approach to the Ellington record date, which unfolded in two sessions (on July 21 and 27, 1955) in the living room/studio of noted engineer Rudy Van Gelder in Hackensack, New Jersey. Keepnews remembers the selection of individual pieces as follows:

> I insisted that Thelonious pick out the specific repertoire, and eventually he requested several pieces of sheet music. But when we finally arrived at the studio, he proceeded to sit down at the piano and hesitantly begin to work out melody lines, as if he were seeing the material for the first time!
>
> (KEEPNEWS 1986A)

In describing the recording process, Keepnews again emphasizes Monk's seeming unfamiliarity with Ellington's music:

> I still recall with painful clarity that a great deal of studio time first had to be spent in basic preparation, with Thelonious sitting at the piano reading sheet music and slowly picking out the notes of the Duke Ellington compositions he had agreed to record. . . . Although Monk began each time as if the tune were totally strange, within a relatively short time he had carved out his own firmly individualized version.   (KEEPNEWS 1986B)

Given the repeated claims made by critics of Monk's close ties to Ellington, it is surprising to imagine the pianist encountering "for the first time" such chestnuts as "Mood Indigo," "Solitude," "Sophisticated Lady," and "Caravan" at his debut session for Riverside. Perhaps, though, he was simply working out new harmonizations at the session—like the arresting beginning to "Black and Tan Fantasy," with its substitute chords, rhythmic displacement, and chromatic inner-voice motion (example 2). On the other hand, Keepnews speculates that Monk may have been dissembling, feigning a lack of preparation as a kind of psychological game to play with his new producer: "I will never know," Keepnews writes, "to what extent he

was actually learning on the spot, but I'm certain that at least in part he was deliberately testing, demonstrating that he was in command, and probing at this new producer to see how he would react" (Keepnews 1986a). A sense of friction also comes across in Keepnews's memory of drummer Kenny Clarke "displaying his own impatience at Monk's making all of us wait for him" by holding up the comics section of a Sunday paper and "[sitting] there behind it, reading and pointedly ignoring the rehearsing pianist" (Keepnews 1986b).

Even if Keepnews has not recounted the strained circumstances of this record date, the performances themselves suggest how problematic the pairing of Monk and Ellington proved to be. Monk sounds uncharacteristically careful and restrained, even tentative in spots, as in the halting, unaccompanied opening to "I Got It Bad (And That Ain't Good)," where midway through the bridge (1.09) he pauses, as if to take his bearings, searching memory for the right melodic path to take. On "Black and Tan Fantasy" Monk begins and ends with thematic material from Ellington's composition, but in the middle he solos on three choruses of the twelve-bar blues without attempting integration; there is an audible separation between the outer, Ellington-derived sections and the Monkian interior—and, for a player who reputedly believed that solos should incorporate themes and motives from the composition, this split-screen approach seems peculiar. It does not help matters much that Clarke's accompaniment throughout the two sessions is dutiful and workmanlike. Fortunately bassist Pettiford sounds more committed to the tunes, some of which he had performed with Ellington himself when serving as bassist in the orchestra in the mid-1940s and for brief stints in 1953 and 1954. It is revealing that Pettiford takes the first solo on the album (on "It Don't Mean a Thing"), an unusual practice in Monk's groups. Overall, compared to the dynamic, energized, imaginative readings of Tin Pan Alley standards on Monk's second

EXAMPLE 3   Thelonious Monk, "Mood Indigo" (1955), introduction and beginning of first chorus.

Riverside album—featuring Pettiford once again but with Art Blakey on drums—the Ellington album sounds flat and listless.

Monk's playing does show flashes of inspiration from time to time, though, and there are moments of haunting beauty, too, as in the solo rendition of "Solitude" and the unusual introduction for "Mood Indigo" (example 3). In the latter, with its surging, syncopated bass lines, Monk offers a clever harmonic gambit: initially E-flat minor appears to be the tonic, followed by moves to the subdominant A-flat major, but in m. 5 Monk suddenly reveals A-flat as the true tonic, thus turning E-flat minor (retrospectively) into an unconventional, minor dominant preparation. Monk launches "I Let a Song Go Out of My Heart" (example 4) with a whimsical introduction based on a motive (taken from the melody) that unexpectedly comes to rest on a "wrong," chromatically altered scale degree (E-natural in the key of E-flat) before the theme begins. Some of Monk's most engaged soloing and comping can be heard on "I Let a Song"; note especially the limber double-time lines he tosses off following Pettiford's solo (beginning at 3.36) and the playful tension between consonance and dissonance he sustains throughout this chorus. And in a few instances Monk does find common ground with Ellington—the insistent repeated-note figures of "It Don't Mean a Thing" (recalling the hammering motive of Monk's own "Thelonious"), the sweet melancholia and gentle left-hand stride of "Solitude," the quasi-"classical" arpeggiated flourishes that punctuate "Sophisticated Lady" (recalling Ellington's grandiose concert hall gestures). Monk's interest in chromatic countermelodies and inner-voice activity, similarly, recalls one of Ellington's chief stylistic hallmarks.

What strikes the listener more than these points of connection, however, is a sense that on some fundamental level Monk is not at home with Ellington's music; missing is that edge of creative urgency and in-the-moment immediacy that char-

159

acterizes so many of his recordings. Perhaps his detachment resulted from not knowing the tunes better, or not playing them often enough over a substantial period of time (as he did with his own compositions and a select group of Tin Pan Alley standards). Contrary to what he would tell Ira Gitler in 1957 (i.e., "I wanted to do it"), Monk may have been ambivalent (or indifferent) about making the Ellington album, but agreed to Riverside's idea believing it might help jump-start his career. Plunging into the jazz "mainstream" this way—after eight years of being able to record, as a leader, exactly what he pleased—was difficult for Monk. His subdued mood on *Thelonious Monk Plays Duke Ellington* may be taken as a form of begrudging protest.

Some writers have taken precisely the opposite view, claiming that the pairing of Monk and Ellington was fortuitous and completely successful. Reviewing the album in 1956, Bill Coss called it "a rewarding adventure" that "should go far toward making friends for Monk" (Coss 1956:27). Gerald Lascelles concurred, pronouncing the combination "as near perfect as one could ever achieve," an "immaculate blend of modern interpretations of classic jazz themes" (Lascelles 1956:24). More recently, jazz pianist and author Laurent de Wilde has echoed the enthusiasm of these earlier critics. "Monk slips on Duke's music like a custom-made glove," he writes. "The music speaks directly to Monk, and is part of his instinctive heritage. . . . It is hard to believe that Monk didn't write any of these compositions . . . a flawless diamond of a session composed almost entirely of first takes—a producer's dream" (De Wilde 1997:104–105).

In the course of his rave review, though, de Wilde does concede that "there is something restrained or modest about this album." Other critics have gone further with this line of criticism. In a broad survey of Monk's recordings, Gunther Schuller observed that the Ellington album suffered from "an over-all dullness"

(Schuller 1958:24). "I think it was an illusion on the part of Orrin Keepnews," Schuller continued, "to think that he could get Monk to reach a wider audience through the use of standard tunes. A musician of Monk's individuality and artistic integrity is never easily accepted by a large audience, and it seems fruitless to try to achieve this—at least on the audience's terms."[9] Nat Hentoff shared Schuller's misgivings about the project: "It does Monk little good to force him to adapt to a program for which he has little empathy as a pianist-writer. . . . I don't think Monk dug this session so much" (Hentoff 1956:24). The British critic Max Harrison wished that Monk had recorded different compositions by Ellington—such as "Rockin' in Rhythm," "The Saddest Tale," or "Ko-Ko"—instead of the "slighter pieces" that appear on the album; Harrison expressed regret that Monk ended up merely improvising on a set of Ellington tunes instead of engaging with them as a composer. He also hinted at the pianist's unfamiliarity with (or distance from) the repertory, noting that "rarely does Monk master any of this material" (Harrison 1959:19–20).

Looking back at the first two albums of standards Monk made for Riverside—the second, *The Unique Thelonious Monk*, was issued in 1956—Orrin Keepnews acknowledged the adverse criticism of those reviewers who charged Riverside with "denying Thelonious full creative freedom." But Keepnews took this reaction as proof that Riverside's strategy to demystify the pianist had succeeded. Phase two of the company's marketing strategy for Monk could commence: "We felt that our first purpose had been achieved. Riverside could now safely turn to recording him with horns, in original compositions" (Keepnews 1986b). The album *Brilliant Corners* (1957), accordingly, contained four originals and only one standard (a piano solo on *I Surrender, Dear*) and featured a quintet with saxophonists Sonny Rollins and Ernie Henry (with trumpeter Clark Terry replacing Henry on one piece). In the liner notes Keepnews stressed not Monk's accessibility but the opposite: "Thelonious Monk remains among the most challenging, provocative, and disturbing figures in modern music. . . . Monk's music is decidedly not designed for casual listening. . . . Monk and his music demand the most difficult thing any artist can require of his audience—attention." In describing the making of *Brilliant Corners*, Keepnews emphasized the challenges posed by Monk's compositions and the demands Monk placed on performers: "These musicians worked hard. . . . Monk is a hard task-master. . . . In the end, [the session] wasn't 'impossible'—merely far from easy" (Keepnews 1957). Now Keepnews, in his dual roles as producer and annotator-publicist, felt no need to position Monk in the continuum of the jazz "tradition" that had produced Morton and Ellington. Instead he re-introduced Monk as the uncompromising jazz modernist. Having displayed mainstream credentials in two albums of standards, Monk was free (once again) to play his own music.

It is tempting to take Keepnews's explanation at face value and to view the Ellington album as part of a successful audience development campaign that helped build a following for Monk during one of the lowest points of his professional career. By 1957, that audience, as Keepnews proudly noted, included "critics, an ever-increasing number of musicians, and a thoroughly hearteningly large number of just plain jazz lovers—willing to make the effort and to reap the rewards of digging Monk" (Keepnews 1957). Both Monk's audience and his reputation would continue to grow after he regained his cabaret card in 1957 and took a long-term engagement at the Five Spot the following year, winning critical accolades in the process.

But the mainstreaming of Monk in the mid-1950s must also be seen as part of the larger transformation of the jazz public occurring during this time. Despite addressing different repertory, Monk himself changed not at all between the Ellington album and *Brilliant Corners*. Instead what was changing was the conception of the mainstream, which by the latter part of the 1950s was becoming broad and deep enough to accommodate Monk's bracing modernism. By exhibiting "communicable emotional expression" and "swing," Monk's music met Stanley Dance's twin criteria for "mainstream jazz" (Dance 1958) even while presenting listeners with more dissonance and complexity than they encountered in the work of many other jazz artists. The political landscape of jazz was shifting: as Monk and the other modernists of his generation moved toward the middle, Dance and the older "swing" artists found themselves pushed right of center.

Beyond its historiographic importance, though, the Ellington album reaffirmed Monk as a strong-willed, free-thinking artist. In its neutral affect and half-hearted delivery, the record conveys a message of resistance—to commercialism, to critical notions of kinship and tradition within the jazz world, and, most of all, to the power leveled by those in the music business who controlled the means of production and distribution. In making the Ellington album bland and unexceptional, Monk announced that he would not be pushed into the mainstream—let the mainstream come to him instead. He challenged anyone to wrest from him the artistic freedom he claimed as his and his alone. Monk realized he could pay no greater tribute to Ellington than to declare absolute musical independence.

NOTES

1. By July 1948 Blue Note had released three recordings under Monk's leadership: "Thelonious"/"Suburban Eyes" (BN 542), "Well, You Needn't"/"Round About Midnight" (BN 543), and "Off Minor"/"Eronel" (BN 547) (Cuscuna 1983). These were likely the sides Nance played for Ellington. A year earlier Ellington had premiered his ultra-dissonant "The Clothed Woman" at Carnegie Hall, a piece that suggests, in the words of critic J. R. Taylor, "an awareness of Thelonious Monk's emerging blues primitivism" (Taylor 1977).

2. "Monk's Dream" (arranged by Strayhorn, according to Dutch musicologist Walter van de Leur) and "Frère Monk" were issued by Ellington collector Jerry Valburn on the LP *Duke Ellington—The Studio Series*, vol. 7 (Up-To-Date 2008) as well as on the compilation *The Private Collection*, vol. 3 (LMR CD 83002).

3. Monk and his quartet recorded the Ellington ballad "I Didn't Know About You" on November 14, 1966, and the following year at a concert in Mexico he was joined by Dave Brubeck in a performance of "C Jam Blues."

4. Although Dance may have played a leading role in popularizing the term *mainstream*, it had already turned up earlier in jazz criticism. In 1948, for example, Orrin Keepnews wrote, "It may serve to clarify Monk's relative position along the main stream of mod-

ern music to point out that he is engaged in developing an essentially original piano style" (Keepnews 1948:5).

5. The full text of Dance's definition—included in a sidebar on the liner notes entitled "MAINSTREAM JAZZ . . . WHAT IT IS"—reads as follows:

> Primarily, it is a reference term for a vast body of jazz that was at one time in some danger of losing its identity. Practically, it is applied to the jazz idiom which developed between the heyday of King Oliver and Jelly Roll Morton on the one hand and that of Charlie Parker and Dizzy Gillespie on the other.
>
> The tag originated during the recent period when jazz seemed to be entirely divided between Traditional (alias Dixieland, alias New Orleans, alias Two-Beat) and Modern (alias Bop, alias Cool, alias Progressive). Among those this division left out in the cold were musicians like Duke Ellington, Earl Hines, Count Basie, Coleman Hawkins and Buck Clayton. Since all good jazz, of whatever kind and era, theoretically swings, "Swing" was hardly an adequate label for them. Hence "Mainstream" for jazz of a "central" kind, a music not inhibited by any particular instrumental combination, but emphasizing the twin virtues of communicable emotional expression and swing. Yes, swing, without which jazz "don't mean a thing." (Dance 1958)

6. See Keepnews 1948.
7. Harry Colomby, though, was not Monk's manager when the Ellington album was recorded. According to writer and Monk expert Peter Keepnews, Colomby assumed this role "in late 1955, probably November" (Keepnews 1999).
8. This was especially important to emphasize for a "modern," postwar jazz musician. Earlier figures were perceived as willing (and expected) to put the public's wishes before their own—part of the accommodating entertainer persona that bebop musicians had rejected.
9. Schuller's view that artistic quality and mass popularity are incompatible is echoed in an anecdote saxophonist Coleman Hawkins related to Bill Grauer and Paul Bacon during a 1956 interview (released by Riverside as one of their Spoken Word Recordings). Discussing his celebrated 1939 recording of "Body and Soul," Hawkins recalled a question Monk had frequently posed to him: "Thelonious Monk said to me . . . he used to say it quite often, back in the 52nd Street days, but about six months ago, he mentioned to me . . . he says, 'You know, you never did explain to me,' [he] said, 'how did these people, these old folks and everybody, go for your record of 'Body and Soul'?' [I] said, 'Monk, I don't know.' . . . He says, 'That's one thing I'll never understand. I don't see how they went for it.' He said now, 'Cause I've listened to the record,' he said, 'and I could understand if you played melody . . . 'cause that's what they like, those kind of people, that's what they like, they like melody.' He said, 'They sure won't listen to anything else that's jazz!' . . . So I just told him, 'That's one of those cases, you know? That's just one of those rare cases'" (Hawkins 1956).

WORKS CITED

Chevigny, Paul. 1991. *Gigs: Jazz and the Cabaret Laws in New York City.* New York: Routledge.

Collier, James Lincoln. 1988. "Mainstream Jazz." In *The New Grove Dictionary of Jazz*, edited by Barry Kernfeld, 2:75. London: Macmillan.

Coss, Bill. 1956. Review of *Thelonious Monk Plays Duke Ellington*. *Metronome Music USA* (February): 27.

Cuscuna, Michael. 1983. "Thelonious Monk: The Early Years. The Blue Note Recordings." Essay in booklet for *The Complete Blue Notes Recordings of Thelonious Monk*, 1–10. Mosaic MR 4101.

Dance, Stanley. 1958. Liner notes, *Coleman Hawkins, the High and Mighty Hawk*. Felsted FAJ 7005.

—— 1981. *The World of Duke Ellington*. New York: Scribner's, 1970. Reprint, New York: Da Capo.

—— 1998. Letter to the author, February 6.

de Wilde, Laurent. 1997. *Monk*. Trans. Jonathan Dickinson. New York: Marlowe.

DeVeaux, Scott. 1999. "Nice Work If You Can Get It": Thelonious Monk and Popular Song." *Black Music Research Journal* 19.2: 41–58.

Gitler, Ira. 1957. "Ira Gitler Interviews Thelonious Monk." *Metronome* 74.3 (March): 19–20, 30, 37.

Gourse, Leslie. 1997. *Straight, No Chaser: The Life and Genius of Thelonious Monk*. New York: Schirmer.

Harrison, Max. 1959. "Thelonious Monk." In *Just Jazz* 3, edited by Sinclair Traill and Gerald Lascelles, 14–22. London: Four Square.

Hawkins, Coleman. 1956. *Coleman Hawkins: A Documentary*. Riverside RLP 12–117/118.

Hentoff, Nat. 1956. Review of *Thelonious Monk Plays Duke Ellington*. *Down Beat* 23, no. 2 (January 25): 23–24.

Keepnews, Orrin. 1948. "Thelonious Monk's Music May Be First Sign of Be-Bop's Legitimacy." *Record Changer* (April): 5, 20. Reprinted in Orrin Keepnews, *The View from Within*, 109–113. New York: Oxford University Press, 1988.

—— 1957. Liner notes, *Brilliant Corners*. Riverside RLP 12–226.

—— [1958]. Liner notes, *Thelonious Monk Plays Duke Ellington*. Riverside RLP 12–201.

—— 1986a. "Thelonious and Me." Essay in booklet for *Thelonious Monk: The Complete Riverside Recordings*. VIJ-5102–5123. (Reprinted in Keepnews, *The View from Within*, 117–126. New York: Oxford University Press, 1988.)

—— 1986b. "The Thelonious Monk Sessions." Essay in booklet for *Thelonious Monk: The Complete Riverside Recordings*. VIJ-5102–5123. Reprinted in Orrin Keepnews, *The View from Within*, 126–144. New York: Oxford University Press, 1988.

Keepnews, Peter. 1999. E-mail to the author, March 8.

Lascelles, Gerald. 1956. Review of *Thelonious Monk Plays Duke Ellington*. *Jazz Journal* 9.10 (October): 24.

Panassié, Hugues. 1942. *The Real Jazz*. New York: Smith and Durrell.

Peck, Ira. 1948. "The Piano Man Who Dug Be-Bop." *P.M.* (February 22). In the clipping file of the Institute of Jazz Studies, Rutgers University-Newark.

Porter, Lewis, Michael Ullman, and Ed Hazell. 1992. *Jazz: From Its Origins to the Present*. Englewood Cliffs, N.J.: Prentis Hall.

Schuller, Gunther. 1958. Review of Monk recordings. *Jazz Review* 1 (November): 22–27. Reprinted in *Jazz Panorama*, edited by Martin Williams, 216–233. New York: Collier, 1967.

Shapiro, Nat, and Nat Hentoff. 1955. *Hear Me Talkin' to Ya: The Story of Jazz by the Men Who Man It*. London: Davis.

Simon, George [T.]. 1948. "Bop's Dixie to Monk." *Metronome* (April): 20, 34–35.

Smith, Charles Edward. 1958. "Madness Turned Out to Be Musicianship." *Nugget* (October): 53, 68, 70.

Stearns, Marshall. 1956. *The Story of Jazz*. London: Oxford University Press.

Taylor, J. R. 1977. Liner notes, *The Duke Ellington Carnegie Hall Concerts, December 1947*. Prestige P-24075.

Voce, Steve. 1985. Excerpt from an interview with Thelonious Monk by Louis Tavecchio. ceol-tmonk-l@loa.com (September 28, 1998).

Williams, Martin. 1963. "Thelonious Monk: Arrival Without Departure." *Saturday Review* (April 13): 32–33, 37.

DISCOGRAPHY

Ellington, Duke. "Monk's Dream/Frère Monk" (1962). Issued on *Duke Ellington: The Studio Series*, vol. 7. Up-to-Date 2008 (1987). LP. Also issued on *Duke Ellington: The Private Collection*, vol. 3. LMR CD 83002 (1987). Compact disc.

Monk, Thelonious. "Bags' Groove" (1954). Issued on *The Smithsonian Collection of Classic Jazz*, rev. ed. Smithsonian Collection of Recordings RD 033 (1987).

———— *Brilliant Corners*. Riverside RLP 12–226/1174 (1957).

———— "C Jam Blues." Issued on *Dave Brubeck: Summit Sessions*. Columbia C 30522 (1968).

———— "I Didn't Know about You." Issued on *Straight, No Chaser*. Columbia CS 9451 (1966–1967).

———— "Off Minor"/"Evonce." Blue Note 547 (1948).

———— *The Complete Riverside Recordings*. VIJ-5102–5123 (1986). (Includes reissues of *Thelonious Monk Plays Duke Ellington*, *The Unique Thelonious Monk*, and *Brilliant Corners*.)

———— *Thelonious Monk Plays Duke Ellington*. Riverside RLP 12–201 (1955).

———— "Thelonious"/"Suburban Eyes." Blue Note 542 (1948).

———— "These Foolish Things" (1952). Issued on the LP *Thelonious Monk: Reflections*, vol. 1. Prestige 7751; reissue, OJC 010. Compact disc.

———— *The Unique Thelonious Monk*. Riverside RLP 12–209 (1956).

———— "Well, You Needn't"/"'Round about Midnight." Blue Note 543 (1948).

Weston, Randy. *Cole Porter: In a Modern Mood*. Riverside RLP-2508 (1954).

JOHN SZWED

The Man

I called him King Tut, and sometimes King John. What else could I call him? He had that royal thing.
—Vernon Davis

Miles is a potentate. He's also a puritan, and the combination can be pretty sadistic.[1]
—Lena Horne

Beyond anything else he might have been, Miles Davis was the sound of his trumpet. It was a sound that was deeply personal to him, and almost mystical in its source and power to project himself through his music. Amiri Baraka once said to poets, "You have to start and finish there . . . your own voice . . . how you sound."[2] Miles, similarly, could tell horn players that sound was everything: "Believe your sound."

"Voice" is a poet's metaphor, of course, an analogy between the speaking voice and the writing voice, conveying the sense that the poet is not only what he or she says, but how it is said. But Miles went further and added an African American dimension to the equation by declaring that the instrumental voice is analogous to the human voice. If poets can bring a vocal, tonal quality to words on a page, then the instrumental voice can signify words through its tonality and timbre. Athough Miles knew the words of all the ballads he played, he had no interest in having a singer with his band: better to have sound alone, he said, so that you could make up your own "attitude," and not be put off by the body, race, age, or sex of a singer.[3] (Love songs with words tell you how someone else makes love, he said, like stories in *Penthouse* or *Playboy*: they're for people who aren't having sex.)

> You know, when a singer sings, he gives you a map of what to think when he sings a ballad with a title. But when we play we don't bother your thoughts. You use your own thoughts. What you think is yours. When you hear someone singing a ballad you have to think what he means. He gives you the route. But when you hear—I hate to say jazz—jazz musicians give you the privacy of your own head.[4]

His sound was not a gift, but something he crafted slowly over time, extracting it like an alchemist from an alloy of breath and metal. Gil Evans was the first to tell him of the importance of that sound and was the biggest defender of him as a stylist:

> He has to exert the most tremendous control to play the way he does. Aside from blowing power, the strength of the embouchure, everything. When he works it's real labor. . . . He couldn't be a musician and sound like anybody else. He didn't know that. That developed. And you go along, you try and start out, you sound like so-and-so—various players like Clark Terry and Freddie Webster.[5]

The first trumpet player who interested Davis as a boy was Harry James—a lead player, a ladies' man, a horseman (and clothes horse), with one foot in the concert hall and the other in the circus tent, a contender for the honor of being one of the first of the cool white men. The second was Louis Armstrong, who was many things—father of modern trumpet (and, not incidentally, Miles' mother's favorite jazz performer), shape shifter, high-C-playing hot dog, modernist, broad comedian, the Walt Whitman of jazz. Miles could benignly ignore Harry James in later life, but Armstrong was a dominating presence in the mythology of jazz, his hugeness and generosity of sound on the trumpet, the richness and inexhaustibility of his ideas, the alluvium of his voice (echoed on his trumpet), the raw countryness of his stage mugging and clowning, all of them forever bound together. Dizzy Gillespie eventually came to terms with Louis the man, as did Miles (though several remarks in his autobiography would make it appear otherwise). On the death of Armstrong in 1970, Davis wrote,

> To me, the great style and interpretation that Louis gave to us musically came from the heart, but his personality was developed by white people wanting black people to entertain by smiling and jumping around. After they do it they call you a Tom, but Louis fooled all of them and became an ambassador of good will.[6]

"Everybody up until Miles Davis played an extension of Louis Armstrong," Gil Evans said. "Even though it may have been camouflaged by high style and all that, it was still the basic sound, it was still based on Louis Armstrong, and Miles Davis changed the sound."[7] Armstrong was either a hurdle to get over or a troubling force of influence to be creatively transformed.

Miles worked hard to get a full, round tone that lurked in the middle register. He practiced across the lake on his father's farm to open his tone up, to get a cornet sound, the sound of Wagner's brass, he said. But some heard it as a naive sound, a beginner's tone on the horn. Even his chosen range was suspected of being the result of his not being able to reach high notes. Davis, however, said it was more a matter of not *hearing* the trumpet in that range, and for Miles, what he heard, like whatever else he felt in his body, determined what he played. The music had to resonate physically before he could articulate it. (In fact, on many records, he can be heard reaching the upper limits of the horn with apparent ease.) Though he described his own playing as free of vibrato—that wavering of pitch that listeners hear as a sign of sincerity or professionalism—he often used some vibrato at the end of long notes and phrases, much as a singer would, and his notes could crack or sob like a singer's. Sometimes the notes seemed not to be quite there, ghosted notes, jazz musicians call them, more implied than played. It was a sound that some described as tragic, vulnerable, the essence of the blues—"a man walking on eggshells" or "a little boy crying in the closet." Kenneth Tynan would call him a "musical lonely hearts club." But there were those, especially among older listeners, who were not so happy with his blues aesthetic. Critic Roger Pryor Dodge, for example, missed the rougher, louder blues of the South and Southwest, and what he heard in modern musicians like Davis was a melodramatic, "decadent" affinity with Billie Holiday and Billy Eckstine—singers he disliked for their "whining intimacy, a merging of blues with the torch song."[8] (In later years, when Miles flirted with rock, some heard his blues in a new way—his singing tone, soft attack, and delayed vibrato, his slurred, sobbed, and bent notes, the buzzing metallic edge of his mute, together suggested to them nothing less than the sound of an electric guitar.)

He took to playing with a Harmon mute in the mid-1950s, a tin device patented in the 1920s by Dave Harmon, owner of the Dreamland Ballroom in Chicago, where trumpeter King Oliver, a great user of mutes to transform his horn's sound, first became famous outside of New Orleans. The Harmon was originally used for "wa-wa" effects, a technologically sophisticated version of the toilet plunger employed by some trumpet players for jokey or exotic sounds. It worked by covering and uncovering the stem, the small tube in the middle, by hand, yet avoided the pitch changes that plagued plunger users. Miles, however, pulled the tube out and played the mute straight, shoving the bell of his horn into the microphone to gain volume and resonance.

The Harmon had a certain mystique to it because it was hard to record.[9] It muted so well, in fact, that trumpet players blew harder, and it subdued the fundamental of the tone, as the engineers might say, giving off high frequency transients that disturbed the lathes that cut the masters and distorted the sound on the records. A punctuated loud note in a fast tune could rattle the metal of the mute and give it the ominous quality of an explosion in the building next door. But Miles used it more cautiously, as a mood-enhancing apparatus. "In the slow ballads," *New Yorker* writer Whitney Balliett once wrote, "Davis, using a mute, buzzes rhythmically and persistently at the melody, like a bluebottle."[10] The effect was not one of calm, but of repressed emotion: "More often than not," Gil Evans observed, "when people play with mutes, everything sounds relaxed; but with Miles there's an extraordinary tension."[11] The mute also allowed Miles to play the way he spoke, in that grainy whisper that compelled others to lean towards him—a wisp of a musical tone that could suggest delicate intimacy but also a force barely under control. And by favoring the mute, Davis stepped back from Armstrong's country brashness and exuberance, softening the gruff voice he shared with Armstrong on both horn and larynx, and thus reinforced the perception of his playing as the essence of black urbanity.

Miles was a master of phrasing—the groupings of notes or words in songs—the nexus where the voices of both the body and the horn are most clearly aligned. Like Billie Holiday, he divided and regrouped notes by means of silences sometimes of such daring length that the audience was left wondering if he had lost his way. Through phrasing and carefully chosen tempos, he could understate a melody to the point where he stripped it of its romantic character ("All of Me"); or giving it a different turn, he could make a straightforward show tune take on a sense of poignancy ("The Surrey with the Fringe on Top"), or, again, play a blues so slowly that it dissolved into a romantic ballad ("Basin Street Blues"). He might erase or hold back some of the notes from the original tune in order to work against its familiarity (as in the four held notes that speak the title of "Bye, Bye, Blackbird," which he effaced after a few years of playing the tune). Even if the song were well known, Miles could make listeners feel as if he were creating its melody afresh.

It was the kind of phrasing that caught the imagination of the literati. When poet Robert Creeley heard Davis' "But Not for Me" in 1954, he wondered how musicians were able to create phrases different from those in the original songs without composing them in advance.[12] In Jack Kerouac's *Visions of Cody*, Jack Duluoz muses over the structure of Miles' phrases (and maybe mimics them as well):

> And meanwhile Miles Davis, like the sun; or the sun, like Miles Davis, blows on with his raw little horn; the prettiest trumpet tone since Hackett and McPartland and at the same time, to flesh some of its fine raw sound, some wild abstract new ideas developed around a growing theme that started off like a tree and became a structure of iron on which tremendous phrases can be strung and hung and long pauses goofed, kicked along, whaled, touched, with hidden and active meanings; to come in, then, like a sweet tenor and blow the superfinest, is mowed enow [more than enough].[13]

Kerouac might be forgiven his excesses, because in Miles' playing the missing note, the auditory ellipsis, the sense of breath being held rather than sounded, the choked-back note . . . all of them *are* literary in feel, something akin to the rhetorical device called meiosis—understatement in the service of something less than the truth, a form of withholding that said that you were being asked to feel something that couldn't be explained literally. It signified that you would have to believe more than what you were being offered. Philippe Lacoue-Labarthe, the author of *Musica Ficta*, a philosophical meditation on Wagner's operas, said that during a performance he had once seen, Miles Davis had stopped, midphrase, to utter an expletive: "In the caesura not of speech but of music, filling in with an empty word for a musical phrase he could not find, Miles shows how music is simultaneously inside the body, of the subject, and beyond."[14]

Frank Sinatra taught me how to phrase, when [he] sings . . . "Night and Day"; the way Orson Welles used to phrase . . . the heavy accent that would stop short.[15]

Orson Welles and Frank Sinatra, two men whose careers began shortly after the development of the microphone, and who knew how to use it like a musical instrument. Before them, most performers used mikes as megaphones, as a means of making themselves heard at a distance. When he was a child, Miles heard Welles' voice on the radio in many roles, as the pure and disembodied voice of the Shadow ("Who knows what evil lurks in the hearts of men?"), the omniscient narrator in *The War of the Worlds* ("We know now that in the early years of the twentieth century this world was being watched closely by intelligences greater than man's."), but also as a speaker in other dramatic settings in which Welles' voice brought a sense of the body with it, making him seem a physical presence. Welles had a powerful, mellifluous voice, and he could use the mike to convey intimacy through whispers and murmurs.

Sinatra, the man they called "The Voice," phrased conversationally, closely, at moderate volume, emphasizing words rather than melody. He stretched vowels and deemphasized consonants, allowing musical phrases to extend beyond their normal length. Moving into and away from the microphone, shifting position in relation to the hearer and the band, Sinatra learned to avoid the sibilants and pops of microphone use. At the peak of his career, he could record in a studio with a twenty-five-piece orchestra and a hundred guests and still make it sound intimate.

Like Welles and Sinatra, Davis grasped the potential of the microphone to set the body free. He sensed that a mike could be used like a close-up lens in motion pictures, focusing and amplifying small gestures and emotions, making histrionics and grand stagecraft unnecessary. With a microphone, singers and musicians could join the new naturalistic stage rhetoric that was developing in the wake of the Russian director Stanislavsky's plea that actors should cease *portraying* emotions to the audience and begin communicating them directly. In the same era when audiences were becoming accustomed to closer and more intimate looks at actors on film, the mike removed the need for musicians and singers to struggle to close the physical distance between themselves and the audience. Performers were finding new ways to position themselves on stage, assuming new attitudes (to use the word with which dancers describe the position of their feet and hands). The strongest position on stage—the three-quarter profile that allows the audience to see actors' expressions while the actors maintain the fiction that there is no audience there—could be replaced by any number of so-called weaker positions, such as performing while walking into the corners of the stage or with the actors speaking with their backs to the audience. (By the beginning of the twentieth century, the actors of the Moscow Art Theater and the Abbey Theater had already redefined dramatic naturalism by performing back-to-audience in the United States.) The concept of a fourth wall could be realized by performing as if there were no audience in the theater at all, an illusion in which the performance element could be concealed.

Musicians and their audiences were slower than those in the theater to grasp the possibilities offered to them by the microphone and new forms of theatrical practice. At the heart of jazz performance was the demand that musicians play for an audience's entertainment, whether for listening, dancing, drinking, or various forms of coupling. They were to come onstage in character, so to speak, dressed in band uniforms or business suits, and play with a lively, expressive stage manner just short of choreography. When not playing, they were to stand in place and engage the audience with eye contact, gracious smiles, perhaps even some clowning.

Miles rejected these shibboleths. He not only resented the show biz elements in Louis Armstrong's performances, but also the clowning of Dizzy Gillespie and the stage foolishness of Charlie Parker. At Juilliard, he had learned what an artist could demand of an audience, and it was he who would correct the music, who would purify it of its brothel and tent show origins, and present it as the art it was. And in an era in which a night's gig in a club could constitute another chapter in the discourse on race and manhood in America, this had the weight of a mission.

He was a small man, five feet six, around 150 pounds, but the way he moved, the short cut of his coats, and his slim profile pants made him seem larger. He dressed like a model and walked with a dancer's grace and economy, but with a detachment that hinted at a secret vulnerability. His large, round eyes seemed never to blink, and it was said by some of those in awe of him that he never closed them as he slept. When he played, he stood motionless, like a still life painting, with knees flexed, head bent forward, indulging in the vanity of the slouch. And unlike other musicians who played their trumpets like weapons, horns erect and at the ready, he pointed his down. In a time when the trumpet player symbolized a certain kind of modern man—a high, loud, and virile player, technically proficient, a master of this piece of instrumental machinery—Miles played soft and low, turning the trumpet into an organic extension of himself, hitting wrong notes along the way as though to remind the audience that it was a human performance and not a didactic essay on modernism. He brought to mind the Hollywood jazz trope in which sexual impotence is symbolized by missed high notes on a horn in movies such as *Young Man with a Horn* or *Mo' Better Blues*.[16] But Davis instead turned such errors (if indeed they were errors) into art, making them seem like sobs and whispers from an introverted, interior monologue being carried out on the bandstand. Despite his *Playboy*-like appearance, there was a cry of loneliness in his music that, even if it came from deep within himself, spoke to a condition many felt in the 1950's.

He abandoned the banter that kept the audience quiet and engaged between pieces and ceased to announce song titles altogether, shocking critic Whitney Balliett, who once complained that it was like a minister neglecting to reveal his chapter and verse. With Davis, there were no smiles, no bows, no recognition that an audience was even present. Nor did he acknowledge applause, at either the completion of a solo or the end of the tune. In fact, he sometimes scarcely allowed time for applause, beginning one piece almost on top of another.

In 1957, a young writer named Joyce Johnson went to the Café Bohemia to see Davis play and to hang out in a club beloved of artists and writers. Afterward, she wrote to her new boyfriend, Jack Kerouac, and described one occasion on which Davis did thank his audience:

> The place was packed, but silent as a cathedral. . . . Then—all of a sudden, a car smacked up across the street between a house and a lamppost. . . . A man at the bar cried "Crazy!" threw up his arms and ran out into the street, followed by everybody except Miles who kept playing. He finished and said quietly, "Thank you for the applause," and walked off. It was like a dream.[17]

Of all Davis' mannerisms, the one that really got to fans and press was what they called "turning his back on the audience." Though he never actually played with his back turned—films from the 1950s show him standing fully forward to the microphone, or at most, playing into it with an actor's three-quarter profile—when he finished a solo, he often walked to the back of the band or left the bandstand for the bar or a table. Jazz singer Eddie Jefferson even immortalized this demeanor by putting words to "So What": "Miles Davis walked off the stage! / That's what folks are saying.")[18] Whatever he *was* doing was enough to have the audience whispering, and the meaning of their reaction was clear: a performer—and a Negro performer, at that—was refusing to follow the fundamental etiquette of performance. He was declining to display graciousness and appreciation for the audience's attention and applause, refusing to acknowledge the special nature of their relationship—refusing to show, in a word, humility.

And what resonance that simple gesture had! During a wind-up doll joke craze in the early 1960s, George Crater, a humorist with *Down Beat* magazine, asked the question: What does a Miles Davis doll do if you wind it up? Answer: It turns its back on you.[19] Even in the global backwaters of the jazz world, they had heard of Miles' behavior. In *Portrait of India*, Ved Mehta describes the vocalist with a Bombay jazz band singing "My Funny Valentine" with her back to the crowd because of the disdain in which she held Indian audiences.[20] When Birdland seemed to be on the verge of eliminating jazz for rhythm and blues in 1964, *New York Daily News* columnist Robert Sylvester quoted bartender Oscar Goodstein on "these icebox artists" who were not entertaining anyone.[21] But if Birdland does close out jazz, Sylvester said, "It's at least one less place in which the arrogant and hostile can turn their backs on people who made them rich and sputter through their sour, slobbering horns." With the civil rights movement beginning in the same era, such a gesture took on added symbolism, that of a refusal to placate whites; and with the appearance of the black arts movement of the early 1960s, Miles could be seen as turning his back on all of Western civilization. Asked about why Miles left the stage after soloing, Dizzy Gillespie once said, "Why don't you ask him? And besides, maybe we'd all like to be like Miles and just haven't got the courage."[22] By the 1990s this gesture was still emblematic, though of what was not so clear by then. Poet Nathaniel Mackey gently mocks the obsession with Davis' behavior by imagining a social scientist who attempts to analyze Miles' movement scrupulously:

> This clicked with an idea Derek had been carrying around for some time—namely that people weren't being precise enough in discussing Miles Davis turning his back on his audiences, that sufficient note had yet to be made of the fact that the angle at which his back addressed the audience tended to vary in relation to a host of contextual factors and coefficients. The upshot was that he set about quantifying and chronologizing based on photographs, films, second-hand accounts and first-hand observation—the positional/propositional variables attendant upon Miles' posture, or, as he himself puts it, the "semitemporal calculus of Miles' postural kinematics."[23]

Journalists began to let readers know whenever Davis turned away from them when they asked for interviews. Newspaper headlines and club marquees now proclaimed Davis "the prince of darkness," "the angry young man of jazz," "the evil genius." "Evil" was a word whose black meanings resonated well beyond the obvious: bad humored, ominous, unnatural, angry, but also thrillingly dangerous. Despite Davis' distrust of most critics and journalists, he offered a select few of them various reasons for his behavior: he turned away from the audience when he wasn't playing because he wanted to hear the band like a conductor; he didn't want to distract from other musicians' solos when he wasn't playing; some spots on the bandstand were better than others for sound; he wanted to be close to the rhythm section; or, while playing at the Village Vanguard, he couldn't stand looking at the flicker of the candles on the tables. Since he normally played with his eyes open, this last explanation is not as strange as it might sound. Musicians who are reading music focus on the page, while those who are playing from memory or improvising have the choice of playing with eyes open or shut. Eyes open in front of an audience presents serious distractions to many players, and Miles' solution was to minimize the presence of the audience.

Charlie Parker often said that Miles was shy,[24] as did Dizzy Gillespie: "You'd never think it, but I've been watching him for so many years. There must always be reasons for actions. So I think that the reasons for some of his actions are a natural result of his being shy."[25] Dizzy told of the time that they were both playing at the Village Vanguard, and Sugar Ray Robinson and Archie Moore walked in the club while Miles' band was on the stand. Miles came over to Dizzy and asked him to introduce them when his set started. Knowing Miles was a huge fight fan, he said, "Hell, you're on now. You introduce them. You've got it."[26] But Miles was too shy to do [it], and left it to Dizzy. Sonny Rollins agreed: "I hate to use that word 'shy,' but he is a shy guy. Which is why he turned his back sometimes, and then people would say, 'Oh, gee, he's arrogant.' Miles wanted to hear the music, and he'd play something that he didn't want the public to hear, because we were getting the music together. It was more the feeling of a workshop, and Miles would take the time to change a note or chord. We were all experimenting, and Miles encouraged it."[27] "Miles sometimes played into the curtain at the Vanguard," according to the club's manager, Lorraine Gordon, "but people didn't seem to mind."[28]

James Baldwin, who said of Miles that he was the only person he knew who was shyer than he, once compared Miles' shyness to Floyd Patterson's reticence, his "will to privacy":

> He lives gallantly with his scars, but not all of them have healed—and while he has found a way to master this, he has found no way to hide it; as, for example, another tough and tender man, Miles Davis, has managed to do. Miles' disguise would certainly never fool anybody with sense, but it keeps a lot of people away, and that's the point.[29]

"Miles' way of coping with shyness," wrote Nat Hentoff, "is to affect fierceness:

> "Like all of us," a musician who has known him for many years explains, "Miles only has a certain amount of energy, and he finds it difficult to meet new people. Rather than subject himself to what is for him a tiring discomfort, he tries to create so forbidding an image of himself that he won't even be bothered."[30]

And Miles could be hurt. In early summer 1956, David Amram was at the bar in Birdland with Gil Coggins, and Miles walked in with his dark glasses and a certain look on his face, and Gil said, "Uh oh, he's not feeling too sociable tonight." David said that "this sort of wave of fear suddenly went through all the musicians, the people who loved him and admired him."

> There was this terrible kind of freeze that used to happen at Birdland. I mean it was a terrible kind of cold feeling, because without Charlie Parker being alive, it was almost like a temple named after some religious figure, and that god had died. At the same time there were these big tables where hustlers and gamblers sat who appreciated jazz. It was a combination of a gangster vibe, along with connoisseurs and snobs—if you can imagine that—all those combined.

> Instead of walking to the expensive tables, Miles went into slow motion and started to go to the outer edges, the cheap seats in the bull pen and the bar where the musicians stood.

> As he got closer, I kind of tried to make myself invisible so I wouldn't of-

fend him. And when he was about five feet away I thought to myself, "I better not even say hello." So he went *really* slow, and just when he got almost right in front of me I saw through the left side of his dark glasses a bloodshot eye, the left eye, and it flashed over for a second. And I didn't make any effort to say hello like I always would. I just acted like I didn't know he was there—and I knew in that millisecond I saw, and I *felt*, this hurt. And it completely freaked me out, because that was the last thing that I thought that I or anybody would be capable of doing, of hurting his feelings or rejecting him since I felt like a nobody in his presence. . . . I understood at that moment why he would often be the way he was when he was rude with people, or when his behavior was erratic: he could actually sense what other people were feeling and thinking. So the point was, that he had a sensitivity that was so acute that it made it impossible for him to let things slide, and they sometimes became unbearable to him. . . . A lot of his toughness on the outside came from a combination of pride, understanding his value as an artist, and not being able to deal with the way he was treated in some of the environnoments that he had to be in.

Whatever Miles meant by leaving the stage, and whether it ultimately derived from his shyness or not, his behavior and his explanations asked the audience to focus on the music, not on the performers or the audience's relation to them.

A joke went around about Miles, David Amram said, one that Miles liked so much he even told it about himself:

> A guy said , "I've been waiting to hear Miles Davis all my life. I've saved up a month's salary just to be able to stay the whole night for all the sets. I go there," he said, "and Miles comes in wearing this beautiful suit, turns his back on the audience for the whole set, doesn't play a note." He said the second set the same thing happened, so he turned to his friend who had introduced him to Miles' music, and said, "He hasn't played a *note*!" He said, "I want my money back. This is a bunch of bullshit." And his friend said, "No, man, it's not what he's *playing*, it's what he's *thinking*!"

Offstage, Miles was a sight to see. Sunglasses worn against the night, he aestheticized his vision, turning himself into an artwork, into a minor deity of some sort, a Greek *daemon* perhaps, silently observing humanity's foolishness from his seat at an empty table or at the end of the bar, or merely observing his band's behavior. Trumpeter Eddie Henderson sat beside him at the Blackhawk in 1961, and whenever saxophonist Hank Mobley squeaked or fluffed a note, Miles would half-humorously feign hitting Hank over the head with a trumpet. Mike Zwerin said that Miles complained to him about the rhythm section one night at Birdland in 1959, "What's Paul doing with the time?" But Zwerin could hear nothing wrong.

Another Miles joke: a jazz fan dies and reaches the other world and meets St. Peter, who takes him to a club with bad lighting, crowded tables, and bored waitresses. But when he sees that the customers include Lester Young, Billie Holiday, Monk, and Bird, he cries out to St. Peter, "This *is* heaven!" Then he notices a figure sitting at the end of the bar, dressed all in black, his back turned to the audience. "Who's that?" asks the fan. "Oh," says St. Peter, "that's God. He thinks he's Miles Davis."

Throughout the 1950s Davis continued to develop a set of distinctive stage gestures, tilting his head to one side, or rocking his head left or right; pressing a forefinger underneith his ear; wiping his tongue with his fingers to dry it; or removing sweat from his brow with a sweep of one finger, flicking it to the floor. A master of the subtext, every move he made was immediately seized on, linked with the others, and studied by fans. Even friends and sidemen puzzled over his behavior and sometimes asked him what he was up to. He told them that he never made the usual announcements because music should speak for itself, or that he might decide to change the tune at the last minute. Besides, classical musicians didn't do stage banter, so why was it required of jazz? He didn't smile or bow because he associated such stage manners with Uncle Tomming, and Tomming for him was a pandering performance style that knew no race lines.

Offstage he could be diffident, aloof, even hostile. (When Coleman Hawkins chided him about his stage manners, Davis reminded him of their time together on 52nd Street, and asked him, "What kind of example were you? Sometimes you didn't show up at all.")[31] He said he didn't like to speak to customers since he was wary of them because of his drug habit and didn't know who to trust. He said he was a musician and nothing more, and in this he was apparently sincere. He seemed never to grasp what people wanted from him other than music, why they cared what he had to say about things, or why they even bothered to talk to him.

If you were insulted by Miles Davis, ignored, or treated rudely, he said it wasn't personal: some days he could answer some questions, some days he couldn't.[32] And when he couldn't, he got angry, and his energy and creativity drained away. After a nasty confrontation, he said he could see the results in the wrinkles in his face. Some of what he felt in these encounters was embarrassment for himself, but also embarrassment for those who approached him—fans, journalists seeking interviews, would-be lovers—they were all the same. Afterwards, he could feel bad for hours, and he went to any length to avoid these skirmishes.

When Miles took up the discipline of boxing, he did so as a corporeal virtue, as a way of expressing masculinity.[33] Like one of his models, Sugar Ray Robinson, Miles was "a sybarite who enjoyed the sensual experience, was indeed a connoisseur of it," as Gerald Early has observed. Yet Davis also sought that most basic of epicurean goals, the avoidance of suffering. And if there was a contradiction for Miles between self-denial and total gratification, it was not apparent. His body was the root of his consciousness, and like a computer directing his mind, he did what it compelled him to do. In bad health and pain for much of his life, addicted in one way or another for more than half of his years, he could suffer as much or more than any pugilist. Davis would muse that he could have been a contender, but he avoided actual fighting so as not to injure his mouth and hands. (Once, though, he said he sparred a few rounds with Roberto Duran, the man with *manos de piedra*, hands of stone.)[34] Like Berry Gordy, who switched from professional boxer to jazz drummer and later became the emperor of Motown, Miles understood that the boxer must finally lose his title, by either retirement or defeat, while the musician can remain king forever. But, again, as Early suggests, boxers and musicians are both itinerant workers in the arena of individualism, both pay the dues of a brutal meritocracy, and though public figures, both are embedded in a shadowy elite with its own code of values under the spotlights.

Before performances, Miles stayed away from others and often drove away anyone who might approach him.[35] Like a boxer preparing for a fight, he denied himself food and sex before playing, believing that a musician should perform hungry and unsatisfied. He said that like Joe Louis and Sugar Ray Robinson, he avoided shaking hands before the main event, or he offered his left hand. In the dressing room before the gig, he worked to get his hands to have the right feel . . . not too dry, not too wet. He wanted nobody else's oil on his hands. And like a fighter, he tied his shoe laces as tightly as he could bear, on shoes that were already a size smaller than his size seven feet, so that he would feel firmly in place. Asked if he had stage fright, he answered that he was afraid of nothing, then allowed that he had "butterflies" before every performance and would often be sick to his stomach before he played. When asked if he was shy, he admitted he was, but not with what he called a white shyness.[36] Rather, it was an artistic shyness, a shyness of those who were aware. He made a similar racial distinction between confidence and arrogance: white people, he said, get confidence mixed up with arrogance.[37] If people of any color other than white are confident, they are called arrogant.

David Amram sometimes ran into Davis at boxing matches at one of the many small boxing clubs of the 1950s:

> Miles didn't go there to be *seen*. He went there to watch—watch the boxing, and to see that *courage* and *loneliness* of what it's like to be doing that, and at the same time the only spontaneity and ensemble sense that you have even in that violent sport that somehow in its own terrible way has a certain beauty and nobility to it. It wasn't so much that he was *pugnacious*, I think, as it was that he was a very proud person.

Boxing could make you graceful, could help shape your body. But more important, boxing and music were intimately connected. Miles played from the legs, bending his knees so as to not break his embouchure. In an interview with *Down Beat* editor Don DeMichael, Miles drew out that connection:

> DAVIS: . . . You notice guys when they play—and this is some corny stuff they play and they breathe in the regular spots; so, therefore they play the regular thing.

DEMICHAEL: You're talking about two- and four-bar phrases, things like that?

DAVIS: Yeah. . . . You're playing in a pattern. Especially if the time is getting mucked up, and you're playing in a pattern, it's going to get more mucked up 'cause you're going to start dropping the time when you drop your horn down, 'cause whoever is playing behind you will say, "Well, he's resting." You never let a guy know when you're gonna rest. Like in boxing, if I jab a guy, I won't relax, 'cause if I jab him, that's a point for me. If I jab him, then I'm gonna do something else. I mean, you've got to keep something going on all the time.

DEMICHAEL: If when you move, you break your embouchure, why move at all?

DAVIS: You keep getting your balance back. Certain things jerk you. Say, like last night I was playing triplets against a fast 4/4. . . . You got to keep getting your balance. . . . The things of music you just finish. When you play, you carry them through till you think they're finished or until the rhythm dictates that it's finished and then you do something else. But you also connect what you finished with what you're going to do next. So it don't sound like a pattern. So when you learn that, you've got a good band, and when the band learns that, it's a good band.

DEMICHAEL: A lot of times you'll let, say, eight bars go by during a solo without playing anything. . . . Doesn't that break the flow you talked about?

DAVIS: It doesn't break the flow because the rhythm section is doing the same thing they were doing before. . . . Whatever's been happening has been happening too long; if it dies out, you can start a whole different thing. . . . Sometimes if you do the same thing [you ended with], it hits the spot.[38]

Though it was not apparent to his audience at first, Davis was slowly turning the bandstand into a stage, changing it from the work area of the help into an expressive and dramatic site. Bandstands had been used as vaudeville stages, as exotic sets, and sometimes even for neo-minstrel shows. But Davis was using his stage in much the way as did a new generation of American male actors who arrived at the same postwar moment—notably Marlon Brando, James Dean, and Montgomery Clift, all midwesterners—actors who learned the principles of Stanislavsky as filtered through the innovations of film directors and American popular style. Practicing what was called the Method, these actors broke with customary theatrical practice and became known for a form of intimate yet emotionally charged acting, carried off with the liberating sense that everything was improvised, and therefore real.[39] Their personae, on stage and off, were often brooding, rude, and inarticulate. Yet their inarticulateness was understood to be part of their rebellion, their unease and restlessness a part of their incomplete commitment to the existing society. And behind a mask that seemed incapable of expressing anything, one sensed sensitivity and strength as well as a deeper level of expressivity. Small gestures, no matter how studied, expressed their awareness of their bodies and drew attention to their provocative sexuality, together conveying a new form of American naturalism.

These gestures, the relaxed posture, the studied inarticulateness, a calculated detachment, a certain angle of descent, merge with elements of the cool, a powerful metaphor for twentieth century life.[40] Cool has its roots in West and Central African philosophy, where beauty and character are joined in self-possession free of anger. But it also resonates with a nineteenth-century European sense of the artful self, the dandy, a type of aristocratic Bohemian intellectual delineated by Baudelaire: "The distinguishing characteristic of the dandy's beauty consists above all in an air of coldness which comes from an unshakeable determination not to be moved; you might call it a latent fire which hints at itself, and which could, but chooses not to, burst into flame."[41] The motivation of the dandy "is the burning need to create for oneself a personal originality. It is the joy of astonishing others, and the proud satisfaction of never oneself being astonished." Rooted in opposition and revolt, the dandy is driven by a need to "combat and destroy triviality." "That is the source in the dandy of that haughty, patrician attitude, aggressive even in its coldness."[42]

It was not always easy for Miles to be cool, to slow down, to wait a few beats to understand better what something meant. He could become angry, violently so, or be hurt by criticism. And cool posture or no, he was not relaxed when he played. There is a school of thought about jazz that honors the physical and sees corporeal effort as an indication of aesthetic greatness. Such players were once rewarded with cries of "Work, man!" or "Sweat, brother!" This is what composer Anthony Braxton has called the phenomenology of the sweating brow, a celebration of the physical through an erasure of the intellect. There was an unmistakable intensity about Davis' playing, but it was not bodily. As saxophonist George Coleman said, "Miles used to sweat profusely—but it was not so much physical energy as it was mental energy. There was lots of concentration."

Being cool did not mean that he could not be verbally hot. Yet he was selective, choosing the moment of his words for maximum effect. Certain men and women among his friends never heard him utter a vulgar word. But others who did, knew him for his sometimes wild and chaotic use of "motherfucker" (or "motherfúcker," since he stressed the third syllable).[43] Charles Mingus, for example, said that in the mid-1940s Miles used it "every other word." A term with complex origins and weight, a noun that can imply the most profane form of address, "motherfucker" can also express an affectionate or collegial relationship, or even serve as a term of praise or a description of a situation of great misfortune or great success. He was not alone in using it, of course, as it can be seen in the writings of Ralph Ellison, Billie Holiday, James Baldwin, William Burroughs, and any number of others in the 1940s and 1950s who sought to bring the language of the streets into their discourse. It was also a word that could get you beaten, or tossed out of a club in those days, and its use in public required considerable daring to pull off. But Miles used it so flagrantly, and vociferously, that he personified it, made it his own, and moved it to a new level of performance. When it was turned on him, however, he could be shocked by its use. Once when a road manager told him to do an encore by yelling, "Get back on the stage, motherfucker!" Miles was incensed: "This wasn't like any motherfucker I'd ever heard before. It was a white motherfucker with too many Rs in it."[44]

Such language clashed violently with his clothing. In the mid-fifties, Miles took to the Ivy League look in fashion, having his clothes made at the epicenter of preppy fashion, the Andover Shop in Cambridge's Harvard Square, where tailor Charlie Davidson dressed him in jackets of English tweed or madras with narrow lapels and natural shoulder, woolen or chino trousers, broadcloth shirts with button-down collars, thin knit or rep ties, and Bass Weejun loafers. It was a look that redefined cool and shook those who thought they were in the know. Some, like *Boston Herald* columnist George Frazier, reacted badly. Calling him "the Whilom War Lord of the Weejuns," he accused Davis of no longer being cool, but of merely showing off . . . in fact, of having become a "fink."[45] But as always with Miles, there was something extra about his clothing, something that the discerning could spot and know that he was set apart from the obvious. For one, his coats were cut with a 3/4 inch higher rise in the back so as to gracefully accommodate the slump he assumed when he played. The chest was cut close, as were the waist and back of the coat; the pockets were piped and slightly slanted; and the buttons on the sleeves buttoned and unbuttoned, allowing for freedom of movement when playing the trumpet, but also exposing their silk lining when turned back. His shirts were high-collared and skin tight, just as his trousers were slim and close, so close that some wondered aloud about his intentions, and whether those intentions could be sustained by his physique. But he had their attention.

He had the attention of the fashion press as well. By 1960, his tastes had shifted toward Italian-made coats of an even trimmer cut, and *Esquire* in its September issue picked him as one of the best-dressed men in America, side by side with Clark Gable and Dean Acheson, as well as two of his boyhood models, Fred Astaire and Cary Grant. And by April 1961, GQ chose him as a "Fashion Personality of the Month," noting that they had never seen a jacket made like the one he wore from Emsley, his New York tailor. There were no seams in the shoulders, and the sleeves and body were cut in one piece; in fact, there were only two seams—under the sleeve and down the jacket's side. It was the sort of thing that gave a press agent inspiration. A press release for the Randall's Island Jazz Festival in 1961, for example, spelled out in loving detail Davis' clothing itinerary for the festival:

> Before his performance, Mr. Davis will wear a single-breasted (one button) beige pongee suit, combining the French and Italian influence on pants and jacket. When Mr. Davis is playing on stage, he will be wearing a double-breasted gray imported silk (two buttons) featuring only two pockets to create an extra slim line.
>
> After his performance, Miles will relax in a pink, single-breasted seersucker jacket with matching pants, hand-made loafers of doeskin, and white sports shirt worn with a pink silk square.[46]

But fame can be as local as it is fickle. "Miles came home to East St. Louis wearing a continental suit," Eugene Redmond said, "but the fashion hadn't reached here yet, and at the Ringside Pool Room they teased him about his clothes being 'country,' coming in there wearing that too-tight jacket and those too-short 'highwater pants'!" And try as he would, color could trump fame in much of America. At his tailors' in Harvard Square, while Miles was being fitted in the finest fabric in the highest style, another customer bet that he could guess Miles' occupation: "tap dancer, right?"

He wore his cars like his clothes—expensive, imported, stylish, and unique. In the 1950s, imported high-performance cars were rare, driven only by the very privileged and elite, not by all of those who might be able to afford them—certainly not by hustlers, players, pimps, and gangsters, who then feared drawing *too* much attention to themselves. But Miles relished the attention and drove fearlessly on streets that could not reasonably accommodate his speed. Running cars to their limits allowed him to focus on the moment, to be free of time, of past and future, free of the body and pain, caught up in the ecstasy of pure speed.[47]

Still, the car offered no antidote to race. As a symbol of wealth and of manhood, in fact, it was something of a red flag to those who would demean him. On one occasion he drove his Ferrari down to Philadelphia (he drove everywhere in those days) and picked up saxophonist Jimmy Heath. As they sped along the wide expanses of Broad Street talking about music, Miles complaining that Sonny Stitt was messing up "So What" every time they played it, he suddenly bet Jimmy that he could make every light. He geared down and the car was whistling past lights at 60-some miles an hour (in a 25 mph zone), when one of the lights suddenly changed and he had to brake. But he knew what the car could do, and when he downshifted, it stopped smartly alongside two undercover narcotics cops in an unmarked car. "It's Miles Davis and Jimmy Heath!" one of them shouted as they jumped out of the car. After a fruitless search for drugs, they grudgingly let them go. In Philadelphia on another occasion, Miles was in the Ferrari with a white woman, when a policeman pulled him over. Before the cop could speak, Miles said, "You take the girl, and I'll keep the car, OK? That's the problem, right?"

Miles was fond of jamming down on the pedal and sending the car into a slow spin. "I drive my yellow [Ferrari] in New York, police don't bother me cause it looks like a cab. *Wssshhhtt!* They figure, Oh shit, that's just a taxi. I did that shit once in front of a brother. I did one of those funny things that only a Ferrari can do. He stopped me and said, '*Goddamn*, Miles, why do you do that shit?' I said, 'What would *you* do if you had this motherfucker?' And he said, 'Okay, go ahead.' The shit was outrageous, though. Only a Ferrari would do that shit. I love a Ferrari, man. The white cops, they all know me by now. Motherfuckers say, 'Oh, that's just him.'"[48] "That car," according to a musician friend, "was his way of saying to white people, 'I'm not supposed to have this, huh?'" "I drive a $58,000 car," a yellow Ferrari, he says, "and white people look at me like I'm crazy. You must be an entertainer. I say no," says Mr. Davis, with a wide-eyed glare. "Are you Miles Davis?" "No," he says, he answers, "I'm a janitor."[49]

The effectiveness of Davis' persona depended on a clash of interests and perspectives, on a series of small but effective offenses, all of which implied that the lines between white and black, male and female, performer and audience might need to be redrawn. In his routine, he often came to work at the last second, parking his sports car in front of the club—once even having it towed to the club when it wasn't running. He entered looking good, better dressed than his audience, dressed so fine yet speaking to no one, heading first to a phone, maybe to call his stockbroker to check on his portfolio. Then, lighting a cigarette, he walked resolutely to the stand, picked up his horn, and quickly moved into the first number, usually the softest of songs, a murmur of a ballad that would halt the cocktail blender, hush the audience, and freeze the whole room. Never for a second did he allow anyone to believe that he was there to entertain. He would never let himself be received as only a black musician, but neither would he permit you to think of him as one who aspired to disappear into white society. (Ornette Coleman once trenchantly acknowledged that although Miles Davis *was* a black man, he lived like a white man.)

On one occasion he might come on with the hauteur of royalty; on another, he might appear as the artist of principled violence, like Howard Roark in Ayn Rand's *The Fountainhead.* Or, turning his shyness into a weapon of strength, he could wilt the audience with the calculated understatement of a mime. "He was jazz's Marcel Marceau," critic Albert Goldman observed:

> With a single gesture he could signal an attitude; with a single note, precipitate a deep mood. Listening to him was like watching Balinese shadow puppets. Everything was a dark profile, a tenebrous outline, a stylized stretch-and-dip that closed into itself with ritualistic finality.[50]

Sometimes that single note was all he would play. Shirley Horn recalls a night when she was opening for Miles at the Village Vanguard in the early 1960s:

> Miles was late. . . . The club was packed and people were spilling out onto the street. I felt bad for Max Gordon, the owner: He kept worrying, pacing back and forth, chewing on his cigar. Then suddenly Miles came in, grabbed his trumpet, and counted off a blues. He played just one note, and went back out the door! As he went past the bar, I asked him, "What's the matter Miles?" He said, "I've got to make a run . . ." And he never came back that night. It was amazing: people sat there, saying to each other, "He only played one note!"

Whatever else it was, it made for good theater of a sort. Ralph Ellison, however, was one of the first to register his complaint against it:

> The result was a grim comedy of racial manners, with the musicians employing a calculated surliness and rudeness, treating the audience very much as many white merchants in poor Negro neighborhoods treat their customers, and the white audiences were shocked at first but learned quickly to accept such treatment as evidence of "artistic" temperament. Then comes a comic reversal. Today the white audience expects the rudeness as part of the entertainment. If it fails to appear the audience is disappointed.[51]

But if things were not right, if the crowd hadn't read his press clippings, or if it wasn't a scene he knew how to control, he could come off as merely cranky, unhappy, bitchy, or an insufferable prick. And as the collective amnesia of the sixties washed away memories of the fifties, some aspects of his persona began to seem oddly dated, and his part like that of an out-of-it hero such as Mike Hammer, the confused, anachronistic private eye in Robert Aldrich's film, *Kiss Me Deadly*. The hero, Emerson said, is at last a bore. But nothing is more boring than a hero left over from an era that people have already forgotten.

Miles' early life stretched across several difficult eras, including the Depression and World War II. By the 1950s, America had become aware of subtle shifts in social and gender roles. Sociologists and psychiatrists were talking about men trapped in gray flannel suits, the age of conformity, the weakening of the superego, the other-directed person. The concern was that a new postwar economy was creating a society in which people were externally motivated, too well adjusted, too sociable. Scarcely concealed behind the jargon of social science was the fear that it was not women who were changing, but men, who were becoming soft, emotional, and expressive—that is, more like women rather than like the rational and task-oriented patriarchs who had built and protected America. More often than not, such ideas were dressed up as if they were the received wisdom of the ages, but their sources were transparently pop.

Elsewhere, *Playboy* magazine was wrestling with the same anxieties and assuaging them with a particular kind of male hedonism, promoting the good life for the single man: money, imported cars, circular beds, top-of-the-line stereos, chicks. And like *Esquire* before it, *Playboy* championed jazz, as a male music, to be sure, but the music of a certain kind of male, as the couture, decorations, and genderized illustrations of the jazz life in its pages made clear. Then there were the Beats, detested by *Playboy*, but sharing some of its fantasies by celebrating freedom, male bonding, drugs, art, and the hip lifestyle, one of their inspirations being the nightlife of the black jazz musician. On another continent, Jean-Paul Sartre was creating an existentialist ethics that pleaded for authenticity and argued against the self-deception of bad faith—the man who impersonates himself or who plays the role in which others cast him. Sartre stood against self-estrangement through the predominance of the Other, or allowing one's past to limit the possibilities of the future.

In the midst of this maelstrom of ideas, these criss-crossed, heightened sensibilities and exaggerated claims for male selfdom, in walked Miles: inner-directed to a fault and authentic as all hell, with the material aspirations of a *Playboy* man and the drive for self-expression of the Beats. There were many at the time who saw such a configuration in Davis, or projected it onto him. Norman Mailer, for one, was drawn to him as a natural existentialist, alienated because of his color, yet out there every night, grabbing his freedom, making choices, risking everything in his solos. Mailer's essay "The White Negro" was one of several in which he purported to understand blackness through the concept of the hip—of which Davis was the avatar.

Miles was becoming the coin of the realm, cock of the walk, good copy for the tabloids, and inspiration for literary imagination. Allusions to him could turn up anywhere. There was the muted post horn, the symbol of the Tristera, the society of isolates in Thomas Pynchon's *The Crying of Lot 49* (a group bound together in part by what they didn't know about each other, and bearing the slogan, "Don't ever antagonize the horn"). Tributes to him sprang up in poems by Langston Hughes ("Trumpet Player: 52nd Street"), and Gregory Corso, and Frank O'Hara, poets who put him on a level shoulder to shoulder with Jackson Pollock, Lana Turner, James Dean, Errol Flynn, and Botticelli.

The breakups of Miles' groups were discussed with the passion of baseball trades, and the radical stylistic shifts that inevitably followed were dissected like great movements in painting. Young people ostentatiously carried his albums to parties and sought out his clothing in the best men's stores. In person, his every action was observed and read for meaning. They watched in silence his whispered comments to sidemen on the bandstand, and when the musicians laughed, they laughed too, envious of that confidence. A discourse developed around him, one that bore inordinate weight in matters of race—Miles stories—narratives about his inner drives, his demons, his pain, and his ambition. Invariably, the stories climaxed with a short comment, crushingly delivered in a husky imitation of the man's voice, capped by some obscenity. Whenever Miles took one of his many respites from work and disappeared from public view, the stories spread in number and variety: he was injured, sick, fat, dead, or dying; he was unable to play; he was in jail; he was coming back with some breakthrough innovation that was more than his fans could bear.

He was the man.

NOTES

1. Lena Horne quoted by Kenneth Tynan, *Holiday*, February, 1963, 103.
2. Amiri Baraka, "How You Sound," in *The LeRoi Jones/Amiri Baraka Reader*, William J. Harris, ed., 2nd edition (New York: Thunder's Mouth, 1999), 16.
3. Author's interview with Vernon Davis; Willie Ruff, *A Call to Assembly* (New York: Viking, 1991), 279; TROUPE COLLECTION.
4. Steve Lake, "Miles Smiles," *The Guardian*, 15 November 1986.
5. Gil Evans interview with Helen Johnson, Institute of Jazz Studies, Rutgers University-Newark, Oral History Project.
6. "Roses for Satchmo." *Down Beat*, 9 July 1970, 19.
7. Gil Evans interview.
8. Roger Pryor Dodge, *Hot Jazz and Hot Dance*, Pryor Dodge, ed. (New York: Oxford University Press, 1995), 274.
9. Keith Nichols, "Muted Bass," *Storyville*, 30 August-September 1970, 203–206; Danny Barker, *Buddy Bolden and the Last Days of Storyville* (New York: Cassell, 1998), 98.
10. Whitney Balliett, *Dinosaurs in the Morning* (London: Jazz Book Club, 1965), 142.
11. Leonard Feather, "The Modulated World of Gil Evans," *Down Beat*, 23 February 1967, 17.
12. Robert Creeley, Preface, *All That Is Lovely In Men* (Asheville, North Carolina: Jonathan Williams, 1955).

13. Jack Kerouac, *Visions of Cody* (New York: McGraw Hill, 1974 [1972]), 323–324.
14. Felicia McCarren, "Translator's Forward," Phillipe Lacoue-Labarthe, *Music Ficta* (Stanford: Stanford University Press, 1994), xiv. (I am obliged to Lance Durenfard who called this to my attention.)
15. John Ephland, "Miles To Go," *Down Beat*, October 1988, 17.
16. Krin Gabbard, "Signifyin(g) the Phallus: Representations of the Jazz Trumpet," *Representing Jazz* (Durham: Duke University Press, 1995), 138–159.
17. Joyce Johnson, *Door Wide Open: A Beat Love Affair in Letters, 1957–1958* (New York: Vintage, 2000), 17.
18. Eddie Jefferson, *Body and Soul*, Prestige 7619 (1968).
19. George Crater," Out of My Head," *Down Beat*, 14 April 1960, 30.
20. Ved Mehta, "Jazz in Bombay," *Portrait of India* (New York: Farrar, Strauss and Giroux, 1970), 67.
21. Ira Gitler, "The Columnist and the Club," *Down Beat*, 21 May 1964, 13.
22. Gene Lees, "Dizzy Gillespie: Problems of Life on a Pedestal," *Down Beat*, 23 June 1960, 17. An odd parallel to the scandal of Miles' back-turning is the outrage that Rod Steiger expressed over Marlon Brando leaving the set as soon as he completed his portion of a critical scene between the two of them in *On the Waterfront*. James Naremore, *Actors in the Cinema* (Berkeley: University of California Press, 1988), 74. Naremore's book was a great help in framing the discussion of Davis' theatrics in this chapter.
23. Nathaniel Mackey, "Blue in Green: Black Interiority," *River City* 16, no. 2 (1995), 122–123.
24. Ira Gitler, "The Man with a Horn," CBC radio series, 1994.
25. Dizzy Gillespie, "Blindfold Test," *Down Beat*, 5 February 1970, 24.
26. Dizzy Gillespie in Ole Brask and Dan Morgenstern, *Jazz People* (New York: Da Capo, 1993 [1978]), 9–10.
27. Conrad Silvert, album liner notes to *June Up*, Prestige P-24077.
28. Lorraine Gordon, "The Man with a Horn," CBC radio series, 1994.
29. James Baldwin, "The Fight: Patterson vs. Liston," reprinted in Gerald Early, *The Culture of Bruising* (New York: Ecco, 1989), 327.
30. Nat Hentoff, *Jazz Is* (New York: Random House, 1976), 137.
31. Stanley Dance, "Coleman Hawkins," *The World of Swing* (New York: Da Capo, 1979 [1974]), 144.
32. Interviews with Miles Davis conducted by Quincy Troupe, housed in the Schomberg Center for Research in Black Culture, New York City.
33. Gerald Early, "The Art of the Muscle: Miles Davis as American Knight and American Knave," *Miles Davis and American Culture* (St. Louis: Missouri Historical Society), 7.
34. Diane Goldsmith, "A Thirst for Pressure, Not Bank Notes, Has Davis Blowing His Horn Live Again," *Atlanta Journal*, 28 August 1981.
35. Interviews with Miles Davis conducted by Quincy Troupe, housed in the Schomberg Center for Research in Black Culture, New York City.
36. *Ibid.*
37. *Ibid.*
38. Don DeMichael, "Miles Davis, 'And in This Corner, The Side Walk Kid . . . ,'" *Down Beat*, 11 December 1969, 32–33.
39. Naremore, *passim*.
40. Robert Farris Thompson, "An Aesthetic of the Cool," *African Arts* 7, no.5 (1973): 41–43, 64–67, 89–92.

41. Charles Baudelaire, *The Painter of Modern Life and Other Essays* (New York: Da Capo, 1986), 29.
42. *Ibid.*, 27–28.
43. Tom Moon, "The Black Saint's Epitaph," *Musician*, June 1985, 64.
44. Moon, 14.
45. George Frazier, "Cool and Otherwise," *The Boston Herald*, 29 May, 1962 (reprinted in Charles Fountain, *Another Man's Poison: The Life and Writing of Columnist George Frazier* [Chester, CT: Globe Pequot, 1984], 174–175).
46. *New Haven Register*, 27 August 1961.
47. Milan Kundera, *Slowness* (New York: Harper, 1995), 1–2.
48. David Breskin, "Searching for Miles," *Rolling Stone*, 29 September 1983, 46.
49. George Goodman, Jr., "Miles Davis: I Just Pick Up My Horn and Play," *New York Times*, 28 June 1981, section 2: 13.
50. Albert Goldman, *Freak Show* (New York: Athenium, 1971), 302.
51. Ralph Ellison, "On Bird, Bird-Watching and Jazz," in *The Collected Essays of Ralph Ellison* (New York: Modern Library, 1995), 259–260. (Originally published in *Saturday Review*, 28 July 1962.)

john szwed

part 2

PENNY M. VON ESCHEN

The Real Ambassadors

In 1955 Felix Belair, Stockholm correspondent for the *New York Times* proclaimed that "America's secret weapon is a blue note in a minor key" and named Louis (Satchmo) Armstrong as "its most effective ambassador." Belair had been in Geneva covering the decidedly unsuccessful East-West conference of November 1955 when Armstrong passed through Switzerland on the triumphant tour that would be commemorated in the album "Ambassador Satch." "What many thoughtful Europeans cannot understand," argued Belair, "is why the United States Government, with all the money it spends for so-called propaganda to promote democracy, does not use more of it to subsidize the continental travels of jazz bands. . . . American jazz has now become a universal language. It knows no national boundaries, but everyone knows where it comes from and where to look for more." The jazz/Cold War metaphor was infectious. In 1956 Armstrong performed before a crowd of more than one hundred thousand in Accra, Ghana. Signifying on the trumpeter's virtuosity and pervasive fears of nuclear disaster, Africa-wide *Drum* magazine quipped, "Satchmo Blows Up the World."[1] If, as Belair suggested, the U.S. government was a bit slow to catch on to the diplomatic value of jazz, the State Department would soon take up Belair's suggestion with a missionary zeal. Beginning with Dizzy Gillespie's 1956 tours of the Middle East and South America, over the next two decades the State Department sent hundreds of jazz musicians on tours of Africa, Eastern Europe and the Soviet Union, Latin America, South America, and Asia.

In the words of the writer and lyricist Iola Brubeck, "The entire jazz community was elated with the official recognition of jazz and its international implications." Yet participants in the world of this African American music were uniquely steeped in the ironies of the export of jazz ambassadors at a time when America was still a Jim Crow nation and civil rights activists were faced with violent resistance and the indifference of the federal government. Following their own tour through Eastern Europe and the Middle East in 1958, Dave and Iola Brubeck addressed these ironies in *The Real Ambassadors*, a 1962 collaboration between Dave and Iola Brubeck and Louis Armstrong.[2] All had participated in the tours; the Brubecks tour in 1958 included trips through Poland, Turkey, India, and an unexpected extension of the tour to Iran and Iraq. Armstrong had recently returned from a twenty-seven-city tour of the African continent during the Congo crisis. With the bands of both musicians coming together for the production, many of the musicians had been on the State Department tours, including drummer Joe Morello, trombonist and vocalist Trummy Young, and pianist Billy Kyle. A jazz musical revue performed to critical acclaim at the Monterey Jazz Festival in September 1962, with Brubeck and Armstrong joined by vocalists Carmen McRae and Dave Lambert, Jon Hendricks and Yolande Bavan, *The Real Ambassadors* satirized State Department objectives, personnel, and protocol and voiced a powerful and unequivocal indictment of Jim Crow America.[3]

As noted above, *The Real Ambassadors* received much praise in the music world for its swinging juxtaposition of disparate musical styles.[4] In this essay I want to revisit the production as an important work of cultural and social criticism and a provocative political intervention. *The Real Ambassadors* brilliantly captured the often complicated if not contradictory politics of the State Department tours in the intersections of the Cold War, African and Asian nation building, and the U.S. civil rights struggle. It also presented a satirical portrayal of the internal politics of the tours. On the one hand, the Brubecks saw many of the State Department cultural personnel with whom they had worked as their allies in the promotion of the arts. For these government cultural workers, like the musicians, the State Department tours offered a unique opportunity to follow in the best traditions of countries like France that made culture, not simply defense, a fundamental part of their foreign relations. In satirizing the tours, Iola Brubeck guessed that "we were saying things a lot of the cultural personnel would probably have liked to say themselves."[5] On the other hand, not all U.S. foreign service personnel were as enlightened as those encountered by the Brubecks. Indeed, with an overarching State Department strategy of supporting civil rights, individual officials abroad often mirrored the racial views of President Eisenhower and his segregationist allies who were profoundly uncomfortable with the presence of African Americans. Thus, honoring the perspectives of the musicians, the Brubecks allude to the ways in which the tours, like world events, could sometimes spin out of the control of the State Department. The satire also focused humorous attention on the deadly serious political tensions revealed by the tours.

Set in a mythical African country, Talgalla, *The Real Ambassadors* opened with the narrator explaining how the hero, modeled on and played by Armstrong, had "spoken to millions of the world's people" through his horn. Yet he and other musicians had "inadvertently served a national purpose, which officials recognized and eventually sanctioned with a program called cultural exchange."[6] Thus, we are reminded that the tours are fundamentally a product of Cold War foreign policy. The foreign policy of the tours as well as the ironic background of racial unrest in the U.S. is captured in "Cultural Exchange."

> Yeah! I remember when Diz was in Greece back in '56.
> he did such a good job we started sending jazz all over the world
>
> The State Department has discovered jazz.
> It reaches folks like nothing ever has.
> Like when they feel that jazzy rhythm,
> they know we're really with 'em
> That's what they call cultural exchange.
>
> No commodity is quite so strange
> as this thing called cultural exchange.
> say that our prestige needs a tonic,
> export the Philharmonic,
> That's what we call cultural exchange!
> . . . when our neighbors call us vermin
> we send out Woody Herman.

Note lyricist Iola Brubeck's telling observation that "no commodity is quite so strange, as this thing called cultural exchange." Indeed, cultural exchange was a commodity that closely pursued the quintessential Cold War commodities oil and uranium. An appreciation of the musicians' critique of the State Department's understanding of cultural exchange must begin with the Brubeck and Armstrong tours. Both artists had participated in the tours; both artists had deliberately been sent into the front lines of major foreign policy crises.

Nothing better exemplifies the infusion of diplomatic bravado into the early tours than the highly chaotic tour of the Dave Brubeck Quartet in 1958. Touring without a State Department escort officer, Brubeck was first sent across the Iron Curtain into East Germany, without a visa, to Poland, Turkey, Afghanistan, Pakistan, India, and Ceylon, and a coup in Iraq.[7] The trip had already lasted 120 days when Secretary of State John Foster Dulles unilaterally canceled their engagements in the U.S. and extended the tour to Iran, and then Iraq and straight into the Middle East crisis of July 1958. Dulles ordered the quartet, Brubeck remembers, "to keep playing way longer than we had planned. They just kept us moving." In Iran the quartet played before elites in Iranian Oil Refinery Co. and United States Information Service cosponsored productions.[8] Although the State Department had not briefed them on national and regional politics, to Brubeck and his band things seemed dangerously amiss when they arrived in Baghdad, Iraq. Deliriously ill with dysentery and ordered by a British physician not to travel, Brubeck nonetheless found a flight out through Istanbul. On July 14, just weeks after their departure, General Abdel Qarem Qassem led a nationalist revolt that overthrew the pro-American Iraqi monarchy and established a regime friendly to the United Arab Republic (UAR), threatening the delicately constructed Baghdad Pact and challenging U.S. oil interests. As Qassem's troops rolled into Baghdad, clearing out the hotel Brubeck had just left, Lebanese president Camille Chamoun responded to the coup with an urgent request for military assistance from the United States.[9] Ironically, alto saxophonist Paul Desmond had left the group as they went to Iraq and had headed to Beirut for what he thought would be a peaceful vacation on the beach. Desmond woke up however, to fourteen thousand American marines wading onto shore amidst the sunbathers, to quiet the threat of civil war in Lebanon and warn the new Iraqi regime that any threat to Western-controlled oil resources in the area would not be tolerated.[10]

Armstrong had recently returned from a twenty-seven-city tour of the African continent. Armstrong's 1960–1961 tour of Africa included stops in the Congo in October and November of 1960. Looking back on the concerts in the midst of a civil war, Armstrong liked to comment that he stopped a war when a truce was called for a day so both sides could hear him perform. However, just as relevant to the politics of the trip was the deep U.S. political and economic interest in the secession crisis in mineral-rich Katanga Province. What Armstrong did not know was that at the time of his visit to Leopoldville at the end of October and to Katanga in November Lumumba had been arrested and was being held and tortured by Tshombe's army with American assistance. He would be assassinated in January of 1961 with CIA assistance while Armstrong and his band were still playing on the continent.[11]

As Iola Brubeck's lyrics indicate, the scope of these programs involved many realms of the performing arts. Yet jazz was the pet project of the State Department. Unlike classical music, theater, or ballet, U.S. officials could claim jazz as a uniquely American art form.[12] Officials and supporters of the arts alike hoped to offset what they expressed as an inferiority complex toward the classical music and ballet of Europeans and the Soviet Union. Moreover, the popularity of jazz in the Soviet Union and Poland, in particular, provided officials with what they viewed as a unique opportunity to fight the cultural Cold War. Just as important to the State Department as the Eastern bloc interest in jazz was the prominence of African American artists in jazz. In high-profile tours by Dizzy Gillespie, Louis Armstrong, Duke Ellington, and many others U.S. officials pursued a self-conscious campaign against worldwide criticism of U.S. racism, striving to build cordial relations with new African and Asian states.

The glaring contradiction in this strategy was that the U.S. promoted black musicians as symbols of the triumph of American democracy when America was still a Jim Crow nation. In *The Real Ambassadors* the Brubecks addressed this contradiction. Brubeck was concerned that Armstrong's contribution to the Civil Rights cause was largely overlooked, even though official attempts to showcase Armstrong as a symbol of racial progress had imploded when Armstrong denounced President Eisenhower during the desegregation crisis at Central High School in Little Rock in 1957. Indeed, the State Department had approved Armstrong for a tour in November of 1955, from the moment of its "sudden discovery" of jazz.[13] But Armstrong's

civil rights militancy as well as the era's tangled international and civil rights politics are revealed in the long road to the State Department actually engaging Armstrong for an official tour. In the excitement of high-profile negotiations for a Soviet tour, Armstrong abandoned his plans for the trip after Governor Orval Faubus of
Arkansas ordered units of the National Guard to surround Central High School in
Little Rock and block the entry of African American students.[14] Armstrong's experiences in a 1956 trip to Ghana and his identification with the southern civil rights
movement provided the context for his strident criticism of Eisenhower during the
Little Rock crisis. Visiting an African nation on the eve of its independence and following the actions of civil rights activists enabled Armstrong to speak out in ways
that would have been unthinkable a decade earlier. For Armstrong, by failing to
support desegregation the government had violated its end of the tacit agreement
that his role as Ambassador Satch was predicated on. Armstrong stated that "the
way they are treating my people in the South, the Government can go to hell." Calling Faubus "an uneducated plow-boy," Armstrong also denounced Eisenhower for
his foot-dragging, accusing the president of being "two-faced" on civil rights and allowing "Faubus to run the government." "It's getting so bad a colored man hasn't got
any country," Armstrong declared. The impact of Armstrong not only denouncing
Eisenhower and refusing to tour for the State Department but announcing that
black people in America had no country sent a very alarmed State Department
scrambling to get "perhaps the most effective un-official goodwill ambassador this
country has ever had" to reconsider.[15] The State Department immediately issued a
statement expressing hope that Armstrong "would not let the segregation issue keep
him from making a musical mission to Moscow." Despite pressure from his manager
to recant, and patronizing attempts to downplay his anger—with manager Pierre
Tallerie nervously telling the *New York Times* that "Louie isn't mad at anybody. He
couldn't stay mad for more than few seconds anyway," Armstrong stood his
ground.[16] A week later, when Eisenhower finally sent in federal troops to uphold integration, Armstrong praised his actions and explanation as "just wonderful." Indicating that he might change his mind about refusing to tour for the government,
Armstrong sent the president a telegram: "If you decide to walk into the schools
with the colored kids, take me along daddy, God bless you."[17] But if Armstrong
could endorse Eisenhower's *change* in policy, against a flurry of attacks and canceled
concerts and television appearances, he continued to express outrage over Little
Rock. He remarked in October 1957 that he'd rather play in the Soviet Union than
Arkansas because "Faubus might hear a couple of notes—and he don't deserve
that."[18]

Yet, as the struggle for equality accelerated, Armstrong was widely criticized as
an Uncle Tom and, for many, compared unfavorably with a younger, more militant
group of jazz musicians.[19] Written as tribute to Armstrong, the production recov-
ered his submerged militancy and paid him homage as a political actor. It also expressed Brubeck's own commitment to desegregation. Throughout the 1950s
Brubeck had refused to play before segregated audiences in the South or accede to
segregationist demands that he replace his African American bassist, Eugene
Wright.[20]

Thus the musical opens with a suggestion of the militancy concealed behind Armstrong's mask, countering the perception that Armstrong hewed to whites' stereotypes of black cheerfulness and docility. The narrator's claim that the hero possesses the gift of the "ability to keep his opinions to himself" is challenged when a voice (Armstrong) declares, "Lady, if you could read my mind, your head would bust wide open." Moreover, the audience learns precisely what was on the hero's mind: "Look here, what we need is a good will tour of Mississippi"; and in a sharp reminder of Armstrong's denunciation of Eisenhower: "Forget Moscow, when do we play in New Orleans!"[21]

Nevertheless, the hero is persuaded to begin yet another tour, and "the morning of their departure, members of the President's Committee . . . for Cultural Exchange appeared to give the musicians a last minute 'briefing.' . . . You represent the USA/So watch what you think and do and say."[22] Here, as well as in the song "Remember Who You Are," the Brubecks evoked and evaluated the briefing they received before embarking on their tours:

> [Armstrong] Remember who you are and what you represent
> Always be a credit to your government
> No matter what you say or what you do
> The eyes of the world are watching you
> Remember who you are and what you represent . . .

> [Trummy Young] Remember who you are and what you represent
> never face a problem, always circumvent
> stay away from issues, be discreet
> when controversy enters, you retreat . . .

Musicians were often quite taken aback by the directives they received. Dizzy Gillespie somehow managed to dodge his briefing, declaring, "I've got three hundred years of briefing." But, for most, briefings were an inescapable part of the tour, providing, in the words of Brubeck, "a long list of how we should act."[23] With briefings so focused on the prevention of potentially embarrassing behavior, the musicians had little warning about the occasionally turbulent politics they often encountered. Aware that they were asked to perform in politically sensitive situations, musicians often felt that their own desires to play music and meet local musicians, as well as their genuine desire to bring jazz to new audiences, "to the people," conflicted with the State Department's near exclusive focus on neocolonial elites as target audiences in tense political circumstances.

The State Department's views of cultural exchange were overtly challenged by members of the Duke Ellington Orchestra on their 1963 tour of the Middle East. When the musicians protested that they were only playing for elites already familiar with jazz when they had expected to play for "the people," Thomas W. Simons, an escort officer assigned to the band, struggled to reconcile his role in the State Department with his sympathy for the musicians' view of "the people." The orchestra members, Simons explained, had a "different conception of what they were to do" than the State Department. Simons reported: "The orchestra members had misunderstood the word 'people,' and were disagreeably surprised."[24] Simons continued: "That we are trying to reach out to those who . . . count[ed]" failed to impress "band members [who] continued to feel that they would rather play for the 'people,' for the men in the streets who clustered around tea-shop radios. . . . They believed that the lower classes, even if unimportant politically, were more worthy of exposure to good western music than the prestige audiences for whom they played."[25]

Expressing a similar frustration with the emphasis on elite audiences, trumpeter Clark Terry, who toured India and Pakistan in 1978, explained that they "coined a phrase to describe the official receptions musicians were expected to attend: "Time for us to go to the grinner." Terry added: "Our escort officer was "very uptight, very strict about time, appearance and behavior. . . . If these guys blow it, it's my neck."[26]

This official concern about appearance and behavior—remembering who you are—led to a battle between Randy Weston and escort officer Harry Hirsch, a man whom Weston described as having a "colonial mentality," on Weston's 1966 tour of North and West Africa. Weston's contract stipulated that American suits be worn during performances and at official receptions. Conflict erupted over the "down time." When Weston and band members wore dashikis, officials protested that they could not readily be identified as Americans, which, for Weston, was precisely their intention.[27] During a 1975 Eastern European tour under the auspices of George Wein and the Newport Festival, Charles Mingus presented yet another problem for officials, who accused him of inserting his politics into his song titles. "This, explained the attaché at the Romanian embassy "would have caused quite a problem had it not been caught in time." The official solution was to change the titles in the Romanian program. "Mingus," the official explained, "doesn't speak Romanian and he'll never know."[28]

Indeed, the last stanza of "Remember Who You Are" alluded to the musicians' allegiance to something other than the American government, namely jazz and the history that gave birth to the music:

> [Armstrong] Remember who you are and what you represent
> Jelly Roll and Basie helps us to invent
> a weapon like no other nation has
> especially the Russians can't claim jazz . . .

Here the artist's burden of representation is to remember Jelly Roll and Basie and to represent jazz, even as the lyrics celebrate the gift of that music to America and proclaim pride in the music's status as a unique Cold War weapon.

Returning to the narrative of *The Real Ambassadors*, as the tour—free of political drama—comes to a close (no coups d'état, no obnoxious escort officers) the hero's story has just begun. In his travels throughout Africa the hero had heard stories of Talgalla, "the newest of new African nations." Talgalla's portrayal in the musical satirizes the political motives for the African tours. "It had been unknown and unrecognized as a nation until the two great superpowers simultaneously discovered its existence. Suddenly Talgalla was a nation to be reckoned with. The Russian technicians built the empty road that lay below them. U.S. equipment had cleared the airfield."[29]

On the one hand, Talgalla is imagined as a product of superpower rivalries. Its mythic status as a repository of "tradition" as well as utopian dreams displaces actual African politics; just as the revue's subplot of the love story displaces the story of U.S. interests in Africa and other formerly colonized areas (Armstrong's actual trip through Africa as well as Brubeck's actual trip through the Middle East). Yet Talgalla is also a place where a new social order can be ushered in: a symbol of democratic and utopian aspirations. The hero has been drawn to Talgalla by tales of an annual ceremony where in this "tiny tribal monarchy" the "social order was turned upside down" for a week. Thus, as they approach Talgalla, the hero dreams of being "King for a Day."[30]

Despite the hero's superficial aspiration to be king, "King for a Day" unfolds as a satire on authority as well as a critique of political (civil rights) gradualism, as the hero affirms a revolution in social relations against a voice that tells him "you're expecting too much too soon." The opening passage illuminates the inspiration for the collaboration between the Brubecks and Armstrong and the fact that the Brubecks wrote the revue specifically for Armstrong. Constantly rewriting the libretto over a period of nearly five years to keep it topical, and writing with Armstrong in mind, the Brubecks incorporated Armstrong's playful statements before embarking on his six-month African tour in 1960. Armstrong was quoted in *Downbeat* commenting on the chance that the trip may extend behind the iron curtain: "Yeah, I'd like to slip under the curtain. Let all them foreign ministers have their summit conferences—Satch just might get somewhere with them cats in a basement session."[31]

penny m. von eschen

> Man if they would just let me run things my way
> The world would be a swinging place!
> [Trummy Young] Pops, what would you do?
> [Armstrong] The first thing I'd do is call a basement session.
> [Trummy Young] Oh Pops, you mean summit conference.
> [Armstrong] Man, I don't mean a UN kind of session.
> I mean a jam session . . .

Presenting jazz as a model for democracy, the lyrics move deftly between civil rights themes and international relations:

> [Armstrong] I'd go and form a swinging band
> with all the leaders from every land.
> [Young] Can't you hear that messed up beat?
> I'll tell you now you'll meet defeat.
> [Armstrong] They'd fall right in a swinging groove
> And all the isms gonna move.
> Relationships is bound to improve.

As the debate between the hero and the skeptic continues, note the play on symbols of monarchy and authority. In the playful discussion of the oppositional black politics of self-naming, Iola Brubeck is referencing bassist Eugene Wright's naming as "Senator," a nickname that stuck from the time of their 1958 tour, as well as riffing on an Armstrong interview where he explained his attitude toward the title of "Ambassador."[32] During his 1960 Africa tour Armstrong told *New York Times* magazine reporter Gilbert Millstein: "We used to call one another that when we were we was broke and hungry. That's where the Duke got his name—Duke Ellington—and the Count—Count Basie."[33]

[Trummy Young] Pops, you got eyes to wear a crown?
[Armstrong] I might enjoy being King
after all Buddy Bolden was King
[Trummy Young] and there's King Oliver
[Armstrong] Count Basie
[Young] and Duke Ellington
[Armstrong] and Earl "Fatha" Hines
[Young] Man quit jiving me—you know that cat ain't no Earl, that's his first name
[Armstrong] No? Man he had me fooled all these years

The United States had recognized the importance of Talgalla by appointing an ambassador, due to arrive momentarily. When the hero arrives—trumpet in hand—as a sign of greeting he blows his horn. Mistaking Armstrong for the officially appointed American ambassador, the Talgallans ask, "You are the American Ambassador aren't you?" The hero replies: That's what they call me, Ambassador Satch." The Talgallans are thrilled that "out of all the Americans such a wondrous man should be chosen as their Ambassador." Everyone is happy for several days, but the arrival of the U.S. ambassador sparks a flurry of confusion as all concerned attempt to discern who the real ambassador is.[34]

In the studio performance of "Who's the Real Ambassador?" Lambert, Hendricks, and Ross make appropriately stiff and sanctimonious State Department personnel, with the lyrics repeated a second time at breakneck tempo, parodying the uptight frenzy perceived by many musicians.[35]

It is evident we represent American society
Noted for its etiquette, its manners and sobriety
We have followed protocol with absolute propriety
We're Yankees to the core
We're the real ambassadors
Though we may appear as bores
We are diplomats in a proper hat

Fortunately, Armstrong steps in and clears up the confusion. But in doing so he challenges the legitimacy of government policy and asserts his authority, grounded in something deeper than mere state sanction.

I'm the real Ambassador
It is evident I wasn't sent by government to take your place
All I do is sing the blues and meet the people face to face
I'll explain and make it plain I represent the human race and don't pretend
no more
Who's the Real Ambassador?
Certain facts we can't ignore
In my humble way I'm the USA
Though I represent the government
The government don't represent some policies I'm for
Oh we learn to be concerned about the constitutionality
in our nation segregation isn't a legality
Soon our only differences will be in personality
that's what I stand for
Who's the real Ambassador? Yeah! The real Ambassador.

With the central political tension of the drama resolved, the narrative turns to a romantic subplot, yet continually revisits the animating theme of civil rights. The poignant "They Say I Look Like God," opens with the lines:

They say I Look like God.
Could God be black? my God!
If both are made in the image of thee,
Could thou perchance a zebra be?

Brubeck praised Armstrong for his ability to transform some of the more trivial lyrics—those written for a laugh—into pathos or political commentary. The Brubecks had written the lines for a laugh, "to show how ridiculous it was" but, Brubeck continued: "Louis had tears in his eyes. He didn't go for a laugh, and the audience followed him away from our original intentions. And all through the night he took those lines that were supposed to get a laugh, and went the other way with it. And at the record session he cried. You can hear it at the end when he says 'Really free' for the last time; he broke down a little."[36] After years of demeaning roles the collaboration in *The Real Ambassadors* offered Armstrong material that was closer to his own sensibility and outlook. And while Armstrong had often managed to rise above racist material by the sheer force of his artistry, the production allowed him a chance to make a statement about a lifelong struggle for control over his own representation that had hardly ended with the Little Rock incident. On the one hand, it is important to see Armstrong as transformed by his experiences in Ghana in 1956 and his ongoing experience of the southern civil rights movement. Visiting an African nation on the eve of its independence and following the actions of civil rights activists clearly inspired Armstrong and enabled him to speak in ways that would have been unthinkable a decade earlier. Those events provided the context for his strident criticism of Eisenhower following Little Rock.

Armstrong's transformation is evident in his 1961 essay in *Ebony Magazine,* "Daddy, How the Country Has Changed." At one level an optimistic endorsement of integration, the essay also provides a scorching indictment of Jim Crow America through candid thick description.[37] Emphasizing the warmth and respect felt between himself and such white performers as Bing Crosby, Armstrong makes clear the limits to this friendship: "But we weren't social. Even in the early days we didn't go cabareting together. I didn't go out with the Hollywood colony then—and still don't. I don't go out with the modern stars, even though I've played with a lot of them—Danny Kaye, Sinatra. I don't even know where they live. In fact, I've never been invited to the home of a movie star—not even Bing's."[38] Discussing the South, Armstrong noted that he still could not play in his hometown of New Orleans, and explained: "I don't socialize with the top dogs of society after a dance or concert. Even though I'm invited I don't go. These same society people may go around the corner and lynch a Negro. But while they're listening to our music, they're not thinking about trouble. What's more, they're watching Negro and white musicians play side by side."[39]

Yet while the boundaries of political expression had widened considerably, to fully appreciate the militancy of Armstrong's 1957 actions as well as the context for the 1962 performance it is just as critical to emphasize the constraints and censorship that continued to limit his choices. The long arm of McCarthyism, with its worst excesses seemingly past, left many singers and actors blacklisted well into the late 1960s. Indeed, after his angry denunciation of Eisenhower, a disavowal of politics while on his later State Department tour may have been the price for continuing to work. As the *New York Times* reported from Naroibi, Kenya in November 1960: "Mr. Armstrong showed his diplomacy when he ruled out political questions from newsmen. 'I don't know anything about it; I'm just a trumpet player,' he said with a laugh in his gravely voice. 'The reason I don't bother with politics is the words is so big by the time they break them down to my size the joke is over.'"[40] If Armstrong expressed veiled cynicism and frustration in suggesting politics was a "joke," it was clearly masked by self-deprecating, if not self-demeaning, humor. For Armstrong freedom remained an aspiration, not an achievement. And the power of *The Real Ambassadors,* performed during the most turbulent years of the civil rights movement, lay in its articulation of that yearning as well as in its satirical wit and musical accomplishments.

After the Monterey Jazz Festival *The Real Ambassadors* was never again performed. (The studio production released in LP and reissued on CD was recorded before the festival.) At Monterey Joe Glaser, Armstrong's longtime manager, disallowed its filming by the TV cameras on hand. Attempts to get it produced, including plans for a Broadway production, failed as it was consistently viewed, at the height of violent resistance to the civil rights movement, as too political and controversial.[41] In the utopian finale of *The Real Ambassadors,* "Swing Bells/Blow Satchmo"—rich with the Old-Testament biblical imagery of black Christianity—the hero's horn ("Joshua had just a horn") had blown in a new world:

Ring out the news! the world can laugh again.
This day, we're free! we're equal in every way . . .

Lift up thy voice like a trumpet
and show thy people their transgressions and their sins . . .
Let thee oppressed go free . . .

Blow Satchmo! Blow Satchmo,
can it really be, that you set all people free?

That day had certainly not yet arrived in 1962—the year marked by the killings and injuries perpetrated by those protesting James Meredith's registration at the University of Mississippi in Oxford. And it would appear no closer in the following year of the dogs and hoses turned on demonstrators in the Southern Christian Leadership Conference's (SCLC) campaign in Birmingham, Alabama and, later, the murder of four children in the bombing of that city's Sixteenth Street Baptist Church.

As the U.S. government recognized the power of jazz and African American culture and tried to harness it to Cold War foreign policy by projecting abroad an image of racial progress, ironically, the State Department jazz tours also provided a global platform from which to celebrate the subversive wit of jazz, and to announce to the world, "been waitin so long for . . . the day we'll be free."[42] Indeed, the international power and appeal of jazz lay, not as the State Department would have it, in representing the music of a free country. Rather, as brilliantly and forcefully articulated in the *The Real Ambassadors*, the jazz ambassador, epitomized by Louis Armstrong, conveyed through his horn and voice hopes and aspirations for freedom in a world where he, like so many of the audiences for whom he played, was still waiting for the day when he was "really free."

NOTES

I am enormously grateful to the late Mark Tucker for generous advice and encouragement on this project and, along with Jim Ketch, for giving me the opportunity to participate in the North Carolina Jazz festivals from 1997–1999. Many thanks to Robert O'Meally for the opportunity to present an earlier version of this paper for the Columbia University Jazz Institute and the Newport Jazz Symposium, and to the other members of the group. Special thanks to Brent Edwards for his close reading, and to Ingrid Monson, George Lipsitz, and Robin D. G. Kelley for their comments. Kevin Gaines's collaboration on interviews with Dave and Iola Brubeck and Randy Weston enlivened the interviews immeasurably, and his suggestions have greatly enriched the paper.

1. Felix Belair, New York *Times*, November 6, 1955, 1; "Satchmo Blows Up the World," *Drum*, August 1956, p.40.

2. Iola Brubeck, liner notes to *The Real Ambassadors*, 1962 Columbia LP. *The Real Ambassadors*, book by Iola Brubeck, music by Dave Brubeck, lyrics by Iola and Dave Brubeck, premiered on September 23, 1962, at the Monterey Jazz Festival in Monterey, California with the following cast: Louis Armstrong, Dave Brubeck, Carmen McRae,

Iola Brubeck, Trummy Young, Dave Lambert, Jon Hendricks, Yolande Bavan, Joe Morello, Eugene Wright, Joe Darensburg, Billy Kyle, Willy Kronk, Danny Barcelona, and Howard Brubeck as musical coordinator. A folio of fifteen songs and related narration from *The Real Ambassadors* was printed in 1963 and formerly published by Hansen Publications. That folio is no longer available. Twenty songs from *The Real Ambassadors* were recorded in September and December 1961 by Louis Armstrong, Dave Brubeck, Carmen McRae, Dave Lambert, Jon Hendricks, Annie Ross, and additional musicians, most of whom later performed at the 1962 premiere. Fifteen of those recorded songs were released by Columbia Records in 1962 on an LP entitled *The Real Ambassadors* (COL CL 5850). That LP is no longer available. In 1994 all twenty recorded songs were released by Sony Music Entertainment on the Columbia/Legacy label on a CD entitled *The Real Ambassadors* (CK 57663).

3. Interview, Penny Von Eschen and Kevin Gaines with Dave and Iola Brubeck, March 13, 1997, Wilton, Connecticut. The Bureau of Educational and Cultural Affairs Historical Collection, held in the J. William Fulbright Papers, University of Arkansas, Fayetteville, Arkansas, contains scant records of these early tours but does have an itinerary for Brubeck's trip. For Brubeck's tours, see also "Dave Brubeck Collection," University of the Pacific, Stockton, California; and Ralph J. Gleason, "Overseas with the Brubeck Klan: Mrs. Dave Brubeck Discusses Jazz Abroad," *Downbeat*, July 10, 1958. The itinerary for Armstrong's 1960–61 tour is held in the Papers of Louis Armstrong, Queens College, Queens, New York, scrapbook 58. See also, scrapbooks 22 and 36 and photos box 30. See also "Armstrong's Akwaaba in Ghana," *Down Beat*, November 24, 1960, 12; "Africa Hears Satchmo's Horn," *Drum*, Dec. 1960, 21–23; Leonard Ingalls, "Armstrong Horn Wins Nairobi, Too," *New York Times*, November 7, 1960, p. 5; "South Africa Bars Armstrong," *New York Times*, September 26, 1960, p. 2; Paul Hoffman, "Satchmo Plays for Congo's Cats," *New York Times*, October 29, 1960, 8.

4. Rave reviews by Leonard Feather (syndicated column), Ralph J. Gleason (*San Francisco Chronicle, Down Beat, Variety,* and the *Saturday Review*), are printed in the 1963 publication *The Real Ambassadors*. For a fuller discussion of the context of the tours, see Penny M. Von Eschen, *Satchmo Blows Up the World* (Cambridge: Harvard University Press, forthcoming).

5. Interview, Von Eschen and Gaines with Brubecks.

6. Interview, Von Eschen and Gaines with Brubecks. Libretto, p. 2, in possession of author.

7. For contemporary coverage of the tour, see "Dave Brubeck: The Beat Heard Round the World," *New York Times Magazine*, June 15, 1958, pp. 14–16; "Warsaw Extols Brubeck Jazz," *New York Times*, March 13, 1958; "Pianist Most Outstanding: Brubeck Concert Captivating," *Times of India*, April 4, 1958. For an account of the 1958 tour, see Von Eschen, *Satchmo Blows Up the World,* chapter 2.

8. Interview, Von Eschen and Gaines with Brubecks. Poster in possession of Brubecks: "The Iranian Oil Refinery Co. in cooperation with the U.S. Information Service presents the Dave Brubeck Quartet: Dave Brubeck, Paul Desmond, Gene Wright, Eugene Wright at the Taj Theater, Abadan, Iran, Sunday, May 4" (1958).

9. For a succinct narrative discussion of the Iraqi coup and Middle East crisis of July 1958, see Walter LaFeber, *America, Russia, and the Cold War: 1945–1990*, 6th ed. (New York: McGraw-Hill, 1980), pp. 201–2.

10. Interview, Von Eschen and Gaines with Brubecks; LaFeber, *America, Russia, and the Cold War*, pp. 212–2.

11. Papers of Louis Armstrong; area and country breakdown, July 1954 through March 1962, p.1, series 4, box 1, Bureau Historical Collection; Hoffman, "Satchmo Plays for Congo Cats"; Madaline G. Kalb, *The Congo Cables: The Cold War in America—from Eisenhower to* Kennedy (New York: Macmillan, 1994); William Blum, *Killing Hope: U.S. Military and CIA Intervention Since World War II* (Monroe, Maine: Common Courage, 1995), pp. 156–62. While it is not clear that U.S. agents were present at the assassination of Lumumba, it is clear that President Eisenhower approved the assassination. For an account of the Armstrong tour, see Von Eschen, *Satchmo Blows Up the World*, chapter 3.

12. Seeking a distinctly American alternative to Soviet and European dominance in the arts, the program committees became venues for debating what was considered "modern" and "uniquely American" in dance, art, and music.

13. Music Advisory Panel, November 15, 1955, p. 2, Bureau Historical Collection.

14. I have related the story of Armstrong and the Little Rock incident in Penny M. Von Eschen, *Race Against Empire: Black Americans and Anticolonialism, 1937–1957* (Ithaca: Cornell University Press, 1997), pp. 179–80. See also Mary Dudziak, *Cold War Civil Rights* (Princeton: Princeton University Press, 2000), p. 131; and Thomas Borstelman, *The Cold War and the Color Line: American Race Relations in the Global Arena* (Cambridge: Harvard University Press, 2001), pp 102–104.

15. "Louis Armstrong Barring Soviet Tour, Denounces Eisenhower and Governor Faubus," *New York Times*, September 19, 1957, p. 23; "Satchmo Tells Off U.S., *Pittsburgh Courier*, September 28, 1957; Gary Giddins, *Satchmo* (New York: Doubleday, 1988), pp. 160–65.

16. "Armstrong May Tour: U.S. Hopes He'll Visit Soviet Despite Segregation Issue," *New York Times*, September 20, 1957, p. 15.

17. "Musician Backs Move, Armstrong Lauds Eisenhower for Little Rock Action," *New York Times*, September 26, 1957, p. 12.

18. Giddens, *Satchmo,* p183.

19. Interview, Von Eschen and Gaines with Brubecks; *Race Against Empire*, pp. 179–180.

20. See "Dave Brubeck's Band Won't Play in Georgia," *New York Post*, February 24, 1959; "22 Colleges Bar Quartet, Bias Charged," *New York Herald Tribune*, January 13, 1960; Ralph Gleason, "Brubeck's Dixie Dilemma," *Pittsburgh Sun-Telegram*, February 6, 1960; Ralph Gleason, "Racial Issue 'Kills' Brubeck Jazz Tour of the South" *San Francisco Chronicle*, February 1959; George E. Pitts, "Give Brubeck Credit for a Slap at Bias" *Pittsburgh Courier*, February13, 1960. Brubeck expressed disappointment that critics have represented his contribution as bringing jazz to white audiences. Understandably uncomfortable with this reductive view of his legacy, he was proud to have topped popularity polls in black newspapers such as the *Pittsburgh Courier*.

21. Brubeck, *The Real Ambassadors*, libretto, pp.21–23.

22. Ibid.

23. Interview, Von Eschen and Gaines with Brubecks.

24. Thomas W. Simons Sr., Effectiveness Report, Ellington Tour 1963, series 2, box 9, pp. 15–17, Bureau Historical Collection.

25. Ibid.

26. Interview, Penny Von Eschen with Clark Terry, February 28, 1997, Chapel Hill, N.C.; Performers, series 2, box 28, Bureau Historical Collection.

27. Penny Von Eschen and Kevin Gaines, interview with Randy Weston, Austin, Texas, October 1998.

28. Charles Mingus, Budapest and Bucharest; To: Department of State from P & C Bucharest, Subject: 1975 American Music Festival, Bureau Historical Collection.

29. Brubeck, *The Real Ambassadors*, libretto, p. 40.

30. Ibid., p. 32.

31. "Armstrong's Akwaaba in Ghana," *Downbeat*, November 24, 1960, p. 12.

32. Interview, Von Eschen and Gaines with Brubecks and liner notes to Columbia CD; Fred M. Hall, *It's About Time: The Dave Brubeck Story* (Fayetteville: University of Arkansas Press, 1996), p. 86.

33. Gilbert Millstein, "Africa Harks to Satch's Horn," *New York Times Magazine*, November 20, 1960, p. 24.

34. Brubeck, *The Real Ambassadors*, libretto, pp. 40, 47–50.

35. In the liner notes for the original LP, Iola Brubeck wrote: "Obviously, no vocal group but Lambert-Hendricks-Ross could manage to sound like a crowd or a full chorus on demand."

36. Chip Stern, liner notes to the 1993 Columbia reissue of *The Real Ambassadors*.

37. Armstrong's stunning range of expression through his voluminous writings and collages have only recently been explored by scholars. See Tom Brothers, *Louis Armstrong in Own Words: Selected Writings by Louis Armstrong* (New York: Oxford University Press, 1999), and Brent Edwards's brilliant "Louis Armstrong and the Syntax of Scat," presented at "Rhythm n' Ning: A symposium on Jazz Culture," May 2000, Columbia University.

38. Louis Armstrong, "Daddy How the Country Has Changed," *Ebony Magazine*, May 1961, p. 84.

39. Ibid., p. 88.

40. Leonard Ingalls, "Armstrong Horn Wins Nairobi, Too," *New York Times*, November 7, 1960, p. 5.

41. Interview, Von Eschen and Gaines with Brubecks.

42. From the finale, "Swing Bells/Blow Satchmo," Brubeck, *The Real Ambassadors*, libretto, p. 66.

KEVIN GAINES

Artistic Othering in Black Diaspora Musics: Preliminary Thoughts on Time, Culture, and Politics

In May of 1995 the jazz vocalist Jimmy Scott concluded an engagement at Tavern on the Green in New York City. Scott was backed by a trio, the Jazz Expressions. Their final set included his usual offering of blues-inflected jazz standards, ranging from impossibly slow ballads to mid-tempo swing grooves. All were performed in his distinctive style in which phrasing, shaped and punctuated by gesticulating hands, literally dramatizes the lyric. Scott's bandstand persona, reinforced by his choice of material, was suffused with a sense of pain and loss. It seemed that everything he did onstage was purposeful. Scott's singing, gestures, and song selection all contributed to a sense of communion between artist and audience. As we will see, Nathaniel Mackey's notion of the "artistic act of othering" draws attention to this intertwining as it plays out in musical performance.

But back to Jimmy Scott. Midway through the set Scott made a point of introducing the backup musicians, all of whom were a generation or two younger than him, as leaders in their own right, thus highlighting the communal act of world making through music. Scott told the audience of their offstage activities as music teachers, or, in the case of the pianist, as the director of the Harlem Boys Choir. This brought the usually perfunctory applause for backing musicians to a warmer level of appreciation. Scott's praise of his fellow musicians went unappreciated by the management, which apparently preferred music to public acknowledgment of the musicians' contributions to the community. From the stage Scott alluded to labor/management tensions, negotiating the situation with playful yet assertive statements of mock-respect: "If the boss will permit. . . ."

Still signifying at several levels, both at the expense of "the boss" and on behalf of the band and attentive members of the audience, Scott announced, with an unmistakable irony, "It's time to go back to work." Scott and the band were reinterpreting the well-known spiritual "Sometimes I Feel Like a Motherless Child" as a very slow blues. If this selection, seldom heard live nowadays in a secular setting, resonated with some, perhaps they took notice as well of the lyric Scott added to the song, "Why did I leave the ones that I love? Why did I run away?" By adapting the lyric Scott reimagined the history of enslavement by embodying the perspective of a fugitive slave. Scott's revision of the spiritual intimated the profoundly tragic dilemma of those condemned to the status of property. Their need to be near loved ones actually solidified their bondage within the very system that, on a whim, would separate and destroy the most intimate familial bonds.

Scott's decision to personify an enslaved person challenged members of his audience to regard themselves in relation to interwoven, continuing histories of slavery and resistance. At the same time, Scott bore witness to consecrated community ideals devised to overcome domination and the market's violations of freedom, artistic or otherwise. Far from an exercise in nostalgia, Scott's performance exemplified a radical situatedness, every gesture and utterance offered as part of a social compact with audiences. It is this relationship between cultural practice and historical consciousness that I want to explore. When asked why he performed that particular song and, moreover, altered its text, Scott replied that it was an obligation—indeed, a cultural imperative—to create, as others had done before him. He identified Paul Robeson, for many an enduring symbol of political and artistic integrity, as such an inspiration. African American culture, for Scott, served, then and now, a material function in its musical, verbal, and historical intertextuality, educating the community and serving as a repository of collective memory. Both on the bandstand and off, Scott sought to preserve an embattled collective memory of oppression and struggle against those forces dedicated to erasing it from the public sphere.[1]

The sense of urgency that Scott summoned in his view of the centrality of creativity for black culture, brings to mind Nathaniel Mackey's discussion of what he calls the *artistic act of othering* through musical creativity. As part of an array of black diaspora cultural practices, artistic othering is the response, if not the antidote, to the social othering, namely, the oppressive commodification and objectification of African Americans within a U.S. society shaped by institutionalized racism. For Mackey jazz improvisation epitomizes artistic othering as an inherently political art, achieving a level of expression and meaning that cannot be codified in Western languages, including musical notation. Jazz performances, including Scott's, involve listeners in a contingent yet structured unfolding of sound and memory, making listeners witnesses to an open-ended dialogue between musicians. Artistic othering by black diaspora musicians and cultural participants resists commodification, contests and refigures racial and social conventions, and, furthermore, produces material and spiritual effects in those within if not beyond its circles. Artistic othering promises to take us out of the sedimented conventions of this world, presaging a transformation not so much in terms of place but, rather, a temporal shift in historical and social relations.[2]

Like Albert Murray, whose writing on jazz can be seen as a precedent for Mackey's view of artistic othering, Mackey's vision of a black diaspora aesthetic emphasizes the formal aspects of black linguistics, literature, music, and other forms of cultural production. Murray also insisted on the formal mastery and rigorous musical training at the heart of the blues idiom, against critics' ill-informed claims that located the blues (standing generally for black culture) in a dehistoricized, primitivist notion of black authenticity. Such critics described the blues as emotionalism, suffering, restlessness—in essence, the raw, unmediated voice of the rural black proletariat.[3] Similarly, for Mackey formalism constitutes a corrective against cultural critics obsessed with content analysis, an approach that, to Mackey, leads to equally racially and socially overdetermined readings such as dogmatic claims of black authenticity in art and literature, a path down which many critics heedlessly plunged in the Black Arts movement of the late 1960s. Then and now claims of black authenticity often derived their criteria of value negatively, more as a repudiation of perceived "white" norms and standards than as an affirmation of black historical and cultural distinctiveness.

While drawing on and seeking to elaborate Mackey's notion of artistic othering, I want to reframe discussions of black culture by questioning the need to emphasize formalism against misguided assertions of black authenticity. My discussion of black diaspora music emphasizes a material and concrete interaction and dialogue between musician and audience. I want to suggest that this dialogue derives meaning from its situatedness within a particular historical moment. In other words, following much recent work that situates jazz within its sociopolitical context,[4] I am concerned with the phenomenological and sociohistorical conditions that shape black diaspora aesthetic and cultural practices and their reception.

Black diaspora musics, including but not limited to jazz, constitute methods of artistic othering that oppose racist attempts to circumscribe black bodies and being. For musicians and audiences jazz as a repository of cultural memory offers the potential to make a difference, that is, literally crafting it musically while undermining oppressive differences. In the following I want to explore the observations and careers of several black diaspora musicians (to call them African American would obscure the broader, black diaspora identities they claimed for themselves): the tenor saxophonist Lester Young, the trumpeter and bandleader Dizzy Gillespie, the pianist and bandleader Sun Ra, and the gospel singer and arranger Marion Williams. Admittedly, the musicians discussed here are just a few of numerous possible examples. They, like so many others, interest me because they embody the apparent tension between music as universal expression and as historically situated practice that, in its aesthetics and performance, claims and constitutes an autonomous refusal of the dynamics of racial domination.

Young, Gillespie, Williams, Sun Ra, Scott, and countless others, were all products of the postwar surge in black political consciousness that participated in and interpreted the overlapping lived experiences of urbanization, migration, mass culture, and antiracist struggles. Their lives allow us to explore the connection between their universalistic aspirations to the status of creative artists and their historically specific and situated racialized identities. They also provide us the opportunity to reflect on the historical, collective, and spiritual dimensions of black diaspora aesthetics and performance styles.

During the period under consideration, artistic othering is deeply concerned with time, modernity, and freedom. It is grounded in historical struggles, past and present. Postwar Afro-diasporic consciousness among musicians and audiences linked African anticolonial and U.S.-based antiracist movements. This global convergence of black freedom struggles was reinforced by migrations of rural southern black Americans, Afro-Caribbean, and African peoples to African American urban communities, including many musicians and performers. In its wartime aspect artistic othering, chiefly within jazz, also suggests a relationship between music, black masculinity, and militarism. Robin Kelley has suggestively written of black urban culture, specifically bebop, as an oppositional culture providing for many men the basis for a refusal to accommodate the wartime demands of the segregationist U.S. state.[5] With military service and patriotic display functioning historically for black men as a rare source of respectability and dignified employment, jazz, specifically the world of the big bands, or the bandstand, provided a public alternative to the culture of militarism and the American nation's longstanding denial of full citizenship to black people. In one sense an outgrowth of military culture, as marching bands and instruments proliferated in black communities in the wake of the Civil War and the Spanish–Cuban American War, jazz ensembles and the big bands, like drill teams, embodied ideals of black organization, cooperation, self-defense, spirituality, and freedom, all filtered through an African-diaspora inflected style and sensibility.[6] While not all black jazz musicians were draft resisters, or were as disaffected as Lester Young, and while many black (and white) servicemen became jazz musicians while in the army,[7] jazz and big bands nevertheless provided for black men, and their communities, an equally disciplined and dignified cultural and material alternative to militarism and military service. One need not overstate claims of jazz as a utopian space to argue that in the postwar period jazz rivaled the military as a field for the assertion of dignified black masculinity. Moreover, as we will see, Sun Ra's big band constituted a revolt against prevailing forms of masculinity, militarism, and American nationalism during the Cold War.

The Politics of Time, Rhythm, and History

These social struggles, paralleling African American cultural traditions of struggle rooted in slavery and segregation, lent political resonance first of all to the rhythmic experience of time as a participatory and universalizing diasporic or pan-African idiom that operated at several levels of meaning. Referring to the rhythmic pulse of the music, Ingrid Monson notes that among musicians "the idea that good time should inspire movement [in audiences] remains fundamental."[8] Good time, I would add, carried a multilayered meaning at this historical juncture, symbolizing black solidarity and freedom. In other words, this pleasurably altered sense of time combined a utopian antiracist potential with an affirmation of black cultural distinctiveness.[9]

African-influenced conceptions of rhythm served as bridges for actual social, cultural, and language differences among peoples of African descent, formed vehicles among audiences for political solidarities, symbolically merged histories of struggle, emancipation, and religious practice separated by enslavement and colonization, and infused secular spaces with spiritual and communal meaning. At the same time, the diasporic cosmopolitanism within the world of jazz musicians facilitated this expansion in the repertoire of Afro-diasporic rhythms available to them. This expanded rhythmic concept, paralleling postwar black liberation struggles, marked a radical shift heralding another time and space that, for the moment, promised the abolition of systems of racial oppression. This sense of immediacy and immanence was highlighted by the rhythmic component of black diaspora musics, which symbolized and signaled an alternative conception of historical movement. Aided by mass communications technologies and consumer activities including radio, records, film, and television, the postwar advent of such black diaspora styles and perspectives, of which rhythm was a constituent part, implied and augmented historical narratives of struggle by virtue of their physical enactment of spirituality during performance. Through a continuum of speech, song, textual meaning, music, dance, and gesture, more traditional elements of African American music (swing) and culture (sorrow songs, or spirituals) were supplemented by newer black diaspora rhythmic forms, bringing to listeners a cosmopolitan historical consciousness and spirit of social advancement that anticipated and accompanied movements for black freedom and social change in the 1950s and 1960s.[10]

How fitting, then, that, the jazz soloist's effectiveness as an improviser was measured by his ability to "tell a story," articulating the gaps in signification between speech and music, or between rhythm and melody, to the satisfaction of audiences. Within this dialogue between musicians and audiences, between creation and reception, seemingly commonplace acts of watching and listening to black subjects in performance become suffused with political importance, as when Billie Holiday, throughout her career, performed and recorded the antilynching song "Strange Fruit." Later, when audiences heard the 1966 hit record "Tell it Like It Is," by Aaron Neville, the ostensible love song might be heard as an injunction to the political establishment to face up to its hypocrisy in its complicity with racial segregation and inequality and its toleration of antiblack violence.[11]

There are numerous other examples of political expression in popular music and culture, complex moments of transcendance and embeddedness in racialized and unequal social and market relations. *Artistic othering* by black musicians is understood here in a profoundly materialist sense as a social struggle realized in two ways: first, as an affirmative othering, or dialogue, between black artists and audiences, with the effect of drawing these two parties together into a musically-enacted community; second, as a form of othering providing black artists and audiences a sanctuary, or refuge, from the white world. Indeed, in the latter case, the white world and its deformed images of self and society are relegated to the status of "other" in relation to the musically complex vision affirmed by black artists and audiences. In addition, artistic othering was in large part the musicians' response to disempowerment within the music industry and restrictions on their mobility and opportunity. Thus innovation and the cultivation of an inimitable sound and style, and the translation of such creativity into community institutions, were essential guards against ubiquitous realities of nonpayment and expropriation. This resolute stance of individuality, of refusing to be spiritually owned or defined by another, as exemplified by the gospel singer Marion Williams, extended to the everyday lives of musicians as well as to the bandstand or the recording studio. Musicians, like other black people, confronted racism on a daily basis and variously responded to its daily indignities in ways ranging from outright defiance, to dissembling, to studied indifference to time and task. Indeed, musical standards of improvisation, invention, and individuality, as challenges to American society's dehumanization of blacks, extended to the realm of everyday life—how one dressed, spoke, carried oneself. How the musicians and members of their audience presented themselves, how they coped with white hostility and unfavorable working conditions, and how they negotiated the dominant society's preoccupation with black bodies, and its hostility to black male success and accomplishment, were manifested in the various modes of being in a world circumscribed by racism that might be loosely categorized as part of an ever evolving black urban style or sensibility.

The tenor saxophonist Lester Young provides but one illustration of artistic othering systematically extended to everyday life and fundamentally shaped by the predicament of being an African American man and artist in Jim Crow society. Not long before his death in 1959 Young is said to have told an audience of young admirers that a musician is an artist, a scientist, and a philosopher, no doubt bestowing upon himself as a member of that calling the stature and recognition seldom forthcoming from American culture. The story of this final encounter speaks volumes as a commitment among musicians to preserving the memory and meaning of Young's life. Young's observation testifies to the universal aspects of musical performance, but, at the same time, his circumstances require us to read the statement attributed to him a bit differently. Young's stylistic innovations and light, airy tone were initially judged inadequate, if not unmanly, by contemporaries, construed as no match for Coleman Hawkins's then popular, putatively "masculine" sound. But Young was a complete nonconformist, dressing comfortably and often playing his horn aloft at an acute angle. In addition, by cultivating his own lexicon dedicated to the articulation of social truths, and bestowing on others the honorific "Lady" regardless of their race or gender, Young subverted dominant codes of whiteness and masculinity. Drafted during World War II at the age of thirty-five, and incarcerated for a time in a military stockade, Young bitterly attributed to racism his confinement to basic training while other white jazz musicians were granted the privilege of performing in uniform. All this suggests that his ostensibly universal reflections on musicianship were fundamentally shaped by his racialized experience.[12]

Changing articulations of black identity and consciousness have rested upon a fairly consistent concern with time and history. Such concern for the recovery of a usable past, however, has often led to an ahistorical preoccupation with a search for origins, leading to reinventions of a mythic past as the basis for authentic black being.[13] Other versions of this popular historicism have often been understood as a distinction between the old and the new. Black writers of the turn of the century countered stereotypes of racial backwardness by stresssing the progress marking the distance the race had traveled from its enslaved past. This particular "New Negro" was distinguished by ideological assertions of his possession of civilization and patriarchal authority, as a proof of his entitlement to citizenship, over against the old Negro, figured as the degraded antithesis of the dominant bourgeois civilizationism that denoted whiteness. The next popular expression of New Negro identity, though as deeply gendered and masculinist as its antecedent, was articulated in the wake of northern urban migrations of poor blacks and whites, blacks' military service in World War I, and an urban epidemic of white mob violence against African Americans. The new New Negro symbolized blacks' willingness to fight back against their racist tormentors as a departure from the Old Negro's purported docility and accommodation. Today popular black historicism is shaped by the systemic failures of public education and the concealment of black historical realities. Afrocentrism and its variants currently vies with the "social othering" of market-imposed images of "authentic" blackness, fixated on hedonism, materialism, and hypersexuality. Contemporary exponents of historicism legitimately seek to address these assaults on black personhood within American political culture, but seldom in terms of their own making. What often results is an invented notion of a "new" normative black identity over against a presumably backward racial consciousness, an assertion that ironically erases a history of black agency and artistic othering. Worse, such forms of black nationalism are politically disengaged, abandoning historical struggles for citizenship and human rights. Many of those who would affirm blackness thus risk unconsciously passing off received stereotypes as their own identity, predicated on presumptions of "the race's" backwardness, "unmanliness," or some similarly abject, pathological condition. The Million Man March of 1995 is a good example of this necessary, albeit, in this case, ultimately disappointing quest for an autonomous group consciousness.

This mentality is similar to what Manthia Diawara has elsewhere described as a conversionist identity often characteristic of contemporary black nationalism, in which black identities are ostensibly rooted in rhetorical appeals to history but remain historically untethered. Against oversimplified conversionist claims about time and identity, I would like to counterpose another sense of time suggested by artistic othering. This sense of time is potentially nonhierachical, not of this world of unfreedom, yet at the same time enabling a sense of being in the world along a continuum of material temporality encompassing the personal and the political, the individual and the communal, and ranging from the most physical and immediate to the global and historical. An approximation of this sense of time is seen in Diawara's reading of *The Autobiography of Malcolm X*, which imagines Detroit Red, before his conversion to Minister Malcolm X, as avidly attuned to the emancipatory possibilities of 1940s black culture: "In his secular imagination, Detroit Red considers such musicians as Duke Ellington, Lionel Hampton, and Billie Holiday as leading Black people toward spiritual, economic, and political fulfillment."[14]

Against the neo-puritanism of black conversionists whose orthodox sense of blackness is informed by a pathologized vision of black culture, Diawara's essay invokes the black entertainment industry in Harlem in the 1940s, emphasizing the vital links between modernity and cultural and economic independence. The career and recollections of John Birks "Dizzy" Gillespie (1917–1993) have much to offer for Diawara's project of "Black cultural specification" and also for the sort of radically situated historical readings of black musical forms and cultural identity that illustrate the convergence of rhythm as both deeply embodied time and, more broadly, herald of historical movement, modernization, and social transformation. Later this multilayered sense of time was crystallized by the popular conviction, frequently broadcast over the airwaves during the 1960s civil rights protests, that a change was imminent.

Gillespie, one of the pioneering figures in bebop, writes of a period surrounding World War II in which the stylistic repertoire of jazz was greatly expanded and advanced. Indeed, Gillespie's account shows that the origins of bebop were more multifaceted than theories of individual creativity allow. The collective contributions of musical visionaries like Gillespie, Charlie Parker, Thelonious Monk, Clyde Hart, Charlie Christian, Mary Lou Williams, Bud Powell, Max Roach, and others were situated in the sociohistorical conditions of wartime, which favored small groups of instrumentalists over the big bands. More important, bebop was the product of the communal culture of the jam session. This was an attempt by primarily, though not exclusively, African American musicians to hone their skills after hours, creating new styles whose harmonic complexity and rapid tempos ensured that they would not easily be copied and thus expropriated. There was also the functional need to conserve the physical energy of drummers by excluding self-indulgently mediocre players from the bandstand. The jam session, while competitive, was also a site of shared cultural values and mutual encouragement, nurturing individual striving, originality, and achievement. These sessions inspired an eclectic search for musical ideas, ranging from Tin Pan Alley standards, to blues tonality, to Egyptian scales, to quotes of Western classical motifs. There were spiritual aspects to this secular site of activity. Here ecstatic younger musicians might receive compliments from their revered idols, encouraging them to reach for new heights of musical skill and expression and surpass themselves.

The wildly allusive virtuosity allowed full reign in the jam session was part of an unprecedented level of cross-cultural exchange and collaboration among jazz musicians from various locations throughout the black diaspora. Gillespie famously merged the already hybrid idioms of jazz with popular musics from Latin America, specifically Afro-Cuban styles, later personally inspiring and assisting many Latin American jazz musicians.

That said, we must acknowledge the complicated American racial dynamics within which the jam session was situated. The jam session, which constituted black musicians' bid for artistic independence, illustrated the extent to which the world of jazz musicians and audiences was integrated, yet hardly egalitarian in its opportunities and rewards. This qualified and ambiguous integration was defined by the exclusion of blacks from the most lucrative opportunities. For example, Gillespie worked as a big band arranger freelancing for popular white bandleaders such as Woody Herman, who confessed that he would have loved to have hired Gillespie in his band if he weren't so dark. If anything, the contradictory experience of black jazz musicians, performing for white audiences while daily confronted with the distinction between respectful, appreciative fans and white racists, intensified the material reality of race. This state of affairs mandated their defensive sense of cultural and political solidarity. Black musicians insisted that they be recognized as dignified artists, not embodiments of white minstrel fantasies.

Thus the creation of bebop or, as Gillespie preferred to call it, modern jazz, in Harlem and New York clubs was deeply informed by black musicians' experience and consciousness of racial oppression, acquired not just in the urban North, but through extensive travel through the South and Southwest. That lived experience was augmented by knowledge of anticolonial struggles in Africa, the legacy of Garveyism, and the reception of black nationalist beliefs among musicians and audiences, including those of the Nation of Islam. In addition, Afro-diasporic cultures enjoyed a heightened visibility in artistic circles as a result of the efforts of such choreographer/dancers as Katherine Dunham and the Trinidad-born Pearl Primus as well as, later, such singer-activists such as Harry Belafonte and the South African artist Miriam Makeba. Indeed, Belafonte helped introduce Makeba to American audiences, following her appearance in the 1959 anti-apartheid film *Come Back Africa*.[15] The impact of such collaborations among musicians, writers, and performers across geographical and cultural differences was immediately felt in modern jazz rhythm sections. Indeed the new music was distinguished by musicians' synthesis of the exacting musical standards set forth by leading swing drummers (Chick Webb, Sidney Catlett, and Jo Jones) with new rhythmic concepts supplied, in part, by the Afro-Cuban drummers who played with small groups. Max Roach recalled playing a concert with Parker and Gillespie at the Hotel Diplomat in New York City with a group of six or seven West African drummers who effortlessly accompanied the jazz musicians' usual bebop repertoire. The incorporation of African-derived polyrhythms posed a challenge for jazz bassists and other instrumentalists, one that occasionally produced cultural tensions among musicians. The Ghanaian percussionist Guy Warren, who led his own groups during the 1950s in recording his pathbreaking fusion of African rhythms and modern jazz, complained of the difficulty of finding musicians who could execute his ideas correctly.[16]

For Gillespie the coming together of different African-derived musics could not have been wholly unfamiliar. He described the connection between his later interest in Afro-diasporic musics and his earliest formative musical expriences. Although he was afraid of being seen, for fear of being considered disloyal to his own Methodist church, Gillespie recalled visiting the Sanctified church in his hometown of Cheraw, South Carolina: "I first learned the meaning of rhythm there and all about how music could transport people spiritually." The drum-based, polyrhythmic Sanctified beat, propelled by the congregation's hand clapping, drew Gillespie to the church's services every Sunday. "Even white people would come and sit outside in their cars just to listen to the people getting the spirit inside," he added. Even so, the endemic violence and deprivation blacks faced in the deep South strengthened his conviction to improve himself musically "to get the hell out of Cheraw. That was all we could do about it."[17]

Gillespie's recognition of the links between his early background and the cosmopolitanism of his cultural affinities reveals the postwar culture of modern jazz as an accretion and fusion of histories of aspiration and struggle as much as musical styles. The political implications of his foregrounding of black diaspora styles as a composer (of such standards as "A Night in Tunisia" and "Manteca"), bandleader, and, later, as "goodwill ambassador" for the State Department were fully appreciated by such intellectuals as the African American historian Lawrence D. Reddick. Gillespie remained a critic of American racism despite the U.S. government's sponsorship of his big band tours of Asia and Latin America. With the impending confrontation between anticolonial movements and a U.S. foreign policy dominated by the Cold War, and the massive resistance waged by segregationist mobs to court-ordered school desegregation, the State Department's deployment of Gillespie and Louis Armstrong to repair the image of American democracy among African and Third World peoples ironically elevated their stature not only as world citizens but as critics of U.S. racism as well. Furthermore, Gillespie testified to the social constraints on black artists, recalling that earlier in the 1950s he had sheltered Billie Holiday from police "hounding her" until she could obtain treatment for her drug addiction. And he fondly remembered an encounter with Paul Robeson, who "reminded [him] of how much further we had yet to go in the struggle" and whom he admired for his "uncontrollable spirit, his superdedication to ideals which he didn't vary one inch."[18]

Gillespie's autobiography afforded him the opportunity to offer his perspective on struggles around race and representation regarding jazz and Afro-diasporic musics and to contest pervasive attempts by critics and rival white musicians, such as Stan Kenton, to minimize his musical innovations. More important, with characteristic wit, Gillespie waived the discretion and reticence on political matters so often imposed on black entertainers.[19] Describing his run for the presidency in 1964, Gillespie reprinted his standard speech, which suggested that his candidacy was more than a mere publicity stunt. Besides promising to staff his cabinet with fellow jazz musicians, as president Gillespie claimed that he would disband the FBI, investigate the Klan's "un-American activities," revoke segregationist Alabama governor George Wallace's citizenship and deport him to Vietnam, and appoint only blacks as U.S. attorneys and judges in the South, "so we can get some redress." For attorney general Gillespie named Malcolm X: "He's one cat we want on our side." Gillespie wrote that as president he would have fought for disarmament, civil rights, and free government-subsidized health care and education. Gillespie articulated his politics as an extension of his Baha'i faith and insisted that the abilities of improvising jazz musicians resulted from their being in tune with God and nature.[20]

Gillespie's book, like Langston Hughes's audacious meditation on the origins of bebop, is a forceful rejoinder to those who would abstract black diaspora musics from their sociocultural origins and ignore the critical debates over their political significance. Hughes's streetwise everyman, Jesse B. Simple, offered a tragicomic account, worth quoting at some length, of the bodily intersection of rhythm and history. Simple posits police brutality and segregation as explanations for the apparent nonsense of bebop lyrics:

"Every time a cop hits a Negro with his billy club, that old club say, 'BOP! BOP! . . . BE-BOP! . . . MOP! . . . BOP!'

That Negro hollers, 'Ooool-ya-koo! Ou-o-o!'

Old cop just keeps on, 'MOP! MOP! . . . BE-BOP! MOP!' That's where Be-Bop came from, beaten right out of some Negro's head into them horns and saxophones and piano keys that plays it. . . . That's why so many white folks don't dig Bop," said Simple. "White folks do not get their heads beat *just for being white*. But me–a cop is liable to grab me almost any time and beat my head–*just* for being colored.

In some part of this American country as soon as the polices see me, they say, 'Boy, what are you doing in this neighborhood?'

I say, 'coming from work, sir.' . . .

Then I have to go into my whole pedigree because I am a black man in a white neighborhood. And if my answers do not satisfy them, BOP! MOP! . . . BE-BOP! . . . If they do not hit me, they have already hurt my soul. *A dark man shall see dark days.* Bop comes out of them dark days."[21]

The career of the African American jazz musician, composer, and big band leader Sun Ra (1914–1993) further illustrates the historical and political consciousness that resides in postwar black diaspora cultural practices. Sun Ra was born as Herman Sonny Blount in Birmingham, Alabama, though in later years he would insist that he came to this world by way of Saturn. Through his refusal of this world Sun Ra undermines parochial understandings of race and national identity on both sides of the black-white divide. His vehement denunciations of American racism contest the ethnocentrism that falsely separates American and African American cultures. Sun Ra's conception of outer space as an imaginary destination for the reformulation of black consciousness not only renounces white supremacy but also its derivative discourses, as seen in problematic conversionist articulations of black nationalism.

As John Szwed and Graham Lock have argued, despite his oft-proclaimed status as an exile from his interplanetary origins on the planet Saturn, Sun Ra's worldview is incomprehensible without reference to its contexts in U.S. racism, specifically Jim Crow, and the popular mass protest among blacks of the 1930s and 1940s represented by urban migration. Sun Ra's philosophy was a blend of black and Judeo-Christian cultural traditions, Afrocentric and antislavery historicist visions, and inspirational messages of spirituality and self-love that are universalistic while speaking to particularly African American concerns. The conviction that nothing less than the soul of the American nation is at stake is further conveyed by Sun Ra's comments in an interview in which he seems to equate his person with the collective status of African Americans: "I'm in human form. If they can't recognize me representing innocence and beauty and sincerity, then they're hypocrites and they don't fit in this omniverse."

The formative experiences of urban migration, and the culture of big bands also informed Sun Ra's interest in the omniverse as an otherworldly realm of freedom. When asked by an interviewer about his lyrics, Sun Ra replied:

> It's all about space. . . . I didn't find being black in America a very pleasant experience, but I had to have something, and where was that something? It was being creative. Something that nobody owned but us. . . . Now I [have] a treasure house of music that no one has. The Arabs [have] oil, the Africans [have] tin. . . . I have music from the creator which is more valuable than anything.

Sun Ra's blunt if understated declaration that "I didn't find being black in America a pleasant experience" marks the source of his unique identity and philosophy.[22] Compared to the Jim Crow South and, for that matter, the de facto segregation and poverty he later encountered in Chicago and Philadelphia, which was his earthly base of operations throughout his later years, outer space and its interplanetary music described a utopian place where, as he once put it, human feet have never trod, one that human eyes have never seen. Indeed, it was outer space that provided the conditions for a truly human existence.

These contentions are positively baffling if viewed in isolation from intellectual and popular discourses of black nationalism or from black cultural practices recalling slavery and resistance. However unconventional, Sun Ra's example affirms the fundamentally American character of black nationalism, including Afrocentrism. In short, Sun Ra's extraterrestrial persona and antinomian spirituality were thoroughly mediated by African-American cultural and historical consciousness.

For someone as concerned with origins as Sun Ra (reflecting popular black nationalist mythmaking, such as that of the Nation of Islam, that seeks to codify the genesis of black oppression and thus prescribe its solution), the musician was notoriously reticent about his own background. But, if it is difficult to determine precisely when he adopted the name of the Egyptian sun god, enough is known of the circumstances of his early life to explain his determined independence, here displayed by the African American cultural phenomenon of renaming, or self-naming, expressing a spiritual and social conversion, as an act of self-determination.

This self-naming illustrates the multiple sources and contexts involved in the production of identity. Indeed, the very situatedness and complexity of his identity demands that scholars move beyond preoccupations with essentialism that, at worst, deny the necessity of human agency in constituting ourselves, for better or worse, as historical and political actors. Upon describing his aesthetics and cosmic philosophy as an expression of "my natural blackness," he claimed that he was able to achieve this state of awareness, which he implicitly considered to be the realization of his human potential, "by isolating myself from Black folks in America and isolating myself from white folks in America. I'm ME and that's more than either one of them can say. So therefore, what I'm playing is just natural." Even the idea of strategic essentialism hardly seems to do justice to Sun Ra's sui generis self-fashioning or to his claim to and assertion of the fundamental right of persons to name and situate themselves, both individually and as members of communities, composing, as it were, their own histories.[23]

Sun Ra's brand of romantic, antimaterialist cultural nationalism, in its disavowal of power politics, wealth, and military might as the basis for nationhood, represents a distinct trend in popular black nationalist discourse, although its religious aspects invite comparison with the Nation of Islam. I want to revisit the question of the significance of gender within nationalist discourses, by quoting Sun Ra on his rejection, once again, of another crucial aspect of black nationalism, namely, its emphasis on reclaiming the image of a heroic black masculinity from the shadow of the humiliations imposed by U.S. patriarchal racism:

> I am not a man. . . . Man is filthy and abominable, and is appointed to die. . . . Man is condemned from the day he is born. I'm an angel, I'm an archangel now, and I'm going to keep on advancing to everything beyond the M-A-N, I guess I don't even want to say it because it's so bad and so horrible, that it just makes me shudder to think of M-A-N.

For Sun Ra the nearest temporal approximation of the utopian possibilities of outer space was the culture of the big bands. Indeed, for many African American men and women, and especially men, big bands held a utopian appeal for both economic and cultural reasons, as employment opportunities and by virtue of their autonomous cultural associations. Besides their value as sites for cooperative economics, the big bands' precision, swing, and excellence, along with a rhythmic force that seemed to inhabit the bodies of dancers and listeners, affirmed for many collective ideals and aspirations to dignity, organization, and power. Along with their promise of leisure and pleasure, big bands offered men a welcome alternative to employment with the segregated U.S. military and with the Pullman Company. Despite being rare occupations in their promise of respectable employment, all three occupations were not without their sacrifices and indignities.[24]

Nevertheless, the big bands were themselves valued sites of modernity. In the first place, they provided autonomous spaces for blacks to revel in a culture of aspiration and freedom. Big bands also symbolized popular ideals of mobility, success, and escape from racist Jim Crow terrain represented by the image of an urban promised land. Indeed, these cultural and economic institutions provided secular sites for African American folk religion and beliefs that served as precedents for newer forms of black diaspora consciousness in the postwar period. For Sun Ra, who played piano briefly with Fletcher Henderson's orchestra during the 1940s, nothing surpassed the big band sound, and he later claimed that the decline of the big bands, so synonymous in his mind with black solidarity, was indicative of a fundamental spiritual declension in the lives of African Americans, if not the nation:

> Unfortunately the Black musician over here has been diverted into playing [popular music] instead of playing the natural things we're supposed to play as black men. Instead of holding their units together to play for their people in an organized way with the big bands, they moved down to trios

and combos. They moved down to duos and the ego. . . . And then, you look at what the Black race did in America and it's not what I can be proud of.

To quote Valerie Wilmer's trenchant assessment of Sun Ra's remarks, which issued from his memory of a time in which big bands were commonplace and widely celebrated, "The big band and the hard work that lies behind its precision, epitomised all that is fine and heroic in black music."[25] Sun Ra remained uncompromising in the face of the commercial marginalization of the big bands, whose appeal for him and many other black men and women was doubtless enhanced, as we have seen, by the rare outlet they provided as material and symbolic sites of employment, liberation, professionalism, and dignified respectability.

The ideal and reality of an institution providing a haven from social turmoil was maintained by Sun Ra's organization, known at one time as the Arkestra, long after the virtual disappearance of big bands. During the 1950s Sun Ra shunned conventional Western dress for the flashy, space-age, Afrocentric costumes and ritualized, carnivalesque performances that embodied the band's visionary artistic othering. Perhaps the Nation of Islam provided a model for his decision to effectively renounce his U.S. citizenship, proclaiming himself instead as a citizen of the Omniverse. In any case, activating the utopian potential of big bands, Sun Ra's musicians and singers joined culture, history, religion, and politics by chanting fragments of the slave spirituals and holding out the collective memory of slavery as a rebuttal to sanitized American myths of national origin. Unorthodox by any stretch of the imagination, the big band Sun Ra led was far more than a professional organization. As an institution bridging sacred and secular ways of living, the band was not unlike a church for its members, and Sun Ra was no less than a spiritual leader for his musicians, who lived and rehearsed with total commitment in a communal situation. Indeed, within its leader's philosophy, outer space functioned symbolically as a pastoral refuge from the dangers of urban poverty and alienation facing African American migrants from the South.

Having recorded his band on countless occasions in both rehearsal and live performance, Sun Ra supported his collective endeavors by releasing the band's works on his own label, Saturn Records, setting an example of independent ownership and creative autonomy against the white-dominated music industry. Paradoxically, then, despite, or possibly because of its decidedly otherworldly outlook, we find Sun Ra and his organization able to survive and function, albeit not without difficulty, within the worldly realm of necessity and the market.

Owing to the vastness and seemingly infinite stylistic range of his musical output, one hesitates to offer generalizations about Sun Ra's music. Nevertheless, there is abundant evidence to contend that his complex figurations of rhythm, time, and diaspora consciousness served the purposes of artistic othering. Sound, style, and message went hand in hand in the radical situatedness of his band's performances. This reflected Sun Ra's fusion of blues, black historical counternarratives, his quest for an intergalactic path out of the racial wilderness of the U.S., and, finally, his utopian appropriation of popular science discourses of outer space throughout the nuclear age in opposition to the Cold War's era's militarization of space. Sun Ra's piano style and arranging, while rooted solidly in African American blues and swing idioms, also embraced avant-garde and electronic experimentation. One might argue as well that political and historical events were reshaping Sun Ra's style, as seen in the band's incorporation of African-derived polyrhythmic effects and dance, reflecting black American jazz musicians identification with anticolonial movements.[26] The rhythmic repetition of melodic phrases and the frequent use of ostinato are echoed in the poetry and lyrics Sun Ra supplied his band members and vocalists with. These texts, reflecting the multilayered sonic textures of the music, often blend intergalactic and Afrocentric meanings and usually issue a direct challenge to the beliefs and values of the listener as, in live performance, they invite audience participation.[27]

The functional and participatory character of much African-derived music makes it difficult to assess its quality apart from its impact on audiences. At the same time, as Paul Gilroy has argued, a consideration of the role of sound recordings and radio as globalizing technologies of cultural transmission and communication is vital to an analysis of the relationship between black culture, politics, and history in the postwar period.[28] Indeed, the black consciousness movements in Jamaica, Brazil, and in West and South Africa sparked by the U.S.-based black freedom movement were fundamentally shaped by mass communications technologies. Thus far, however, the present discussion has largely dwelled on audiences' experiences of live music and on the immediacy of the spectacle, gesture, and sound of performers. I have distinguished between live and recorded music, with the implied loss of immediacy from one to the other, to illuminate the struggle waged by black diaspora peoples and their cultural practices of collective memory against the malignant practices of social othering and their imposition of antiblack distortions, if not outright forgetting, of history. It bears repeating that rhythm-based black diaspora musics, or artistic othering, bridge and ultimately transcend the distinction between time immediately experienced and a more global historicism. This in turn encourages us to regard the diaspora, a historical and geographical product of enslavement, colonization, and the dispersal of African-descended peoples, also as a symbolic space for culture building. At the same time, the unfinished project of social emancipation and the reproduction of forms of social alienation and historical amnesia have resulted in a chilling postcolonial, post–civil rights alienation and a fear for the survival of communities of resistance that animates the efforts of people such as Jimmy Scott.

We have discussed the spiritual dimension of time and history in black diaspora music and culture, and it is this spiritual vision that has pointed away from a world of oppressive social relations toward visions of human freedom to which we turn in a consideration of the gospel singer Marion Williams (1927–1994). Unlike the drum, whose force and immediacy cannot be reproduced in sound recordings, such is the level of Williams's virtuosity and musicianship that it is difficult to imagine anything more to be desired by listeners to her recordings. That timelessness is a fortunate thing, since a supreme and profoundly significant artist the like of Williams is gone, no longer to be seen or heard in the flesh.

Born in Miami to Bahamian parents, Williams was a musical prodigy, singing with several local Sanctified churches. Her father, a barber, whom she remembers campaigning for Franklin D. Roosevelt, died when she was nine, forcing her to leave school to help support her mother, a laundress. Williams's youth was spent working "from sun-up to sun-down," until she began singing professionally, joining the Clara Ward Singers in 1947 while not yet out of her teens. With a style deeply grounded in blues tonality and jazz improvisation, Williams exhibited the ability to sing anything. She immediately became the main attraction, recording million sellers and expanding the group's reputation outside gospel circles. In 1960 Williams left the Ward Singers and formed her own group, the Stars of Faith. With that group Williams joined the cast of Langston Hughes's play *Black Nativity*, in 1961, a vehicle for showcasing her talents and the distinctive cultural style and sensibility of black gospel. The revue enjoyed critical and popular success for four years, touring the United States and Western Europe. After 1965 Williams performed as a soloist, touring Africa in 1966 under the auspices of the State Department.[29]

Enormously successful within the limited market of gospel, Williams's career as a recording artist and performer was characterized by her struggle to maintain the integrity of her religious mission. Williams became as legendary for her refusal of lucrative offers to record secular popular music for major record companies as she was renowned for her electrifying performances. By this time much in demand outside religious circles at jazz festivals all over the world, Williams consented to recording projects only on her own terms. The jazz bassist Ray Brown, who sought Williams as a guest vocalist after seeing her in *Black Nativity*, wrote that she refused to record any popular music, jazz, or blues for his collaboration with the vibraphonist Milt Jackson released in 1964 as *Much in Common*. Williams sang only spirituals, including, at Jackson's suggestion, "Sometimes I Feel Like a Motherless Child." When she made several recordings on Atlantic Records in the early 1970s, Williams stuck to songs with socially conscious, spiritual themes such as Stevie Wonder's "Heaven Help Us All."

Although her recorded output is consistently of a high caliber, the record that she produced and arranged for Epic in the mid-1960s with the Stars of Faith is particularly exemplary of the radical situatedness of black diaspora musics, whose assertions of black style and spirituality carry unmistakably topical and political resonances. Williams included an arrangement based on West Indian calypso rhythms and an interpretation of one spiritual that deploys exquisitely controlled fury in denouncing war, segregation, and colonialism:

I want to know, my brothers, why are you fighting for man?
God's got the whole world in His hands, and He owns this whole land. . . .
He's got the country of France in His hands, Yeah! And England, too, in His hands, He's got Belgium, Yeah! In His hands . . .
And another thing, He's got Alabama, yes He has, in His hands, (Oooo!)
Louisiana, child, in His hands, He's got, Oh! Mississippi! In His hands, He's got the whole wide world in His hands.[30]

By virtue of her stylistic and technical mastery alone, even Williams's less overt revisions of the text of spirituals and gospel standards are compelling. Her intricate rhythmic and harmonic solo improvisations create the effect of total freedom within a developing musical structure, resolving effortlessly with impossibly high notes after providing antiphonal effects and emphasis with her own wordless vocal interjections as well as with the quartet's backup vocal arrangements. In other words, Williams's is an emphatically Afro-diasporic style.[31]

Williams's creative interventions with time and history occurred at the visual level, as well, visible in the photographic portraits that she and other gospel women made of themselves. Whether or not she originated the practice, several accounts of Williams attribute to her intensely posed, stylized portraits in which the gospel diva, resplendent in a regal pompadour hairdo, looks not into the lens of the camera but gazes upward, beatifically, with eyes fixed on some object off in the distance outside the frame of the picture.[32] As the pictures may well suggest a refusal to submit to an objectifying male gaze, or her resistance to market forces and commodification, they crystallize the act of artistic othering as the refusal of the temporal world as it is.

The singular creative personalities of Williams, Sun Ra, Gillespie, Scott, and others all affirm the social and spiritual dimensions of postwar black diaspora cultures as pathways not merely to individual conversion but as utopian sites of historical transformation. By way of the tension between the universal call that music invokes and the historical situation of black artists evolving Afro-diasporic traditions, these musicians make the flawed conditions of human encounter in a racist world felt. At the same time, and as in Jimmy Scott's final set, their mingling of historical and sensorial experience continually recreates the occasion for resistance and transformation.

NOTES

1. On Jimmy Scott, see David Ritz, *Faith in Time: The Life of Jimmy Scott* (New York: Da Capo, 2002).

2. Nathaniel Mackey, "Other: From Noun to Verb," in Krin Gabbard, ed., *Jazz Among the Discourses* (Durham: Duke University Press, 1995), pp. 76–99.

3. Albert Murray, *Stomping the Blues* (New York: Vintage, 1982).

4. For example, see A. D. Spellman, *Four Lives in the Bebop Business* (New York: Limelight, 1966); Valerie Wilmer, *As Serious as Your Life: The Story of the New Jazz* (London: Serpent's Tail, 1992); Robert O'Meally, *Lady Day: The Many Faces of Billie Holiday* (New York: Arcade, 1991); Mark Tucker, *Ellington: The Early Years* (Urbana: University of Illinois Press, 1991); Mark Tucker, *The Duke Ellington Reader* (New York: Oxford, 1993); Ronald Radano, *New Musical Figurations: Anthony Braxton's Cultural Critique* (Chicago: University of Chicago Press, 1993); Samuel A. Floyd, *The Power of Black Music* (New York: Oxford, 1995); Ingrid Monson, *Saying Something* (Chicago: University of Chicago Press, 1996); Scott DeVeaux, *The Birth of Bebop* (Berkeley: University of California Press, 1997); John Szwed, *Space Is the Place: The Lives and Times of Sun Ra* (New York: Pantheon, 1997); Ronald Radano and Philip Bohlman, eds., *Music and the Racial Imagination* (Chicago: University of Chicago Press, 2000);

Sherrie Tucker, *Swing Shift: "All-Girl" Bands of the 1940s* (Durham: Duke University Press, 2000); Graham Lock, *Bluetopia: Visions of the Future and Revisions of the Past in the Work of Sun Ra, Duke Ellington, and Anthony Braxton* (Durham: Duke University Press, 2000); Farah Jasmine Griffin, *If You Can't Be Free, Be a Mystery: In Search of Billie Holiday* (New York: Free, 2001); Eric Porter, *What Is This Thing Called Jazz* (Berkeley: University of California Press, 2002); Penny Von Eschen, *Satchmo Blows Up the World: Jazz Musicians Play the Cold War* (Cambridge: Harvard University Press, 2004).

5. Robin D. G. Kelley, "The Riddle of the Zoot: Malcolm Little and Black Cultural Politics During World War II," in *Race Rebels: Culture, Politics, and the Black Working Class* (New York: Free, 1994).

6. Jack V. Buerkle and Danny Barker, *Bourbon Street Black: The New Orleans Black Jazzmen* (New York: Oxford University Press, 1973), p. 14.

7. Ronald M. Radano's biography of Anthony Braxton discusses Braxton's period in the army as central to his development as a musician. See Radano, *New Musical Figurations*. On white jazz musicians and the reinforcement of their "outsider" status by their alienation from military discipline, see Lewis Erenberg, "Things to Come: Swing Bands, Bebop, and the Rise of a Postwar Jazz Scene," in Lary May, ed., *Recasting America: Culture and Politics in the Age of Cold War* (Chicago: University of Chicago Press, 1989), pp. 236–37.

8. Monson, *Saying Something*, p. 28.

9. Erenberg has made a similar point about the utopian possibilities of swing music in the 1930s. See "Things to Come," pp. 227–233.

10. For an insightful history of the civil rights movement through an account of the era's popular music, see Craig Werner, *A Change is Gonna Come: Music, Race, and the Soul of America* (New York: Plume, 1999).

11. See Werner, ibid., pp. 27, 36, for discussions of the popular political readings of songs without an overt political message.

12. Murray has noted the significance of Young's offstage demeanor as an extension of his musical creativity: "The ever-so-casual speech, dress, and movements of Lester Young . . . were no less stylized and ceremonial than the traditional formalities of the rhetoric, vestments, and bearing of a member of any priesthood." See *Stomping the Blues*, p. 230. For several perspectives on Young, including transcriptions of interviews, see Lewis Porter, *A Lester Young Reader* (Washington, D.C.: Smithsonian Institution Press, 1991). I am indebted to Phil Schaap for the story of Lester Young's last remarks. One of the young musicians present who passed this story on was the late, legendary African American drummer, teacher, and activist Willie Jones.

13. Paul Gilroy, *The Black Atlantic: Modernity and Double Consciousness* (Cambridge: Harvard University Press, 1993), pp. 83–84.

14. Manthia Diawara, "Malcolm X and the Black Public Sphere: Conversionists Versus Culturalists," *Public Culture*, 7.1 (Fall 1994): 35–48, 46.

15. A contemporary profile of Pearl Primus mentions her collaboration with West African and Haitian drummers and devotes considerable space to Primus's account of her aesthetics and politics. See Mary Bragiotti, "Democracy in Rhythm," *Negro Digest* (November 1944): 73–75. Belafonte coproduced and wrote the liner notes for Makeba's debut album in the States, *The Many Voices of Miriam Makeba* (Kapp Records, KL-1274), featuring songs from South Africa, Brazil, the West Indies, the Congo, and the Americas. Belafonte's status as a contemporary of the modern jazz revolution comes

through clearly in Dom Cerulli, "Belafonte: The Responsibility of an Artist," *Down Beat*, March 6, 1957, pp. 17–18.

16. Gillespie, *To Be or Not to Bop*, p. 233. Later, Warren, whose groups had performed in the African Room, a New York nightclub, was dismayed that the music industry and American musicians and audiences passed him over for the relatively unskilled Nigerian Michael Olatunji. Guy Warren, *I Have a Story to Tell* (Accra: Guinea Press, 1963).

17. Gillespie, *To Be or Not to Bop*, pp. 30–31.

18. Reddick tells of befriending Gillespie partly because "he had a very good perspective on the social implications of music." Ibid., p. 363. On the participation of Gillespie, Armstrong, and others in State Department tours during the Cold War, see Penny M. Von Eschen, *Satchmo Blows Up the World* (Cambridge: Harvard University Press, forthcoming). On Robeson and Holiday, see Gillespie, *To Be or Not to Bop*, p. 412.

19. The critic Ralph J. Gleason's favorable review of Gillespie's mid-1950s big band is noteworthy for its portrayal of Gillespie as an "entertainer," "comedian," and "Court Jester." As for the band, Gleason asserted, possibly seeking to deflect political pressure from Gillespie at the height of the Cold War, "This is no angry band. This is a happy band, having a ball." See "Perspectives," *Down Beat*, March 6, 1957, p. 8.

20. Gillespie, *To Be or Not to Bop*, pp. 452–61, 473–75. For a recent biography of Gillespie, see Alyn Shipton, *Groovin' High: The Life of Dizzy Gillespie* (New York: Oxford, 1999).

21. Langston Hughes, "Bop," in Abraham Chapman, ed., *Black Voices: An Anthology of Afro-American Literature* (New York: New American Library, 1968), pp. 104–5.

22. All subsequent quotes, except where noted, are taken from a 1987 interview with Sun Ra conducted by Phil Schaap, rebroadcast in March 1993 on 89.9 mhz, WKCR-FM, New York.

23. The jazz historian Valerie Wilmer has written that Sun Ra's emphasis on percussion in his big bands, combined with chants set up by the musicians, "was the first sign of *conscious* Africanisms to appear in the music since Gillespie's Afro-Cuban period." Sun Ra is quoted in Wilmer's brilliant chapter on him in *As Serious as Your Life*, pp. 80, 90.

24. As instrumentalists rather than singers women's participation in touring big bands was extremely rare. Gillespie hired the trombonist and arranger Melba Liston in his mid-1950s big band. The pianist, composer, and arranger Mary Lou Williams worked with his late 1940s band and performed her *Zodiac Suite* with the 1950s band. The church-trained Sarah Vaughan established her reputation as a nonpareil musician, vocalist and pianist, in the Billy Eckstine big band in the early 1940s, along with Gillespie, Charlie Parker, Miles Davis, Art Blakey, Dexter Gordon, Gene Ammons, and others.

25. Sun Ra is quoted in Wilmer, *As Serious as Your Life*, pp. 87–88.

26. For examples of jazz recordings inspired by African independence movements, including works by Art Blakey, Sonny Rollins, Max Roach, and others, see Radano, *New Musical Figurations*, pp. 64–65, note.

27. For detailed analyses of Ra's lyrics, see Szwed, *Space Is the Place*, and Lock, *Bluetopia*.

28. Gilroy, *The Black Atlantic*.

29. See Anthony Heilbut, "Marion Williams," in Darlene Clark Hine, Elsa Barkley, Brown, Rosalyn Terborg-Penn, eds., *Black Women in America: An Historical Encyclopedia* (Bloomington: Indiana University Press, 1993), pp. 1261–62.

30. *The Great Gospel Voice of Marion Williams, Accompanied by the Stars of Faith*, n.d. (Epic-BN 26175).

31. In her appearance on the PBS documentary *Amazing Grace With Bill Moyers*, Williams

introduced her rendition of the hymn with the statement that she delivers it in the "black way of singing." See Walter Goodman, "A Hymn in the Hearts of So Many for So Long," *New York Times*, September 12, 1990, C-18.

32. This view is attributed to Anthony Heilbut in John Rockwell, "Tracing Little Richard to the Source," *New York Times*, February 1, 1989, B-29.

TIMOTHY R. MANGIN

Notes on Jazz in Senegal

The study of jazz in the African diaspora has tended to focus on the retention of Africanisms in African American music[1] and the versioning of Africa in jazz.[2] The reverse influence of how U.S. jazz affects music and culture in West Africa[3] has been less well documented. Since World War II Senegalese musicians and fans have borrowed, internalized, and incorporated jazz into their popular music and culture as a way of figuring Senegalese modern identities. As former French colonial subjects, Senegalese modern identities are intertwined in complex historical and contemporary situations exacerbated by globalization processes that increasingly link Senegalese to new and different cultural, social, and political ideas from distant places. These identities are bound with Senegal's postcolonial situation, which involves the mediation of precolonial, colonial, and national histories and current relationships to the West, Middle East, and other African countries (Diouf 2002). Achille Mbembe further characterizes the postcolony as containing multiple public spaces, each with its own internal logics that engage with other logics, requiring the postcolonial subject to "bargain in this conceptual market place . . . [and] to have marked ability to manage not just a single identity, but several—flexible enough to negotiate as and when necessary" (Mbembe 2001:104). I examine how these multiple identities are mediated in the cities of Dakar and Saint-Louis, Senegal, through the appropriation of New World musics into Senegalese musics.[4]

This article is concerned with how the appropriation of U.S. jazz has been and continues to be a vital element in the representation, practice, and living of Senegalese modern identities through the mimetic performance of U.S. jazz and its internalization into Senegalese popular musics. My aim is to illuminate the ways in which local cosmopolitans learn and interpret jazz in Senegal. I shall argue that jazz is a living and vital force in Senegalese music and culture because of sustained Senegalese appropriations from French and U.S. sources since the mid-twentieth century and from local versionings of jazz in the Senegalese popular music scene. I analyze jazz events in Saint-Louis and Dakar in an attempt to illustrate how Senegalese negotiate and portray their modern identities. Further, my goal is to describe concrete processes of globalization that occur in Senegal through the lens of cosmopolitanism based on ethnographic research I conducted in Senegal (1999–2000).

Features of cosmopolitanism refers to "objects, ideas, and cultural positions that are widely diffused throughout the world and yet are specific only to certain portions of the populations within given countries" (Turino 2000:7). This dispersion of cultural products and knowledge is achieved, in part, through the spread of new technologies, media, and individuals. Travelers who have immersed themselves in different cultures share their experiences and ideas with people when they return home—and with those whom they encounter abroad (Hannerz 1996:267–41). Cosmopolitans who have not traveled outside their country are able to broaden their cultural and worldview knowledge through encounters with traveling cosmopolitans, experience with media, and use of new technologies. These interactions enable locals to imagine, contemplate, and make associations with localities beyond their immediate environment (Tomlinson 1999:194). This paper concentrates on Senegalese cosmopolitans recognition and meditation of similarities and differences of interests with people from the African diaspora.

The term *African diaspora* is distinguished from the wider debate on diaspora (which addresses issues such as migration, dispersion, exile, and postcolonialism) by emphasizing discussions on race and racial oppression such as pan-Africanism, black nationalism, and essentialism (Monson 2000a:1). African diaspora also invokes the notion of African heritage and the desire and political need for blacks outside of Africa to discover their African cultural roots as a response to racism that denied the historical and cultural value of the black experience (Gilroy 1993:112). In this essay my use of *African diaspora* concentrates on black cultures of the Caribbean, U.S., and France.

By examining how Senegalese cosmopolitans interpret and integrate U.S. black music and cultural forms we can better understand globalization processes in Africa where there is a strong ideological allegiance to U.S. blacks. The following description of a play that took place within a larger international jazz festival in Senegal will illuminate aspects of Senegalese self-perceptions within a pan-African imaginary sustained through cosmopolitan networks.

The Billy Jones Odyssey

I am in West Africa and the setting is Saint-Louis, Senegal; the date June 3, 2000. The occasion is the Saint-Louis Jazz Festival, an event spanning five days that celebrates Saint-Louis's long association with jazz in West Africa. An open-air drama called *L'Odyssée des origines* was performed by a local youth troupe from the primary and secondary schools and colleges in Saint-Louis. The play was authored and conceived by Madame d'Aquino, who collaborated with the students. Professional musicians, actors, and theater professionals accompanied these youth. The story's main character is Billy Jones, an African American jazz musician invited to perform at the festival. Jones's journey becomes a transformative experience for him in which he discovers his musical and cultural roots by immersing himself in Senegalese music, art, and culture. Scenes enacted to music, drama, and dance take place in different locations in Saint-Louis. Between scenes a *sabar* ensemble (an indigenous drum group) and *tama* drummer (an hourglass-shaped tonal drum that can mimic speech) lead a procession of Senegalese, European, and West African spectators to the different places where an act will be performed. Actors, a forty-foot-long cloth and mask serpent; performers in costumes of *moderne* and *traditionnel*[5] instruments also attend the procession, thus dissolving the space between spectacle and reality (performer and audience). Jones carries a clarinet and is dressed in a Western suit. During one of these processional interludes between scenes I am walking beside a tama player who praises and welcomes me, an African American, to Saint-Louis. I reciprocate his praise by giving him a crisp bill, in accordance with Senegalese cultural practice.

The story begins with Jones's arrival by train when peddlers sell him a drum and take him on a tour of the city. They encounter a festival of masks led by the costumed serpent and followed by a round dance, which is accompanied by sabar drumming. Jones enters a cave described in the program as a "rhythmical space" where he hears a ballad in the "universe of Saint-Louisian jazz" that suggests an "attractive and magnificent unknown." Jones is drawn further into the culture and history of Saint-Louis when a procession of *signares*[6] performs a dance honoring Mame Coumba Bak, a princess who lived near the water and yearned to know its mysteries. One day she was swallowed by an enormous shell and joined "a nothing which allows her to reach the imperceptible. Since this time, she sometimes comes out of the waters under various forms and brings protection and support to Saints-Louisians."[7]

The dance has a mesmerizing affect on Jones, and he is pushed by the performers toward the house of a signare where he sees in the "cracked walls a secret immaterial atmosphere which intoxicates this musician to look for his origins." The past and present are conflated, and Jones meets a signare from the past and an old man who was a friend of his grandfather, who relate the history of Saint-Louis. Bedazzled by the encounters, Jones goes to the river to seek solace. At this juncture the actors, dancers, and musicians perform sabar, folk (a Senegalese term for indigenous music), salsa, jazz, and fusion songs. In the finale Jones calls forth the water spirit, Mame Coumba Bak, by playing his clarinet. Upon her arrival they are joined in the acknowledgment that Jones has discovered his past and can move confidently into the future.

Inside the Odyssey

The blending of indigenous and modern cultural signs, time, and music in the play illuminates the Senegalese's perception of themselves and African Americans within the pan-African imaginary that includes the African diaspora and Africa. Characters are costumed in Senegalese *mbubb* (a dress or robe), Western suits, and as musical instruments (e.g., *kora,* bass, electric guitar, *djembe,* and sabar drums). Mythical figures such as Mame Coumba Bak, signares, and the giant serpent interact with the contemporary Jones character. Time and place are conflated to express connections across the Atlantic and continuity between the past and present in several ways. For example, Jones tours the city's historically colonial places (the governor's mansion, the signare's house, and the train station) and spiritual sites (the waterfront and the cave) where he interacts with figures and myths in the present, precolonial, and colonial past. Indigenous and Western-derived musics are combined to reveal contemporary Senegalese identities. For example, the sabar played at the round dance signifies the present and past in that it is a historical genre still vital in contemporary Senegalese culture. When sabar is combined with the rhythm section of electric bass, piano, and guitar to perform songs in salsa, jazz, and fusion styles, a major characteristic of Senegalese cosmopolitanism and modernity is invoked—the appropriation of New World styles into Senegalese music.

Jones's odyssey demonstrates the long interest Senegalese have had in jazz. Senegalese recognize the American origin of jazz but also assert their own version and ability to contribute to a pan-African jazz consciousness. For example, the program notes refer to jazz as "Afro-American," and the production itself is based on an American jazz musician discovering his African roots. When Jones enters the cave and hears a ballad from the "universe of Saint-Louisian jazz," it is an affirmation of a distinctive Senegalese jazz voice. This claim of a Senegalese jazz consciousness is based on acknowledging the African contribution to jazz and the ongoing practice of borrowing and internalizing African American music into Senegalese popular music and culture. The figure of Jones is cast as a world savvy jazz musician. He is a fictitious character based on Senegalese experiences with U.S. jazz musicians involved in the Saint-Louis Jazz Festival. The festival is an annual event in Senegal that invokes the memory of Saint-Louis as a major jazz center in West Africa from 1945–1957. There are actually two main characters here, Jones and Saint-Louis. Jones is that traveling cosmopolitan who attains awareness of his place in the world through the tutelage of Saint-Louisians; Saint-Louis is portrayed as a postcolonial city whose nexus is jazz. Complex transatlantic histories and contemporary relationships between the U.S., France, and Senegal are illuminated in the narrative, music, and dance. Saint-Louisians assert their agency as citizens of the world and decenter jazz from its U.S. base.

I now turn to a historical overview of jazz in Senegal in order to untangle complex cultural, social, and global processes that are embedded in the Billy Jones Odyssey. The following survey will examine the role of cosmopolitans in spreading, performing, and producing jazz in Senegal. I review how festivals contribute to establishing jazz as part of Senegal's urban and national character. I then analyze jazz performances in Dakar to reveal the way in which cosmopolitan interactions help to fashion a jazz voice.

Historical Overview

Early Influences (World War I–1950s)

Senegalese living in France during World War I and the interwar years were the first cosmopolitans to encounter jazz. It is likely that during World War I the music of the forty-four-piece 369th Infantry Regiment (known as the Harlem Hellfighters) jazz band, led by bandmaster James Reese Europe and drum major Noble Sissle, was heard by French and Senegalese soldiers stationed in France who returned to Senegal with jazz recordings and experiences of Reese's performances. Further, France provided an opportunity for cultural and social interactions between the French, American, and Senegalese since there were over 135,000 soldiers from French West Africa and nearly 200,000 U.S. black soldiers (Stovall 1996:1–24). During the interwar years Paris[8] became a center for jazz and meeting ground for African Americans, African Caribbeans, and French West Africans. In the 1920s jazz was extremely popular and expatriate black Americans began to make the Montmartre section of Paris home. Parisians patronized dozens of jazz clubs in Montmartre where they danced the Charleston and Black Bottom.

By the 1930s an expatriate U.S. black community was established, and many artists, writers, painters and musicians involved in the Harlem renaissance visited this community. French musicians, who were experimenting with jazz in the 1920s and sitting in with African American musicians, began to form their own groups in the 1930s. For example, in 1935 Stéphane Grappelli, Django Reinhardt, Coleman Hawkins, and Benny Carter recorded an album, *Coleman Hawkins and Benny Carter* (Stovall 1996:96). Additionally, in the1930s black students and intellectuals from French West Africa, the French West Indies, and the U.S. were meeting and exchanging ideas about art, culture, and politics in Africa, Europe, the Caribbean, and Americas. For example, Léopold Senghor wrote of the "literary salon" (1929–1934) of Jane and Andrée Nardal where he met "African negroes, West Indians, and American Negroes" (Stovall 1996:107). At these gatherings the Nardal sisters would play U.S. jazz, dance, and discuss the writings of the Harlem Renaissance (e.g., Langston Hughes, Countee Cullen, and Claude McKay), racism, and other topics. The exchange of ideas at events such as these inspired young black writers like Senghor and Aimé Césaire to found their own literary and cultural journal, *L'Etudiant Noir* (March 1935). This publication signaled the beginning of *negritude* (blackness), a philosophical black humanist movement whose driving force was to spread the knowledge of black culture and history in the world and in so doing better humankind. As Tyler Stovall (1996) notes, negritude "was a creation of French-speaking black intellectuals"(105) in a Parisian cosmopolitan community where African Americans and blacks from the French colonies interacted in jazz clubs (e.g., Bricktop's), nightclubs that featured music from the French Caribbean (e.g., Bal Négre in Montparnasse), and parlors (Stovall 1996: 82–118). Thus, in Paris, Senegalese cosmopolitans such as Senghor were broadening their cultural horizons and began to identify with an African diaspora (i.e., blacks from the U.S. and French West Indies) and develop strategies for asserting agency against racism and colonialism. Jazz was part of Senegalese students social and cultural life in Paris. This music and their political activities would play prominent roles in affecting the urban character of Senegal upon their return. For the 1940s I turn to Senegal, where Saint-Louisians and Dakaroise appropriated jazz.

In 1942 the U.S. military occupied the port city of Dakar with detachments quartered in Thiés and Saint-Louis. Sailors stationed in Dakar brought with them instruments, records, and dance styles from the U.S.. Percussionist Gana M'Bow recalls:

> I was not yet 20 years old and at that time lived in Dakar. My best friend was the chauffeur of a grand marabout.[9] When he was free my friend would come pick me up in the marabout's gigantic black Cadillac and we ploughed through the city, in every sense, to listen to this insane music which leaked out of the dashboard's radio and which "Voice of America" used to broadcast. This is how I came to know jazz. A little time after in 1943, the first contingents of the American army arrived and I constantly approached these orchestras of black American musicians to see at last who was making this crazy peoples' music and to be able to touch them and to speak with them. (LENORMAND 1996:36)[10]

M'Bow's experience with the soldiers, musicians, and U.S. radio programs led him to pursue a career as a percussionist with jazz musicians. In 1948 he moved to France and performed in Paris with French and Americans such as Pierre Michelot, René Urtreger, Percy Heath, and Kenny Clarke. M'Bow would later work in the U.S. with artists such as Max Roach and Sonny Stitt. Through the radio and interaction with soldiers, M'Bow interpreted, learned, and performed jazz. His quest led him through Paris, New York City, and Boston where he acquired new experiences and knowledge from master musicians that would change his worldview.

Saint-Louis, like Dakar, was a key center for jazz. Between 1945 and 1957 the capital of Senegal, Saint-Louis, became a major jazz hub of West Africa. It was the economic, political, and artistic center, where intellectuals, artists, businessmen, colonial administrators, soldiers, journalists, Mauritanians, Senegalese, Arabs, sabar ensembles, and griots filled the streets and clubs listening and dancing to jazz bands and orchestras. Saint-Louisian musician and local historian Marious Gouané (2002), recalls that in 1945 U.S. troops in Saint-Louis played marches and fanfares in the town square. After these pieces the band would play jazz. According to Gouané the first Saint-Louisians to begin performing jazz were the griots, who were particularly attracted to the blues and up-tempo dance pieces.

Photographs and register records from the 1940s indicate that bands such as Amicale Jazz, Saint-Louisien, and Sor Jazz (whose typical instrumentation included banjos, accordion, snare and bass drum, alto saxophones, guitar, and trumpets) imitated the performance style of New Orleans music (Lenormand 1996). Saxophonist Abdoulaye N'Diaye (son of Saint-Louisian saxophonist Barud N'Diaye) recalls "they dressed exactly like the New Orleans style. They were serious in music with the dress, ensemble, cravat and they have the same drums you see. One sock cymbal you know, that was the same you see in New Orleans" (N'Diaye 2000).

This early borrowing of music, dress, and instrumentation of New Orleans jazz style indicates three key aspects in this Senegalese appropriation. Jazz was an urban music that resonated with Saint-Louisian pride in their cosmopolitan status. Second, jazz was a music created by U.S. blacks and not French colonials. Thioub and Benga (1999:218–221) argue that the appropriation of jazz was a rupture from French hegemony and not an overt political act of resistance. These authors also claim that the colonials favored the tango, *paso doble*, French song, and waltz in their segregated clubs. However, I have shown that there are other French connections through Senegalese Parisian experiences. Finally, jazz was an urban dance music that appealed to Senegalese in the cities. In rural Senegal dance music revolves around the sabar, a drumming ensemble that features the layering of repeated interlocked rhythms. A lead drummer who will play distinct lead patterns on top of the groove directs the overall rhythmic drive. The lead drummer often solos and communicates with dancers who enter the circle, establishing a dialogue based on traditional dances and new gestures created by participants. Improvisation by the lead drummer (and dancers) consists of drawing upon an established vocabulary of patterns, which are varied and modified with new elements. New Orleans jazz and sabar are entirely different genres. However, I wish to emphasize that dance is an important part of life in Senegal and opens a space for discovering and experiencing different cultures. For example, sabar is primarily a Wolof dance, though it may incorporate rhythms of the Fulani and Serer of Senegal.

By the 1950s Senegalese were playing their version of bebop. Groups such as Star Jazz and the All Stars emerged, with talented soloists including saxophonists Baraud N'Diaye, Papa Samba Diop, and Abou Sy, trumpeter Mustapha Diop, guitarist Cheik Tidiane Tall, vocalist Aminata Fall, and bassist Ady Seck. Photographs of Senegalese bop and swing groups show ensembles of men dressed in sharp Western attire, in contrast to the New Orleans groups with their identical uniforms. The audience dressed in the same manner as the bop band members, with women in both indigenous African and Western styles. Images of African American musicians in Paris and the U.S. were shown in periodicals such as the West African magazine *Bingo*, which ran features and photographs on Lionel Hampton, Lil Armstrong, Louis Armstrong, Don Byas, Duke Ellington, Sidney Bechet, Charlie Parker, and Mary Lou Williams. The awareness by Senegalese of Western clothing style demonstrates an additional layer of monitoring of American cultural products and style as the reality of independence came closer.

In 1958, after Charles de Gaulle had come to power in France, Senegal became an autonomous republic within the French Community (the French Republic, overseas territories, overseas departments, and six independent African republics). Under the leadership of the soon to be president Léopold Sédar Senghor, Senegalese political leaders transferred all administrative and governmental business to Dakar. Due to the withdrawal of patronage by elites and government workers from Saint-Louis, the economy and jazz scene deteriorated. Between 1958–1960 Senegal was becoming an independent nation while maintaining close ties to France. Senegalese national identities were being negotiated within the dual constructs of a French allegiance and pan-Africanism. Inspired by the writings and activities of W. E. B. Du Bois and Aimé Césaire, Senghor promoted the ideologies of pan-Africanism and his concept of negritude, which emphasized *African* values and culture as a positive ideology that could benefit humanity as opposed to the negative paternal constructions of a "primitive Africa" espoused in colonialist discourse. He realized his views through his art and political career. For example, the instructions in some of Senghor's poems called for the use of traditional and modern instruments such as clarinet and *balafon,* or "jazz orchestra" (Bender 1991:32). Senegalese who had lived in Paris such as politicians Blaise Diagne and Tiémoko Garan Kouyaté (who had collaborated with pan-Africanist George Padmore) were simultaneously exposed to jazz and other black intellectuals involved in pan-African and nationalist movements. These Senegalese and soldiers returned to Senegal with burgeoning black Atlantic ideologies and experiences with jazz that they shared with family and friends.

Jazz, Salsa, Variété (1940s–1970s)

As Senegal began to form as a nation, African diasporic popular musics were more widely incorporated into Senegalese popular culture. Since the 1940s not jazz but Latin music such as the *cha-cha-chá, pachanga, rumba, paso doble, charanga, bolero, mambo* became popular with Senegalese who since the 1960s often refer to these styles as salsa. These styles were found throughout French West Africa and diffused by the record company Electrical and Musical Industries (EMI),[11] which had absorbed England's Gramophone Company Ltd. and the American company Victor. After World War II the "GV" or "Spanish" records from Havana in the 1940s and 1950s contained over two hundred titles, most of which were recorded before the war and later reissued as a bid to boost sales. It was the tune "El Manicero 'The Peanut Vendor,'" composed by Moises Simon, who combined *son* and *pregón* rhythms, that captured the imagination of Senegalese and many West African bands (Mukunda 2000:109). Additional *sones* released included "Sacudiendo mis Maracas" by Sexteto Habanero as well as other styles such as the bolero "Elixir de la Vida" by guitarist Miguel Matamoros and his Trio Matamoros and the samba "Madalena" from Banda Rico Creole. A wider range of styles were later released, such as calypsos and African popular musics from artists such as Shake Keane and the West African Swing Stars, which covered E. T. Mensah songs (Stapleton and May 1987:21).

Senegalese bands in the 1940s and 1950s such as Sor Jazz, St. Louisien Jazz, and Orchestre du Grand Diop at the Moulin Rouge nightclub in Dakar played jazz rumbas, marches, and waltzes for elites with strong cultural ties to France. By the 1950s and through the 1960s Cuban and jazz music dominated most nightclubs in Senegal's urban centers, solidifying these genres in the tastes of the general population. By the late sixties the style and repertoire of the group Khalam signaled the way in which jazz would be used in Senegalese music. Young musicians who had grown up hearing jazz and salsa now blended *traditionnel* melodies and rhythms into their songs. Eventually the practice of playing sets that combined *traditionnel*, soul, rock, salsa, African pop, and Senegalese popular music became known as *variété*. Jazz in Senegal became associated with a wider range of genres outside of what Americans would term jazz.

As the sixties progressed, 45-rpm records of popular music were brought into the country by elites who had been living in Europe. On the back of these discs were illustrations of dance steps corresponding to that record's popular music style. Thus, with the help of the traveling cosmopolitan, new dances were appropriated by Senegalese youth who turned to three styles of music. For example, Saint-Louisian Khalil Gueye recalls that parties in his youth featured three genres. First, the "long hair" kids listened to pop and rock 'n' roll played by the Doors, Rick Nelson, Johnny Hallyday, and Creedence Clearwater Revival. Second, the "slick hairs" enjoyed soul music played by such artists as Etta James and Otis Redding. Third, youth dressed in Latin American styles favored Cuban music by groups such as Orchestra Aragon, Bravo, and Ray Baretto.[12] Of these three genres salsa had proved the most resilient in sustaining a prominent space in Senegalese popular music and culture.

However, Senegal's independence in 1960 inspired Senegalese to create their own national popular music. In the late 1960s, during nightclubs' *variété* sets, Senegalese instruments were added to the prevailing instrumentation of guitar, keyboards, electric bass, horns, drums, and timbales. Sabar drums were foregrounded and their rhythms played on the keyboards and guitars, which transformed these harmonic instruments into tonal percussion. Senegalese from all social classes were drawn to the new sound. This was the birth of *mbalax*, which was the creolized expression of these genres featuring sabar rhythms. Mbalax represents a national identity based on the internalization of foreign genres (jazz, Latin music, soul, highlife, and Afro-Beat)[13] blended with indigenous music and performance practice styles to mark a cosmopolitan formation of Senegalese identity. The integration of jazz within mbalax reflects the intersection of French and African diasporic circuits maintained through musicians, elites, and cosmopolitans inflecting their experiences onto local scenes that operate on Senegalese cultural principles. As the popularity of mbalax rose as a national dance music, U.S. jazz became associated with foreign musics and was seen as a listening music.

Institutionalizing Jazz (1960s–1990s)

In 1966 the Senegalese government, led by Léopold Senghor, hosted the Festival of Negro Arts, which featured Duke Ellington,[14] Josephine Baker, Marian Anderson, Louis Armstrong (the first major U.S. jazz artist to visit Senegal in early 1960s), Ella Fitzgerald, and Catherine Dunham. The aim of the festival was to celebrate the diversity and unity of Africans and people of African descent, promote negritude, commemorate Senegal's peaceful transition to independence, and encourage a pan-African unity agenda among the newly independent African nations. The festival was a success and has continued under various names in different countries. Under Senghor's direction the government participated in sponsoring jazz musicians such as Phil Woods, Frank Foster, Irene Reid, and the All-Star

Big Band directed by Billy Taylor that featured Frank Foster, Jimmy Owens, Kenny Rodgers, and Slide Hampton playing music by Ellington and Basie. Additional sponsorship by African American organizations such as the Jackie Robinson Foundation reflected the economic and political link between African American and African institutions.

The U.S. State Department likewise sponsored jazz events, to promote American culture, with artists such as Dizzy Gillespie, Duke Ellington, Louis Armstrong, and Pharaoh Sanders. The U.S. government continues to promote jazz in Senegal through lectures, concerts, mass media events, and the Jazz Ambassador Program of International Cultural Exchange. Begun in 1998, this program is a collaboration between the John F. Kennedy Center for the Performing Arts and the United States Information Agency (USIA). The program blends the Kennedy Center's mission, "the provision of opportunities for people of all ages and backgrounds to learn about and to experience the performing arts" though "its commitment to the recognition and celebration of the rich heritage of the American people," and USIA's goal to promote "mutual understanding between the United States and other countries through a series of educational and cultural exchange activities" (Kennedy Center 1999). In 1999–2000 the group chosen for the West African leg of the Jazz Ambassadors program was a trio from Mississippi whose repertoire (e.g., Ellington, Paul Webster, John Lewis, and originals) reflected that year's theme honoring Duke Ellington's one hundredth birthday. Concerts were held at the U.S. ambassador's home and at the French Cultural Center. The group conducted a master class at the American Cultural Center and an arranged television appearance was canceled because of the station's inability to provide the necessary technical support for broadcast. Their official itinerary was restricted to venues accessible to the middle class and elite of Dakar.[15] Likewise, France promotes jazz in Senegal through its Centres Culturels Français (CCF). This program hosts many jazz, salsa, and blues concerts, providing access to literature, films, and lectures, but reaches a restricted audience.

Shortly after the Jazz Ambassadors' performance, the British and Italian embassies sponsored jazz concerts showcasing their nation's performers. The goal of these events was to promote cultural and business ties. Recognizing Senegal's history with jazz, the British and Italian embassies sought to expand Senegalese identification of the genre with a wider international arena. This was achieved by sponsoring jazz concerts in public venues with low entrance fees and programming that included collaboration between Senegalese and European musicians based on jazz-fusion styles more accessible to Senegalese. Additionally, British officials related to me that jazz was chosen to dispel Senegalese notions of Great Britain as a country without a black presence.

These instances of musical exchanges through workshops and collaborations enhance Senegalese knowledge of jazz performance practice from the West and demonstrate another example of jazz infusion. However, an ironic tension exists in that the European nations' goal of promoting their distinctive character relies on jazz's ability to articulate a pan-African black consciousness. For example, the

British use jazz as a means to advertise Great Britain's racial diversity and inclusivity. However, in the group that performed in Senegal there was only one black member. Therefore, it was the musical elements grounded in transnational exchanges and the racialized overtone of jazz that overrode the actual enactment.

Saint-Louis International Jazz Festival (1990–2000)

In 1990 Xaaban Thiam, Badou Sarr, Pape Laye Sarr, Abdu Aziz Seck, and Abdu Diallo founded the Saint-Louis Jazz Festival as a way to resuscitate the city's cosmopolitan status and in the hopes of promoting tourism and the city's international reputation through the development of cultural and artistic life in Saint-Louis. The first concert was in a garage and was followed by official Senegalese recognition and financial help from the Saint-Louis Centre Culturel Français (CCF) in 1991. In 1992 the CCF took over the festival, which created discontent among Senegalese because ticket prices rose beyond the general population's ability to pay and the five founders' input was reduced. In response to popular pressure and press criticism, an alliance was formed in 1993 between the Senegalese organizers and the CCF. In 1999 complete control was given to a newly formed Senegalese association. The founders' goal of creating an internationally recognized institution that would revitalize the economic and cultural life of Saint-Louis was partially realized, but because of the CCF financial and administrative pull-out the festival suffered from the lack of technical support, sponsorship, and organizational experience.

During the festival hotels are filled to capacity, and families rent out space to visitors at elevated prices, thus boosting the local economy. Attendees are largely Europeans, nongovernmental organization employees working in West Africa, Senegalese and returned Senegalese immigrants, students, bureaucrats, professionals, and academics. Nightclubs and restaurants with names such as the Blue Note and Marco Jazz provide venues for off-duty musicians to collaborate.

The festival lasts three days between late May and early June in order to coincide with school and European vacations. Performances are spread throughout the island Ndar (Saint-Louis), with headlining acts confined to the "in," or main stage, where tickets are required, and all other performances to the "off" stages, which are free to the public. For Senegalese it is crucial to have an American artist present. American guests in the past have included Jack DeJohnette, Herbie Hancock, Archie Schepp, McCoy Tyner, Jimmy Johnson, Hal Singer, Joe Zawinul, Steve Coleman, Johnny Griffin, Liz McComb, Elvin Jones, and David Murray. Other nations, primarily from the francophone countries, supply the bulk of performers, such as groups led by Lorraine Desmarais (Quebec, Canada), Nathalie Loriers (Belgium), Hervé Meshinet (France), Olivier Temime (France), Robert Jeanne (Belgium), Manu Dibango (Cameroon/Paris), Xabaan Thiam (Senegal), Ray Lema (Zaire), and Moncef Genoud (Switzerland). The use of many European and white performers instead of black artists indicates a paradox to my argument. This situation reflects a wider imagining that "authentic" jazz is best performed by African Americans. However, contemporary jazz is a global phenomenon performed by many people, as is evidenced by the presence of numerous European artists in the festival. Further, I suggest that it is the image of jazz as a sign of African American allegiance with Africa and these musical links that are relevant in this context.

Main stage concerts begin at 9:00 P.M., while *off* stage performances (free to the public) are held throughout the day and feature local mbalax, fusion, jazz, and Afro-Beat groups. Programming foreign performers on the main stage and Senegalese on the off stage caused tension among Senegalese musicians and patrons. Organizers respond that the *création*, collaboration between African, American, and European artists, sometimes based on a few days of rehearsals, is a sufficient answer to this criticism. *Créations* have included collaborations of African musicians with the African Project in 2000; Olivier Temime Quartet (France), Kayou Band (Cameroon), and Yande Codou (Senegal) in 1999; Harmattan (Senegal) in 1998; and Steve Coleman and the Five Elements with members of Afro-Cuba de Matanzas and conguero, Miguel "Anga" Diaz in 1997.[16] Collaboration also occurs in workshops and jam sessions in Dakar and Saint-Louis between festival musicians and Senegalese. These informal settings provide an opportunity for the exchange of knowledge about African and international styles, rhythmic concepts, as well as Western jazz performance practice. Jazz for Senegalese becomes an international music that can be appropriated, commodified, and used to express their modern voice among francophone countries as well as a pan-African imaginary that includes French West Africa, America, and Europe. For Senegalese, then, jazz is "world music," an international phenomenon that provides a nexus in which to participate in the global sphere.[17]

Additionally, these collaborations illustrate how cosmopolitans from afar broaden the cultural and musical horizons of local cosmopolitans. As John Tomlinson states "the first characteristic of cosmopolitanism, then is a keen grasp of a globalized world as one in which 'there are no others'"(Tomlinson 1999:194). Distance between different cultural and musical positions is diminished by the use of jazz as a musical medium. The performers rely on musical elements such as syncopation, polyrhythms and rhythmic complexity, collective improvisation, repetition, and a vocal and melodic quality associated with the blues.[18] Wedded to these musical elements are similar performance practice dynamics that vary according to locale yet retain core features important to musicians and audiences such as the layering of grooves to maintain improvisatory and musical space for communication between instrumentalists and audience.

The inclusion of francophone circuits in understanding the formation of Senegalese modern identities (e.g., colonial policies, an elite with close ties to France that disseminates jazz and pan-African ideology, and the inclusion of francophone musicians and concomitant political clashes in the Saint-Louis Jazz Festival) broadens Paul Gilroy's conceptualization of the black Atlantic (1993), which focuses on the construction of black, modern, transnational identities of Britain, North America, and the Caribbean. For Gilroy one aspect of black modern identity elaborates the way in which the residual horrors of slavery and imperialism expressed in black music "contribute to historical memories inscribed and incorporated into the volatile core of Afro-Atlantic cultural creation" (73). This resonates with Hervé Lenormand and the Association Saint-Louis Jazz's history of jazz in

Senegal (1996:7–13), which cites a history of violence as one of the primary factors for the birth of jazz in the U.S. and its dissemination into Senegal, where locals understood the genre's relationship to slavery, racism, colonialism, and wars. Further, the expansion of jazz into popular Senegalese culture as a result of U.S. military occupation, influence of elites, government sponsorship, and integration into nightclub performances demonstrates a musical continuum that harkens back to Senegambians shipped to French Louisiana in the seventeenth century.[19] As new technologies and media facilitate the spread of information and travel between global cities increases, jazz in Senegal becomes a way to negotiate evolving modern identities in the African diaspora in the twenty-first century.

Interpreting Jazz

Three performance types characterize the live jazz scene in Dakar: jazz is included during a *variété* set,[20] small jazz ensembles perform bop, post-bop, blues, modal, and fusion standards, and the most widespread diffusion of jazz takes place in the first three to four songs an mbalax group will play (usually originals and fusion such as Joe Zawinul's "Mercy, Mercy, Mercy") before their lead singer enters the stage, after which the band plays solely mbalax tunes. Additional jazz has been disseminated through television programs, movies, radio, CDs, LPs, and cassettes. In the following sections I focus on Senegalese musicians' interpretations of American jazz, Senegalese imaginings of jazz, and the influence of cosmopolitans in the Dakar jazz scene.

Jazz and Sabar: Jammin' at Club Alizé

Jazz in Dakar nightclubs is influenced by locally trained musicians and cosmopolitan Senegalese who travel, work, and study abroad, accumulating social and cultural knowledge that they internalize and, upon return to Senegal, share with local cosmopolitans. Nightclub manager Tanor Diang explains the spread of jazz as involving

> people who were studying overseas, I mean France or in the States or the intellectual people used to listen to jazz music for a long long time before the sixties. In the time of Billie Holiday or Louis Armstrong, those kinds of great musicians since then they listened to jazz. And a lot of jazz musicians from the States came and performed here. People listened to it and the students at the University when they listen to music it is mostly jazz and that's why jazz is very expansive here. Dakar is the capital of jazz in West Africa. . . . Having friends all over the world wherever they play jazz they bring the CD or cassettes. You never get into a car with a cassette without listening to jazz music. (DIANG 2000)

Diang identifies a cosmopolitan network between France, Senegal, and the U.S., which is traversed by musicians, students, elites, and intellectuals. Senegalese cosmopolitans in this network listen, internalize, and then share their knowledge of jazz among friends and family in Dakar, contributing to the development of a Senegalese jazz sensibility.

Diang continues:

> We feel like jazz belongs a little bit to us. It seems like it was coming from here. The way the *beat* is, the complaint, the singers. We feel close to jazz, we feel it when we listen to jazz. Even if 99% don't speak English, they don't know what the singer is saying, what is interesting is that they feel the beat of jazz. Dixieland or any type of jazz, they feel it. (DIANG 2000)

Diang recognizes jazz as a transnational phenomenon with African roots and voice.[21] Diang's emphasis on the beat and melodic qualities of jazz as musical elements Senegalese can associate with (beyond an understanding of song texts) demonstrates an understanding of Senegal's incorporation of jazz into their popular music over time and to historic syncretic practices from the New World based on West African music elements such as those embedded in the ring shout (Floyd 1995:7, 35–48). A brief biographical sketch of Diang will illuminate characteristics of a Senegalese cosmopolitan influencing the Dakar jazz scene.

In the 1970s Diang attended New York University and immersed himself in the jazz culture of Greenwich Village. Diang vividly recalls the night he attended a jazz club on Seventh Avenue in New York City, where the headlining act was Stan Getz. Later in the evening Jimmy Owens walked in and jammed with Getz's band. The magic of that night and similar ones remained with Diang, and thus he has instituted a nightly live music jam session at his nightclub Alizé. His idea was to have an "after-work" party modeled on the U.S. "happy hour." The goal was to provide an environment in which people could relax, socialize, and negotiate business. "The Senegalese beat [mbalax] is too jumpy, you see. And to make those people relax and so on, jazz was the real music I felt like giving to them. In my own opinion the best music to relax to is jazz, it's a listening music. I've been into jazz a long long time" (Diang 2000). Diang created an environment in which musicians could improvise, experiment with new forms, and have regular gigs, thus addressing his and some musicians' resentment of mbalax's "stranglehold" over musical life in Dakar. Diang's after-work party is a result of his elite cosmopolitan experience in New York that in turn influences local Senegalese cosmopolitans' awareness of practices abroad and fosters an environment for interchanges that further the sharing of knowledge.

Mbalax's domination in popular music in Senegal stemmed from the creation of the genre as an articulation of Senegal's independence. The genre is based on sabar rhythms blended with Cuban, jazz, and Afro-pop styles. Sabar embodies the history of feasts, harvests, and celebration of life cycle events. It is most frequently performed at women's events where community issues can be mediated. Men dance to sabar at wrestling matches (*lamb*) and community youth events (*simb*). In the nightclub the dynamics and utility of sabar changes under the rubric of mbalax. Men dance with women and no longer are individuals restricted to dancing specific dances to sabar rhythms.

In Diang's club jazz evenings become forums for improvisatory experiments in which different styles are blended, syncretized, and developed. For example, Tuesday nights at Alizé are called *Soirée Senegalaise* and feature mbalax. The evenings begin around 8:30 P.M. with cocktails and recorded jazz on the stereo. Usually upper-middle-class businessmen, government workers, Senegalese who have been living abroad, and young women socialize. At 9:00 P.M. a jazz or improvisation ensemble performs. The musicians are most often members of popular mbalax bands who have formed ensembles to explore jazz. The repertoire from one such group, Fenni Fare (mbalax musicians in Omar Pene's band), includes tunes frequently heard in Dakar such as "Billie's Bounce," "Donna Lee," "Misty," and a funk tune. Often Senegalese musicians substitute chord progressions during the solo sections, as, for example, blues changes played during the solo passages of "Donna Lee."

In general there is a lack of knowledge of U.S. jazz theory and repertoire. Senegalese bandleaders who have studied and performed under knowledgeable musicians such as Americans Sam Sanders and David Murray improvise close to a song's chord changes, and sets consist of diverse repertoire. For example, Abdoulaye N'Diaye's sets consisted of a twelve-bar blues "I Remember April," "Stella by Starlight," "All Blues," "Fifth House," "Impressions," "Darn that Dream," "Beautiful Love," "Body and Soul," "Nardis," and some free improvisation. N'Diaye learned U.S. approaches to jazz through his apprenticeship with the U.S. jazz musicians Murray and Sanders when they visited, worked, and performed in Dakar. N'Diaye and other musicians take this knowledge from their sessions with the Americans and share it with other local musicians who have similar but different experiences, thus creating a local habitus that will share some similar characteristics with other jazz locals.

By 12:00 A.M. patrons dressed in both indigenous and Western-style clothing arrive for the mbalax set which feature dancing to the recorded hits of Senegal's popular stars. At 3:00 A.M. the dance floor clears and an MC entertains the audience with jokes and announcements followed by a popular salsa, mbalax or rap artist who lip-synchs a song they are promoting. Around 3:30 A.M. sabar drummers enter and perform a combination of standard sabar repertoire (e.g., *ceebu gen*) with modern instrumentation such as a keyboardist playing jazz riffs and melodies lines from Dave Brubeck's "Take Five" in duple time as opposed to the original's meter in five/four. As the evening progresses a circle forms, standard sabar repertoire is performed without electronic accompaniment, and dancers from the audience enter the space one at a time, usually in *mbubb*. When women are in European clothing they borrow a wrap for their hips. The dancing involves one person locked in dialogue with one drummer. Successive dancers comment or compete on previous dancer's performance via more energetic or expressive movements, often creating new dances and gestures. This is a re-creation of the sabar circle (*guew bi*) in which *tassu* (a partially improvised praise singing), dancing, and drumming is involved throughout Senegal.

This example demonstrates a particular way in which jazz becomes part of Senegalese popular culture. The sabar drummers and musicians influenced by the early jazz set and recordings played at Alizé take these influences, alter them according to their own aesthetics, and then experiment with them within traditional sabar performance practice aesthetics. The nightclub is a liminal space in which patrons may or may not transgress boundaries and moral codes, such as prohibitions against smoking and drinking in a country that is 91 percent Muslim. Later these experiences are internalized and incorporated in varying degrees in sabar and mbalax performances inside and outside the club. Diang's after-work party allows musicians to experiment with American jazz repertoire, incorporate that knowledge into their playing, and develop their own styles. These musicians then perform in different venues and reach a wider audience in the network of the Dakar nightclub scene. For example, within walking distance to Alizé are three nightclubs that cater to a less affluent audience and wider network of musicians that often includes players from Alizé. In this scene Senegalese musicians who have been traveling abroad with mbalax bands on the world music circuit frequently sit in and jam with various groups. These musicians and those from Alizé will collaborate and share their knowledge within a more culturally and musically restrained club scene that caters and adheres to the working-class Senegalese who do not desire too much innovation.

Cosmopolitans such as Senegalese elites, soldiers, and musicians spread jazz and their cultural knowledge of foreign places in Dakar and Saint-Louis thus influencing Senegalese popular culture and music. However, in the nightclubs jazz was blended with local music styles and other African American musics to create mbalax, which emerged as the primary signifier of Senegalese national identity. Today Senegalese claim jazz as both part of their heritage and as a vital link to modernity in the black Atlantic. Local cosmopolitan musical and cultural horizons are expanded because of the frequent collaborations in the nightclubs of Dakar and events such as the Saint-Louis jazz festival. These collaborations amongst Senegalese musicians and U.S. musicians are mediated within working-class clubs that foreground Senegalese musical and cultural tastes. In the following section I focus on jazz performances in the Dakar nightclubs Toolu Buur and Sunrise Jazz. I reveal how complex historical processes contribute to contemporary performances of jazz through cosmopolitan interactions.

Jazz and Mbalax: Sunrise Jazz Club

Near Alizé are three nightclubs: Sahel, Toolu Buur, and Sunrise Jazz. In the 1970s Sahel was the first modern nightclub built to accommodate the emerging mbalax groups, as it still does today, although it also accommodates hip hop and other dance musics. Connected to Sahel is Sunrise Jazz club, a small space that features jazz, *variété*, Afro-pop, and mbalax. Toolu Buur is across the parking lot and is known for salsa, salsa/mbalax, and mbalax. Unlike Alizé, the clientele is lower to middle class, since these clubs have lower entrance fees and free admission on certain nights. This zone attracts and books a wide range of artists. The atmosphere in the area welcomes musicians to sit in on each others' sets. One group where musicians frequently sit in is Dieuf Dieul.

Dieuf Dieul named their style "Mandingo mbalax," yet fans refer to it as "jazz mbalax." Dieuf Dieul is influenced by Afro-Beat and musicians such as Jimi Hendrix, George Benson, Lee Ritenour, David Murray, and Miles Davis. The following narrative from my fieldwork typifies the flow of events at a Dieuf Dieul performance. The set begins with a quartet of bass, drums, keyboard, and guitar playing original compositions characterized by theme statement, solos, and another theme statement. Solos are not improvised within fixed song forms (e.g., AABA or AAB) but begin and end with statements of themes by the lead instruments when the soloist within the collective communicates sufficient tension or trajectory signaling the conclusion of his solo.[22] After two songs, alto saxophonist Abdoulaye N'Diaye joins the group, utilizing phrases and patterns found in U.S. jazz.[23] By the fifth song, the "jazz set" is over and the emphasis is now on mbalax, when a vocalist and two sabar drummers join the group. The sabar players fuse *modern* grooves with traditional rhythms based on mbalax. The singer's vocals (mostly in Tukulor) are melismatic and slightly nasal, reflecting Senegal's long association with the Arab north. A tama player joins the ensemble and the overall sound emphasizes the percussion over harmonic progressions that are reflected in audience members dancing improvised steps in duet with the lead drummer. The evening's energy level increases as more dancers engage the percussionists, particularly when a sabar plays a *bakk,* the highly demarcated solo passage in which the player improvises and "says something." Throughout the night guest musicians and singers sit in adding their voices to the collective while appreciative audience members give money to the singers and drummers who have taken them to higher levels.

This performance reveals nuances of Senegalese perceptions of jazz. When the sabar drummers began, the other instrumentalists considered the jazz set finished because they were relegated to performing mostly accompanying repetitious phrases. However, audience members still considered the mbalax jazzy because the instrumentalists occasionally took lengthy improvisatory solos and used dissonant harmonies such as diminished chords as opposed to other mbalax groups who refrain from extended solos and dense chords. Additionally, there were performance characteristics common to U.S. jazz used during the mbalax set such as repetition of phrases, riffs, call and response, extensive use of hemiolas, polyrhythms, musicians sitting in, and intense communication between dancers and drummers. Further, Senegalese drummers, musicians, and dancers were engaged in musical dialogues reminiscent of U.S. tap dancers and big bands and lindy hopping in ballrooms (Malone 1998).

How do Senegalese musicians perceive jazz? Dieuf Dieul's musical director and keyboardist Nankou Sembene explains:

> Jazz is more complete than other music. The possibility of jazz. Senegalese music depends mainly on the rhythms, percussions. With the rhythms, par exemple, the instruments do not really really express [things] because there are rhythms and the singers on it. Because there is not very very long times when people in Senegal started to know piano, organ, guitar. Before we know the *balafon,* the *kora,* the *xalam,* the flute. Even today there are instruments that we cannot play well, that's why, because of this, a young country, jazz [is important], we need to listen, to listen to jazz . . . to learn

and, with this knowledge, to join with African music. We can show to all the people, you know. With this we can have a nice knowledge.

(SEMBENE 2000)

For Sembene jazz is a music whose meanings are submerged (compared to mbalax) under dense harmonies and performance practices not common to Senegalese popular music.[24] When these jazz practices are blended with indigenous music a fusion can emerge that expresses a modern Senegalese identity characterized by the historical and present ambitions to incorporate music and cultural dimensions from the African diaspora into local cultural expressions.

Dieuf Dieul and David Murray

The Dieuf Dieul performance analyzed above followed a concert for the UNESCO summit on education held in Dakar. Many of the musicians for that concert were members of Dieuf Dieul and guest soloists at Sunrise Jazz. U.S. composer, band leader, and saxophonist David Murray, who has been collaborating with Senegalese musicians since 1996, selected, rehearsed, and directed the musicians for the April 28 UNESCO date. Instrumentation included a *kora* (twenty-one-string harp-lute), *balon* (five-string bass harp), a Fulani flute, Wolof and Jola sabar drums, guitar, voice, and alto and soprano saxophone. Matters of tuning and strategies for leaving space open for performers during solos were based on Murray's aesthetic as a jazz musician. For example, since there were indigenous African instruments with limited tuning ranges blending with chromatic instruments, issues of tuning were complex. For Murray the instruments were "out of tune," whereas for the other musicians texture and rhythm took precedence over intonation. Murray's consistent guidance on the nuances of tuning during the UNESCO rehearsals resulted in the musicians who performed later that evening at Sunrise Jazz taking additional time to tune up. This example represents one way in which a U.S. jazz musician influences practice at the local level.

There is a tension between the primacy of rhythm, as an essential cultural marker of Senegalese identity,[25] and harmony as an identifying marker of jazz and transatlantic modernity. For Senegalese, rhythms can represent specific aspects of their lives, since drumming occurs at multiple community events and is entrenched in performances that negotiate and articulate people's existence. For example, the tonal character of drums such as the tama may imitate speech as well as convey messages. In sabar performances I have witnessed, tamas immediately repeat the sonorities and rhythms of spoken text by griots. In griot recordings such as *Keepers of the Talking Drum* (see Mangin 1999) or on cassettes by Salam Diallo such as *Soirée Senegalaise* one can hear drums repeating spoken phrases.[26] This close relationship between rhythm and meaning marks a nuanced similarity and difference between jazz and Senegalese popular music that Murray conceptualizes in terms of "language" and "languageness":

We [African Americans] have a language inside of our music. In most African music the rhythms are words, expressions, meanings, and codes. Our language [U.S. English]—maybe because our language was never our own—is not in our music, especially now in jazz . . . so we are *mixing a languageness with a music that is language*. Like, there we have big similarity and a great big difference. The differences are bigger than the similarities in that regard. (MURRAY 2000; EMPHASIS MINE)

For Murray, Senegalese rhythms contain more direct referential meanings to society and culture, which differs from U.S. jazz, which communicates ideas further divorced from spoken language. Murray's "languageness" in U.S. jazz is in fact an aspect of the complex relationship between language and music used to mediate and express twentieth-century African American and American culture and society (see Monson 1996).

Further, when Murray clams that the "language was never our own" there is resentment and a sense of loss over the disconnection from Africa due to violence and racial oppression from the New World slave trade—a condition that many black cultures across the Atlantic share (Gilroy 1993:80–81).

Murray broadens his discussion of similarities and differences in his experiences with Senegalese musicians to improvisation. He continues:

A lot of times the concept of improvisation in African music is not as far advanced as in jazz. Like a guy will play what he knows in African music, but not so much, they won't play what they don't know. In jazz we'll play the stuff we know, but great improvisers will jump off a cliff and go into an area that he don't know nothing about and land on his feet. I'm trying to get the African musicians to jump off that cliff too. . . . I want them to build a world around themselves. It would be great if they could do that more often. . . . The drummers build a base for us to build our improvisation on. In the end sometimes it ends up being that. And then you bring them into it by doing that. After awhile it becomes infectious and then they might get it that way. Once they hear something they can copy it and say "Yeah, OK." But a lot of African people want to tell you that this is a rhythm from this country and we have to play it right and they don't want to mess it up. "This rhythm is from Mali." You talk to Mor Thiam, or somebody like that, "This rhythm is from the Ivory Coast, and this rhythm is from South Africa." And their language is [in] that, but don't mess it up. So, me, I wanna mess it up. (MURRAY 2000)[27]

Recognizing that Senegalese and American musicians take a different approach to performing, Murray descends into the music and drumming with his "languageness," communicating on sonic levels created from different perceptual origins but relying on the percussionists to establish a common ground for improvisations. When mutual understanding is achieved, ideas are presented, copied, and varied. In this instance rhythm is used as a way to bridge different conceptions of performing jazz and facilitate the influence of U.S. jazz into contemporary Senegalese music. Additionally, two goals within this black Atlantic exchange are actualized. First, Senegalese musicians can realize their desire to explore international musics and second, Murray is able to pursue his artistic and political agendas. He aims to create

> African American music mixed with African music to come together to make a meeting point, not something that is a slogan but something real . . . something that is totally different than what we could do alone. Joint forces. I'm looking for a total meeting. I don't want to fuse, I've tried other fusions, but to me that would be the most powerful music that I can think of, the best African music with the best jazz. I'm not interested in going to Cuba and mixing, I mean that's been done. I'm not from Cuba; I'm from somewhere in Africa. I'd just like to find that place and know that I've touched home. Look, I went to a place where I'm supposed to be from. I went to find the face of my mother, the face of my father, and to find out where the fuck I'm coming from, doing the roots. Doing the roots thing trying to find out where my people are coming from. Just like what you're doing. You're trying to find out where you come from and then when you see the face of your mother you say, "OK I probably came from here." You see the face of your grandmother, you see and say, "Oh yeah. maybe I came from here, all right."   (MURRAY 2000)

Africa as home is a powerful idea in African American culture. U.S. jazz musicians have been mediating this and other aspects of Africa imaginings in music from accounts of musicians who remember Congo Square in New Orleans to musicians who visit and live in Africa or mediate the idea of Africa in their music today (Weinstein 1993). Even though Murray was born in the U.S. and now lives in France, Africa remains a powerful imaginary home, his "roots," where he seeks the knowledge and connection to his origins that Billy Jones found in Saint-Louis or that Senegalese feel in their mbalax and sabar rhythms. Murray's spiritual, political, and personal quests provide an example of contemporary transnational flows centered on the idea of a black Atlantic realized through music. Through performing a mixture of Senegalese music and jazz, recording the CD, *Fo Deuk Revue* (Where are you from), traveling and working in Senegal, and equitably distributing publishing rights among the composers of *Fo Deuk,* Murray aims to create an idiom that reflects the current situation of cosmopolitans in the African diaspora and West Africa, an idiom informed by greater access to information through new technologies and media. Likewise, musicians in Dakar, Senegal, are involved in similar processes of collaborations with U.S. artists such as Murray and in the appropriation of New World musics such as jazz to articulate their modern identities.

This essay explores multiple ways that Senegalese have borrowed, interpreted, and incorporated jazz in their popular music and culture. Examination of historical and contemporary appropriations reveals complex mediations of Senegalese modern identities (e.g., black, French, African, and cosmopolitan). Additionally, jazz has become more than just a genre; it is an imaginary where the ideas of roots, pan-Africanism, and connection to the West are celebrated. With its institutionalization by governmental organizations and national festivals, jazz is identified with Senegalese society and the world of nations. Through cosmopolitan interactions in Saint-Louis and Dakar, jazz continues to be integrated into local pop musics, such as mbalax, and performed as a distinctive genre in its own right. In this way Senegalese musicians not only enhance their musical knowledge but introduce new material to the public. Today Senegalese claim jazz as both part of their heritage and as a vital link to modernity in the black Atlantic.

NOTES

1. Africanisms in American music and culture has long been a topic in ethnomusicology (cf. Dauer 1985; Floyd 1995; Herskovits 1941; Maultsby 1990; Nketia 1974a; Waterman 1952; Wilson 1974).

2. See for example, Monson (2000b) and Weinstein (1993).

3. Scholarship on jazz in Africa has concentrated on the Southern hemisphere (cf. Ballantine 1993; Coplan 1985; Turino 2000). For recent scholarship on jazz in Senegal, see Benga (2002) and Thioub and Benga (1999).

4. Ethnomusicological writings have discussed one aspect of appropriation in popular music from the stance of Western pop stars using world music in respect and admiration while benefiting financially and professionally from an unequal power relationship afforded through major recording artists under contract with large music corporations (cf. Born and Hesmondhalgh 2000; Feld 1994a, 1994b; Taylor 1997). I use appropriation from the reverse flow, that is, Senegalese musicians incorporating Western musics to their benefit and as a way to articulate their cultural identies.

5. In this work I use italics and French spellings to indicate Senegalese common usage of the terms *moderne* and *traditionnel* to distinguish between new and Western-derived items (e.g., the synthesizer) and older indigenous items (e.g., the *kora*). These issues point to a rich discourse on the modern/traditional dichotomy (cf. Coplan 1991; Turino 2000; Waterman 1990b) that I cannot address here because of lack of space.

6. Senegalese métisse women from the colonial period were renowned for their beauty and entrepreneurship. *Signares* were often the partners of colonial administrators estranged from their wives in Europe.

7. "Au hazard des rues chargées d'histoire et de culture, / il est plongé dans une rêverie fantastique où se mêlent l'éphémère, / le chimérique et l'énigmatique empreint d'histoire. Un soir, presque ivre de tant de jouissances, il joue un morceau de musique. Soudain, il voit, il entend, émergeant des eaux, une très belle femme. C'est peut-être la mythique Mame Coumba Bak! En ce temps là et ce temps là est très loin, Mame Comba Bak, la déesse des eaux protectrice de la ville de N'Dach n'était autre qu'une jeune princesse. Elle vivait entre ocean et fleuve. Tiraillée entre le désir de découvrir le monde du silence et l'insoutenable légèreté de la vie terrestre, elle est brusquement avalée par un énorme coquillage. Elle se retrouve alors dans un univers merveilleux et fascinant. Elle a enfin rejoint le rien, ce rien qui lui permet d'atteindre l'insaisissable. Depuis ce temps, elle sort parfois des eaux sous différentes formes et apporte protection, soutien aux Saints-Louisiens. Billy Jones pourra-t-il la rencontrer? Sa musique est un

appel, une complainte mélancolique, une plainte qui enivrera même l'incroyable, l'in- saisissable Mame Coumba Bak." R. D'Aquino, program notes, *L'Odyssée des origines*, June 3, 2000, Saint-Louis, Senegal.

8. Much of the material discussed in this section comes from Tyler Stovall's *Paris Noir* (1996).

9. Marabout is a Senegalese Islamic leader.

10. "Je n'avais pas vingt ans et je vivais à ce moment là à Dakar. Mon meilleur ami était le chauffeur d'un grand marabout. Dés que ce dernier le libérait, mon ami passait me prendre avec le gigantesque Cadillac noire du marabout et nous sillonnions la ville en tous sens, pour écouter cette musique insensée qui sortait de la radio du tableau de bord et que diffusait "La Voix de l'Amérique". C'est ainsi que j'ai connu le jazz. Peu de temps aprés, en 1943, sont arrivés les premiers contingents de l'armeé américaine, et je n'ai eu de cesse d'appocher ces orchestres de musiciens noirs américans, pour voir, enfin ceux qui faisaient cette musique de fous et pouvoir les toucher, leur parler." Lenormand 1996:36.

11. EMI was formed during the Great Depression in June 1931 from a merger between the Columbia Graphophone company and the Gramophone Company Ltd., both of which were British registered but mostly owned by American interests such as RCA Victor. These labels had already absorbed the French Pathe label, Lindstrom (owner of the Par- lophone label), and other Latin American companies in the 1920s as well as the famous logo of a dog listening to a gramophone, a trademark known as "His Master's Voice."

12. Personal communication of Khalil Gueye, radio DJ, television host, and producer, and communications director for USIS. Similar comments were made to me by Senegalese during fieldwork.

13. Afro-Beat arose in the 1960s as a blend of Ghanaian and Nigerian dance band highlife, jazz, and soul. In the 1970s Nigerian Fela Anikulapo Kuti and his group Africa '70 de- veloped Afro-Beat by infusing it with deep Yoruba phrases and political critique. Afro- Beat became a powerful national popular music that reached far beyond Nigeria's bor- ders.

14. See Ellington (1973:337–39) for his description of performance. Lenormand (1996:26) suggests repertoire such as "Ko Ko," "Black, Brown, and Beige," "Black Beauty," "Black and Tan Fantasy," "A Drum Is a Woman," "Creole Rhapsody," "Sophisticated Lady," "Ebony Rhapsody," and "Liberian Suite." Likewise, Ousman Socé (1955/93) and Weinstein (1993:37–47) provide insightful fictional accounts of Ellington's relation- ship to Africa.

15. Unofficially, the group visited but did not perform at Sunrise Jazz.

16. Other collaborations have included the 1996 performance of the Conservatoire Na- tional de Musique Douta Seck Orchestra, trained by guitarist Pierre van Domaël (France) and saxophonist Pierre Vaïana (Belgium) in 1994–1995.

17. There is an emerging literature and discourse on world music that examines the cultur- al politics, marginalization, and commodification of non-Western music in the global market (cf. Feld 1994a; Feld 1994b; Meintjes 1990; Taylor 1997). Also, *world music* is popularly used as a marketing term for non-Western music or music of ethnic minori- ties. My use of and play on *world music,* in this case, is broad and intended to describe how jazz allows Senegalese to engage with musicians and musics throughout the world.

18. See Kubik (2000) for a detailed discussion regarding U.S., Caribbean, and Africa con- nections on the blues.

19. Senegambians during the trans-Atlantic slave trade refer to people from the Greater

Senegambian region that includes present-day Senegal, Guinea Bissau, Gambia, and parts of Mali, Mauritania, and Guinea Conakry. Boubacar Barry argues that any investigation of Senegal during the slave trade must be contextualized within this Senegambian zone (Barry 1998).

20. For example, vocalist and drummer Pape Niang sets include "Ruby My Dear" (resembling Thelonius Monk's version), an instrumental, Roberta Flack's version of "Killing Me Softly" sung in English with a reggae back beat, Stevie Wonder's "I Just Called to Say I Love You," "When the Saints Go Marching In," sung in imitation of Louis Armstrong, a *mbalax* tune, an acapella intro with a 2 + 3 clave beat followed by *sabar* drumming.

21. One way of viewing this phenomenon is described by Samuel Floyd as cultural memory (1995:8–10). Floyd defines cultural memory as "a repository of meanings that comprise the subjective knowledge of a people, its immanent thoughts, its structures, and its practices; these thoughts, structures and practices are transferred and understood unconsciously but become conscious and culturally objective in practice and perception" (8). However, as I have shown, Senegalese have been listening to jazz, rhythm and blues, soul, salsa, and blues since the 1940s; therefore the vocal "sentiments" and feelings that Diang refers to include the appropriations of U.S. black music as they work in Senegalese black Atlantic imaginations.

22. Most urban popular musicians are male.

23. N'Diaye's first studied under his father Baraud N'Diaye, a jazz saxophonist influenced by Ben Webster and Lester Young. Subsequent studies were at the Ecole National des Artes (with an unnamed Russian), followed by intense tutelage under Detroit saxophonist Sam Sanders where N'Diaye learned Charlie Parker solos ("Billie's Bounce," "Donna Lee," "Confirmation," "Dewey Square," and "Yardbird Suite"). N'Diaye also learned John Coltrane solos (by ear and from books) and remarked to me during a rehearsal how he was influenced by Coltrane's rhythmic variations of melodic phrases.

24. In general Senegalese musicians do not read music or intensively study Western jazz harmony and performance practices. However, Sembene (and Senegalese musicians who have studied under Sam Sanders) constantly seek information on jazz performance from locals and visiting artists.

25. There is a plethora of scholarly material that discusses how music and rhythms are integral to West African society and culture (cf. Bebey 1975; Chernoff 1979; Nketia 1974b; Waterman 1990a).

26. For an analysis of drumming and speech in *sabar* see Patricia Tang (2001).

27. See Robert Kauffman's essay on African rhythm for analysis of Leopold Senghor's use and conceptualization of rhythm in African life (Kauffman 1980:401).

WORKS CITED

Ballantine, Christopher. 1993. *Marabi Nights: Early South African Jazz and Vaudeville*. Johannesburg.

Barry, Boubacar. 1998. *Senegambia and the Atlantic Slave Trade*. Cambridge: Cambridge University Press.

Bebey, Francis. 1975. *African Music: A Peoples Art*. New York: Hill.

Bender, Wolfgang. 1991. *Sweet Mother: Modern African Music*. Chicago: University of Chicago Press.

Benga, Ndiouga Adrien. 2002. "Dakar et ses tempos: Signification et enjeux de la musique urbaine (c. 1960–années 1990)." *Le Sénégal contemporain, hommes et sociétés*. Edited by M.-C. Diop, pp. 289–308. Paris: Karthal.

Born, Georgina, and David Hesmondhalgh, eds. 2000. *Western Music and Its Others: Differences, Representation, and Appropriation in Music*. Berkeley: University of California Press.

Chernoff, John Miller. 1979. *African Rhythm and African Sensibility: Aesthetics and Social Action in African Muiscal Idioms*. Chicago: University of Chicago Press.

Coplan, David. 1985. *In Township Tonight! South Africa's Black City Music and Theatre*. London: Longmans.

——— 1991. "Ethnomusicoloy and the Meaning of Tradition." *Ethnomusicology and Modern Music History*. Chicago: University of Illionois Press.

Dauer, A. M. 1985. *Tradition afrikanischer Blasorchester und Entstehung des Jazz*. Graz: Akademische Druck- u. Verlagsanstalt.

Diang, Tanor. 2000. Interview by author. Dakar. May 1.

Diouf, Mamadou. 2002. "Des Cultures Urbaines entre Traditions et Mondialisation." *Le Sénégal Contemporain, Hommes et Sociétés*. Edited by M.-C. Diop, pp. 261–88. Paris: Karthala.

Ellington, Duke. 1973. *Music Is My Mistress*. New York: Da Capo.

Feld, Steven. 1994a. "From Schizophrenia to Shismogenesis: On the Discourses and Commodification Practices of 'World Music' and 'World Beat.'" *Music Grooves: Essays and Dialogues*. Edited by C. Keil and S. Feld, pp. 257–89. Chicago: University of Chicago Press.

——— 1994b. "Notes on 'World Beat.'" *Music Grooves: Essays and Dialogues*. Edited by C. Keil and S. Feld, pp. 238–46. Chicago: University of Chicago Press.

Floyd, Samuel A., Jr. 1995. *The Power of Black Music: Interpreting Its History from Africa to the United States*. New York: Oxford University Press.

Gilroy, Paul. 1993. *The Black Atlantic: Modernity and Double Consciousness*. Cambridge: Harvard University Press.

Gouané, Marious. 2002. Interview by author. Saint-Louis. June 6.

Hannerz, Ulf. 1996. *Transnational Connections*. New York: Routledge.

Herskovits, Melville. 1941. *The Myth of the Negro Past*. Boston: Beacon.

Kauffman, Robert. 1980. "African Rhythm: A Reassessment." *Ethnomusicology* 24:393–416.

Kennedy Center, The. 1999. "The Jazz Ambassadors Program of International Cultural Exchange." Edited by U.S.I. Agency, pp. 2. http://kennedy-center.org/programs/jazz/ambassadors/information.html: Kennedy Center Jazz.

Kubik, Gerhard. 1999. *Africa and the Blues*. Jackson: University Press of Mississippi.

Lenormand, Hervé. 1996. *Saint-Louis Jazz: Histoires de Jazz au Sénégal*. Nantes: Joca Seria.

Malone, Jacqui. 1998. "Jazz Music in Motion: Dancers and Big Bands." *The Jazz Cadence of American Culture*. Edited by R. G. O'Meally, pp. 278–97. New York: Columbia University Press.

Mangin, Timothy R. 1999. "Ethnomusicology On Line CD Review. Keepers of the Talking Drum: Tama Walo." http://www.research.umbc.edu/efhm/5/mangin.

Maultsby, Portia K. 1990. "Africanisms in African-American Music." *Africanisms in American Culture*. Edited by H. E. Holloway, pp. 185–210. Bloomington: University of Indiana Press.

Mbembe, Achille. 2001. *On the Postcolony*. Berkeley: University of California Press.

Meintjes, Louise. 1990. "Paul Simon's *Graceland*, South Africa, and Mediation of Musical Meaning. *Ethnomusicology* 34:337–73.

Monson, Ingrid. 1996. *Saying Something: Jazz Improvisation and Interaction.* Chicago: University of Chicago Press.

——— 2000b. "Art Blakey's African Diaspora." *The African Diaspora: A Musical Perspective, Critical and Cultural Musicology.* Edited by Ingrid Monson, pp. 329–52. New York: Garland

Monson, Ingrid, ed. 2000a. *The African Diaspora: A Musical Perspective.* New York: Garland.

Mukunda, Kazadi wa. 2000. "Latin American Musical Influences in Zaïre." *The Garland Handbook of African Music.* Edited by R. M. Stone, pp. 107–12. New York: Garland.

Murray, David. 2000. Interview by author. New York. January 8.

N'Diaye, Abdoulaye. 2000. Interview by author. Dakar. April 13.

Nketia, J. H. 1974a. "African Roots of Music in the Americas: An African View." *Black Perspective in Music* 2:82–88.

——— 1974b. *The Music of Africa.* New York: Norton.

Sembene, Nankou. 2000. Interview by author. Dakar. February 1.

Socé, Ousman. 1955/93. "An African View of Ellington (1955)." *The Duke Ellington Reader.* Edited by M. Tucker, pp. 289–90. New York: Oxford University Press.

Stapleton, Chris, and Chris May. 1987. *African All-Stars: The Pop Music of a Continent.* London: Quartet.

Stovall, Tyler. 1996. *Paris Noir: African Americans in the City of Light.* Boston: Houghton Mifflin.

Tang, Patricia. 2001. Masters of the Sabar: Wolof Griots in Contemporary Senegal. Ph.D. diss., Harvard University.

Taylor, Timothy D. 1997. *Global Pop: World Music, World Markets.* New York: Routledge.

Thioub, Ibrahima, and Ndiouga A. Benga. 1999. "Les Groupes de Musique 'Moderne' des Jeunes Africains de Dakar et de Saint-Louis, 1946–1960." *Fêtes urbaines en jeunes africains: Espaces, identités et pouvoirs, hommes et sociétés.* Edited by O. Goerg, pp. 213–27. Paris: Karthala.

Tomlinson, John. 1999. *Globalization and Culture.* Chicago: University of Chicago Press.

Turino, Thomas. 2000. *Nationalists, Cosmopolitans, and Popular Music in Zimbabwe.* Chicago: University of Chicago Press.

Waterman, Christopher. 1990a. *Jùjú: A Social History and Ethnography of an African Popular Music.* Chicago: University of Chicago Press.

——— 1990b. "Our Tradition Is a Very Modern Tradition." *Ethnomusicology* 34:367–80.

Waterman, Richard A. 1952. "African Influence on the Music of the Americas." *Acculturation in the Americas.* Edited by S. Tax, pp. 207–18. Chicago: University of Chicago Press.

Weinstein, Norman C. 1993. *A Night in Tunisia: Imaginings of Africa in Jazz.* New York: Limelight.

Wilson, Olly. 1974. "The Significance of the Relationship Between Afro-American Music and West African Music." *Black Perspective in Music* 2:3–22.

DIEDRA HARRIS-KELLEY

Revisiting Romare Bearden's Art of Improvisation

As a child who loved to draw, I was fortunate to have Romare Bearden as my uncle. My Aunt Nanette would invite a few of my cousins and me to come from Staten Island and spend weekends at their loft in Manhattan. "Romie," as family and friends called him, was always there making art, cutting, painting, putting pieces over pieces. Jazz records often played in the background, and he often told stories of growing up surrounded by music. The music seemed to make him happy, putting him in the mood to create.

It wasn't until I grew up and became an artist myself that I became aware of my uncle's stature in the art world. To me he was just "Uncle Romie," the man who would ask us to draw the four seasons. Once I learned more about his work, I was struck by the frequent connections critics made between jazz and his collage. Of course, such connections made perfect sense given his love of the music and my own memories of hearing jazz in his loft on Canal Street. But the more I learned about how artists make work, both by studying other artists and by painting myself, the more I questioned the easy analogy between playing jazz and making visual art. While I do think there are profound links between Bearden's approach to collage and jazz improvisation, I also think the analogy doesn't account for differences in genre and technique. By not accounting for these differences, we risk obscuring more about Bearden's process than we might reveal. We might even miss what is most "jazzlike" about his work.

Bearden himself insisted that he structured his paintings and collages as if they were jazz compositions. Certainly Bearden is not the first artist to take the principles of one art form and apply them to another. He is part of a long line of artists who have tried to make conceptual ideas visible. Since the turn of the century artists like Wassily Kandinsky were trying to make art based less on nature and more on their own vision. Cubists like Pablo Picasso and Georges Braque emphasized the basic significance of organization through experimentation and analysis. As a result some art became more abstract. Although Bearden had little formal training, he was a scholar of cubism and studied the Dutch masters for keys to good composition and form. His friend Carl Holty once told him that what made Picasso's and Matisse's work so solid was their attention to structural form, which many American artists' work lacked. I imagine that must have made Romie even more determined to master these concepts.

He was one of those people who could do just about anything to which he set his mind. He was an arts education major at NYU, a philosophy student in Paris, a cartoonist, a pretty good baseball player, and a self-taught art historian. He took up songwriting because he thought he could write a hit song and make enough money to go back to Paris. He did publish about twenty songs with Larry Douglas and Fred Norman, even managing to get a hit, "Seabreeze," recorded by Billy Eckstine in 1954. He claims at the time that he didn't know anything about musical structure, but he'd been around music all his life.

When we think of Bearden, we often think of jazz. In the seventies and eighties he created images of jazz singers and ensembles. His most popular pieces include *At the Savoy, Johnny Hudgins Comes On, Sunday Night Session, Alto Composite, Show Time*, and *Wrapping It Up at the Lafayette*. In some of these works the rich hues blending with hazy, smoldering washes may evoke a smoky blues joint. We see bursts of paint spurting out from the end of a horn, infusing a painting like music spilling out into the street and following us home in our heads. Romie could get the figures just right, too. The lean of a sax man, the tilted head of the bass player, the shifted weight in attitude of the singer as she pauses to cue the piano man. These people are no clichés. They feel individual and specific, yet familiar. It's enough to make you remember, even if you weren't there.

Romie had a way of putting some viewers in situations that felt like home. In ways his experiences were universally felt. He was there in Harlem, living next to the Apollo Theatre, hanging out with musicians, and inhaling the atmosphere. He often said that an artist must be like a whale swimming with its mouth open, taking everything in, then selecting out what he needed to create his own thing. When he was there, Harlem was a hip place to hear jazz, where, as he would say, "people lived outside" on the street. They did a lot of living outside, and he took it all in.

How Bearden incorporated jazz in his work wasn't always about representing jazz musicians or employing titles referring to the music. Given his broad knowledge of American culture, it seems logical to me that he was thinking of the fundamentals of this very radical, very modern American music and how it could be applied to his work. Critics interested in the relationship between painting and jazz frequently quote Bearden on how listening helped him make use of the spaces between the shapes. When quoted in a *New Yorker* article by Calvin Tomkins he said,

"I take a sheet of paper and just make lines while I listen to records. A kind of shorthand to pick up the rhythm and intervals." Then he goes on to say that he was encouraged by Stuart Davis, an American painter working in a cubist way, who listened a lot to Earl Hines. And he said he listened to Hines for the intervals. Tomkins notes then, "Hines made the pauses between notes into something important. The silences were as expressive as the sounds." Romare said he would listen to Earl Hines on piano for hours, until he couldn't hear the melody, only the spaces between the notes. The spaces between the notes . . . what does that mean to me as an artist? It could mean many different things musically. In between the notes could refer to rhythm or rhythmic phrasing. In a visual sense it may translate into the way he places blocks and strips of color between the figures, sort of like rests (quarter note, eighth note) between the phrases.[1]

In the piece *At Connie's Inn* his ideas about space are evident in the use of large areas of color. The broad blue patch on top looks like a solid color perhaps, but it is really very modulated. He went through with steel wool rubbing the pieces to get a more unified surface. So when I am looking at this piece and thinking about the way Bearden creates spaces, I'm wondering where to start. I can enter at the top where I see a band of color above the stage with a rhythmic pattern going on. Then there's an area of blue that slows you down. Is that what he means by space? Moving down, there's this circle motif, looping to the left, gathering into a sunlike circle, where yellow color spills out over the musicians in the center. Here I feel the tempo picking up. The band figures are cut smaller and into more varied, dynamic shapes, thus giving us a sense of picking up the rhythm. So perhaps we can say we moved into a different section, a different movement of the music. Below the band is a quieter space with larger figures and fewer details. The colors from separate forms move into one another; it's a slower rhythm that gathers at the bottom right corner into a spiral leading up again. As an artist I don't always read paintings in this way, but know that it is important to find ways to navigate through the work. When we are thinking about our viewer, we may ask ourselves, where will they look first? How are they going to move, and at what pace? Where are their eyes going to rest, and what do we want them to see when they get there?

Wrapping It Up at the Lafayette is an example where the rhythm or the spacing is different. Most areas in *At Connie's Inn* are muted and softened by similar tones blending together. The rhythm here is a sharper contrast, to me like a drum beat. Here Romie divides the painting into quarters. I have to wonder if he is trying to give four very different moods, movements, or scenes of a stage setting. Different rhythms develop as the contrast in the elements change from quarter to quarter. I don't always want to chop it up or read it in pieces like that, but it helps me to understand the artist's intent. That's what I do in the first two minutes of looking at a piece of artwork. I want to figure out what it is, and how it was made. I go to the side of a painting and check out the surfaces. It is important to me, for instance, that he rubbed the surface to unify it—because then I can, after those two minutes, marvel at what was done with the materials and how the artist transformed it. I then try to figure out why he chose to do that, and how form might relate to the content. Why did Romie border the space in *Wrapping It Up at the Lafayette* like a frame and have this rhythmic movement with the legs differ from right to left? Is that what he means by interval?

I doubt Bearden was only thinking about rhythm and silences between the notes. I think he was also speaking of tonal intervals as well. In the film *Bearden Plays Bearden* Romare is pictured with writer and critic Albert Murray and they are talking on a rooftop. He starts to sketch the houses across the street. As he sketches he describes the buildings and the stacking up of them as a piano keyboard. I don't know if he was sketching for *The Block*, but, like that famous collage, he was looking at each building as if they were parts of a composition. Perhaps each of the buildings act as an instrument taking solos and playing together in an ensemble? But when I think of the placement of the buildings in tonal terms, I see the pink building on the left sounding a chord in the high register. It moves to the gray, deeper tone, then the lighter gray, to the dynamic phrase in the middle, all as one instrument. So I think Bearden was talking about intervals moving through different pitches.

We might link "tonal" more directly with color. The leaps in tone can refer to shifts in color. Romie had a wonderful way of using gray, too. He would use it with such confidence, sometimes to move from one area of explosive color to the next as a way of holding the bright color in balance. As a neutral color gray tends to heighten everything else. It is important to make the space around shapes as interesting as the shapes themselves. These shapes are interdependent, interlocked, and control the tension. To me as an artist this concept is still so profound. I can remember learning it in my first semester drawing class and I haven't looked at forms the same way since. What a revelation I felt when I realized I could draw the shape of the space around the subject, and the subject would appear. I could draw all the black shapes around the white form, without even drawing the outlines of the white form, and it would appear because they were interlocking.

Artists call the space around the figure the ground. But when I talk about figure-ground relationship and Bearden's use of gray here, I'm talking about the balance of color and of how gray shapes support the other shapes. In other words, a painting full of only intense colors will compel your eyes to dart from one bright color to the next. You're bound to look in many different directions. However, the gray locks you there and keeps you from falling out of the painting. That's what I think composition is all about.

For example, in *Patchwork Quilt* there is a gray area on the right, by the door; it just looks nondescriptive overall. I think it's essential to the composition because on top there's this bright blue strip that causes the window below, to the left, to float in space. A diagonal of mostly middle tone colors comes from behind the window, attaching it to the wall. The movement leads our eyes down toward the center of the collage. Maybe Romie wants us to go directly down to the female figure. Our eyes slide down this diagonal and rest at the brightly colored figure. But almost immediately I'm drawn to an even lighter patch to the right, the pitcher, that for me points to or transitions into the sort of "gray" to the right. It's not gray meaning

FIGURE 11.1   *At Connie's Inn.* 1974.
Collage with acrylic and lacquer on board, 49 7/8 × 39 15/16″.

FIGURE 11.2 *Wrapping It Up at the Lafayette.* 1974.
Collage with acrylic and lacquer on board, 44 × 36".

FIGURE 11.3 *The Block* (detail). 1971.
Collage of cut and pasted paper and synthetic polymer paint on masonite, 48 × 216″ overall.

FIGURE 11.4   *Patchwork Quilt.* 1969.

Collage of paper and synthetic polymer paint on composition board, $9 \times 11 \ 7/8''$.

FIGURE 11.5   *The Train.* 1974.
Collage on paper, 15 1/4 × 19 1/4″.

FIGURE 11.6 *The Piano Lesson.* 1983.
Oil with collage, 40 × 31″.

black and white gray, it's a grayed tone of tan. And in that is another figure I don't see at first—he is quietly camouflaged. I rest at this, before my eye picks up on another diagonal movement up through the chair, leading me to the bright staccato pattern of the quilt in the center, framed strongly by the gray blocks around it. It leads up to the window again by the little hanging curtain. I'm caught up in the repetition and rhythm of the glass panes, and then, boom, I hear that red block singing a high note. I step back a bit and notice how much that red was singing throughout, with the other reds, the pinks, the oranges. The grays kept it all in balance. That bolt of red might even be the starting point for some viewers, because it leads up and around again.

What's interesting about *The Train* is his use of grays. There are intervals of space; he literally slices things up. It is a good demonstration of his use of rhythm through vertical lines and patterns. Some are created by the pieces of paper coming together and not quite meeting where he leaves a gap. In some places there are clear lines. We are confronted with a march of rectangles, from a small blue one in the sky, to a bigger one that makes up the wood paneling, to the biggest rectangle that creates the whole interior wall. The blue is repeated here and there down to the bottom. The real intense color comes from the sunset in the window to the right, made more intense when peeking through the gray walls.

Bearden's approach to structure is most interesting to me as an artist. The possibilities of flipping those relationships and holding elements together so they don't fall out of your painting are endless. But can we say that these are the same reasons for the pauses in between the notes in music? I don't know. Are the notes interdependent this way? Bearden seems to use them in what was part of his improvisational process. Starting with a theme, but having no real idea of how he would lay things down, he chose colors according to what was already down. He'd lay in a large piece of color, then arrange pieces down on top of that. He would work from one section to the next. There may have be an idea of what he wants to depict, maybe a theme, but *how* he was painting was very improvisational. He would work off of whatever was there.

In an interview with biographer Myron Schwartzman, Andre (Teabo) Thibault, Romare's assistant, talks about this process. Romare, who was quite a virtuoso with color, would choose colored pieces that Teabo thought shocking. He would glue them down and then move to the adjacent parts. He would step back occasionally and look at the overall structure, making sure it was holding together. I think he put those brilliant colors down because he knew he was going to chop them up. He knew that he would lay other things down on top and was performing improvisation more like a conductor than a single instrumentalist. When I think of him listening to Earl Hines and talking about the spaces, I think he's the piano player playing this phrase, and then he leaves a space, plays another set of notes, followed by another section. But then maybe he is the leader of a big band and has a lot of pieces/instruments he's orchestrating, pulling some in and easing others back. He would apply large vibrant colors—colors that seemed to dominate the space—early on. He knew that they would have to compete against all those other pieces that would come in, toning them down, and that they would have to stand their ground. That's the way he worked with the background, using one flat color or a couple of large blocks of color, then reasserting them in different quantities throughout.[2]

Bearden explored many different systems of composition while studying the work of Pieter Bruegel, Jan Vermeer, and Pieter de Hooch. He was interested in ways to stabilize the space. One thing he learned from them was the repeated use of rectangles of similar proportion to the picture plane, the outer edges. Now what that means is, if you were working on a canvas and it was a vertical rectangle, you might use rectangles throughout, in varying sizes but in the same proportion. If it were a two-to-one rectangle, you would repeat that, making reference to its form and stabilizing the composition so the parts stay together.

In describing his process to create *Piano Lesson*, Romare said, "I've seen some of Goya's paintings where the underneath ground predominated over half the painting, and then he would, say, weave a certain blue color here and develop those things that he wanted highlighted." Romare goes on to say,

> So I would let the ground play through and then what I put there, the things I lay down, I try to put in proportion to the overall size-in the same ratio. And then in this, I did something that I don't usually do. You see I tipped it to lay the piano in a kind of perspective going this way, and to compensate for that, I had to bring things back onto the frontal plane.[3]

254

diedra harris-kelley

We can see how this process is employed in *Piano Lesson*. He lays down big rectangles of color: purple, orange, green, and blue. The smaller ones in the shutters, the blue window panes, the picture frame, the wardrobe, the rug, and up to the center through the long pole between the figures. He placed the blocks around in various sizes that seem to march down into the space. Then there is the big diagonal caused by the piano (a rectangle in perspective) that shoots you right back into the deeper space of the room. He does get back to the frontal plane by using those bright blues in the window, then repeats them down through the carpet, up into the figure's shoes, then finally to the center of attention, the player's shoulder. He says he does this so he can make things flat because that was the aesthetic he was after.

Using rectangles to structure the space in a painting is very classical, but it can restrict the movement. His treatment of color in the *Piano Lesson* also makes the piece more static and "quieter." It's quiet and stable compared with *At Connie's Inn*, where color is allowed to spread into other areas. Romie said it was silent, he had to drag or track color "because that's another kind of movement. . . . But I feel you have to do something like that to get something of that jazz feeling." I take this to mean dynamic movement and rhythms. From this quote one might get the impression that he employed music aesthetics only when doing a jazz piece. But we can find the same practices in any number of the Mecklenburg collages, and certainly in many of the "Projections" and interiors of the sixties. For example in *The Train*, mentioned above, a staccato rhythm is created by the flickering of white tones throughout, and the small bits of color sing through the grays.

In conclusion, how far do we want to go with musical analogies? It seems impossible to make direct correlations without really understanding the different forms and production techniques, even when artists insist on these correlations. Without an understanding of technique on both sides of the analogy, we end up making easy links that hide more than they reveal. As much as artists might draw on musical ideas and concepts, playing jazz is not painting. I can occupy myself for hours with these kinds of puzzles, but the creative process is still mysterious and magical. I pursue this because this is what I do. I love to think about how things are made, but, in the end, the more important thing may be what we feel about what is in front of us.

NOTES

1. Calvin Tomkins, "Profiles: Putting Something Over Something Else." *New Yorker*, November, 28 1977, pp. 53–58+.
2. Myron Schwartzman, *Romare Bearden: His Life and Art* (New York: Abrams, 1990), 200–1.
3. Ibid., 34.

JORGE DANIEL VENECIANO

Louis Armstrong, Bricolage, and the Aesthetics of Swing

Louis Armstrong kept thousands of photographs in his home in Corona, Queens. Some were publicity photos taken by studio professionals; many were taken by fans, media photographers, and friends. Consequently, he appears in a majority of them, smiling back at the camera. The vast panoply of images spilled into various quarters of the home itself, becoming part of his living environment. Armstrong had one of these photographs—a studio portrait in expressionistic key lighting from a 1935 Vanity Fair spot—reproduced as a painting and displayed prominently as a formal portrait in his living room. Other images he cut up, lifting heads and torsos, and reconfiguring the iconic fragments in collage and montage arrangements.

Armstrong assembled his collage and photomontage work[1] in scrapbooks and on the front and back covers of hundreds of commercial boxes of reel-to-reel audiotape, which contain his collection of personal recordings. The boxes are small, just under eight by eight inches square and less than an inch deep. Their diminutive scale notwithstanding, they provide effectual canvases, like miniature paintings, for the composition of formal elements. The fact of their existence in sufficient abundance is enough to open a barrage of questions about their relationship to other dimensions of Armstrong's life work. A fundamental question pursued in these pages concerns Armstrong's operative aesthetics as developed in the photo-collages and as evidenced by his professional endeavors, especially in music and published writings.

Armstrong had begun his photo-collage work by the early 1950s, when collage was an acceptable form of artistic and commercial advertising practice. Yet there are distinctive qualities to be found in his photo-collages, certain formal insistences, that annunciate something of a counteraesthetic stance in relationship to either form of production. On the whole Armstrong's photo-collages aspire to neither the status of high art nor the propagandistic function of advertising. Yet impulses borrowed from each orientation course their way through the collages. He referred to them, however, as a hobby. And, indeed, they seem to play disinterestedly along the same liminal divide between art and entertainment that Armstrong made a career of crisscrossing as musician and performer—performing a kind of double-crossing that vexed many fans and critics of the jazz-as-art denomination, even as it won multitudes the world over.

Very little is known about the photo-collages. Less than a handful of boxes were featured in the extensive 1994 exhibition *Louis Armstrong: A Cultural Legacy*, organized by Marc H. Miller and the Queens Museum of Art. Miller was the first, outside of the Louis Armstrong House and Archives, to show and write about the collages. In the exhibition's catalogue, he writes, "His collages, tenuously held together by cellophane tape, were probably not viewed by Armstrong as significant works of art."[2] Given its much broader purview, the catalogue consigned only two paragraphs to the subject. Setting aside (for the moment) Miller's speculation about their relation to "art," we can surmise from the work itself that Armstrong did take a playful, leisured, and avocational approach to photo-collage as a hobby—an understandable relegation of task for a man whose principle vocation lay in the world of music. Nevertheless, it is precisely their *significance* as works of formal creation, produced in response to recognizable aesthetic practices, and under the orchestrating hands of an intermedia artist, that should compel us to consider them at greater length than they yet have been. Perhaps, for Miller, it is the tenuousness with which the collages are held together that has a mitigating effect on their significance. It may be argued, however, as this essay does, that it is the same condition of tenuity that sustains an aesthetic distinct from, and in some ways counter to, those of the fine arts tradition, while at the same time engaging them. It is an aesthetic that plays the contingent and the provisional against the archival and the museum standard, one that we cannot help viewing as consistent with the syncopated musical aesthetic of jazz improvisation that characterizes the broader range of Armstrong's work.

The pianist Marty Napoleon once observed that Armstrong was always "carrying a pair of scissors around with him and constantly cutting up newspapers, *Jet* and *Life* magazines and anything that he wanted to remember. He would cut out pictures, words, headlines, etc. and paste them all together in little notebooks that he carried around. It was a hobby of his. We'd see him in between sets—cutting and pasting these bits together."[3] Miller reads Napoleon quite literally when he assesses that Armstrong made the collages "primarily as memory aids." But the collages also illuminate Armstrong's predilection for redeploying mottoes, sayings, advertising phrases, and colorful sound bites, all of which defy mnemonic necessity. Repositioned into collage constructions, they take on something of the force that Kenneth Burke attributed to proverbs: the force of dispensing metaphorical medicine—i.e., strategies or *attitudes* for dealing with life's challenging situations.

Proverbs are designed, according to Burke, to impart instruction on matters of human welfare, to provide solace or vengeance, admonition or exhortation, and so on.[4] For Armstrong, however, the dispensary was never not at the same time tongue-in-cheek.

Another way to read Napoleon's observations, as a careful look at the collages will bear out unmistakably, is to take them to mean that Armstrong assembled these materials not simply in an effort to remember what they represented but, more important, to commemorate the events and people they identify: to celebrate, document, and organize the grand and nominal events that held some significance in his world (see figure 12.1).[5] To a man whose preferred mode of written communication was autobiographical and anecdotal, the collages offer iconic (photographic) representations and personally symbolic interpolations of a life and its celebrity world (see figure 12.2). They constitute autobiography by other means: in the visually fractured form of cubism (containing nonlinear, multifaceted elements) and the impulsive orchestrations of witticism (the irrepressible touch of Armstrong's humor; see figure 12.3). Some collages allow Armstrong to explore sexual subjectivity, something denied him as an object of representation in film and publicity images.

What Napoleon appears to describe is the work of a would-be archivist, not an artist. Another hobby of Armstrong's was the collecting and archiving of media reportage on the events and phases of his career. This documentary objective was better served, in fact, by the many volumes of scrapbooks he and his wife, Lucille, organized over their years together than by the collages, which also served, arguably, aesthetic objectives.

In a letter to a friend to whom he had mailed a collage piece, Armstrong wrote: "I guess you've wondered why all the regalia (the photo) that I sent you . . . huh? Well, you know my hobby (one of them anyway) is using a lot of scotch tape. . . . My hobby is to pick out the different things during what I read and piece them together and making a little story of my own."[6] Armstrong was emphatic about using household Scotch tape throughout the fabrication process, as 1. a vehicle for fixing collage elements into units of re-arrangeable relationships, 2. a means of fastening the phraselike units onto the box covers, and 3. a laminating devise for the box covers themselves.

Making a "little story" of his own was only one creative objective, one that correlated with some of the events documented on the audiotapes: backstage stories, personal anecdotes, and off-color jokes. The audiotapes also contain recordings of favorite songs and concerts, radio and television programs, performances by friends, his own performances, and occasionally his trumpet accompaniment to any of these (see figure 12.4). The ability to tell "stories" in music has, of course, been prized among jazz artists, especially those who honor the music's first marriage to the blues. It is an ability to communicate life experiences without the use of words and, hence, without a traditional narrative. Armstrong's photo-collages bring together fragments of story elements that similarly eschew linear narrativity. They are "stories" only in that they are fictive constructions. The storytelling effect, in its creative function, runs consistently through Armstrong's music, writing, conversational manner, and photo-collages and thus provides a point of comparison between his musical and visual art.

However, it is the seemingly anti-aesthetic practice, marked by the locution "using a lot of scotch tape," that inspires this comparative review of Armstrong's work. His predilection for mass-produced domestic adhesive tape is eminently suggestive of a number of practical and aesthetic lines of interconnection. For one, he does not refer to his work as collage but as a hobby involving something of a signature style to be identified by the prodigious *use* of various household tapes. He refers therefore not to an artistic product but to a *practice*. Second, the primary reference to "scotch tape" identifies the centrality of a nonart material to his practice. Third, the emphatic reference to "*a lot of* scotch tape" reveals a conscious, counteraesthetic drive behind the use of nonart materials as integral to his compositions.

Armstrong made use of a range of household-variety tape: transparent cellophane tape in sizes from 3/8" to 2" (packaging tape), masking tape of comparable widths, fabric tape that might have been stored for bandaging or first aid, and plastic graphics tape of bright red, blue, and green. The collages, produced during a period of about twenty years (to just days before his death in 1971), were consistently constructed with these household tapes. They convey, therefore, a persistent and decidedly makeshift quality, as signified in their domestic-material presentation. Their consistency of style is sufficient to indicate the pursuit of an idiosyncratic practice: a craft or art form with its own formal principles, its own peculiar form of aesthetics. Just what kind of aesthetic we can call it falls into question. Picking up this trail of the tape, as it were, and pursuing its culturological consequences, becomes the quest.

I shall contend that the collages offer new grounding from which to assess Armstrong's aesthetic pursuits with respect not only to his visual work but also to the energy they suffuse over the broader spectrum of his creative endeavors. The photo-collages provide a visual, plastic (material) dimension to the artist-musician's oeuvre, which included voice, instrument, acting, and language-based arts. What remains compelling about the collages is their unrelenting argument with the aesthetics of Western traditions; specifically, they sustain a twenty-year dialogue with the artistic practice of collage. This examination focuses on what the photo-collages can tell us about Armstrong's aesthetic practices across disciplines rather than on the interpretation of the collages themselves.

Starting with the pragmatist-inflected jazz writings of Albert Murray and working backward, historically, we find an articulation of Armstrong's musical-aesthetic practices in the context of a cultural history of American pragmatism. In *The Blue Devils of Nada*, Murray argues, squarely in the tradition of American exceptionalism, that Armstrong's innovations and improvisations are rooted in and function as "*emblems for a pioneer people who require resilience as a prime trait*."[7] He dresses this brand of resiliency in jazz musical metaphors, calling it an "ability to maintain equilibrium through swinging and improvising." It is ability representative of jazz in the dynamics of the vamp, the riff, and the break—though one may also think of boxing maneuvers, in this vein. Murray asserts, overarchingly, Armstrong's stature as the culture hero who provided "indispensable existential equipment for the survival of humanity."[8] The notion of equipment in the cultural arena provides a key trope for the current analysis.

While swinging and improvising are not synonymous, in Armstrong's case, especially in his published writings about swing, one becomes a species of the other, and vice versa. Murray's pragmatist concept-metaphor of existential *equipment* conveys a debt to the philosophical writings of Martin Heidegger and to the literary criticism of Kenneth Burke. In his essay "Literature as Equipment for Living" Burke claimed, "Art forms like "tragedy" or "comedy" or "satire" would be treated as *equipments* [sic] *for living,* that size up situations in various ways and in keeping with correspondingly various attitudes."[9] For Murray, Armstrong's music came to symbolize "the very spirit of exploration and readjustment that [were] so indispensable for survival"[10]—especially in the civilly less stable times of segregation in which he lived. Armstrong himself made a comparable claim about the power of music, in a *Life* magazine interview where he recalls his formative experiences and the sustaining, inspiriting effect of music: "I sure had a ball there growin' up in New Orleans as a kid. We were poor and everything like that, but music was all around you. Music kept you rolling."[11] Surely this brand of survival equipment is what Murray has in mind for Armstrong's own impact on a now broader swath of listeners.

Murray finds support for his jazz-pragmatist metaphor in the work of American studies scholar Constance Rourke, who identifies the roots of the so-called American character in a composite image of the "legendary Yankee peddler with his shrewdness and ingenuity, the equally legendary backwoodsman, the Indian-modified gamecock of the wilderness with his ever eager disposition to adventure and exploration, his skill at improvisation and innovation and thus his adaptability."[12] He also cites John A. Kouwenhoven's *Made in America* for its pragmatic approach in plumbing the aesthetic significance of American cultural production. Kouwenhoven's analysis, in terms of "learned/vernacular interaction," registers a synthesis between antecedent European traditions and what Murray sees as "improvised and homespun solutions and devises evolved from or inspired by frontier situations indigenous to the United States."[13] For Murray, Duke Ellington was primus exemplar of the synthesis of these traditions.

The blues tradition, Murray argues, is an extension of the American frontier tradition, which reached into the plantations and cities, as it did into the so-called wilderness. Shared are the requisite qualities of endurance and an obstinate disposition to situations of adversity. Contributing to the blues heritage is the very crucible that is the South itself—the "down-home source." The blues statement in turn became elemental to the originary constitution of jazz. When "fully orchestrated," in Murray's terms, the blues statement becomes a "highly pragmatic and indeed fundamental device for confrontation, improvisation, and existential affirmation: a strategy for acknowledging that life is a lowdown dirty shame and for improvising or riffing on the exigencies of the predicament."[14] We may add here the attendant qualities of contingency and provisionality, which are also fundamental to the blues statement—states of affairs always being subject to ironic volatility in a blues song.

As a novelist himself, Murray excavates the downhome source for the rooting and uprooting of his own fictional characters. He states, "It is precisely such southern 'roots' that will dispose and also condition my protagonist to function in terms of the rootlessness that is the basic predicament of all humankind in the contemporary world at large."[15] In the fictive junction between jazz and storytelling we may note a certain reverberation, a tension in the dynamic between root and rootlessness, that characterizes jazz music as well as jazz fiction, such as in Murray's *Train Whistle Guitar*. Whether we are looking at Armstrong's photo-collage as telling a "little story" of its own or Murray's novels as grounded in and departing from the musical and fictional soil of "down-home stuff," there is in each instance an interpretive play between the source or grounding and the flight or improvisation. There is the structure of a scoring and a swinging—in the world of music and, for Murray, in "the contemporary world at large." It is the rhetoric of adaptability and makeshift solutions that ties Murray's discussions to the visual strategies of Armstrong's photo-collages.

To tell stories about one's life—an indefatigable bent of Armstrong's—is necessarily to interpret that life, to inquire about what makes it *significant*. "The very asking of this question," wrote Martin Heidegger, "is an entity's mode of *Being*." "This entity which each of us is himself and which includes inquiring as one of the possibilities of Being" is the subject of *Being and Time*, wherein Heidegger asserts that there is a fundamental, self-interpreting aspect to human being, i.e., a human *way* of being.[16] The rootlessness that marks the human predicament for Murray is, for Heidegger, constituent of human existence. It creates a comparable feeling of being unsettled (*unheimlich*) in the world, and it calls for constant self-interpretation as something peculiar to human being.

Concerned with the everydayness of human activity, Heidegger's treatise posits a specialized sense of self-interpretation in which one finds oneself in a "world" not simply of physical space, but one that involves or implies any of the multifarious relationships that makes up *one's own* world—one's historically specific environment. This sense of embeddedness in one's surroundings lends itself to a pragmatic interpretation of the objects in one's world as being immediate, integral, and meaningful elements of that world. It is in this respect that objects in one's environment assume what Heidegger calls the quality of "equipment": they are *ready-to-hand*, taken at one's ready disposal for use and, as such, taken as equipment in the service of one's life projects. We are surrounded by things we take daily as tools and opportunities.

Heidegger's sense of "equipmental" pragmatism should be distinguished from the concerns with meaning, truth, and belief that have preoccupied American pragmatists such as C. S. Peirce and William James and from the nationalist enterprise and Sartrean existentialism of Albert Murray. There is, of course, sufficient room in the pragmatism running through Armstrong's swing aesthetic to find, as Murray does, a mirror of the fabled American buoyancy of self-creation (through improvisation, in this case): a reflection of a sociohistorical malleability through which, it is said, one's life can be recast. The vital play between this mythic "American" strain in pragmatism and the Old World incumbencies in tradition and community (both European and African), *we* can say, preordains the jazz-inflected play between "rootlessness" and "root," which is the essential play of swing in floating a recast melody above its scored rhythm.

Swing is Armstrong's imperative mode of "being-in-the-world." He set out to explain the phenomenon of swing in his 1936 book *Swing That Music*. An early passage captures the artistic attitude with which Armstrong lived his life. In an image reminiscent of Jean Toomer's poetical work *Cane*, he recalls the salience of the magnolia tree's balm "when it comes out in late spring, in Louisiana. Those big white flowers do swing their scent. They let it loose on the warm air and it spreads out over the whole county, and lies in the air for weeks, heavy and sweet."[17] With this introductory image Armstrong extends the poetics of swing to encompass a fundamental aesthetic attitude toward the world, whether natural or social in dominion. Swing becomes an interpretive activity that moves its celebrants in the world. Amiri Baraka's *Blues People* comes to a similar conclusion about the importance of attitude in relation to one's worldview. Jazz's (traditionalist) worldview, Baraka reminds us, signifies a specifically blues attitude. "Music . . . is the result of thought perfected at its most empirical, i.e., as *attitude, or stance*."[18] In Burkean and Heideggerian fashion, *Blues People* insists, "Negro music can be seen as the result of certain attitudes, certain specific ways of thinking about the world (and only ultimately about the *ways* in which music can be made)."[19] Baraka wants to classify a mode of being, living the blues and waging its requisite attitudes, as anterior to the practical and cultural effects of the blues, the making of music and art, and to align this mode with a historically racial group.

Being-in-the-world, for a jazz musician, is a matter of imbricate relationships to a world of jazz music, musicians, recording sessions, club *scenes*, and bus tours, and not to a world of a simple location in physical or geographical space. In *Swing That Music*, the first book written by an African American on the subject of jazz, Armstrong explains the *manual*-like function of the book and the role of language in identifying the jazz musician's world:

> I mention here that there are more than four hundred words used among swing musicians that no one else would understand. They have *a language of their own*, and I don't think anything could show better how closely they have worked together and how much they feel that they are apart from "regular" musicians and have *a world of their own* that they believe in and that most people have not understood. I hope this book will help to explain it a little—it is the real reason I have tried to write it and kept on after I found out what hard-going writing was for man who has lived all of his life mostly with a trumpet, not a pencil, *in his hand*.[20] (Emphasis added)

The third-person phrasing of the last passage suggests an editor's touch on the partial truism it speaks.[21] Armstrong had, in fact, been using a typewriter, which he took on road tours, to correspond with friends since 1922. The passage does points out, however, that language distinguishes the swing musician, sets him apart by equipping him with the empowering, metaphorical tools of self-naming and self-referencing. The passage essentially marks jazz as a discourse: as a network of linguistic and extralinguistic references to the world of jazz. In Armstrong's case these references included, by 1936, recordings, performances, sheet music and book publication, film and cartoons, and publicity memorabilia, any one of which might appear, however fragmented, as cultural material in later works of collage. In this multiplicity of modes for *articulating one's world* we find an example of what Heidegger means by self-interpretation as something integral to the condition of being-in-the-world.

Armstrong had developed an "equipmental" attitude toward the things around him and, consequently, a need to keep things "ready-to-hand," even when on the road. The typewriter was one of them. And as Heidegger had stressed, equipment functions in sets, not in isolation. When an interviewer asked Armstrong if it was true that he carried a dictionary and a book of synonyms and antonyms in his brief case wherever he went, Armstrong replied: "Certainly is. I learned to use them when I was writing the book, and I keep 'em handy now for my letter writing."[22] He also had a traveling cabinet custom designed to house two reel-to-reel tape players and a record player so that he could keep this extended set of equipment (for leisure, hobby, and documentation) with him when he went on tour. The central piece of equipment in his life, of course, was the trumpet. Max Jones, one of Armstrong's biographers, writes:

> He believed that music, and more specifically the trumpet, controlled his destiny. "That horn is my boss," he claimed, "because it is my life." The Selmer [his trumpet] was seldom far away from him for long. At home or in a hotel room it was customarily nearby, in the open case on a table or a desk, or at his feet, perhaps, where he could look down and see it. It was the centerpiece of sundry small rituals: the pouring through of hot water, the drying and oiling, the fingering of valves, the renewing of acquaintance each day.[23]

Still other rituals involved photographs as objects of routine handling in Armstrong's professional world. Since the early days of jazz promotion, "Publicity photos were placed outside theaters, reproduced in newspapers, used on sheet music covers, and given out to friends and fans—often with an autograph."[24] The handling of photographs in this way became an unrelenting exigency for Armstrong: "Greeting and signing sessions, like the hours he spent autographing pictures to send to letter-writers, were part of his world for years."[25] In addition to these sessions, throughout his life, on the road, after performances and public appearances, the trafficking of photographs and autographs resumed unabated (see figure 12.5). Photographs, by the thousands, accumulated in Armstrong's Corona home.

The photo-collages make use of this seemingly inexhaustible resource. They bring diverse elements together: Scotch tape, audiotape boxes, photographs, and fragments of other materials, transforming them into a new product of practical (everyday) as well as aesthetic (contemplative, affective) purpose. They are decorative yet functional as audiotape box covers, archivally numbered and filed in his studio bookcases, not on display. The ability to regard (envision) objects with the kind of (materialist) *circumspection*[26] that sees in them a readiness-to-hand is the ability of the "handyman," or what the French call *bricoleur,* a term that best compares with Armstrong's handiness at *collage*—two terms that share etymology: *coller,* French, to glue.

In "The Science of the Concrete" Claude Lévi-Strauss elaborates a theoretical distinction between the *bricoleur* and the engineer in his effort to distinguish "mythical thought" from scientific modes of thinking. The old French verb *bricoler,* Lévi-Strauss explains, was used to refer to "some extraneous movement [*un mouvement incident*]: a ball rebounding [*rebondit*], a dog straying [*qui divague*] or a horse swerving [*qui s'ecarte*] from its direct course to avoid an obstacle." He adds, "And in our own time the 'bricoleur' is still someone who works with his hands and uses devious means [*des moyens détournés*] compared to those of the craftsman."[27]

The term's original sense of deviation (incidental movement) from a straight course, together with its secondary, more contemporary sense of indirectness (*détourné*), recommend the comparison, proposed here, between the activities of bricolage and swing music as Armstrong described it. In *Swing That Music,* for instance, he puts forth a lexicon of swing that includes the phrase "goin' to town." It means, he explains, "cuttin' loose and takin' the music with you, whatever the score may call for. . . . It takes a swing player, a real good one, to be able to leave that score and to know, or 'feel,' just when to leave it and when to get back on it."[28] Rudy Vallee, who wrote the introduction to Armstrong's book, describes in similar fashion the bricolage dynamic of swing: "Compare a record by Crosby, in which he departs from the 'straight' form of the melody and lyric, and then listen to an Armstrong record and discover whence must have come some of his ideas of 'swinging.'"[29] Later, Armstrong, swing lexicographer, goes on to define *hot* (an early term meaning *improvised* or *improvisation*): "as swing musicians use the word, [it] does not necessarily mean loud or even fast. It is used when a swing player gets warmed up and 'feels' the music take hold of him so strong that he can break through the set rhythms and the melody and toss them around as he wants without losing his way."[30] The ability to stray or swerve from the "straight form of the melody and lyric"—to perform 'incidental movements' around the melody line—describes, in the older sense of *bricoler,* the very activity of swing in jazz music.

Lévi-Strauss identifies the bricoleur, who is restricted to an availability of materials and tools at his disposal, by distinguishing him from the engineer, who can more freely avail himself of the resources that allow him to follow through with the conception and procurement of requisites for a particular project. We recognize in this distinction a mediation of ideas that reminds us of Heidegger's sense of embeddedness-in-the-world and of equipmentality, on the one hand, and of Murray's pragmatic imperative of improvisation, on the other. For example, Lévi-Strauss stipulates that the bricoleur's "universe of instruments is closed and the rules of his game are always to make do with 'whatever is at hand.'"[31] The bricoleur collects and retains his materials "on the principle that 'they will always come in handy.'"[32] For Armstrong the true swing musician is someone with a faculty for making do with whatever (musical and visual) materials are at hand. The rules of his game call upon an ability to transform the material of an exhausted pop song, for example, into an aesthetically reinvigorated piece of music; this was done—*performed*—by "play[ing] away from the score"—by "cuttin' loose and takin' the music with you."

The structuralist concept of language, from Saussurean linguistics, provides the theoretical metaphor in Lévi-Strauss's analysis of bricolage. "The elements which the 'bricoleur' collects and uses are 'pre-constrained' . . . the possible combinations of which are restricted by the fact that they are drawn from the language where they already possess a sense."[33] Musicologists approach music as a language when they speak of phrasing and quoting in the structure of a composition. Paul Berliner, for example, in his extensive study *Thinking In Jazz: The Infinite Art of Improvisation*, takes a long, serious look at jazz improvisation in general linguistics terms. Commenting on the selection of musical material that a jazz musician traditionally has had at his disposal, he enumerates the following: "Primary materials for the jazz artist's vocabulary also include excerpts of jazz pieces, popular songs, Western classical compositions, and compositions from other musical traditions."[34] He interviews vocalist Carmen Lundy, who describes what is arguably bricolage-style deviation: "There's a little improvisation technique in which you learn to pull things from other songs and insert them into what you're singing at the moment. Someone like Ella Fitzgerald will often use quotes from other songs in the middle of a song. She'll sing a few lyrics and then she'll scat sing, taking you into another song."[35] Jazz lore has it that Armstrong brought scat singing to jazz music with the 1926 recording of "Heebie Jeebies." It's a good piece of lore, given that scat singing represents the alembic of Armstrong's bricolage aesthetics. The activity of singing weds language to music and lends phonetic contour to the music's audio-temporal figure. On this structural figure, scat performs its circumlocutionary, incidental movement of syllables around language. Scat syllables are audible fragments collaged into a song—word debris, or *des morceaux,* in Lévi-Strauss's terminology. As such, they not only circumnavigate the scored rhythm of the music, but they *swing* the "song" right off its lyrical tracks.

The melody of a popular song can also function as a kind of text or language from which a jazz composition draws its motives, "figures," and "phrases": these are elements "pre-constrained" (in Lévi-Strauss's sense) by the melodic significance they already possess and carry into a new composition. Berliner notes that "each figure has a particular history of usage and transformation—its own track record of applications—both within the artist's own performing experience and within the larger musical tradition."[36] Musical (as well as visual) elements, *cut* from their contexts, carry something of the embedded associations that surrounded them. Bricolage is the art of creating new arrangements from scrap elements. Bricolage, for Lévi-Strauss (as jazz improvisation, for Berliner), "builds up structured sets . . . by using the remains and debris of events: in French 'des bribes et des morceaux,' or odds and ends in English, fossilized evidence of the history of an individual or a society."[37] In the reconstitution of materials "it is always earlier ends which are called upon to play the part of means: the signified changes into the signifying and vice versa."[38] This exchange in signification constitutes an essential aspect of the activity of bricolage.

The process of rearrangement constituent to both collage and swing improvisation, even as it involves play with familiar elements, effects a degree of defamiliarization. Structuralism recognizes that the choice of element (linguistic, musical, or visual) inserted in a particular place in a sentence or (improvised) composition depends in part on "the possibility of putting a different element there instead, so that each choice which is made will involve a complete reorganization of the structure, which will never be the same as one vaguely imagined nor as some other which might have been preferred to it."[39] Armstrong describes this process in jazz when he explains the difference between a swing orchestra and a "regular" orchestra:

> When you listen to a swing band, you will begin to recognize that all through the playing of the piece, individual instruments will be heard to stand out and then retreat and you will catch new notes and broken-up rhythms you are not familiar with. You may have known the melody very well but you will never have heard it played just that way before and will never hear it played just that way again. Because the boys are "swinging" around, and away from, the regular beat and melody you are used to, following the scoring very loosely and improvising as they go, by ear and free musical feeling.[40]

Like bricolage, swing appears to be inherently metaphorical and thus ineluctably mythopoetic. It transports the participant (artist or audience) to new insight, away from the known melody, the standard meaning of the lyrics, and the fixed score. A good swing band "sends me," Armstrong would say. It swings the melody and the sense anew; or, as Lévi-Strauss observed, "earlier ends . . . are called upon to play the part of means: the signified changes into the signifying."[41] What was an end in itself as a popular song becomes the springboard for new arrangement and improvisation. That this process is not terminal but repeatable endlessly is the theoretical insight of poststructuralism and the practical, historical insight of jazz as a tradition that has continually called into question the structurality of the structures it quotes, mimics, and signifies.

In "The Science of the Concrete" Lévi-Strauss does broach the subject of art, situating it "half-way between" the engineer's scientific knowledge and the bricoleur's mythical thought. He does not, however, countenance modern art very well. Cubism and impressionism, he believed, were "successive stages" collaborating by distortion in an attempt to prolong the prevailing yet threatened modes of painterly expression. Collage, in this scenario, held the status of "intermittent fashion . . . originating when craftsmanship was dying, [and] could not for its part be anything but the transposition of 'bricolage' into the realms of contemplation."[42] He was right to recognize the contemplative potential and enterprise that collage work represents; he was aesthetically conservative to contrast it, pejoratively, to craftsmanship. In Armstrong's case the photo-collages appear to be constructed for the purpose of a practical contemplation: one of *commemoration* and adornment (see figure 12.6).

Comparisons between Lévi-Strauss's notion of bricolage and Armstrong's swing aesthetic are useful to a point: e.g., in drawing out shared aspects of a practical-materialist aesthetic. But other distinctions between the bricoleur and the "engineer," upon which Lévi-Strauss's analysis depends, do not hold up to internal, theoretical scrutiny, and they do not compare to parallel distinctions in the domain of jazz or other forms of music. For instance, Lévi-Strauss distinguishes the bricoleur as someone who submits to the constraints of his social environment while the engineer always tries to supersede such impositions. This distinction breaks down when applied to jazz bricoleurs who adopt irony, for example, and parody or satirize the very social environment in which they find themselves obliged to work. In such instances the bricoleur adopts the role of the critic, challenging the staid presuppositions of sociopolitical or cultural "engineering."[43] The political themes in Charles Mingus's music offer obvious counterexamples in this regard, but one might also think of Armstrong's public criticisms of segregation in Little Rock as well as instances in his music. For example, his version of "(What Did I Do to Be So) Black and Blue," according to Ralph Ellison, transforms the Broadway song into a meditation about social invisibility.

The contemplative and, hence, transformational potential of collage received its primary attention and emphasis in the work of European avant-garde artists and theorists who introduced it into the discourse of the "high arts." Peter Bürger has written that a theory of the avant-garde would have to begin with the concept of montage and its history, traceable to the first cubist collages of Picasso and Braque. What was radically different about their work, against the reigning perspective of illusionistic techniques developed since the Renaissance, was the innovation of incorporating "reality fragments" into a painting, which in turn signaled "the destruction of the unity of the painting as a whole."[44] An objective of the avant-garde formal principle with respect to collage and montage was to sustain an attack on the bourgeois institution of high art by introducing into it elements of the everyday world. The avant-garde principle called for an offensive on the concept of the autonomous work of art and its theorized separation from social life. "Avant-garde aesthetic praxis . . . aimed to intervene in social reality."[45] The concept of praxis here retains its broader, Marxist orientation toward sociocultural revolutionary action.

Recalling the early history of jazz music in the United States, and Armstrong's years in New Orleans during this time, invites comparison between them and the contemporaneous advent of the European avant-garde: all three emerging in the early years of the twentieth century. Any comparison, however, should begin with an important distinction between the two general movements, the European avant-garde and American jazz, in their early development. A critical difference between them, which should color subsequent comparisons, lies in their respectively disparate origins: the distinctive sociohistorical contexts of their beginnings. We might imagine their origins, in avant-garde terms, as being situated at opposing ends of a continuum of intervention between art and social reality. Hence, while each movement can be characterized as reaching toward a middle ground, producing, in the interfusion, an effect of comparability—an effect of blurring the separation between the spheres of art and social reality—they converge upon this shared terrain from diametrical directions. For instance, modernism, in Gustave Courbet's realist vein of painting, was concerned with introducing events of ordinary life into the subject matter of academic easel painting. Later, in Paris, Pablo Picasso, following Edouard Manet's lead, advances not only the brothel but representations of Africanicity into his inherited tradition of heroic painting. At the same time in history, early jazz, and Armstrong's formative experiences, on the other side of the Atlantic, found their beginnings literally *in and around* the milieu of the brothels and the emphatic Africanicity of Congo Square. In Armstrong's New Orleans, with its standing tradition as an operatic venue, it was the gramophonic voice of Enrico Caruso, and that of other opera luminaries, that was introduced amid the older traditions of the "good-time houses." As avant-gardist class crossings, these introductions were initiated from counterdirections. While such gestures of sociocultural converging produced somewhat comparable results, they were necessarily at variance ideologically. The ideological difference naturally owes to the particular historical climate of class, race, and geography that situated a distinctive praxis of life for avant-garde artists in Europe and their jazz counterparts in the United States. That is to say, any comparison of transatlantic avant-gardes must acknowledge historical conditions that begin at geopolitical variance.

When we consider the practical imperatives outlined in the writings of Murray and Lévi-Strauss, and we use them to frame our understanding of early American jazz as a counterpart statement to the European avant-garde aesthetic, we come up with an approach to cultural production that we can call bricolage aesthetic praxis. It is a distinctive approach to the interfusion of art and social reality; borrowing from notions of pragmatism, it is also culturally transformational. It represents an aesthetic practice that is de facto revolutionary in the cultural sphere, as indeed jazz has been, and transformative in the broader Marxian sense of individual and social force of change. But its origin would derive from a pragmatic-historicist rather than traditional-Marxist imperative. Not that the two imperatives are mutually exclusive, but they imply different theoretical and historical starting points. Bricolage aesthetic praxis begins not in the world of art, not with the presumptions of high art as the subject of appeal, as avant-gardism in Europe did—a world in which reality fragments are to be subversively imported. Instead, it begins in the social world of coal-peddling manual work in houses of sexual labor, as it did in Armstrong's world—a world in which aesthetic principles and practices are dispersed to ironic, if subtler, effects. While the goal of historical avant-garde movements was to revolutionize the praxis of life, the alternate "American" imperative, which Murray and Kouwenhoven characterize as *vernacular*, is one that stems from *strategies* (or "attitudes," according to Heidegger, Burke, and Baraka) for surviving

FIGURE 12.1   Box 376 (*front*) features the image that appears on the 1955 Columbia Records album cover *Ambassador Satch:* trumpet and briefcase in hand, traveling the world as goodwill and cultural ambassador. The collage is a self-reflective acknowledgment of the cultural-diplomatic status Armstrong achieved at home and abroad beginning in the mid 1950s.
Louis Armstrong House and Archives at Queens College/CUNY.

FIGURE 12.2 Box 491 (*front*) was assembled in the last year of Armstrong's life, after the presentation ceremony for the New York Summer Festival at Rockefeller Center, June 11, 1970, at which Armstrong received a silver platter with the inscription "Satchmo / New York Loves You / New York Summer Festival." The hostess is Lauren Bacall and the festival president is G. S. Eyssell. This box is primed with wide masking tape, as gesso on canvas, before the individual elements are added on to the surface with Scotch tape. The white fabric tape indicates the reel is empty. What is interesting about this composition is the perfect triangulation of the gaze of the three figures—each looks at the other in perfect circularity. Each is caught in the act of turning to his or her left, in the act of some sort of appeal, of an indirection—Eyssell (seemingly) lecherously to Bacall, Armstrong warily to Eyssell (as if possessive of Bacall), and Bacall admiringly to Armstrong. None returns the gaze. The oblong object below the Armstrong torso is a side view of the inscribed platter. Its symbolic register as memento mori and phallus is like that of Holbein's enigmatic anamorphasis in *The Ambassadors*. The visual-linguistic pun here is on what the "eye" has to "sell": desire of the other. *Louis Armstrong House and Archives at Queens College/CUNY*.

FIGURE 12.3   Box 359 (*front*) showcases a sensuous photograph of Armstrong's wife, Lucille, in a satin evening dress. "Pops" was Armstrong's more respectful nickname among friends. "Brown Sugar" was his nickname for Lucille. The collage contains a line drawing of a trumpet on Lucille's lap and a floating head of Armstrong himself over the trumpet. The postscript, "No 'cracks' as to the position of the 'trumpet,'" bespeaks the sexual symbolism of the trumpet and, by extension, the same for the placement of his head. Like the bawdy jokes recorded on some of the tapes these boxes house, this collage tells its own in visual-linguistic form. The setting suggested is the Plaza Hotel, Buenos Aires. *Louis Armstrong House and Archives at Queens College/CUNY.*

FIGURE 12.4 Box 9 (*back*) contains a list of recorded contents and is also decorated with collage elements. The list includes items "12-Bing Crosby (Radio Show)," "14-Lazy Bones. (Bing & Satch," "29-The Westerner / As told by- / Mrs Lucille / (Brown Sugar / (Armstrong) / 30-W.Winchell," and "38-L.Armstrong / (Tells one)." They feature musical performances as well as joke and storytelling. The collage elements display an iconography of places encountered on the road: Johnny's Big Red Grill in Ithaca, New York ("A Cocktail Lounge for Those Moments of Relaxation"), Narragansett Hotel in Providence, Rhode Island ("Where the Guest is KING"), and the company emblem for Swiss Kriss ("Herbal Laxative"). Each slogan bears some quality of the Burkean proverb: solace coupled with instruction, attitude, and exhortation. *Louis Armstrong House and Archives at Queens College/CUNY.*

FIGURE 12.5 Box 195 (*back*) features a photograph of the bed of a fan on which various Armstrong album covers, vinyl discs, and what look like fan and publicity photographs are arranged. The makeshift crown lends the ensemble a "King Louis" theme, as also suggested by the Columbia Records album cover on the upper right. Armstrong has added the cutout heads over the vinyl discs, suggesting a kind of formal synonymy between the two, creating an iconographic category of "jazz heads": the musician (Armstrong himself), the DJ (man in glasses), and the fan (perhaps the female fan who sent the photo). The placement of the heads also suggests that they are distinguished by a jazz nimbus or glory and, hence, the canonization not only of a king but a "Saint" Louis. This redoubling of photographic imagery occurs within an economy of material exchanges between Armstrong and his fans, including photographs, letters, and other memorabilia. *Louis Armstrong House and Archives at Queens College/CUNY.*

FIGURE 12.6   Box 109 (*back*) constructs a valentine collage out of premade elements such as printed fabric (the rose), a photograph (the stand-in valentine), and lines of text cut from a valentine card, each individually taped—obviously so—and thus bringing back in a visible yet transparent way traces of the artist's loving hands. *Louis Armstrong House and Archives at Queens College/CUNY.*

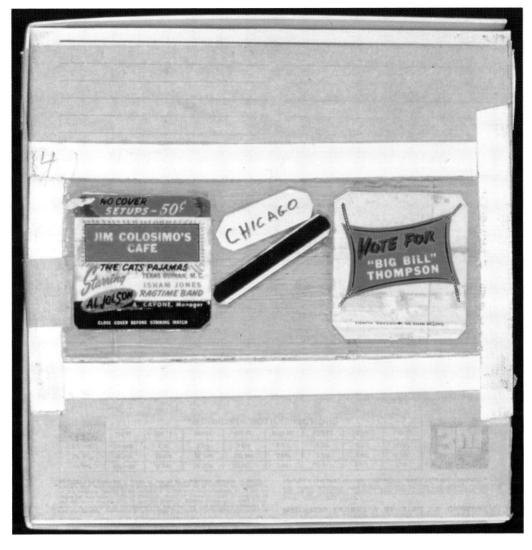

FIGURE 12.7   Box 518 (*back*) contains a matchbook cover that encrypts a minor history of mob-era Chicago. Jim Colosimo operated a chain of bordellos, bars, and gambling houses in the early 1900s. His syndicate passed on to his nephew, Johnny Torrio, then to Al Capone, who is listed as manager of the café. Many star orchestras and acts performed at the café-restaurant, including, here, Al Jolson. Between the two covers Armstrong places the strike strip pointing one end at Al Capone's name and the other to the political promo for "Big Bill" Thompon. Three-time mayor of Chicago, Thompon was known to receive gifts from the mob and to turn his back on Prohibition enforcement. His family fortune was enabled, in a sense, by the Great Chicago Fire. It was in Chicago that Armstrong met his lifelong manager, Joe Glaser, who managed the Sunset Café under the protection of Capone. Jazz was a beneficiary of mob business during Prohibition, and vice versa. This simple collage, framed in first-aid tape, apparently has too much to say to on its own to warrant extraneous elements. *Louis Armstrong House and Archives at Queens College/CUNY.*

a series of peculiarly homegrown historical conditions—conditions, however, that are not exclusive to the U.S. It is in relation to surviving these circumstances that an operative bricolage aesthetic praxis can be said to have contributed to revolutionizing not just the cultural life but also the praxis of life in the U.S. and in other regions.

In Armstrong's work (musical, visual, or otherwise) the improvisatory imperative that Murray describes carries—for the artist as producer and his audiences as consumers—an insistence on strategies for suffusing the aesthetic dimension through the praxis of life. The consistency of creative attitude with which Armstrong performed in the comedic, literary, musical, verbal, and visual arts marks a consistency in his approach to life, a strategy that renders the multiple media at his disposal as so much "equipment for survival," all subsumable within the range of bricolage aesthetic praxis. As a socially grounded, pragmatic aesthetic, this bricolage imperative distinguishes itself from the avant-garde insistence on the collaging of social reality *back* into art. It is clear from Armstrong's writings that his sense of aesthetics developed at an early age, as witnessed in his observations of the world around him, observations numerously recounted in autobiographical writings. The related mediums of collage and photomontage served Armstrong's objectives well in visually symbolizing the nexus between the worlds of art and everyday life. It remains to be seen how a bricolage aesthetic finds embodiment in Armstrong's musical work, as the creation of someone for whom the bourgeois distinction between art and social reality was always to be taunted, sometimes with a trumpet.

In his essay "The Quoter and His Culture" Krin Gabbard dubs the ironic, often "signifying" practice of quoting musical fragments among bebop jazz musicians as an "avant-garde gesture," a phrase that refers to the visual and literary avant-garde theorized in Peter Bürger's study.[46] Gabbard advances the idea that the use of quotation practiced among beboppers produced an effect tantamount to collage. Among the examples he reviews is one in which Armstrong quotes George Gershwin's "Rhapsody in Blue" in a 1929 solo of "Ain't Misbehavin"; he also refers to Armstrong's occasional quotation of passages from advertising jingles. With regard to their entertainment value, Gabbard adduces that Armstrong's use of musical quotation "was less complicated by conflicting messages" than were the later instances of quotation among beboppers. The inherent ironies, notwithstanding, of Armstrong quoting Gershwin—who infused jazz and other black cultural and musical references in symphonic compositions—it was, instead, in performances interspliced with advertising jingles that audiences registered the fragments of commercial (social) reality.[47] It is with such citations that Armstrong's own musical collages compare to avant-garde gestures in resisting the unitary aestheticization associated with bourgeois forms of art. By tethering to his virtuosic flights on the trumpet the kind of kite tail playfulness of popular jingles and parodic quotation, Armstrong created musical collages that, collectively, insist on a demotic musical statement. The insistence is affirmed again in the photo-collages, especially in those containing advertising slogans from magazines or product labels: a practice that echoes the quoting of recognizable jingles (see, for example, figure 12.4). Other types of mass-media, ready-made elements collaged onto the boxes, include cut-out text and design graphics from greeting cards, post cards, printed invitations, and commemorative certificates (see figure 12.7).

Though collage juxtapositions may seem at times surprising or trivial—more or "less complicated"—the practice of quoting, in music or collage, is never entirely haphazard; it requires competence in a musical or visual vocabulary. As noted above, such a structural requirement does not preclude the possibilities of play or critical insight. And, as Lévi-Strauss observed of bricolage, juxtapositions require an interrogation of "all the heterogeneous objects of which [the bricoleur's] treasury is composed to discover what each of them could 'signify.'"[48] With respect to quoting in bebop, Gabbard makes the point—consonant with Lévi-Strauss on the inherent limits of the bricoleur's "treasury"—that bop quotation provides "the best example of how jazz artists have used the limited means at their disposal to question their culture's institutionalization of art."[49] Examples cited in this vein include the few bars of Chopin's "Marche Funebre" heard at the end of Duke Ellington's "Black and Tan Fantasy" and Rossini's "William Tell Overture" in Freddie Jenkins' solo for the recording of "In the Shade of the Old Apple Tree." This kind of quotation breaks with the illusion of organic art—the intrusion working against both the seamlessness of the performing musician and the composition vamped. Other collage effects can be created by the introduction of "seemingly nonmusical material" such as bird noises and imitations of human conversation. All of these gestures, according to Gabbard, add up to an undermining of the traditionally received autonomy and integrity of art. The intended effect of such subversion, according to avant-garde theory, is to have audiences question their relationship to their culture.

On the other hand, an interrogation proceeding from the praxis of bricolage aesthetics would involve the bricoleur in a kind of cross-examination of his own resources: a "dialogue with the materials and means of execution."[50] The practice of quotation and collage become musical and visual means of engaging in or *performing* a dialogue. Traditional jazz is, after all, essentially dialogic, not simply between performing ensemble musicians but also, and precisely, between musicians and their "materials and means of execution": i.e., with the music, songs, instruments, rhythms, and orchestrations of Western and African musical traditions.

In his study "Louis Armstrong and Opera" Joshua Berrett is concerned with those occasions in which operatic influences and strains find expression in the thick of Armstrong's improvisations. Among *des bribes et des morceaux* that Berrett offers are those he calls the "operatic sound bites" of, for instance, *Rigoletto*, which appears on two separate Armstrong recordings: one with Johnny Dodds's Black Bottom Stompers, "New Orleans Stomp," and the other a 1930 recording of "Dinah," also containing quotations from Gershwin's "Lady Be Good!"[51] With exegetical circumspection Berrett examines Armstrong's 1930 recording of "Tiger Rag." It enfolds quotations from "Irish Washerwoman," "Singing in the Rain," and a *Pagliacci* fragment from the aria "Vesti la giubba" associated with Enrico Caruso, one of Armstrong's favorite tenors. Berrett cites Gunther Schuller's dismissive appraisal of these quotations in "Tiger Rag": "Its sturdy ragtime changes did not warrant gagging it up with no less than three banal quotes, playing for audience titters."[52] Berrett convincingly answers Schuller's skepticism by unpeeling the layered richness of personal and professional significance that Schuller apparently missed in the *Pagliacci* passage, with its special relevance to Armstrong's professional life and hence its autoreflective instantiation in "Tiger Rag."

Yet, for the purpose of this analysis, the recognition of banalities in quotation becomes most interesting and most relevant not in Schuller's pejorative sense but in a demotic-satiric sense enabled by a bricolage aesthetic praxis. This form of praxis brings something of the quotidian to the nominal world of art: something of the nightclub to Broadway to opera, performed in tandem, as much for irony as for titters. Thus the attendant leveling of the field of musical hierarchies follows implicitly. And at Armstrong's threefold insistence, in "Tiger Rag," we hear the *active*, para-aesthetic function of the banal. Berrett cautiously notes that Armstrong "never superimposed hierarchies of 'highbrow' or 'lowbrow' on his musical taste."[53] He compares Armstrong to Charles Ives in this regard, for their "underlying egalitarian attitude toward the source of musical material."[54] A question that follows: From where does this the egalitarian will to level musical hierarchies come?

In a passage commensurate in some ways with the avant-gardist critical tradition, Armstrong explains the way in which swing music runs a course antithetical to the Western classical tradition, before converging with it. In *Swing That Music* he writes of the early New Orleans jazz musicians (exaggerating their innocence to make a point):

> I had been brought up with a group of great musicians. They didn't know Bach from Beethoven, or Mozart from Mendelssohn, and maybe hadn't even heard of them, and, strange as it may sound, I think that is exactly why they became great musicians. Not knowing the classical music, and not many of them having proper education in reading music of any kind, they just went ahead and made up their own music . . . they created swing. . . . If those early swing musicians had gone to music schools and been taught to know and worship the great masters of classical music and been told it was sacrilegious to change a single note of what was put before them to play, swing music would never have been born at all. They would have got the idea that written music, whether it is a great classic or just a popular air, is something sacred that must never be touched, especially by a beginner.[55]

The passage contains some key ideas on education later supported in *Satchmo: My Life in New Orleans*. For example, in *Satchmo* Armstrong contrasts the Kid Ory band of his teen years with the trained "music-reading musicians" of contemporaneous Creole bands. He recounts an incident involving the older and self-assuming Robechaux band during a funeral parade, after the burial, a moment when "they struck a ragtime march which required swinging from the band. And those old fossils just couldn't cut it. That's when we Ory boys took over and came in with flying colors."[56] He concludes: "We'd proved it to them that any learned musician can read music, but they can't all swing."[57] His point is that swinging (performatively "signifying" on scored music) did not develop within a system of formal education in reading music. Armstrong goes on to describe a parallel educational system of apprenticeship in the early (and persisting) tradition of jazz education. He characterizes swing's antithetical strain to written music when he writes, "swing *can* be written down by someone listening to it, but if the players continue to follow it the way it is written down, very soon swing becomes set and regular and then it is not swing any more and that is what almost happened later when jazz tunes became so popular."[58] Armstrong weaves his reflections about written music into a critique of the commercialization of the form: its devolution to a "regular" form of swing, to which he wants to contrast his brand of "hot," active swing. "The very soul and spirit of swing music is free improvisation, or 'swinging' by the player."[59] In Armstrong's sense of *hot*, "swinging" becomes the performative principle of jazz swing— to perform the essential *activity* of free, circumnavigatory improvisation.

Perhaps because it receives soft-coded treatment in the editorially permitted language of *Swing That Music,* the radicality of Armstrong's critical claims about swing aesthetics, vis-à-vis the Western musical tradition, has not received the appreciation it merits from Armstrong's commentators. It should be self-evident, however, that in his writings Armstrong articulates the idea that blindness to academic strictures has permitted certain cultural innovation and insight, and that this phenomenon accurately describes the historical circumstance that contributed to the advent of New Orleans jazz. He refers, in his comments, to the factual lack, not to mention denial, of access to formal musical education among this cadre of innovators. And while Armstrong does not write in theoretical parlance, his meaning is unmistakably clear. He names the historical predicament of denied access to formal education as having generated a cultural response—i.e., internally generating its own antithesis. That response challenged the sanctity of the very educational resources denied, which, we may add, in turn threatened, to the minds of reactionary classicist critics, to undermine the musical achievements of Western civilization. Just as Hegel had found an ethnocentric embodiment of dialectical progress in his contemporary German civil society, Armstrong claimed that the American swing of his era was an exemplary resolution to the historical tension between the "very strong and vital" yet "crude and not 'finished'" jazz of its early beginnings in New Orleans and the European tradition of classical music and training (previously withheld). "And it is very true that the swing music we have today is far more refined and subtle and more highly developed as an art because the swing men who learned to read and understand classical music have brought classical influences to it."[60] What was in its own way radical (avant-gardist) for the historical moment of its 1936 publication was Armstrong's sociocritical comments on access to musical education. It necessarily implied a critique of racial segregation. And coupled with a claim for the consequentially integrative power of swing aesthetics to break down the social barriers that institutionalized the denial of access, the critique anticipates claims about jazz's democratizing power, later promulgated by writers and musicians from Ralph Ellison and Stanley Crouch to Wynton Marsalis.

The synthesis that Armstrong proposes in *Swing That Music* seems all the more striking when we stop to consider that the book was intended, among other things, to appease a contemporary white patronage. As William Kenney points out in his study of Armstrong's autobiographies, this element of appeasement, or apology, was consistent with political motivations surrounding the publication of the book.[61] Armstrong's travels to Europe and his experiences with European critics in the early thirties confirmed for him what his domestic experiences could not: that jazz was considered "a music that is truly American, [and] that will surely take its place, in time, alongside of the great and permanent music of other countries."[62] Interestingly, Armstrong points out the European origin of the notion of a national music and its permanence. In approbating this European construct he anticipates Ellison's claims about the American national character of jazz as well as what Murray was to refer to, in a more practical vein, as the "Ellington Synthesis": "the very best of all contemporary soundtracks for the nation's workaday activities."[63] The idea of permanence in jazz, however, is paradoxical, as jazz would become susceptible to the kind of "regular" form of swing that Armstrong derided as commercialized. In his later years Armstrong performed iterations of his music, almost to the day he died, never bowing to permanence, not even the permanence of his numerous recordings.

The conflicted prospect of rendering permanence to a music based on impermanence is the challenge of the bricoleur's aesthetic praxis—putting the provisional to work. Armstrong's predilection for Scotch tape and for making it not invisible but manifest in the overlapping layers in his photo-collages constitutes the use of the material in both a proper and improper way. Like the elements in a dream that sustain a relation of contradiction, the Scotch tape, itself a prominent signifier in the photo-collages, is transparency made visible; it *fixes* elements *impermanently*. The cellophane tapes yellow and lose their adhesive capacity after many years. The collages, in turn, refused to become static objects. In his lifetime Armstrong saw the effects of aging on the collages, but he chose to compensate for their fraying condition by adding yet more tape. He did not change his production techniques in the face of chemical changes that altered the color and translucency of collaged elements. He remained consistent in his formal strategies and thus in his attitude toward the demotic aesthetic statement he preferred. It is the paradoxical condition of their physical tenuity that sustains the photo-collages in a bricolage aesthetic that is "grounded" in the play of contingency and provisionality. Armstrong maintained a creative regard for using materials of everyday life, in contradistinction to "high-art" standards, yet in resonance with the syncopated musical aesthetic of jazz improvisation.

If the photo-collages present a "little story" of their own, they do so in the way that dreams present their "stories." Their function compares to that of a rebus: to "speak" in pictures is to remain linguistically enigmatic. And, as with "the productions of the dream-work," Freud has written, they "*are not made with the intention of being understood*"[64]—despite an analyst's intent to interpret them. In this sense dreams, too, are provisional and improvisatory. They serve to represent the exigency of a psychic moment: expressing an unconscious thought, a picture-thought, which, Freud notes, "stands nearer to unconscious processes than does thinking in words."[65] Surrealists came to exploit this pictographic phenomenon most fully.

Today new media technologies vie to usurp the dream-work's throne of visual surreality. Collage in itself has long since its avant-garde introduction ceased to be effectively subversive, though the technique retains something of the potential. Its ability to shock, however, diminishes with the proliferation of new media visual effects, which render photomontage digitally ubiquitous. What collage continues to do functionally, if arcanely, is to transfer material from one context to another. In this manner Armstrong's photo-collages allowed him to intervene in the construction of his public media representation. His montages do not repeat those forms of representation, even though they borrow fragmentary elements excised from popular media sources; instead they alter aspects of a former representation by recontextualizing snippets of images. Under Armstrong's arrangement the collages permit another perspective from which to access aesthetic sensibilities that suffuse a spectrum of creative endeavors. They do so in evidencing a visual correlative to an already developed musical sense of swing aesthetic.

jorge daniel veneciano

NOTES

My thanks to Michael Cogswell and Peggy Alexander of the Louis Armstrong House for their time and assistance with the Armstrong photo-collages.

1. Photomontages juxtapose primarily photographic images, whereas collages mix the media they contain. Armstrong produced both types, but his preferred medium for collage was the photograph, in the form of fragments from actual prints or from reproductions found in popular media sources. This preference, or general tendency, should permit us, when referring to the overall body of his visual work—i.e., containing both collage and photomontage—to use the term *photo-collage*. For more exacting distinctions among the terms applicable here, see Ulrich Weisstein, "Collage, Montage, and Related Terms: Their Literal and Figurative Use in and Application to Techniques and Forms in the Various Arts," *Comparative Literature Studies* 15 (1978): 124–39.

2. Marc H. Miller, ed., *Louis Armstrong: A Cultural Legacy* (Seattle: University of Washington Press, 1994), p. 209.

3. Ibid., p. 209.

4. Kenneth Burke, "Literature as Equipment for Living," in *The Philosophy of Literary Form* (Berkeley: University of California Press, 1973), pp. 293–304.

5. Box numbers refer to the numbering system of the Louis Armstrong Archives and not to Armstrong's own notations.

6. Miller, *Louis Armstrong*, p. 212.

7. Albert Murray, *The Blue Devils of Nada* (New York: Vintage, 1996), p. 53.

8. Ibid., p. 53.

9. Burke, "Literature as Equipment," p. 304.

10. Murray, *The Blue Devils*, p. 72.

11. Richard Meryman, "An Interview with Louis Armstrong," *Life*, April 15, 1966, p. 96.

12. Murray, *The Blue Devils*, p. 78.

13. Ibid., p. 65. That such situations were not indigenous to the U.S. is not Murray's concern. Armstrong's own mythogenic accounts, e.g., that he was born on July 4, 1900, lend themselves to nationalist appropriations.

14. Ibid., p. 14.

15. Ibid., p. 17.

16. Martin Heidegger, *Being and Time*, trans. John Macquarrie and Edward Robinson (New York: Harper and Row, 1962), p. 27.

17. Louis Armstrong, *Swing That Music* (New York: Da Capo, 1993), p. 2.

18. Amiri Baraka, *Blues People: Negro Music in White America* (New York: William Morrow, 1963), p. 152.

19. Ibid., p. 153.

20. Armstrong, *Swing*, pp. 77–78.

21. For valuable insight on the question of editing and ghosting in Armstrong's writings, see William H. Kenney III, "Negotiating the Color Line: Louis Armstrong's Autobiographies," in *Jazz in Mind: Essays on the History and Meanings of Jazz*, ed. Reginald T. Buckner and Steven Weiland (Detroit: Wayne State University Press, 1991), pp. 38–59.

22. Louis Armstrong, *Louis Armstrong, in His Own Words: Selected Writings*, ed. Thomas Brothers (New York: Oxford University Press, 1999), p. xi.

23. Max Jones and John Chilton, *Louis: The Louis Armstrong Story* (Boston: Little, Brown, 1971), p. 193–94.

24. Miller, *Louis Armstrong*, p. 185.

25. Ibid., p. 186.

26. The term for Heidegger's *Umsicht*: "a kind of awareness in which one looks around before one decides just what one ought to do next," editor's footnote, Heidegger, *Being and Time*, p. 98.

27. Claude Lévi-Strauss, *The Savage Mind*, trans. George Weidenfeld (Chicago; University of Chicago Press, 1966), pp. 16–17; all English language translations are from this edition; French passages are from Claude Lévi-Strauss, *La pensée sauvage* (Paris: Plon, 1962), p. 26.

28. Armstrong, *Swing*, p. 30.

29. Ibid., p. xvii.

30. Ibid., p. 31.

31. Lévi-Strauss, *The Savage Mind*, p. 17.

32. Ibid., p. 18.

33. Ibid., p. 19.

34. Paul F. Berliner, *Thinking in Jazz: The Infinite Art of Improvisation* (Chicago: University of Chicago Press, 1994), p. 103.

35. Ibid., p. 103.

36. Ibid., p. 196. Berliner draws this insight from Alan Perlman and Daniel Greenblatt, "Miles Davis Meets Noam Chomsky: Some Observations on Jazz Improvisation and Language Structure," in *The Sign in Music and Literature*, ed. Wendy Steiner (Austin: University of Texas Press, 1981). Perlman and Greenblatt insist not only on the notion of linguistic competence in music but also on linguistic performance as providing a homology to jazz improvisation.

37. Lévi-Strauss, *The Savage Mind*, pp. 21–22.

38. Ibid., p. 21.

39. Ibid., p. 19.

40. Armstrong, *Swing*, p. 33.

41. Lévi-Strauss, *The Savage Mind*, p. 21.

42. Ibid., p. 30.

43. In "Structuralism and Literary Criticism" Gérard Genette takes up the critical function of the bricoleur in relation to literary criticism, *Figures of Literary Discourse* (New York: Columbia University Press, 1982). Another problem with the engineer-bricoleur distinction arises when Lévi-Strauss makes the claim that the engineer works "by means of concepts and the 'bricoleur' by means of signs" (20). This is a fabulous distinction, the impossibilities of which have been famously reviewed by Jacques Derrida in "Structure, Sign, and Play in the Discourse of the Human Sciences." Similarly, one might argue that the failure of Lévi-Strauss's distinction parallels the impossibility of an essential distinction between jazz and other forms of music. However, if we were to take the distinction as a matter of degree rather than kind, we might find a useful metaphor for an evolutionary relationship wherein jazz would stand in "scientific" relation to the bricolage aesthetic of its precursor, the blues—i.e., as a (musical) theory-based stylization of the blues (to borrow a note here from Albert Murray).

44. Peter Bürger, *Theory of the Avant-Garde* (Minneapolis: University of Minnesota Press, 1984), p. 77.

45. Ibid., p. xxxix.

46. Krin Gabbard, "The Quoter and His Culture," in *Jazz in Mind: Essays on the History and Meaning of Jazz,* ed. Reginald T. Buckner and Steven Weiland (Detroit: Wayne State University Press, 1991). The present essay owes measurable inspiration to Gabbard's article.

47. The significance of Armstrong's quotation of George Gershwin is heightened by the fact that Gershwin was someone who also blurred the boundaries between popular entertainment and "serious" art. A study of Armstrong's diverse uses of quotation, and the richness of their semiotic aesthetic implications, would benefit from a broader frame of reference, expanding the one that Gabbard provides here, thereby allowing greater complexity to enter the much debated artist/entertainer question with regard to Armstrong's career. An extensive discussion of this debate can be found in Gary Giddens, *Satchmo* (New York: Da Capo, 1998), and a broader discussion of jazz as art in Krin Gabbard, *Jammin' at the Margins: Jazz and the American Cinema* (Chicago: University of Chicago Press, 1996).

48. Lévi-Strauss, *The Savage Mind*, p. 18.

49. Gabbard, *Jammin'*, p. 102.

50. Lévi-Strauss, *The Savage Mind*, p. 29.

51. Joshua Berrett, "Louis Armstrong and Opera," *Musical Quarterly*, 76.2 (Summer, 1992): 222–23.

52. Ibid., 225. See also Gunther Schuller, *The Swing Era: The Development of Jazz, 1930–1945* (New York: Oxford University Press, 1989), p. 170.

53. Berrett, "Opera," 236.

54. Ibid., 237.

55. Armstrong, *Swing*, pp. 72–73.

56. Louis Armstrong, *Satchmo: My Life in New Orleans* (New York: Da Capo, 1954), p. 142.

57. Ibid., p. 143.

58. Armstrong, *Swing*, p. 73.

59. Ibid., p. 73.

60. Ibid., pp. 74–75.

61. Kenney, "Negotiating the Color Line."

62. Armstrong, *Swing*, p. 75.

63. Murray, *Blue Devils*, p. 81.

64. Sigmund Freud, *The Interpretation of Dreams* (New York: Avon, 1965), p. 377.

65. Sigmund Freud, *The Ego and the Id* (New York: Norton, 1962), p. 11.

ROBERT G. O'MEALLY

Checking Our Balances:
Louis Armstrong, Ralph Ellison, and
Betty Boop

What the black actor has managed to give are moments—indelible moments, created, miraculously, beyond the confines of the script: hints of reality, smuggled like contraband into a maudlin tale, and with enough force, if unleashed, to shatter the tale to fragments
—James Baldwin

But if all this seems too pessimistic, remember that the antidote to hubris, to overweening pride, is irony, that capacity to discover and systematize clear ideas. Or, as Emerson insisted, the development of consciousness, consciousness, consciousness, a more refined conscientiousness, and most of all, that tolerance which takes the form of humor, for when Americans can no longer laugh at each other, they have to fight one another.
—Ralph Ellison

The key figure in the creation of the instrumental jazz solo, of the quality of inevitable-seeming momentum that the world calls swing, and of the relaxed, playful impulse to reinvent a song that is called jazz singing, Louis Armstrong is one of the inventors of jazz, a true revolutionary in art.[1] Harder to evaluate with certainty are Armstrong's cultural politics, the varied offerings and takings of his image and music, his significances as an American icon. Here I refer to "Ambassador Satch," the tireless worker for the State Department and the one who stood up to Dwight Eisenhower at Little Rock; the man who surprised his white agent by saying angrily that Eisenhower, waffling in sync with Governor Faubus, had two faces and *no heart.* At the same time, I refer to the familiar comic image Armstrong began to offer the public as early as the 1930s. What do we make of Armstrong's semicircular, shining smile? His signature flourish of a blazing white handkerchief? If in these familiar scenes what he wears is a comic *mask*, then what does it conceal? And how do we understand the meaning of the mask (or, as Constance Rourke might say, the "double-mask") itself?[2] What can Louis's smiling face tell us about the man who took his stand against a U.S. president? How does this complexly evocative face affect the way we hear his music? Is the comic act something he transcends in his creation of high art music—as the received wisdom would insist—or is the comedy part and parcel of a sometimes blatantly contradictory artistic whole?[3] Looking closely at Armstrong's appearances, in Ralph Ellison's *Invisible Man*—where Armstrong plays a very important role, and, perhaps surprisingly, in a Betty Boop cartoon of the 1930s—where a smiling Armstrong plays an unforgettable cameo role—I shall explore some of the meanings of Armstrong's complicated place in American cultural iconography. In this essay I shall try to read a great man's telltale smile.

This exploration will feature Ralph Ellison's theories of comedy as a set of lenses—both for telescopic perspective and for the close reading of invisible (or, as Ellison once put it, "ambivisible") signs. With this strategy I also hope to see how understanding Armstrong's manifold art can shed light on the world according to Ellison's own art as a writer. How can Louis's sound and smile make us see, and perhaps hear, Ellison's writing more clearly? (Invisible Man asks, "Could this compulsion to put invisibility down in black and white be thus an urge to make music of invisibility?")[4] Perhaps, too, Ellison's sharp eye can help us to understand Armstrong's appearance in Betty Boop—and, if we are really listening, to hear a bit of boop-boop-a-doo in his trumpet playing.

I choose Ellison as critical guide because before becoming a writer, and indeed even in his first years of trying to write fiction, the future author of *Invisible Man* defined himself in his "heart of hearts" as a musician. He was a trumpet player who, by day, paid his dues to Bach and Sousa (as a college boy one of his jobs every morning was to wake the campus with reveille, after which he would blow sustained tones to increase his sound), but who by night was practicing the phrasing and timbre of such blues singers as Ida Cox and, most emphatically, of the singing and trumpet playing of Louis Armstrong and his imitators. "Let that boy blow," Ellison recalls a neighbor's saying of his fledgling efforts on horn. "He's got to talk baby talk on that thing before he can preach on it. . . . Now, try and make it sound like ole Miss Ida Cox sings it."[5]

Ellison's main ambition while in college was to master European classical music sufficiently to write symphonies with an African American accent, sounding the depths of the spirituals and the blues. And it is interesting to consider that Ellison held onto that ambition, only transferring the mode of expression to writing fiction that was thick with black talk and song: the trumpet player as novelist, his novel as Black New World Symphony.

Through most of his childhood Ellison (b. 1914) lived on or near Oklahoma City's Second Street, nicknamed Deep Second or Deep Deuce, which was a smaller version of Kansas City's famous Twelfth and Vine, that city's buckle of the black belt. Like Kansas City, Ellison's home town specialized in hard-dancing big band blues that were alive with what Ellison always termed a *frontier* aspect, a lighter, more hopeful ring not as characteristic of, say, Muddy Waters or other blues artists of the Deep South.[6]

He grew up knowing the singer Jimmy Rushing and the guitarist Charlie Christian (with whom he had gone to school), and particularly favored the Armstrongian trumpeter/singer Hot Lips Page, that famously inventive, full-throated shouter of the blues. In his essays Ellison remembers vividly the day in 1929 when Lester Young appeared in the local shoe shine parlor, waiting in one of those elevated chairs to have his shoes done, wearing a heavy white sweater and a blue stocking cap and holding his "up-and-outthrust silver saxophone" and playing his magically fluid lyrical lines[7]—clearly inspired by fellow-New Orleanian Armstrong—upsetting the town. Elsewhere Ellison also recalls first seeing Armstrong, also in 1929, as he performed in a black dance hall in Oklahoma City. The scene produced a memorable lesson in what Ellison has termed American "segregated democracy."[8] "Suddenly the place was filled with white women," he said. "Nothing like that had ever happened in our town before. His music was our music but they saw it as theirs too, and were willing to break the law to get to it. So you could see that Armstrong's music was affecting [the broad community's] attitudes and values."[9] If this scene gave a hint of Armstrong the subtle civil rights activist to be, perhaps it also indicated some of the power of his comical art against the absurd world in which he found himself: irony versus hubris.

Beginning in the late 1940s, when it already had become commonplace to criticize Armstrong's public persona as pandering to whites, Uncle Tomming, Ellison steadily and staunchly defended him. Indeed, Armstrong may be called the hero of Ellison's 1964 book of essays (the book which the novelist Paule Marshall has brilliantly termed Ellison's true second novel), *Shadow and Act*. Armstrong also opens and closes *Invisible Man*; in its prologue he appears as that novel's most complexly evocative artist as direction giver: the one inside whose art the most discerning reader may hear a highly charged history of black Americans and indeed of the nation. From the vantage point of decades later, it interesting to consider these sell-out charges against Armstrong and to watch Ellison's defenses of him in light of the sudden onslaught of anti-Ellison criticism from black students and artists of the 1960s and 1970s, for whom, like Armstrong, Ellison began to look suspiciously detached, elitist, and Uncle Tommish.[10] (Doubtless one reason for Ellison's failure to complete his ultimately unfinished novel was the shock of finding himself classified by his friends' college-age children and their classmates as some sort of racial opportunist.)

Let us consider some of Ellison's defenses of Armstrong's comic smile:

1. It was the entertainer's style to wear a smile on stage, simple as that. Armstrong's was a generation, before Charlie Parker's, that was less abashed about the entertainer's role as joy bringer, good-time roller. "By rejecting Armstrong they thought to rid themselves of the entertainer's role. And by way of getting rid of the role, they demanded, in the name of their racial identity, a purity of status which

by definition is impossible for the performing artist."[11] In the end, as Dizzy Gillespie's extroverted performance style clearly indicated, the beboppers were entertainers too—even when, as eventually in Miles Davis's case, audiences came to see him turn his back on them, performing disdain in perfect shirts and slacks.

But entertainment with a smile has a distinctive social value, says Ellison. Especially in times of national stress, we depend upon the good work of such musical joy bringers. During the Great Depression, for instance, jazz served the general welfare by helping to lift the spirits; and through the twentieth century, Ellison adds, black American art often gave the whole nation a lift.[12] Moreover, in an interview of 1976, the writer proclaimed "Ellison's law": if blacks could laugh (even if only laughing to keep from crying), who could dare to frown?[13] (A sobering corollary, he also said, was that "whatever happens to blacks will accrue eventually, one way or another, to the nation as a whole. This is their dark-visioned version of the broader 'American Joke.'")[14]

2. Indeed, Ellison's take on Armstrong's deeply humorous art does recall Henry James's famous assessment of the American joke as a secret definitive national gift, "that American humor of which of late years we have heard so much."[15] We live, Ellison once wrote, in the "United States of Jokeocracy,"[16] "a land of masking jokers."[17] What could be more definitively American than Louis Armstrong, smiling? If it is a national gift, this great good humor, perhaps it is in line with Kenneth Burke's idea of the comic frame of reference in art as the wide window on the world through which one could see the most: comedy as the clearest view of salvation. "Comedy," writes Burke, "should enable us to be *observers of ourselves while acting*. Its ultimate end would not be *passiveness* but *maximum consciousness*. [It should allow] one to 'transcend' himself by noting his own foibles . . . [and should] provide a rationale for locating the irrational and the non-rational."[18] The Armstrongian smile as an American icon of optimism, an emblem of good cheer and "maximum consciousness."

Nor, in this view, is such American humor necessarily a shield of deflection or avoidance. Writing about the Americanness of Duke Ellington's slyly humorous habits of spoken and musical expression in a way that brings Armstrong to mind, Ellison gives insight into humor in jazz, and perhaps into defining a process that helps power the creation of much U.S. art as an indigenous form. Ellington's sense of humor, Ellison says, is as full of mockery

> as the dancing of those slaves who, looking through the windows of a plantation manor house from the yard, imitated the steps so gravely performed by the masters within and then added to them their own special flair, burlesquing the white folks and then going on to force the steps into a choreography uniquely their own. The whites, looking out at the activity in the yard, thought they were being flattered by imitation, and were amused by the incongruity of tattered blacks dancing courtly steps, while missing completely the fact that before their eyes a European cultural form was becoming Americanized, undergoing a metamorphosis through the

mocking activity of a people partially sprung from Africa. So, blissfully unaware, the whites laughed while the blacks danced out their mocking reply.[19]

This is an American process of creating art through a dynamic system of exchanges—including what Henry Louis Gates terms "signifyin(g)" and what Robert Farris Thompson terms "dances of derision"—that often comes with a coolly aloof but calculated smile. Armstrong's smile, then, as a heap of signifying, in the African American way: an Armstrongian dance of derision.

In a masterful essay called "An Extravagance of Laughter," Ellison's studies "the blackness of Negro laughter" as he riffs hilariously on the old "folktales" of the colored citizen's "laughing barrel." According to many a tale, laughing barrels were strategically placed in the walkways of southern towns so that if a Negro felt too urgent a gale of laughter coming on, he or she could howl down into one of these laughing barrels and thus avoid disrupting the general civic peace.

> The barrels [writes Ellison] were by no means an elegant solution of what whites regarded as a most grievous and inelegant problem. After all, having to observe the posture of a Negro stuck halfway into a laughing barrel . . . rising and falling . . . was far from an aesthetic experience. Nor was that all, for often when seen laughing with their heads stuck in a barrel and standing, as it were, upside down upon the turbulent air, Negroes appeared to be taken over by a form of schizophrenia which left them even more psychically frazzled than whites regarded them as being by nature. . . . It appeared that in addition to reacting to whatever ignorant, harebrained notion had set him off in the first place, the Negro was apt to double up with a second gale of laughter, triggered, apparently, by his own mental image of himself laughing at himself laughing upside down. It was, all whites agreed, another of the many Negro mysteries with which it was their lot to contend, but whatever its true cause, it was most disturbing to a white observer.[20]

Here then, one might view Armstrong's jazz as a rippling, subversive comic art, deflating self and others in a cake-walking communal celebration and bash.[21] Riffing on Du Bois's thesis of doubleness and clairvoyance, in "Extravagance" Ellison also notes that the view from inside the laughing barrel was ironically such that "when a Negro had his head thrust into a laughing-barrel he became endowed with a strange form of extrasensory perspective—or second sight."[22]

These passages about laughing barrels, Ellington, and, it seems to me, also about Armstrong, suggest that American-style comedy offers modes of self-reflection, ways of seeing ourselves and others without taking ourselves too seriously. And it is one of the mightiest engines producing unself-conscious American art—art that is most characteristically American: Armstrong, looking at the lead sheet of a song like "Shine," or "Otchi-Tchor-Ni-Ya," laughing at what's expected of him, seeming to comply, then mocking the expectation and the falsely accommodating self, winking at his audience, laughing as he helps create a new form of American expression and art. Here is Armstrong employing a rich comedy indeed: comedy as our national artistic strategy and, in James's term, truly our national "gift."[23]

3. Harder to embrace is Ellison's contention that we Americans need this highly charged comic process *sometimes even when it means putting up with offensive racial stereotypes*. Through American history, Ellison said, "The northerner found the southerner strange. The southerner found the northerner despicable. The blacks found the whites peculiar. The whites found the blacks ridiculous. Some agency had to be adopted which would allow us to live with one another without destroying one another, and the agency was laughter, was humor. If you can laugh at me, you don't have to kill me. If I can laugh at you, I don't have to kill you."[24] And in the process of laughing at the comic dupe, a human identification is made—something perhaps more important, Ellison says, than eliminating the offending comic image or its perpetrator. Recall Invisible Man's comically thwarted effort to discard the metal bank in the stereotypical shape of a grotesquely smiling "Negro" head;[25] even in shards, the heavy load can't be thrown away by the young black man because, offensive as it is, it is nonetheless part of his American cultural luggage. Earned or unearned, wanted or not, the stereotyped black face is one of his most densely significant *gifts*. What the young man learns is that if he can anticipate the uses by his enemies of racist images like this one, maybe he can deploy them for his own strategic purposes—to "overcome 'em with yeses, undermine 'em with grins, agree 'em to death and destruction," as his grandfather advised.[26]

4. Ellison implies that Louis's laughter might be taken as part of a strategy to create a freer space in which to make art: a way to "make poetry out of being invisible," as Invisible Man puts it, extolling Armstrong's art. Mistaken as clown or fool, Armstrong himself is an invisible man and thus ironically freer to experiment with his art, freer from the pressures that typically go with the official recognition of "high art."

Furthermore, deriving from African, European, and Native American people, with their many traditions of mask wearing, and specifically from multinational New Orleans where masquerade is intrinsic to carnival (and where in 1949 Armstrong came home to the Crescent City as the painted and highly decorated King of the Zulus, the Afro-Indian monarch of mockery), no wonder Armstrong the performer was a masked man. As such, he operated in the American/African American tradition of wearing one face while concealing another: of Benjamin Franklin playing Europe as a primitive, Ellen Craft made up to look like her slave husband's white master, Richard Wright pretending, at a whites-only library, to be a white man's errand boy and hangdog black dunce. Like Rinehart's hat in *Invisible Man*, Louis's face that resembled a stereotyped happy darky's grin permitted him to express his own complex sense of life through his music without ruffling the feathers of those who preferred to think him less than he was.

5. It is very important that Ellison calls Armstrong not just a masked man but a *trickster*. With his "sweat, spittle and facial contortions," writes Ellison, Armstrong was "the trickster" who "emphasizes the physicality of his music as he per-

forms the magical feat of making romantic melody issue from a throat of gravel; and [who] some few years ago was recommending to all and sundry his personal [medicine] 'Pluto Water,' as a purging way to health, happiness and international peace."[27] All in good fun, as through the trickster's mask he projected "romantic melody"[28] and sublime elegance. ("Elegance turns up in every aspect of Afro-American culture," says Ellison, "from sermons to struts, pimp-walks and dance steps. . . . And if Louis Armstrong's meditations on the 'Potato Head Blues' aren't marked by elegance, then the term is too inelegant to name the fastidious refinement, the mastery of nuance, the tasteful domination of melody, rhythm, sounding brass and tinkling cymbal which marked his style.")[29]

"We wear the mask," Ellison writes, *"for purposes of aggression as well as for defense."*[30] Does this indicate a more aggressive side to Armstrong's trickster-play? Consider Ellison's short story "A Coupla Scalped Indians," where the improvised music in the distance is heard as the art of coping with chaos in the form of white antagonists: The trumpet is a soldier, Buster says, "'Cause he's slipping 'em in the twelves and choosing 'em, all at the same time. Talking 'bout they mamas and offering to fight 'em. Now he ain't like that ole clarinet; clarinet so sweet-talking he just eases you in the dozens." Buster tells his friend that he will emulate the instruments' ways of dealing with enemies with the switchblade subtlety of the signifying dozens ("the twelves"): "You have to outtalk 'em, outrun 'em, or outfight 'em and I don't aim to be running and fighting all the time."[31] But one way or the other, "our life is a war," as the Invisible Man's grandfather said before he died,[32] and the music a call to arms, a set of strategies for battle. "This familiar music had demanded action," says Invisible Man, listening to Armstrong's "Black and Blue."[33]

This idea of Armstrong's more aggressive humor is hinted at in a 1957 letter from Ellison in Rome to his friend Albert Murray. Ellison writes:

> Here, way late, I've discovered Louis singing Mack the Knife. Shakespeare invented Caliban, or changed himself into him—Who the hell dreamed up Louie? Some of the bop boys consider him Caliban but if he is he's a mask for a lyric poet who is much greater than most now writing. That's a mask for [the critic] to study, me too. . . . Hare and bear [are] the ticket; man and mask, sophistication and taste hiding behind clowning and crude manners—the American joke, man. . . . The only time he ever comes out from behind that mask is when he's cornered—that's when you have to watch him. Unless, of course, he's Mose, who has learned to deal with a hell of a lot more pressure.[34]

Louis as Brer Hare and Brer Bear (trickster and strongman), clowning while, behind the mask, he continued to assert his values with "sophistication and taste." But also, very tellingly: Armstrong as Caliban the New World slave learning Old Master's language well enough to curse him with it, Armstrong/Caliban cursing as he laughs.

6. As a consummate player and singer of the blues, Armstrong was involved, day in and day out, with the comedy at the edge of tragedy that defines the funda-

mental blues mode—wherein typically the performer counts the teeming troubles of the world and then laughs at them, the tragic facts typically trumped by an ironically comic punch line. As a form the blues is characterized by "unobtrusive irony" and a staunch refusal to be sentimental or mawkish, however lovelorn the lyrics or moods. The "great human joke" in the blues, wrote Ellison in 1954, is that "though we be dismembered daily we shall always rise up."[35] For Ellison, at its best this joke's dark blue laughter offers not just release but a rush of perspective by incongruity[36] and revelation—which helps explain the strangely violent outbursts of cathartic laughter in "Flying Home," "On Being a Target of Racism," "An Extravagance of Laughter," and *Invisible Man*.[37]

In 1966, Ellison told a group at Langston University what he meant by the blues as a tragicomic frame of mind:

> I refer not simply to the song form, but to a basic and complex attitude toward experience. It is an attitude toward life which looks pretty coldly and realistically at the human predicament, and which expresses the individual's insistence upon enduring in the face of his limitations, and which is in itself a kind of triumph over self and circumstance. . . . I can only say that there is a part of my temperament which finds its expression in this crazy mixture of modes.[38]

This Ellisonian perspective on the blues as funny and sad but still triumphal is congruent with Albert Murray's sense of the Saturday Night Function as functional indeed: a ritual floor wherein one confronted the tragic facts of life at the same time that one sought to drive the blues-troubles away with hard-partying to blues music; the blues as an intrinsic part of a rite of purification and of courtship and fertility—a comic victory of spring over winter, a bluesy laugh and shout as we rise again.[39] Listen to Armstrong sing the "St. James Infirmary Blues"[40]—as much a chilling meditation on the death of a young lover stretched out on a cold white table as it is a reflection on the singer's own death. Twice in the midst of one performance recorded in 1959, Louis cracks up laughing, as if the blues can squeeze humor out of (and thus help singer and listener to confront) the most inscrutable of losses, not excluding the destruction of a lover and even of the self.

With these various ideas about the Armstrong's art—and in particular its comic arc—let us consider the prologue to *Invisible Man* where the protagonist, hiding in his underground basement, says he owns one record player but plans to get five of them, all broadcasting Armstrong's "Black and Blue" at the same time. Ellison uses that song as his character's Proustian madelaine or *lieu de memoire*: sweet site of memory and spur to cultural excavation and consciousness. Beneath the surfaces of that song, he hears a wide variety of sounds, recalling Ellison's statements about the modern artist's bold play of references, which Ellison admired both in Armstrong and T. S. Eliot. In both cases the impulse to quotation "grows out of a similar and quite American approach to the classics, just as Armstrong and any other jazz musician of that period would take a theme and start improvising. Then he would pay his respects to *Aida,* to any number of operas, to light opera, or to religious music. All this . . . in the course of the improvisation."[41] Invisible Man hears a whole symphony of songs and stories—including the sounds of an old ex-slave woman whose sons laugh eerily because their white father, whom she loved and hated, is dead; and who for her own part explains, *"I laughs too, but I moans too"*—folded inside that tragic and (though we usually forget this part) uncannily *comical* song, "What Did I Do (to Be so Black and Blue?)"

Standing, for a moment more, outside the novel, what on earth are we to make of "Black and Blue" itself, this strange dirge of 1929 often called the first racial protest song in the United States? "Black and Blue" was written by the black song-writing team of Andy Razaf and Thomas "Fats" Waller in response to a specific order by the gangster Arthur Flegenheimer (a.k.a. Dutch Schultz) that the new, all-black show he was bankrolling have "something with a little colored girl singing how tough it is being colored."[42] In its original setting for that show, *Hot Chocolates,* "Black and Blue" offered what appeared at first blush to be just what Dutch had in mind: a conventional piece of staged racial pathos. "Even a mouse, / ran from my house," go the lyrics. "Feel like old Ned, / Wish I was dead."

But there is a carefully anticipated twist of black laughter located here. Instead of jerking tears from whites about "how tough it is to be colored," Razaf conceived "Black and Blue" as a mock-pathetic joke by a dark-skinned woman who reclines on a fluffy white bed shining with white satin sheets in a room washed in white light, and who sings about how Negro men preferred light-skinned women. The line "browns and yellers," delivered with a mock-pathetic pout by the show's original singer, Edith Wilson, *"all have fellers,"* got the show's biggest laugh. And while the line "I'm white inside, but that don't help my case," offends our ears in 2003, in 1929 these words stopped the laughter for a moment; they were so bold an upend-ing of what white U.S. audiences generally expected of a "colored" show tune (pathos, humor, sex) Razaf later said that, at the show's opening, only the (white) audience's tumultuous extravagance of laughter—and then its spirited standing ovation—kept Schultz from shooting him on the spot! One rule in this world, Razaf later said, seemed to be that you did not kill a man who had just written you a hit song.[43]

With Razaf's own agenda of subtle subversion in mind, it is easy to wonder if "Black and Blue" may have been conceived for Louis Armstrong, who did appear in the show and evidently was present while the song was being created. Armstrong recorded "Black and Blue" that same year, 1929, now editing it to erase the intraracial theme and boomeranging stage comedy as he turned it into his own tragedy-haunted meditation on white racism and—beyond the issue of race in the United States—a philosophical reflection on the meaning of inevitable human suffering: What did any of us do to be so bruised by life, so beaten *black and blue?*

Listening to Armstrong's "Black and Blue" (smoking a reefer) and wishing he had five record players to hear it properly, Invisible Man was struck by Armstrong's way of singing with and against the music's expected steady cadences—his way of swinging the song. You felt you were "never quite on the beat," Ellison's character says. "Sometimes you're ahead and sometimes behind. Instead of the swift and imperceptible flowing of time, you are aware of its nodes, those points where time stands still or from which it leaps ahead. And you slip into the breaks and look around. That's what you hear vaguely in Louis' music." Of course swinging (one thinks of Malcolm X's "we need to stop singing and start *swinging*") can have its aggressive as well as its pleasingly musical side, its *elan vital*.[44] To make this point, Ellison has Invisible Man listen to "Black and Blue" at the same time that he recalls seeing a prizefighter boxing a yokel, landing a hundred scientifically timed blows while the yokel can only recoil in stunned helplessness. "But suddenly the yokel, rolling about in the gale of boxing gloves, struck one blow and knocked science, speed and footwork as cold as a well-digger's posterior," writes Ellison. "The yokel had simply stepped inside his opponent's sense of time." Between the breaks in this intense but nonetheless swinging performance of "Black and Blue," Invisible Man hears the instruments as characters in a story: "The unheard sounds came through," he says, "and each melodic line existed of itself, stood out clearly from all the rest, said its piece, and waited patiently for the other voices to speak. That night I found myself hearing not only in time but in space as well. I not only entered the music but descended, like Dante, in its depths."[45]

In a novel often criticized for being masculinist, Invisible hears a song first staged as a woman's song inside which he also hears an old woman who sings a spiritual *"as full of Weltschmertz as flamenco, and beneath that lay a still lower level on which I saw a beautiful girl the color of ivory pleading in a voice like my mother's as she stood before a group of slaveowners who bid for her naked body."* While the old singer of spirituals tells her story and moans[46] of love and hate for the white man she has killed to gain her freedom, her sons upstairs howl an uncanny laughter. Typical Ellison, and true to "Black and Blue," the scene is mixed with tragedy and comedy. *"I laughs too,"* the woman says, *"but I moans too. He promised to set us free but he never could bring hisself to do it. Still I loved him."*[47]

Before Ellison began to work his magic on "Black and Blue" the song was a site of contestation over the meaning of black expression and history. Schultz called for minstrel-show-style Negro pathos and received, from Razaf, a protest song gently ribboned in humor; Armstrong edited out the humor to intensify the protest song's racial edge and tragic thrust; and Ellison edited it still further, eliminating the song's dated language about "house" and "mouse" and "I'm white, inside"—compressing it to the bare, bluesy ten words of the song's title, "What did I do / To be so black and blue?" But what fascinates me most here is that Ellison's character's reflections on the song return to the idea of the song as a woman's plaint and moan, mixed with strange, ambiguous laughter and a secret knockout punch. That in the novel Armstrong is made to deliver the lines only adds more force to the meaning: It is a trickster's song, deep and wide with meaning and moaning (certainly it is significant that the modern English word *moan* derives from an Anglo-Saxon word meaning "to tell" and "to mean"), but not without the edged, angular anger of Ellison's novel: the blackness of Negro laughter.

An Ellisonian perspective on Armstrong's humor can also help us confront the strange Betty Boop cartoon of 1932 in which, three years after his recording of

"Black and Blue," Armstrong makes brief but captivating appearances. Before turning to this cartoon, called "I'll Be Glad When You're Dead, You Rascal, You," we should pause to note that Ellison sometimes referred to comics (he wrote about comic books but I believe his analyses could also apply to cartoons) as revealing much about the values and mythologies informing American life. In *Invisible Man*, as the hero begins to sense the significance of black leadership from the periphery, he sees three quiet black boys on a subway platform who are studying comic books "in complete absorption." "Who knew," thinks Invisible Man,

> they might be the saviors, the true leaders, the bearers of something precious. . . . What if history was not a reasonable citizen, but a madman full of paranoid guile and these boys his agents, his big surprise! His own revenge? For they were outside, in the dark with Sambo, the dancing paper doll; taking on the lambo . . . running and dodging the forces of history instead of making a dominating stand.[48]

These readers of comics are in touch, according to Ellison's view of American popular culture, with truths about the United States's usually invisible history.

In the cartoon, "I'll Be Dead When You're Dead, You Rascal, You," we first see Armstrong and his band in a prefatory film clip, without animation.[49] The ten-piece band plays the quick, jaunty lines of "High Society," with Armstrong the sharply dressed leader playing trumpet and mock-conducting the other instrumentalists through the cool, nonchalant flexing of his arms and upper-body. After an animated clip introduces Betty Boop as the cartoon's star, again with Armstrong's "High Society" as sound track, the story line unfurls with Betty "on safari" in "the jungle" with her friends Bimbo the Dog and Koko the Clown, as her "white hunters" carrying her on a kind of stretcher that floats and bumps her along in an erotic dance that keeps dog, clown, and even the stretcher itself giggling as they go. As if to confirm racialist fears and wishful fantasies dating back at least to the seventeenth century, Betty's trip into the heart of the forest's darkness has rendered her skin color noticeably darker than in the introductory trailer.

Eventually the grotesquely androgynous "black" "natives," who stalk the intruders at every step, snatch Betty from her protectors and take her prisoner. Here again another centuries-old American fear and fantasy is evoked: that of the "white" girl being led by dark people into the dark forest to face unspeakable temptations against her dearest values and, most pressingly, against her sexual purity.[50] What ensues is a fantastic chase, with Bimbo and Koko strut-dancing at top speed into the quickly darkening night, pursued by a lone "savage," who moves to ("I'll Be Glad When You're Dead), You Rascal, You"—the song, performed by the Armstrong band. Soon the dark chaser morphs into an animated head that floats on air—an immense and menacing stereotyped black primitive, though bodiless—which chases Bimbo and Koko while singing the lyrics of the song in Armstrong's voice! The disembodied floating head then melts into a film image of Louis Armstrong's own smiling head, singing the lyrics with more of a laugh than a real threat as it makes its way in hot pursuit![51]

Then, as if it were a filmic variety show,[52] the animated cartoon rolls up like a curtain to reveal more film footage of the Armstrong band, this time playing "Chinatown, My Chinatown," the leader now directing his men by flapping his arms as if he were still some sort of (temporarily grounded) creature of the sky. "Looks like these cats're trying to cut me here sure 'nough," says Armstrong as a stage aside—suggesting that the band's music, too, is about a chase or competition—"Oh, but I'm ready," he says, "*I'm ready!*" To top things off, before Betty is rescued, and the "savages" blown up by a volcano, Armstrong's drummer Alfred "Tubby" Hall makes a solo cameo appearance—Hall, too, changing from musician into rhythm-intoxicated but jolly "savage" who stirs the pot in which the other "natives" evidently plan to stew Miss Betty. At the very end of "I'll Be Glad," Armstrong has the last word, delivered in front of his band with a kind of roar in the middle of the chorus and with an explosive grunt at the end: "I'll be glad when you're dead , *Oooooh,* I'll be glad when you're dead, you rascal you. . . . *NNyuhnn!!*"

There's much to consider here: the sharp-edged song itself, perhaps related in spirit to the ironically passive-aggressive slave secular "Massa's in the Cold, Cold Ground"; Armstrong's presentation of the song in other contexts;[53] the Fleischer Brothers' brilliant uses of jazz in other cartoons, particularly in those with Cab Calloway, where the producers' innovative process called "rotogravure" permitted the Calloway characters to sing and dance with astonishing musicality and subtly precise rhythm;[54] the Fleischers uses of jazz, here and elsewhere, not as conventional soundtrack but as starting point from which the action is derived—the cartoon's action narrativizing original recorded music, not the other way round; the cartoon's intriguingly jazzlike methods of production, with a band of writers and illustrators working alone and together to create an improvised whole cartoon; this particular cartoon's pointed racial comedy, paralleling vaudeville, minstrelsy, and other sites of raw American racial mythology—suggested everywhere here but especially by the "blacks" and by Koko the Clown, who runs out of his "black" clown-suit to reveal that he is "white" underneath; the markings then of Koko as Jewish as while he runs he hits speeds recorded first in miles per hour and then by a phrase in Hebrew letters; Betty's "race"—"white," sometimes "Jewish," sometimes shaded "black," always tantalizingly ambiguous; her ambiguity, for that matter, as a sexy grown-up whose head makes up about one-third of her body, marking her as some sort of outsized baby as well as big-girl vamp; Betty's first screen incarnations as a dog, Bimbo's love interest, she whose signature loop earrings were floppy puppy ears; Betty's wink, here in "I'll Be Glad" and then throughout her career, as if she and her audience understood all this complex business as part of a joke shared in secret together.[55]

And then—as we turn back toward the question of Louis Armstrong—there is the fascinating problem of the vocal lineage of Betty herself, whose flapper curls and boop-oo-pa-doo act were copied so directly from the popular white singer Helen Kane, as the Fleischers Brothers later admitted, that Kane took them to court for stealing her act and income. In a dramatic (Ellisonian) turn of events, the Fleischers Brothers defended themselves by appearing in court with a series of five different singers—all of whom used the boop-oop-a-doop riff in their acts and all of whom had played the part of Betty in Fleischer cartoons at one time or another. All five disclaimed Kane as their model—even Mae Questel, who as a teenager had won a Helen Kane look-alike contest and who, for her faithfulness to the Kane model, was the singer most often cast in the role of Betty. Still, Max Fleischer boldly declared in court that Betty Boop was not a copy of any one singer but instead was a figment of his imagination, enacted by many singers that he hired.

The climax of the case (a further Ellisonian twist) came when the court viewed archival film brought in by the defense—footage shot in the early days of sound, featuring yet another singer, this time a black cabaret artist billed as Baby Esther, who on film performed a song that contained the heavily debated phrase, "boop-boop-a-doop." The Fleischers' lawyers further surprised the court with testimony from Baby Esther's manager, Lou Walton, claiming that Helen Kane and her manager had heard Baby Esther sing in a cabaret in 1928. The point of course was that even if the Fleischers' singer(s) had copied Kane to create Betty Boop, Kane herself, if the evidence could be believed,[56] was an imitation of black Baby Esther.[57] In other words, Boop herself was an imitation of an imitation and had, as it were, a black grandmother in her background.[58]

And, of course, *she also had a black grandfather.* For who else but Mister Louis Armstrong, the grand old man of scat singing—from his work on "Heebie Jeebies" (1926), widely regarded as the first scat song to reach a wide audience, to his many other immensely popular and influential early scat performances[59]—could be Betty's true secret granddaddy? And yes, it is wonderful to think of Louis Armstrong, cast by the Fleischers as stereotyped "savage" or, at best, as novelty showman, standing behind the signature style of their "white" singer Betty Boop: Satchmo, the true progenitor of her act. Maybe *that* explains, at least in part, the toothiness of his smile in this cartoon—his extravagance of laughter!

Indeed, given all this tremendously ironical background drama, the role played by Armstrong in "I'll Be Glad When You're Dead, You Rascal You," is that much more intriguingly layered. Cast as a primitive among primitives, he nevertheless appears, too, as the highly polished leader of a band for which he is the conductor, singer, and principle soloist. And his song, despite its "fried chicken" lyrics and foolishness, is unmistakable in its aggressive declarations that its singer will be glad when "*you*"—the "whites" in the cartoon? Betty? the producers? the audience?—are all dead.

Of course Armstrong agreed to make the cartoon as a promotional short subject in order to advertise his traveling band and the best-selling record he had ever made up to that time.[60] But, in so doing, he also advertised a point of view that might be termed Ellisonian: that through all the comedy, which can seem so simplistically stereotyped, the trickster with his trumpet projects his complicated cultural message. As with "Black and Blue" in Ellison's novel, through this cartoon and this song, including Armstrong's smiling disembodied head and song of revenge—a whole cultural history may be detected. Nor is the Armstrong role fully defined in terms of the simple transcendence of the artist over Hollywood and New York, as Albert Murray, Gary Giddins, and Ken Burns have argued.[61] No, rather it seems to me that Armstrong's is an indivisibly double or triple role—genius, clown, and aggressive warrior, salesman in the racial marketplace, actor, and revolutionary giving no quarter when the moment for war arrives.[62] "I'll Be Glad" has its transcendent and aggressive sides. With this said, it also is important to admit the embarrassing foolishness of this cartoon, the racial travesty in which Mr. Armstrong is complicit. With this admission freely made, the history told here is that much richer, for it does not lie about American racism and the roles to which even our most brilliant black artists have been consigned.

In his novel, *Juneteenth*, Ellison's main character is Rev. A. Z. Hickman, a trombone-playing bluesman who has been converted and called to preach. His adopted son, Rev. Bliss, is an unreliable narrator, but he does get it right when he implies that what we need as a nation are the values of jazz, not finished stasis but a will to improvise. Here's Bliss:

> We seek not perfection, but coordination. Not sterile stability but creative momentum. Ours is a youthful nation; the perfection we seek is futuristic and to be made manifest in creative action. . . . Born in diversity and fired by determination, our society was endowed with a flexibility designed to contain the most fractious contentions of an ambitious, individualistic and adventurous breed. . . . Yes, and as we check our checks and balance our balances, let us in all good humor balance our checks and check our balances, keeping each in proper order, issuing credit to the creditable, minus to plus, and plus to minus.[63]

What Bliss and Invisible Man, who calls himself a "bungling bugler of words," and Armstrong, the trumpeter known for what Ellison terms his "rowdy poetic flights"—what they all recommend are the qualities of resiliency and spiritual equipoise, which define the blues along with the music's awareness that "the real secret of the game is to make life swing."[64] And swinging, as we have seen, is an extremely complex business: with its aggressive and defensive aspects, swinging may be regarded as a fiercely comic mode, a game of coordinating checks and balances, defenses and aggressions.

As a coda, let us look for a moment at Ellison looking at Armstrong, and—as if to confirm the difficulty of getting a fix on the great musician's public image—completely misreading the situation. In a letter to Albert Murray Ellison reports on his impression, evidently from newspaper accounts, of the 1957 Newport Jazz Festival, where Armstrong's band appeared briefly. After performing a few songs, Armstrong hammered out a quick "Star-Spangled Banner" as a farewell song and Bronx salute; then he marched his band off stage, not to reappear. Loud talk backstage was heard by reporters. "Louis was wearing his ass instead of his genius," wrote a disappointed Ellison to Murray.[65]

What Ellison did not know is that on that day, George Wein, the director of Jazz at Newport, had arranged with Armstrong's manager, Joe Glazer, that Armstrong's fifty-seventh birthday, the day of the concert, would feature guests associated with Louis's career, including Ella Fitzgerald, who would replace Armstrong's regular singer Velma Middleton for the evening. No one told (or asked) Armstrong about these surprise plans, however. And his longstanding agreement with his manager was that he alone, Armstrong, would make all such artistic decisions while leaving bookings and payments to Glazer. What Ellison read were newspaper speculations about what had made Louis take off in a huff. No one seemed to get the story straight. Instead of "showing his ass"—embarrassing himself by acting unprofessionally, for no good reason—Louis had been standing up for his own artistic program and colleague, even though doing so meant a showdown with powerful white men with whom he long had done business. Behind the stage smile on that day was a world of trouble, misread by those who were there and even by his best reader and defender, Ralph Ellison.[66]

Louis's smiling face is the slipperiest of cultural masks to interpret. What lies behind it? Sometimes it is political anger, sometimes another, more genial smile; sometimes it's a story of artistic integrity defended. Sometimes it is a wink or moan that deflates arrogance, racial or otherwise, as it shatters a maudlin tale to fragments. Sometimes it seems to say that not only is the real secret to make life swing, but to make life swing *hard,* and with a smile. In other words, Armstrong's smile often indicates a secret but highly effective assertion of power. So watch out, for what Ellison said of himself evidently was just as true of Mr. Armstrong, too: When he was laughing the hardest, *he was usually preparing a punch for somebody!*

NOTES

1. See Robert G. O'Meally, liner notes to "Louis Armstrong Hot Fives and Sevens," Columbia CDs, 2001.
2. See Constance Rourke, *American Humor: A Study of the American Character* (1931) reprinted by Harcourt, Brace (1959).
3. For superb new discussions of Armstrong and stereotypical racial humor, see Krin Gabbard's "Actor and Musician: Louis Armstrong and His Films," in *Jammin' at the Margins: Jazz and the American Cinema* (Chicago: University of Chicago Press, 1996), pp. 204–38, 310–28; and Brent Hayes Edwards's "Louis Armstrong and the Syntax of Scat," *Critical Inquiry* (Spring 2002): 618–49. For the canonical readings of Armstrong's image, see Gary Giddins's *Satchmo* (New York: DaCapo, 1998); and Albert Murray's *The Blue Devils of Nada* (New York: Vintage, 1996).
4. Ralph Ellison, *Invisible Man* (New York: Vintage, 1972 [1952]), pp. 13–14.
5. Ralph Ellison, "Living with Music," *High Fidelity* (1955), reprinted in Ralph Ellison, *Living with Music* (New York: Modern Library, 2001), p. 9.
6. See Ralph Ellison, "Remembering Jimmy" (1958), reprinted in Ellison, *Living with Music.*
7. Ellison writes of Lester Young in "The Charlie Christian Story" (1958), and in "The Golden Age, Time Past" (1959), both reprinted in *Living with Music.*
8. This phrase is used in Ellison's personal essay called "On Being the Target of Discrimination," *New York Times Magazine,* April 1989, reprinted in *The Collected Essays of Ralph Ellison* (New York: Modern Library), p. 821.

9. "Ralph Ellison's Territorial Vantage," an interview by Ron Welburn, *Grackle* (1977–1978), reprinted in Ellison, *Living with Music*, pp. 28–29.

10. See James McPherson, "Indivisible Man," *Atlantic Monthly* (December 1970), reprinted in *Conversations with Ralph Ellison*, pp. 173–191.

11. Ralph Ellison, "On Bird, Bird-Watching, and Jazz," *Saturday Review* (1962), reprinted in *Living with Music*, p. 69.

12. Ellison discusses this in "Homage to Duke Ellington," *Washington Star* (1969), reprinted in *Living with Music*, pp. 77–86.

13. Ellison said this in conversation with the author in May 1976.

14. Ralph Ellison, "An Extravagance of Laughter," in *Going to the Territory* (1986), reprinted in *The Collected Essays of Ralph Ellison*, pp. 185–86.

15. Henry James, "Nathaniel Hawthorne" (1905), reprinted in *Henry James: Literary Criticism, Essays on Literature, American Writers, English Writers* (New York: Library of America, 1984), p. 352.

16. Ralph Ellison, "It Always Breaks Out," *Partisan Review* (Spring 1963), p. 16.

17. Ralph Ellison, "Change the Joke and Slip the Yoke," *Partisan Review* (Spring 1958), reprinted in *The Collected Essays of Ralph Ellison*, p. 109.

18. These lines from Burke's *Attitudes Toward History* (New York: New Republic, 1937), pp. 220–21, are quoted in Ellison, "An Extravagance of Laughter," p. 185. The italics are Burke's, the brackets and elipses Ellison's.

19. From "Homage to Duke Ellington on His Birthday," *Washington Star* (1969), reprinted in Ralph Ellison, *Living with Music*, p. 84.

20. Ellison, "An Extravagance of Laughter," pp. 651–52.

21. With all this going on in this music, small wonder Plato had his doubts about the place of *musika* in his republic: pouring so directly into the soul, how easily music could lead the unsuspecting student astray.

22. Ellison, "An Extravagance of Laughter," p. 191.

23. "Verbal comedy was a way of confronting social ambiguity," wrote Ellison in 1980.

Being familiar with racial violence—we were living in the aftermath of the race riots that followed World War I, remember—we learned quite early that laughter made the difficulties of our condition a bit more bearable. We hadn't read Henry James at that time, but we realized nevertheless that American society contained a built-in joke, and we were aware, even if James wasn't (or did not choose to admit), that this joke was in many ways centered in our condition. So we welcomed any play on words or nuance of gesture which gave expression to our secret sense of the way things really were. Usually this took the comic mode, and it is quite possible that one reason the popular arts take on an added dimension in our democracy lies in an unspoken, though no less binding, agreement that popular culture is not to be taken seriously. Thus the popular arts have become an agency through which Americans can contemplate those aspects of our experience that are deemed unspeakable.

Perhaps that is what it was left to such comedians as Redd Foxx to notify us that since the 1950s a major change has occurred in our attitudes toward racial minorities. Thus when he, a black comedian, makes remarks about ugly white women which once were reserved only for black women, he allows us to bring attitudes and emotions that were once tabooed into the realm of the rational, where, protected by the comic mode, we may confront out guilt and prejudices and perhaps resolve them.

"Going to the Territory," *Carleton Miscellany* (Winter 1980), reprinted in The *Collected Essays of Ralph Ellison*, 607–8.

24. Ralph Ellison, "American Humor," p. 148.
25. One source of the image of the undiscardable item may have been "Abu Kasem's Slippers," in Joseph Campbell's *The King and the Corpse: Tales of the Soul's Conquest of Evil* (Princeton: Princeton University Press, 1971[1948]), pp. 9–25.
26. Ellison, *Invisible Man*, p. 16.
27. Ellison, *The Collected Essays of Ralph Ellison*, pp. 106–7.
28. Ibid.
29. "Study and Experience: An Interview with Ralph Ellison," *Massachusetts Review*, 1977, reprinted in *Conversations with Ralph Ellison*, ed. Maryemma Graham and Amritjit Singh (Jackson: University Press of Mississippi, 1995), p. 329.
30. Ellison, "Change the Joke and Slip the Yoke"(emphasis mine).
31. Ellison, "A Coupla Scalped Indians," *New World Writing* (1956), reprinted in Ellison, *Living with Music*, pp. 186–87.
32. Ellison, *Invisible Man*, p. 16.
33. Ibid., p. 12.
34. From *Trading Twelves: The Selected Letters of Ralph Ellison and Albert Murray*, ed. Albert Murray and John F. Callahan (New York: Modern Library, 2000), p. 166.
35. Ralph Ellison, "Introduction to Flamenco," *Saturday Review* (1954), reprinted in Ellison, *Living with Music*, p. 100.
36. This phrase is Kenneth Burke's, from *Attitudes Toward History*, reprinted in *Perspectives by Incongruity*, ed. Stanley Edgar Hyman (Bloomington: Indiana University Press, 1964), pp. 94–99.
37. Note also the explosion of laughter in chapter 10 of *Invisible Man* where the protagonist is asked to sing a Negro spiritual at a party of political activists.
38. Unpublished transcription of a talk at Langston University, 1966, p. 5
39. See Albert Murray, *Stomping the Blues* (New York: McGraw-Hill, 1976).
40. The version of "St. James Infirmary" to which I refer appears on a CD called *Doctor Jazz, Louis "Satchmo" and His All Stars*, Blue Moon 3067, recorded 1959.
41. "An Interview with Ralph Ellison," Richard Kostelanetz, *Iowa Review* (Fall 1989; the interview was conducted in 1965), reprinted in Graham and Singh, *Conversations with Ralph Ellison*, p. 90.
42. Barry Singer, *Black and Blue: The Life and Lyrics of Andy Razaf* (New York: Schirmer, 1992), pp. 216 ff.
43. Ibid., p. 219.
44. This is the phrase used by Andre Hodeir in his landmark discussion of the meaning of swing, in *Jazz: Its Evolution and Essence* (New York: Grove, 1956).
45. Ellison, *Invisible Man*, pp. 7–9.
46. As we consider the woman's laughter, let us not forget her moans: A "moan," according to the *OED*, is a sympathetic lamentation, an expression beyond words, associated with OE maenan, "to have in mind, to mean." It is a sound of what Nathaniel Mackey has termed "telling inarticulacy," an expression that, for all its difficulty to interpret, has its own truth value and precision.
47. Ellison, *Invisible Man*, pp. 10–11.

48. Ibid., p. 431.

49. Several other Betty Boop cartoons feature film footage of musicians; for example, Cab Calloway, Don Redman, and Ethel Merman all make appearances as themselves, performing.

50. See Richard Stotkin, *Regeneration Through Violence: The Mythology of the American Frontier, 1600–1860* (Middletown: Wesleyan University Press, 1973).

51. See the article in this volume by Daniel Veneciano on Armstrong's own uses of floating heads in his collage work. Was he remembering this cartoon's weird presentation of his own caricatured image?

52. The Fleischer Brothers' training in show business led them to reproduce many elements of vaudeville or variety theater. Virtually every scene contains some sort of gag, to keep the show from flagging. See Leslie Cabarga, *The Fleischer Story* (New York: DaCapo,1981 {1976]).

53. Bruce Rayburne gave a paper, at an Armstrong conference in New Orleans in 2002, looking closely at Armstrong's presentation of this song in situations that were racially combustible.

54. See "Minnie the Moocher," "Snow White," and "The Old Man of the Mountain"—all Betty Boop cartoons featuring Cab Calloway.

55. See Cabarga, *The Fleischer Story*; and Charles Solomon, *The History of Animation: Enchanted Drawings* (New York: Knopf, 1989).

56. Cabarga, *The Fleischer Story*, makes clear that this evidence might very well have been cooked up by the Fleischers to discredit Kane, whom they later admitted to have been their model for Betty Boop.

57. See Klaus Stratemann's *Louis Armstrong on the Screen* (Copenhagen: JazzMedia, 1996), pp.17–26.

58. One can only wonder if there was some sort of sideline deal with Mr. Walton. Was Ms. Esther paid for *her* presumed loss of revenue?

59. This does not mean that Armstrong was the first person to scat sing, or to record a scat performance. Armstrong was the first master of the form to make records heard around the United States, and then the world: He was the most influential of the progenitors of the form.

60. This song by the black songwriter Sam Theard was an important one for Armstrong. The 1931 recording for Okey was Armstrong's biggest-selling item to date. In 1950 he rerecorded it as a duet on Decca with Louis Jordan—who had also recorded "Let the Good Times Roll" and "You Can't Get That No More"—both by Sam Theard; Armstrong then recorded it again for Decca with his own band, in 1957.

61. At this point my argument owes something to David Yaffee, who, at the Modern Language Association meeting in 2000, gave a paper linking Ken Burns's film series *Jazz* and its insistence on Armstrong's transcendence, over debasing materials, to Giddins, Murray, and Ellison

62. In his article Brent Edwards forcefully argues for the acceptance of this Armstrongian doubleness, the figure of unresolved but nonetheless intriguing contradictions.

63. Ralph Ellison, *Juneteenth* (New York: Random House, 1999), pp. 20–21.

64. This phrase, Ellison's, comes from his essay, "What America Would Be Like Without Blacks" (1970), reprinted in *Going to the Territory* (New York; Random House, 1986), p. 110.

65. Murray and Callahan, *Trading Twelves*, p. 175.

66. This version of what happened on that night at Newport comes from an August 2000

conversation with George Wein, who received his information first-hand and from Armstrong himself.

DISCOGRAPHY

Armstrong, Louis. "Elder Eatmore's Sermon on Generosity." *Louis and the Good Book, 1938–1959*. Verve 549593, 1938.

———— "I'll Be Glad When You're Dead, You Rascal, You." *You're Drivin' Me Crazy*. Columbia/Legacy CK 48828, 1931.

———— "Otchi-Tchor-Ni-Ya." *I Love Jazz*. Decca/Verve 314 543 747–2, 1958.

———— "Shine." *Louis Armstrong and His Sebastion New Cotton Club Orchestra*. Classics 547, 1931.

———— "St. James Infirmary." *Doctor Jazz*. Blue Moon BMCD 3067, 1959.

Ellington, Duke. "Half the Fun." *Live at Monterrey 1960: The Unheard Recordings*. Status DSTS 1008, 1960.

Ellison, Ralph. *Living with Music*. Columbia/Legacy CK85935, 2002.

The Jazz Singers. Smithsonian RD 113, RJ 0040, A5–28978, 1998.

Kane, Helen. *The Original "Boop-Boop-a-Doop" Girl*. Robert Palmer CD-323.

Morton, Jelly Roll. "Hyena Stomp." *The Jelly Roll Morton Centennial: His Complete Victor Recordings*. RCA 2361–2-RB, 1927.

Terry, Clark. "Trumpet Mouthpiece Blues." *Daylight Express*. Chess Reissue 0007, 1957.

KRIN GABBARD

Paris Blues:
Ellington, Armstrong, and Saying It with Music

With overlapping careers that dominated jazz throughout its most turbulent years, Duke Ellington (1899–1974) and Louis Armstrong (1901–1971) had surprisingly little interaction. They spent the most time together when they stayed in the same hotel in Paris during the shooting of the film *Paris Blues* (released in 1961) and then a few months later when they followed up on conversations begun in Paris and recorded together back home. Specifically, Armstrong and Ellington worked together in Paris during the last weeks of 1960 and the first week of 1961.[1] Their recording session took place at the RCA studios in New York on April 3 and 4, 1961.[2]

The Dignity of the Trickster

The Great Summit, the title of the Armstrong/Ellington recording session in its most recent reissue, solved the problem of bringing together two performers with well-established musical traditions of their own by first placing Ellington in the pianist's chair in Armstrong's sextet. Producer Bob Thiele then saw to it that the band recorded nothing but Ellington's compositions. The band belonged to Louis, but the music was Duke's. According to those who were present, the musicians were both tired at the time of the recording session, and not surprisingly, the music is a bit ragged in places. There are also moments of the brilliance that one would expect when the two men do what they do best. Ellington creates new versions of his compositions for a sextet that also included Barney Bigard, the clarinetist and saxophonist who had been a key member of the Ellington orchestra from 1928 until 1942. Ellington's piano work with Armstrong's group is consistently dependable and at times even surprising as he finds new ways of working through his old material. At one point he even seems to be alluding to the style of Thelonious Monk.

Armstrong is also himself at *The Great Summit*, deploying his usual exuberance as a singer and a trumpeter as he struts through the Ellington canon. As always, Armstrong is a quick study, in full control even when he is playing tunes for the first time. Anyone who knows the lyrics to Ellington's songs, however, can hear Armstrong making significant departures from what was originally written. On "I'm Beginning to See the Light," for example, the original lyrics read, "But now that your lips are burning mine, I'm beginning to see the light." Armstrong, however, sings, "Now that your chops are burnin' mine." Later, instead of ending a phrase with the complete lyric—"I'm beginning to see the light"—Armstrong suggests a broader range of meaning by abbreviating the phrase and inflecting it as: "I'm beGINnin'!"

In short, Ellington plays the dignified leader and Armstrong plays the trickster. Armstrong's tricksterisms were an essential part of his performance persona. On one level, Armstrong's grinning, mugging, and exaggerated body language made him a much more congenial presence, especially to racist audiences who might otherwise have found so confident a performer to be disturbing, to say the least. When Armstrong put his trumpet to his lips, however, he was all business. The servile gestures disappeared as he held his trumpet erect and flaunted his virtuosity, power, and imagination. Even in one of his earliest appearances on film, *A Rhapsody in Black and Blue* (1932), a nine-minute short subject in which he is costumed as a grotesque caricature of an African native, he is not always a comic figure. And at those moments in the film when he seems most eager to please with his vocal performances, his mugging is sufficiently exaggerated to suggest an ulterior motive. Lester Bowie has suggested that Armstrong is essentially "slipping a little poison into the coffee" of those who think they are watching a harmless darkie. (The crucial scenes from *A Rhapsody in Black and Blue* as well as Bowie's commentary appear in *Satchmo* (1988), a video documentary directed by Kendrick Simmons and Gary Giddins.) Throughout his career in films, Armstrong continued to subvert received notions of African American identity, signifying on the camera while creating a style of trumpet performance that was virile, erotic, dramatic, and playful. No other black entertainer of Armstrong's generation—with the possible exception of Ellington—brought so much intensity and charisma to his performances. But because Armstrong did not change his masculine presentation after the 1920s, many of his gestures became obsolete and lost their revolutionary edge. For many black and white Americans in the 1950s and 1960s, he was an embarrassment. In the early days of the twenty-first century, when Armstrong is regularly cast as a heroicized figure in the increasingly heroicizing narrative of jazz history, we should remember that he was regularly asked to play the buffoon when he appeared on films and television.

Paris Blues would have been a remarkable film simply for the participation of Ellington and Armstrong. The film is all the more remarkable for providing Armstrong with a rare opportunity to display some dignity. The film effectively begins when Wild Man Moore (Armstrong) arrives in Paris, and it ends when he departs. Cheering throngs of musicians serenade him as he arrives at the train station. When a small band performs for him (they play a composition written specifically for the film by Ellington and Billy Strayhorn), Moore/Armstrong extends his trumpet out of the window of the train and magniloquently inserts his own phrases into the music. Moments later the film's protagonist, Ram Bowen (Paul Newman), walks onto the train and is greeted warmly by Moore. Although they joke amiably ("This town agrees with you. What is it? The chicks or the wine?" "Oh, it's both, man."), Moore is in no way the obsequious dark companion of the white hero. In fact, Bowen has come to see Moore to ask for his help. As an aspiring composer of "serious" music, Bowen hopes to gain an audience with René Bernard (played in the film by André Luguet), a grand old man of classical music in Paris. With Bernard's help, Bowen seeks to have his own music played in a concert setting. So great is the reputation of Wild Man Moore that he has the power to intercede with Bernard on behalf of a young acolyte. The jazz trumpeter's special relationship with a character based on Nadia Boulanger, the great teacher of aspiring composers, may reflect Armstrong's interactions during his European travels in the 1930s and afterward, when he regularly mixed with the conservatory-trained musicians who recognized his special talents as a musician. At least in *Paris Blues*, these interactions bear fruit. Before the film is over, Moore has arranged a meeting between Bernard and Bowen.

Ellington never appears in *Paris Blues*, but his music is everywhere. We hear Ram Bowen's band playing complete versions of "Mood Indigo" and Billy Strayhorn's "Take the A Train." When Bowen plays a recording of his own music, it is a composition by Ellington and Billy Strayhorn. And numerous scenes are backed up by gorgeous performances of an expanded Ellington orchestra playing Ellington and Strayhorn's music. The two composers, however, use their music to engage in a dialogue with the film at a few crucial moments. At one point, Ellington may even be engaging in a dialogue with Strayhorn. In *Paris Blues*, Ellington actually plays the trickster. At least in this film, Armstrong and Ellington have traded places.

The Studio Changes Its Mind

Although he worked in films as early as 1929, during his fifty years as a composer Duke Ellington wrote soundtracks for only four feature-length films. Of the four, Ellington had the most control over the score for *Paris Blues*. Working also with Strayhorn, Ellington wrote his first soundtrack for Otto Preminger's *Anatomy of a Murder* (1959). Ordinarily, a film composer is handed an edited copy of a film and then given approximately six weeks to write and record a synchronized soundtrack.[3] Preminger, however, persuaded Ellington and Strayhorn to spend time in Ishpeming, Michigan, while the film was being shot.[4] He also convinced the two to write a great deal of music even though they could not have known exactly how it would be used. Some of this music appeared on the soundtrack album for the film and has also been widely praised. For the actual film of *Anatomy of a Murder*, however, Ellington and Strayhorn's music was given to music editor Richard Carruth, who used only a small portion of what was written.[4] There is no music at all in the film's long courtroom scenes. When the music is actually heard on the soundtrack, it occasionally sounds extraneous, and in some cases, even inappropriate.

Shortly after *Anatomy of a Murder* was released, Ellington admitted that he was less than satisfied with his work as a composer for films. He is quoted in an article in the *American Weekly Entertainment Guide*: "Music in pictures should say something without being obviously music, you know, and this was all new to me. I'll try another one and then I'll show them" (*DEDBD*, p. 407). Ellington has accurately characterized the theory and practice of film music. As Claudia Gorbman has suggested, a Hollywood film's extradiegetic score is almost always "invisible and 'inaudible,'" and the musical sounds are supposed to be "just there, oozing from the images we see."[5]

For *Paris Blues*, Ellington and Strayhorn used what they learned from *Anatomy of a Murder*, showing real competence with the conventions of scoring for classical Hollywood. They would never again have such an opportunity. In Ellington's scores for two subsequent films, *Assault on a Queen* (1966) and *A Change of Mind* (1969), the music was as extensively edited as it was for *Anatomy of a Murder*. Only Ellington and not his band were contracted for *Assault*, and although Ellington revived several of his classic compositions for *A Change of Mind*, the film features only fragments of extradiegetic music, much of it obscured by dialogue. But, for *Paris Blues*, producer Sam Shaw gave Ellington and Strayhorn the same stature ordinarily granted to established film composers. What one hears on the screen is exactly what the two intended.

Billy Strayhorn played a central role in composing the music for *Paris Blues* from the outset. *Paris Blues* was an ideal project for Strayhorn, an openly gay composer and pianist who worked consistently in the shadow of Ellington. From 1939 until his death in 1967, Strayhorn had a hand in the majority of Ellington's most important works. As his biographer David Hajdu has observed, Strayhorn was a major figure among expatriate American jazz musicians in Paris and regularly traveled to Paris, where he spent time with pianist Aaron Bridgers, who had been his lover in the 1940s.[6] Bridgers moved to Paris in 1948 and eventually became the house pianist at the Mars Club, a tiny Paris cabaret where on any given night "the clientele was nearly half gay."[7] Bridgers actually appears in *Paris Blues* as the pianist in Ram Bowen's band, although Ellington and Strayhorn are the only pianists heard on the soundtrack. The presence of Bridgers as well as the gay couples who appear in the opening scene of *Paris Blues* suggest that the club in the film may have been at least in part inspired by the Mars Club.

Other aspects of *Paris Blues* must have appealed to Strayhorn, at least at first. The film's attempt to place jazz within an art discourse was probably as important to Strayhorn as it was to Ellington. Strayhorn worked closely with classical musicians in Paris, and one of the few LPs released under his own name, *The Peaceful Side*, was recorded in Paris with a string quartet. His solo compositions were always much closer to the classical mainstream than were Ellington's; Strayhorn's "Suite for the Duo," recorded for the Mainstream label by the Mitchell/Ruff Duo in 1969, is an excellent example of his ability to fuse jazz with more European forms. Some of the early work on the music for *Paris Blues* was in fact directed by Strayhorn, who arrived in Paris a month before Ellington. A close inspection of the scores for *Paris Blues*, most of them in the Smithsonian Institution, reveals that a large portion of the music is in Strayhorn's hand.

Most of what Ellington and Strayhorn wrote and recorded during the *early* stages of their work on *Paris Blues* was for the actors who play musicians on camera. Paul Newman and Sidney Poitier, who plays the tenor saxophonist in Ram Bowen's band, convincingly mime playing their instruments because they could practice with recordings supplied to them before rehearsals began in Paris. This music was probably recorded in Hollywood during the summer of 1960 and in Paris later that year. In May 1961, when all filming had been completed and Ellington had resumed touring with his band, Ellington and Strayhorn received an edited copy of the film and quickly wrote the score for *Paris Blues*. A few days later they took an expanded version of the Ellington orchestra into the Reeves Sound Studios in New York and recorded about thirty minutes of extradiegetic music.

Paris Blues was based on a novel written in 1957 by Harold Flender.[8] The main character in the novel is an African American tenor saxophonist named Eddie Jones who plays regularly in a Paris nightclub. Entertaining no desire to be anything other than a working musician, he plays mostly Dixieland and traditional jazz. He meets and gradually falls in love with a black American schoolteacher, Connie, who is vacationing in Paris. Even though Eddie has been living happily in Paris for several years and appreciates its tolerance for blacks, at the end of the novel he decides to return to the States and marry Connie. The novel also introduces the trumpet player Wild Man Moore, who is clearly modeled after Louis Armstrong, long before he was cast in the film. While in Paris, Moore offers Eddie a job that he first refuses, but after Eddie decides to follow Connie he knows that he can work with the Wild Man when he returns. The film takes almost all of this directly from the novel.

The film of *Paris Blues* retains the black saxophonist Eddie, but it greatly expands the novel's character Benny, a Jewish pianist in his fifties who is a member of Eddie's band. In the novel, when Connie arrives in Paris with a large group of tourists, she rooms with Lillian, a middle-aged, white, unmarried schoolteacher. When Lillian insists on accompanying Connie to hear Eddie perform at his club, Benny does Eddie a favor by latching on to Lillian so that Eddie can devote all of his attention to Connie. A little drunk and filled with the desire to *épater la bourgeoise*, Benny shows the wilder side of Paris to Lillian. He even takes her to an all-night nudist swimming club where she is titillated almost as much as she is offended. Although Benny later says that he regrets his crude treatment of Lillian and wants to apologize, nothing comes of the relationship. Lillian goes back to the States alone.

Benny, the minor character in the novel, becomes Ram Bowen the handsome young (Jewish?) trombonist played by Paul Newman, and Lillian the old maid schoolteacher becomes Lillian the beautiful young divorcée played by Joanne Woodward. Eddie Jones the handsome young black saxophone player and Connie the beautiful young schoolteacher make the transition from the novel relatively unscathed—in the film they are played by Sidney Poitier (as Eddie *Cook*) and Diahann Carroll. The adaptation of the novel by Lulla Adler and the screenplay by Jack Sher, Irene Kamp, and Walter Bernstein also include the significant addition of Ram Bowen's desire to become a "serious" composer. Although he has enlisted Eddie as his arranger, it is also clear that Ram Bowen is the leader of the group and much more an "artist" than Eddie.

Ellington probably did not know about these aspects of the script when he signed on to do the music. He had been told that the film would dramatically depart from the novel by romantically pairing Paul Newman with Diahann Carroll and Sidney Poitier with Joanne Woodward. The vestiges of this romance are still present in an early scene when Ram is much more interested in Connie than in Lillian. Even earlier, during the opening credits, the film seems to be preparing audiences for interracial romance by repeatedly showing nontraditional couples in the Paris nightclub where Ram Bowen's band performs. We see people of all ages and ethnicities, including male and female homosexuals, interracial couples, and a young man with a much older woman. Intentionally or not, this multiply integrated scene was also an idealized reflection of the milieu inhabited by Billy Strayhorn. As the progress of the film's script should make clear, however, the Hollywood of 1961 was not prepared to accept so much tolerance for nontraditional romantic pairings.[9] In a scene that takes place about twenty minutes into the film, the camera again pans the faces in the club, but there are absolutely no interracial or same-sex couples. There are not even any older people. This sequence was shot after the decision had been made to dispense with the interracial love affairs.[10]

Ellington agreed to cancel a number of appearances and fly to Paris to do the film's music largely because he was attracted to a story about romance between the races. Sam Shaw said, "Duke thought that was an important statement to make at that time. He liked the idea of expressing racial equality in romantic terms. That's the way he thought himself."[11] For similar reasons he later agreed to write music for *A Change of Mind*, a film about a black man who has the brain of a white person inserted into his skull. Ellington was upset when the executives at United Artists lost their nerve and color coded the couples in *Paris Blues* according to more conventional standards.[12] Billy Strayhorn may have been disappointed for similar reasons, including the transformation of the nightclub from a tolerant, heterogeneous space into a club with more conventional clientele.

Is Jazz Art?

I also suspect that Ellington and Strayhorn were upset by the film's suggestions that jazz lacks the "seriousness" of classical music. The final print of *Paris Blues* preserves the opening credits sequence with its daring mix of couples, but in the larger context of the film's conservatism the club in this early scene might just as well represent a degraded milieu that the trombonist hero hopes to escape by becoming a serious composer. The dedication of Ram Bowen (Rimbaud? Ram [a trom]Bone?) to art—and Eddie Cook's lack of interest in "serious" music—is established in the first scene after the credits. As the owner, Marie Séoul (Barbara Laage), descends into her cabaret after an early morning trip to the market, Ram is playing a melodic phrase that will later be established as the "Paris Blues" theme. With Eddie, Ram has been working all night on his composition. Asserting that the melody is too heavy, Eddie says that he will score it for an oboe. Ram protests what he considers a criticism of his music and insists that Eddie tell him whether or not he really likes the composition. Eddie seems more interested in calling it a night. In an intriguing reference to this exchange, Ellington and Strayhorn (probably Strayhorn alone) score the "Paris Blues" theme for an oboe when it appears later in the film.

This first stretch of background music, including the oboe solo, is not heard until thirty minutes into the film. Lasting approximately six minutes, the music quickly reveals how thoroughly Ellington and Strayhorn had learned the craft of composing for films after their mixed success with *Anatomy of a Murder*. Like all background music from classical Hollywood, the softly soothing version of the "Paris Blues" theme creates an appropriate mood, even before the audience knows exactly what to feel. As Kathryn Kalinak has observed, film composers have always struggled to find the right moment to introduce a segment of extradiegetic music.[13] Often a composer will "sneak" the music in softly where the audience is unlikely to notice its appearance. This is exactly what Ellington and Strayhorn accomplish with the early stirrings of romance between Ram Bowen and Lillian. The same music continues as the camera picks up the romance between Eddie Cook and Connie and climaxes when we see Lillian the next morning in Ram's apartment wearing his dressing gown. Each of the transitions between the two sets of couples is clearly marked in the music. Ellington and Strayhorn have even written somewhat "funkier" music for the black couple. When the camera first moves to Poitier and Carroll after the two couples have separated, Ray Nance can be heard making the kind of vernacular, growling sounds on his trumpet that were originally associated with Ellington's "jungle music" in the 1920s.

Documents in the Smithsonian show that Ellington and Strayhorn knew exactly where each moment of their music would fit in the final film. There are several pages from the shooting script that are carefully marked with timings suggesting that someone (the handwriting is not Ellington's or Strayhorn's) had stopwatched parts of the film so that the music could be precisely correlated with the action. At one point in the script, when Connie is telling Ram about her affection for Eddie, Ellington has written next to her line, "Pretty," a concise description of what happens in the extradiegetic score during her speech.

The choice of an oboe for the "Paris Blues" theme is significant in a score so closely tailored to the dialogue and action.[14] Ellington and Strayhorn had not used an oboe since 1946 when they wrote the score for *Beggar's Holiday*, a musical adaptation of John Gay's *The Beggar's Opera*. The show opened in New York at the Broadway Theater on December 26, 1946, to mixed reviews and closed after fourteen weeks and 108 performances.[15] (Walter van de Leur has pointed out that the section of the score for oboe, strings, French horn, and harp is entirely in Strayhorn's hand.)[16] The connection between a line of dialogue about an oboe and the presence of the instrument in the extradiegetic version of the same music suggests that Ellington and Strayhorn were blurring the distinction between the diegetic and extradiegetic scores. In the script, Ram Bowen is writing a composition called "Paris Blues" that he wants to see performed as a concert piece. When the film is approximately half over, Bowen puts on a record of his "Paris Blues." He is in his apartment with Lillian, who has asked to hear something that he has written. The audience then hears the same theme by Ellington and Strayhorn that has been extradiegetically featured throughout the film. (The actual music we hear on Ram's record was written and recorded *after* the scenes with Newman and Woodward had been shot and edited.)

On the one hand, the matching of diegetic and extradiegetic music is completely consistent with classical Hollywood practice: it is common in the many biographies about composers, and movies often introduce a theme diegetically before it becomes a part of the extradiegetic score. In *Casablanca*, for example, Max Steiner repeatedly used phrases from "As Time Goes By," but only after the song had been sung on camera by Dooley Wilson. On the other hand, Ellington and Strayhorn could be using an oboe to wink at those in the audience who recall that Eddie Cook, the black musician, had suggested an oboe as a way of correcting the heaviness of a theme that a white musician had played on his trombone.

According to *Paris Blues*'s producer Sam Shaw, director Martin Ritt made few demands on Ellington, but he specifically requested that Ram Bowen's trombone have a smooth sound with a strong vibrato in the tradition of Tommy Dorsey.[17] Shaw did not speculate on why Ritt made this stipulation except to say that Ritt liked this kind of sound. Perhaps Ritt was not familiar with the work of Lawrence Brown or did not know that Brown had rejoined the Ellington orchestra during the summer of 1960. (Brown had earlier been with Ellington between 1932 and 1951.) Although Brown played an American trombone with a wide bore, he could surely have produced the mellow, singing sound we associate with a trombonist such as Dorsey, who played on a French trombone with a more narrow bore. Perhaps Ritt was aware of the striking difference between the role of the trombone in jazz as opposed to the more classical sound associated with the instrument outside of jazz and essentially brought back into jazz by Tommy Dorsey. Ellington's growling, talking trombonists, such as Charlie Irvis, Joe "Tricky Sam" Nanton, and Booty Wood, had their roots in the vaudeville traditions of early jazz when the trombone was a novelty instrument. Farting, belching, and braying, the trombone was often the clown of the instrument family. In the first jazz recordings of 1917 by the Original Dixieland Jazz Band, trombonist Eddie Edwards provides many of the appropriate sounds for tunes such as "Livery Stable Blues" and "Barnyard Blues." A man like Dorsey was able to restore a certain stateliness to the sound of the instrument, even though one could argue that Lawrence Brown and numerous other African American musicians had already brought a great deal of artistry to the instrument from within a jazz context.

Ritt's preference for the "white" Dorsey sound may be another example of the color anxiety that drove the filmmakers to back away from interracial romance as *Paris Blues* took shape. It may also have reflected the needs of a script in which Ram Bowen hopes to transcend jazz and write classical music. Tommy Dorsey might have seemed a more likely candidate for advanced study in harmony and counterpoint than would, say, Tricky Sam Nanton. At any rate, the white trombonist Murray McEachern was brought in early to play the first solos that Paul Newman mimes. (To further complicate Ritt's distinction between white and black trombonists, McEachern would later become a regular member of the Ellington orchestra.) McEachern's trombone can later be heard at a key moment in the film's final background music. Trombonist Billy Byers, who is also white, dubbed in solos during location shooting in Paris while he was working as the film's "musical adviser" (*DEDBD*, p. 433). Since the film insists on the strict separation of jazz and classical music, and since this division is embodied in the character of Ram Bowen, Ellington and Strayhorn may have found a place where they could have their say. Since both composers would have rejected the kinds of distinctions between jazz and classical music that are central to the ideology of *Paris Blues*, they may have adopted the introduction of an oboe into their score because it is recommended by a musician who has no pretensions about art.[18] They accepted a musical choice spoken on screen in a spirit of creative pragmatism by a character played by Sidney Poitier, even though the choice was effectively made by the screenwriters.

The film's attitude toward jazz and art is articulated explicitly and with great authority by René Bernard when Bowen is finally ushered into his quarters toward the end of the film. Although Bernard says that he has long admired Bowen's work as a jazz trombonist, he is only guarded in his praise of the written score that Wild Man Moore delivered to him. When he characterizes it as a "jazz piece of a certain charm and [pause] melody" he sounds uncomfortable. Pushed by Bowen to declare whether or not his work is any good, Bernard tells him that there is a great deal of difference between what a jazz musician can write and "an important piece of serious music." He urges the young trombonist to devote a few years to developing his craft in Paris, studying "composition, harmony, theory, counterpoint." The scene ends with Bernard giving Bowen some small encouragement that he might someday become "a serious composer" instead of a "lightweight," Bowen's self-description after he hears Bernard's faint praise for his jazz tunes.

In *Paris Blues*, jazz cannot be an art form even if it has been written by Duke Ellington and Billy Strayhorn. Many in the classical music community of Paris in 1961 would probably have agreed with Bernard—jazz can be charming and melodic but not truly serious.[19] If we are to accept the film's message, then Ellington and Strayhorn simply have a "gift for melody." In *Paris Blues*, that melody is the one the audience has been hearing all along, the "Paris Blues" theme, both diegetically from Ram Bowen and extradiegetically on the soundtrack.

Thoroughly discouraged by his conversation with René Bernard, Bowen arrives at Lillian's hotel to tell her he is prepared to return with her to the United States immediately. In the States he will simply play his horn and abandon his dream of becoming a great composer. Eddie independently arrives at the decision that he too will return and join Connie a few weeks after she leaves Paris. Later, at a party with his musician friends, Ram tells Eddie what Bernard has said about his music. In a moment that is, at least for the purposes of this essay, charged with significance, Ram brushes aside Eddie's attempts to question Bernard's authority. The logical argument that the old Frenchman has used an inappropriate aesthetic to judge jazz in general and Ram's "Paris Blues" in particular is raised only to be rejected. With a noticeable lack of conviction, Eddie says, "He's longhair, and he doesn't always know what he's talking about." Ram replies definitively, "He knows," and the film's debate on cultural aesthetics comes to an end.

On the one hand, the chickens have come home to roost for the view that Ellington belongs within the European musical tradition where some critics—beginning in the 1930s with R. D. Darrell and Constant Lambert—have sought to place him.[20] As Scott DeVeaux has written, the particular art discourse for jazz that emerged in the 1950s could only succeed if jazz was ultimately regarded as "an immature and imperfectly realized junior partner to European music."[21] A more Afrocentric view of jazz, such as Amiri Baraka would forcefully present two years later in his *Blues People*, was not yet widely available.[22] At least it did not seem to be known to the writers of *Paris Blues*. On the other hand, Ellington never saw himself as part of the European tradition and even ridiculed those who claimed that he was.[23] Nevertheless, almost the entire Ellington discography stands as a refutation of René Bernard's argument that a "jazz piece" cannot be "an important piece of serious music."

In the final scene of *Paris Blues*, Lillian is waiting for Ram at the train station along with Eddie and Connie. When Ram arrives shortly before the train is due to depart, Lillian can tell from his face that he has decided not to leave with her. Directly behind them, workmen are papering over the poster that depicts the laughing face of Wild Man Moore. As alto saxophonist Johnny Hodges and the Ellington orchestra play the "Paris Blues" theme behind his words, Ram explains that he has decided to follow the advice of Bernard and remain in Paris to study: "Lillian, I got to follow through with the music. I got to find out how far I can go. And I guess that means alone." After an emotional farewell speech, Lillian rushes to her train. The solo statement of the theme is now taken over by the trombone of Murray McEachern, whose sound has been associated throughout with the character of Ram Bowen. The music swells as Eddie bids farewell to both Lillian and Connie. Then a new theme emerges, one that recalls Ellington's many train songs, including "Lightnin'" (1932), "Daybreak Express" (1933), and "Happy-Go-Lucky Local" (1946). Unlike the more lyrical, almost mournful "Paris Blues" melody, the new theme is fast, dissonant, and dominated by percussion. While "Paris Blues" is primarily the work of Strayhorn, the new train theme is almost surely the work of Ellington. The "Paris Blues" theme is not entirely erased by the train tune, however. McEachern's trombone can still be heard playing fragments of "Paris Blues" on top of the now dominant train theme. This juxtaposition continues for about sixty seconds as the train departs and Eddie and Ram leave the station. In the film's final shot, the poster with Wild Man's face has been almost entirely papered over with a new billboard.

I would suggest a number of interpretations for this final scene in *Paris Blues*. First, the closing music can be imagined as emanating from the screen, "oozing from the images we see"[24] as an expression of the conflicting emotions of the characters. The "Paris Blues" theme might represent the feelings that the lovers have for each other, while the train theme looks toward the future and the need for the characters to get on with their lives. This final music could also be what Ram Bowen will write once he has transcended the pain of his experiences with Lillian and completed his study of "composition, harmony, theory, counterpoint" as recommended by René Bernard. This interpretation combines a rationalist belief in conservatory training with the romantic myth of suffering as the key to artistic creation. Bowen will, according to this reading, write music that will cover over the "charming" but "lightweight" jazz exemplified by Wild Man Moore/Louis Armstrong, whose image is erased as Bowen sets off to become a "serious" artist. Appropriately, the new billboard that is covering over the face of Armstrong is an advertisement for the Librarie Larousse, the leading French publisher of canonical literature at that time. The jazz of Ram Bowen and Wild Man Moore, the film tells us, will be replaced by something more established and more literate once Bowen emerges as a serious composer.

I strongly suspect, however, that Ellington wrote the music that ends *Paris Blues* as an answer to the statements of René Bernard. Remember that Bernard had said he liked the melody of "Paris Blues" but little else. So Ellington gives us Strayhorn's melody in all its glory as played by the trombonist, but he audaciously covers it over with another entire piece. The pretensions of the white musician who wants to rise above jazz is overwhelmed with rousing African American rhythms and harmonies. This is the composer's response to the demand that the trombone sound be color coded as white. It is also a response to the film's squeamishness about mixing black and white as well as jazz and classical.

But the music is also a key to understanding the dynamics of the long collaboration between Ellington and Strayhorn. At the finale of *Paris Blues*, the lovely Parisian music of Strayhorn—at its most ravishing thanks to the alto saxophone of that single greatest interpreter of Stayhorn's music, Johnny Hodges—is overpowered by the Ellington Express. In scrupulously chronicling the evolving relationship between Ellington and Strayhorn, Hajdu has found strains of ambivalence even where there was a great deal of love and respect. Although he is circumspect about the issue throughout his biography, Hajdu implies that Strayhorn willingly gave up his identity as a composer and musician to protect his privacy as a gay man. He would never have been able to lead the uncloseted life he embraced had he become "Billy Strayhorn and his Orchestra." He knew and accepted the price for ensuring his privacy, but Strayhorn often resented the extent to which Ellington took credit for his work. The opening credits for *Paris Blues*, for example, simply read "Music by Duke Ellington." Conversely, Ellington must have felt vulnerable by relying on Strayhorn to provide beautiful compositions and arrangements that had become essential to the success of the Ellington orchestra. In Paris, where Strayhorn was right at home but Ellington was a stranger, Ellington was even more dependent on Strayhorn, who often disappeared for days at a time to enjoy himself with friends.[25] At least on an unconscious level, Ellington may have used the last moments of *Paris Blues* to establish a degree of independence from Strayhorn by drowning out his composing partner's music with his own. Of course, Ellington would become extraordinarily prolific and creative after Strayhorn's death in 1967, but when he was writing music for *Paris Blues*, in 1961, Ellington had no way of knowing what his music would be without the contributions of Strayhorn.

It must be remembered, however, that the final musical moments in *Paris Blues* were entirely conceived and executed as part of a film score. None of the Ellington orchestra's subsequent recordings of material from the film includes the juxtaposition of the trombone solo and the train theme. The music is unique to the film. Regardless of the degree to which Ellington and Strayhorn worked together or at cross-purposes in *Paris Blues*, they managed to express themselves politely but sharply. By pulling out all the stops at the end of *Paris Blues*, the composers surely made the filmmakers happy at the same time that they subtly destroyed the film's dichotomies of jazz and art.

The "stylistic excess" of the Ellington/Strayhorn composition that ends *Paris Blues* can be understood in terms of an argument that Caryl Flinn makes in her discussion of music in film noir and melodrama: "Stylistic excesses and unconventional formal practices have often been identified as the purported means by which cinematic content (e.g., story lines) can be politicized and rendered subversive."[26] Accordingly, the critique of *Paris Blues* that I hear in the film's final music depends on the excesses of a music that completely overwhelms every other aspect of the film, including the "Paris Blues" theme itself.

When *Paris Blues* was released in November 1961, the critics were mostly dismissive. John Tynan wrote in *Down Beat*, for example, that it was "dramatic nonsense."[27] As has always been the case with the film scores credited to Ellington, critics have chosen to write only about the music for *Paris Blues* as separate from the film. Through this one film score, however, the real achievement of Ellington and Strayhorn can only be appreciated within the film's specific context.

Ellington was capable of sending out ambiguous messages, inviting the hip members of his audience to decode in ways unavailable to the rest. I would argue that his achievement in *Paris Blues* was foreshadowed by the effect he created with "Goin' Up," the composition he wrote specifically for *Cabin in the Sky*.[28] The film was released in 1943, just after the great Carnegie Hall concert where Ellington compellingly combined the sacred and the vernacular in *Black Brown and Beige*. Like *Green Pastures* before it, however, *Cabin in the Sky* was built on the old idea that African Americans must choose between the church and the dance hall. Ellington surely knew what he was doing when he wrote "Goin' Up" for *Cabin in the Sky*. Although the tune is played in a dance hall, it features a preacherly trombone solo by Lawrence Brown. The congregation of dancers even engages in some churchly call and response with the trombonist. The music undermines the film's naive dichotomies by joyously fusing the sacred with the profane. One could cite numerous if less flamboyant examples of Ellington's irony and his subtle habit of "signifying" on those who would hold him to standards other than his own. His droll deflections of extravagant praise for his composing skills are a typical example. Ellington's conventionalized assurance to his audiences that he and "all the kids in the band love you madly" is also typical as is the ironic "finger-snapping, earlobe-tilting bit" with which he often closed his concerts in his last decades.[29]

Louis Armstrong also signified on audiences, filmmakers, and the classical repertoire. Like Ellington, he was able to send out a variety of messages, some of them more easily decoded by certain groups than by others. In almost all his film appearances, the trickster Armstrong presents the face of the seemingly obsequious jester at one moment and the heroic sound of the trumpet king at the next. In *Paris Blues*, however, Armstrong speaks as the peer of classical musicians despite the fact that his music is subsequently denigrated; he is denied the opportunity to play the trickster. Ellington, by contrast, was not to be denied. It is Ellington who becomes the trickster, signifying on filmmakers who lost their nerve when faced with the controversy of interracial romance and then forswore the claim that jazz is art. *Paris Blues* tells us that there is a difference between the jazz musician and the serious artist. Both Armstrong and Ellington, however, spent their long careers revealing the absurdity of that distinction.

NOTES

I am extremely grateful for the contributions that Robert O'Meally, Farah Jasmine Griffin, Brent Edwards, David Hajdu, Stanley Crouch, Tom Harris, Mark Tucker, Steven B. Elworth, Lewis Porter, Bob Mirandon, and Dan Morgenstern have made to this essay, which revises and expands material in the Ellington and Armstrong chapters of my book, *Jammin' at the Margins: Jazz and the American Cinema* (Chicago, 1996). I also thank the members of the Jazz Study Group at Columbia University for many hours of inspirational conversation about jazz and American culture.

1. For the details of the Ellington/Armstrong collaboration in *Paris Blues*, see Klaus Stratemann, *Duke Ellington Day by Day and Film by Film* (Copenhagen, 1992), pp. 429–36 (hereafter abbreviated *DEDBD*).

2. Originally issued on LP, the music from the session has been on reissued on two compact discs with additional material on Roulette Jazz 7243 5 24546. The CD set includes an essay by Dan Morgenstern that touches on the few occasions when Armstrong and Ellington had less productive interactions.

3. For the classical film score, see Irving Bazelon, *Knowing the Score: Notes on Film Music* (New York, 1975); Roy Prendergast, *Film Music: A Neglected Art* (New York, 1977); Hanns Eisler and Theodor Adorno (uncredited), *Composing for the Films* (New York, 1947). The practice of film music is theorized most completely in Claudia Gorbman, *Unheard Melodies: Narrative Film Music* (Bloomington, 1987).

4. Otto Preminger, *Preminger: An Autobiography* (Garden City, N.Y., 1977), p. 156.

5. Walter van de Leur, who has exhaustively catalogued the three boxes of music now in the Smithsonian Institution that Ellington and Strayhorn composed for *Anatomy of a Murder*, says that only shards of the music were used in the final print of the film (personal communication, June 8, 1994).

6. Gorbman, *Unheard Melodies*, pp. 73, 75.

7. David Hajdu, *Lush Life: A Biography of Billy Strayhorn* (New York, 1996).

8. Ibid., p. 144.

9. Harold Flender, *Paris Blues* (New York, 1957).

10. Not until 1968 did Sidney Poitier became the first major black star in a Hollywood film to be romantically linked with a white person in *Guess Who's Coming to Dinner*. For a discussion of the racial dynamic of Poitier's career, see Thomas Cripps, *Making Movies Black: The Hollywood Message Movie from World War II to the Civil Rights Era* (New

York, 1993), pp. 284–94. For the treatment of homosexuals in Hollywood film, see Vito Russo, *The Celluloid Closet: Homosexuality in the Movies* (New York, 1987), which includes as an appendix a "necrology" cataloging the numerous films in which gay characters die on screen.

11. Sam Shaw, personal communication, August 17, 1994.

12. Shaw quoted in Hajdu, *Lush Life*, p. 207.

13. Mercer Ellington, with Stanley Dance, *Duke Ellington in Person: An Intimate Memoir* (Boston, 1978), p. 183.

14. In *Settling the Score*, Kalinak quotes a contemporary of Erich Wolfgang Korngold, Herbert Stothart: "If an audience is conscious of music where it should be conscious only of drama, then the musician has gone wrong" (99).

15. The oboe solo in the score for *Paris Blues* is played by Harry Smiles, one of nine musicians added to the Ellington orchestra for a recording session held in New York on May 1, 1961 (*DEDBD*, p. 434).

16. John Edward Hasse, *Beyond Category: The Life and Genius of Duke Ellington* (New York, 1993), p. 293.

17. Walter van de Leur, personal communication, June 8, 1994.

18. Sam Shaw, personal communication, August 17, 1994.

19. Ellington himself frequently rejected the term *jazz,* largely because it limited his options as a composer. See his many statements on the subject in Mark Tucker, ed., *The Duke Ellington Reader* (New York, 1993), pp. 324–26, 332–38, 364 ff.

20. When George Gershwin met Maurice Ravel in 1928 and asked if he could study with him, Ravel refused, adding, "You might lose your *melodic* spontaneity and write bad Ravel" (Victor I. Seroff, *Maurice Ravel* [New York: 1953], p. 248, emphasis added). Nevertheless, Ravel shared an enthusiasm for jazz with composers such as Milhaud and Stravinsky, just as Ansermet had expressed delight at a performance of Sidney Bechet as early as 1919. Members of the conservatory, however, such as the fictional René Bernard, were more likely to police the confines of what is and is not "serious art."

21. Tucker, *The Duke Ellington Reader,* pp. 33–40, 57–65, 110–11.

22. Scott DeVeaux, "Constructing the Jazz Tradition: Jazz Historiography," *Black American Literature Forum* 25 (Fall 1991): 547.

23. Amiri Baraka (as LeRoi Jones), *Blues People: Negro Music in White America* (New York, 1963). I name Baraka's book because it was widely read by white intellectuals in the 1960s. Needless to say, a variety of writers, most notably Langston Hughes and Ralph Ellison, made eloquent pleas for understanding jazz outside of a Eurocentric aesthetic many years before Baraka's book appeared.

24. When he was asked in 1935 about Constant Lambert's lavish praise for his music, including the claim that he was in the same league as Ravel and Stravinsky, Ellington responded, "Is that so? Say, that fellow Lambert is quite a writer, isn't he?" When he was praised for the "texture" of his records, Ellington told of transposing a piece to a different key so that it would sound better when recorded by "a goofy mike" with a "loose plunger." After the interviewer read a phrase that compared Ellington's music to "the opalescent subtleties of Debussy," he responded, "Opalescent subtleties. Don't those London fellows push a mean pen?" See Tucker, *The Duke Ellington Reader,* p. 113.

25. Gorbman, *Unheard Melodies,* p. 75.

26. Hajdu, *Lush Life,* p. 210.

27. Caryl Flinn, *Strains of Utopia: Gender, Nostalgia, and Hollywood Film Music* (Princeton, 1992), p. 116.

28. Tynan, "Paris Blues," *Down Beat*, November 23, 1961, p. 16.

29. Gabbard, *Jammin' at the Margins*, pp. 177–84.

30. A good example of this routine has been preserved on a CD of a November 26, 1969 concert in Manchester, England, on Sequel Jazz NED183. Ellington was by no means the only jazz artist to engage in some version of signifying. Jed Rasula has written: "Because Ellington was perceived as debonair, his (much noted) strategies of verbal evasion were regarded as displays of inscrutable charm, where corresponding strategies on the part of other musicians tended to be seen as dissimulation, insolence, capriciousness, or a simple inability to speak standard English (or, as in the case of Lester Young, symptomatic of some alleged mental fatigue). It would be more accurate to see Ellington as the norm rather than the exception here, practicing a strategically contrapuntal speech intended to glance off and otherwise evade the dominant code" (Rasula, "The Media of Memory: The Seductive Menace of Records in Jazz History," in Krin Gabbard, ed., *Jazz Among the Discourses* [Durham, N.C., 1995], p. 155).

WILLIAM J. HARRIS

"How You Sound??":
Amiri Baraka Writes Free Jazz

A true tradition is not the witnessing of a past closed and finished; it is a living force that animates and informs the present. —Igor Stravinsky

And Rhythm and Blues is "new" as well. It is contemporary and has changed, as jazz has remained the changing same. —Amiri Baraka

This essay is taken from a work in process on the contemporary black avant-garde writers Amiri Baraka and Ishmael Reed and their developing conceptions about race and ethnicity, racial politics, racial art, racial poetics and racial aesthetics.[1] This selection comes from a chapter on jazz, dealing with the highly individual ways in which these two authors utilize, emulate, and translate this African American expressive form into another: African American literature. They draw on the jazz tradition to expand, modernize, and vitalize the black literary tradition. I will restrict my discussion to Amiri Baraka's relationship to free jazz, a 1960s experimental music. Although this dissonant and seemingly chaotic music is based on no "predetermined, underlying harmonic structure" (Carr 174)—that is, no traditional chord progressions—it is still rooted in the familiar sounds of black music, especially the earthy and funky sounds of blues and gospel. Some of the major musicians and/or composers of free jazz movement are John Coltrane, tenor sax; Albert Ayler, tenor sax; Cecil Taylor, piano; Archie Shepp, tenor sax; Ornette Coleman, alto sax; Sun Ra, keyboards; Henry Grimes, bass; and Sonny Murray, drums. Like white avant-garde contemporary music, free jazz self-consciously incorporates noise; however, this noise originates in the black tradition. Unlike white avant-garde music, which is self-consciously arbitrary—free jazz is rooted in the African American audio past; that is, more specifically, it is rooted in the shouts of the black church and the hollers of the field, sounds saturated with the history of slavery. Furthermore, from its inception to the present, extramusical sounds, such as shouts, screams, and grunts, have been associated with the black musical tradition; in fact, they have been an integral part of that tradition, from the anonymous singers of the spirituals to James Brown to Albert Ayler to almost any contemporary black pop singer. In essence, the music is a contemporary way into African American history and tradition, into ethnic identity through sound and form, into what Baraka has called "the changing same," that cultural continuity that persists in changing forms; what Eliot calls "the present moment of the past, " (*Selected Essays* 11).[2]

Although rich with the sounds of the African American past, free jazz provides the contemporary black voice that Baraka in the 1960s wanted to incorporate into his art. Baraka says of free jazz: "The new music reinforces the most valuable memories of a people but at the same time creates new forms, new modes of expression, to more precisely reflect contemporary experience!" (*Black Music* 267). Baraka believes that black music captures the ever changing voice of the black masses in its forms. It is there in the music that one finds the current vernacular of the African American people. In the 1960s Baraka's project became the translation of the black free jazz voice into one for his poetry, a project similar to that of Langston Hughes. Throughout his career, Hughes kept changing verse styles—first blues, then bebop, and then free jazz—to catch the transmuting voice of the African American masses.

Moreover, this essay examines Baraka's actual performances of his poems, his speaking and reading voice, his delivery style; in short, what Charles Bernstein calls the "audiotext . . . the poet's acoustic performance" (13) instead of the imagined "sound" of the written page, the conventional subject of literary analysis. In other words, I analyze how Baraka literally sounds: his actual voice, his voicing of poems, his changing sound over the course of his career, and the reasons for these changes. Since, like jazz performances, no two readings are exactly alike, I am concentrating on specific performances of Baraka's work. To demonstrate the radical shift in Baraka's sound, let us compare the sound of the early "BLACK DADA NIHILISMUS" (1964) to the later "Dope" (1978). From these performances we can gauge the impact of jazz and the vernacular on Baraka's art. The African American oral tradition offers a number of performance styles; styles that embody traditions and values, not because of an essential nature but because of associations over time.

The reading of "Black Dada Nihilismus," published in *The Dead Lecturer* (1964), occurred at a writer's conference at Asilomar in Monterey, California in August 1964, shortly after the publication of this new volume of poetry. Clapping politely after each poem, the audience for the reading was mostly white, including such luminaries as Kenneth Rexroth, Harvey Swados, Nat Hentoff and the then unknown young black poet and novelist Al Young. Even though the purpose of the poem was to attack white Western institutions, it uses Eliotic language, rhythms, and imagery to accomplish this end. Elegiac lines like "in this place, a window on a dark / warehouse" and "Where the minds packed in / straw" (*Reader* 72) echo the Eliot of *The Waste Land* and *The Hollow Men*. In other words, it seems he is using the master's tools to dismantle the master's house, using the King's English to slay the king.

At this point there is the question of audience for the poem. Because it is a high modernist allusive poem, it is not likely that it would incite the masses into the street, since they would not know the allusions. It seems, instead of inciting the masses, at best, the poem identifies the enemy. Perhaps, since the poem is ambiguous (even though it identifies with the black masses, it does not want to kill the whites: "we beg him [John Paul Sartre] die, / before he is killed" [*Reader* 71]). It does not embrace the black vernacular; it moves toward the black chant and is more rhythmic than the other poems in *The Dead Lecturer* volume yet it is written in white standard English, the language of power and literature. The closest it comes to the vernacular is "got it, Baby!" (*Reader* 73). Even though, in the poem, he mentions, the "Black scream / and chant" (*Reader* 72), he does not employ these black forms in this poem. He has not found "the huge black voice," the voice informed by the vernacular, the chant and scream. Moreover, perhaps, ironically, the performance style drew heavily on white middle-class literary and verbal conventions of the time. That is, Baraka's reading is virtually indistinguishable from any other mainstream literary writer of the time—he manifests no black ethnic markers: in essence, he reads just like a white man, the literary model of the period.

Interestingly, even though he read "Black Dada" on November 26 that same year, with the New York Art Quartet, a free jazz group par excellence, brimming with the new sound, Baraka's sound doesn't change: there is no visible impact on the poetry by the music; the music has not penetrated the words. In fact, the reading is even more subdued and less rhythmic, less chantlike than the Asilomar reading. In short, it is not a call to action. I am not suggesting that black writers must employ an ethnic vernacular to be authentic but that Baraka mounts his attack without any ethnic markers, indicates an alienation from the very tradition, history, and ethnic community that he desires to a part of.[3] This poem shows the same formal contradictions one finds in Claude McKay's poetry. In the 1920s in such poems as "If We Must Die" McKay attacks the white man in the white man's form, the English sonnet and in conventional nineteenth-century diction. He asserts: "Like men we'll face the murderous, cowardly pack, / Pressed to the wall, dying, but fighting back!" (Randall 63). McKay has not made the sonnet his own, has not incorporated either his personal or cultural voice. In the 1960s Baraka attacks white institutions in white avant-garde forms, conventions, and diction. In part Baraka was drawn to the white avant-garde because of their rebellion against white middle-class society, but they were using white forms and ideology for their revolt. At this point Baraka has not found the right black form and ideology for his rebellion. In 1966, when Baraka is a cultural nationalist, he boldly observes, "Form and content are both mutually expressive of the whole. . . . We want different contents and different forms because we have different feelings. We are different peoples" (*Black Music* 185).

Baraka's later poem, "Dope" (the version we are examining was recited in 1978 at Columbia University) is both written and delivered in a black style. In this poem Baraka renders his Marxist message in the sermonic style of the black Baptist preacher, drawing on a black performance style. Unlike the 1981 rendition of "Dope," with David Murray and Steve McCall, there is no musical accompaniment. Baraka says, "You can be the music yourself. You don't have to have a band" (Feinstein 77). Even though the David Murray version enhanced the poem with musical nuance, by underscoring musical themes, Baraka's reading without music embodied the black musical style; that is, at this point, he has internalized it. The key question here is why does he move from one performance style to another? And what is the significance of black music, especially, free jazz, in this transformation? Why did he move from "The Black Dada Nilhilismus" sound to the "Dope" sound? What does this change in sound mean?

In his major Beat poetic statement of 1959, "How You Sound," Baraka observes that "HOW YOU SOUND?? Is what we recent fellows are up to. How we sound" (*Reader* 16). Significantly, in 1959 all these recent fellows—the "we," Baraka speaks of—are Philip Whalen, Gary Snyder, Michael McClure, Frank O'Hara, Robert Creeley, Allen Ginsberg, etc. (*Reader* 17). That is, all of these fellows are white avant-garde poets, unconsciously creating a white avant-garde sound, a sound that Baraka decides, over time, does not express his true self, that is, his black ethnic self; hence does not reflect his and his people's history. Elsewhere, I have discussed Baraka's need to cast off the white self, the white sound, the white voice, and achieve a black self and sound.[4] Reflecting on his past, Baraka observes: "Having read all of whitie's books, I wanted to be an authority on them. Having been taught that art was 'what white men did,' I almost became one, to have a go at it" (*Home* 10). In other words, studying white literature has turned him into a white man, somebody with white attitudes. Moreover, Baraka says more specifically about the Beat days: "Yeh, I was some colored bohemian liberal living on the Lower East side in heaven, yet I could not sound like that" (*Autobiography* 278). For Baraka "sound" is a sign of authenticity, of place: where you come from; he no longer wants to sound white, to come from that place. In the culture nationalist essay collection, *Raise Race Rays Raze* (1971), Baraka states, "American poetry reflects American lives. The various kinds, in America, from whatever voices. Each voice is a place, in America, in the totality of its image" (17). Furthermore, Baraka says of black music:

> Only Negro music because, perhaps, it drew its strength and beauty out of the depths of the black man's soul, and because to a large extent its traditions could be carried on by the 'lowest classes' of Negroes, has been able to survive the constant and willful dilutions of the black middle class and the persistent calls to oblivion made by the mainstream of the society.
>
> (*BLUES PEOPLE* 131)

Baraka was trying to shed his black middle-class self, which he felt did not include the voice of the people, the unassimilated voice of the black masses. For him this is not a battle that began with the white avant-garde; this is a battle that began back in his childhood. Commenting on his adolescence, Baraka observes, "Having been the only 'middle-class' chump running with the Hillside Place bads, I was 'saved' from them by my parents' determination and the cool scholarship game which turns stone killers pure alabaster by graduation time" (*Home* 10). His parents, especially his mother, the traditional figure of indoctrination, and the academic system wanted to turn Baraka into a white man. This is not terribly different from the colonial system, through its schools, turning its subjects into little Englishmen or little Frenchmen. In *Black Skin, White Masks* (1967) the third world theorist Frantz Fanon observes:

> The black schoolboy in the Antilles, who in his lessons is forever talking about "our ancestors, the Gauls," identifies himself with the explorer, the bringer of civilization, the white man who carries truth to savages—an all-white truth. There is identification—that is, the young Negro subjectively adopts a white man's attitude. . . . Subjectively, intellectually, the Antillean conducts himself like a white man. (147, 148)

In "Uncle Tom's Cabin: Alternate Ending," from the short story collection *Tales* (1967), Baraka explores the social and ethnic significance of middle-class pronunciation. Louise McGhee, the middle-class and college educated mother in this semi-autobiographical story, is on the one hand fighting racism, defending her son against racist teachers, but, on the other, enforcing the values of white-middle class society by insisting on white middle-class pronunciation and behavior. She asks her son,

"Is Miss Orbach the woman who told you to say sangwich instead of sammich," Louise McGhee giggled.

"No, that was Miss Columbe."

"Sangwich, my Christ. That's worse than sammich. Though you better not let me hear you saying sammich either . . . like those Davises."

"I don't say sammich, mamma."

"What's the word then?"

"Sandwich" (39).

In this story the protagonist is carefully drilled by his mother to pronounce white and become white, take on white values. A language, dialect, embodies a way of life—what Baraka would call "an attitude" about the world. In another story, from *Tales*, "The Death of Horatio Alger," Baraka discusses the consequences of another middle-class mother's imposed education. The main character, Mickey, does not want to be the thing that his unnamed mother has made. Being middle class has deprived him of his manhood. In a schoolyard fight he does not fight back but simply curses, uses words, that is, is an artist. His father encourages him to fight back, be a man. His mother "stopped the fight finally, shuddering at the thing she'd made" (48), a white writer who can curse but not act. In the early years Baraka could only envision the bourgeois artist as ineffectual. It is not until the Black Art and Marxist periods that he came to the idea of the artist as effectual, acting in the political world.

In the novel *The System of Dante's Hell* (1965), in a black bar in the South, the autobiographical protagonist observes: "Of course the men didn't dig two imitation white boys come in on their leisure. And when I spoke someone wd turn and stare, or laugh, and point me out. The quick new jersey speech, full of italian idiom, and the invention of the jews. Quick to describe. Quicker to condemn" (128). In *Tales* Mickey declares, "I vaguely knew of a glamorous world and was mistaken into thinking it could be gotten from books. Negroes and Italians beat and shaped me, and my allegiance is there" (45). Of this time he has spoken of writing defensively to escape the influence of the white avant-garde, his ex-friends he ironically calls "his friends." Moreover, he also wanted to escape his whitened black middle-class heritage, to escape their content and form. He observes, "I literally decided to write just instinctively, without any thought to any form or to any kind of preunderstanding of what I was shaping" (Benston, "Amiri Baraka" 305). Baraka says of the writing of the time: "It wasn't the little, stylized, Creeley-esque stuff that I was doing at the time; it began to be my own kind of sound, my own voice" (ibid.). In short, he rejected the Robert Creeley sound because it did not reflect his voice and history. I argue that this intuitive, and not so intuitive, reshaping draws heavy on free jazz forms and traditions because they provide the avant-garde ethnic sound he desires, while leading him back to self, ethnic self, and ethnic history.

Free jazz not only provided a connection with Baraka's ethnic past but also provided an avant-garde form that was not beholden to the white world. It provided a sound that could connect him with his tradition, with the idealized black self, the self that is larger than the individual, the self that Hughes delineates in "The Negro Speaks of Rivers," when he presents in the first person the continuity of the black soul across time: "My soul has grown deep like the rivers"(*Poems* 23). When James Baldwin says of himself, "I was the son of a slave" (*Nobody* 4), which is not literally true, he is partaking of a symbolic self, speaking from a self larger than the personal one. Before, Baraka had accepted the William Carlos Williams model to connect him with the local, with the speech of New Jersey. Allen Ginsberg argues, "Williams's practice. It brought Jones [Baraka] back to Newark, in a sense. If any literary influence had tended in that direction, Williams's influence tended to bring Jones back home to his own speech and to his own soul and to his own body and to his own color and his own town" (*Spontaneous Mind* 269). But real Newark speech was not pure enough, not black enough; it was not only the speech of blacks but also the speech of Italians and Jews, mixed speech.

To gain the idealized speech he must turn to free jazz. Since free jazz embodies both the present and the past of a people, its forms provide both real and idealized black identities. Free jazz allowed Baraka into the archetypical world of idealized blackness, a world stripped of whiteness, a world at once real and ideal. Here the black voice is purged of whiteness: actual but reified, no trace of the accents of Italians and Jews, only pure black sound. The purified black identity, where the black voice issues from, must be based on the real, on actual history and the local scene, to connect Baraka to the African American tradition. The creation of black identity cannot be arbitrary: there must be something real behind the ideal, a cultural continuity. In other words, since Baraka is not Irish American, he could not connect to an idealized Irish history because he has no cultural connection to that tradition. The 1960s cultural nationalists, including Amiri Baraka, made a similar idealistic move when they found Mother Africa nestled on every street corner in the great American black cities. The idealized African Village could not be a total fiction; it had to be based on a real city, such as Newark, to provide connections with the African American psyche. Furthermore, some, let's say, Melville Herskovits, the anthropologist, Robert Farris Thompson, the art historian, and Randy Weston, the jazz pianist, would argue—an argument that I am ambivalent about—that Newark, no matter how tenuously and spiritually, had to have a trace of the real African Village, that there must be some retention of the Old World.[5]

Before we look at Baraka's utilization of black music, it would be helpful to look at his and two other distinguished black writers, James Baldwin's and August Wilson's employment of the great blues singer, Bessie Smith. All three address the meaning of black music to them in the person of Bessie Smith. In "The Discovery of What It Means to Be an American," from *Nobody Knows My Name* (1961), in Switzerland, away from the black world, Baldwin discovers that "it was Bessie Smith, through her tone and her cadence, who helped me to dig back to the way I myself must have spoken when I was a pickaninny, and to remember the things I had heard and seen and felt" (5). The blues singer helps Baldwin recapture the cadence of Negro speech and the lost world of his Negro youth and therefore recapture himself. In "Preface" to *Three Plays* (1991) Wilson says: "With my discovery of Bessie Smith and the blues I had been given a world that contained my image, a world at once rich and varied, marked and marking, brutal and beautiful, and at crucial odds with the larger world that contained it and preyed and pressed it from every conceivable angle" (*The Jazz Cadence* 564). Like Baldwin, the singer gave Wilson a rich image of himself that he hasn't found elsewhere. It is odd that a writer so conscious of both black music and language would discuss images of blacks instead of sounds. In "the myth of a 'negro literature,'" from *Home* (1966) Baraka declares: "It would be better if such a [n aspirant black] poet listened to Bessie Smith sing *Gimme A Pigfoot*, or listened to the tragic verse of a Billie Holiday, than be content to imperfectly imitate the bad poetry of the ruined minds of Europe" (113). These singers provide a more precise poetic model for a black writer than the European one because they not only share a common language but also a common experience. They provide a vernacular model, reflecting the African American experience in the New World.

Baraka notes: "The blues is so basic because it is black speech at its earliest complete articulation as a New World speech. The speech of black people native to the Western world! . . . The blues is the actual secular day-to-day language given the grace of poetry" (*The Music* 262). Thus all three writers see Smith and the blues as entrances into the black world. Since the blues speaks black vernacular English, it tells the stories of the tribe, revealing African American identity. Therefore to learn to write the blues is to write the actual speech of African Americans. All three feel that the blues artist has captured the actual speech of the people in a way that the literary artist haven't. In "Words" Baraka has said: "In the closed circle I have fashioned. In the alien language of another tribe. I make these documents for some heart who will recognize me truthfully" (*Tales* 90). He wants to speak and write in the language of his own tribe: he wants to be a blues artist; he wants to use that basic form, which is behind most post-spiritual black music in this country.

To achieve this black sound, to find a black language, Baraka turns to free jazz because it contains the sound of the blues, the black voice, the black memory, in its most contemporary form. Baraka argues in several places that blues contains the cultural memory of black people (*Black Music* 180 and 183, *The Music* 263). In fact, Baraka finds his black voice through black music and free jazz, in particular. Baraka says:

> Blues and jazz have been the only consistent exhibitors of "Negritude" in formal American culture simply because the bearers of its tradition maintained their essential identities as Negroes; in no other art (and I will persist in calling Negro music, Art) has this been possible. Phyllis Wheatley and her pleasant imitations of eighteenth-century English poetry are far and, finally, ludicrous departures from the huge black voices that splintered southern nights with their *hollers, chants, arwhoolies,* and *ballits.*
>
> (HOME 106)

Baraka turned to free jazz musicians because they are the African American generational equivalent to white avant-garde artists, that is, they produce an art as sophisticated as the whites. Elsewhere I have concentrated on the power of the new music to destroy the old. Following Baraka's lead, I used the figure of John Coltrane for this task: he embodies the force, the energy, to destroy the old forms.[6] Here, however, I want to concentrate on the power of the new sound to enable Baraka to create both a new and an old sound, what he refers to as "the changing same," the revision and extension of the tradition. Free jazz allows him to find new forms that contain the old voice. In the end it is Albert Ayler, not Bessie Smith, who allows Baraka to find his voice, because Ayler embodies the contemporary black sound. Baraka insists it is the artist's mission to transmit the contemporary: "If it is honest it must say something new" (*The Music* 266).

It is not arbitrary that Baraka is drawn to the black avant-garde. What the black avant-garde has that the white one doesn't is the black oral tradition as well as an advanced style of expressing that tradition. The music critic Frank Kofsky says:

> It has been written so often as to be a cliché that the avant-gardists are striving to simulate the sound of human speech in their playing. Even a casual audit of a few of their recordings will illustrate the validity of this dictum; but what has not been stated is the kind of discourse that is being reproduced. . . . What one will hear in the music of John Coltrane, Eric

Dolphy, Sam Rivers, John Tchicai, and especially Archie Shepp is not speech "in general," but the voice of the urban Negro ghetto. . . . That Archie Shepp's growling, raspy tenor saxophone locutions, for example, distill for your ears the quintessence of Negro vocal patterns as they can be heard on the streets of Chicago, Detroit, Philadelphia, Harlem, or wherever you choose. Although the speech-like attributes are conceivably less palpable in their work, this is also the significance of Coltrane's eerie shrieks and *basso profundo* explosions, the jagged clarinet squeals of Eric Dolphy, even the more stately and oblique lamentations of John Tchicai: all invoke, to one degree or another, those cadences and rhythms that are unique to the lives of black people in the city millieu.

(BLACK NATIONALISM 134–135)

Kofsky is right about the voice of the people in the free jazz, but he is only working in the present tense of this music: there is also the sound of the past time, which includes the field holler and the church shout as well as the voice of the urban proletariat. It is a black way to "make it new" and, at the same time, "make it old," that is, to continue "the changing same." The black musical tradition has always issued from the black voice, but free jazz expresses the contemporary as well as actively expressing the past; it is the history of the music as well as its present tense.

It is of the first order of importance that free jazz includes the traditional sounds of spirituals and the blues as well as the more radical and dissonant sounds of contemporary music. These forms allowed Baraka to connect with the African American expressive past, which is profound, and also with the most avant-garde sounds of the time. We get a sense of this when we hear Albert Ayler's "Down by the Riverside," from *Goin' Home* (February 24, 1964). Baraka perceptively says of Ayler: "The music sounds like old timey religious tunes and some kind of spiritual march music. . . . Albert's music, which he characterizes as 'spiritual,' has much in common with older Black-American religious forms. An openness that characterizes the 'shout' and 'hollers'" (*Black Music* 193). The folk religious sound provides a profound underpinning and meaning to the music. Baraka using this technique in his art is not unlike Philip Roth using the Jewish joke, Yiddish, and Yiddish-inflected English to enrich his English prose. And it is not unlike John Zorn, in his Masada project, fusing Jewish folk music with Ornette Coleman-like free jazz. All three are connecting with tradition, something larger than the individual self, a cultural continuity and resonance. Moreover, as we have seen above, Baraka not only uses the blues sound of the new music but the church sound as well—to invoke Gwendolyn Brooks's term, the preachment sound, "the sermonic mode" of the black oral tradition. In "Dope," discussed above, Baraka adopts the preacher sound, the preacher performance style, to preach his sermon of communism.

Baraka was not only seeking an individual past but also a collective one, seeking the past of the tradition. Baraka states: "An expression of culture at its most un-self- (therefore showing the larger consciousness of a *one* self" (*Black Mu-*

320

william j. harris

sic180). Interestingly, this sounds like a classical vision of self; like T. S. Eliot's in "Tradition and Individual Talent" where he observes that the individual must "surrender . . . himself as he is at the moment to something which is more valuable [the tradition]," (*Selected Essays* 7). Elsewhere Baraka declares: "Find the self, then kill it" (*Black Music* 176). Kill the individual self to achieve the collective voice of the tradition; moreover, kill the individual black middle class voice to find the black mass one. Finally, distance yourself from the white individualistic "Cult of Themselves," (*Raise Race* 22) of white American civilization. For Baraka to "kill the self" means to kill the white Western self, the overly assimilated self, not the black individual self purged of whiteness.

Baraka's new sound came together with his major and controversial poem-manifesto, "Black Art." Significantly, it was first published in the *Liberator* in January 1966 but it was performed on Sonny Murray's *Sonny's Time Now* in November 1965, that is, the spoken word predates the written one. In addition to free jazz player Sonny Murray, Albert Ayler, Don Cherry, and Henry Grimes are on the record; liner notes are by Baraka himself. Baraka says that this album is new, free, spiritual and innovative—that is black avant-garde.

In this poem Baraka learned to speak in a distinctive African American voice, or at least one fully informed by the African American sound tradition. Baraka takes on the voices and sounds of the entire African American sound tradition. Baraka observes, "Poetry, first of all, was and still must be a musical form. It is speech musicked. . . . And the clearer I got on my own legitimate historical and cultural sources, the more obvious it became that not only was the poetry supposed to be as musical as it could be, but that reading with music would only enhance and extend its meanings and give new strength to its form" (*Black Music* 243, 244). Hence his voice is larger than a personal voice but embodies the voice of the tradition. This is different from the voice of "Black Dada," which embodied the voice of another tradition and therefore another history.

"Black Art," fuses the screams and cries of the music and poetry. Baraka says:

> Black poetry, in its mainstream, is oracular, sermonic; it incorporates the screams and shouts and moans and wails of the people inside and outside of the churches; the whispers and thunder vibrato and staccato of the inside and the outside of the people themselves.   (BLACK MUSIC 244)

Baraka's screams are wild and free—free jazz screams. Baraka asks, "Can Robert Lowell scat??" (*Raise Race* 26). At this point, scatting is alien to the white mainstream poetic tradition. Here Baraka employs the scream, a jazz form. In this recording he imitates, even competes with the free jazz musicians' screams, linking him to the scream of the church and the tradition. This is an amazing performance where Baraka does not only imitate the players but the players imitate him: Baraka screams and they scream back. The sound is wonderful and chaotic, resembling sirens, machine guns, and horns: "rrrrrrrrrrrrrrrr / rrrrrrrrrrrr . . . tuhtuhtuhtuhtuh-tuhtuhtuhtuh" (*Reader* 219). It sounds like a divine catfight where Baraka has learned to speak the passionate language of the scream, connecting him with both the church, the Holy Roller, and popular entertainment, James Brown. He has learned to make divine noise, has found black energy, leaving the white vehicular language behind. Baraka has screamed and hollered himself into the tradition. As this aggressive music creates black consciousness, it wipes out the white world.

Baraka muses, "Players like Coleman, Coltrane, and Rollins literarily scream and rant in imitation of the human voice, sounding many times like the unfettered primitive shouters" (*Blues People* 227). Then Baraka says, "The hard, driving shouting of James Brown identifies a place and image in America. . . . James Brown's screams, etc., are more 'radical' than most jazz musicians sound, etc. Certainly his sound is 'further out' than Ornette's. And that sound has been a part of Black music, even out in them backwoods churches since the year one" (*Black Music* 185, 210).

The jazz singer Abby Lincoln's scream in "Triptych," on Max Roach's *We Insist! Freedom Now Suite* (1960), seems controlled in contrast. The three sections of "Triptych" are "Prayer / Protest/ Peace." It is in the middle section, "Protest," that Lincoln screams, but it is not a free jazz scream; it is melodic, musical, and structured—in fact, pleasing; it is protest, not revolt. Perhaps this is the difference between the civil rights scream and the black power scream. The civil rights' scream ends in peace and the free jazz one ends in rebellion. Baraka says, "Coltrane's cries are not 'musical,' but they *are* music and quite moving music. Ornette Coleman's screams and rants are only musical once one understands the music his emotional attitude seeks to create. This attitude is real, and perhaps the most singularly important aspect of his music" (*Black Music* 15). Therefore from the new music one is not only learning technique but also attitudes toward the world. Baraka sheds white attitudes for black ones.

Significantly, "Black Art" ends, after a great verbal explosion, poetic screams with these lines

> We want a black poem. And a
> Black World.
> Let the world be a Black Poem
> And Let All Black People Speak This Poem
> Silently
> Or LOUD. (*Reader* 220)

The poem ends in the imperative mood, ends with speech, with sound. Bell hooks says, in the essay "Talking Back," that "for us, true speaking is not solely an expression of creative power; it is an act of resistance, a political gesture that challenges politics of domination that would render us nameless and voiceless. As such, it is a courageous act—as such, it represents a threat. To those who wield oppressive power, that which is threatening must necessarily be wiped out, annihilated, silenced" (*Talking Back* 8).

In summary, free jazz enabled Baraka to develop a new-old African American voice, the changing same, simultaneously his own personal and ethnic voice. Free jazz allowed Baraka access to both traditional African American expressive forms and new radical contemporary ones and allowed him to come into a fuller sense of self, allowed him to be "in the tradition": [in the] Tradition / of Douglas / of David Walker / Garnett / Turner / Tubman / of ragers yeh / ragers / (of Kings, & Counts, Dukes / of Satchelmouths & SunRa's (*Reader* 303). It allowed him to be part of a persistent yet changing tradition; it allowed him both a musical and racial continuity in the discontinuity of the multiplicity of black sound.

NOTES

1. Here are a few words about racial identity. Before advancing to Baraka and Reed, it is perhaps helpful to know my position on this issue. I do not find either *social construction* (the belief that identity is a linguistic fiction) or *essentialism* (the belief that identity is static and transhistorical), including *strategic essentialism* (the belief that identity is a useful fiction), particularly useful terms. I want to say race is real not in terms of skin color but in terms of shared cultures, histories, traditions, ideologies, and experiences. Moreover, for me, racial identity, is fluid, always adjusting to the current moment but historically and culturally grounded, always responding to a residue of personal experiences and cultural memories; that is, racial identity is persistent; however, it is highly influenced by factors beyond itself. Looking at race in its historical and cultural context, my larger project will compare and contrast the changing definitions of race in the sixties, with the example of Baraka, and in the seventies, with the example of Reed. Wanting to escape the homogenization of white American culture, Baraka became a cultural nationalist, affirming black culture and rejecting white culture; and Reed, wanting to escape the homogenization of black culture by cultural nationalists, including Baraka, became a multiculturalist, affirming all minority cultures and rejecting black nationalism. There are a number of philosophers and theorists trying to move beyond the categories of social construction and essentialism. A book that tackles this theme is Moya and Hames-Garcia's *Reclaiming Identity and the Predicament of Postmodernism.*

2. I want to thank my colleagues and friends Jeff Nealon and Paul Youngquist for reading this article with care and rigor. I feel very lucky to have belonged to the lively and productive intellectual community at Penn State.

3. For other discussions of Baraka's performance of "BLACK DADA NIHILISMUS" with the New York Art Quartet, see Nielsen's *Black Chant* (190–95) and Benston's *Performing Blackness* (220). These interpretations very nicely fill out the description of the performance. Nielsen provides the fullest account, depicting its understatedness, and Benston finds the recording a breakthrough to a new ethnic sound.

4. The need to cast off white identity to achieve black identity is one of the main themes of my entire study, *The Poetry and Poetics of Amiri Baraka,* but especially see chapter 3, "The Failure of the White Postmodernists" (67–90).

5. For their ideas about African retentions, see Thompson's *Flash of the Spirit* and Herskovits's *The Myth of the Negro Past* and listen to any number of Randy Weston's CDs, such as *Tanjah* and *African Cookbook.*

6. See chapter 1, "The Jazz Aesthetic," of my *The Poetry of Amiri Baraka* for a full discussion of the transformative powers of the new music, especially 14–16.

WORKS CITED

Baldwin, James. *Nobody Knows My Name: More Notes of a Native Son*. New York: Delta, 1961.

Baraka, Amiri. *The Autobiography of LeRoi Jones/Amiri Baraka*. New York: Freundlich, 1984.

———— *Black Music*. New York: Apollo, 1968.

———— *Blues People: Negro Music in White America*. New York: William Morrow, 1963.

———— *Home: Social Essays*. New York: William Morrow, 1966.

———— *The LeRoi Jones / Amiri Baraka Reader*. Ed. William J. Harris. New York: Thunder's Mouth, 2000.

———— *The Music*. New York: William Morrow, 1987.

———— *Raise Race Rays Raze: Essays Since 1965*. New York: Random House, 1971.

———— *The System of Dante's Hell*. New York: Grove, 1965.

———— *Tales*. New York: Grove, 1967.

Benston, Kimberly W. "Amiri Baraka: An Interview." *Boundary 2* 6 (Winter 1978): 303–16.

———— *Performing Blackness: Enactments of African-American Modernism*. London and New York: Routledge, 2000.

Bernstein, Charles. "Introduction." *Close Listening: Poetry and the Performed Word*. Ed. Charles Bernstein. New York: Oxford University Press, 1998.

Carr, Ian. "Free Jazz." *Jazz: the Essential Companion*. Ed. Ian Carr, Dighy Fairweather, Brian Priestly. New York: Prentice Hall, 1987. 173–74.

Eliot, T. S. *Selected Essays*. New York: Harcourt, Brace and World, 1964.

Fanon, Frantz. *Black Skin, White Masks*. New York: Grove, 1967.

Feinstein, Sascha. "Better You Say It First: An Interview with Amiri Baraka." *Brilliant Corners* 4 (Winter 1999): 67–85.

Ginsberg, Allen. *Spontaneous Mind: Selected Interviews, 1958–1966*. Ed David Carter. New York: Harper Collins, 2001.

Harris, William J. *The Poetry and Poetics of Amiri Baraka: The Jazz Aesthetic*. Columbia: University of Missouri Press, 1985.

Herskovits, Melvile. *The Myth of the Negro Past*. Boston: Beacon, 1958.

Hooks, bell. *Talking Back: Thinking Feminist, Thinking Black*. Boston: South End, 1989.

Hughes, Langston. *The Collected Poems*. Ed Arnold Rampersad. New York: Knopf, 1995.

Kofsky, Frank. *Black Nationalism and the Revolution in Music*. New York: Pathfinder, 1970.

McKay, Claude. "If We Must Die." *The Black Poets*. Ed Dudley Randall. New York: Bantam, 1971. 63.

Moya, Paula M. L., and Michael R. Hames-Garcia, eds. *Reclaiming Identity: Realist Theory and the Predicament of Postmodernism*. Berkeley: University of California Press, 2000.

Nielsen, Aldon. *Black Chant: Languages of African-American Postmodernism*. Cambridge: Cambridge University Press, 1997.

Thompson, Robert Farris. *Flash of the Spirit: African and Afro-American Art and Philosophy*. New York: Vintage, 1983.

Wilson, August. "Preface to 'Three Plays.'" *The Jazz Cadence of American Culture*. Ed. Robert G. O'Meally. New York: Columbia University Press, 1998.

DISCOGRAPHY

Ayler, Albert. *Goin' Home*. Black Lion. ASIN: B0000015R6, 1995.

Baraka, Amiri. "Dope." *Every Tone a Testimony*. Smithsonian Folkways, SFW CD 47003, 2001.

———— *New Music-New Poetry*, with David Murray and Steve McCall. India Navigation, 1048. 1981.

———— "BLACK DADA NIHILISMUS." *Poetry with Jones*. Pacifica Archive, BB 1910.02. 1964.

Murray, Sonny, *Sonny's Time Now*. Diw-355. 1965.

Roach, Max. *We Insist! Freedom Now Suite*. Candid, CCD 9002 Stereo. 1960.

Rudd, Roswell. *The New York Art Quartet*. Calibre, ESP cd 1004. 1965.

Weston, Randy. *African Cookbook*. Koch Jazz, Koc CD 8517. 1972.

———— *Tanjah*. Verve, 314 527 778–2. 1973.

BRENT HAYES EDWARDS

The Literary Ellington

One of the main assumptions in thinking about African American creative expression is that music—more than literature, dance, theater, or the visual arts—has been the paradigmatic mode of black artistic production and the standard and pinnacle not just of black culture but of American culture as a whole. The most eloquent version of this common claim may be the opening of James Baldwin's 1951 essay "Many Thousands Gone": "It is only in his music, which Americans are able to admire because a protective sentimentality limits their understanding of it, that the Negro in America has been able to tell his story. It is a story which otherwise has yet to be told and which no American is prepared to hear."[1] Eleven years later Amiri Baraka put it even more forcefully, excoriating the "embarrassing and inverted paternalism" of African American writers such as Phyllis Wheatley and Charles Chesnutt, and claiming flatly that "there has never been an equivalent to Duke Ellington or Louis Armstrong in Negro writing."[2] Such presuppositions and hierarchical valuations have been part of the source of a compulsion among generations of African American writers to conceptualize "vernacular" poetics and to strive toward a tradition of blues or jazz literature, toward a notion of black writing that implicitly or explicitly aspires to the condition of music.

I want to start by juxtaposing these stark claims with an early essay by one of the musicians they so often cite as emblematic. Duke Ellington's first article, "The Duke Steps Out," was published in the spring of 1931 in a British music journal called *Rhythm*. "The music of my race is something more than the 'American idiom,'" Ellington contends. "It is the result of our transplantation to American soil, and was our reaction in the plantation days to the tyranny we endured. What we could not say openly we expressed in music, and what we know as 'jazz' is something more than just dance music."[3] This would seem to be in keeping with an assumption that black music articulates a sense of the world that could not be expressed otherwise—that it "speaks" what cannot be said openly. Yet Ellington, in moving on to describe the African American population of New York City, offers a somewhat different reading of the music that was being produced in that context, specifically in relation to the literature of the Harlem Renaissance that had exploded into prominence in the previous decade. He writes:

> In Harlem we have what is practically our own city; we have our own newspapers and social services, and although not segregated, we have almost achieved our own civilisation. The history of my people is one of great achievements over fearful odds; it is a history of a people hindered, handicapped and often sorely oppressed, and what is being done by Countee Cullen and others in literature is overdue in our music.

Here what we so often suppose to be the dynamics of influence between black music and literature is inverted—in Duke's view the achievements of the literary Renaissance are a model for his own aspirations in music. He continues: "I am therefore now engaged on a rhapsody unhampered by any musical form in which I intend to portray the experiences of the coloured races in America in the syncopated idiom." In a remarkably early reference to his lifelong ambition to compose a "tone parallel" to African American history—an ambition that would find partial realization in later works like *Black, Brown, and Beige* and *My People*—Ellington makes no apologies for his desire to "attribut[e] aims other than terpischore to our music."[4] Indeed, he adds, "I am putting all I have learned into it in the hope that I shall have achieved something really worth while in the literature of music, and that an authentic record of my race *written by a member of it* shall be placed on record." My aim here is not of course to undermine the importance of black music, or to crudely promote the literary at its expense, but to begin to challenge some of our assumptions about the relations between aesthetic media in black culture. Looking at the literary Duke, at Ellington as writer and reader, I want to reconsider just what that provocative phrase—"the literature of music"—might mean.

It is well known that Duke Ellington based a number of his compositions on literary sources. One thinks of the 1943 *New World A-Comin'*, based on the Roi Ottley study of the same name; Ellington's aborted plans to adapt South African novelist Peter Abrahams' *Mine Boy* (1958); *Suite Thursday* (1960), the Ellington–Billy Strayhorn suite based on John Steinbeck's novel *Sweet Thursday*; and the so-called Shakespearean Suite, also known as *Such Sweet Thunder* (1957).[5] There are many more compositions that involve narrative written by Ellington and/or Strayhorn (either programmatic, recitative, or lyric) in one way or another, including *A Drum Is a Woman* (1956); *The Golden Broom and the Green Apple* (1963); *The River* (1970); and of course the *Sacred Concerts* in the 1960s.[6] Barry Ulanov has commented that "Duke has always been a teller of tales, three-minute or thirty. . . . He has never failed to take compass points, wherever he has been, in a new city, a new country, a redecorated nightclub; to make his own observations and to translate these, like his reflections about the place of the Negro in a white society, into fanciful narratives."[7]

What is remarkable, in this wealth of work, is the degree to which Ellington was consistently concerned with "telling tales" in *language*, not only in sounds—or, more precisely, in both: spinning stories in ways that combined words and music. Almost all of the extended works were conceived with this kind of literary component, even though Ellington's attempts at mixing narrative with music were for the most part dismissed by critics. The bizarre and misogynist vocal narration performed by Ellington himself on *A Drum Is a Woman* was mocked as "monotonous" and "pretentious" and as "purple prose," with even favorably disposed reviewers like Barry Ulanov complaining that "there is no point in analyzing the script. Such banality, such inanity, such a hodgepodge does not stand up either to close reading or close listening."[8] And yet Duke's desire to write remained constant. Asked to speak to a black church in Los Angeles in 1941 on the subject of Langston Hughes's poem "I, Too," Ellington commented that "music is my business, my profession, my life . . . but, even though it means so much to me, I often feel that I'd like to say something, have my say, on some of the burning issues confronting us, in another language . . . in words of mouth."[9]

Ellington also wrote poetry. He showed some of his writing to Richard Boyer, who in 1943 was preparing a now legendary portrait of Ellington for the *New Yorker*: "New acquaintances are always surprised when they learn that Duke has written poetry in which he advances the thesis that the rhythm of jazz has been beaten into the Negro race by three centuries of oppression. The four beats to a bar in jazz are also found, he maintains in verse, in the Negro pulse. Duke doesn't like to show people his poetry. 'You can say anything you want on the trombone, but you gotta be careful with words,' he explains."[10] Nevertheless, some of Ellington's poems are collected in *Music Is My Mistress* (MM 39–40, 212–13), and there are even a few recordings of Ellington reciting poetry in concert. Some of these performances are whimsical, couched as a humorous interlude to the music, as when Duke recites a short, colloquial quatrain at a Columbia University date in 1964 and prefaces it with the nervous disclaimer that "I wanted to tell it to Billy Strayhorn the other day in Bermuda, and he went to sleep. . . . So I still haven't done it":

> Into each life some jazz must fall,
> With after-beat gone kickin',
> With jive alive, a ball for all,
> Let not the beat be chicken![11]

Another example is a poem entitled "Moon Maiden," which Ellington recorded in a session for Fantasy Records on July 14, 1969. He plays celeste on the thirty-six bar tune and recites (in an overdub, since he is snapping his fingers as well) two brief stanzas before taking a solo:

Moon Maiden, way out there in the blue
Moon Maiden, got to get with you
I've made my approach and then revolved
But my big problem is still unsolved
Moon Maiden, listen here, my dear
Your vibrations are coming in loud and clear
Cause I'm just a fly-by-night guy,
But for you I might be quite the right "do right" guy
Moon Maiden, Moon Maiden, Lady de Luna[12]

In the liner notes Stanley Dance comments that this "unique" selection originated when Ellington's imagination "had been stimulated by the thought of men walking around on the moon, and he had not uncharacteristically visualized their encountering some chicks up there." These lyrics comprise only one among a number of works that reflect Ellington's fascination with the space race, like "The Ballet of the Flying Saucers" in *A Drum Is a Woman* (1956), "Blues in Orbit" (1958), "Launching Pad" (1959), and unperformed lyrics like the undated "Spaceman," with its more lascivious reveries: "I want a spaceman from twilight 'til dawn / When the chicks say there he is he's really gone / . . . . Give me a spaceman on a moonlit nit [sic] / Who can fly further than he'll admit / One whose cockpit is out of this world / Been around so much he's even had his stick twirled."[13]

THE LITERARY ELLINGTON

Stanley Dance writes that the "felicitous internal rhymes" of "Moon Maiden" come off Duke's tongue "as though phrased by plunger-muted brass," but surely it is important that Ellington conceives the piece as a vocal recitation, not an instrumental number or a sung lyric. Indeed, he had "recorded the number twice as an instrumental, and with at least a couple of singers, but each time he remained dissatisfied." At one concert around this time, Ellington introduced the piece by saying that "*Moon Maiden* represents my public debut as a vocalist, but I don't really sing. I'm a pencil cat. My other number will be, *I Want to See the Dark Side of Your Moon, Baby*. . . . Extravagance going to the moon? Extravagances have always been accepted as poetic license."[14] In other words, Ellington was deliberately seeking a kind of rhetorical—and apparently libidinal—excess that he considered to necessitate a poetic form, one in which "extravagances" would be accepted.

I want to focus briefly on what we might term this literary imperative in the Ellington oeuvre, which is not by any means limited to Duke's efforts at programmatic narrative or poetry. In his brilliant autobiographical suite, *Music Is My Mistress*, Ellington writes of a more general narrative or "story-telling" impulse behind the very process of creating music, arguing for the necessity in music of "painting a picture, or having a story to go with what you were going to play." He goes on to claim (like a number of other jazz musicians) that soloists could "send messages in what they play," articulating comprehensible statements to one another on their instruments while on the bandstand. "The audience didn't know anything about it, but the cats in the band did," he adds.[15] But he also noted that "stories" were

sometimes necessary to the composition and arrangement process, and often ver-
balized in language—with Duke talking the band through a new or unfamiliar tune
with the guidance of a tall tale or two. The band seldom turned to collaborative
arrangements (with all the musicians contributing to the construction of a song),
but the anecdotes of that process are legendary, and fascinating for just this reason.
Ellington describes it this way:

> Still other times I might just sit down at the piano and start composing a
> little melody, telling a story about it at the same time to give the mood of
> the piece. I'll play eight bars, talk a bit, then play another eight and soon
> the melody is finished. Then the boys go to work on it, improvising,
> adding a phrase here and there. We don't write like this very often and
> when we do it's usually three o'clock in the morning after we've finished a
> date.
>
> But this is a little off the point. What I am trying to get across is that
> music for me is a language. It expresses more than just sound.[16]

A more vivid description of the same process is provided in Richard Boyer's "The
Hot Bach," which is worth quoting at some length:

> The band rarely works out an entire arrangement collectively, but when it
> does, the phenomenon is something that makes other musicians marvel.
> This collective arranging may take place anywhere—in a dance hall in
> Gary, Indiana, in an empty theatre in Mobile, or in a Broadway night club.
> It will usually be after a performance, at about three in the morning. Duke,
> sitting at his piano and facing his band, will play a new melody, perhaps, or
> possibly just an idea consisting of only eight bars. After playing the eight
> bars, he may say, "Now this is sad. It's about one guy sitting alone in his
> room in Harlem. He's waiting for his chick, but she doesn't show. He's got
> everything fixed for her." Duke sounds intent and absorbed. His tired band
> begins to sympathize with the waiting man in Harlem. "Two glasses of
> whiskey are on his little dresser before his bed," Duke says, and again plays
> the two bars, which will be full of weird and mournful chords. Then he
> goes on to eight new bars. "He has one of those blue lights turned on in
> the gloom of his room," Duke says softly, "and he has a little pot of incense
> so it will smell nice for the chick." Again he plays the mournful chords,
> developing his melody. "But she doesn't show," he says, "she doesn't show.
> The guy just sits there, maybe an hour, hunched over on his bed, all
> alone." The melody is finished and it is time to work out an arrangement
> for it. Lawrence Brown rises with his trombone and gives out a compact,
> warm phrase. Duke shakes his head. "Lawrence, I want something like the
> treatment you gave in 'Awful Sad,'" he says. Brown amends his suggestion
> and in turn is amended by Tricky Sam Nanton, also a trombone who puts
> a smear and a wa-wa lament on the phrase suggested by Brown. . . . Now
> Juan Tizol grabs a piece of paper and a pencil and begins to write down the

orchestration, while the band is still playing it. Whenever the band stops for a breather, Duke experiments with rich new chords, perhaps adopts them, perhaps rejects, perhaps works out a piano solo that fits, clear and rippling, into little slots of silence, while the brass and reeds talk back and forth. By the time Tizol has finished getting the orchestration down on paper, it is already out of date. The men begin to play again, and then someone may shout "How about that train?" and there is a rush for a train that will carry the band to another engagement.[17]

It is not at all unusual for collaborative musicians and dancers to give each other epigrammatic or narrative clues during the compositional or choreographic process. Here, though, the arrangement seems to *start off* from the narrative, with Duke's self-accompanied performance—the tired band members are drawn into the creative process by the scene Duke sketches as he speaks. Here, in the middle of the night, at the core of what drives the band's extraordinarily creative cohesiveness, is an intimate call and response between words and music, narrative instigation and the subsequent musical contextualization of a melody. It is almost a commonplace by now to describe Ellington's music with superlative literary analogies, as a "drama of orchestration" or a "theatre of perfect timing."[18] Some critics have gone so far as to write about the "Shakespearean universality" of Ellington's music, contending that it is akin to the Bard's plays "in its reach, wisdom, and generosity, and we return to it because its mysteries are inexhaustible."[19] But part of what I am suggesting is that the literary is less an *analogy* for Ellington's music than an inherent element in his conception of music itself and a key formal bridge or instigating spur in his compositional process.

It seems that Ellington was particularly attracted to the Stratford Shakespeare Festivals in Ontario partly because of the complex creative connections between literature and music fostered there in the late 1950s. The festival was unique in that it featured not only Shakespeare performances but also extensive musical lineups, in effect proposing a dialogue or consonance between aesthetic media. In 1956 the festival presented Benjamin Britten's opera *The Rape of Lucretia* as well as the Ellington band, Dave Brubeck, the Modern Jazz Quartet, Willie "the Lion" Smith, and the Art Tatum Trio; in 1957 it premiered Britten's *The Turn of the Screw* and programmed Ellington's *Such Sweet Thunder* as well as Count Basie, Billie Holiday, Gerry Mulligan, and the Teddy Wilson Trio; in 1958 John Gay's *The Beggar's Opera* was presented next to the Maynard Ferguson Orchestra, Carmen McRae, the Billy Taylor Trio, the Dizzy Gillespie Orchestra, and Henry "Red" Allen and his All Stars, who performed with the poet Langston Hughes. In the program notes to *Such Sweet Thunder* Ellington commends the 1957 festival's "awareness" of the "parallel" between Shakespeare and "top-grade jazz" and comments:

> There is an increasing interrelationship between the adherents to art forms in various fields. . . . It is becoming increasingly difficult to decide where jazz starts or where it ends, where Tin Pan Alley begins and jazz ends, or even where the borderline lies between classical music and jazz. I

feel there is no boundary line, and I see no place for one if my own feelings tell me a performance is good.

In the final analysis, whether it be Shakespeare or jazz, the only thing that counts is the emotional effect on the listener. Somehow, I suspect that if Shakespeare were alive today, he might be a jazz fan himself—he'd appreciate the combination of team spirit and informality, of academic knowledge and humor, of all the elements that go into a great jazz performance. And I am sure he would agree with the simple and axiomatic statement that is so important to all of us—when it sounds good, it is good.

(MM 193)

Here, Ellington slyly pulls the rug out from under the critics who applaud the "Shakespearean" qualities in his music. If anything, in this description of boundary-crossing, Shakespeare is revealed to be an Ellingtonian before his time. What unites jazz and Elizabethan drama, for Ellington, is above all a common concern with capturing the vibrant complexity of a particular social milieu. As Billy Strayhorn added in an interview, "Duke also said that the only way Shakespeare could have known as much about people as he did was by hanging out on the corner or in the pool room. He says that if William Shakespeare were alive today, you would surely find him down at Birdland listening to jazz."[20]

In 1956, the first time that the orchestra was invited to the festival, Ellington and Strayhorn had been less inspired, offering a set of mainly old hits like "I Got It Bad (and That Ain't Good)" and "Take the 'A' Train." They did offer one selection, though, that seemed geared for the theatrical environs and toward an interest in the "interrelationships" between art forms: "Monologue," also known as "Pretty and the Wolf" (which had first been recorded in 1951). The piece features Ellington with Jimmy Hamilton, Russell Procope, and Harry Carney. The record not only captures Duke's "vagabond syntax" (in Barry Ulanov's description) but also might be heard as an attempt to capture the feeling of one of those late-night arranging session narratives, with Duke narrating a piece to the band. One might hear "Pretty and the Wolf" as a kind of orchestration of that ephemeral process, a version of one of those casual tales spun to incite elaboration and embellishment.

Like the tale Ellington tells the band in the rehearsal recounted in the Boyer article, like "Moon Maiden," and indeed like much of Ellington's writing, "Pretty and the Wolf" is a parable of seduction as well as an insouciant reflection on African American urban migration (figure 16.1). "Once upon a time," Duke opens as the three reeds unfurl behind him, "there came to the city a pretty little girl—a little country, but pretty; a little ragged, but a pretty little girl. There she met a man, a city man—smooth—handsome—successful—cool. A well-mannered type man. And since she was pretty, he saw fit to give her an audience, so he talked to her for quite a while." The Wolf, standing on the corner casually twirling his "diamond-studded gold chain," agrees to assist the pretty girl in her ambition to "get somewhere." (The piece's simple conceit turns on the two meanings of the phrase: in other words, the narrative sets up an analogy between sexual conquest and material success.) She obsequiously purrs "Yes, Daddy" at his every suggestion. "And so agreed, they danced," Ellington intones, as Jimmy Woode and Sam Woodyard enter on bass and drums, falling into an infectious swing. But the dynamics of the seduction switch during the dance, a "mad whirl" that leaves the seemingly unflappable city dweller in an amorous "spin." By the end of the two-and-a-half-minute piece, it is no longer the Wolf, but the "pretty girl" who twirls the gold chain. As she "enumerates the various conditions and ways for him to get somewhere, you can hear him say, 'Yes, Baby. Yes, Baby. Yes, Baby.'"[21] It is as though Ellington is attempting to perform that singular arranging technique—the music shifting with the bandleader's narrative, taking on shape as his "Monologue" develops. The reeds "spin" in chromatic triplets as the Wolf twirls his chain, rock into rhythm when the characters start dancing, and later wheeze at the close of the piece, punctuating the Wolf's "Yes, Baby" with resignation.

Deeply impressed by the 1956 festival, Ellington and Strayhorn promised to return the next year with a new composition specifically for that context. The result was *Such Sweet Thunder*, which premiered in New York in the spring of 1957 at the Music for Moderns series at Town Hall, and then was performed in Stratford that summer. Ellington explained that "the idea of writing a Shakespearean suite occurred to me during a visit to Anne Hathaway's cottage when we first toured England in 1933. I have often wondered, had I been asked to play for the Bard, what devices I would have used to impress him. Consequently, I was very pleased when it was suggested that I compose a work for the Shakespearean Festival in Stratford, Ontario, since I found Shakespeare as performed there to be a thrilling experience."[22] The suite is constructed around "parallels" to the stories of a number of Shakespearean characters, including Othello, Julius Caesar, Henry V, Lady Macbeth, Puck, Hamlet, and Romeo and Juliet.

"It was the preparation that was tremendous," Billy Strayhorn told Stanley Dance later. "We read all of Shakespeare!"[23] He told another interviewer that

> you have to adjust your perspective, you know, as to just what you're going to do, and what you're going to say, and what you're going to say it about, and how much of it is supposed to be coming . . .—and this included also consultations with two or three Shakespearean actors and authorities, you know. We'd sit down and discuss for hours. . . . And it was a matter of just deciding finally [that] on one album we're not gonna parallel any, you know, anything of Shakespeare. . . . You need a thousand writers and a thousand years to do it . . . to cover Shakespeare. So, we'll say well we'll just devote one number to one Shakespearean word, or one Shakeapearean phrase, you know, something like that. Just like "Lady Mac," you know.[24]

Ellington described the process more figuratively—and with characteristic irreverence: "I kept thinking what a dandy song Lady Macbeth would make. The girl has everything. Noble birth, a hot love story, murder—even a ghost. Then there's Othello and Desdemona. There's a swinging story for you. What a melodrama! What a subject for the blues. Blues in the night!"[25]

FIGURE 16.1 Two pages from one of Ellington's draft scores for "Pretty and the Wolf." *Duke Ellington Collection, Archives Center, National Museum of American History, Smithsonian Institution, Washington, D.C.*

FIGURE 16.1   Continued

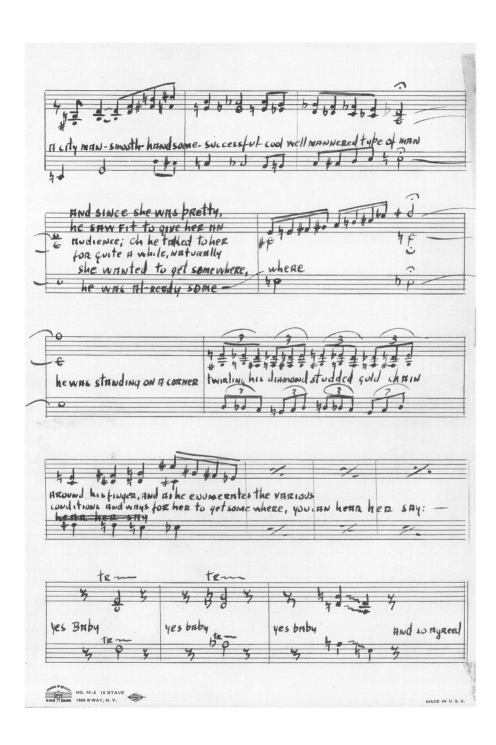

I would argue that this transformation of Shakespeare is doing work very different from other black expressive appropriations one might assume are similar, like Langston Hughes's poem "Shakespeare in Harlem":

> Hey ninny neigh!
> And a hey nonny noe!
> Where, oh, where
> Did my sweet mamma go?
> Ney ninny neigh
> With a tra-la-la!
> They say your sweet mama
> Went home to her ma.[26]

Ellington and Strayhorn do not place Shakespeare *in* Harlem, challenging our preconceptions about "high" and "low" art in the process.[27] Instead, *Such Sweet Thunder* is above all a *reading* of Shakespeare—perhaps *from* Harlem—and an elaborate reading at that. In the liner notes to the album, Duke describes the title cut (featuring Ray Nance on trumpet) as "the sweet and singing, very convincing story Othello told Desdemonda. It must have been the most, because when her father complained and tried to have her marriage annulled, the Duke of Venice said that if Othello had said this to his daughter, she would have gone for it too."[28] The point is that the speech of seduction is not given in the play itself: here the music fills the silences or interstices of Shakespeare's work. It imagines what cannot be or is not given in the written language—aiming to capture in sound the enthralling effect of Othello's violent and bloody tales of his life as a soldier. And, to do so, the music "rhymes" *Othello* with an entirely different moment from another play, as Barry Ulanov has noted:

> On stage Ellington introduces each "major work" with a vagabond syntax that makes one wonder why he bothers. But if one listens carefully, both to the words and the music, one discovers why. One finds, for example, that in titling a piece about *Othello* with a quotation from *A Midsummer Night's Dream* ("I never heard so musical a discord, such sweet thunder"), he has gone right to the root of Othello's problem. His blunt and jazzy explanation is probably closer to the substance of the play than the long and involuted commentaries of most Shakespearean scholars.[29]

David Hajdu has commented that the Ellington-Strayhorn suites, even when inspired by literary characters, are in no way "traditional descriptive music."[30] Ellington writes in a press release for the Stratford Festival that "in the suite I am attempting to parallel the vignettes of some of the Shakespearean characters in miniature . . . sometimes to the point of caricature."[31]

Indeed, Ellington seems to choose the word *parallel* carefully to describe the way *Such Sweet Thunder* interprets the Shakespearean texts. It is a term that Ellington used more than any other to describe his longer works, such as the 1951 "(A

Tone Parallel to) Harlem," the 1943 *New World A-Comin'*, which he called "a parallel to Roi Ottley's book,"[32] and *Black, Brown, and Beige* (1943), which was originally titled "A Tone Parallel," and which Ellington described as "a tone parallel to the history of the American Negro" (MM 181). Whereas before *Black, Brown, and Beige* Ellington and Strayhorn sometimes speak more loosely about music "portraying" the world, or about the necessity to "translate" experience into the arena of sound, by the mid-1940s they begin use the term *parallel*, seemingly in order to specify the effects and requisites of *musical* transcription, without relying on reference to another art form (as in *tone poem, portrait*, or *translation*). The term is sometimes used in a sense that connotes a kind of mimesis, aesthetic reflection, as in *Music Is My Mistress*, where Ellington says that "composers try to parallel observations made through all the senses" (MM 457). Elsewhere, in sketching a history of black music, he describes the "Negro musician" as "strongly influenced by the type of music of his time, and the black beat was his foundation. . . . The music of his time—and sound devices—were always parallel to the progress of science, medicine, and labor. When you pick the jazz musician of any period, if he happens to be one of the many unique performers, you may be sure he always reflects what's happening in his time" (MM 413). But Ellington's use of the term usually avoids formalizing whatever that artistic reflection might involve. *Parallel* has interesting implications for an Ellingtonian understanding of the relation between music and literature in particular, since it offers a metaphor not of crossing, transferral, or import—much less grafting or mixing—but instead of simultaneous and equivalent movement through space and time. Ellington and Strayhorn seem to favor this sense of an exact match in development, a structure of reflection without primacy, in a term that implicitly respects the distances between expressive media.

Ellington also seems to understand the term *parallel* in a structural sense, indicating the "musical" use of a literary form. The four pieces called sonnets, for instance ("Sonnet for Caesar," "Sonnet for Hank Cinq," "Sonnet in Search of a Moor," and "Sonnet for Sister Kate") are "different in mood, orchestration, and rhythm, but have in common, as Ellington scholar Bill Dobbins points out, fourteen phrases of ten notes each, musically mirroring the fourteen lines of iambic pentameter (ten syllables) that make up the literary sonnet Shakespeare favored."[33] This effect is particularly marked in Jimmy Hamilton's stately clarinet melody in "Sonnet for Caesar" and Jimmy Woode's plucked bass statement in "Sonnet in Search of a Moor"—both of which are woven out of a series of ten-note two-measure phrases. But it is also apparent in the theme in A-flat (framed by two blustery blues choruses) played by trombonist Britt Woodman in "Sonnet to Hank Cinq." Ellington's pencil manuscript for "Sonnet for Sister Kate" (which characteristically identifies the trombone solo simply with Quentin Jackson's nickname, "Butter") actually numbers the two-bar phrases of the melody from one to fourteen.[34] Of course, this is an odd and somewhat convoluted way to "parallel" the Shakespearean texts, since the dialogue in the plays is not in sonnet form. It is a bit like writing a book of short stories inspired by Beethoven's symphonies and calling some of the stories "etudes" or "sonatas." Still, the choice evidences the attempt by Ellington and Strayhorn to structure their portraits or caricatures by deliberately adopting the phrasing structure required by a literary stanza form. The parallel is staged, in other words, both on a level one might term representational, or even interpretive (the bass suggests the gravity of Othello, perhaps; or a medium-tempo blues indicates the swagger of "Hank Cinq"), and simultaneously on a structural level.

The other way that *Such Sweet Thunder* "reads" Shakespeare is a strategy that Ellington and Strayhorn take with most of their tone parallels. Particularly in the titles of the pieces, they play with puns and homonyms, not just for humorous effect but also in order to highlight the phonemic registers of the Shakespearean text. Strayhorn told one interviewer that "Sonnet in Search of a Moor" was "triple entendre, because it was, you know, you had to decide whether we were talking about Othello, or whether we were talking about love [that is, *amour*], or whether we were talking about the moors [the Scottish lowlands] where the three witches were, you know."[35] This is a familiar practice, when one examines the discography: John Steinbeck's novel *Sweet Thursday* becomes *Suite Thursday*, embedded in *Toot Suite* is the French for "right away" (*tout de suite*), and likewise I would suggest that we are asked to hear "suite" in "Such Sweet Thunder." This operation privileges the sound of words over the particular ways they are written on the page. Again, it underlines the specific parameters of a musical parallel, an interpretive mode that reads by "hearing" phonemically at a certain distance from the literary source text (divining thereby, for instance, that the proper musical form to represent Steinbeck's novel is a suite). It brings sound to the fore, as it were, places sound before sense, in a spirit of semantic disturbance or "fugitivity" that Nathaniel Mackey, among others, has argued is endemic to black traditions of literate and musical expression alike.[36]

This effect is related to what is sometimes considered to be a "trick" that Ellington trumpet players resorted to in performance: playing "words" on their horns in a manner to imitate the relative pitch of English pronunciation.[37] The most famous example is Cootie Williams's exclamation of "Harlem!" on his trumpet in the 1951 composition "(A Tone Parallel to) Harlem" (MM 189). But in *Such Sweet Thunder* there's another, in the section called "Up and Down, Up and Down (I Will Lead Them Up and Down)," based on *A Midsummer Night's Dream*. Puck, played by Clark Terry in this rendition, comments on the foolish love tangles of the couples (Jimmy Hamilton and Ray Nance on clarinet and violin and Russell Procope and Paul Gonsalves on alto and tenor saxophones) by "pronouncing" on his trumpet what is perhaps the most famous quotation in the play: "Lord, what fools these mortals be" (3.2.115). To take up an Ellingtonian vocabulary, one might say that, in this sense, the suites strive to "insinuate the sonic dimension" in the literary.

To come to terms with Ellington's sense of the "literature of music," it is necessary to consider in more detail that work he announced so grandly in 1931, the "rhapsody unhampered by any musical form" designed to parallel the "experiences of the coloured races in America in the syncopated idiom." As I argued at the outset of this essay, for Ellington the literary is not only a medium to parallel in sound, or a poetic mode that allows the expression of libidinal excess; in addition, especially in the compositions he came to call his "social-significance thrusts" (MM 183), the literary is closely bound up with Ellington's sense of the historical.

Ellington had spoken in the 1930s of a "tone parallel to the history of the American Negro" (MM 181) with five sections, tracing a trajectory of diaspora starting with the African past and moving through the experience of slavery, the role of blacks in the development of the United States (particularly in the Revolutionary War and the Civil War), the great migration to the urban centers of the north in the early twentieth century, and the future. The piece that came closest to embodying this project, though, the 1943 *Black, Brown, and Beige*, which premiered on January 23, 1943, at Carnegie Hall in a benefit concert for Russian war relief, comprised only three movements.[38] "Black" focused on slavery, drawing on early work songs and spirituals, "Brown" "recognized the contribution made by the Negro to this country in blood" (MM 181), and "Beige" followed the rise of a black community in Harlem. Ellington gave spoken introductions to each section, which form the basis of his description of the suite in *Music Is My Mistress* (181–82).[39] One programmatic narrative, the introduction to "Emancipation Celebration," one of the short dances in *Brown*, was preserved on the recording of the second Carnegie Hall concert in December 1943 when the orchestra played selections from the composition:

> And now another short portion of "Brown" which represents the period after the Civil War, where we find many young free Negroes who are happy with so much opportunity in front of them, and just behind them a couple of very old people who are free but have nothing and no place to go, and of course it's very dark for them. And we find a duet representing the old people and the solos representing the younger people. This is "The Lighter Attitude."[40]

As Brian Priestly and Alan Cohen point out in the first detailed musicological analysis of *Black, Brown, and Beige*, the relationship between such a programmatic introduction and the music that follows is not necessarily transparent: thus it is not easy to track, in listening to "Emancipation Celebration," a particular moment in the music when one hears the entrance of "a couple of very old people who are free but have nothing and no place to go."[41] The point is that the narrative is not simply intended to elucidate the development of the music, nor simply to "sell" the grand sweep of the piece to a potentially resistant audience. Ellington's statement here, in fact, may not deserve the designation *programmatic* at all, at least in any straightforward sense of the term (that is, a narrative that drives the musical composition, providing an audible motivation for its structure). Although the language here gestures toward the historical ("the period after the Civil War"), it also engages in a register of sometimes playful metaphor and double entendre ("This is 'The Lighter Attitude'") and rhetorical obliquity ("of course it's very dark for them") that cannot be easily categorized as a historicist, fact-driven representation of the past. In other words, Ellington's narrative introductions are not at all glosses, or the uneasy discursive cement between weakly linked segments—they are integral to the structure of *Black, Brown, and Beige*, providing a literary component to the performance that is constitutive because outside or beyond (but "parallel" to) the music itself.

Critic Graham Lock, in his excellent recent book *Blutopia*, has considered in more detail the ambitions of Ellington's music as history. Lock contends that, for Ellington, music serves as "an alternative form of history" in a mode of creative expression that might be termed "Blutopia": "a utopia tinged with the blues," a mode "where visions of the future and revisions of the past become part of the same process, a 'politics of transfiguration,' in which accepted notions of language, history, the real, and the possible are thrown open to question and found wanting."[42] Placing Ellington's work in what some music historians would consider unfamiliar territory (in juxtaposition to the music of Sun Ra and Anthony Braxton), Lock reveals the innovative futurism that is a sometimes overlooked element in Ellington's aesthetic, while at the same time demonstrating the engagement of Ra and Braxton with supposedly "traditional" issues of historical representation and racial politics. In the process, Lock offers a number of fresh readings of the Ellington-Strayhorn oeuvre, from the "jungle music" of Ellington's early period in Harlem in the late 1920s (78–91), to a number of the later extended works, including *Jump for Joy* (93–97), *The Deep South Suite* (97–101), *Black, Brown, and Beige* (102–18), and *A Drum Is a Woman* (137–41).

Here I will question only one component of Lock's theoretical framing, a presupposed antidiscursivism that reduces Ellington to a position that "music can be used to say that which cannot be stated openly" (78). Lock takes this antidiscursive stance in the very subtitle of his opening chapter on Ellington's music, called "In the Jungles of America: History Without Saying It" (77). Lock makes this argument most forcefully in his reading of the purely instrumental *Deep South Suite*, which premiered in 1946 at Carnegie Hall, and which for Lock was driven by a "more pointed subtext" of racial protest than was apparent in Ellington's discussions of the suite, or even in his description of it nearly thirty years later in *Music Is My Mistress* (MM 184). In the autobiography Ellington recounts an anecdote about a party after the concert, where William Morris Jr. approached him to complain that the piece was too timid in its protest. Ellington writes: "'You should've said it plainer,' he kept insisting. 'You should have said it plainer!' He was for out-and-out protest, but as with *Jump for Joy*, I felt it was good theatre to say it without saying it. That is the art" (MM 185).

Lock assumes that the notion of a history "without saying it" was one of Ellington's "guiding aesthetic principles" (95). But even given the *Deep South Suite* anecdote, this would seem a difficult argument to make about a great deal of Ellington's oeuvre. Indeed, a number of the scholars who have traced Ellington's musical development, including Mark Tucker, have noted the prevalence of programmatic, narrative, and multimedia work among his key influences.[43] Tucker stresses not just Ellington's exposure to innovative and hybrid forms such as the Cotton Club revues and Lew Leslie's Blackbirds shows that dominated the New York musical theater scene in the late 1920s but also Ellington's upbringing in Washington, D.C. Tucker notes Ellington's exposure to "Negro history" and heritage programs early in his childhood and speculates in particular that the elaborate pageants that were produced in black communities throughout the country in the teens and twenties greatly affected Ellington's sense of the way that history should be depicted in artistic expression. These included sweeping allegorical works like *The Evolution of the Negro in Picture, Song, and Story* (which played at the Howard Theater in 1911), *The Open Door* (which played at Carnegie Hall in 1921, with music featuring the Clef Club Orchestra), and especially W. E. B. Du Bois's magisterial pageant *The Star of Ethiopia*, a performance that premiered in 1913 and was reprised in 1915 in Washington. *The Star of Ethiopia* attempted nothing less than to encapsulate "10,000 years of the history of the Negro race."[44] Du Bois drafted the spectacle as an outdoor, participatory lesson in the African diaspora, what biographer David Levering Lewis has described as an almost unimaginably grandiose "three-hour extravaganza in six episodes, featuring a thousand creamy-complexioned young women and tawny, well-built men, and flocks of schoolchildren marching through history." The music featured not only two selections from Verdi's *Aida* but also new pieces from a number of black composers, including Bob Cole, Rosamond Johnson, and Samuel Coleridge-Taylor. The range of historical information condensed into the pageant was itself mind-boggling: three young women dressed to represent the regal African past (Sheba, Ethiopia, and Meroe) were "serially replaced center stage by a pharaoh, Mali's fourteenth-century Islamic ruler Mansa Musa, Columbus's pilot Alonzo; moaning slaves in chains; Spanish lancers; Toussaint L'Ouverture; Sojourner Truth; Frederick Douglass; and, to the accompaniment of rolling drums, the Massachusetts regiment of Colonel Robert Gould Shaw; followed by children, the professions, and the working class." A narrator extolled Africa's gifts to the world, including iron and fire, the great civilization of Egypt, and then a parade of spiritual values, with performers meant to portray "Faith in Righteousness, then Humility, and the gift of 'Struggle Toward Freedom' and finally 'the Gift of Freedom for the workers'—all this in 'a great cloud of music that hovered over them and enveloped them.'"[45]

Certainly Ellington's work that led most directly to *Black, Brown, and Beige* (discussions of writing his tone parallel with journalists in the 1930s, the film *Symphony in Black* in 1935, the musical revue *Jump for Joy* in 1941) evidences an interest in explicit and discursive history, pointing toward the literary and narrative experiments that would become such an integral part of his music. For instance, the film *Symphony in Black: A Rhapsody of Negro Life* was produced in December 1934 and early 1935 at Paramount's Eastern Service Studios in Astoria. Especially compared to the early film appearances of other African American musicians such as Bessie Smith and Louis Armstrong,[46] *Symphony in Black* is remarkable if for no other reason than the unprecedented and dignified depiction of Ellington as a black composer commissioned to perform a "symphony" in a concert hall. But one should not overlook its clear narrative and allegorical aspirations. The film opens with a carefully planned shot of Ellington at his piano, composing music for the premiere of the "symphony" in pencil on a manuscript score. After this thirty-second introduction, the film segues through four sections indicated by handwritten titles that the film implies are written on Ellington's manuscript: "The Laborers," with a theme based on work songs played in accompaniment to sharply angled and heavily shadowed "images of black men shoveling coal into blast furnaces and carrying bales on a river wharf,"[47] a second set-piece called "A Triangle," portraying a lover's betrayal in three movements ("Dance," "Jealousy," and "Blues"—featuring a version of "Saddest Tale" sung memorably by Billie Holiday in her first film appearance), a "Hymn of Sorrow," portraying a black minister leading his congregation in a stylized mourning ceremony, and "Harlem Rhythm," shot with the Ellington orchestra in a nightclub apparently based on the Cotton Club, with the dancer Earl "Snakehips" Tucker. What is notable even in this early composition, again, is Ellington's insistence on a narrative framing—here one that interestingly combined the sentimental romance of much of Ellington's poetry and short prose (in the section called "A Triangle") with the emblematic historicism of "The Laborers" and the near ethnographic expressionism of the scenes of contemporary Harlem nightlife.

Nearly ten years later, *Black, Brown, and Beige* marked a narrowing of this programmatic frame into a register of historical representation. Indeed, the so-called *Black, Brown, and Beige* controversy emerged only partly around Ellington's foray into the concert hall and the debate over whether jazz could provide the foundation of long-form musical composition.[48] It was most explicitly articulated in terms of the way *Black, Brown, and Beige* "says it": the suite's programmatic form, its attempt to "parallel the history of the American Negro" by combining spoken narrative, song lyrics (in the "Blues" in *Brown*), and the instrumental music itself. Almost all the major critics castigated not just the piece's length (many snidely suggested he restrain himself to the length of a record side: "Mr. Ellington can make some two dozen brief air-tight compositions out of *Black, Brown, and Beige*. He should.") but more specifically its literary components and historicist baggage. Mike Levin opined sourly that "I don't think the music needs any such 'programmatic' prop," and Paul Bowles, reviewing for the *New York Herald-Tribune*, reserved his most dismissive words for the work's "ideological" frame, claiming that "presented as one number it was formless and meaningless. In spite of Mr. Ellington's ideological comments before each 'movement,' nothing emerged but a gaudy potpourri of tutti dance passages and solo virtuoso work."[49] In fact, Barry Ulanov was one of the few critics who later countered that a listener's "understanding and appreciation of the work will, however, be considerably heightened if you bear Duke's program in mind while listening to the music."[50] Ulanov's spirited defense of the programmatic ambition of Ellington's composition is worth quoting here:

> The fact that [*Black, Brown, and Beige*] is not written in the sonata form and therefore is not a symphony, the fact that it is programmatic, these are not limitations from Duke's point of view or from that of sympathetic auditors whose listening experience in some way duplicates Ellington's. Duke, contrary to the arrogant dismissal of his musical equipment and knowledge, could have written. . . . a symphony or string quartet or oratorio or opera; he chose, instead, to write a "tone parallel," in which jazz virtuosi, in solo and in section and in band ensemble, gave vigorous inter-

pretation to his phrases, some rough, some tender, all colorful and all directed to a narrative point.[51]

Lock adopts the phrase "without saying it" directly from Ellington, in a passage from *Music Is My Mistress* devoted to the revue *Jump for Joy*, where he writes: "I think a statement of social protest in the theatre should be made without saying it, and this calls for the real craftsman" (MM 180). But *Jump for Joy*, a vibrant West Coast production that involved collaborators such as Langston Hughes, Mickey Rooney, Dorothy Dandridge, Big Joe Turner, and lyricist Paul Webster, was a compilation of sketches, dances, and songs expressly designed "to correct the race situation in the U.S.A. through a form of theatrical propaganda" (MM 175). Lock himself admits that it "was possibly the most outspoken project [Ellington] was involved in" (95). Ellington pens the sentence about social protest not in reference to the discursive content of the show (its song lyrics and spoken sketches—many of which were openly ideological) but in reference to a debate about whether the comedians in the show should put on blackface:

> I had stopped all the comedians from using cork on their faces when they worked with us. Some objected before the show opened, but removed it, and were shocked by their success. As the audience screamed and applauded, comedians came off stage smiling, and with tears running down their cheeks. They couldn't believe it. I think a statement of social protest in the theatre should be made without saying it, and this calls for the real craftsman.
> (MM 180)

This is a much more subtle point about the strategy of critiquing racist stereotypes in theatrical representation: it asks, if anything, for a certain subtlety in the manipulation of specifically *visual* signifiers, without coming anywhere near demanding a simple reticence or shying away from linguistic expression. As I have already pointed out, this passage in no way dampens Ellington's continuing conviction that an effective mode of "propaganda" had to combine art forms—and specifically, that it had to include a literary element.

Ellington seems to have decided, in the wake of the journalistic criticism of *Black, Brown, and Beige*, that the programmatic mix of narrative and instrumental music was not successful, and, as Lock points out, he never performed the entire suite again in public. Yet this traumatic rejection became the impetus for Ellington to write *more*, not less. Ellington penned a never published manuscript (thirty-eight typed pages) that seems designed to parallel the music of *Black, Brown, and Beige*, following the progress of an African slave named Boola from bondage to freedom, and (in the *Beige* section) into Harlem, the modern black metropolis. In Ellington's verse narrative the music—work songs, spirituals, blues, and finally jazz—charts the drive to emancipation and modernity among New World black populations: "Out of this deep dream of freedom / Evolved the blessed release / Of freedom of expression in song."[52] But, in the end, the narrative also argues that the music is *not* enough, that the "song" of the American Negro does not tell the

whole story—that the music has been "categorized," perverted, and commercialized to the degree that it doesn't speak for the full wealth of black modernity:

> HARLEM! Black metropolis!
> Land of mirth!
> Your music has flung
> The story of "Hot Harlem"
> To the four corners
> Of the earth!
>   . . .
> The picture drawn by many hands
>   For many eyes of many races.
>   But did it ever speak to them
>   Of what you *really* are?
> Did it say to them
>   That all your striving
> To take your rightful place with men
>   Was more than jazz and jiving?
>   . . .
> It can't be true
>   That all you do . . .
> Is dance and sing
>   And moan!
> Harlem . . . for all her moral lurches
> Has always had
> LESS cabarets than churches![53]

Interestingly, the proposition here would seem to be that the music is inadequate,
alone—that by itself it is open to misinterpretation ("But did it ever speak to
them / Of what you *really* are?"). Even though the music has "flung / The story of
"Hot Harlem" / To the four corners / Of the earth," it cannot transport the truth of
black strivings for political justice and historical retribution. If anything, it remains
mired in easy racist stereotype and cliché ("jazz and jiving"). In a startling apostro-
phe, departing from the allegorical narrative of Boola to address its own historical
referent and end point ("HARLEM"), here Ellington's verse narrative announces
its own indispensable "parallel" role in the project of *Black, Brown, and Beige*.

Ellington's difficulty, in other words, was ultimately methodological: how does
one stage such a parallel? How does one bring such a verse narrative into conjunc-
ture with a musical composition, without falling into a mode of expression that
would be heavy-handed or unwieldy or scattered? This is a problem that Ellington
does not solve. It haunts all his larger works after *Black, Brown, and Beige*—all of
which are at least in part motivated by an attempt to unearth the elusive definition
of that suggestive phrase "the literature of music." Duke continued to yearn for the
proper structure, even as he declined to perform *Black, Brown, and Beige* in full
again. In June 1943 *Variety* reported that Ellington was even going to attempt to

literalize his aesthetic of parallel, placing narrative and music (score) into one publication:

> Duke Ellington is preparing a book explaining the story behind his much-discussed composition, "Black, Brown and Beige," which he debuted during his orchestra's recent Carnegie Hall, N.Y. concert. Leader [*sic*] feels that detailing the thoughts which motivated the work will help toward a better understanding of it: to this end the story will be printed on the upper half of each page in the book, with the music related to each portion below on the same page so that readers with a knowledge of music can follow both at the same time.[54]

In 1956 Ellington told another interviewer that he had "almost completed" *Black, Brown, and Beige* "as a stage presentation: songs and narration and all that. . . . Now I want to do *Black, Brown, and Beige* with a narration and tell all the things about the Negro in America—the Negro's contributions and so on." When the interviewer asks him to explain the scope of the piece, Ellington hesitates, and then says: "Maybe you should *read* it." "You got a script?" the interviewer responds, and Ellington says, "I have a thing I wrote a long time ago—some of it might be changed now." Even here he seems uncertain of the status of his writing in the larger composition, calling it variously a "screenplay," a "script," and "annotations" to the music. Ellington adds that he's trying to add song lyrics for the spiritual theme (most likely "Come Sunday," which was recorded in 1958 with Mahalia Jackson singing the lyrics), the work song, and the "Emancipation Celebration" section; but he doesn't know yet if the words he's written are "adequate."[55]

It is only appropriate that by the end of his life Ellington consistently projected this effort to practice a "literature of music" into the realm of eschatology.[56] Both the tortured quest for compositional form and a spiritual register are evident, for instance, in Ellington's only book, the autobiographical suite *Music Is My Mistress*, published in 1973. Mercer Ellington has commented wryly on the "undoubtedly unique" composition of his father's "autobiography," which Duke wrote slowly and haphazardly while on tour, scribbling fragments "on hotel stationery, table napkins, and menus from all over the world."[57] (The book was subsequently "deciphered," thoroughly edited, and assembled by jazz critic and biographer Stanley Dance, who nonetheless would only let Ellington give him a minor credit in the book's acknowledgments.) In this sense the composition of the vignettes and portraits that make up the book can also be read as a diffuse travel itinerary, recording the places the Ellington orchestra passed through in the late 1960s and early 1970s (figures 16.2 and 16.3). Reading the fragments and notes gives a sense not just of the intermittent travails of Duke's memory but also of the incredibly diverse variety of the scenes where he wrote, especially the hotels that allowed brief moments of literary work in his hectic concert travels. For example, Ellington's description, near the beginning of *Music Is My Mistress*, of Frank Holliday's poolroom on T Street near the Howard Theatre in Washington, D.C. (23), is written on stationery from the D.C. Hilton Hotel. A section of the faux "interview" that closes

FIGURE 16.3   Page from Ellington's notes for *Music Is My Mistress. Duke Ellington Collection, Archives Center, National Museum of American History, Smithsonian Institution, Washington, D.C.*

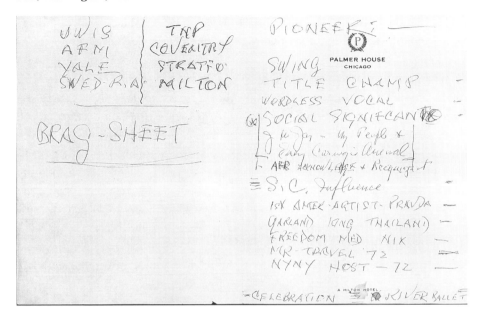

the book (455), where he considers the value of "new music" in the sixties, appears on pages from the Fairmont Hotel in Dallas. In another stolen moment, Duke jots down a few paragraphs on the great stride pianist Luckeyeth Roberts (104) on a pad from the Waldorf-Astoria in New York. His proud description of the band's concert at the 1966 World Festival of Negro Arts in Dakar is composed on paper from the Desoto Hilton in Savannah, Georgia, in a thick black felt-tip scribble. The opening fable used as the book's prologue ("Once upon a time a beautiful young lady and a very handsome young man feel in love and got married. They were a wonderful, compatible couple, and God blessed their marriage with a fine baby boy" [x]) appears on stationery from the Baltimore Hilton. On paper from the Steigenberger Park Hotel in Düsseldorf, Germany, Duke scrawls portraits of Al Hibbler (223–24) and Johnny Hodges (116–19), while he pens the section about his early days in New York with lyricist Joe Trent (70–71) and the anecdote about his 1962 recording session with Max Roach and Charles Mingus (242–44) under the letterhead of the Ambassador Hotel in Chicago.

During this period Ellington was increasingly concerned with spiritual matters. He channeled much of his religious sensibility into the three *Sacred Concerts*, but it also became more and more part of his daily life, as he collected religious readings and meditations during the band's tours. His papers contain an assortment of Bibles that fans and correspondents had given him, as well as religious broadsides and pamphlets from various sources—Jewish prayer books, programs from Catholic masses, Unitarian tracts, and an assortment of more obscure literature.[58] He seems not to have paid close attention to the majority of this material, taking

347

what was presented to him, and studying his personal copy of the Bible with the deepest care. One of the few other items that Ellington read assiduously in these years was a pocket-sized pamphlet called *Forward Day by Day*, a "manual of daily Bible readings" published by the Forward Movement in Cincinnati, Ohio, which he received in periodic installments from the summer of 1968 until the spring of 1973.

Ellington seldom underlines the texts of these readings, and, when he does, he usually highlights quotes from the scriptures that have to do with music. In the *Forward Day by Day* selection for March 17, 1973 (figure 16.4), for example, when the band was playing an extended gig at the Royal York Hotel in Toronto, Ellington only underlines one phrase, "who gives songs in the night," from an epigraph from the Book of Job: "Men cry out; they call for help. . . . 'Where is God my maker, who gives songs in the night?'"[59] This is not to say that Duke leaves the books pristine, though: in fact, he pen-marks these daily prayer books heavily, with busy crosshatches, long vertical lines, corner flourishes, and brackets that swirl around the margins of the texts. This odd, even compulsive graphicity must be read as concurrent with or concomitant to his reading but not directly reflective of

FIGURE 16.4   A page from Ellington's personal copy of *Forward Day by Day*, February 1–April 30, 1973 (Cinncinnati, Ohio, 1973). *Duke Ellington Collection, Archives Center, National Museum of American History, Smithsonian Institution, Washington, D.C.*

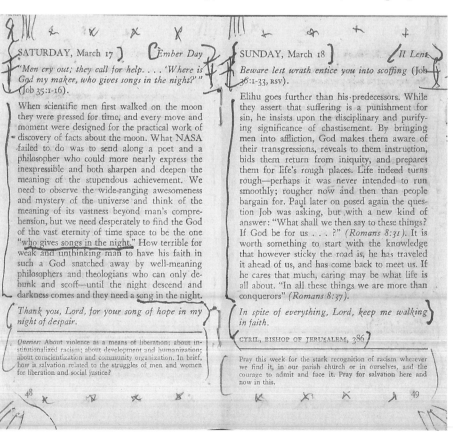

it—the markings have a consistency day to day and through the months that seems to have little to do with the texts he's reading. One might understand this graphicity as parallel to his reading, then, in the Ellingtonian sense of the term. The marks don't represent or translate the words he reads as much as they move alongside the text, filling the margins, with what might be closer to a "musical" form of inscription than a linguistic one. Duke's recourse to the pen could even be called a *scoring* of the books, in at least two senses: both as a marking or incision that interrupts or cuts the words on the page and as the record of a kind of rhythm, a graphic suggestion of "beat" (through the spacing and iteration of the marks) that registers, subdivides, or accompanies the time of reading.

In March 1969 the Ellington orchestra played a three-week engagement at the Casbar Lounge in the Sahara Hotel in Las Vegas.[60] In the *Forward Day by Day* for Wednesday the 19th, the reading is taken from I Corinthians 14: "Aspire above all to excel in those [gifts of the spirit] which build up the church," which the book explicates in terms of the "ministry" of "what we say" in daily conversation and informal speech (figure 16.5). The page ends with a prayer: "Direct and bless, we beseech thee, Lord, those who in this generation speak where many listen, and write

FIGURE 16.5   A page from Ellington's personal copy of *Forward Day by Day*, February 1–April 30, 1969 (Cinncinnati, Ohio, 1969). *Duke Ellington Collection, Archives Center, National Museum of American History, Smithsonian Institution, Washington, D.C.*

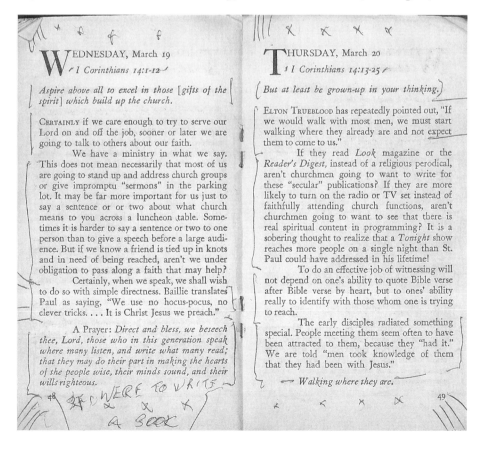

what many read."[61] Ellington brackets the prayer, as usual, but, for once, he adds his own marginal note at the bottom of the page, amidst his usual "X" scorings, in a somewhat feeble-looking uppercase script:

IF I WERE TO WRITE
  A BOOK

A strange and poignant subordinate clause to hang at the foot of a plea. It is important that this phrase isn't simply past tense ("If I wrote a book") or declarative ("I want to write a book")—much less some kind of glancing reinterpretation of the call to bless those who "speak where many listen, and write what many read" (if Ellington had written instead, for instance: "I write music" or "I *play* where many listen"). Neither is it an allusion to the well-known Rogers and Hart popular standard, "I could write a book," with its playfully amorous proclamations of literary agency. The phrase "If I were to write a book" expresses a kind of desire, but it is desire couched in the subjunctive, in the realm of a shakily contingent possibility rather than a prediction or a promise or a counterclaim.

   If the subjunctive mood denotes an action or state as conceived and not as a fact, then the phrase articulates in this personal and meditative space Ellington's sense of the literary. That Ellington would describe his "book" in this mood, as contingent and hypothetical, as an open-ended, unlikely, but imagined prospect, is not surprising given that he was struggling to write *Music Is My Mistress* during this period. "He dragged his feet," Mercer Ellington commented later,

> and grumbled about the progress. He would have Stanley [Dance] go to places like Toronto and Houston when he had long engagements, but often they would sit up all night watching dog-assed movies and not work at all. It was the same when he was at home. Stanley would come to work, but after hours of Perry Mason and shoot-'em-ups, Ellington would be too tired for anything but criticisms and promises. It was a miracle the book was ever finished.[62]

"If I were to write a book": it is appropriate, then, that Ellington comes to express that struggle as a fragile possibility, in a religious pamphlet titled to evoke daily progress "forward."

   But, in a broader sense, one might also read this subjunctive as the mood of all Ellington's grand racial programmatic ambitions, the desire to write a "tone parallel to the history of the American Negro" that in different ways animated his "social significance" works: *Jump for Joy* and *Black, Brown, and Beige* in the 1940s, *A Drum Is a Woman* in the 1950s, and *My People* in the 1960s. To write an extended composition about the Negro, the work that "tells his story," in Baldwin's phrase. "If I were to write": the desire, and the vulnerability, in the phrase might also in part be Ellington's conviction that his great work had to combine music and language, somehow, as I have already suggested—melody and text "parallel" to each other in voice-over narration, programmatic verse, and song lyrics—in order to capture the full richness of that history. Only such a work, an achievement in what he had called many years before "the literature of music," might offer an "authentic record" of African Americans. "If I were to": the contingency, the open-endedness, would seem unavoidable. In *Music Is My Mistress* Ellington writes that he felt the rather "unfinished ending" of the first section of *Black, Brown, and Beige* "was in accordance with reality, that it could not be boxed, and stored away when so much else remained to be done" (MM 181). Part of the project's "authentic record," then, is precisely its open-endedness, parallel to the unfulfilled hopes of the African American. And it is likewise as though Duke could only conceive and desire his combination of words and music as a prospect, in the uncertainty of the subjunctive, only in an intimate space of reflection. For Ellington, the literature of music trembles at the margin of a prayer.

NOTES

1. An early version of this essay was first presented at a symposium on Duke Ellington at the North Carolina Jazz Festival in February 1999. The late Mark Tucker invited me to that event, and I only hope that the expanded piece honors to some degree the model of his own pathbreaking scholarship on Ellington. I am also grateful for the extraordinarily generous assistance of Krin Gabbard, David Hajdu, and David Lionel Smith and for the comments and suggestions of Katherine Bergeron and the anonymous readers for *Representations*. At the Archives Center in the National Museum of American History, Annie Kuebler helped with my research on a number of occasions, and Reuben Jackson and Jeff Tate were invaluable when it came time to obtain reproductions. In particular, I thank Robert O'Meally, who asked me to present a revised version of the piece as the inaugural lecture in the Lecture Series on Jazz and American Culture at the Center for Jazz Studies, Columbia University, in November 1999, and who shared both his personal Ellington archive and his extensive knowledge of the music with me throughout the writing process.

   James Baldwin, "Many Thousands Gone," *Partisan Review* (November/December 1951), collected in James Baldwin, *Collected Essays*, ed. Toni Morrison (New York, 1998), 19.

2. Leroi Jones (Amiri Baraka), "The Myth of a 'Negro Literature'" (1962), in *Home: Social Essays* (New York, 1966), 106–7.

3. Duke Ellington, "The Duke Steps Out," *Rhythm* (March 1931): 20–22, collected in *The Duke Ellington Reader*, ed. Mark Tucker (New York, 1993), 49.

4. This is not the only such reference. In 1930 a Manhattan reporter wrote: "At present [Ellington] is at work on a tremendous task, the writing, in music, of 'The History of the Negro,' taking the Negro from Egypt, going with him to savage Africa, and from there to the sorrow and slavery of Dixie, and finally 'home to Harlem.'" Florence Zunser, "'Opera Must Die,' Says Galli-Curci! Long Live the Blues!" *New York Evening Graphic Magazine* (December 27, 1930), collected in *The Duke Ellington Reader*, 45.

5. See Ellington's own description of the impetus for *New World A-Comin'* in Ellington, *Music Is My Mistress* (Garden City, N.Y., 1973), 183. Subsequent page citations from this work will be cited parenthetically in the text with the initials MM.

6. A number of these texts are available: *The Golden Broom and the Green Apple* (MM 200); *The River* (MM 201–2); "Program Outline for the Sacred Concert" (MM

270–79); *My People* (1963), eight-page typescript, Duke Ellington Collection, Subseries 4B: Scripts, Box 8, Folder 7, Archives Center, National Museum of American History, Smithsonian Institution.

7. Barry Ulanov, "The Ellington Programme," in *This Is Jazz*, ed. Ken Williamson (London, 1960), 168.

8. Barry Ulanov, "Thumps Down," in "Two Thumps on 'A Drum,'" *Downbeat* (June 27, 1957): 18.

9. Ellington, "We, Too, Sing 'America,'" a talk delivered on Annual Lincoln Day Services, February 9, 1941, Scott Methodist Church, Los Angeles, *California Eagle*, (February 13, 1941), collected in *The Duke Ellington Reader*, 146.

10. Richard O. Boyer, "The Hot Bach," *New Yorker*, (June 24–July 8, 1944), collected in *The Duke Ellington Reader*, 239.

11. Duke Ellington, "Into Each Life Some Rain Must Fall (Duke's Poetry)," concert at Columbia University, May 20, 1964, *The New York Concert* (MusicMasters CD 01612–65112–2, 1995). This poem plays with the title of a song made famous by Ella Fitzgerald, "Into Each Life Some Rain Must Fall."

12. Duke Ellington, "Moon Maiden," recorded July 14, 1969, *The Intimate Ellington* (Pablo/Fantasy OJCCD-730–2, 1977). I am grateful to David Lionel Smith for alerting me to this rendition and for helping me to track it down at short notice. Ellington's manuscript for "Moon Maiden" is located in the Duke Ellington Collection, Subseries 1A: Manuscripts, Box 229, Folder 8, Archives Center, National Museum of American History, Smithsonian Institution. George Avakian, who was present at the recording session, confirms that Ellington recites in an overdub; personal communication, November 2000.

13. Duke Ellington, "Spaceman," Duke Ellington Collection, Series 5: Correspondence, Box 6, notes, undated, Archives Center, National Museum of American History, Smithsonian Institution. See also Ellington's unpublished essay, "The Race for Space" (ca. 1957), in *The Duke Ellington Reader*, 293–96.

14. Liner notes, *The Intimate Ellington*. Duke's claim notwithstanding, "Moon Maiden" is in fact not the first Ellington recording to feature his abilities as a vocalist; that distinction belongs to the obscure and odd version of "The Saddest Tale" that the band recorded in 1934. Another song under this title would be recorded in 1935 (with Billie Holiday singing) for the film *Symphony in Black*; but the 1934 studio "The Saddest Tale" features Ellington himself, speaking a short lyric ("Saddest tale told on land and sea / Was the tale when they told the truth about me") over an instrumental backdrop.

15. Ellington uses this phrase in recounting a "cutting contest" between Sidney Bechet and Bubber Miley: "Call was very important in that music. Today, the music has grown up and become quite scholastic, but this was au naturel, close to the primitive, where people send messages in what they play, calling somebody, or making facts and emotions known. Painting a picture, or having a story to go with what you were going to play, was of vital importance in those days. The audience didn't know anything about it, but the cats in the band did" (MM 47).

16. Ellington, "Swing Is My Beat!" *New Advance* (October 1944): 1, 14, collected in *The Duke Ellington Reader*, 249.

17. Boyer, "The Hot Bach," in *The Duke Ellington Reader*, 226.

18. Ulanov, "The Ellington Programme," 169.

19. Gary Giddins, "Duke Ellington (Part 3: At the Pulpit)," in *Visions of Jazz: The First Century* (New York, 1999), 501. The phrase "Shakespearean universality" was used by

a London critic reviewing Ellington's first appearance at the Palladium; it is quoted in Boyer,"The Hot Bach," in *The Duke Ellington Reader*, 216.

20. Strayhorn interview with Sinclair Traill and Gerald Lascelles, *Just Jazz* 3 (London, 1959), quoted in David Hajdu, *Lush Life: A Biography of Billy Strayhorn* (New York, 1996), 156.

21. "Monologue (Pretty and the Wolf)" was originally recorded for Columbia Records on May 24, 1951. The live version appears on *Duke Ellington Live From the 1956 Stratford Festival* (Berkeley: Music and Arts CD-616, 1989). Ellington performed this recitation frequently in concert. There is even a version in the telecast *Music '55*, broadcast that summer by CBS, where Ellington recites "Pretty and the Wolf" seated at the piano against the backdrop of a series of drawings by Andy Warhol (specially commissioned for the program), which scroll across a screen from left to right. See Klaus Stratemann, *Duke Ellington Day by Day and Film by Film* (Copenhagen, 1992), 358.

22. "Music Press Release no. 6 (for Saturday morning release, April 13, 1957)," Stratford Shakespearean Festival, Ontario, Canada (April 10, 1957). Ellington clippings file, Institute for Jazz Studies, Rutgers University.

23. Stanley Dance, *The World of Duke Ellington* (New York, 1970), 32.

24. Bob Smith interview with Strayhorn, Vancouver (November 1, 1962). I thank David Hajdu for making this interview available to me.

25. Beatrice Washburn, "The Duke—'I Hear Music All the Time,'" *Miami Herald* (January 12, 1958).

26. Langston Hughes, "Shakespeare in Harlem," in *Shakespeare in Harlem* (New York, 1942), collected in Hughes, *Collected Poems of Langston Hughes*, ed. Arnold Rampersad (New York, 1994), 260.

27. Rebecca Walkowitz has argued convincingly that Hughes's poem offers "a contrast not between two different *traditions* but between differences *within* traditions—Shakespeare or Harlem—that are thought to be undifferentiated. As 'Shakespeare in Harlem' points to Shakespeare's bawdy songs, it represents not 'low' Shakespeare so much as Shakespeare's own conjunction of high and low cultures." See Rebecca Walkowitz, "Shakespeare in Harlem: *The Norton Anthology*, 'Propaganda,' Langston Hughes," *Modern Language Quarterly* 60, no. 4 (December 1999): 515.

28. Irving Townsend, liner notes to Duke Ellington and his Orchestra, *Such Sweet Thunder* (Columbia CL 1033, 1957).

29. Ulanov, "The Ellington Programme," 171. The phrase is taken from Hippolyta's speech in act 4, scene 1 of the play: "I never heard / So musical a discord, such sweet thunder" (lines 120–21).

30. Hajdu, *Lush Life*, 161.

31. "Music Press Release no. 6."

32. Stratemann, *Duke Ellington Day by Day and Film by Film*, 239.

33. Stanley Crouch, Program Notes, Classical Jazz Series Concert, Alice Tully Hall, Lincoln Center for the Performing Arts (August 10, 1988), collected in *The Duke Ellington Reader*, 441.

34. "Sonnet for Sister Kate," Duke Ellington Collection, Series 1A: Music manuscripts, Box 363, Folder 6, Archives Center, National Museum of American History, Smithsonian Institution.

35. Bob Smith interview with Strayhorn, Vancouver (11/1/62).

36. Nathaniel Mackey, "Other: From Noun to Verb," in *Discrepant Engagement: Dissonance, Cross-Culturality, and Experimental Writing* (New York, 1993), 269–70. It would

be a mistake to underestimate the role of humor in this fugitive mode—the way that *Such Sweet Thunder* is composed not just of "parallels in miniatures" but also *caricatures*. This is equally an element in Ellington's own writings. For example, *The Afro-Eurasian Eclipse*, recorded in 1971 in the wake of Ellington's travels on U.S. State Department tours in the 1960s, was apparently inspired by Marshall McLuhan's claim in the late 1960s that the world was "going oriental, and that nobody will be able to retain his or her identity—not even the orientals" (MM 4). But Ellington's spoken introduction to the suite's opener, "Chinoiserie" (which he repeated word-for-word at each performance) only glancingly takes up McLuhan's proposition, preferring to jaunt through a self-deprecating run of alliteration and association that matches its rhetoric of pseudo gallantry with its tongue-in-cheek allusion to "the piano player": "In this particular segment, ladies and gentlemen, we have adjusted our perspective to that of the kangaroo and the dijiridoo, which automatically puts us Down Under or Out Back. From this viewpoint, it is most improbable that anyone can tell who is enjoying the shadow of whom. Harold Ashby has been inducted into the responsibility and obligation of scraping off a tiny chip of the charisma of his chinoiserie, almost immediately after the piano player completes his riki-tiki . . ." It is crucial to read this as serious play, though: to suggest, in other words, that the fugitive poetics of Ellington's language (its slippage along what Roman Jakobson would call the axis of equivalence) actually *enacts* McLuhan's proposition that the contemporary world is characterized by cultural mixing without progeniture—a state in which "it is most improbable that anyone can tell who is enjoying the shadow of whom." *The Afro-Eurasian Eclipse: A Suite in Eight Parts* (Fantasy Records OJCCD-645-2, 1975).

37. Albert Murray has gone much further, arguing that this effect is not at all exceptional, but instead that the entire Ellington band must be heard as one orchestrated "extension of the human voice." He writes:

> Such was the vocal orientation of Duke Ellington's genius that in addition to achieving the most highly distinctive overall instrumental orchestral sound (made up of instrumental voice extensions), he not only played his orchestra as if it were a single instrument (to an extent that cannot be claimed for any other composer or conductor) but expressed himself on it as if the three-man rhythm section, three trombones, four to six trumpets, five woodwinds (plus occasional strings) were actually the dimensions of one miraculously endowed human voice.

Albert Murray, *Stomping the Blues* (New York, 1976), 114.

38. Duke Ellington and His Orchestra, *Black, Brown, and Beige, The Duke Ellington Carnegie Hall Concerts, January 1943* (Prestige Records 2PCD-34004-2, 1977).

39. See also the summary of Ellington's verbal introductions in Barry Ulanov, *Duke Ellington* (New York, 1975), 254–55.

40. Quoted in Brian Priestly and Alan Cohen, "Black, Brown, and Beige," *Composer* 51 (Spring 1974): 33–37; 52 (Summer 1974): 29–52; 53 (Winter 1974–1975): 29–32; collected in *The Duke Ellington Reader*, 195–96.

41. Priestly and Cohen, while demurring about any easy links between music and narrative, do offer some examples of the ways the suite format of *Black, Brown, and Beige* may have arisen "from the demands of the programmatic motivation itself. In other words, . . . the fragmentation and development of short thematic motifs in 'Black'

is intended to represent musically the fragmentation of African tradition on American soil; similarly, the conflict during 'Work Song' between motifs referring to the blues scale . . . and those affirming the major mode . . . may just be a metaphor for the clash between two cultures." Priestly and Cohen, "Black, Brown, and Beige," in *The Duke Ellington Reader*, 188–89.

42. Graham Lock, *Blutopia: Visions of the Future and Revisions of the Past in the Work of Sun Ra, Duke Ellington, and Anthony Braxton* (Durham, 1999), 2–3. Further references will be indicated parenthetically in the text.

43. Mark Tucker, "The Genesis of *Black, Brown, and Beige*," *Black Music Research Journal* 13.2 (Fall 1993): 67–86.

44. Mark Tucker, *Ellington: The Early Years* (Urbana, 1991), 7–8.

45. David Levering Lewis, *W. E. B. Du Bois: Biography of a Race*, Vol. 1: *1868–1919* (New York, 1993), 460. See also W. E. B. Du Bois, "The Star of Ethiopia," *Crisis* 11 (December 1915): 91–3; Du Bois, "The Drama Among Black Folk," *Crisis* 12 (August 1916): 169–73; Du Bois, *A Pageant* (a four-page leaflet issued in 1915), in *Annotated Bibliography of the Published Writings of W. E. B. Du Bois*, ed. Herbert Aptheker (Millwood, N.Y., 1973), 543.

46. Krin Gabbard compares Ellington's dignified role as a bandleader in his debut film, *Black and Tan* (1929) with Bessie Smith's role as a victimized woman in the film *St. Louis Blues* (1929). See Gabbard, *Jammin' at the Margins: Jazz and the America Cinema* (Chicago, 1996), 161–62. Gabbard follows Gary Giddins in arguing that Armstrong was able to "transcend the racist trappings" of his early films, such as the infamous *Rhapsody in Black and Blue* (1932); ibid., 210–11; Gary Giddins, *Satchmo* (New York, 1988), 36.

47. Stratemann, *Duke Ellington Day by Day and Film by Film*, 121.

48. Ulanov, *Duke Ellington*, 258.

49. Robert Bagar, quoted in Ulanov, *Duke Ellington*, 257. Of course this complaint had been common in reviews of Ellington as soon as he began to experiment with longer forms: Ulanov quotes Constant Lambert, who in 1934 wrote: "Ellington's best works are written in what may be called ten-inch record form. . . . Into this three and a half minutes he compresses the utmost, but beyond its limits he is inclined to fumble" (259). Mike Levin, "Duke Fuses Classical and Jazz!" *Down Beat* (February 15, 1943): 12–13, collected in *The Duke Ellington Reader*, 169. Paul Bowles, "Duke Ellington in Recital for Russian War Relief," *New York Herald-Tribune* (January 25, 1943), collected in *The Duke Ellington Reader*, 166. On the critical reception of *Black, Brown, and Beige*, see more generally Scott DeVeaux, "*Black, Brown, and Beige* and the Critics," *Black Music Research Journal* 13.2 (Fall 1993): 125–146; Andrew Homzy, "*Black, Brown, and Beige* in Duke Ellington's Repertoire, 1943–1973," *Black Music Research Journal* 13.2 (Fall 1993): 87–110; Priestly and Cohen, "Black, Brown, and Beige," in *The Duke Ellington Reader*, 185–204.

50. Ulanov, *Duke Ellington*, 260.

51. Ibid., 259.

52. Duke Ellington, "Black," in *Black, Brown, and Beige*, undated typescript 8, Duke Ellington Collection, series 4: Scripts, Box 3, Archives Center, National Museum of American History, Smithsonian Institution. I should note that scholars are still uncertain about the dating of this document. The typescript (based on an earlier handwritten draft), with the character Boola, would seem related to Ellington's plans to write an

"opera" of the same name in the later 1930s. The question remains, of course, whether this script was written before or after the premiere of musical *Black, Brown, and Beige* in 1943.

53. Duke Ellington, "Beige," in *Black, Brown, and Beige*, undated typescript 8, Duke Ellington Collection, series 4: Scripts, Box 3, Archives Center, National Museum of American History, Smithsonian Institution, 1, 3.

54. "Duke's Book Will Explain His Carnegie Hall Symph," *Variety* (June 9, 1943): 2, quoted in Lock, Blutopia, 110.

55. Carter Harman, audiotape interview of Ellington, Las Vegas (1956), Oral History Collection 422, tape 1, Archives Center, National Museum of American History, Smithsonian Institution.

56. Janna Tull Steed has also recently suggested that Ellington approaches the literary through a spiritual focus in this period. See her reading of another untitled Ellington manuscript, written on stationery from a Zurich hotel (the poem opens "His Every Day Cracked Up / in Empty Day / With Promises of only the Blackest / Stormy Night") in Steed, *Duke Ellington: A Spiritual Biography* (New York, 1999), 152.

57. Mercer Ellington with Stanley Dance, *Duke Ellington in Person: An Intimate Memoir* (New York, 1978), 171.

58. On Ellington's turn to religion, see Ellington, *Duke Ellington in Person*, 110–11.

59. *Forward Day by Day* (February 1–April 30, 1973) (Cinncinati, 1973), 48. Duke Ellington Collection, Series 14: Religious Materials, Box 2: Pamphlets, Archives Center, National Museum of American History, Smithsonian Institution. The Ellington itinerary is taken from Stratemann, *Duke Ellington Day by Day and Film by Film*, 653.

60. Stratemann, *Duke Ellington Day by Day*, 584.

61. *Forward Day by Day* (February 1–April 30, 1969) (Cincinnati, 1969), 48. Duke Ellington Collection, Archives Center, National Museum of American History, Smithsonian Institution.

62. Ellington, *Duke Ellington in Person*, 172.

TRAVIS A. JACKSON

"Always New and Centuries Old": Jazz, Poetry, and Tradition as Creative Adaptation

Writers concerned with African American literatures and musics have returned over and over to questions about the nature and meaning of "tradition." Kimberly Benston, Houston Baker, and Henry Louis Gates as well as musicians and music critics like Wynton Marsalis, Keith Jarrett, Albert Murray, and Kevin Whitehead have confronted that concern with different strategies and divergent aims.[1] In some cases tradition, like ritual,[2] has been associated with the timeless and unchanging, viewed either as an Eden to which one must return or a wasteland from which one must escape. In other cases it has been celebrated as a productive and energizing base on top of which one can erect new structures. The former position draws strict boundaries—live with tradition or depart from it—while the latter encourages a more fluid, even nomadic, relationship to tradition—go where you will but remember whence you came. In either case tradition is a strategic, referential invention, a constructed version of the past used as a charter to authorize (or invalidate) present-day cultural and artistic practices.[3]

In the realm of jazz writing, the issue of tradition and its proper understanding is perhaps the trope of tropes. With each seeming artistic revolution (bebop in the 1940s, "free" or "action" jazz in the 1960s, fusion in the 1970s) the debate has been joined anew. Is the new musical style a break from tradition that points toward the future, a logical extension of all that preceded it, or an aesthetic dead end? And, in any event, how are those people confronting the new style to understand its relation to the past? What exactly are contours of "the tradition" emerging from the past? Which outstanding musicians, stylistic nuances, or performance practices allow us to see those contours more clearly?[4] The Marsalis/Murray answer to such questions centers on the "fundamentals" of blues and swing audible in the work of musicians like Ferdinand "Jelly Roll" Morton, Louis Armstrong, Duke Ellington, Count Basie, and John Coltrane. Any music that is a legitimate heir of the tradition emerges from intense study of the music's masters and their masterworks. One cannot and perhaps need not move any further "forward" until she has thoroughly understood and mastered the music composed and recorded by these figures, their argument goes.[5] While the contrasting vision of Jarrett and Whitehead also focuses our attention on individual musicians, its emphasis is on the degree to which those figures have had a vanguardist outlook. In other words, the tradition, such as it is, is primarily a function of change and innovation.

A particularly compelling meditation on these issues emerges from a 1981 poetry and music collaboration between poet, essayist, and playwright Amiri Baraka, multireed instrumentalist and composer David Murray, and percussionist Steve McCall. The poem that furnishes the title for the collaboration, "In the Tradition," has been printed with slight alterations several times since it first appeared in the *Greenfield Review* and is, as a result, much better known than the live recording of it on Amiri Baraka's *New Music—New Poetry*.[6] Many commentators have expressed admiration for the poem, with one describing it as "a masterpiece of political art and a major statement on the interpenetration of culture and politics."[7] Few, however, have commented on Baraka's inspiration for the poem, on the recorded and various live performances of it, or the role played by David Murray and Steve McCall as collaborators. Indeed, despite the attention given to African American poetry from the 1960s forward as performed utterance informed by vernacular and popular cultural elements, the recording of this poem and many others has been strangely ignored, with a few notable exceptions to be discussed below. One cannot gain a full understanding of how the recording—both the poem and the music—articulates a vision of tradition, however, without examining what inspired it and how the poet/performer and musicians realized their goals.

On the recording and in printed versions Baraka dedicates the poem to alto saxophonist, composer, and arranger Arthur Blythe and takes the poem's title and "positive inspiration" from *In the Tradition*, Blythe's second album for Columbia Records.[8] *In the Tradition* features Blythe, pianist Stanley Cowell, bassist Fred Hopkins, and drummer Steve McCall performing pre-1960s compositions by Fats Waller ("Jitterbug Waltz"), Duke Ellington ("In a Sentimental Mood"), Juan Tizol ("Caravan"), and John Coltrane ("Naima"). Included alongside those examples of music apparently in the tradition are two compositions by Blythe: "Break Tune" and "Hip Dipper." By titling his recording and selecting material for it as he did, Blythe was perhaps making a statement about what the jazz tradition meant for many performers who, like him, had developed their skills beginning in the late 1960s as participants in what came to be known as New York City's "loft scene" as well as similar ones in Chicago, St. Louis, and Los Angeles. Along with the loft proprietor/performers Sam Rivers, Rashied Ali and Ornette Coleman, Blythe was celebrated as a performer capable of producing wide-ranging, exploratory music that often fell outside the stylistic parameters that club owners and record executives thought profitable to promote and market. Despite the freedom that loft performances afforded, many musicians found themselves, as the 1970s drew to a close, reexamining musics that had flourished before the 1960s almost as though they were trying to actualize the Art Ensemble of Chicago's credo, "Great Black Music—Ancient to the Future." David Murray and Henry Threadgill, among others, undertook projects during that time that were as much about embracing the past as they were about breaking away from it. With his octet Murray experimented with different forms for improvisation and group interplay, while Threadgill's trio Air recorded a series of avant-gardist versions of classic ragtime themes.[9]

As a descriptor, then, the phrase *in the tradition* became a multivalent signifier. In the simplest sense it denoted the respectful embrace of past musical practices by a number of musicians who were typically regarded as "outside" players. Beyond there, it accrued associations over time that Blythe may not have anticipated:

> When Arthur Blythe formed a quartet . . . and began mixing tunes by Ellington, Waller, Monk, and Coltrane in with his originals, he gave a movement—or more precisely, a moment—its name and unintentionally became its figurehead. Any performance that swings or follows a chord sequence or makes an overt reference to the past is now said to be in the tradition. And any performance which doesn't do any of those things isn't.[10]

And while Blythe performed and recorded in a variety of contexts and with differing groups of musicians, he added another layer of signification by using "In the Tradition" to designate the touring ensemble that performed on the recording. For close followers of the jazz scene, then, the late 1970s and early 1980s were a period of time that, like that in the mid-1970s when media attention centered on Anthony Braxton,[11] focused on an unlikely figure as a savior for jazz. Columbia's signing, promotion and marketing of Blythe was partially intended to bring jazz powerfully back into the marketplace. In the end, the label's efforts on Blythe's behalf were less successful than those for Wynton Marsalis. As a result, much 1980s and early 1990s writing has stressed the degree to which Marsalis and a pride of other "young lions" were returning jazz to "the tradition,"[12] though it should be clear that this process was well underway when Marsalis arrived in New York in 1979.

When asked about his turn toward tradition in an interview published in 1980, Blythe stated that his desire to record *In the Tradition* "was not an attempt to be part of any trend, because several players are going back to the tradition, but [came from the sense] that now the feeling would be right for an album like this."[13] His further comments speak to a conception of tradition as a foundation, a malleable source for creativity, rather than as a foil to innovation:

> The music on *In the Tradition* is basic and fundamental to so-called jazz. If you don't acknowledge anything of that nature, then what are you doing? . . . I think, too, that this might be a period when a synthesis of what has preceded and more recent concepts is coming into being. Everything that was good, and is good, is cool. And if it is good, then do it! . . . A bit of the pressure to be innovative is off. People don't have to be innovative to

be creative. For a while everybody was trying to be innovative, but everybody isn't. I've always felt that the innovative thing comes about when one does his homework being creative. That's where people get ideas—"Hey, maybe that can go over there instead of where it was." So I think it's going back to a creative situation where everything is possible. You don't have to reject everything that has been dealt with already and go look for the new horizons, because you could be out in the dark where you don't see shit.[14]

Rather than regarding tradition as a set of outdated practices that one must abandon or revere uncritically, he sees it as a developing resource, one still in the process of becoming. The tradition extends into the present and, as the inclusion of his own compositions on the recording indicates, has his own work as the latest addition to it.

As public figures and performers embedded in the late 1970s New York scene, Baraka, Murray, and McCall were certainly aware of the layered meanings attached to the phrase *in the tradition*. They used Blythe's recording, his implicit philosophy, and the feeling he captured in his work as the "positive inspiration" for the two imaginings of tradition on the recorded version of "In the Tradition": one poetic, the other musical. Their "negative inspiration," according to Baraka, was a late 1970s television show called *The White Shadow* whose plotlines centered around a paternalistic but liberal white basketball coach who, like Gabriel Kaplan's character on *Welcome Back, Kotter,* was capable of solving the problems of troubled African American and Chicano youth.

The poetic and musical visions of "In the Tradition" have a complex relationship to one another that is poorly addressed by descriptions of the music as "background" or "accompaniment" or any suggestion that the music "amplifies" the meaning of the poem. A number of terms might be used for the recording in question with "jazz poetry" being the most obvious. That term, however, makes little distinction between poems *about* jazz or jazz musicians, poems *by* jazz musicians, poems that use jazz performance practices as resources, and poems meant *to be read to* jazz.[15] Too often, those writing about jazz poetry restrict themselves to poems in the first three categories and, by neglecting study of music, overlook the ways in which jazz might be an integral component of poetic performance rather than a vaguely articulated influence.[16]

One writer who has tried to make finer distinctions between these understandings of the poetry-jazz nexus is Aldon Nielsen, who, in discussing recordings made by poets like Kenneth Rexroth and Jack Kerouac in the late 1950s, observes that poetry read to jazz often sounds somewhat haphazard:

Too frequently, enamored of the ideal of improvisation, poets simply took to the stage or to the studio to declaim their creations, trusting the spirit of the moment and the musicians' ability to anticipate the text's direction, often sorely trying the sympathy of their audience. . . . The Beat poets' relationship to the music was . . . contingent. Rexroth and Kerouac certainly knew a lot about musicians and listened with a keen ear to jazz, but they evidenced little clear understanding of how the music was put together, and thus their approach to locating their own lines within the music was generally intuitive. The music was . . . more frequently background (or even distraction) than equal partner in a new genre.[17]

In contrast, jazz/poetry *collaborations* for him tend to be much more deliberate. He singles out Baraka's work on the New York Art Quartet's 1964 debut recording as a watershed moment in the development of the genre.[18] The group, consisting of drummer Milford Graves, alto saxophonist John Tchicai, bassist Lewis Worrell, and trombonist Roswell Rudd, comprised musicians already familiar to Baraka. For Nielsen Baraka's delivery, particularly on Roswell's composition "Sweet V," doesn't possess the fiery energy of his later work but does have a power of its own:

> Baraka's work with the New York Art quartet builds its terrifying tensions out of the dissonance between the apocalyptic words of the poem and the almost overly calm fashion in which Baraka reads it. In fact, Baraka's rendition of the poem with the New York Art Quartet is nearly identical to his cool and suspense-filled performance, without music, recorded at an August 1964 Asilomar conference taped by Pacifica Radio.[19]

It is difficult to understand how the similarity between Baraka's performances with and without music supports the notion that his work with the New York Art Quartet constitutes a true collaboration. Difficult, that is, until one understands that by "collaborative" Nielsen means that the musicians knew the poem ahead of time and improvised responses to the calls issued by the poet.[20] The music therefore remains secondary or decorative: it moves beyond being background or distraction only to the degree that it enhances or underscores the meaning of the poetic text.

Something closer to an ideal of collaboration can be found on the 1958 Verve recording *The Weary Blues,* which features Langston Hughes reading his poetry to music composed by Leonard Feather on side 1 and then to music by Charles Mingus on side 2.[21] The differences between the settings are instructive: the Feather-Hughes side presents jazz as atmosphere, as background, almost as mood-setting support for a voiceover. It, like Baraka's work with the New York Art Quartet, seems a clear example of "poetry read to jazz." Feather nearly acknowledges as much in his liner notes for the recording:

> Most of the blues-directed material and all the gospel-related poems were assigned to a traditional-style group, for which I wrote a few 12, 16, and 8-bar blues themes or patterns, a couple of gospel-type numbers for *Testament,* and co-ordinated solos by the sidemen. For the second side, Charles Mingus wrote or improvised suitable material, always with a sensitive ear to the content and meaning of Hughes' statements and questions . . . .

Mingus's genius for controlling a group of men was never clearer than on this session, as he set changes of mood, tempo and theme, often quite spontaneously.

The Mingus side, however, does more than respond to Hughes's reading: it demands something of him. Not only does Mingus's music follow the dramatic and narrative contours of Hughes's poetry, it also elicits a more emotive, dynamic reading from Hughes, especially on poems like "Big Ben" where the poet's normally laconic delivery takes on greater tonal nuance in response to the music.

In a sense, then, one might characterize as jazz/poetry collaboration those situations in which both poet and musicians have to make adjustments and in which auditors have to attend to the meaning of the music as well as that of the poetic text. A useful analogy can be made to jazz performance practice without poetry: to the degree that musicians' privilege allowing each member of an ensemble to "bring something to the music," the best performances or recordings result from situations where each performer contributes to the impact of the event. Composers write material that leaves room for other players to improvise within and play with the conventions of jazz performance, bandleaders choose musicians on the basis of their individual sounds and ability to complement and challenge one another musically, and all performers ideally approach their task as one of simultaneous performance, listening, and interaction.[22] The implications for jazz-poetry collaborations couldn't be more clear: the musicians don't provide accompaniment for the poet any more than the poet is merely a "lyricist" adding interest to a musical work.[23] Instead, all involved work toward creating something greater than either musical performance or poetry alone might accomplish.

On the recording the three performing participants had something to bring to the collaboration by virtue of their lives as performers in their respective genres. In a chameleonic career, Baraka, for example, has gone from being a Greenwich Village bohemian poet, to being an antiwhite, antisemitic cultural nationalist, and, more recently, to being a committed Third World Marxist. Along the way, he has produced an interesting and challenging body of work concerned with the relation and responsibility of the poet to his predecessors, contemporaries, and successors.[24] Since the 1960s his poetry has frequently been "written" with oral performance, musical collaboration, and nonprint media such as recordings in mind.[25] Likewise, following the lead of Larry Neal, Baraka adopted a different style of reading in the late 1960s, one indebted to a number of vernacular sources: "street" language, black preaching, scatting, and gospel and rhythm and blues singing.[26] Many commentators on his work, while acknowledging the changes in his delivery as well as that of other black poets, have been content merely to analyze the "jazz influence" in his work and have significantly neglected his collaborative aims. In any event, Baraka brought to the event a wide-ranging understanding of history, literature, politics, and music—all filtered through his then Marxist worldview as well his prior attempts to have standing ensembles (like his Advanced Workers group in the 1970s) with which to *perform* his poetry rather than merely to publish it in textual form.

In his own work David Murray has explored a broad expanse of the black musical landscape. During his childhood he studied piano and alto saxophone and performed in various churches as well as in rhythm and blues groups. He turned to free jazz while attending Pomona College, where he befriended Arthur Blythe and Stanley Crouch (then a drummer and poet) before moving to New York City in the mid-1970s. As he developed as a performer, rather than abandoning any of the styles that were part of his musical education, Murray embraced them all. In writing for and playing in his celebrated Octet and Big Band as well as the World Saxophone Quartet, he has drawn upon all the musics one might describe as "African American": from the "free" improvisations of the 1970s loft scene to "in the tradition" work based on rhythm and blues classics, the work of Duke Ellington, and collaborations with Senegalese drummers and with poets like Harry Lewis.[27] Moreover, he has continued to work with Baraka since recording *New Music—New Poetry*, most recently on a 1996 recording.[28] Likewise, a number of reviews and concert announcements in the *New York Times* indicate that Baraka and Murray (with McCall) collaborated on several projects between 1980 and 1984 including a jazz musical called *Primitive World*.[29]

Likewise, Steve McCall, before his untimely death in 1989, explored terrain at least as expansive as Murray's. In the 1960s he was a member of the Experimental Band, the group that laid the foundation for the Association for the Advancement of Creative Musicians (AACM), a musical collective of which McCall was a charter member. In addition, he performed and recorded in a variety of other contexts in the years that followed: with blues musicians in Chicago, with Arthur Prysock, with Anthony Braxton, with tenor saxophonist Dexter Gordon, with Murray's Octet, with Arthur Blythe (on *In the Tradition*), and, most famously, with the collaborative trio Air. The latter group covered the same range of musics as Murray's groups, focusing on updatings of ragtime, march music, rhythm and blues, bop-derived styles, and free, post-1960s styles.[30] Like his two contemporaries, then, McCall had experience in nearly all aspects of vernacular African American music and was admired for his skill, taste, and versatility. Indeed, McCall was a member of three of the major "avant-gutbucket"[31] ensembles performing in the late 1970s: David Murray's Octet, Air, and In the Tradition/the Arthur Blythe Quartet (see table). His wide-ranging affiliations document the degree to which he was perhaps most eminently suited to be the drummer on this recording—for his knowledge of Blythe, his experience playing with Murray, and his immersion in the various musics embraced by Air.

Together, then, Murray and McCall came to the recording of "In the Tradition" with a deep knowledge of one another's performing styles, and, one assumes, Baraka came fully aware of them as well. Baraka's writing in the recording's liner notes make clear that the musical component of this project was conceived as collaborative rather than simply accompanimental: "We wanted the music and the words to extend to each other, be parts of the same expression, different pieces of a whole." The collective work toward that end resulted in a meditation on tradition that moves along two parallel tracks, each reinforcing the same basic point. Though the poet and the musicians have divergent strategies for presenting their

David Murray Octet	Air	Arthur Blythe Quartet	In the Tradition
Murray, ts, bcl			Murray, ts, bcl
Henry Threadgill, as, bfl	Henry Threadgill, as, fl		
		Arthur Blythe, as	
Olu Dara, tpt			
Butch Morris, cornet			
George Lewis, trb			
Anthony Davis, p			
		Stanley Cowell, p	
	Fred Hopkins, b	Fred Hopkins, b	
Wilbur Morris, b			
Steve McCall, d	Steve McCall, d	Steve McCall, d	Steve McCall, d

Note: as = alto saxophone; b = bass; bcl = bass clarinet; bfl = bass flute; d = drums; fl = flute; p = piano; ts = tenor saxophone; trb = trombone; tpt = trumpet.

visions of tradition, those visions are in the end mutually complementary and more powerful by virtue of their being combined.

An insightful analysis of the poem by William J. Harris identifies "naming" as one of the critical components of Baraka's poetic strategy:

> Baraka . . . drew on the tradition of naming that, in this country, has had its exemplars in Walt Whitman and Allen Ginsberg. While Baraka has always named, he never before so completely used naming as the main poetic device of a poem. As if it is a magic formula, he names the people in *his* tradition to counter those in the *other*.[32]

In the course of the performance, as if to answer the question "What is this tradition Basied on[?]," [33] Baraka names historical figures, musicians, writers, sculptors, painters, songs and musical styles as both positive and negative examples of the tradition he seeks to describe and celebrate:

> Tradition
> of Douglass
> of David Walker
> Garnett
> Turner
> Tubman
> of ragers yeh

ragers
(of Kings, & Counts, & Dukes
of Satchelmouths & SunRa's
of Bessies & Billies & Sassys
& Mas
Musical screaming
Niggers
yeh
tradition
of Brown Welles
& Brown Sterling
& Brown Clifford
of H Rap & H Box (200–1)

In using naming as a strategy, Baraka also calls into question the nature of American music and American literature: what are their relations to European music and literature? To Anglo-American music and literature?

where's yr american music
gwashington won the war
where's yr american culture southernagrarians
academic aryans
penwarrens & wilburs
say something american if you dare
if you
can
where's yr american
music
Nigger music?

(Like englishmen talking about *great* britain stop with tongues
lapped on their cravats you put the irish on em. Say shit
man, you mean irish irish Literature . . . when they say about
they
you say nay you mean irish irish literature you mean, for the
last century you mean, when you scream say nay, you mean
yeats,
synge, shaw, wilde, joyce, ocasey, beckett, them is, nay, them is
irish, they's irish, irish as the ira)

you mean nigger music? don't hide in europe—"oh that's
classical!"
come to this country
nigger music?

you better go up in appalachia
and get some mountain some coal mining
songs, you better go down south in our land
& talk to the angloamerican national minority
they can fetch up a song or two, country & western
could save you from looking like saps before the world (206–7)

Throughout the recording Baraka's delivery makes the names he intones and recites even more powerful. In addition to naming the exemplars of his tradition, he embodies certain aspects of that tradition by drawing on black vernacular language, especially the techniques and resources of ecstatic black preaching. His tone at the beginning is almost conversational, like that of a preacher introducing his/her topic and scriptural basis for a sermon. Also like a preacher, Baraka utilizes other voices and other characters (his repetitions of "Hey coah-ch!" in the first section of the poem are one instance) to make his chosen examples more clear and lively. As he moves through his reading, he continues in the preacherly vein, gradually raising the level of loudness and intensity of his words, breaking up and worrying his lines, occasionally singing recognizable songs (e.g., "C.C. Rider") or improvising scatted lines that work much better in recitation than they do on the printed page. Moreover, his repetitions of the word *tradition*, like those drawn from a key biblical verse, continually accumulate power, for all the names he mentions in tandem with his repetitions make that tradition something one can feel:

                    in the tradition thank you arthur for playing & saying
                reminding us how deep how old how black how sweet how
        we is and bees
        when we remember
        when we are our memory as the projection
        of what it is evolving
        in struggle
        in passion and pain
        we become our sweet black
        selves

        once again,
          in the tradition
          in the african american
            tradition
              open us
              yet bind us
              let all that is positive
              find
              us
                        (208–9)

At several points, lest his "sermon" reach its climactic point too soon, Baraka pulls back from a high level of intensity to begin again conversationally (e.g., after the words "elegant as skywriting" on page 201 or his first scatted lines on page 202). Indeed, it is difficult not to imagine Baraka (pictured on the album cover holding a microphone) moving animatedly about the stage adding meaning to his words and their sound with his gestures.

While the strategy of "naming" may not seem readily transferable to the realm of music making, there is a sense in which the tradition constructed by Murray and McCall is also predicated on that strategy. The music they play and improvise here "names" foundational styles and practices that one might use to construct an African American musical tradition. It is significant that Baraka (205) refers to Ellington's *Black, Brown, and Beige* in the poem, for what the musicians perform is a condensed version of African American musical history with similar contours to those in Ellington's work (which names work songs, spirituals and blues, among other styles, as part of African American musical history).[34] Over the nearly fourteen-minute span of "In the Tradition," Murray and McCall play—in order—a work song, "Amazing Grace," a slow, bluesy shuffle, a 1920s-style small group jazz piece, Count Basie's riff-based "One O'Clock Jump," Charlie Parker's "Now's the Time," a section with Afro-Latin rhythms (nicely keyed to Baraka's naming of the Puerto Rican styles *bomba* and *plena*), and a free-bop workout on Murray's composition "The Fast Life."[35] They handle the transitions from piece to piece in different ways: the work song begins with an anacrusis from Murray and ends with an emphatic snare drum hit from McCall, for example, while the slow shuffle section begins with McCall's insistent snare drum (synchronized with the last word of the line "I thought I heard Buddy Bolden say," 201). In other words, the musicians take turns asserting leadership with regard to their portion of the collaboration.

Similarly, they share authority for the performance's pacing with Baraka. The beginnings of some of their tunes coincide with major sections in the poem, but not all of them do. A close examination of the recording makes it difficult to support the contention that the musicians are merely accompanying Baraka, particularly when changes in musical style seem to take precedence over the structure of the poem. A reading of the printed poem would not necessarily suggest, for example, that there should be any break between the lines "like the Art Ensemble" and "like Miles's Venus DeMilo" (205), since they are the second and third items in a series. But Baraka stops after the word *Ensemble* when Murray and McCall are coming to the end of a chorus of "One O'Clock Jump." Murray punctuates the poet's silence with the remnants of a riff from that tune and then moves with McCall into "Now's the Time." Only in the third bar of the Parker tune does Baraka finish the series and continue his recitation.

While all three performers rely on naming strategies, they use them in different ways. The aspects of tradition named by Murray and McCall are presented in a linear, chronological fashion, while those presented by Baraka are more "improvisational," less tied to chronology than to his moment to moment concern with naming the figures of his tradition. Because of its ordering, one might be tempted to read a narrative of progress into the musical presentation, for it starts with what many assume to be the first manifestations of music making by Africans on the North American continent and moves chronologically forward. Such a reading, however, would be misguided for at least three reasons. One, Murray and McCall make no attempts to play idiomatically in each of the styles. Rather than presenting a history lesson, they are picking and choosing elements from that history, and are, like Baraka, commenting on them musically. Approximately eight minutes and forty seconds into the recording, after they have played the melody of "Now's the Time" twice, Murray and McCall start to move away from performing the tune the way Parker's late 1940s quintet or other bebop musicians might have. Beginning with the third solo chorus, they play in a way that has more affinities with the kinds of performances they themselves might have done in nightclub or on record, independent of Baraka or a narrative program. Just as Baraka has been gradually raising the level of intensity throughout his recitation and then pulling back, Murray and McCall here deploy specifically musical intensification strategies. Murray's pitch choices, for example, grow increasingly distant from the harmonies implied by a twelve-bar blues in F. Likewise, McCall's drum fills have the effect of obscuring the form more than reinforcing our understanding of it. Indeed, in the sixth solo chorus it becomes nearly impossible to discern the contours of the blues form or to know whether Murray and McCall are still following it.

Two, the musicians make no attempt to be comprehensive or all-inclusive in their survey, for we hear no hardbop, soul, or funk in their parade of African American musical styles. As is the case with Baraka (or anyone else constructing a tradition), they are selective. One might say that, rather than tell us the entire history of African American music in all its particulars, they give us a series of snapshots that powerfully suggest that history's shape. And three, they, like Baraka, have no difficulty playing with the details of the history they invoke or its relation to their conception of tradition. In the climactic section that closes the performance, where they play Murray's "Fast Life" (beginning approximately at the eleven-minute mark), they make clear they consider themselves to be the latest manifestation of the tradition whose elements they are naming—a gesture that recalls Blythe's strategy on *In the Tradition*. In other words, they present a view of tradition as something still in process, a process of which they are part and in which they participate. Baraka's naming of himself at various points in his presentation functions in the same way: "in the tradition of all of us in the positive aspect / cut zora neale & me & and a buncha other folks in half. My brothers and sisters in the tradition" (205). The same can be said of his invocation of Murray's work with the World Saxophone Quartet at the beginning of this climactic portion of the recording (207).

In the end, Baraka's question "What is this tradition Basied on[?]" receives multiple answers. On one hand, with his words and his delivery he responds by naming the exemplars of his tradition as well as paying homage to some of the ways in which they have communicated that tradition verbally, musically and politically. On the other, Murray and McCall answer by "naming" the styles and embodying the practices of the musics in their tradition. Both answers, one improvisational and the other linear, are mutually reinforcing, partially because they draw on a much larger notion of tradition than either letters or music making might indicate: Baraka's performance style emerges in part from the residue of the African American past contained in musical performance, while the work of Murray and McCall emerges from their own work with musics inspired by African American vernacular speech and spirituality.

In either case, tradition represents for all of them less a closed canon than it does an energizing, inspirational base: a series of exemplars, foundational figures, and sustaining practices. While it may have (uncomfortable) contacts with them, "the tradition" is not based on the aesthetic principles of elite European cultures, on "classical" music, or strict imitation of one's forbears. It is instead the kind of synthesis that Blythe saw as characteristic of the 1980s when he made *In the Tradition*: one that drew lovingly from the past and used it to chart a course into the future. For all of them tradition—"always new and centuries old" (209)—has to be seen as a process, an act of struggle and creative adaptation. If the two visions of tradition on this recording authorize or validate anything, they draw our attention to the collective power of different people and musical styles brought into an open, collaborative space. They constitute a reading of the past that escapes the confines of seeing tradition as static or compelling relentless innovation in favor of seeing it as an opening of the way: to both the past and the future.

NOTES

1. Baker, *Blues, Ideology, and Afro-American Literature*; Benston, "Ellison, Baraka, and the Faces of Tradition"; Crouch, "Wynton Marsalis: 1987"; Elie, "An Interview with Wynton Marsalis; Gates, *The Signifying Monkey*; Jarrett, "Categories Aplenty"; Murray, *The Omni-Americans* and *Stomping the Blues*; Whitehead, "Death to 'the Avant Garde,'" "Jazz Rebels," and "Off Minor."

2. Bell, *Ritual Theory, Ritual Practice*; Kelly and Kaplan, "History, Structure, and Ritual"; Smith, *To Take Place*.

3. Appadurai, "The Past as a Scarce Resource"; Hobsbawm and Ranger, *The Invention of Tradition*; Trouillot, *Silencing the Past*.

4. For very different examinations of these questions, see DeVeaux, *The Birth of Bebop*, pp. 1–29; Jost, *Free Jazz*, pp. 8–16; and Watrous, "A Jazz Generation and the Miles Davis Curse."

5. For a lengthy exploration of the Marsalis/Murray position, see Porter, *What Is This Thing Called Jazz?* pp. 287–384.

6. *New Music—New Poetry* (LP, India Navigation IN 1048, 1981) was recorded at Soundscape, a performance space established by Verna Gillis located at 500 W. 52d Street. The recording has long been out of print, and now that India Navigation has ceased operation it is unclear whether the recording will ever be distributed again. The label was founded by Bob Cummins in 1972. He spent the majority of the 1970s and 1980s recording musicians, both avant-garde and mainstream, who were frequently ignored by major labels or larger, better-distributed independent labels. As a serious fan of the music, Cummins dedicated himself to recording the musicians he liked and getting their music out to the public. See Ben Ratliff, "Bob Cummins, 68." Both Arthur Blythe and David Murray made their first recordings as leaders for India Navigation. The label

effectively ceased operation in the spring of 2001, less than a year after Cummins's death.

7. Smith, "Baraka and the Politics of Popular Culture," p. 236.

8. Arthur Blythe, *In the Tradition* (LP, Columbia JC 36300, 1979).

9. David Murray Octet, *Ming* (LP, Black Saint BSR 0045, 1980); Air, *Air Lore* (CD, Bluebird 6578-2-RB, 1979). The overlapping connections between the musicians who played in these ensembles will be discussed later in this essay.

10. Davis, *In the Moment*, pp. 194–95.

11. Radano, *New Musical Figurations*.

12. Pareles, "Jazz Swings Back to Tradition"; Sancton, "Horns of Plenty."

13. Bob Blumenthal, "Arthur Blythe: Refreshing Traditions," p. 64.

14. Ibid.

15. For further discussion, see Feinstein and Komunyakaa, "Preface," in *The Jazz Poetry Anthology*, pp. xvii–xx. A useful though somewhat skewed overview of meetings between jazz musicians and poets is Wallenstein, "Poetry and Jazz. A more exhaustive survey is Nielsen, *Black Chant*.

16. Perhaps the most incomprehensible example comes from Ellison, "Jazz in the Poetry of Amiri Baraka and Roy Fisher" p. 117. She writes, with no apparent irony, "[Poets like Amiri Baraka and Roy Fisher] employed the language of jazz: the blue notes, the atonality, the polyrhythms, the extended harmonies, the melisma, the microtones, and the celebratory rhythm of swing. Simple syncopation was supplemented by the complex backbeat and shifting rhythms of the kind employed by a drummer or boogie pianist." While some of her arguments regarding rhythm and syncopation might be taken at face value, it is more difficult to understand—and she does not explain—how atonality, extended harmonies, melisma, and polyrhythms might be employed. She seems to be operating more on received wisdom here than on any solid analysis of their work.

17. Nielsen, *Black Chant*, 177.

18. *New York Art Quartet* (LP, ESP 1004, 1965).

19. Nielsen, *Black Chant*, 191.

20. Ibid., 195.

21. Langston Hughes, Charles Mingus and Leonard Feather, *The Weary Blues* (CD, Verve 841 660-2, 1990), recorded March 18, 1958, New York, New York.

22. Jackson, "Jazz Performance as Ritual," pp. 45–51.

23. Charles Mingus's recorded versions of "The Clown" and "The Chill of Death" are both good examples of how this kind of work might be realized, though neither reaches the level of the Baraka-Murray-McCall recording. The former can be found on *The Clown* (CD, Rhino/Atlantic R2 75590, 1999), recorded February 13, and March 12, 1957, New York, New York, while the latter is on *Let My Children Hear Music* (LP, Columbia PC 31039, 1972 [?]), recorded September 23 and 30, October 1, and November 18, 1971, New York, New York. Better examples of such collaboration, partially inspired by Baraka, can be found in the work of individuals like Nathaniel Mackey and Jayne Cortez.

24. Harris, *Jones/Baraka Reader*, xxvii–xxx.

25. Harris, "An Interview with Amiri Baraka," p. 27; Smith, "Baraka and the Politics of Popular Culture."

26. Stephen E. Henderson, "Worrying the Line," pp. 62–63, 77–78; Sollors, "Does Axel's Castle Have a Street Address?" 408.

27. Various Artists, *Wildflowers 4: The New York Loft Jazz Sessions* (LP, Casablanca/Douglas NBLP 7048, 1977); David Murray Octet, *Home* (LP, Black Saint BSR 0055, 1982); World Saxophone Quartet, *Rhythm and Blues* (CD, Elektra/Musician 60864, 1989), *Plays Duke Ellington* (CD, Nonesuch 79137, 1986) and *Four Now* (CD, Justin Time 83, 1996). For the curious, Crouch's drumming (with Murray on tenor saxophone, Olu Dara on trumpet and fluegelhorn, and Fred Hopkins on bass) can be heard on "Shout Song" from *Wildflowers 4*.

28. *Fo deuk Revue* (CD, Justin Time JUST 94–2, 1997). Baraka joins Murray's ensemble on "Evidence" and "Chant Africain."

29. Charles, "Sono Artists' Colony"; Palmer, "Music Is Living in a Loft on 10th Ave"; Pareles, "The Village Becomes a Jazz Festival" and "'Primitive World.'" For the text of *Primitive World,* see Harris, *Jones/Baraka Reader,* pp. 400–49.

30. Joseph Jarman, *Song for* (LP, Delmark 410, 1966); Creative Construction Company, *Creative Construction Company* (2 LPs, Muse 5071 and 5097, 1970); Gene Ammons and Dexter Gordon, *The Chase* (LP, Prestige 10010, 1970); David Murray Octet, *Ming* (see note 9).

31. Pareles, "Jazz Swings Back to Tradition," 68.

32. Harris, *The Poetry and Poetics of Amiri Baraka,* p. 115.

33. Baraka, *Transblucency,* p. 203. Hereafter all references to the poem will be noted parenthetically in the text.

34. *The Duke Ellington Carnegie Hall Concerts, January 1943* (3 LPs, Prestige P-34004, 1977. Recorded 23 January 1943, New York, New York).

35. One can find the octet version of this tune on *Ming.* See note 9 for discographical information.

REFERENCES

Appadurai, Arjun. "The Past as a Scarce Resource." *Man* 16 (1981): 201–19.

Baker, Houston A., Jr. *Blues, Ideology, and Afro-American Literature: A Vernacular Theory.* Chicago: University of Chicago Press, 1984.

Baraka, Amiri (LeRoi Jones). "'Not a White Shadow.'" *Greenfield Review* 8.3–4 (1980): 38–46.

——— *Transblucency: The Selected Poems of Amiri Baraka/Leroi Jones (1961–1995).* Ed. Paul Vangelisti. New York: Marsilio, 1995.

Bell, Catherine. *Ritual Theory, Ritual Practice.* New York: Oxford University Press, 1992.

Benston, Kimberly W. "Ellison, Baraka, and the Faces of Tradition." *Boundary 2* 6.2 (1978): 333–54.

Blumenthal, Bob. "Arthur Blythe: Refreshing Traditions." *Down Beat,* April 1980, pp. 25–26, 64.

Charles, Eleanor. "Sono Artists' Colony." *New York Times,* August 2, 1981, p. 11:5.

Crouch, Stanley. "Wynton Marsalis: 1987." *Down Beat,* November 1987, 16–19, p. 57.

Davis, Francis. *In the Moment: Jazz in the 1980s.* New York: Oxford University Press, 1986.

DeVeaux, Scott. *The Birth of Bebop: A Social and Musical History.* Berkeley: University of California Press, 1997.

Elie, Lolis Eric. "An Interview with Wynton Marsalis." *Callaloo* 13.2 (1990): 271–90.

Ellison, Mary. "Jazz in the Poetry of Amiri Baraka and Roy Fisher." *Yearbook of English Studies* 24 (1994): 117–45.

Feinstein, Sascha, and Yusef Komunyakaa. "Preface." In *The Jazz Poetry Anthology*, ed. Sascha Feinstein and Yusef Komunyakaa, pp. xvii–xx. Bloomington: Indiana University Press, 1991.

Gates, Henry Louis, Jr. *The Signifying Monkey: A Theory of African-American Literary Criticism*. New York: Oxford University Press, 1988.

Harris, William J. "An Interview with Amiri Baraka." *Greenfield Review* 8.3–4 (1980): 19–31.

——— *The Poetry and Poetics of Amiri Baraka: The Jazz Aesthetic*. Columbia: University of Missouri Press, 1985.

Harris, William J., ed. *The Leroi Jones/Amiri Baraka Reader*. New York: Thunder's Mouth, 1991.

Henderson, Stephen E. "Worrying the Line: Notes on Black American Poetry." In *The Line in Postmodern Poetry*, ed. Robert Frank and Henry Sayre, pp. 60–82. Urbana and Chicago: University of Illinois Press, 1988.

Hobsbawm, Eric, and Terence Ranger, eds. *The Invention of Tradition*. Cambridge: Cambridge University Press, 1983.

Jackson, Travis A. "Jazz Performance as Ritual: The Blues Aesthetic and the African Diaspora." In *The African Diaspora: A Musical Perspective*, ed. Ingrid Monson, pp. 23–82. New York: Garland, 2000.

Jarrett, Keith. "Categories Aplenty, But Where's the Music?" *New York Times*, August 16, 1992, p. 2:19.

Jost, Ekkehard. *Free Jazz*. Graz: Universal, 1974.

Kelly, John D., and Martha Kaplan. "History, Structure, and Ritual." *Annual Review of Anthropology* 19 (1990): 119–50.

Mackey, Nathaniel. "The Changing Same: Black Music in the Poetry of Amiri Baraka." *Boundary 2* 6.2 (1978): 355–86.

Murray, Albert. *The Omni-Americans: Some Alternatives to the Folklore of White Supremacy*. New York: Outerbridge and Dienstfrey, 1970.

——— *Stomping the Blues*. New York: McGraw-Hill, 1976.

Nielsen, Aldon Lynn. *Black Chant: Languages of African-American Postmodernism*. Cambridge: Cambridge University Press, 1997.

Palmer, Robert. "Music Is Living in a Loft on 10th Ave." *New York Times*, November 28, 1980, p. C12.

Pareles, Jon. "Jazz Swings Back to Tradition." *New York Times Magazine*, June 17, 1984, pp. 22–23, 54–55, 61–63, 66–68.

——— "'Primitive World,' a Jazz Musical." *New York Times*, January 20, 1984, p. C3.

——— "The Village Becomes a Jazz Festival." *New York Times*, 26 August 1983, C1, C22.

Porter, Eric C. *What Is This Thing Called Jazz? African American Musicians as Artists, Critics, and Activists*. Berkeley: University of California Press, 2002.

Radano, Ronald M. *New Musical Figurations: Anthony Braxton's Cultural Critique*. Chicago: University of Chicago Press, 1993.

Ratliff, Ben. "Bob Cummins, 68, a Producer in New York's Loft-Jazz Scene." *New York Times*, September 10, 2000, p. 54.

Sancton, Thomas. "Horns of Plenty." *Time*, October 22, 1990, pp. 64–71.

Smith, David Lionel. "Amiri Baraka and the Politics of Popular Culture." In *Politics and the Muse: Studies in the Politics of Recent American Literature*, ed. Adam J. Sorkin, pp. 222–38. Bowling Green, Ohio: Bowling Green State University Popular Press, 1989.

Smith, Jonathan Z. *To Take Place: Toward Theory in Ritual.* Chicago: University of Chicago Press, 1987.

Sollors, Werner. "Does Axel's Castle Have a Street Address, or, What's New?: Tendencies in the Poetry of Amiri Baraka (Leroi Jones)." *Boundary 2* 6.2 (1978): 387–413.

Trouillot, Michel-Rolph. *Silencing the Past: Power and the Production of History.* Boston: Beacon, 1995.

Wallenstein, Barry. "Poetry and Jazz: A Twentieth-Century Wedding." *Black American Literature Forum* 25 (1991): 595–620.

Watrous, Peter. "A Jazz Generation and the Miles Davis Curse." *New York Times*, October 15, 1995, p. 2:1, 40.

Whitehead, Kevin. "Death to 'the Avant Garde'." *Village Voice*, March 21, 1995, pp. 63–68.

———— "Jazz Rebels: Lester Bowie and Greg Osby." *Down Beat*, August 1993, pp. 16–20.

———— "Off Minor." *A Gathering of the Tribes* 4.1 (1994): 37.

HERMAN BEAVERS

A Space We're All Immigrants From: Othering and Communitas in Nathaniel Mackey's *Bedouin Hornbook*

How to divert interpretation (rereading) into invention(aberrant readings)?
—Michael Jarrett, Drifting on a Read

Space is the place.
—Sun-Ra

1

Readers of Nathaniel Mackey's *Bedouin Hornbook* might be surprised to find that the Deconstructive Woodwind Chorus (soon to become the East Bay Dread Ensemble and later the Mystic Horn Society) chooses to spend their formative moments as a band engaged in a series of discussions, "some of them quite heated," on the subject of duende. As Edward Hirsch observes, Federico García Lorca understood duende to be evocative of "the obscure power and penetrating inspiration of art" in the presence of death.[1] Lorca saw duende as both spirit and thought, rising "through the body . . . cours[ing] through the blood and break[ing] through the poet's back like a pair of wings" (11). Ultimately, then, duende has much to do, Hirsch suggests, with "the power of wild abandonment . . . an art that touches and transfigures death, that both woos and evades it" (11). Duende is a matter as "serious as a heart attack," and so we have to regard the Deconstructive Woodwind Chorus as musicians of a different sort; for them music is anything but mere entertainment. This group of musicians views music as an exercise in intellectual and performative leaps that grow bolder with each set they play.[2]

Bedouin Hornbook takes the form of a series of letters written by a musician and composer designated simply as N, addressed to his intellectual coconspirator, antagonist, and artistic collaborator who goes by the unlikely moniker of the Angel of Dust. The letters span a period of three years and three days, running from June 14, 1978, to June 17, 1981. They describe N's exploits as a member of a band known as the Mystic Horn Society. But, in the process, the letters deal with N's struggle to come to terms with some thorny musicological or performative problem.

In light of N's penchant for correspondence and reflection, I want to call attention to Victor Turner's notion of communitas as a crucial aspect of the discussion surrounding *Bedouin Hornbook* in part because N struggles to embrace it as an artistic credenda but also because communitas represents a substantive *break* from social convention. The significance of this is to be found in Turner's analysis of the cultural importance of carnival, which he insists is a moment "severed from ordinary historical time, even the time of extraordinary secular events." As Turner describes it, carnival "is the denizen of a place which is no place, and a time which is not time" (123). Moreover, he continues, what

> we are seeing is society in its subjunctive mood—to borrow a term from grammar—its mood of feeling, willing, and desiring, its mood of fantasizing, its playful mood; not its indicative mood, where it tries to apply reason to human action and systematize the relationship between ends and means in industry and bureaucracy. (123)

Turner attributes to carnival the power to reverse social polarities, and thus, following on Maria Goldwasser's work, concludes that carnival is the embodiment of antistructure, an instance of communitas, a "shared flow."[3]

Though it has the power to expand what we mean when we use a term like *cultural diversity*, communitas constitutes such a powerful re-ordering of spatial priorities that it can be likened, as Turner argues, "to death, to being in the womb, to invisibility, to darkness, to bisexuality, to the wilderness, and to an eclipse of the sun or moon" (95). As such, we can think of communitas as the site of what Nathaniel Mackey recommends as an amendment to how we conceptualize otherness. In his view:

> When we speak of otherness we are not positing static , intrinsic attributes or characteristics. We need instead to highlight the dynamics of agency and attribution by way of which otherness is brought about and maintained, the fact that other is something people do, more importantly a verb than an adjective or a noun. (265)

Mackey draws a powerful distinction between what he calls "artistic othering" and "social othering." In his view, the former

> has to do with innovation, invention, and change, upon cultural health and diversity depend and thrive. Social othering has to do with power, exclusion, and privilege, the centralizing of the norm against which other-

ness is measure, meted out, marginalized. My focus is the practice of the former by people subjected to the latter. (265)

N finds himself caught up betwixt and between these forces in his role as musician and composer, which dramatizes the relationship between these two modalities and by virtue of this, we can see that *Bedouin Hornbook* seeks to make the liminality of the African American artist into fictional subject matter. I want to suggest further, however, that Mackey wants to postulate that the liminality of the African American fictional subject *matters*.

The performances of the band are nothing if not moments where they engage in the "shared flow" that comes from trying to recover the "excluded middle," rather than reaching an aesthetic plateau. Thus, N articulates his particular brand of otherness when he states, "I confess to a weakness for these amphibious, in-between, both/and advances." We get a sense of what he means early on in the novel, when the band spends an afternoon roller-skating at Venice Beach, where N notes that "I haven't seen so many bodies on display in one place in I can't remember how long" (57). Though there is no reason not to take N at his word, I want to suggest that Mackey's intentions are a bit more circumspect. N's comment is provocative on at least two levels. First, his description of the scene in Venice evokes the slave auction, with its black bodies on display as commodities whose value can be speculated upon before they are purchased. That N "can't remember how long" suggests the transparency of Mackey's hope that the reader will suture the historical "text" to the moment at Venice Beach.

What we also have to note, however, is that N is set to "thinking along lines that . . . put [him] to work on a new composition" (57). Looking at the men and women wearing cut-off shorts, "cut short enough to expose at least an inch of the rounded base of each buttock," N concludes that he is seeing nothing short of a "quantum increase in public access to 'private' parts" (57). This is particularly the case when he observes a couple skating by wearing what N describes as "cellophane jumpsuits," clinging to their bodies "like a sort of Saran Wrap," each plugged into a radio-cassette player, "utterly oblivious to every outside presence . . . thoroughly and absolutely absorbed in their respective maneuvers" (57). Able to see through "the blatantly transparent affairs" clinging to the couple's bodies, N notes he can see everything about them—"body hair, balls, asses, breasts, labia, the whole works" (57).

N recalls a piece called "No Tonic Prez," which is distinguished as a musical composition because the "head" of the tune "doesn't have a tonic or definite key resolution." What makes this significant is that N and Penguin have engaged in a debate over whether the goings-on in Venice have a "Carnival air" about them. Penguin argues that they do not, noting "that the word 'carnival' etymologically has to do with bidding the flesh farewell," which he insists doesn't "seem to apply to what was going on around" the group. But N insists that carnival is distinguished by its ability to "take solace in the flesh" (58). The tune N recalls leads him to think about "Carnival's refusal to resolve into fixed, unequivocal meaning." He concludes:

What I saw, as though for the first time in fact, was the body's dichotomous desire to both extinguish and extend its own mystique, to reveal itself without relinquishing its ruse. What I saw was that ruse's ability to survive exposure. "The body as open secret," I heard myself mutter.   (59)

What Mackey accomplishes here is a move that allows N's "destination" to coincide with the link we can draw between bodies on display at Venice Beach and the slave auction. N's decision to title his composition "The Slave's Day Off" intimates that the blurring between public and private, when viewed as reflections of the carnivalesque, leads us away from the obvious conclusion that bodies on display must always , in a capitalist system, represent diminished or circumscribed capacity. N's conjecture that the "body [can function] as open secret" argues that bodies in a state of nullification and mystification occupy a liminal space that refutes capitalism's propensity [particularly in advertising and cinema] to fragment human bodies into consumable parts. Hence the couple wearing the cellophane jumpsuits, though they are Otherized by their unique form of bodily adornment (which is simultaneously a lack of adornment), are equally representative of an alternative space, one that leads N to see them as an analogy for "our present predicament." The analogy he draws serves to suggest the ways in which *Bedouin Hornbook* sees that "predicament" as one involving the struggle to sustain liminality, to resist closure.

The body as open secret takes on a different aspect in a letter dated January 2, 1981, where N informs the Angel of Dust that he is writing from a hospital bed, beset "by dizzy spells—relapses or attacks brought on by the bits of glass planted in [his] brow by the Crossroads Choir" (108). With each "attack" N hears Ornette Coleman's version of "Embraceable You," playing "like a subcortical muzak" in his head. Though he has been subjected to a variety of tests, the doctors can find no name for N's affliction, but he describes it as a

> wheeling, drenched or drunken intensity in which aberrant flight answers aberrant fall. The attacks tend to come on as an inverse gravity in which *I'm cut loose from every anchoring assumption*, a giddy index if not an indictment of a tipsy world. I feel it as a weightlessness, a radical, uprooting vertigo, a rash, evaporative aspect of myself.   (108–9; MY EMPHASIS)

As Jay Wright might put it, "there is a blessing in [N's] disrupted blood." For here, N finds himself Otherized, prone to "trancelike interludes" where he experiences cravings for odd things like orange-flavored aspirin. "Tangled up with 'Embraceable You,'" he observes, "I tend to hear my own heartbeat, amplified and coming at me from outside" (109). He feels as if his heart is a

> ventriloquist of sorts, throwing its voice at an ever more obtruse angle so as to exact an acoustical shell from the surrounding air. It's an eerie feeling to be engulfed by one's own heartbeat, put upon by the heat of one's own stolen pulse like a vulnerable flame palpitating in a draft. The heart's

thrown voice, it seems, moves as a mutable window or a "mute" succession of windows, the transparent advance of an elliptical witness to a many-tongued yet unmentionable, all the more audacious truth. (109)

N's body, as "mutable window" is at once syncretic object—e.g., his body ceases to be his own when fused with Coleman's version of a jazz standard—and also unreadable text. Falling as he does outside the realm of conventional diagnosis, N is nonetheless the embodiment of "public access." In light of this, N's description of his ailment suggests the collapse of his subjectivity, where he becomes a signifier of lack. Recalling the opening letter of the novel in which N has denounced "the ontology of loss," N finds himself the victim of an "illness" that is both disembodiment and disposition. Thus, when he remarks, "It's as if the stolen pulse fed the amputated hand with which one might one day stroke the ribs of a ghost" (109)" he articulates the way that the "heart's thrown voice," testifies to the value of loss. If liminality can be viewed as a "fall" from grace, N's condition insists that it is just as easily an instance of heightened self-awareness. Earlier in the letter N describes his spells as "animistic sculpture": on one level an oxymoron but, for our purposes here, indicative of Mackey's insistence that our apprehension of art—even that which is rendered as commodity by the marketplace or as monument by the body politic—is always already an instance when we ascertain, if only momentarily, spiritual force that assumes physical form. In N's case the "body as open secret" is illegible within the context of medical inquiry but manifest as "between-ness, " able to move between worlds, the embodiment of matter and spirit.

It is while he is recuperating in the hospital that N receives an invitation from an old friend to present at a symposium dealing with "Locus and Locomotivity in Postcontemporary Music." The friend, who teaches at Cal Arts, has been inspired by Joseph Jarman (a member of the Art Ensemble of Chicago) and his notion of the "instrumentalist as sculpture" (111). Such a comment recalls N's description of his condition. In his letter, dated January 6, 1981, N informs the Angel of Dust that the tape he is sending contains music from Chad. The music is played by a wind orchestra composed of ten men, "nine of whom form a counterclockwise-moving circle, at the center of which the tenth player stands" (112). N describes its effect as an "acoustic trace tantamount to a chorus having cast a mounded shadow, a banked, elliptical silhouette" (112). The music offers him "an implied poetics," which he decides to build his talk around. He finds himself drawn to the way the horns in the music "traffic in fractures they otherwise alchemize or mend (113)." And he concludes, "I'm fairly convinced . . . that the counterclockwise rotation asserts a solidarity with the far-flung heavens. Each player, looked at in this way, might be said to stand in for a star" (113).

We need to pay close attention to Mackey's use of wordplay here. To be sure, N's comment can be read as an honest description, but it also denotes a radical departure from Western popular music. N notes that the piece is played at harvest time, which suggests that it functions within the space of a ritual practice that coincides with the Earth's diurnal movement. Hence his comment that each player can be said "to stand in for a star," speaks to the ways that the musician need not be seen simply as one who entertains. Rather, the musician is at once the embodi-ment of the cosmos and the force driving its renewal. Moreover, the ensemble's counterclockwise movement invokes Turner's notion that the liminal moment is outside of time, here, because they travel in opposition to the hands of the clock around a fixed point, varying the "tempo of the music by altering the speed at which the circle revolves." What Mackey proposes here is that symmetricality, a by-product of mechanization and routinization, offers but one way to structure what we know as "the everyday". Rather than attempting to explain the music in a technical language, N's letter moves through a succession of metaphors. He re-turns, for example, to the "thrown voice" as a trope that recalls his ailment but casts the ensemble's music as a metaphor for the ensemble's "loss of alignment," an instance amounting to "a looped or ventriloquized harvesting by which the voice is no sooner flung than fetched" (114). Realizing that the Toupouri wind en-semble is susceptible to "any number of allegorizations," N ruminates on what "thread to pursue" in his composition. Most interesting, then, is his conclusion, when he notes that "a) we can't help but be involved in fabrication, b) a case can be made for leaving loose ends loose, and c) we find ourselves caught in a rickety confession no matter what" (116). N appends to the letter a diagram for the Toupouri wind ensemble's Harvest Song, which once more points to all the ways that Mackey presents alternatives for considering musical discourse: visually, not as notes on a measure but as a mapping of the player's movements during the song's performance.

N's decision to end his correspondence with a visual referent meant to supple-ment an aural text is poignant in light of the visit he receives from the band in the hospital, which is described in a letter dated January 19, 1981. He begins by thank-ing the Angel of Dust for the tape she or he has sent in response to the Toupouri Harvest Song. It contains a recording of Thelonious Monk's "In Walked Bud," a version that features Johnny Griffin on tenor saxophone. Though N is "puzzled for days" at the Angel's response to the tape, he comes to recognize it as a form of sub-tle agreement. Thus when N recalls the cover of Bob Marley's *Exodus* album, which features lions carrying red, gold, and green banners (evocative of the Ethiopian flag), which he suggests "might as well be wings" (118), it reiterates Lor-ca's attempt to create a visual metaphor for duende, which provides Mackey with a way to link musical endeavor to death at a basic level but also articulates the musi-cal composer's dilemma: how to make something new, in light of all that has come before.

Noting that his condition "hasn't radically changed," N finds himself still "subject to invasions or visitations, put upon from all sides by a whirlwind embrace as by an orbiting 'absence' (half muse, half menace)" (118). He describes a dream in which he asks one of his doctors about his chances of dying of a heart attack like his father. The doctor replies, "The chances of a first strike . . . are 400 to 1," at which point N awakens. The next day the band visits and performs a version of "Embraceable You," with Penguin on alto sax, Lambert on tenor, Djamilaa on trumpet, and Aunt Nancy on violin. They proceed to play, but because they are in a hospital they mime the fingerings on their instruments "while making sure no sound [comes] out." Because he finds himself "deprived of ears," N is forced to confirm visually that they are playing "Embraceable You." So intense is his connection to the band's "performance," he states, "I can truthfully say that I *heard* it in fact, so after my own heart was the mixed pace at which they took it (part waltz, part funeral march)" (119). Here Mackey demonstrates that "lack"—represented by the "performed" silence of the band—is rendered as a presence because N's ability to "read" the fingerings makes it so. Thus, he states,

> It was like hearing my lush, longstanding absorption in "absence" at last harvested or come home to roost—a concert or a concept, as I've already said, after my own heart. The mute withholding imposed on the band by the surroundings made for a music fueled with a feeling of loss or lack.
>
> (120)

The passage above clearly demonstrates Mackey's propensity for puns, both aural and visual. Note as well his use of alliteration, indicated by the words "like," "lush," "longstanding," "last," "loss," and "lack" as well as "absorption," "absence," "already," and "after." Though *Bedouin Hornbook* is perhaps best thought of as prose fiction, Mackey's use of poetic devices subverts our propensity to read from "inside" the plot. Rather, part of the novel's "argument" is that reading should incorporate a methodology of error, one that posits acts of perception displaced by misperception that proceed through the reader's impulse to revise their misperception in order to return to the original perception. Mackey's fictional discourse depends, however, on the "trace" left by misperception, and it suggests that if music can leave an "echo" behind—if only in our heads—then prose can do the same thing. That N is "healed" by the band's performance suggests Mackey's investment in music as a force that can reinvigorate not only the aural terrain occupied by global music but the visual as well. And moving through the novel one finds that he embraces acts of dyslexic reversal where he inverts or expands words, leading us from "limb" to "liminal," "word" to "wered," "concert" to "concept," "lifted" to "lofty," and thus makes it possible for the reader to move into a space that is as much about heuretics as hermeneutics.[4] Othering, as Mackey would have it, is a creative act. It is ecological in that it preserves meaning, but, in his predilection for homonyms, puns, and inversions, it is also an intervention on an exigent posture toward language. The result is an imprecision that yields up connections, not necessarily generated at the conscious level, that point to the contingent nature of reading.

2

Bedouin Hornbook constitutes an object of such intense critical interest, in part, because Mackey works throughout the text to privilege issues of space over the temporal concerns so often associated with the novel.[5] Mindful as I am of the proliferation of *spatial* metaphors in literary and cultural studies, I posit the term in this instance because Mackey's novel is so insistent in its effort to undermine music and performance as temporal events.[6] As Ngugi wa Thiong'o has argued, the spaces in which performance occurs (in the form of its material qualities) is to be distinguished from performance space and its relation to audience. In such an instance he points toward the immaterial, "the outline formed by the audience in what is otherwise an open space" (12). Rather than being merely a set of props, lights, and shadows, Thiong'o argues that "these levels and centers acquire their real power in relationship to the audience. The entire space becomes a magnetic field of tensions and conflicts" (12). For him "the real politics of the performance space may well lie in the field of its external relations; its actual or potential conflictual engagements with other shrines of power."

In his assessment of Mackey's work, Michael Franco sees *Bedouin Hornbook* as a primer, "an emerging Alphabet of primary puns acknowledgements Placements and apprenticeships addressed to the *deep Songs* of those Masters who call to us from outside ourselves touching that place of response which the heart knows as recognition" (71). If *Bedouin Hornbook* can be considered a primer, it thus stands as an example of what Jody Berland refers to as "cultural technology." The function of the primer, of course, is to instruct us in how to negotiate a system of codes and to subsequently maneuver in that system. Primers can in no way, Toni Morrison intimates in *The Bluest Eye*, be considered outside the realm of ideology; pedagogical circumstance is nothing if not iterative of what we should know, when it is appropriate to display certain forms of knowledge. As cultural technology, then, the primer is the materialization of power and location, and so I agree with Berland's insistence that "we need to situate cultural forms within the production and reproduction of capitalist spatiality" (39).[7]

Berland conceives spatiality as one of the underlying assumptions in a world characterized by difference sustained through hegemonic force. However, I want to suggest that African American literature offers any number of examples of a spatialized subject. What makes this important is the way spatiality can contain acts of social critique even as its collisions with temporality generate a friction we cannot ignore. Hence we can regard poems like Michael Harper's "Here Where Coltrane Is" and Paul Laurence Dunbar's "When Malindy Sings" as examples where spatial politics can reimagine what it means to be "othered." In the latter we have a persona intent on marking the differences between music rendered by "lines an' dots" and that which is the product of "genuine" feeling. Further, it moves the speaker into a space where she can discriminate between Malindy's voice and the sounds produced by an "edicated band," as if the hierarchies produced by white supremacy are rendered inert. Though the title of the poem suggests that its subject is temporal, that is, these things happen *when* Malindy sings, I want to argue that the poem's subversiveness arises in Dunbar's insistence that African American expressive culture is evocative of an authority powerful enough to intervene on what the plantation recognizes as the "everyday." Unlike Dunbar's poem, which moves forward from the sound of the human voice, Harper's poem places at its center the act of playing John Coltrane's "Alabama" on a record player. At the outset the poem's persona understands that "soul" and "race" are "private dominions" and thereby open to individual interpretation, making them terms evincing whimsicality as easily as difference. However, playing Coltrane's "Alabama," marks the creation of a liminal space, beset on one side by the discursive properties of race, but on the other by the maintenance of kinship ties, a larger, encompassing form of human intimacy. This is not to suggest that either of these poems can be regarded as necessarily historical but rather that they engage in the kind of "othering" Mackey describes above. Thus, even as both poems reference instances of social othering—in the Dunbar poem the plantation, in the Harper poem the Birmingham bombing—they also insist that people occupying subaltern status can invent spaces in which they have autonomy and subjectivity. The "when" and the "here" in the poems are not, as we might assume, references to purely temporal locations. Rather they gesture toward spatial coordinates that denote the carnivalesque—instances where the finite nature of both scenarios serves nonetheless to highlight reversals of hierarchical arrangements, pointing to what Morrison scholar Marilyn Sanders McKenzie refers to as a "third space."

Interestingly, that "third space" takes a form that leads Mackey's N to assert a desire for undifferentiation, a recombinant attitude. In the first letter from N to the Angel of Dust (that appears under the title "Song of the Andoumboulou: 6" and has no date) N asserts:

> We not only can but should speak of "loss" or, to avoid, quotation marks notwithstanding, any such inkling of self-pity, speak of *absence* as unavoidably *an inherence in the texture of things* (dreamseed, habitual cloth). You really do seem to believe in, to hold out for some first or final gist underlying it all, but my preoccupation with origins and ends is exactly that: a pre- (equally post-, I suppose) occupation. (50; MY EMPHASIS)

The turn of language here invokes artistic othering. The "texture of things" cannot, in N's view, be divorced from absence. If it seems, however, that I am positing *Bedouin Hornbook* as a text in which liminality is a central concern, let me suggest that this concern is reflected elsewhere, in other texts by African American writers, in a variety of genres. Having noted this, it important to point out that Mackey's literary career crystallizes in the mid-eighties as a poet and cultural critic. Hence we could easily regard N as Mackey's literary alter ego or we could propose that N is an alternative to the realist (and racialist) subject. As such, we could argue that N is the embodiment of the cultural anxiety associated with the idea of nomenclature; this is especially credible due to the fact that so many of his letters evince a preoccupation with acts of naming. In light of this, however, consider Mackey's propensity to utilize scholarly texts to clarify N's thinking. In a letter dated October 14, 1980, N quotes the musicologist Victor Zuckerkandl from his book *Sound and Symbol*. Zuckerkandl's words help to clarify N's artistic credenda:

> The space experience of eye and hand is basically an experience of places and distinctions between places. The ear, on the other hand, knows space only as an undivided whole; of places and distinctions between places it knows nothing. The space we hear is a space without places.
>
> (82; MY EMPHASIS)

N's use of Zuckerkandl's scholarship serves to suggest that even as he goes about citing song titles, trying to postulate descriptive language for what he hopes to accomplish as a musician and a composer, he is likewise concerned with *erasing* distinctions, evincing an *othering* of music's visual content. This raises questions about form, particularly in light of Mackey's decision to render *Bedouin Hornbook* as a one-sided correspondence. Do N's acts of othering also work to defamiliarize our relationship to music? Does his propensity to "narrativize" the band's performances somehow let us off the hook in terms of understanding how difficult it is to *play* music? And, finally, does the exchange between he and the Angel of Dust operate on such an intimate level that we cannot ascertain the "crux" of their intellectual sparring?

The epistolary form makes these questions just as important for us as they are for N and the Angel of Dust. And as we move from one letter to the next, we forget that we are looking at private correspondence that the novel portrays as public. Indeed, the reader is placed in the position of "reading over the shoulder" of the Angel of Dust." Hence, as the Angel of Dust reads N's writing the narrative presses forward,[8] producing a narrative doubling where the Angel of Dust becomes a doppelganger for the reader.

This doubling is manifested in *Bedouin Hornbook* in two ways. First, the novel's epistolary discourse is opened up by N's constant use of musical examples (often complete with the album label and number). He embeds aurality into the text and thus shapes our reading of it because we can listen to Shepp or Coltrane or Bob Marley or Al Green and essentially share (if only tenuously) the aural kinship he shares with the Angel of Dust. As an aural text *Bedouin Hornbook* forces the reader to struggle with the referential field N's letters create and sustain. For example, after receiving a tape from the Angel of Dust, N reports, "It's as though we shared a single set of ears" (138). And then he continues:

> It's not only that I'd already heard the piece you sent (I have the record it's on in fact), but it's the very cut I like the most on the album and, to my hearing, one of the most awesome things Wayne's ever done. I especially like the way the soprano integrates itself into all that percussion (which is exactly, I realize, why you sent it). (138)

Second, then, is that N points up the gap between the actual reader and the implied reader of this text because "we" are given credit for prescience that we cannot legitimately claim even if we are familiar with Wayne Shorter's *Super Nova* and his particular version of "Dindi." In this instance knowing the song—I think most often of versions done by Sarah Vaughan and John Lucien—will not necessarily help us; not knowing Shorter's version means that we cannot resist sliding into a space where Mackey is signifying on us. Further, the epistolary form mocks the fact that even if we know the song we cannot claim space within the Angel of Dust's intent. Thus Mackey calls our attention to the gap formed between our readerly desire to understand, to empathize with N's writing and that possessed by the Angel of Dust. The next letter from N, dated two days later, suggests that he moves their "dialogue" in another direction, one that both encompasses and evacuates the territory engaged in the previous letter.

Mackey drives home the ways that temporality is beset by spatiality (and perhaps vice versa) by dramatizing the anxieties generated when New Critical techniques of interpretation are called into question. In a particularly funny moment The Mystic Horn Society decides "it [is] time to confront [its] critics face to face." They send out invitations and "reserve some space down at Rhino Records." Though N warns us that he writes "not so much to play Proust" as to tell the Angel of Dust about the press conference, it is clear that Mackey wants to suggest the ways spatiality and temporality function in proximity, indicated by his use of Rhino Records, a label that has developed a niche market by reissuing recordings that have been out of print, a technologically biased enterprise that markets the aural legacy of the past, producing records that serve as a "remembrance of things past." The proceedings open with a local radio personality declaring that though he is "somewhat uninformed on recent developments in music the trouble he has with [the band's] compositions is their tendency to . . . go off on tangents," insisting that the music not "be made easier exactly, 'just more centered somehow.'"

The radio personality's remarks elicit applause from "three people back towards the budget classical section," which suggests the ways that his comments can be located within the realm of Eurocentrism and thus reveals them to be theoretically suspect. Lambert, who plays tenor and alto sax, replies "that all the talk of being 'more centered' [is] just that, talk." And, as N relates, Lambert goes on to argue that

> he wasn't sure anyone had anything more than the mere word "center," that it didn't simply name something one doesn't have and thus disguises a swarm of untested assumptions about. Then he shifted his argument a bit, saying that if our music does have a center, as he could argue it indeed does, how would someone who admits being "somewhat uninformed" recognize it. (11)

Applause for Lambert's remarks come from the folk imports section of the store after he concludes that the dj is asking for "nothing if not an easier job, that your work be done by someone else, that our music abandon its center and shuffle over to yours" (11). What makes this such an effective set piece is the way that Mackey essentially reproduces the debate that surrounded recordings like John Coltrane's *Interstellar Space*. At root the talk about making the music "more centered" is ultimately about the ability to listen to the Mystic Horn Society and achieve some measure of closure with regard to the "meaning" in their music.

A woman N describes as a "fortyish, not bad looking lady from one of the neighborhood weeklies," with a "lazy way of speaking," wonders how the band can "place the music within the context of the *whole* culture, rather than just African, Asian, and generally Third World reference(12)." Aunt Nancy's response (note how close the name is to Ananse) reveals humanism's blind spots when she states, "All I can say . . . is that the culture you're calling 'whole' has yet to assume itself to be so except at the expense of a whole lot of other folks, except by presuming that what they were up to could be ignored at no great loss" (12). This time the applause comes from "some people over near the reggae bin," and it indicates, once more, both the quality of discourse in the so-called culture wars as well as the locations from which countercritiques such as Aunt Nancy's emanate. But what is also interesting is that Mackey foreshadows the visual and homonymic punning we see in later sections of the novel, implying that "whole culture" as the woman constructs is revealed by Aunt Nancy to be a "hole culture," one that excludes that which it finds either disruptive or distasteful, an instance of social othering.

The press conference plays out the issues surrounding canonicity. The scene reveals the struggles to revise the canon to be more than the correction of literary history gone awry. The project of canon reform or, as one might have it, canon displacement, is informed by spatiality. Even though the band's decision to "confront [their] critics face to face" does not center necessarily around records, we are nonetheless invited to consider—through Mackey's act of calling our attention to the variety of responses from different sections of the record store—that music, no less than literature, is organized into categories that are meant to fix notions of the "appropriate" and the "popular" and invoke responses from specific locations within geopolitical space.[9]

This points at some *Bedouin Hornbook*'s larger concerns with space, as it takes the form of "shrunken" or "diminished" or "compromised" spaces, the kinds of settings that have long been objects of concern in African American expressive culture. Thinking about jazz music as "America's Classical music," while a novel idea, ultimately serves to plane off the rough hewn edges produced by a jazz historiography which attends to the conditions under which musicians had to work, the circumstances—negative and positive—which affect their playing. As Mackey's letters between N and the Angel of Dust indicate, the wrangling about issues of origin and closure are ultimately counterproductive since they rest so often on essentialized notions of identity. Thus, in attempting to produce master narratives that are both "historically accurate," "inclusive," and "representative," Mackey suggests, we merely reproduce cultural technologies whose main drawback is that they do not orient us to break down the categorical barriers used to create safe havens for those economic and political concerns that thrive by adhering to simple binaries.

Mackey's novel, with its multiple references to music from all over the world, culled from a variety of musical settings ranging from the popular to the sacred, the obscure to the banal, suggests that aurality of the sort we find in *Bedouin Hornbook* is, as Victor Turner suggested in his study of Ndembu rituals, recombinatory. In other words, the novel takes seriously liminal space as a place where barriers collapse, where closure is anathema.

3

In a letter dated October 13, 1980, N relates his feelings about a solo played by saxophonist Pharoah Sanders during a version of John Coltrane's "My Favorite Things," which can be found on his *Coltrane Live at the Village Vanguard* album.

Though he has lots to say about the solo, what I find most intriguing about his remarks is N's observation regarding Sanders's ability to "make a virtue of imprecision(79)." Earlier in the letter N describes a dream in which he finds himself a poet, giving a reading in a large domed arena. "Instead of reading poems, though," he states, "what I did was sing an extended version of 'Someone to Watch Over Me'—Arthur Prysock's version, which I was quite taken with while in my teens" (78). When he reaches his favorite line in the song, however, N finds that his voice "breaks," as if he is entering puberty. Try as he might, he cannot finish the song. When he awakes N realizes that the dream has a cautionary theme, aimed at his aspirations as a composer:

> Even as the dream was still in progress I knew I was being warned against a threat of excess, that I was being warned against sentimentality as a possible lapse into (to use a word you seem to like so much) overdetermination. I was being accused of stacking the cards or gilding the lily or however else one might want to put it. I awoke to the even more radical realization that its not enough that a composer skillfully covers his tracks, that he erase the echo of "imposition" composition can't help but be haunted by. (78–79)

Realizing that to do so "only makes matters worse," N concludes that a composer must find a way "to invest in the ever so slight suggestion of 'compost,'" which he derives from the word "composer." The dream contains a number of motifs carried through in the succeeding pages. First, it establishes the relationship that inheres between authorship and ventriloquism. Second, it suggests that the "authorial gloss" composers spin around their compositions as a way to assert their "originality" is a delusion; it is an act of overdetermination in its insistence that creativity and purity are coincidental. As the failed ventriloquism motif of the dream suggests, other voices impose themselves upon the authorial moment. Which means that the third piece of the dream's cautionary aspect is that N's broken "voice" reveals the process of song-making to be an exercise in the imperfect. As a composer, N is "trying [following the example of John Coltrane] to work out a kind of writing that will allow for more plasticity, more viability, more room for improvisation in the statement of the melody itself" (78).[10]

As *Bedouin Hornbook* conceptualizes it, composition has a great deal to do with collaborations with the dead, what N refers to as "composting." Thus compos[t]ers are working to "maneuver their basic materials into a textual heap from which other texts can grow." It is important to recognize, then, that the correspondence between N and the Angel of Dust centers on N's "compositions." This forces us to ponder the significance of Mackey's decision to create a respondent called the Angel of Dust. In keeping with the notion of "composting," the Angel of Dust might suggest refuse, remains, or, in fact, decomposition. Indeed, the juxtaposition of immortality and virtue (i.e., an angel) and decomposition once more points to Mackey's deep concern with the ways spatiality can trump temporality, which leads N to remark, in the novel's second letter, "it all reduces to waste" (7). Here, "dust" with its potential reference to death and obsolescence likewise suggests that the idea of "originality" is "as much a myth as the idea of permanence." Viewed in a spatial context, originality and permanence are rhetorical devices that serve to obscure the intersubjectivity underlying acts of creation.

The implication I wish to draw attention to is that composers work within the context of language, which is always already a *social* space. As Kathleen Kirby has argued, "Language . . . can be described as a loose unrealized network (langue) organized by relative distances, proximities, connections, and chasms between terms" (23). Thus, when Coltrane seeks to integrate "more plasticity" and "more room for improvisation," he is not interested in a form of writing that privileges "originality." Rather, he wants to give himself (and the musicians that play with him) greater access to whatever materials they wish to bring to bear on the performative act. But, as N's lingering preoccupation with duende supposes, *writing*, as the deployment of language, is about transversing the "distances, proximities, connections, and chasms" that separate one subject from another as well as those that separate the living and the dead.

N takes this seriously enough to include for our perusal a number of his compositions. What is striking, however, is that rather than appearing in the form of musical notation, each of the compositions is rendered in the form of narrative. Further, N has no qualms about radical revision. Thus the piece he plans to present at the "Locus and Locomotivity" symposium, entitled, "The Creaking of the Word," goes through a number of permutations. In the first version, which N describes as a "metalecture," we find Mackey distorting the distinction between interior and exterior, performer and audience, in addition to the epistemological assumptions that accompany the act of conveying information in the lecture format. Thus, the "metalecture" begins with Jarred Bottle, N's compositional alter ego, stepping up to the podium at the symposium. In the revised "composition," however, we find the piece opening with the words "Djamilaa stood at the window." In what N now refers to as "an after-the-fact lecture/libretto," we find that Djamilaa has supplanted Jarred Bottle as the "protagonist" of the piece. Moreover, it has moved from "metalecture," a clear act of acknowledging the boundaries between lecture and performance even as it flouts them, to "lecture/libretto," which means that N has elided the distance between the lecture's epistemological project and its operatic pretensions. In keeping with the symposium's concern with "locus and locomotivity," N's title for his composition, "The Creaking of the Word," is prescient. For here we can think of all the ways "creaking" can devolve, via an act of misreading, or Freudian slip, into "cracking" or "croaking," which takes us from obsolescence to dissolution or from motion (creaking representing the sound made when someone walks, say, over an old floor) to sound or self-propulsion to death.

Ultimately, the difference between the two lectures is not really a difference so much as an intensification. . N's "revision" merely incorporates the concerns of the metalecture and places them within the larger frame of the after-the-fact lecture/libretto. Hence, Djamilaa's suspicion that a "band of aliases ha[s] blown into town, with the band having changed its name from Jarred Bottle to Flaunted Fifth, is linked to the letter she receives from DB (Djarred Bottle) informing her that he is slated to give a lecture on the blues at a symposium at Cal Arts. In the original Jarred Bottle feels himself caught up on an asymptotic slope, ruminates on the metaphysics of the Gap Band's hit "I Can't Get Over You," concluding that the song is "a shorthand treatise whose namesake brooding had to do with an ontic, unbridgeable distance, a cosmogonic, uncrossable gap" (149), and travels through an odd array of puns, linguistic echoes, catchphrases, and song titles, ending with the words "I'm here" as his hands rap on the lectern. At the end of the revision Djamilaa is listening to a Walkman with the volume up so loud that she cannot hear the phone ringing in her apartment; it turns out to be Flaunted Fifth (aka Jarred Bottle), who has been picked up for "public exposure." She never hears the phone, which rings "like an endlessly repeated note on a scratched record, the opening note of a blocked opera she and Flaunted Fifth would sing their hearts in for days."

Rather than trying to "interpret" Mackey's prose, I want to suggest that the elisions and slippages in both versions are meant to spur readers to reverie and wordplay, to push them toward a heuretic "solution" rather than a hermeneutical one. And we are left with invention because Mackey destabilizes the epistemological assumptions till the "interiority" that a lecture might possess is "emptied" of content. All we know is that the Angel of Dust receives a letter, dated June 17, 1981, that thanks her for the "flattering letter," which we can infer contains a positive response to N's composition/performance. Hence, in a move that reminds us of the "endless improvisation" in jazz, N's "success" at the symposium has already begun to shift its form, moving from presentation to an "outline, a skeletal draft of a possible opera," one that demonstrates that N "really has the future in mind."

We are left with the question, then, what does a text like *Bedouin Hornbook* accomplish? Rather than answer in any sort of definitive fashion, let me point to two moments earlier in the text that might help us [re]gain our bearings. After the band's press conference, Lambert, the band's alto and tenor player, is invited to give a solo concert. Instead of a concert, he presents a piece called "Eventual Elegy" whose highlight is the disassembly and reassembly of a saxophone, which is conducted by a woman wearing Red Wing boots and overalls, referred to as Polyhymnia. Lambert himself never appears on stage. Instead, he calls from in front of a Kentucky Fried Chicken restaurant across the street from the theater and proceeds to deliver a monologue as Polyhymnia works. Polyhymnia is putting the "very last turn on the very last screw" just as Lambert quotes the words of an exslave from the Georgia Sea Islands, "Notes is good enough for you people, but us likes a mixtery" (39). When he delivers the very last word of his monologue, *mixtery*, the performance ends.

Compare this to another moment, when the band is walking on Sutter Street in San Francisco. There Lambert notices some words scribbled in pencil on the wall of a boarded up store. They read, "Mr Slick and Mr. Brother are one of the two most baddest dude in town, and Sutter Street." Penguin comments on the graffitti's "enabling confusion concerning the singular and the plural" and "its vacillations between the claims of the one and the counterclaims of the other." Aunt Nancy dismisses Penguin's interpretation as "outmoded" and "condescending" and attributes the words to "bad schooling." Noticing that a crowd has gathered around the band and concerned about the mutterings from the crowd that that they are engaged in nothing more than "elitist mystification," N nonetheless proceeds to offer his analysis, which reads the words "most baddest" as "a novel, rule-abandoning technique for intensification" (27).

Lambert's concert is a clear instance of heuretics at work; the "concert" is not a musical performance so much as an attempt to recontextualize music. The disassembly and reassembly of the saxophone is certainly Mackey's way of sending up what it means to "deconstruct" a text, but it is also a creative act because it enacts the transformation of the saxophone from an instrument designed for European classical music, which becomes an important piece in marching bands, to an instrument associated with jazz music. Conversely, the band's venture into hermeneutics is an instance in which the paradox of the graffiti is juxtaposed by the parataxis of interpretation, the lateral arrangement of "readings" in a democratic sequence. Ultimately, then, one "interpretation" is as good as the next, a condition often obscured by our propensity to see interpretation and representation as discrete enterprises.

But here it might be useful to consider the apocryphal story about Louis Armstrong's famous reply to a request (posed by a socialite) to define jazz. Armstrong's retort, "Lady, if ya gotta ask what it is, you'll never know" is instructive because, as Michael Jarrett asserts, it suggests that "jazz prefers to speak for itself." However, Armstrong may not have been trying to be as dismissive as we might presume. Rather, he may have been inviting the socialite to generate her own definition. While this might constitute a recipe for disaster, it also has the potential to be an act of "othering." What this means for those of us who work in literary studies, where our purpose is, ostensibly, to "interpret, categorize, and map" the numerous attempts to represent a viable African American subject, is that we might abandon—or at the very least recontextualize, make space for—what Jarrett refers to as a heuretical project that could function alongside the hermeneutical project that dominates, is privileged, in the teaching of literature. In other words, rather than viewing African American literary texts as figurations of African American subjectivity, as acts of *embodiment* located on a purely temporal grid, we might also use them as opportunities to *improvise on* what it means to occupy such a space. Let me insinuate that this essay is a "vamp," a cyclical progression where I'm either improvising or—to carry the definition in another direction—engaged in the act of refurbishment. If *Bedouin Hornbook* is an important text, it might be because of the way that it equates music with the "book of the dead" and concludes that nothing is ever lost. If, as N (echoing Sun Ra) suggests, "space is the place," then it must be that the best thing for us to do in the classroom is to reconsider our propensity to see literary texts as *acts* of voice and rather see them as the *ax* of voice. In so doing we might find ourselves, like Tod Clifton's puppet, Ellison's narrator, and the Angel of Dust, dancing to a music of the excluded middle on the mothership of verb.

1. Edward Hirsch, "A Mysterious Power," *The Demon and the Angel* (New York: Harcourt, 2002), p. 10.

2. In an attempt to distinguish the Mystic Horn Society from other jazz musicians, Mackey quotes from an interview with the members of the eighties fusion group Spyro-Gyra, who announce (with what seems to be a total lack of irony), "It's not intellectually intensive. . . . We dance around and smile. We feel good. We're not pensive black men who have suffered. We're happy white kids. We don't have a heavy cosmic message that we're trying to get across" (64). Mackey's use of the quote not only suggests that *Bedouin Hornbook* is an example of fictional bricolage, but it also points to the ways that jazz continues to be a music that exists under the weight of racial inflection. However, the growth of the "smooth jazz" format in radio markets across the country intimates the ways in which the marketplace can render the familiar as the strange. *Bedouin Hornbook*. All further references to the text will appear parenthetically.

3. Turner cites Goldwasser when she notes:

   Antistructure is represented here by Carnival, and is defined as a transitional Phase in which differences of (pre-Carnival) status are annulled, with the aim of creating among the participants a relationship of communitas. Communitas is the domain of equality, where all are placed without distinction on an identical level of social evaluation, but the equivalence which is established among them has a ritual character. In *communitas* we find an inversion of the structured situations of everyday reality marked by routinization and the conferment of structural status. The status system and communitas—or structure and antistructure—confront one as two homologous series in opposition.

   In an epiphany that strikes me as relevant here, I recall that my students often refer to a party as a "flow." Equally striking is their propensity to use it as both noun and verb. Hence we can argue that notions of the carnivalesque are to be found in the realm of everyday expression.

4. In his book *Heuretics* Gregory Ulmer argues that "'heuretics' . . . functions at the same level of generality as 'hermeneutics.'" In his view, heuretics "contributes to what Barthes referred to as 'the return of the poetician'—one who is concerned with how a work is made. This concern does not stop with analysis or comparative scholarship but conducts such scholarship in preparation for the design of a rhetoric/poetics leading to the production of new work" (4).

5. Here I am thinking about the insistence so often put forward regarding the novel's purpose as an artistic medium whose preeminent purpose is to highlight change. Though one could argue just as easily that the novel is a fictional vehicle used to explore issues of identity, what becomes clear is that it is most often thought of as cultural technology whose purposes are located in a temporal context.

6. As Kathleen Kirby, in "Thinking Through the Boundary," suggests, the "language of space is everywhere in theory today," And she continues:

   It "underwrites" current critical discussion: ideas about space form a kind of philosophical palimpsest for descriptions of politics, epistemology, and subjectivity; they are theory's substrate or foundation, upon which the whole critical edifice stands; but they provide a kind of "guarantee," a solid referent outside language to which the intended line of argument can refer for stability, credibility, substantiality. At the same time, the language of space "overwrites" critical arguments, appearing as mere ornamentation or as dispensable rhetorical device. But even in such "supplemental" uses of spatial language, the idea of space to a degree "overdetermines" (1).

7. As a piece of cultural technology, Mackey's novel must be read as a strategic enterprise where, as Harryette Mullen has suggested, "the historical fact of slavery is associated explicitly or implicitly with constraints on freedom of the contemporary African American artist" (37).

8. As Elizabeth Campbell has observed, the epistolary novel revolves around a set of conventions where "the writing itself is action and plot, action and plot which refuse the kind of closure informing other narratives" (333). She continues: "Epistolary writing is subjective and emotional; it reaches out as it looks inward, opening up and presenting a consciousness to a specific sympathetic listener. While it appears to be stream-of-consciousness writing, the reader of the epistolary novel is aware that within its boundaries there is another reader" (336).

9. As Jody Berland, in "Angels Dancing," suggests, with her insistence that we think of books and recordings as cultural technology rather than mere diachronic events, "such conditions of power and location are materialized not only in the reception of these stories, but in their production itself" (40).

10. In *Drifting on a Read* Jarrett argues that musical composition is analogous to digging in a pile of manure; in so doing he enacts a radical break from the kinds of categorical thinking undergirding the critical project by asserting that writers of music, no less than writers of theory are, as N supposes, composters. Hence, Jarrett observes, "Composting, like deconstruction, is the discourse equivalent to reversing the direction of sublation (the lifting up of the 'sensible' into the conceptual)." And he continues:

> For example, when N. detects the ever-so-slight whiff of "compost" in the word "compose," he has, in fact, begun the work of returning composition, a master trope of Western thought, to the bodily image (or alloseme) from which the concept (or philosopheme) grew. What distinguishes composting from deconstruction, then, is mainly a matter of connotation. Composting is a way to picture in one word both aspects of grammatology. (20)

WORKS CITED

Berland, Jody. "Angels Dancing: Cultural Technologies and the Production of Space." *Cultural Studies*. Lawrence Grossberg, Cary Nelson, Paula A. Treichler, eds. New York: Routledge, 1992. pp. 38–55.

——— "Radio Space and Industrial Time: Music Formats, Local Narratives, and Technological Mediation." *Popular Music,* April 1990, pp. 179–92.

Campbell, Elizabeth. "Re-visions, Re-flections, Re-creations: Epistolarity in Novels by Contemporary Women." *Twentieth Century Literature* 41.3 (Fall 1995): 332–48.

Donahue, Joseph. "Sprung Polity: On Nathaniel Mackey's Recent Work." *Talisman* 9 (Fall 1992): 62–65.

Ellison, Ralph. "The Charlie Christian Story." *Shadow and Act.* New York: Vintage, 1964; rpt. 1972. pp. 233–40.

Foster, Edward. "An Interview with Nathaniel Mackey." *Talisman* 9 (Fall 1992), pp. 48–61.

Fabrijancic, Tony. "Space and Power: Nineteenth-Century Urban Practice and Gibson's Cyberworld." *Mosaic* 32.1 (March 1999), pp. 105–30.

Franco, Michael. "Bedouin Hornbook: 'You should have heard me in the dream.'" *Talisman* 9 (Fall, 1992), pp. 71–73.

Funkhouser, Christopher. "An Interview with Nathaniel Mackey." *Callaloo* 18.2 (Spring 1995), pp. 321–34.

Jarrett, Michael. *Drifting on a Read: Jazz as a Model for Writing.* Binghamton: State University of New York Press, 1999.

Kirby, Kathleen M. *Indifferent Boundaries: Spatial Concepts of Human Subjectivity.* New York: Guilford, 1996.

―――― "Thinking Through the Boundary: The Politics of Location, Subjects, and Space." *Boundary 2* (Summer 1993): 173–89.

Lefebvre, Henri. *The Production of Space.* Trans. Donald Nicholson-Smith. Oxford: Blackwell, 1974; rpt. 1991.

Libby, Anthony. "Conceptual Space: The Politics of Modernism." *Chicago Review* (Spring 1984), pp. 11–26.

Mackey, Nathaniel. *Bedouin Hornbook.* Charlottesville: University of Virginia Press, 1986.

―――― *Discrepant Engagement: Dissonance, Cross-Culturality, and Experimental Writing.* Tuscaloosa: University of Alabama, 1993.

―――― *Eroding Witness.* Urbana: University of Illinois Press, 1985.

―――― *School of Udhra.* San Francisco: City Lights, 1993.

―――― *Whatsaid Sarif.* San Francisco: City Lights, 1998.

Mobilio, Albert. "On Mackey's *Bedouin Hornbook:* Hearing Voices." *Talisman* 9 (Fall 1992), pp. 69–70.

Mullen, Harryette. "Phantom Pain: Nathaniel Mackey's *Bedouin Hornbook.*" *Talisman* 9 (Fall 1992), pp. 37–43.

Naylor, Paul. *Poetic Investigations: Singing the Holes in History.* Evanston: Northwestern University Press, 1999.

O'Leary, Peter. "An Interview with Nathaniel Mackey." *Chicago Review* (Winter 1987), pp. 30–46.

Thiong'o, Ngugi wa. "Enactments of Power: The Politics of Performance Space." *Drama Review* 41.3 (Fall 1997), pp. 11–30.

Turner, Victor. *The Anthropology of Performance.* New York: PAJ, 1988.

―――― *The Ritual Process: Structure and Antistructure.* Hawthorne, N.Y.: Aldine de Gruyter, 1969; rpt. 1995.

Ulmer, Gregory L. *Heuretics: The Logic of Invention.* Baltimore: Johns Hopkins University Press, 1994.

Wright, Jay. "The Abstract of Knowledge/The First Test." *The Selected Poems of Jay Wright.* Princeton: Princeton University Press, 1987. pp. 179–89.

VIJAY IYER

Exploding the Narrative in Jazz Improvisation

Tell a story. This oft-repeated directive for an improvised solo has become a cliché of jazz musicology. Its validity is unarguable, having been restated in various forms by countless artists from Charlie Parker to Cecil Taylor. But we seem to lack the analytical tools to describe in detail how, under what circumstances, or indeed whether this wordless spinning of yarns even *could* happen, let alone what the content might be. In the constellations of jazz lore, the storytelling imperative seems to hang there, fixed in the firmament, along with "If you have to ask, you'll never know" and other hip tautologies.

In a renowned piece of jazz musicology, Gunther Schuller asserted that the musical "coherence" of a jazz solo—present, he claimed, only in the work of figures such as Louis Armstrong, Coleman Hawkins, and Charlie Parker—could be proven using the standard "reduction" tools of Western music analysis.[1] Brian Harker echoes this sentiment, stating that the coherence of an Armstrong improvisation amounts to a kind of "story."[2] For Harker the hallmarks of this story seem to include demonstrable relationships among musical phrases (a trait that seems more reminiscent of verse than narrative) and the gradual build to a climax. But perhaps we can view purely musical coherence as just one facet of a larger, richer, and more complex narrative structure.

George Lewis furnishes a provocative description of African American improvised music as the encoded exchange of personal narratives.[3] Some guiding questions then become: What is the nature of these exchanged narratives, and how are they rendered musically? In the 1990s a wave of important scholarship on African American music addressed some of the ways in which meaning is generated in the course of jazz improvisation.[4] Much of this work focuses on the crucial role of interactivity and group interplay in the dialogical construction of multiplicities of meaning. Here one draws on a notion of communication as process, as a collective activity that harmonizes individuals rather than a telegraphic model of communication as mere transmission of literal, verbal meanings. For example, the musical notion of antiphony, or call and response, can function as a kind of communication, and nothing need be "said" at the literal level to make it so. What definitely *is* happening is that the interactive format, process, and feeling of conversational engagement are enacted by the musicians. In a context like jazz the presence of this kind of dialogical process is constant throughout a performance, as *sustained antiphony*.

But musical dialogue forms only part of the whole story. In the outtakes to John Coltrane's "Giant Steps," there emerges a revealing, poignant moment of candor among the musicians.[5] While rehearsing the precipitously difficult piece in the studio, John Coltrane can be heard saying to his struggling colleagues, "I don't think I'm gonna improve this, you know . . . I ain't goin be sayin nothin, (I goin do) tryin just, makin the *changes*, I ain't goin be, tellin no *story*. . . Like . . . tellin them *black* stories." Amidst the confounded mumbles of assent from his bandmates, one colleague rejoins, "Shoot. Really, you make the changes, *that*'ll tell 'em a story." Surprised by this idea, Coltrane responds, "You think the changes're the story!" Overlapping him, a second bandmate riffs, "(Right) . . . that'll change *all* the stories (up)." His voice cracking with laughter, Coltrane admits, "I don't want to tell no lies (on 'em)." After a group laugh, the second colleague trails off in a sort of denouement, "(The) changes *themselves* is *some* kind of story (man I'm tellin you)."[6]

These few seconds of banter could yield a symposium's worth of exegesis; the antiphonal, multilayered, Signifyin(g) exchange suggests striking notions of how musical stories can be told. "Making the changes"—i.e., negotiating the harmonic maze that forms the piece's improvisational structure—forms just one facet of the real-time construction of an improvised statement in this idiom. A list of other conventional ingredients might include conveying a steady rhythmic momentum ("swinging"), displaying a strong and personal timbre, constructing original melodic phrases, and amassing these phrases into a compelling "whole." From his concern that he isn't "tellin' no story," it is easy to suppose that Coltrane was thinking along these lines, trying to create a "coherent," Schulleresque narrative arc over the scope of a given saxophone solo. However, his hint at larger concerns of cultural connection ("tellin' them black stories") suggests that his intentions transcend the étudelike nature of this clever harmonic progression, and even rise above this compositional idea of coherence. With these four words he seems to reach for musical statements in which no less than his whole community could hear its inexhaustible narrative multiplicity reflected. Indeed, his dogged pursuit of such an ideal is documented over the course of dozens of takes.

Moreover, his is a quest for veracity: "I don't want to tell no lies on 'em." One might wonder what notes, chords, and rhythms have to do with evaluations of truth, and one might be tempted to interpret the laughter that this comment elicits as an affirmation of the absurdity of this idea. But in fact this construction is common usage among jazz musicians, and the group outburst just might be a laugh of assent. Just weeks ago I heard a fellow musician criticize a bandmate for "telling lies" onstage; according to my colleague, his bandmate was playing what he thought their bandleader wanted to hear instead of following the general directive to make his own statement. For Coltrane, telling musical lies might have meant playing in an overly self-conscious, premeditated, or constructed fashion that rang false to his ears. This comment suggests that Coltrane strives to create an authentic representation of his community through telling his story as truthfully as he can. This trope of truthfulness has broad implications for the politics of authenticity and its role in the narrativity of black music; there is a clear connection between "telling your story" and "keeping it real."

My main interest in Coltrane's extemporaneous exchange with his quartet lies in his sideman's observation, "Really, you make the changes, *that*'ll tell 'em a story." Perhaps Coltrane's bandmate means to locate the kind of narrativity his leader seeks not only at the level of a philosophical imperative placed "on" the music but also precisely "in" the moment-to-moment act of making the changes. The sheer fact of Coltrane's maintenance of his musical balance in the face of such arduous challenges tells a compelling, even richly symbolic story. For what one hears is necessarily the result of much effort, time, and process—in short, of *labor* (meant with all of this word's attendant resonances).

This notion really does "change all the stories up": it implies a shift in emphasis from top-down notions of overarching coherence to bottom-up views of narrativity *emerging* from the minute laborious acts that make up musical activity. And given its focus on these acts and the rigors that they presuppose, the comment could also be read as a celebration of the athletics of black musical performance (or perhaps the performativity of black musical athletics). An improvisor is engaged in a kind of highly disciplined physical activity, of which we only hear the sonic result. If we embrace this fact, we are led to consider the storytelling implications of this physical labor that we hear as music; surely the rigors of this embodied process tell "*some* kind of story."

In this vein, I would like to discuss what I call *traces of embodiment* in African-American music, and suggest what we might learn from them: how musical bodies tell us stories. I propose that the story that an improvisor tells does not unfold merely in the overall form of a "coherent" solo, nor simply in antiphonal structures, but also in the microscopic musical details, as well as in the inherent structure of the performance itself. The story dwells not just in one solo at a time, but also in a single note, and equally in an entire lifetime of improvisations. In short, the story is revealed not as a simple linear narrative, but as a fractured, exploded one. It is what we take to be the shifting, multiple, continually reconstructed subjectivities of the improvisors, encoded in a diverse variety of sonic symbols, occurring at different levels and subject to different stylistic controls. Taking a similarly exploded form, this paper may seem fragmented. Indeed it must be, because it is only through this process of examining the puzzling shards of these exploded narratives that we may reveal a mosaic with a discernible underlying pattern.

Hearing the Body

In my previous work I develop the claim that music perception and cognition are embodied, situated activities.[7] This means that they depend crucially on the physical constraints and enablings of our bodies and also on the ecological and sociocultural environment in which our music listening and producing capacities come into being. I argue that rhythm perception and production involve a complex, whole-body experience and that much of the musical structure found in rhythm-based music incorporates an awareness of the embodied, situated role of the participant. I show that certain kinds of rhythmic expression in African-derived music are directly related to the multiple roles of the body in making music and to certain cultural aesthetics that privilege this role.

Recent neurological studies have affirmed the cognitive role of body motion in music perception and production. According to these researchers, a perceived rhythmic pulse is literally an imagined movement; it seems to involve the same neural facilities as motor activity, most notably motor sequence planning.[8] Hence the act of listening to music involves the same mental processes that generate bodily motion. One might suppose that musical elements might be more efficacious in eliciting sympathetic behavior if they represent aspects of human motion somehow. Such sounds might include the dynamic swells associated with breathing, the steady pulse associated with walking, and the rapid rhythmic figurations associated with speech. Note that each of these three examples occurs at a different timescale. In fact, it is interesting to observe the rhythmic correspondences among these groups of behaviors:[9]

Bodily activities	Musical correlates	Timescale
Breathing, moderate arm gesture, body sway	Phrase, meter, harmonic rhythm, dynamics, vocal utterances	1–10 seconds
Heartbeat, walking, and running, sexual intercourse, head bob, toe tap	Pulse, "walking" basslines, dance rhythms	0.3–1 second (approximately 60–180 beats per minute)
Speech, lingual motion, syllables, rapid hand gesture, finger motion	Fast rhythmic activity, "bebop" melodies, etc.	0.1–0.3 second (3–10 notes per second)

It is plausible that musical activity on these three timescales might exploit these correspondences.

A variety of truisms support this view. For example, most wind-instrument phrase lengths are naturally constrained by lung capacity. Indeed, any instrument that produces sustained tones can be used to evoke the human voice. The throbbing of urban dance music often makes sonic references to foot stomping and to sexually suggestive slapping of skin. Blues guitarists, jazz pianists, and *quinto* players in Afro-Cuban *rumba* are said to "speak" with their hands and fingers. All such instances involve the embodiment of the musical performer and the listening audience.

A recent review by Shove and Repp highlights the often overlooked fact that musical motion is, first and foremost, audible human motion.[10] To amplify this view, Shove and Repp make use the "ecological level" of perception as suggested by J. J. Gibson.[11] At this level "the listener does not merely hear the *sound* of a galloping horse or bowing violinist; rather the listener hears a *horse galloping* and a *violinist bowing.*" In this ecological framework the source of perceived musical movement is the human performer, as is abundantly clear to the listener attending a music performance. We connect the perception of musical motion at the ecological level to human motion. This suggests that musical perception involves an understanding of bodily motion—that is, a mutual embodiment. For musical performers the difference between rhythmic motion and human motion collapses; the rhythmic motions of the performer and of the musical object are essentially one and the same.[12] Dance is then a natural response to the movement that music represents.

Kinesthetics

The term *kinesthetics* refers to the sensation of bodily position, presence, or movement resulting from tactile sensation and from vestibular input. We rely on such awareness whenever we engage in any physical activity; it helps us hold objects in our hands, walk upright, lean against walls, and guide food into our mouths. In these cases there is a strong interdependence between the kinesthetic and visual senses. Similarly, in the playing of musical instruments we must treat sonic and kinesthetic dimensions as interacting; we must bear in mind the spatiomotor mode of musical performance.[13] For musicians, musical competence involves the bodily coordination of limbs, digits, and, in the case of wind instruments, breathing.

John Blacking raised the issue of kinesthetics in musical performance by comparing two types of kalimba ("thumb piano") music among the Venda community of South Africa.[14] One very physical type, practiced by amateur boys, featured complex melodies that appeared to be secondary artifacts of patterned thumb movements; the regularity of the movements generated the jagged melodic result. The other type, a more popular style practiced by professional musicians, had simpler melodies with small intervals and flowing contours, directed more by an abstract melodic logic than by a spatiomotor one.

From my experience with jazz improvisation on the piano, I have found that the kinesthetic or spatiomotor approach and the melodic approach form dual extremes of a continuum. We augment our aural imagination by exploring the possibilities suggested by the relationship between our bodies and our instruments, and we judge the result of such experimentation by appealing to our musical ear and aesthetics. Among pianists who have exploited this relationship in jazz, Thelonious Monk has been the most influential. His compositions and improvisations provide an exemplary nexus of kinesthetics and formalism. Often his pieces contained explicitly pianistic peculiarities, including the repeated use of pendular fourths, fifths, sixths, and sevenths (as in "Misterioso" and "Let's Call This"), whole-tone runs and patterns ("Four in One"), major- and minor-second dyads ("Monk's Point," "Light Blue"), and rapid figurations and ornamental filigrees ("Trinkle, Tinkle").[15] All of these idiosyncrasies fit, so to speak, in the palm of the pianist's hand, while often wreaking havoc for horn players (or, even worse, vocalists). Such physical patterns are simpler and apparently more primal for finger coordination than any nonconsecutive pattern. Monk was able to place these simple patterns in unconventional rhythmic and melodic relationships to yield new compositional and improvisational possibilities. The embodied-cognition viewpoint suggests that a musician's internal representations of music are intimately tied to his or her connection with the instrument, which forms part of the music-making environment. The musician's relationship with the instrument can leave its trace on the music itself—that is, it can be communicated musically as Monk demonstrates so vividly.

Aesthetics of the Body

Again, when we speak of cognition via the body and its interaction with its physical environment, we must also discuss the social and cultural forces that construct the concept of the body. An important conceptual distinction between European and African musics involves precisely this status of the body—the degree to which the physical situatedness of the music-making or listening body is acknowledged. The above discussion of Thelonious Monk suggests that his highly experimental musical techniques emerged in an environment where he felt perfectly at ease exploring the relationship between his body and the piano, even allowing his musical ideas to be subject to this relationship. It attests to the idea that African-American music often features an embodied approach to music-making. By this I mean that one does not regard the body as an impediment to ideal musical activity, and that instead, many sophisticated musical concepts develop as an extension of physical activities, such as walking, strumming, hitting, cutting, scratching, or more figuratively, *speaking*.

Speech

As is commonly observed, jazz improvisation bears metaphorical attributes of speech and conversation. Ingrid Monson's book *Saying Something* provides an elaborate discussion of this metaphor. One often hears instances of the metaphor in African-American musical pedagogy, where "'to say' or 'to talk' often substitutes for 'to play.'"[16] Such usage underscores what musical performance does have in common with speech as an activity or behavior, as well as what music has in common with language as a symbolic system. Among the traits that link musical performance to speech, we see that:

- Like speech, musical performance is a *process*, a salient mental and physical activity that takes place in time.
- Like speech, musical performance is interactive, characterized by dialogue, call-and-response, and collective synchronization.
- Like speech, music has *semiotic* dimensions, which enable sonic symbols to refer actively to other parts of the same piece, to other music, or to contextual and extramusical phenomena—as with the rhythmic correspondences between finger motion and speech itself.

Note that these aspects of speech and performed music are not restricted to the domain of semantics; that is, they are not solely concerned with the "intrinsic" meanings of words or notes. Rather, these specific aspects depend upon the act of performance.

Performativity

Similarly one might imagine that visual and other contextual factors in a musical performance co-articulate musical meaning along with the sonic trace. We may call these elements *performatives*. In an essay entitled "The Grain of the Voice," Roland Barthes pointed out that performance of composed music also carries this "extra" dimension.[17] In addition to the meaningful intramusical dynamics, supplemental meaning is generated by the presence of a music-making body, and the sonic traces it leaves behind. Hence the "grain" of the voice, by announcing the vocalist's physical presence, signifies a rupturing of the disembodied, self-contained world of the classical work. The personhood of the performer insinuates its way into (for Barthes, European classical) music performance through its roughness, its resistance, its departure from the ideal disembodied musical object. The physicality and resistance of the voice point to its producer, the performer, and to the act of it being produced. The grain of a musical performance reminds the listener of the physical sensation of using the voice, or other parts of the body: "The 'grain' is the body in the voice as it sings, the hand as it writes, the limb as it performs."[18] These physical encodings in musical performance have intensely expressive powers. The meaning of a vocal utterance is constituted not simply by its semantic content or its melodic logic, but also by its *sonorous* content.

Sound

Tellingly, among many jazz musicians, a most valued characterization is that a certain musician has his or her own, instantly recognizable *sound*, where "sound" means not only timbre, but also articulation, phrasing, rhythm, melodic vocabulary, and even analytical methods. Generally it came to mean a sort of "personality" or "character" that distinguishes different improvisors. Though it is a complement if someone tells you that you "sound like Coleman Hawkins," it is even higher praise to be described as "having your own sound." Trombonist and improvisor George Lewis writes,

> "[S]ound," sensibility, personality and intelligence cannot be separated from an improvisor's phenomenal (as distinct from formal) definition of music. Notions of personhood are transmitted via sounds, and sounds become signs for deeper levels of meaning beyond pitches and intervals.[19]

This view supports the widespread interpretation of improvisation as personal narrative, as that which gives voice to the meaningful experiences of the individual.[20] Cecil Taylor wrote of John Coltrane,

> In short, his tone is beautiful because it is functional. In other words, it is always involved in saying something. You can't separate the means that a man uses to say something from what he ultimately says. Technique is not separated from its content in a great artist.[21]

Often, then, an improvisor's original playing style is bound up with his or her (possibly idiosyncratic or self-styled) technique. In many cases the autodidactic approach plays a large role for improvisors, for whom the creation of music is embodied in one's relationship to one's instrument. Hence the inseparability of "sound," or embodied creative approach, from a "phenomenal definition of music"—a personal sense of what music is and what it is for.

The notion of personal sound functions as an analytical paradigm, a kind of down-home biographical criticism. An individual's tone, rhythmic feel, and overall musical approach are seen as an indicator of who he or she "is" as a person. Musicians' interactive strategies in music might be seen as an indicator of their interpersonal behavior; their rhythmic placement ahead of or behind the beat may reflect how "fiery" or "cool" their temperaments run; their melodic inventiveness and harmonic sophistication might parallel their offstage urbanity and wit. Admittedly, such stereotypical characterizations beg to be broken down; rarely does a musician's offstage personality fit such conventional wisdom. Indeed, one could also view "musical personality" as a kind of *mask* that the performer wears onstage, Signifyin(g) on his or her offstage identity as well as on performance itself. But in either case, the notion of personal sound, relating musical characteristics to personality traits, reveals much about how music, life, and personal narrative can be conceptualized together. In this sense, Sound provides a kind of Afrological animation of the "grain" in European performance.

Many have tried to establish "motivic development" in Coltrane's individual improvisations as that which creates structure and hence meaning.[22] But it seems to me that such structure is merely a consequence of a greater formation—Coltrane's "sound," his holistic approach to music, which yields these elements. I do not wish to imply that Coltrane had no mind for "structuring" an individual solo; but these sorts of analyses stem from the critical tools of the *listener* rather than the improvisor. As a musician, I personally believe that the improvisor is concerned more with making individual improvisations relate *to each other*, and to his or her conception of personal sound, than he or she might be with obeying some standard of coherence on the scale of the single improvisation.

Temporality of Musical Performance

Yet another fundamental consequence of physical embodiment and environmental situatedness is the fact that *things take time*. In intersubjective activities, such as speech, musical performance, or rehearsal, one remains aware of a sense of mutual embodiment, a presupposition of "shared time" between the listener and the performer. This sense is a crucial aspect of the temporality of performance. The experience of listening to live music is qualitatively different from that of reading a book. The former requires a "co-performance" on the part of the audience, one that must occur within a shared temporal domain.[23]

The performance situation might be understood as a context-framing device. In his study of music in South Africa, John Blacking wrote, ". . .Venda music is distinguished from nonmusic by the creation of a special world of time. The chief function of music is to involve people in shared experiences within the framework of their cultural experience."[24] There is no doubt that this is true to some degree in all musical performance, but we can take this concept further in the case of improvised music. The process of musical improvisation in a jazz context can be seen as one specific way of framing the shared time between performer and audience. Time framed by improvisation is a special kind of time that is flexible in extent, and in fact carries the inherent possibility of endlessness. Instances like Paul Gonsalves's 27 choruses (over 6 minutes) of blues on Ellington's "Diminuendo and Crescendo in Blue" and Coltrane's sixteen-minute take on "Chasin' the Trane"– significantly, both live recordings—attest to the power that the improvisor wields as framer of time, deciding both the extent and the content of the shared epoch.[25]

The experience of listening to music that we know to be improvised differs significantly from listening knowingly to composed music. A main source of drama in improvised music is the visceral fact of the shared sense of time: the sense that the improvisor is working, creating, generating musical material at the same time in which we are coperforming as listeners. As listeners, we seem to experience any music as an awareness of the physicality of the "grain," and a kind of *empathy* for the performer, an understanding of effort required to create music. In improvised music empathy extends beyond the concept of the physical body to an awareness of the performers' coincident physical and mental exertion, of their "in-the-moment" *process* of creative activity and interactivity. Listening to Coltrane on "Giant Steps," one cannot help but agree with his colleague, who suggested that the breathtaking *reality* of Coltrane improvising and creating his way through this maze tells quite an awesome story indeed, one that at the very least elicits our empathy.

Exploding the Narrative

In these and many other ways the embodied view of music facilitates a nonlinear approach to musical narrative. Musical meaning is not conveyed only through motific development, melodic contour, and other traditional musicological parameters; it is also *embodied* in improvisatory techniques. Musicians tell their stories, but not in the traditional linear narrative sense; an *exploded narrative* is conveyed through a holistic musical personality or *attitude*. That attitude is conveyed both musically, through the skillful, individualistic, improvisatory manipulation of expressive parameters in combination, as well as *extramusically*, in the sense that these sonic symbols "point" to a certain physical, social, and cultural comportment, a certain way of being embodied. Kinesthetics, performativity, personal sound, temporality—all these traces of embodiment generate, reflect, and refract stories into innumerable splinters and shards. Each one of these fragments is "saying something." The details of what the music is saying, and of how it does so, are as infinitely variable as are the individuals who enact and embody it.

In concluding, it is worth reminding ourselves that representations of African American culture have been plagued by racist mythologies surrounding the idea of the body. Historically, African American cultural practice has been seen by mainstream Western culture as the realm of the physical, the sensual, and the intuitive, in diametric opposition to the intellectual, the formal, and the logical. As Susan McClary and Robert Walser have argued, I must stress that "to discuss the bodily aspects of cultural texts or performances is not to *reduce* them" but rather to elevate the crucial role of embodiment in all aspects of cultural and perceptual activity.[26] An enlightened treatment of embodiment gets beyond that old mind-body binary, particularly in its racialist manifestations; and it also happens to affirm the African American aesthetics that gave birth to this powerfully embodied music.

NOTES

1. Gunther Schuller, "Sonny Rollins and the Challenge of Thematic Improvisation," in *Musings: The Musical Worlds of Gunther Schuller* (New York: Oxford University Press, 1986), pp. 86–97, reprinted from *Jazz Review* (November 1958).

2. Brian Harker, "'Telling a Story': Louis Armstrong and Coherence in Early Jazz," *Current Musicology* 63 (1999): 46–83.

3. George E. Lewis, "Improvised Music Since 1950: Afrological and Eurological Forms," *Black Music Research Journal* 16.1 (Spring 1996): 91–119.

4. See, e.g., Samuel Floyd, *The Power of Black Music* (New York: Oxford University Press, 1995); Robert Walser, "'Out of Notes': Signification, Interpretation, and the Problem of Miles Davis," in *Jazz Among the Discourses*, ed. K. Gabbard (Durham: Duke University Press, 1995), pp. 165–188; Ingrid Monson, *Saying Something: Jazz Improvisation and Interaction* (Chicago: University of Chicago Press, 1996); George Lewis, "Singing Omar's Song: A (Re)construction of Great Black Music," *Lenox Avenue*, 4 (1998): 69–92.

5. John Coltrane, *The Heavyweight Champion*, compact disc compilation (Los Angeles: Atlantic Records, 1995), disc 7, track 1, originally recorded in 1959.

6. Transcribed by Steve Coleman and Vijay Iyer, 2000.

7. Vijay Iyer, "Microstructures of Feel, Macrostructures of Sound: Embodied Cognition in West African and African-American Musics," Ph.D. thesis, University of California at Berkeley, 1998; "Embodied Mind, Situated Cognition, and Expressive Microtiming in African-American Music," *Music Perception* 19.3 (2002): 387–414.

8. B. Carroll-Phelan and P. J. Hampson, "Multiple Components of the Perception of Musical Sequences: A Cognitive Neuroscience Analysis and Some Implications for Auditory Imagery," *Music Perception* 13 (1996): 517–561; Neil Todd, C. Lee, and D.

O'Boyle, "A Sensory-Motor Theory of Rhythm, Time Perception, and Beat Induction," *Journal of New Music Research* 28 (1999): 5–29.

9. Paul Fraisse, "Rhythm and Tempo," in *The Psychology of Music*, ed. D. Deutsch (New York: Academic, 1982), pp. 149–180; Neil Todd, "The Auditory 'Primal Sketch': A Multiscale Model of Rhythmic Grouping," *Journal of New Music Research* 23 (1994): 25–70.

10. Paul Shove and Bruno Repp. "Musical Motion and Performance: Theoretical and Empirical Perspectives," in *The Practice of Performance*, ed. J. Rink (Cambridge: Cambridge University Press, 1995), pp. 55–83.

11. James J. Gibson, *The Ecological Approach to Visual Perception* (Boston: Houghton Mifflin, 1979).

12. Shove and Repp, "Musical Motion and Performance," pp. 59–60.

13. See John Baily, "Music Structure and Human Movement," in *Musical Structure and Cognition*, P. Howell, I. Cross, and R. West, eds. (London: Academic, 1985), 237–258.

14. John Blacking, *How Musical Is Man?* (Seattle: University of Washington Press, 1973).

15. Recordings of all of these compositions can be found in the compact disc compilation *Thelonious Monk: The Complete Riverside Recordings* (Berkeley: Riverside Records, 1986), originally recorded 1955–1961.

16. Monson, *Saying Something*, p. 84.

17. Roland Barthes, "The Grain of the Voice," in *Image, Music, Text*, S. Heath, ed. and trans. (New York: Hill and Wang, 1977), pp. 179–189.

18. Ibid., p. 188.

19. Lewis, "Improvised Music Since 1950," p. 117.

20. Ibid.

21. Cecil Taylor, "John Coltrane." *Jazz Review*, January 1959, p. 34.

22. Roger Dean, *New Structures in Jazz and Improvised Music Since 1960* (Philadelphia: Open University Press, 1992); Ekkehard Jost, *Free Jazz* (New York: Da Capo, 1981), pp. 92–94.

23. See A. Schutz, "Making Music Together," in *Collected Papers II: Studies in Social Theory* (The Hague: Martinus Nijhoff, 1964), pp. 159–178.

24. Blacking, *How Musical Is Man?* p. 48.

25. Duke Ellington, *Ellington at Newport (1956)*, compact disc reissue (New York: Columbia Records, 1990), track 3; John Coltrane, *The Complete 1961 Village Vanguard Recordings*, compact disc compilation (New York: Impulse Records, 1997), disc 3, track 1.

26. Susan McClary and Robert Walser, "Theorizing the Body in African-American Music," *Black Music Research Journal* 14.1 (Spring 1994): 80.

ROBIN D. G. KELLEY

Beneath the Underground: Exploring New Currents in "Jazz"

About thirty years ago a California radio host asked the legendary jazz pianist/composer Thelonious Monk what he thought about the violin in jazz. "Well, I like all instruments, played right." Yeah, it was a dumb question. But what if we could ask Monk what he thought about turntables and digital samplers in jazz? The question is a bit more complicated since recording and playback devices are rarely thought of as "instruments." In fact, virtually every movement to "electrify" jazz has had to face massive resistance, beginning with the jazz purists who dismissed Miles Davis's experiments in the 1970s (i.e., *Bitches Brew* and *On the Corner*) to the current neo-bop renaissance whose defense of acoustic instruments borders on reverence. It is hard to imagine, for example, Jazz at Lincoln Center hiring a DJ as a sideman.[1]

But times might be changing. Trumpeter Russell Gunn not only incorporates hip hop samples on his recent release *Ethnomusicology Vol. 1*, but employs DJ Apollo as a member of his eclectic, funk-inspired jazz band. Even high-brow jazz composers are hiring turntablists and programmers as accompanists. Just last year the Uri Caine Ensemble released a two-CD tribute to Gustav Mahler that included DJ Olive on turntables and live electronics. And these examples represent merely the tip of a giant iceberg, and not even the most innovative tip at that. Anyone with their ear to the underground will discover a world where instrumentalists and turntablists, programmers, and poets have begun to revolutionize improvisational music. Artists such as Graham Haynes, Lawrence D. "Butch" Morris, Melvin Gibbs, Craig Taborn, Steve Coleman, performance poet Tracie Morris, and a gang of DJs, to name but a few, are pushing technology to new limits and crushing all distinctions between genres. They are not simply adding "electronic flavor" to familiar jazz styles; they are figuring out new ways to improvise, compose, and experience the music. The "new jazz underground," embraces contemporary dance rhythms of drum n' bass, trip hop, hip hop, world beat, and electronica's ambient soundscapes. Some artists have even discarded the old rhythm section concept (piano, bass, and drums) for something more dynamic, more expansive, adopting turntables, digital samplers, electronic percussion, effects pads, computer programs, while maintaining the avant-garde tradition of incorporating ancient instruments from the precolonial world—tablas, koras, ouds, water drums.

Like all new underground movements, this one has deep roots in earlier musical developments. For at least a half-century a handful of renegades from the jazz world have experimented with electronic music, from Sun Ra's space music in the 1950s, to the crossover efforts by Miles Davis and Herbie Hancock in the early 1970s, to the more recent funky-ancient-futuristic explorations of composer/producer Bill Laswell. Less known are the avant-garde composers who not only embraced new technology but stand among its most important and original innovators. George Lewis, virtuoso trombonist and composer who came up through the rigorous training of the Chicago-based Association for the Advancement of Creative Musicians, began experimenting with electronic and computer-based music around 1975, after he met composer Richard Teitelbaum. He was also listening to minimalist composers such as La Monte Young, Terry Riley, and Philip Glass, in part because he found in their music affinities to John Coltrane. "The thing to remember about this 1970s period," Lewis recalled,

> is that everybody I know was trying to listen to everything that was out at the time. Everyone in the AACM was very supportive of this direction, so for me, I could follow up the rather obvious and the subtle connections between Stockhausen and La Monte Young and Coltrane and Roscoe Mitchell and Derek Bailey and Sam Rivers and John Zorn and Gil Evans and Randy Weston and Yuji Takahashi and Kaija Saariaho all at the same time, and all of that could emerge in my work. I just didn't see why I had to choose, and plus, the criteria for choosing seemed so absurdly race-based when they came out in print or in conversations.

After learning how to improvise on a Micromoog monophonic analog synthesizer, Lewis began his own form of "sampling" with cheap cassette recorders "that I would hotwire to make sound-on-sound (overdub) recordings." The effect can be heard on the first movement of Lewis's "Imaginary Suite," a duo he recorded with saxaphonist Douglas Ewart in 1979. One can also hear the effect of this kind of sampling on Ewart and Lewis's live recording of "Chicago Slow Dance" (1980), where Lewis employed endless loop cassettes on three tape recorders to "sample" Ewart's solo in real time, and then played them back all at once through an analog delay, orchestrating and multiplying Ewart's phrases as he continued to improvise over the playback.

By the early 1980s Lewis's interests shifted from performance-based electronic manipulations of his trombone to constructing interactive computer programs that could create musical dialogues. He developed technologies that enabled him to create improvised transformations of sound in real-time, including a program that analyses an improviser's performance and immediately generates a complex musical response. In other words, the computer listens to musicians and plays along. This led to significant changes in Lewis's approach to improvisation. "I tried to harness that [electronic] energy within the formal constraints suggested by the sonic possibilities. Just playing standard licks didn't sound very good with the electronics, for any number of reasons—in fact, just playing standard licks never sounds good." Indeed, one hears in Lewis's "Homage to Charles Parker," recorded with Douglas Ewart (sax), Anthony Davis (piano), and Richard Teitelbaum (synthesizers), a precursor to what some contemporary experimental turntablists are trying to achieve through distortion, drones, environmental sounds, and other kinds of "noise." "I suppose that I became a bit of a DJ myself," mused Lewis. "My computer became the DJ, providing me with shifting textures that were quite directed and formally coherent, yet totally interactive with my playing and that of the other musicians. I arrived at a point where the computer could play most of the concert by itself, pretty much without supervision. The musicians with whom I collaborated, such as Roscoe Mitchell and Douglas Ewart, began to feel confident that the computer would fairly consistently do the right thing in a totally open improvisational setting. But I would say that even among computer artists, this totally open-ended relationship with independently functioning musical computers is still considered pretty extreme—'pushing the technology to its limits,' one might say." His recent CD *Endless Shout* opens with "North Star Boogaloo," an interpretation of Quincy Troupe's poem of the same name performed between computer and drums. It incorporates sampling, hip hop grooves, and a computer-driven reconstruction and reshuffling of Quincy Troupe's sampled voice.

Lawrence D. "Butch" Morris is, among other things, another pioneer of the new underground, and his influence has been enormous since many of the artists central to this movement have worked with him at one time or another. An innovative cornetist (who can be heard with George Lewis on David Murray's stunning album *Ming*) and composer, Morris is the creator of the theory and practice of "conduction," a system of conducted improvisation whereby the conductor "may compose, (re)orchestrate, (re)arrange and sculpt with notated and non-notated music." Utilizing a series of learned signs and gestures, Morris can direct entire orchestras to create the music he hears without notation, although many of his pieces are indeed notated. What he has been able to create defies all genres, despite his own moorings in the jazz tradition. A conduction, he insists, "is not jazz, this is not classical—not free, it is what it is. . . . The one thing it does have, no matter where it's done, that makes it akin to jazz is combustion and ignition. To me this is the essence of swing."

Morris was one of the first of his cohort to see the possibilities of employing DJs as instrumentalists. In the early to mid-1980s, he worked with Christian Marclay, a pioneer in experimental turntablism. Marclay not only explored distortion and ambient sounds but was known for placing objects on records to generate new sonic textures or an added rhythmic pulse. Morris also employed Marclay on his first conduction, "Current Trends in Racism in Modern America," performed in 1985, and he continued to explore electronics, turntablism, and live sampling through collaborations with J. A. Deane, Yoshihide Otomo, Paul Miller (DJ Spooky), and Beth Coleman (DJ M. Singe).

Of course, the hip hop revolution is responsible for the integration of DJs into the world of improvisational music. While dozens of artists have deliberately set out to fuse jazz and hip hop, notably Guru's "Jazzamatazz," the Brand New Heavies, Digable Planets, Giant Step, the DJ project Us3, Greg Osby, Steve Coleman, Courtney Pine, Branford Marsalis's Buckshot LaFonque, and most recently in Buckshot alumni Russell Gunn, the distance between these two genres was never so great. Indeed, both Gunn and fellow trumpeter Roy Hargrove have recorded with hip hop/soul singer D'Angelo. Jazz has been an enduring musical staple for hip hop's beat library from its inception a quarter-century ago. Hip hop artists embraced jazz as part of a larger repertoire of music for the taking. Indeed, some of the most innovative uses of jazz by hip hop DJs were never packaged as fusion, as evident in the debut albums by groups like the Pharcyde, A Tribe Called Quest, and Mad Kap—a short-lived California trio that included the talented young trumpeter/DJ Joseph Leimberg, aka Dr. Soose. Leimberg had been playing beautiful improvised trumpet lines over sampled tracks well over a decade ago.

DJs have the potential for dramatically altering improvised music because they play an instrument that simultaneously mirrors and deconstructs improvisational practices we associate with jazz. Turntablists literally make new music from old records by mixing, cutting, and altering original sounds, manipulating records by hand to change pitch, create rhythmic effects, and milk the groove itself for new sounds by "scratching" (back cuing). The most innovative DJs, the cut-creators of what is now called "illbient" music (a kind of ambient-meets-funky abstraction), can bring a John Coltrane or a Claude Debussy back from the dead, altering original passages or placing them in new sonic contexts. Sonny Rollins' tenor can become a drum, Art Blakey's drum roll a horn or a drone. Writer/musician Greg Tate, a follower of and participant in this movement who always seems to know what's coming around the corner, insists that

> the best of the illbient DJs have created a new jazz instrument. And they've done it by having an encyclopedic approach to improvisation, one that is analogous to the Art Ensemble of Chicago or Henry Threadgill. Where you try to create an improvisational/compositional form that allows you to reference the total history of music to that point. . . . The turntables and the human beat box are the jazz instruments of now. They are creating a voice that didn't exist, and new possibilities for improvisation.

The new "jazz" underground is drawn to the illbient DJs precisely because they resist music labeling, embrace experimentalism, and are willing to take risks. Paul Miller (aka DJ Spooky), one of the best known illbient DJs on the scene today, performs with live jazz musicians, spins and remixes records from all subgenres of "jazz," and occasionally picks up the upright bass. A fine example of Miller's imagination and "jazz" sensibilities is his "Piano Roll Blue" remix of "Object Unkown," featuring MC's Kool Keith and Sir Menelik. For Miller and other like-minded artists, established musical genres are pretty meaningless. All music is theirs for the taking, as evidenced by his most recent album *Riddim Warfare*, which incorporates Brazilian underground music ("Quilombo Ex Optico") as well as jazz, funk, blues, classical, ambient, drum n' bass, folk, and organized sounds for which we have no names. If you don't believe me, just listen to his three-part cut, aptly titled "Dialectical Transformation."

DJ Logic (aka Jason Kibler) has developed an improvisational style fiercely attentive to pitch, rhythm, and space. Somewhat of a veteran on the jazz scene—having appeared on Graham Haynes's 1995 release *Transition* and Medeski, Martin, and Wood's 1998 CD *Combustication*—Kibler treats the bands he plays with "like my third turntable" and sees his role as an ensemble member to create "some nice colors to match or blend with what's going on." And he avoids unnecessary displays of virtuosity. His debut album *Project Logic* (1999) might be described as the ultimate turntablist jazz record. A collaboration with bassist Melvin Gibbs and drummer Skoota Warner, Logic is joined by an all-star cast of musicians and poets including Graham Haynes, guitarists Vernon Reid and Brandon Ross, and Medeski, Martin, and Wood. On cuts such as "Mnemonics," Logic lays down a spare yet richly textured carpet for Casey Benjamin's soprano sax solo, while on the slower, plodding "Gig 1" we get density beneath Haynes's electronically altered cornet. Logic turns minimalist on "Kinda Bleu," where saxophonist Daniel Carter executes a Marion Brown-like solo over an incredibly funky bass line by Melvin Gibbs. Drummer Billy Martin sustains the groove while Logic fades in and out with strings, drones, and wind sounds.

Another young voice on the horizon is Carl Craig, a leading DJ/producer out of the Detroit techno scene. He conceived his 1999 release *Programmed* as a kind of electronic avant-garde jazz album. Joined by Francisco Mora on drums and Craig Taborn on keyboards, not to mention a host of guest artists, Craig combines the best of seventies instrumental funk, the space-age futurism of Sun Ra and his Arkestra, the eclecticism of the Art Ensemble of Chicago, with twenty-first-century techno. This is not music driven by backbeat rhythms; rather, on tunes like "Eruption," "Basic Math," and "Bug in the Bass Bin," Mora explores different time signatures, often beating out a waltz over standard 4/4 time. As a "programmer" rather than just an instrumentalist, Craig is able to manipulate volume and layer tracks at will in the studio—a kind of postproduction conduction. I'm not talking about cutting and pasting or even remixing, but using levels to determine when instruments enter the soundscape, like DJs manipulating two turntables, digital samplers, CD players, and other playback devices. "Bug in the Bass Bin," for example, opens on 4/4 time until the drum track is "turned up" and we hear Mora playing in waltz time, shifting the accent on us in a delightful trickster move.

Craig Taborn's improvisations are ingenious. A versatile pianist who is as comfortable playing the music of Sun Ra or Thelonious Monk as he is with Sly Stone or Jimi Hendrix, Taborn showcases his impeccable rhythmic sensibilities on the immensely danceable "Timing." His phrasing demolishes the bar line, contracting and expanding to create rhythmic tensions without ever losing the crowd. He also displays a sensitivity to sound textures, not just key or pitch—a necessity in the world of electronic music. On cuts where he plays over a dense backdrop of "noises" and drones, he selects a more wiry tone with a rounded, less determinate pitch. One of the most compelling pieces on the album is "Blakula," which feels like a nine-minute jazz/techno/hip hop opera. Opening with a digital steel drums simulation over Michael Smith's violin playing diminished and minor scales, the dramatic entry of Francisco Mora's marching snare drum reminds you that there is a story here. Ultimately, it is the transformation of rhythm, not melody, that drives the story, as Blakula rises from the dead to "show his skills" to a funky beat.

Two of the most sought after turntablists among New York's new "jazz" underground are DJ Mutamassik (Guilia Loli), known for her funky reconfigurations of North African music, and DJ M. Singe (Beth Coleman) who is regarded as one of the master stylists of illbient. Coleman has performed with countless jazz and experimental artists, including the Swiss free jazz trio, saxophonist Ilhan Ersahin, Lawrence D. "Butch" Morris, and Graham Haynes. She is comfortable playing improvisational music with live ensembles because she treats "turntablism as an instrumentation." "I have no reason to say to somebody," she adds, "that a harp is an instrument and a turntable is not. Especially to somebody who gets in and digs in there and works." And hard work it is. Coleman explains that innovative turntablism requires an extensive musical knowledge, quick reflexes, a sensitive ear not just to pitch and rhythm but to textures, colors, moods, and space. Even in Coleman's solo performances, one can hear how musically attuned she is to creating ensemble-based improvisations. One hears this in a recent recording of a performance at PS 1, where she lays one up-tempo drum track in 5/4 time over another track in 4/4, which drifts in and out of audibility. She then adds a drone from a horn and incorporates recorded voices, which she speeds up or slows down, depending on the tonal or rhythmic effect she is trying to produce. Her work doesn't always "swing" in the traditional sense, but rather takes the concept of polyrhythms to another level. By refusing to coordinate (or discipline?) recorded sounds into a single time signature, her work seems reminiscent of Sun Ra.

As with any improviser in an ensemble setting, knowing when to lay out is often more important than virtuosity. "My greatest experience ever working with live musicians was working with Butch Morris," Coleman recalled. "The only thing Butch asks of you is complete focus. So you have to play *and* focus on the conductor. . . . He'd give a gesture about tempo or a gesture about vibe and then I could come in with something. You have to work fast and know your material, but I love playing like that." But Morris is rare in the world of "jazz." Not many instrumentalists are open to the idea that turntablists are fellow musicians, and they do not always grant much space, let alone respect. As Greg Tate observes, "Jazz, like any art form, is inherently conservative. Turntablists have to do the most to prove that they have a place in traditional jazz performance space." Coleman found that even some of the more experimental artists did not consider turntablists "real" musicians, and being female in a man's world adds yet another obstacle.

Coleman is also cofounder, with Howard Goldkrand (MC Verb), of Soundlab Cultural Alchemy, a New York-based multimedia environment dedicated to creating location-specific performances of sound and visual art. By bringing together many different artists who otherwise might not engage each other, Soundlab has been central to the development of new music. Graham Haynes credits Soundlab for the artistic direction of his 1996 release *Tones for the Twenty-First Century*, a tightly woven quilt of sound effects, textures, drones, and samples layered over Haynes's beautiful, electronically altered horn. "*Tones* is a meditation record," he explained. "I deliberately tried to make music very minimalist and very trance-like, which is why there is no percussion on this record." *Tones* was not just about sound; it was an effort to change musical experience. Although he had been experimenting with altering performance spaces before (e.g., playing from a balcony rather than the stage), when he performed the music from *Tones* he incorporated visuals (film, slides), removed chairs, burned incense, darkened the room, and really challenged his audiences to engage the music differently.

Yet, for all of his interest in the ambient, abstract sounds of electronica, Haynes has been equally drawn to jazz, blues, and hip hop. Indeed, he grew up in a world that knew no musical boundaries. His mother listened to Frank Sinatra and his father, the legendary jazz drummer Roy Haynes, accumulated an extensive record collection that included artists as diverse as Ravi Shankar and Richie Havens. Graham's older brother Craig turned him on to the Beatles at a very young age and later introduced him to Sly and the Family Stone, whose startling combination of psychedelic rock, free improvisation attracted the ten-year-old Graham to the guitar.

Thanks to an uninspired guitar teacher, Graham turned his attention to the trumpet and studied formally. His two years at Queens College studying composition, harmony, and theory spurred his interest in classical and electronic music and introduced him to composers such as Brian Eno, John Cage, and Stockhausen. Like many of his predecessors in the world of jazz, he furthered his education at jam sessions throughout the city, appearing frequently at Studio We, Barry Harris's Jazz Cultural Theater, the Lickety Split in Harlem, and the Village Door in Queens. There he met and played with an earlier generation of giants, including Tommy Turrentine, Junior Cook, Bill Hardman, Clifford Jordan, and Lonnie Smith, as well as younger musicians interested in cross-genre experimentation—notably trumpeter Tom Browne ("Jamaican Funk"), bassist Marcus Miller, and keyboardist Bernard Wright. Haynes also became a regular on the downtown loft scene— places like the Lady's Fort, Ali's Alley, the Jazz Forum—where the music was bold and experimental.

Then in 1979 he found an artistic soul mate in alto saxophonist Steve Coleman. Besides nightly forays into the jam scene, Haynes and Coleman formed a band called the Five Elements, which ultimately evolved into the collective M-Base—Coleman's vision of improvisational music—whose members included pianist Geri Allen, vocalist Cassandra Wilson, and drummer Marvin "Smitty" Smith. Coleman's musical conception as a composer and improviser, his use of odd time signatures, complex layering of polyrhythms and harmonies, and the angular-ity of his writing and phrasing, deeply influenced Haynes. He started composing, building on Coleman's efforts to revolutionize the rhythm section by writing out very complicated drum and percussion parts. Rhythm was fundamental, for in the heady days of the early 1980s, "jazz" bands such as Sun Ra and his Arkestra were playing New Wave dance clubs like Dancetaria. And Haynes, Coleman, and others in their collective had their eye on the experimental jazz/funk/rock groups on the scene: namely DeFunkt, James White and the Blacks, and Ronald Shannon Jackson. Five Elements moved in a similar direction, creating an eclectic mix of funk and "free bop," laid over complicated and shifting rhythms, but gigs were few and far between.

By the late 1980s Haynes formed his own band and recorded his debut album, *What Time It Be?* (1990). His exposure to the World Music Institute at Symphony Space in New York, where he used to moonlight as an usher and ticket taker, introduced him to a wide range of African, Arabic, and South Asian musics. Inherent in these musics were the rhythms he had been trying to create in his own compositions. So after meeting drummer Brice Wassy, who was then playing with the great Malian vocalist/composer Salif Keita, and trumpeter Don Cherry, Haynes set off on a new journey across the Atlantic. In 1990 he moved to Paris to seek out the city's African, Arabic, and Indian music scene. After spending three years in Paris recording with African musicians and releasing his highly acclaimed album, *The Griots Footsteps* (1994), he returned to New York to find hip hop the dominant force. "Sampling became a big thing by then. It was a new sound, a new instrument, a whole new way to make music." At the same time, he was engaged in an ongoing conversation with Vernon Reid, formerly of the band Living Color, and writer/critic Greg Tate, about doing a nineties version of Miles Davis's 1972 album *On the Corner*. "We wanted to bring together the killingest musicians on the scene, write some sketches, put them in a room, and just record them in one or two days." The result was *Transition* (1995), a stunning display of musicianship that drew on the talents of saxophonist Steve Williamson, guitarists Vernon Reid, Jean-Paul Bourelly, and Brandon Ross, keyboardist Cheick Tidiane-Seck, bassist Lonnie Plaxico, and a host of others. More significantly, Haynes hired DJ Logic and incorporated the digital sampler and the turntable as instruments in the ensemble. *Transition* captured the free funk/jazz sensibilities of seventies Miles, the hybrid Africanisms of *The Griots Footsteps*, and the very essence of hip hop. The hip hop bug bit: after *Transition* Haynes played briefly with Giant Step, a gathering of musicians, DJs, and MCs dedicated to fusing jazz and hip hop, and he appeared on The Roots' first two albums, *Do You Want More?!!!??!* (1995) and *Illadelph Halflife* (1996).

Haynes's 2000 release, *BPM* ("beats per minute"), stands out as an exemplar of the new music, perhaps even a new jazz manifesto. It grew from his interest in "drum n' bass," which in the mid-1990s was called "Jungle" and could only be found in underground raves. He began sitting in with DJs and learned how to play against the rapid fire, stop-go tempos. For Haynes it offered a challenge: "With drum n' bass, you actually have improvisation in the groove itself. It creates fresh possibilities for improvisation. But part of the problem with drum n' bass is that there isn't much going on harmonically. So as a soloist you have to figure out another way to play. . . . In order to achieve the kinds of tone colors I heard over the groove, I started adding alot of effects to my horn." Not every cut on *BPM* is a drum n' bass song. "Red Zone" is a free, illbient exploration of electronic sound punctuated by Haynes's enhanced cornet and the voice of the late Don Cherry reminding us that "jazz music has always been for dancing." "Inn a Most" is drum n' bass at its kinetic best. Built on an infectious rhythm created by sounds of glass breaking, random tones, sampled and enhanced vocals, drums and sitar, the song is a danceable yet lissome rhythm collage. "Variations on a Theme by Wagner" and "Variations II" are genuine masterpieces. The first "Variations" samples several measures from Wagner's last opera, *Parsifal,* which serve as a cyclical melodic statement. When the sample drops out, the theme is taken up by the drummer and Haynes improvises on cornet supported by sustained chords played on keyboards. In other words, like a DJ without a turntable, he transforms Wagner's melodies into rhythm, remixing nineteenth-century opera and twenty-firtst-century dance music to create new contexts for improvisation.

The aesthetic emerging out of DJ practice and digital sampling has also reshaped live improvisation in some profound ways. Greg Tate's latest project, Burnt Sugar (the Arkestra Chamber), is *the* big band of the new millenium. Flexing at times to over a dozen on the bandstand, Burnt Sugar is a kind of gypsy band of young musical masters who mess with all manner of electric and acoustic instruments—Vernon Reid, Michael Morgan Craft, Rene Akhan, Kirk Douglass, Shoshanna Vogel, among the electric guitarists, Nioka Workman and Julia Kent working the cello, Suphala on tablas, drummers Swiss Chris. Qasim Naqvi, Vijay Iyer on piano, Bruce Mack synthesizing, bassists Jason di Matteo, Jared Nickerson, Maximina Juson, Lewis Flip Barnes on trumpet, Micah Gaugh on tenor, a flock of floutists including Atiba Wilson, Monet Dunham, Satch Hoyt, and various vocalists—singers, poets, moaners, and hummers –ranging from Justice X, Lisala Beatty, Eisa Davis, Shariff Simmons, Latasha Natasha Diggs, and still too many musicmakers to mention.

As Tate has said on many occasion, this band is his extension of *Bitches Brew,* what we might call his homage to Miles Davis. And he is committed to building on what Miles started in the late 1960s—groove-based, funky, free improvisation rooted in a true musical conversation rather than a dozen cats all talking at once. Surprisingly, Tate has not employed a DJ or used sampled music, and yet all the essential aesthetic principles are evident. Tate, who plays some guitar but primarily occupies the conductor's spot, works his band like a DJ. While building on Butch Morris's system of conduction, Tate moves his musicians in and out of the groove in the manner of a DJ or engineer adding and dropping tracks at certain points in the song. What the artists bring to the groove, however, is improvised, generating fresh spontaneous responses from other instrumentalists/voices as well as from Tate himself. We can hear the process so clearly on "Sirens of Triton" from Burnt Sugar's debut album, *Blood on the Leaf* (2001). After calling for Vijay Iyer's spare, funky acoustic piano solo, Tate gradually surrounds him with rich, thick textures from electric guitars, synthesizer, and electronic and acoustic percussion. "Gnawalickenlallibella" opens in 6/4 time with Iyer's steady arppegios overlaid with "choked" staccato lines from electric guitar and synthesizer, giving the song the feel of needle on vinyl. Three minutes later here comes Swiss Chris banging out drum n' bass beats, until Tate moves the band into another mode where the guitars sound like sitars playing scales reminiscent of an Indian raga. (Is this what we might call a live sample?) Perhaps more than any other cut, "Beloved" seems most directly related to Miles electric funk—particularly in their ingenious use of the repeated motive and the critical role of percussion as the prime engine for improvisation. It has a chantlike quality, which never seems repetitive over Quasim Naqvi's vedic drumming. The amazing thing about Tate's concept is the way it draws on aesthetics of sampling yet is completely improvised instrumental music. Except for the title track there are no scores, no prearranged chord progressions or modes, just music invented on the spot. As Tate put it in the liner notes, "anything that sounds like it was orchestrated befored-hand was actually improv-ed and conducted into being on the spot, on the fly, off the cuff, in the raging, bloody-impromptu moment."

Burnt Sugar's follow-up three-CD release, *That Depends on What You Know*, has really thrown a wrench into the increasingly calcified "jazz canon." It proved that *Blood on the Leaf* was more than a temporary, experimental jam session. Continuing to build on the concept of completely improvised groove-based conduction, many of the tracks here deserve the kind of study given to Coleman Hawkins's "Body and Soul" or Coltrane's "Giant Steps." "Two Bass Blipsch" from disc 1 (an obvious reference to John Lewis and Dizzy Gillespie's "Two Bass Hit"), opens with Vijay Iyer playing the piano strings with such rhythmic precision that it sounds like it's been "looped"; once Tate brings the drums in percussion becomes the improvisational driving force. While everything is improvised, Tate uses conduction to create particular conversations and dialogues, as in the way he brings out Eisa Davis's voice interpolating triplet figures.

Iyer, like Craig Taborn, is a masterful improviser on the keyboards who always seems to know what to play and how much to play. Himself a composer and bandleader who draws on anything that comes his way, particularly South Asian and African American traditions, Iyer has worked with many, many different artists with some kind of association with "jazz," including Steve Coleman, Roscoe Mitchell, Imani Uzuri, Cecil Taylor, George Lewis, and Amiri Baraka. Iyer brings all of this history to bear on their Burnt Sugar's interpretation of Thelonious Monk's "'Round Midnight" (disc 3). This can hardly be called a "cover." Tate says it best in the program notes: "Monk in dub. Rufus in VERSION. What this world is coming to. Depending on what you know." (And if you haven't figured it out yet, what these cats "know" is monk spelled backward with the "w" inverted.) Over a heavy reggae beat, Iyer launches into a funky, haunting single-note interpretation of the A section of the melody in Gb minor, followed by Lewis Flip Barnes who plays the first four bars of the theme in Eb minor (the key in which Monk originally wrote "Round Midnight"). Whether or not this was deliberate, it generates a very Monkish sound of surprise while underscoring the band's transformation of a thirty-two-bar AABA song form into an open-ended "round"—a witty musical pun Monk himself would have loved. The groove allows band members to enter with the melody at any point and it sounds just right. They noodle around with the theme for eight minutes and then switch gears with a kind of R&B/disco remix version.

The masterpiece in all this innovative music is their thirty-eight-minute "Fubractive Since Antiquity Suite." Built on a repeated North African-sounding chant that is "remixed" or rather "reconducted" several times over in different rhythms, tempos, instrumentation, it too is completely improvised while conveying a kind of turntablist texture or sensibility. Tate understands that rhythm is everything, it's the lifeblood of the music; it's the rhythm that drives the entire suite. Part 3, for example, is an exciting contrapuntal marriage between drum n' bass rhythms, piano obligato, Vernon Reid's monster solo, nicely interrupted by a bass line that travels from the Dirty Dozens brass band to old school (read: Negro) 50s Rock and Roll to heavy funk to heavier metal. Segue into part 4, a dense funk groove with a lot of conduction going on. As a result, we hear in the final section of the suite what Miles always tried to achieve when he told his band members to improvise by asking a question and then answering it. We also hear something else: that sampled music and computer programs will never replace live musicians playing tonal instruments, for the spontaneity, experimentation, imagination, and the wonderful mistakes improvisation generates can never be replaced. New technology can certainly enrich possibilities for new modes of improvisation, and it has already shaped the way musicians with open ears have approached improvisation. But there's no substitute for the raw, natural smell of burnt sugar.

Coda

In a recent interview with me, Graham Haynes once described his latest release *BPM* as the new "jazz for the twenty-first century" and in the same breath pronounced jazz dead. "You can't really say that jazz exists now. It can't be what it was because those days are gone. The social settings that made Coltrane's music, that made the Jazz Messengers, that made Louis Armstrong simply don't exist. We are in a different time and place. If there is jazz, then what I'm trying to do would be it." This may seem like a contradiction, but it makes perfect sense if we think of "jazz" as improvised music created in and for its own time and place, a music that draws on the sounds and sensibilities of the moment. At the very least, these artists are not rejecting jazz so much as critiquing it for failing to move forward. They are embracing new technologies and milking them for rhythms and timbres, colors and textures they have never heard before. They are not only crossing musical genres and using new instrumentation; they are *thinking* differently about improvisation, composition, sound. Haynes himself underscores the point by "sampling" no less an authority than the great tenor saxophonist Lester Young. He closes out the final track on *BPM* the way I will end this essay—with the gauntlet-throwing question "Fuck what you played back in '49. What the fuck you gonna play today?"

NOTE

1. Of course, the use of "sampled" or prerecorded music in jazz is not new, nor is it necessarily innovative. On several occasions contemporary musicians have played over recorded music, sometimes creating collaborations between living and dead artists. The best known examples include Natalie Cole's duet with her late father, Nat King Cole, and the soundtrack for Clint Eastwood's *Bird*, on which a contemporary rhythm section played beneath actual recordings of Charlie Parker. The rationale for this arrangement, ironically, was to maintain the integrity of the original recordings. The worst example of this kind of technological ghosting is Kenny G's horrid overdub of Louis Armstrong's "What a Wonderful Life."

REFERENCES

Adams, Sam. "Sounds on the Fringe," *Philadelphia City Paper*, August 29, 1997.

Coleman, Beth. Interview with the author, July 28, 1999.

Eshun, Kwodu. *More Brilliant Than the Sun: Adventures in Sonic Fiction* (London: Quartet, 1998).

Fitzpatrick, Rob. "Gallic Symbols," *Melody Maker* 76.41 (October 16, 1999).

——— "Programmed," *Melody Maker* 76.31 (August 7, 1999).

Haynes, Graham. Interview with the author, January 2, 2000.

"Illbient Nation," *Urb* (July 1996).

Joyce, Mike. "Jazz with Snap, Crackle and Pop," *Washington Post*, May 13, 1999.

Lewis, George. Communication with the author, December 9, 1999.

McDonnell, Evelyn. "Why Aren't More Geeks with the Gizmos Girls?" *New York Times*, April 12, 1998.

Miller, Paul D. "Uncanny/Unwoven: Notes towards a New Conceptual Art," www.djspooky.com.

Norfleet, Dawn M. "The (Not So) Secret Relationship Between Jazz and Hip-Hop," part 1, *Quarterly Black Book Review* (August 2000).

Owen, Frank with Tricia Romano. "Women Step Up to the Decks," *Village Voice*, December 2, 1997.

Pareles, Jon. "Happy Disorientation Under the Bridge," *New York Times*, July 15, 1996.

Robicheau, Paul. "Putting a New Spin on Jams," *Boston Globe*, October 22, 1999.

Robinson, Greg. "Graham Haynes: Healing Power," *Jazz Times* (March 1996).

Shapiro, Peter. "Entering the Empty Quarter," *Wire Magazine* (October 1997): 54–55.

Strauss, Neil. "At the Clubs, Murmurs and Ambient Music," *New York Times*, March 8, 1996.

Tate, Greg. *Flyboy in the Buttermilk* (New York: Simon and Schuster, 1992).

——— Interview with the author, October 12, 1999.

DISCOGRAPHY

Coleman, Beth, and Howard Goldkrand. *Mobile Stealth Unit—Pink Noise 002* (Soundlab Records, 2000).

Burnt Sugar (the Arkestra Chamber). *Blood on the Leaf—Opus 1* (Trugoid, 2000).

——— *That Depends on What You Know* (Trugoid, 2002)

Carl Craig's Innerzone Orchestra. *Programmed* (AstralWerks/Planet E, 1999).

Davis, Miles. *The Complete Bitches Brew Sessions* (Columbia, 1998).

———— *On the Corner* (CBS/Sony, 1972).

———— *Panthalassa: The Music of Miles Davis, 1969–1974—Reconstruction and Mix Translation by Bill Laswell* (Columbia, 1998).

DJ Logic. *Project Logic* (Rope-a-Dope, 1999).

Guru. *Jazzamatazz: Volume 1* (Chyrsalis, 1993).

Haynes, Graham. *BPM* (Knitting Factory, 2000).

———— *The Griots Footsteps* (Verve Antilles, 1994).

———— *Transition* (Verve Antilles, 1995).

———— *Tones for the Twenty-First Century* (Polygram, 1996).

———— *What Time It Be!* (Muse, 1990).

Laswell, Bill. *Sacred System: Chapter 1* and *Chapter 2* (Reachout International, 1997).

Lawrence D. "Butch" Morris, *Testament: A Conduction Collection* (New World, 1995).

Lewis, George. *Endless Shout* (Tzadik, 2000).

———— *Homage to Charles Paker* (Black Saint, 1979).

———— *Voyager* (Disk Union, 1993).

Mad Kap. *Look Ma Duke, No Hands* (RCA, 1994).

Mandel, Howard. *Future Jazz* (New York: Oxford University Press, 1999).

Medeski, Martin, and Woods. *Combustication* (Blue Note, 1998).

Soundlab. *Flav-o-Pac: Memeograph 1—Live Fragments from Cultural Alchemy's Soundlab* (Soundlab, 1999).

Uri Caine Ensemble. *Gustav Mahler in Toblach—"I Went Out This Morning Over the Countryside"* (Winter and Winter, 1999).

Us3. *Hand on the Torch* (Blue Note, 1994).

Volume 10. *Hip Hopera* (RCA, 1993).

Contributors

Herman Beavers is associate professor of English at the University of Pennsylvania. He did his undergraduate work at Oberlin College and his graduate work at Brown and Yale, where he received his doctorate in American Studies in 1990. He is the author of two books, *A Neighborhood of Feeling* (Doris, 1986), a chapbook of poems, and *Wrestling Angels Into Song: The Fictions of Ernest J. Gaines and James Alan McPherson* (University of Pennsylvania Press, 1995). He is currently at work on *And Bid Him Sing*, which examines representations of susceptibility and shame in twentieh-century African American writing by black male writers, and he has completed a collection of poems entitled "Still Life with Guitar." In the summer of 2001 he was a distinguished visiting scholar at the University of Kansas. He was a visiting fellow in African American Studies at Princeton University for the 2001–2 academic year. Born and raised in the Cleveland, Ohio area, he now lives in Burlington, New Jersey with his wife, Lisa, their son, Michael, and their daughter, Corinne.

Brent Hayes Edwards is associate professor in the Department of English at Rutgers University. He is the author of *The Practice of Diaspora: Literature, Translation, and the Rise of Black Internationalism* (Harvard University Press, 2003). Coeditor of the journal *Social Text*, he also serves on the editorial boards of *Transition* and *Callaloo*.

Krin Gabbard is professor of Comparative Literature and English at the State University of New York at Stony Brook. He is the author of *Black Magic: White Hollywood and African American Culture* (Rutgers University Press, 2004) and *Jammin' at the Margins: Jazz and the American Cinema* (University of Chicago Press, 1996) and the editor of *Jazz Among the Discourses* and *Representing Jazz* (both Duke University Press, 1995).

Kevin Gaines teaches in the history department and the Center for Afroamerican and African Studies at the University of Michigan. He is the author of *Uplifting the Race:*

Black Leadership, Politics and Culture During the Twentieth Century. His forthcoming book is *Black Expatriates in Nkrumah's Ghana* (University of North Carolina Press).

John Gennari is assistant professor of English and director of ALANA U.S. Ethnic Studies at the University of Vermont. His book *Canonizing Jazz: An American Art and Its Critics* is forthcoming from the University of Chicago Press. He is also at work on a study of cultural interaction, exchange, and tension between African Americans and Italian Americans. He has received fellowships from the National Endowment for the Humanities, the W. E. B. Du Bois Institute at Harvard, and the Carter G. Woodson Institute at the University of Virginia.

Farah Jasmine Griffin is professor of English and Comparative Literature at Columbia University. She received her B.A. from Harvard (1985) and her Ph.D. from Yale (1992) Professor Griffin's major fields of interest are African American literature, music, history, and politics. The recipient of numerous honors and awards for her teaching and scholarship, in 1996–97 Professor Griffin was a fellow at the Bunting Institute of Radcliffe College. She is the author of *Who Set You Flowin'? The African American Migration Narrative* (Oxford University Press, 1995), the coeditor (with Cheryl Fish) of *Stranger in the Village: Two Centuries of African American Travel Writing* (Beacon, 1998), and the editor of *Beloved Sisters and Loving Friends: Letters from Addie Brown and Rebecca Primus* (Knopf, 1999). Her most recent book, *If You Can't Be Free Be a Mystery: In Search of Billie Holiday*, was published in 2001 by the Free Press.

William J. Harris is associate professor of English at the University of Kansas in Lawrence, where he teaches American literature, African American literature, creative writing, and jazz studies. Author of numerous scholarly articles and of poetry in many magazines and anthologies, he has published a critical study, *The Poetry and Poetics of Amiri Baraka: The Jazz Aesthetic*, and two books of poetry, *Hey Fella Would You Mind Holding This Piano a Moment* and *In My Own Dark Way*. As well as being the editor of *The LeRoi Jones/Amiri Baraka Reader*, he is coeditor of *Call and Response: The Riverside Anthology of the African Literary Tradition*, and a special issue on Amiri Baraka of the *African American Review* (Summer/Fall 2003). Currently he is at work on a history of African American poetry, under contract with Cambridge University Press.

Diedra Harris-Kelley is a full-time painter who has taught at University of Michigan, NYU, and the Parsons Studio program. She also works with the Romare Bearden Foundation coordinating their exhibition space, conducting workshops, and lecturing on the artist's work. She lives in New York City.

Vijay Iyer is a New York–based pianist, composer, and occasional scholar. His most recent recordings include *Blood Sutra, In What Language?* (with poet Mike Ladd), and *Your Life Flashes* (as the trio Fieldwork). Iyer has performed around the world as a leader and in collaboration with Roscoe Mitchell, Amiri Baraka, Steve Coleman, Miya Masaoka, George Lewis, Butch Morris, Will Power, and Greg Tate. He holds a B.S. from Yale College and a Ph.D. in Technology and the Arts from the University of California at Berkeley. He received the 2003 CalArts Alpert Award in the Arts.

Travis A. Jackson is associate professor of Music at the University of Chicago. His scholarly interests include jazz, rock, ethnography, urban geography, and recording technology. He is the author of *Blowin' the Blues Away: Performance and Meaning on the New York Jazz Scene*, forthcoming from the University of California Press.

Robin D. G. Kelley, a professor of Anthropology and African American Studies at Columbia University, has written widely on jazz, hip hop, electronic music, musicians' unions, and is completing a biography of Thelonious Monk. His latest book is *Freedom Dreams: The Black Radical Imagination* (2002).

George Lewis, improvisor-trombonist, composer, and computer/installation artist, studied composition with Muhal Richard Abrams at the AACM School of Music and trombone with Dean Hey. The recipient of a MacArthur Fellowship in 2002, a Cal Arts/Alpert Award in the Arts in 1999, and numerous fellowships from the National Endowment for the Arts, Lewis has explored electronic and computer music, computer-based multimedia installations, text-sound works, and notated forms. A member of the Association for the Advancement of Creative Musicians (AACM) since 1971, Lewis's work as a composer, improvisor, performer, and interpreter is documented on more than 120 recordings. His forthcoming book, *Power Stronger Than Itself: The Association for the Advancement of Creative Musicians*, will be published by the University of Chicago Press. In fall 2004 Lewis will become the Edwin H. Case Professor of Jazz and American Music at Columbia University.

George Lipsitz is professor of American Studies at the University of California at Santa Cruz. He edits the Critical American Studies series at the University of Minnesota Press and his publications include *American Studies in a Moment of Danger*, *The Possessive Investment in Whiteness*, and *Time Passages*.

Timothy Mangin is a doctoral candidate in the Music Department at Columbia University, completing a dissertation about Senegalese urban popular music. He is the 2003–4 Jeffery Campbell Fellow at St. Lawrence University.

Robert G. O'Meally is the Zora Neale Hurston Professor of Literature at Columbia University. Since 1999 he has been the director of Columbia's Center for Jazz Studies. He is the author of *The Craft of Ralph Ellison* (1980), *Lady Day: The Many Faces of Billie Holiday* (1991), and the principal writer of *Seeing Jazz* (1997), the catalogue for the Smithsonian's exhibit on jazz painting and literature. He has coedited two volumes, *History and Memory in African American Culture* (1994) and *The Norton Anthology of African American Literature* (1996), and edited *The Jazz Cadence of American Culture* (1998) and *Living with Music: Ralph Ellison's Essays on Jazz* (2001). He wrote the script for the documentary film *Lady Day* and for the documentary accompanying the Smithsonian exhibit, *Duke Ellington: Beyond Category* (1995). He received a Grammy nomination for his work as coproducer of the five CD box set *The Jazz Singers* (1998).

John Szwed is Musser Professor of African American Studies, Anthropology, Music, and Film Studies at Yale University, and in 2003–4 he was Louis Armstrong Visiting Professor at Columbia University. His books include *Afro-American Anthropology*, *Space Is the Place: The Lives and Times of Sun Ra*, *Jazz 101*, and *So What: The Life of Miles Davis*. He is currently at work on a biography of Alan Lomax.

Mark Tucker (1954–2000) was a professor in the Music Department at the College of William and Mary. His publications include the book *Ellington: The Early Years* (University of Illinois Press, 1991) and Garvin Bushell's as-told-to autobiography, *Jazz from the Beginning* (University of Michigan, 1998). He also edited *The Duke Ellington Reader* (Oxford University Press, 1993).

Jorge Daniel Veneciano is a doctoral candidate in the English and Comparative Literature department at Columbia University, writing on aesthetic ideology in American modernism. He is former curator of African American art at the Studio Museum in Harlem, where he organized, among other exhibitions, *Norman Lewis: Black Paintings, 1946–1977*. His publications encompass arts and media criticism in journals including *Afterimage* and *New Art Examiner*. He has taught in the areas of literature and visual culture at the Rhode Island School of Design, Columbia, and the California State University, Los Angeles.

Penny M. Von Eschen is associate professor of History and African American Studies at the University of Michigan. She is the author of the forthcoming *Satchmo Blows Up the World: Jazz Ambassadors Play the Cold War* (Harvard University Press, 2004) and *Race Against Empire: Black Americans and Anticolonialism, 1937–1957* (Cornell University Press, 1997).

Salim Washington is a New York–based saxophonist, flutist, and composer. He is also assistant professor of Music at Brooklyn College.

"Cultural Exchange" (Brubeck), 191
Cyrus, Gerald, 4

d

Dafora, Asadata, 13
Dakar (Senegal), 229, 236–44
dance, jazz and, 1, 2, 4, 13, 15–16, 22–23, 59, 226, 238, 327
Dance, Stanley, 151, 153, 329, 345, 350
Davis, Anthony, 52
Davis, Miles, 5, 112, 113, 116–18, 135, 166–84, 405; and boxing, 177–78; and cars, 181; and fashion, 180–81; Harmon mute of, 168–69; on human voice, 166, 169; and phrasing, 169–70; on sexuality, 167; shyness of, 174
Dawson, Daniel, 4
Delany, Beauford, 2
DeVeaux, Scott, 5, 306
Diawara, Manthia, 210
Dixieland, 34, 51
DJs, jazz and, 407–9
Dodds, Baby, 14
Dolphy, Eric, 33, 36, 38, 44
Dorf, Michael, 144–45
Dorsey, Tommy, 13, 304–5
Douglass, Frederick, 109
Down Beat, 34, 37, 71, 140, 142, 177–78, 196
Du Bois, W. E. B., 112, 113, 113, 114–15, 231, 341
Duchesne, Miguel Angel, 13
Dunbar, Paul Laurence, 107, 111–12, 113–14, 381

e

Early, Gerald, 176–77
Eckstine, Billy, 15
education, jazz and, 1, 3, 15, 18, 55
Ellington, Duke, 3, 5, 11, 13, 30, 31, 33, 34, 35, 36, 37, 72, 74, 75, 120, 133, 197, 232, 273, 281, 326–51; as composer of film scores, 299–300, 305–8, 341–42; autobiography of, 328, 329, 340, 345–47; and literary sources, 327; and Monk, 150–51, 156; at the Newport Jazz Festival, 134–35, 138, 151, 401; on music as "tone parallel," 327, 336–339, 349; and *Paris Blues*, 297–309; poetry of, 328–29, 343–44; and religion, 348–51; on Shakespeare, 331–32, 335–38; U.S. State De-

partment tours of, 194–95, 233; writings of, 326–27, 434–44, 348–51
Ellison, Ralph, 2, 3, 108, 133, 136, 137, 139, 182, 267, 273, 278, 279, 287, 288; on Armstrong, 280–85, 291, 292; on Ellington, 281; on comedy, 279–85, 287, 293n23
Europe, James Reese, 13, 77
Evans, Gil, 167, 169

f

"Fables of Faubus" (Mingus) *See* "Original Fables of Faubus"
Fanon, Frantz, 316
Feather, Leonard, 37, 132, 136, 361–62
Flender, Harold, 301
Floyd, Samuel, 51, 123n18
France, 14, 52, 61–62, 230–31, 233
Franklin, Aretha, 21, 102, 144
free jazz, 51, 53, 55, 64, 72, 80, 85, 312–13, 320, 321
Freeman, Chico, 58–59, 62, 66, 70, 75

g

Garcia, Louis ("King"), 13
Gabbard, Krin, 6, 269
Garrison, Lucy Kim, 106, 113
Gayle, Charles, 32, 33
Gennari, John, 5
Giddins, Gary, 66–67, 70, 71, 72
Gillespie, Dizzy, 13, 21, 37, 131, 132, 173, 206, 211–13, 331; autobiography of, 213–14; U.S. State Department tours of, 28, 153, 189, 233
Gilmore, Samuel, 63–64
Gilroy, Paul, 12, 235–36
Gonsalves, Paul, 134–35, 401
Goodman, Benny, 140
Great Summit, The (recording), 297–98
Griffin, Farah Jasmine, 13, 29, 86

h

Hamer, Fanny Lou, 102, 103
Hammond, John, 132–33, 138
Hampton, Lionel, 11, 14, 18
Harding, Vincent, 24
Harker, Brian, 393
Hatch, Jim, 4
Hardt, Michael, 90–91
Harlem Renaissance, 46n12, 73, 327
Harper, Michael, 381–82

424

index